Index of American Periodical Verse: 1977

by
Sander W. Zulauf
and
Edward M. Cifelli

The Scarecrow Press, Inc.
Metuchen, N.J. & London
1979

Preparation of this volume was made possible by a Research Grant from the National Endowment for the Humanities.

Library of Congress Catalog Card No. 73-3060

ISBN 0-8108-1169-3

Manufactured in the United States of America

CONTENTS

iii

PREFACE

The seventh annual Index of American Periodical Verse lo-
cates the poems of more than 4000 poets published in the 201 peri-
odicals selected for inclusion in 1977. Our addition of 35 titles this
year was accomplished through the assistance of a Research Grant
from the National Endowment for the Humanities. The methods used
for selecting these periodicals for inclusion are noted in the Preface
to the 1976 coverage volume. As in the past, our goal is to be
widely representative of contemporary poetry; we wish to be useful
and reliable to poets, writers, readers and libraries.

The format of the 1977 volume follows that of its predeces-
sors. The first section lists the title abbreviations of all publica-
tions indexed and gives the complete journal name, plus editorial and
subscription information. Following this is the alphabetical index of
poets and their published poems, with a citation to where the poem
appeared following each title. This typically includes the underlined
abbreviation for the magazine--"OhioR" (for Ohio Review); the vol-
ume and/or number of the issue in parentheses--"(3:1)" signifying
volume 3, number 1; the date of the issue--"Sum 77" for an issue
dated summer 1977; and the page number on which the poem appears
or begins.

Two magazines indexed this year deserve special attention.
Poetry Now published a single 200-page Bicentennial Issue (combin-
ing issue numbers 14/18) instead of four separate issues. In addi-
tion to the hundreds of poets represented in those pages, a special
portfolio, including photographs, of American poets from William
Cullen Bryant through James Wright is included. This explains the
presence of Poe, Whitman, Longfellow, Emerson and others in this
year's Index. Also, Denver Quarterly produced a 400-page Asian
issue (volume 12, number 2, summer 1977), which made available
in translation the poetry of some 250 Chinese, Japanese, Korean,
and Vietnamese poets. While it is true that these remarkable is-
sues of Poetry Now and Denver Quarterly were unique in scope and
design, we believe that their existence indicates the overall vitality
of poetry and the "little magazine" in America today.

In addition to the National Endowment for the Humanities,
many individuals helped us prepare this volume. We are pleased to
acknowledge our debt to Marion Zulauf, who alphabetized most of
the poems and poets included in this year's Index. Furthermore,
we received a great deal of support from County College of Morris.

In particular we would like to thank deans Judith Raulf and Walter Schroeder who understood the requirements of this project from the outset and solved problems for us as they arose. The librarians who helped us this year were Dorothy Souchack and the periodicals staff of the Sherman H. Masten Learning Resources Center at County College of Morris, Randolph; Robert H. Milford, head of the periodical department of the Friendship Library at Fairleigh Dickinson University, Madison; and the librarians at the Mahoney Library of St. Elizabeth's College, Convent Station. The editors of the magazines included this year also deserve special recognition. Without their cooperation, understanding, and generosity, the Index could not exist. We thank them once again and add special thanks to the growing number of periodicals which told their readers that the poems published by them were indexed by us. We also thank our editors and publishers, the fine people at Scarecrow Press who clear the decks to receive this monstrous manuscript and make it into a book. Finally, we acknowledge the patience, moral support, and love of Madeline and Bobbi, as well as the children: Lisa, Michael, Laura, Mary Beth, and Scott. They manage to get us through the rough spots.

S. W. Z.
E. M. C.

Succasunna, New Jersey
July 1978

ABBREVIATIONS

ad.	adaptation
arr.	arrangement
Back:	back-issue copy price
Ed. (s.)	Editor(s)
Exec.	Executive
(ind.)	price for individuals
(inst.)	price for institutions
(lib.)	price for libraries
p.	page
pp.	pages
Po. Ed.	Poetry Editor
Pub.	Publisher
Sing:	single copy price
SI	Special Issue
(stud.)	price for students
Subs:	subscription price or address
tr.	translation
U	University
w.	with
$7/yr	seven dollars per year
(19)	number 19
(7:7)	volume 7, number 7

Months

Ja	January	Jl	July
F	February	Ag	August
Mr	March	S	September
Ap	April	O	October
My	May	N	November
Je	June	D	December

Seasons

Aut	Autumn, Fall	Spr	Spring
Wint	Winter	Sum	Summer

PERIODICALS ADDED

Aieee

Ann Arbor Review

Big Deal

Bits

Carousel Quarterly

Chelsea

Chomo-Uri

Columbia

Cornell Review

Cutbank

DeKalb Literary Arts
    Journal

En Passant

The Falcon

Gravida

Green River Review

Handbook

Hills

Montemora

New Collage

New River Review

Nimrod

Obsidian

Open Places

Pigiron

Poets in the South

Portland Review

Quarterly West

Samisdat

Second Coming

Some

Stone Country

Stonecloud

Three Rivers Poetry Jour-
    nal

U.S. 1 Worksheets

Waters

PERIODICALS DELETED

Apple

Books Abroad

Corduroy

Etc.

Granite

Okike

Saltillo

Twelve Poems

Unicorn Journal

AAUP
AAUP BULLETIN
R. K. Webb, Ed.
Suite 500
One Dupont Circle, N. W.
Washington, DC 20036
  (63:1-4)
  Subs: $10/yr

Aieee
*AIEEE
Jack Grady
Orlan Cannon, Eds.
Alphaville
Box 3424
Charlottesville, VA 22903
  (5/6)
  Sing: $2

AAR
*ANN ARBOR REVIEW
Fred Wolven, Ed.
Washtenaw Community College
Ann Arbor, MI 48106
  (27)
  Subs: $6/3
  Sing: $2.50
  Back: $3

Agni
AGNI REVIEW
Sharon Dunn
Askold Melnyczuk, Eds.
Box 349
Cambridge, MA 02138
  (7)
  Subs: $7/2 yrs
           $4/yr
  Sing: $2.50

AmerPoR
AMERICAN POETRY REVIEW
Stephen Berg, et al., Eds.
Temple U Center City
1616 Walnut St.   Room 405
Philadelphia, PA 19103
  (6:1-6)
  Subs: $13/3 yrs
           $9/2 yrs
           $5/yr
  Sing: $1

AmerR
THE AMERICAN REVIEW
Theodore Solotaroff
Richard Howard, Eds.
666 Fifth Avenue
New York, NY 10019
  (26)
  Final issue.

AmerS
THE AMERICAN SCHOLAR
Joseph Epstein, Ed.
1811 Q St., N. W.
Washington, DC 20009
  (46:1-4)
  Subs: $20/3 yrs
           $14.50/2 yrs
           $8/yr
  Sing: $2

AndR
THE ANDOVER REVIEW
William H. Brown, Ed.
Erica Funkhouser, Po. Ed.
Phillips Academy
Andover, MA 01810
  (3:1-2) (4:1)

*New titles added to the Index in 1977.

Subs: $6/yr
Sing: $3

Antaeus
ANTAEUS
Daniel Halpern, Ed.
1 West 30th St.
New York, NY 10001
(25/26-27)
Subs: $12/yr
Sing: $3.50

AntR
ANTIOCH REVIEW
Paul Bixler, Ed.
Ira Sadoff, Po. Ed.
Box 148
Yellow Springs, OH 45387
(35:1-4)
Subs: $8/yr
Sing: $2

Aphra
APHRA
Elizabeth Fisher, et al., Eds.
Box 893
Ansonia Station
New York, NY 10023
(-)
Subs: $5.50/4
Sing: $1.50
Back: $1.75

AriD
ARION'S DOLPHIN
Stratis Haviaras, Ed.
Box 313
Cambridge, MA 92138
(-)
Subs: $4/4
Sing: $1

ArizQ
ARIZONA QUARTERLY
Albert Frank Gegenheimer, Ed.
U of Arizona
Tucson, AZ 85721
(33:1-4)
Subs: $5/3 yrs
$2/yr
Sing: $.50

ArkRiv
THE ARK RIVER REVIEW
Jonathan Katz
A. G. Sobin, Eds.
Wichita State U
Wichita, KS 67208
(3:4/4:1)
Subs: $4/4
Sing: $1

Ascent
ASCENT
Daniel Curley, et al., Eds.
English Dept.
U of Illinois
Urbana, IL 61801
(3:1-2)
Subs: $3/yr
Sing: $1

Aspect
ASPECT
Edward J. Hogan, Ed.
12 Rindge Avenue
Cambridge, MA 02140
(69-70)
Subs: $6/yr
Sing: $1.50

Aspen
ASPEN ANTHOLOGY
Kurt Brown, Ed.
Bruce Berger
Donna Disch, Po. Eds.
Box 3185
Aspen, CO 81611
(3-4)
Sing: $2.50

Atl
THE ATLANTIC
Robert Manning, Ed.
Peter Davison, Po. Ed.
8 Arlington St.
Boston, MA 02116
Subs: Box 1857
Greenwich, CT
06830
(239:1-6) (240:1-6)
Subs: $30/3 yrs
$22.50/2 yrs
$13/yr
Sing: $1

BallSUF
BALL STATE UNIVERSITY
FORUM
Merrill & Frances M. Rippy,
  Eds.
Ball State U
Muncie, IN 47306
  (18:1-4)
  Subs: $5/yr
  Sing: $1.50

BelPoJ
THE BELOIT POETRY JOUR-
NAL
Robert H. Glauber, et al., Eds.
Box 2
Beloit, WI 53511
  (27:3-4) (28:1-2)
  Subs: $11/3 yrs
           $4/yr
  Sing: $1

BerksR
BERKSHIRE REVIEW
Michael Davitt Bell
Charles Karelis, Eds.
Williams College
Box 633
Williamstown, MA 01267
  (12:1-2) (13:1)
  Subs: $1/yr
  Sing: $.50

BigD
*BIG DEAL
Barbara Baracks, Ed.
Box 830
Peter Stuyvesant Station
New York, NY 10009
  (5)
  Subs: $21/6 (inst.)
           $18/6 (ind.)
  Sing: $3.50 (inst.)
           $3 (ind.)

BirdE
BIRD EFFORT
Robert Long
Josh Dayton, Eds.
25 Mudford Ave.
East Hampton, NY 11937
  (-)
  Sing: $1

Bits
*BITS
Dennis Douley, et al., Eds.
Gutenberg Annex
Dept. of English
Case Western Reserve U
Cleveland, OH 44106
  (6)

BlackF
BLACK FORUM
Revish Windham
Horace Mungin, Eds.
Box 1090
Bronx, NY 10451
  (2:1)
  Subs: $3/yr
  Sing: $2
  Back: $1.25

Bleb
BLEB
Geoffrey Gardner, Ed.
Box 322
Times Square Station
New York, NY 10036
  (12)
  Subs: $1.50/yr
  Sing: $.75

BosUJ
BOSTON UNIVERSITY JOURNAL
Paul Kurt Ackermann, Ed.
775 Commonwealth Avenue
Boston, MA 02215
  (25:1-3)
  Subs: $6/yr
  Sing: $2

Bound
BOUNDARY 2
William V. Spanos
Robert Kroetsch, Eds.
Dept. of English
SUNY--Binghamton
Binghamton, NY 13901
  (5:2-3) (6:1)
  Subs: $7/yr
  Sing: $3

Box
BOXSPRING
Scott Haas, et al., Po. Eds.

Hampshire College
Amherst, MA 01002
  (5)
  Subs: $3/yr
  Sing: $1.50

Broad
BROADSIDE SERIES
Dudley Randall, Ed.
Broadside Press
1265 Old Mill Place
Detroit, MI 48238
  (-)
  Subs: Limited Editions--
           prices on request.

CalQ
CALIFORNIA QUARTERLY
Elliot L. Gilbert, Ed.
100 Sproul Hall
U of California
Davis, CA 95616
  (11/12)
  Subs: $5/yr
  Sing: $1.50

CarlMis
CARLETON MISCELLANY
Keith Harrison, Ed.
Carleton College
Northfield, MN 55057
  (16:1/2) (17:1)
  Subs: $10/2 yrs
           $5.50/yr
  Sing: $2

CarolQ
CAROLINA QUARTERLY
Robert Gingher, Ed.
Rex McGuinn, Po. Ed.
Box 1117
Chapel Hill, NC 27514
  (29:1-3)
  Subs: $4.50/yr
  Sing: $1.50
  Back: $2

CarouselQ
*CAROUSEL QUARTERLY
Jay B. Isaacs, Ed.
Box 111
Mt. Laurel, NJ 08054
  (2:1-3)
  Subs: $10/yr

CEACritic
CEA CRITIC
Elizabeth W. Cowan, Ed.
English Dept.
Texas A&M U
College Station, TX 77843
  Subs: Paula J. Barthel
           Oakland Community
           College
           Auburn Heights, MI
           48057
  (39:2-4) (40:1)
  Subs: $15 (inst.)
           $12 (ind.)

CentR
CENTENNIAL REVIEW
David Mead, Ed.
Linda Wagner, Po. Ed.
110 Morrill Hall
Michigan State U
East Lansing, MI 48824
  (21:1-4)
  Subs: $5/2 yrs
           $3/yr
  Sing: $1

Chelsea
*CHELSEA
Sonia Raiziss, Ed.
Gerard Malanga, Guest Po. Ed.
Box 5800
Grand Central Station
New York, NY 10017
  (36)
  Subs: $4.50/2
  Sing: $2.50

ChiR
CHICAGO REVIEW
David Shields
Mary Ellis Gibson, Eds.
Richard Hagman, Po. Ed.
Faculty Exchange
Box C
U of Chicago
Chicago, IL 60637
  (28:4) (29:1-3)
  Subs: $21.95/3 yrs
           $15.95/2 yrs
           $8.95/yr
  Sing: $2.45

Chomo
*CHOMO-URI
Annette Townley, et al., Eds.
506 Goodell Hall
U of Massachusetts
Amherst, MA 01003
  (3:3) (4:1-2)
  Subs: $10/3 yrs
         $7/2 yrs
         $4/yr
  Sing: $1.50

Chowder
CHOWDER REVIEW
Ron Slate, Ed.
2858 Kingston Drive
Madison, WI 53713
  (8-9)
  Subs: $5/3
  Sing: $1.75

ChrC
THE CHRISTIAN CENTURY
James M. Wall, Ed.
407 S. Dearborn St.
Chicago, IL 60605
  (94:1-43)
  Subs: $34/3 yrs
         $25/2 yrs
         $15/yr
  Sing: $.50

CimR
CIMARRON REVIEW
Clinton C. Keeler, Ed.
208 Life Sciences East
Oklahoma State U
Stillwater, OK 74074
  (34) (38-41)
  Subs: $10/yr
  Sing: $4

ColEng
COLLEGE ENGLISH
Donald Gray, Ed.
Dept. of English
Ballantine Hall
Indiana U
Bloomington, IN 47401
  Subs: 1111 Kenyon Rd.
          Urbana, IL 61801
  (38:5-8) (39:1-4)
  Subs: $15/yr
  Sing: $2

Columbia
*COLUMBIA
John Plaskett, Ed.
School of the Arts
Writing Division
404 Dodge
Columbia U
New York, NY 10027
  (1)
  Sing: $2

Comm
COMMONWEAL
James O'Gara, Ed.
John Fandel, Po. Ed.
232 Madison Avenue
New York, NY 10016
  (104:1-26)
  Subs: $17/yr
  Sing: $.75

ConcPo
CONCERNING POETRY
Ellwood Johnson, Ed.
Robert Huff, Po. Ed.
Dept. of English
Western Washington State College
Bellingham, WA 98225
  (10:1-2)
  Subs: $4/yr
  Sing: $2
  Back: $2

Confr
CONFRONTATION
Martin Tucker, Ed.
English Dept.
Brooklyn Center of
Long Island U
Brooklyn, NY 11201
  (14-15)
  Subs: $10.50/3 yrs
         $7/2 yrs
         $3.50/yr
  Sing: $2
  Back: $2

CornellR
*CORNELL REVIEW
Baxter Hathaway, Ed.
108 North Plain St.
Ithaca, NY 14850
  (1-2)

Subs: $25/3 yrs
        $18/2 yrs
        $10/yr
Sing: $3. 50

CutB
*CUTBANK
Lex Runciman
Rick Robbins, Eds.
Dept. of English
U of Montana
Missoula, MT 59812
  (8-9)
  Subs: $6. 50/2 yrs
          $3. 50/yr
  Sing: $2

DacTerr
DACOTAH TERRITORY
Mark Vinz, Ed.
Moorhead State U
Box 775
Moorhead, MN 56560
  (14)
  Subs: $2. 50
  Sing: $1. 50

DeKalb
*DeKALB LITERARY ARTS
JOURNAL
William S. Newman, Ed.
DeKalb College
555 N. Indian Creek Drive
Clarkston, GA 30021
  (10:1-4)
  Sing: $1. 50

DenQ
DENVER QUARTERLY
Leland H. Chambers, Ed.
U of Denver
Denver, CO 80208
  (11:4) (12:1-4)
  Subs: $14/2 yrs
          $8/yr
  Sing: $2

Drag
DRAGONFLY
Duane Ackerson, Ed.
Eaton Hall
Willamette U
Salem, OR 97301

(16)
Final issue.

EngJ
ENGLISH JOURNAL
Stephen N. Judy, Ed.
Richard Calisch, Po. Ed.
Box 112
East Lansing, MI 48823
  Subs: 1111 Kenyon Rd.
          Urbana, IL 61801
  (66:5) Poetry published in
          May issue annually.
  Subs: $20/yr
          $5/yr (stud.)
  Sing: $2. 50

EnPas
*EN PASSANT
James A. Costello, Ed.
1906 Brant Rd.
Wilmington, DE 19810
  (4-6)
  Subs: $6/yr
  Sing: $1. 75

Epoch
EPOCH
James McConkey
Walter Slatoff, Eds.
245 Goldwin Smith Hall
Cornell U
Ithaca, NY 14853
  (26:2-3) (27:1)
  Subs: $4/yr
  Sing: $1. 50

Epos
EPOS
Evenly Thorne
Jean West MacKenzie, Eds.
Rollins College
Crescent City, FL 32012
  (-)
  Subs: $3/yr
  Sing: $1

Esq
ESQUIRE
Clay S. Felker, Ed.
488 Madison Avenue
New York, NY 10022
  Subs: 1255 Portland Place

Boulder, CO 80302
(87:1-6) (88:1-6)
Subs: $15. 95/yr
Sing: $1. 25

Falcon
*THE FALCON
W. A. Blais, Ed.
Belknap Hall
Mansfield State College
Mansfield, PA 16933
 (14-15)
Subs: $4/yr
Sing: $2

Field
FIELD
Stuart Friebert
David Young, Eds.
Rice Hall
Oberlin College
Oberlin, OH 44704
 (16-17)
Subs: $7/2 yrs
          $4/yr
Sing: $2

Focus
FOCUS/MIDWEST
Charles L. Klotzer, Ed.
Dan Jaffe, Po. Ed.
928a N. McKnight
St. Louis, MO 63132
 (12:74-77)
Subs: $19/5 yrs
          $9/2 yrs
          $5/yr
Sing: $. 85

FourQt
FOUR QUARTERS
John J. Keenan, Ed.
Joseph Meredith, Po. Ed.
20th & Olney Avenues
Philadelphia, PA 19141
 (26:2-4) (27:1)
Subs: $5/2 yrs
          $3/yr
Sing: $. 75

GeoR
GEORGIA REVIEW
Stanley W. Lindberg

U of Georgia
Athens, GA 30601
 (31:1-4)
Subs: $5/2 yrs
          $3/yr
Sing: $1. 50

Glass
GLASSWORKS
Betty Bressi, Ed.
Box 163
Rosebank Station
Staten Island, NY 10305
 (2:2/3)
Subs: $6/yr (lib.)
          $4/yr (ind.)
Sing: $1. 50

Gra
*GRAVIDA
Ina Chadwick Wilde, et al. , Eds.
Box 76
Hartsdale, NY 10530
Subs: Box 118
          Bayville, NY 11709
 (12-13)
Subs: $4/yr
Sing: $1. 25

GRR
*GREEN RIVER REVIEW
Raymond Tyner, Ed.
SVSC Box 56
University Center, MI 48710
 (8:1-3)
Subs: $6/yr

GreenR
THE GREENFIELD REVIEW
Joseph Bruchac III, Ed.
Greenfield Center, NY 12833
 (6:1/2)
Subs: $4/2 double issues
Sing: $2

Hand
*HAND BOOK
Susan Mernit
Rochelle Ratner, Eds.
72 Spring St.
Delaware, OH 43015
or
50 Spring St.

New York, NY 10012
(1)
  Subs: $12/2 yrs
          $6/yr
  Sing: $4

HangL
HANGING LOOSE
Robert Hershon, et al., Eds.
231 Wyckoff St.
Brooklyn, NY 11217
(29-31)
  Subs: $15/12
          $10/8
          $5.50/4
  Sing: $1.50

Harp
HARPER'S MAGAZINE
Lewis H. Lapham, Ed.
Two Park Avenue
New York, NY 10016
  Subs: 1255 Portland Place
          Boulder, CO 80323
(254:1520-1525) (255:1526-
1531)
  Subs: $9.98/yr
  Sing: $1.25

HarvAd
HARVARD ADVOCATE
John McCullough, President
April Bernard, Po. Ed.
21 South St.
Cambridge, MA 02138
(110:3-5) (111:1-2)
  Subs: $5/yr
  Sing: $1

Hills
*HILLS
Bob Perelman, Ed.
1220 Folsom
San Francisco, CA 94103
(4)
  Sing: $1.50

HiramPoR
HIRAM POETRY REVIEW
David Fratus, Ed.
Box 162
Hiram, OH 44234
(22-23)

  Subs: $2/yr
  Sing: $1

HolCrit
THE HOLLINS CRITIC
John Rees Moore, Ed.
Box 9538
Hollins College, VA 24020
(14:1-5)
  Subs: $4/yr

Horizon
HORIZON
Shirley Tomkievicz, Ed.
10 Rockefeller Plaza
New York, NY 10022
  Subs: 381 West Center St.
          Marion, OH 43302
(19:1-3)
  Subs: $32/yr
  Sing: $7.50

Hudson
THE HUDSON REVIEW
Frederick Morgan
Paula Deitz, Eds.
65 East 55th St.
New York, NY 10022
(30:1-4)
  Subs: $26/3 yrs
          $18/2 yrs
          $10/yr
  Sing: $2.50

Humanist
HUMANIST
Paul Kurtz, Ed.
M. L. Rosenthal, Po. Ed.
SUNY at Buffalo
Amherst, NY 14260
  Subs: 923 Kensington Ave-
          nue
          Buffalo, NY 14215
(37:1-6)
  Subs: $27/3 yrs
          $20/2 yrs
          $12/yr
  Sing: $2

Icarus
ICARUS
Margaret Diorio, Ed.
Box 8

Riderwood, MD 21139
  (5:1-2)
  Final issue.
  Sing: $1

Iowa
IOWA REVIEW
Thomas R. Whitaker, Ed.
William Matthews, Po. Ed.
EPB 321
U of Iowa
Iowa City, IA 52242
  Subs: Publications Order
           Dept.
           U of Iowa
           Iowa City, IA 52242
  (8:1-4)
  Subs: $7. 50/yr
  Sing: $2

JnlONJP
JOURNAL OF NEW JERSEY
POETS
Walter Cummins, et al. , Eds.
Dept. of English
Fairleigh Dickinson U
Madison, NJ 07940
  (1:3, parts 1 & 2)
  Subs: $3/3
  Sing: $1

JnlOPC
JOURNAL OF POPULAR CUL-
TURE
Ray B. Browne, Ed.
U Hall
Bowling Green U
Bowling Green, OH 43403
  (10:4) (11:1-2)
  Subs: $15/yr
           $7. 50/yr (stud.)
  Sing: $4

Juice
JUICE
Stephen S. Morse
Judy L. Brekke, Eds.
5402 Ygnacio
Oakland, CA 94601
  (4-5)
  Subs: $4/yr
  Sing: $2. 50

KanQ
KANSAS QUARTERLY
Harold Schneider
Ben Nyberg, Eds.
Dept. of English
Kansas State U
Manhattan, KS 66506
  (9:1-4)
  Subs: $14/2 yrs
           $7. 50/yr
  Sing: $2. 50
  Back: $2. 50

Kayak
KAYAK
George Hitchcock, Ed.
Marjorie Simon, Associate Ed.
325 Ocean View Avenue
Santa Cruz, CA 95062
  (44-46)
  Subs: $4/4
  Sing: $1

LaB
La-BAS
Douglas Messerli, Ed.
Box 431
College Park, MD 20740
  (5-8)

LadHJ
LADIES' HOME JOURNAL
Lenore Hershey, Ed.
Mary Elizabeth Guimares, Po.
Ed.
641 Lexington Avenue
New York, NY 10022
  Subs: Box 1697
           Des Moines, IA
           50306
  (94:1-12)
  Subs: $6. 99/yr
  Sing: $. 95

LitR
THE LITERARY REVIEW
Martin Green
Harry Keyishian, Eds.
Fairleigh Dickinson U
Madison, NJ 07940
  (20:3-4) (21:1-2)
  Subs: $9/yr
  Sing: $3. 50

LittleR
THE LITTLE REVIEW
John McKernan, et al. , Eds.
Box 205
Marshall U
Huntington, WV 25701
(12)
Missing (11).
Subs: $2.50/yr
Sing: $1.25

Lynx
LYNX
Robert Abel, et al. , Eds.
Box 800
Amherst, MA 01002
(-)
Subs: $3.50/yr
Sing: $1

Madem
MADEMOISELLE
Edith Raymond Locke, Ed.
Mary Elizabeth McNichols,
Po. Ed.
Condé Nast Building
350 Madison Avenue
New York, NY 10017
Subs: Box 5204
         Boulder, CO 80323
(83:1-12)
Subs: $25/3 yrs
         $18/2 yrs
         $10/yr
Sing: $1.25

Madrona
MADRONA
Charles Webb, Ed.
4730 Latona Avenue, N.E.
Seattle, WA 98105
(4:13/14)
Subs: $5

MalR
THE MALAHAT REVIEW
Robin Skelton, Ed.
U of Victoria
Box 1700
Victoria, B.C.
Canada V8W 2Y2
(41-44)
Subs: $21/3 yrs
         $8/yr

Marilyn
MARILYN
Jeffrey Wells-Powers
P. Schneidre, Eds.
150 W. Ninth St.
Claremont, CA 91711
(-)
Subs: $3.50/yr
Sing: $1.95

Mark
MARK TWAIN JOURNAL
Cyril Clemens, Ed.
Kirkwood, MO 63122
(-)
Subs: $3/yr
Sing: $1

MassR
THE MASSACHUSETTS REVIEW
Lee Edwards, et al. , Eds.
Memorial Hall
U of Massachusetts
Amherst, MA 01002
(18:1-4)
Subs: $9/yr
Sing: $2.50

MichQR
MICHIGAN QUARTERLY REVIEW
Laurence Goldstein, Ed.
3032 Rackham Building
The U of Michigan
Ann Arbor, MI 48109
(16:1-4)
Subs: $18/3 yrs
         $13/2 yrs
         $7/yr
Sing: $2
Back: $2.50

MidwQ
THE MIDWEST QUARTERLY
V. J. Emmett, Jr. , Ed.
Michael Heffernan, Po. Ed.
Pittsburg State U
Pittsburg, KS 66762
(18:2-4) (19:1)
Subs: $4/yr
Sing: $1.50

MinnR
THE MINNESOTA REVIEW

Roger Mitchell, Ed.
Box 211
Bloomington, IN   47401
  (NS8-NS9)
    Subs: $9/2 yrs (inst.)
               $6. 50/2 yrs (ind.)
               $5/yr (inst.)
               $3. 50/yr (ind.)
    Sing: $2

MissR
MISSISSIPPI REVIEW
Bernard Kaplan, Ed.
D. C. Berry, Po. Ed.
Center for Writers
English Dept.
Box 37 Southern Station
U of Southern Mississippi
Hattiesburg, MS 39401
  (6:1-3)
    Subs: $3/yr
    Sing: $1. 50

ModernPS
MODERN POETRY STUDIES
R. E. Braun
Jerome Mazzaro, Eds.
147 Capen Boulevard
Buffalo, NY   14226
  (8:1-3)
    Subs: $7. 50/3
    Sing: $2. 50
    Note: (7:3) was indexed
               in 1976 volume.

ModR
MODULARIST REVIEW
R. C. Morse, Ed.
Wooden Needle Press
65-45 Yellowstone Boulevard
Forest Hills, NY   11375
  (-)
    Subs: $3/yr
    Sing: $3

MontG
MONTANA GOTHIC
Peter Koch, Ed.
Jane Bailey, Associate Ed.
190 S. 3rd West
Missoula, MT   59801
  (5-6)
  Final issue.

Montra
*MONTEMORA
Eliot Weinberger, Ed.
The Montemora Foundation, Inc.
Box 336
Cooper Station
New York, NY   10003
  (3)
    Subs: $9/yr
    Sing: $3. 50

MoonsLT
MOONS AND LION TAILES
H. Schjotz-Christensen, Ed.
Linda Beth Cantor, Assistant Ed.
Lake Street Station
Box 8434
Minneapolis, MN   55408
  (2:3)
    Subs: $6/4 (inst.)
               $5/4 (ind.)
    Sing: $1. 95

Mouth
MOUTH OF THE DRAGON
Andrew Bifrost, Ed. /Pub.
342 E. 15th St.
New York, NY   10003
  (11/12-13)
    Subs: $10/5
    Sing: $2. 50

Mund
MUNDUS ARTIUM
Rainer Schulte, Ed.
U of Texas at Dallas
Box 688
Richardson, TX   75080
  (10:1)
    Subs: $10/yr (inst.)
               $8/yr (ind.)
    Sing: $4. 50
    Special Arabic Issue: $6

Nat
THE NATION
Victor Navasky, Ed.
Grace Schulman, Po. Ed.
333 Sixth Avenue
New York, NY   10014
  (224:1-25) (225:1-23)
    Subs: $37/2 yrs
               $21/yr
    Sing: $. 60

NegroHB
NEGRO HISTORY BULLETIN
J. Rupert Picott, Ed.
Thelma D. Perry, Exec. Ed.
1401 14th Street, N. W.
Washington, DC 20005
  (40:1-6)
  Subs: $8/yr
  Sing: $1.50
  Bound: $12/yr

New
NEW
John Gill, Ed.
The Crossing Press
Trumansburg, NY 14886
  (-)
  Final issue due.
  Sing: $2.50

NewC
*NEW COLLAGE
A. McA. Miller, Ed.
5700 North Trail
Sarasota, FL 33580
  (7:2-3) (8:1-2)
  Subs: $3/yr
  Sing: $1

NewL
NEW LETTERS
David Ray, Ed.
U of Missouri--Kansas City
5346 Charlotte
Kansas City, MO 64110
  (43:3-4) (44:1-2)
  Subs: $40/5 yrs (lib.)
           $25/5 yrs (ind.)
           $18/2 yrs (lib.)
           $12/2 yrs (ind.)
           $10/yr (lib.)
           $8/yr (ind.)
  Sing: $2.50
  Back: Prices on request.

NewOR
NEW ORLEANS REVIEW
Marcus Smith, Ed.
Loyola U
New Orleans, LA 70118
  (5:3)
  Subs: $14/12
           $10/8

          $6/4
Sing: $1.50

NewRena
THE NEW RENAISSANCE
Louise T. Reynolds, Ed.
Olivera Sajkovic, Po. Ed.
9 Heath Road
Arlington, MA 02174
  (9)
  Subs: $6/3
  Sing: $2.65

NewRep
NEW REPUBLIC
Martin Peretz, Ed.
Robert Fitzgerald, Guest Po. Ed.
Roger Rosenblatt, Lit. Ed.
1220 19th Street, N. W.
Washington, DC 20036
  Subs: 205 W. Center St.
           Marion, OH 43302
  (176:1/2-26) (177:1-26/27)
  Subs: $24/yr
           $17/yr (stud.)
  Sing: $1

NewRivR
*NEW RIVER REVIEW
Charles L. Hayes
Philip Pierson, Eds.
Highlands Press
Radford, VA 24142
  (2:1)
  Sing: $2

NewWR
NEW WORLD REVIEW
Marilyn Bechtel, Ed.
Jessica Smith, Chairman,
Editorial Board
Suite 308
156 Fifth Avenue
New York, NY 10010
  (45:1-6)
  Subs: $5/yr
  Sing: $1

NewYRB
THE NEW YORK REVIEW OF
BOOKS
Robert B. Silvers
Barbara Epstein, Eds.

250 W. 57th St.
New York, NY 10019
   Subs: Subs. Service Dept.
          Box 940
          Farmingdale, NY
          11737
  (23:21/22) (24:1-21/22)
   Subs: $14.50/yr
   Sing: $.85

NewYorker
THE NEW YORKER
Howard Moss, Po. Ed.
25 W. 43rd St.
New York, NY 10036
  (52:46-52) (53:1-45)
   Subs: $40/2 yrs
          $24/yr
   Sing: $1

Nimrod
*NIMROD
Francine Ringold, Ed.
U of Tulsa
Tulsa, OK 74104
  (21:2/22:1)
   Subs: $4/yr
   Sing: $3.50/double issue

NoAmR
NORTH AMERICAN REVIEW
Robley Wilson, Jr., Ed.
Peter Cooley, Po. Ed.
U of Northern Iowa
Cedar Falls, IA 50613
  (262:1-4)
   Subs: $8/yr
   Sing: $2

Northeast
NORTHEAST
John Judson, Ed.
Juniper Press
1310 Shorewood Drive
LaCrosse, WI 54601
  (3:3-4)
   Subs: $10.50
          Includes four chap-
          books.

NowestR
NORTHWEST REVIEW
Michael Strelow, Ed.

John Ackerson, Po. Ed.
U of Oregon
Eugene, OR 97403
  (16:1/2-3)
   Subs: $5/yr
   Sing: $5/Kesey issue
          $2

Obs
*OBSIDIAN
Alvin Aubert, Ed.
English Dept.
State U College
Fredonia, NY 14063
  (3:1-3)
   Subs: $5.50/yr
   Sing: $2

OhioR
Wayne Dodd, Senior Ed.
Stanley W. Lindberg, Ed.
Ellis Hall
Ohio U
Athens, OH 45701
  (18:1-3)
   Subs: $7.50/yr
   Sing: $2.50

OP
*OPEN PLACES
Eleanor M. Bender, Ed.
Box 2085
Stephens College
Columbia, MO 65201
  (23-24)
   Subs: $7/2 yrs
          $4/yr
   Sing: $2

Paint
PAINTBRUSH
B. M. Bennani, Ed.
Comparative Literature
SUNY at Binghamton
Binghamton, NY 13901
  (-)
   Subs: $5/yr
   Sing: $2.50

Pan
PANACHE
David Lenson, Ed./Pub.
Candice Ward, Assistant for Po.

Box 77
Sunderland, MA 01375
   (18)
   Sing: $2.50

ParisR
THE PARIS REVIEW
George A. Plimpton, Ed.
Michael Benedikt, Po. Ed.
45-39 171 Place
Flushing, NY 11358
   Poetry: 541 E. 72nd St.
            New York, NY
            10021
   (69-71)
   Subs: $11/6
   Sing: $2.25

PartR
PARTISAN REVIEW
William Phillips, Ed.
John Ashbery, Po. Ed.
1 Richardson St.
New Brunswick, NJ 08903
   (44:1-4)
   Subs: $25/3 yrs
            $17.50/2 yrs
            $9/yr
   Sing: $2.50

Paunch
PAUNCH
Arthur Efron, Ed.
123 Woodward Avenue
Buffalo, NY 14214
   (46/47-48/49)
   Subs: $7/yr (lib.)
            $4/yr (ind.)
            $3/yr (stud.)
   Sing: $4 (lib.)
            $3 (ind.)
   Back: Prices on request.

Peb
PEBBLE
Greg Kuzma, Ed.
The Best Cellar Press
118 South Boswell Avenue
Crete, NE 68333
   (14/15-16)
   Subs: $10/4 (lib.)
            $8/4 (ind.)
   Sing: $4/double issue
            $2

Pequod
PEQUOD
David Paradis
Mark Rudman, Eds.
Box 491
Forest Knolls, CA 94933
   Poetry: Mark Rudman
            282 W. 4th St.
            New York, NY
            10014
   (2:2-3)
   Subs: $12/3 yrs
            $9/2 yrs
            $5/yr
   Sing: $3

Perspec
PERSPECTIVE
Washington U
Box 1122
St. Louis, MO 63130
   (-)
   Subs: $4/yr
   Sing: $1

Phylon
PHYLON
John D. Reid, Ed.
Atlanta U
Atlanta, GA 30314
   (38:1-4)
   Subs: $7/yr
   Sing: $2

Pig
*PIGIRON
Jim Villani, Ed.
Terry Murcko, Po. Ed.
Media Arts
Box 237
Youngstown, OH 44501
   (3)
   Subs: $9/6
            $5/3
   Sing: $3

Playb
PLAYBOY
Hugh M. Hefner, Ed./Pub.
919 N. Michigan Avenue
Chicago, IL 60611
   (24:1-12)
   Subs: $14/yr
   Sing: Varies.

Ploughs
PLOUGHSHARES
DeWitt Henry
Peter O'Malley, Directors
Box 529
Cambridge, MA 02139
  (3:3/4) (4:1)
  Subs: $8/4
  Sing: $2.95

Poem
POEM
Robert L. Welker, Ed.
Box 1247
West Station
Huntsville, AL 35807
  Subs: Box 919
           Huntsville, AL
           35804
  (29-31)
  Subs: $5/yr

PoetC
POET AND CRITIC
Richard Gustafson, Ed. (1964-
77)
David Cummings, Associate Ed.
203 Ross Hall
Iowa State U
Ames, IA 50011
  Subs: Iowa State U Press
           Press Building
           Ames, IA 50011
  (10:1)
  Subs: $5/2 yrs
           $3/yr
  Sing: $1

PoetL
POET LORE
Miriam Andrews, Exec. Ed.
Heldref Publications
4000 Albemarle St. N.W.
Washington, DC 20016
  (72:1-2)
  Subs: $10/yr
  Sing: $2.50

Poetry
POETRY
John Frederick Nims, Ed.
1228 N. Dearborn Pkwy.
Chicago, IL 60610

(129:4-6) (130:1-6) (131:1-3)
  Subs: $18/yr
  Sing: $2
  Back: $2.25

PoNow
POETRY NOW
E. V. Griffith, Ed./Pub.
3118 K St.
Eureka, CA 95501
  (14/18)
  Subs: $12/18
           $9/12
           $5/6
  Sing: $1.25
  Back: Bicentennial Issue,
           $5

PoetryNW
POETRY NORTHWEST
David Wagoner, Ed.
4045 Brooklyn Avenue N.E.
U of Washington
Seattle, WA 98105
  (18:1-4)
  Subs: $5/yr
  Sing: $1.50

Poets
*POETS IN THE SOUTH
Willie Reader
Center for Writers
LET 141
U of South Florida
Tampa, FL 33620
  (1:1)
  Subs: $10/2 yrs
           $6/yr
  Sing: $2

PortR
*PORTLAND REVIEW
Art Homer, Ed.
Katherine Prunty, Managing Ed.
Portland State U
Box 751
Portland, OR 97207
  (23)
  Subs: $5/2 yrs
           $3/yr
  Sing: $3

PraS
PRAIRIE SCHOONER
Bernice Slote, Ed.
201 Andrews Hall
U of Nebraska
Lincoln, NE 68588
(51:1-4)
Subs: $15/3 yrs
$10.50/2 yrs
$6/yr
Sing: $1.75

QRL
QUARTERLY REVIEW OF
LITERATURE
T. Weiss and Renêe Weiss, Eds.
26 Haslet Avenue
Princeton, NJ 08540
(-)
Back: $13/cloth
$6/paper

Qt
QUARTET
Richard Hauer Costa, Ed.
1119 Neal Pickett Drive
College Station, TX 77840
(57/58)
Subs: $10/3 yrs
$4/yr
Sing: $2

QW
*QUARTERLY WEST
Andrew Grossbardt, Ed.
Richard Iacovoni, Managing Ed.
312 Olpin Union
U of Utah
Salt Lake City, UT 84112
(2-4)
Subs: $5/3
Sing: $1.50
Back: $2

Rapp
RAPPORT
Patricia Petrosky, Ed.
James Bertolino, Guest Ed.
923 Highview St.
Pittsburgh, PA 15206
(10)
Subs: $3.50/2
Sing: $2

RemR
REMINGTON REVIEW
Dean Maskevich, Po. Ed.
Joseph A. Barbato, Fiction Ed.
505 Westfield Avenue
Elizabeth, NJ 07208
(5)
Subs: $3/yr
Sing: $2.50

RusLT
RUSSIAN LITERATURE TRI-
QUARTERLY
Carl R. Proffer
Ellendea Proffer, Eds.
Ardis Publishers
2901 Heatherway
Ann Arbor, MI 48104
(-)
Subs: $25/yr (inst.)
$15.95/yr (ind.)
$12.95/yr (stud.)
Back: Prices on request.
Cloth: Add $10/yr to above
prices.

St. AR
ST. ANDREWS REVIEW
Malcolm C. Doubles, Ed.
St. Andrews Presbyterian Col-
lege
Laurinburg, NC 28352
(-)
Subs: $4/yr
Sing: $3

Salm
SALMAGUNDI
Robert Boyers, Ed.
Skidmore College
Saratoga Springs, NY 12866
(36-38/39)
Subs: $20/2 yrs (inst.)
$10/2 yrs (ind.)
$12/yr (inst.)
$6/yr (ind.)
Sing: $2.50

Sam
*SAMISDAT
Merritt Clifton, Ed.
Box 231
Richford, VT 05476

or
Box 10
Brigham, Quebec
Canada JOE 1JO
 (51-62)
  Subs: $10/500pp.
     $5/250pp.
  Sing: Varies.

SeC
*SECOND COMING
A. D. Winans, Ed.
Box 31249
San Francisco, CA 94131
 (5:1-2)
  Subs: $5.75/yr (lib.)
     $4/yr (ind.)
  Sing: $2

SenR
SENECA REVIEW
Jim Crenner
Bob Herz, Eds.
Hobart and William Smith Colleges
Geneva, NY 14456
 (8:1-2)
  Subs: $5/yr
  Sing: $2.50

Seventies
SEVENTIES
Robert Bly, Ed.
The Seventies Press
Odin House
Madison, MN 56256
 (-)
  Subs: $3/4
  Sing: $1

SewanR
SEWANEE REVIEW
George Core, Ed.
U of the South
Sewanee, TN 37375
 (85:1-4)
  Subs: $9/yr (inst.)
     $7/yr (ind.)
  Sing: $3 (including postage)
  Back: $3.50

Shen
SHENANDOAH
James Boatwright, Ed.
Richard Howard, Po. Ed.
Box 722
Washington and Lee U
Lexington, VA 24450
 (28:2-4) (29:1)
  Subs: $8/2 yrs
     $5/yr
  Sing: $1.50
  Back: $2.50

Sky
SKYWRITING
Martin Grossman, Ed.
511 Campbell St.
Kalamazoo, MI 49007
 (-)
  Sing: $4 & $2

SmF
SMALL FARM
Jeff Daniel Marion, Ed.
Box 563
Jefferson City, TN 37760
 (6)
  Subs: $4/yr (lib.)
     $3/yr (ind.)
  Sing: $2

SmPd
SMALL POND
Napoleon St. Cyr, Ed./Pub.
10 Overland Drive
Stratford, CT 06497
 (14:1-3)
  Subs: $3.75/yr
  Sing: $1.50

Some
*SOME
Harry Greenberg, et al., Eds.
309 W. 104th St.
Apt. 9D
New York, NY 10025
 (7/8)
  Subs: $9/yr (inst.)
     $5/yr (ind.)
  Sing: $2.50

SoCaR
SOUTH CAROLINA REVIEW

Richard J. Calhoun
Robert W. Hill, Eds.
Dept. of English
Clemson U
Clemson, SC   29631
  (9:2) (10:1)
  Subs: $2/yr
  Sing: $1.50

SoDakR
SOUTH DAKOTA REVIEW
John R. Milton, Ed.
Box 111
U Exchange
U of South Dakota
Vermillion, SD   57069
  (15:1-4)
  Subs: $10/2 yrs
        $6/yr
  Sing: $2

SouthernHR
SOUTHERN HUMANITIES
REVIEW
Eugene Current-Garcia, Ed.
9088 Haley Center
Auburn U
Auburn, AL   36830
  (11:1-4)
  Subs: $6/yr
  Sing: $2

SouthernPR
SOUTHERN POETRY REVIEW
Robert Waters Grey, Ed.
Dept. of English
U of North Carolina at Char-
lotte
Charlotte, NC   28223
  (16:SI) (17:1-2)
  Subs: $4/yr
  Sing: $2

SouthernR
SOUTHERN REVIEW
Donald E. Stanford
Lewis P. Simpson
Coeditors
Drawer D
U Station
Baton Rouge, LA   70893
  (13:1-4)
  Subs: $13/3 yrs

      $9/2 yrs
      $5/yr
  Sing: $1.50

SouthwR
SOUTHWEST REVIEW
Margaret L. Hartley, Ed.
Southern Methodist U Press
Dallas, TX   75275
  (62:1-4)
  Subs: $12/3 yrs
      $9/2 yrs
      $5/yr
  Sing: $1.50

Sparrow
SPARROW
Felix and Selma Stefanile, Eds.
103 Waldron St.
West Lafayette, IN   47906
  (33-34)
  Subs: $3.50/yr (inst.)
      $3/yr (ind.)
  Sing: $1.50

Spirit
THE SPIRIT THAT MOVES US
Morty Sklar, Ed.
Box 1585
Iowa City, IA   52240
  (2:2/3)
  Subs: $3.75/yr
  Sing: $3.50 & $1

Stand
STAND
Jon Silkin, Ed.
Ed Brunner
Robert Ober, American Eds.
59 Clarendon St.
Boston, MA   02116
  Subs: 19 Haldane Terrace
      Newcastle upon Tyne
      England NE2 3AN
  (18:2-3)
  Subs: $5.50/yr
  Sing: $1.25

StoneC
*STONE COUNTRY
Judith Neeld, Ed.
20 Lorraine Road
Madison, NJ   07940

(77:1-3)
Subs: $3. 75/3
Sing: $1. 50
Back: $1. 25

Stonecloud
*STONECLOUD
Dan Ilves, Ed.
1906 Parnell Avenue
Los Angeles, CA 90025
(6)
Subs: $8. 95/3
Sing: $2. 95

SunM
SUN & MOON
Douglas Messerli
Howard Fox, Eds.
4330 Hartwick Road #418
College Park, MD 20740
(4)
Subs: $15/4 (inst.)
          $7/4 (ind.)
Sing: $3

TexQ
TEXAS QUARTERLY
Miguel González-Gerth, Ed.
Box 7517
U Station
U of Texas
Austin, TX 78712
(19:4) (20:1-4)
Subs: $4/yr
Sing: $1. 50

13thM
13th MOON
Ellen Marie Bissert, Ed.
Box 3
Inwood Station
New York, NY 10034
(3:2)
Subs: $9/3 (inst.)
          $4. 50/3 (ind.)
Sing: $1. 75

Thought
THOUGHT
Joseph E. Grennen, Ed.
Fordham U Press
U Box L
Bronx, NY 10458

(52:204-207)
Subs: $12/yr
Sing: $4

ThRiPo
*THREE RIVERS POETRY
JOURNAL
Gerald Costanzo, Ed.
Box 21
Carnegie-Mellon U
Pittsburgh, PA 15213
(10)
Subs: $5/4
Sing: $1. 50

TransR
TRANSATLANTIC REVIEW
J. F. McCrindle, Ed.
33, Ennismore Gardens,
London SW7 1AE
England
(58/59-60)
Final issue.

TriQ
TRIQUARTERLY
Elliott Anderson, Ed.
1735 Benson Avenue
Northwestern U
Evanston, IL 60201
(38-40)
Subs: $30/3 yrs
          $20/2 yrs
          $12/yr
Sing: $4. 25
Back: Prices on request.

UnmOx
UNMUZZLED OX
Michael Andre, Ed.
Box 840
Canal Street Station
New York, NY 10013
(15)
Subs: $10/12
          $8/8
          $5/4
Sing: $2. 25

US1
*U. S. 1 WORKSHEETS
US1 Poets' Cooperative, Eds.
21 Lake Drive

Roosevelt, NJ 08555
(9-10)
Subs: $4/9
Sing: $.50

UTR
UT REVIEW
Duane Locke, Ed.
U of Tampa
Tampa, FL 33606
(5:2)
Sing: $2

Vaga
VAGABOND
John Bennett, Ed.
Box 879
Ellensburg, WA 98926
(25-26)
Subs: $6
Sing: $2

VirQR
VIRGINIA QUARTERLY RE-
VIEW
Staige D. Blackford, Ed.
Gregory Orr, Po. Consultant
One West Range
Charlottesville, VA 22903
(53:1-4)
Subs: $15/3 yrs
$12/2 yrs
$7/yr
Sing: $2

Waters
*WATERS
Rocky Karlage, Ed.
Box 19341
Cincinnati, OH 45219
(5-6) (Supplement #1)
Note: Supplement published
as More Waters.
Subs: $9/8
$5/4
Sing: $2

WebR
WEBSTER REVIEW
Nancy Schapiro, Ed.
Jerred Metz, Po. Ed.
Webster College
Webster Groves, MO 63119

(3:1-4)
Subs: $5/yr
Sing: $1.25

WestHR
WESTERN HUMANITIES RE-
VIEW
Jack Garlington, Ed.
U of Utah
Salt Lake City, UT 84112
(31:1-4)
Subs: $10/yr (inst.)
$6/yr (ind.)
Sing: $2

Wind
WIND
Quentin R. Howard, Ed.
RFD Route #1
Box 809K
Pikeville, KY 41501
(24-27)
Subs: $5.50/4 (inst.)
$4.50/4 (ind.)
Sing: $1.25

WindO
THE WINDLESS ORCHARD
Robert Novak, Ed.
English Dept.
Indiana-Purdue U
Fort Wayne, IN 46805
(27-30)
Subs: $7/yr
$4/yr (stud.)
Sing: $2

Women
WOMEN/POEMS
Celia Gilbert
Pat Rabby, Eds.
23 Merriam St.
Lexington, MA 02173
(-)
Sing: $1.50

WorldO
WORLD ORDER
Firuz Kazemzadeh, Ed.
2011 Yale Station
New Haven, CT 06520
(11:2-4)
Subs: $11/2 yrs

$6/yr
Sing: $1. 60

WormR
WORMWOOD REVIEW
Marvin Malone, Ed.
Ernest Stranger, Art. Ed.
Box 8840
Stockton, CA 95204
  (65/66)
  Subs: $12/4 (patrons)
            $5. 50/4 (inst.)
            $3. 50/4 (ind.)
  Sing: $2/double issue
            $1. 50

Xa
XANADU
George William Fisher, Ed.
1704 Auburn Road
Wantagh, NY 11793
  (4)
  Subs: $2. 50/2
  Sing: $1. 50

YaleLit
THE YALE LIT
Paul Richard Foote III, Ed.
Box 243A
Yale Station
New Haven, CT 06520
  (145:3-5) (146:2) (146:4/5)
  (147:1-2)
  Missing (146:3)
  Subs: $18/3 yrs
            $14/2 yrs
            $7. 50/yr
  Sing: $2

YaleR
THE YALE REVIEW
J. E. Palmer, Ed.
250 Church St.
1902A Yale Station
New Haven, CT 06520
  (66:3-4) (67:1-2)
  Subs: $12/yr (inst.)
            $10/yr (ind.)
  Sing: $3
  Back: Prices on request.

YardR
YARDBIRD READER

Ishmael Reed, Ed.
Reed, Cannon and Johnson Co.
2140 Shattuck Ave.
Room 311
Berkeley, CA 94704
    Volume 5 (1976 Index) was
    final issue. Continued as
    Y'Bird.

YellowBR
YELLOW BRICK ROAD
Robert Matte, Jr.
Paul Cook, Eds.
Emerald City Press
107 W. 7th St.
Tempe, AZ 85281
  (8-9)
  Subs: $5. 50/3 (inst.)
            $4/3 (ind.)
  Sing: $1. 50

Zahir
ZAHIR
Diane Kruchkow, Ed.
53 Lime St.
Newburyport, MA 01950
  (-)
  Sing: $1
  Back: $2

THE INDEX

AAL, Katharyn Machan
"Five Poets Travel To and From a Poetry Reading Two Hours
     Away. " 13thM (3:2) 77, p. 66.
"Regions. " Chomo (3:3) Spr 77, p. 10.

AARON, Howard
"The Cards. " OhioR (18:2) Spr-Sum 77, p. 78.
"Cold Duck & Leftovers. " Chowder (8) Spr-Sum 77, p. 39.
"From Illness. " SouthernPR (17:2) Aut 77, p. 44.

ABBIATI, Wendy
"at 20. " Juice (4) 77.
"Poem #1. " Juice (4) 77.
"Poem #2. " Juice (4) 77.
"Poem #3. " Juice (4) 77.

ABBOTT, Anthony S.
"After Such Love. " SouthernHR (11:2) Spr 77, p. 125.

ABBOTT, Keith
"The John Calvin Tag Team Poetry Match. " LaB (9) N-D 77,
     p. 5.

ABBOTT, Nell
"'For an Old Bitch Gone in the Teeth. '" Poem (30) Jl 77,
     p. 20.
"Up around Tate. " Poem (30) Jl 77, p. 19.

ABBOTT, Stephen
"Final Bar Poem" (for Thom Gunn). Mouth (11/12) Mr-Je 77,
     p. 71.

ABDELLATIF, Najla
"I am fat but I am try to be very skiny so everybody like me. "
     AAR (27) 77, p. 122.

ABRAMS, Doug
"Ambivalence. " EnPas (5) 77, p. 36.
"The Conclusions. " Wind (24) 77, p. 3.
"Credences the Saplings Know. " Poetry (130:3) Je 77, p. 133.
"Freezes. " Poetry (130:3) Je 77, p. 132.
"Grievance. " Chelsea (36) 77, p. 54.

23

"Lengthening." SoCaR (10:1) N 77, p. 43.
"Lyric of the Essential Willow." SmPd (14:3) Aut 77, p. 19.
"The Man Who Would Not Speak." Wind (24) 77, p. 2.
"Maples in Flight." Wind (24) 77, p. 1.
"Marginal." EnPas (5) 77, p. 35.
"The Marshes." Poetry (130:3) Je 77, p. 131.
"Rigging." WebR (3:4) Aut 77, p. 59.
"Speculation." LitR (21:1) Aut 77, p. 78.
"Sunset." EnPas (5) 77, p. 37.
"Wind Factors." DeKalb (10:2) Wint 77, p. 1.

ABRAMS, Mark
"Lovers." Mouth (11/12) Mr-Je 77, p. 86.
"Small Pains." Mouth (11/12) Mr-Je 77, p. 88.

ABRAMS, Sam
"The Laws." ParisR (71) Aut 77, p. 82.

ABREU, Enriquillo Rojas
"God" (tr. by Edith Rusconi Kaltovich). WebR (3:4) Aut 77, p. 15.

ABSHER, Tom
"Resting place." Ploughs (3:3/4) 77, p. 150.

ACKER, Paul
"A Nordic History." DenQ (12:2) Sum 77, p. 344.

ACKERMAN, Diane
"Digging Holes." RemR (5) 77, p. 62.
"Insomnia." RemR (5) 77, p. 65.
"Lakebed." NewL (43:4) Sum 77, p. 38.
"New House." Iowa (8:3) Sum 77, p. 31.
"Romancing the Grey Horse." CornellR (1) Spr 77, p. 72.
"Song of the Banyan Tree." RemR (5) 77, p. 64.
"Song of the Trilobite." RemR (5) 77, p. 63.
"Sweep Me through Your Many-Chambered Heart." NewL (43:4) Sum 77, p. 39.
"Vespers." PoNow (14/18) 77, p. 2.

ACKERSON, Duane
"DNA." Drag (16) 77.
"Full Moon." PoNow (14/18) 77, p. 3.
"The Glass Blower." WebR (3:1) Wint 77, p. 50.
"Mechanized Farming." Drag (16) 77.
"The Starman." Drag (16) 77.
"Train Poem." Drag (16) 77.

ACKROYD, Peter
"'The Great Sun....'" PartR (44:2) 77, p. 263.
"On Any Kind of Novel." PartR (44:2) 77, p. 264.
"'There Are So Many....'" PartR (44:2) 77, p. 262.

ACUFF, Gale G. , Jr.
"Appling. " Poem (29) Mr 77, p. 57.
"Fresh Skin. " Poem (29) Mr 77, p. 59.
"A Lot of Beef. " Poem (29) Mr 77, p. 60.
"Touch of Life. " Poem (29) Mr 77, p. 58.

ADAME, Leonard
"black and white. " AmerPoR (6:3) My-Je 77, p. 29.
"el dolor de invisibilidad. " AmerPoR (6:3) My-Je 77, p. 29.
"la verdad" (for Neruda). AmerPoR (6:3) My-Je 77, p. 29.

ADAMO, Ralph
"The Child's Room. " FourQt (26:2) Wint 77, p. 22.
"Homecoming" (for G.). SoCaR (10:1) N 77, p. 88.
"Human Love. " Falcon (15) 77, p. 19.

ADAMS, Betsy
"Celebration. " Stonecloud (6) 76, p. 144.
"Dear Thumping Bunny: A Maudlin Poem" (This poem is dedi-
    cated to Deborah Richardson). Stonecloud (6) 76, p. 126.
"Making the Path. " EnPas (4) 76, p. 33.
"The Visit. " GRR (8:1/2) 77, p. 142.

ADAMS, David J.
"the visit. " PoetL (72:2) Sum 77, p. 70.

ADAMS, Hazard
"Uncle Sam Spends an Evening at Home. " NewOR (5:3) 77,
    p. 201.
"Why There Are Birds. " NewOR (5:3) 77, p. 202.

ADAMS, Jeanette
"Long Distance Laughter. " Nimrod (21:2/22:1) 77, p. 1.

ADAMS, Michael L.
"Centerfield. " BlackF (2:1) Wint 77-78, p. 24.

ADAMSON, David
"The Traveler. " WestHR (31:2) Spr 77, p. 144.

ADCOCK, Betty
"Joel. " SouthernPR (17:2) Aut 77, p. 5.
"Spell. " SouthernPR (17:1) Spr 77, p. 53.
"Surviving the Wreck. " SouthernPR (16:SI) 77, p. 7.
"Twentieth Anniversary. " SouthernPR (17:2) Aut 77, p. 6.

ADCOCK, Edgar H. , Jr.
"Anniversary Curtain. " CarolQ (29:1) Wint 77, p. 73.

ADDIEGO, John
"Mars/Color and Afterimage. " Drag (16) 77.

ADLER, Jeremy
 "Ea. Lacrimae. " GRR (8:1/2) 77, p. 109.
 "In the Teeth of the World. " GRR (8:3) 77, p. 173.
 "The Line and the Circle. " GRR (8:1/2) 77, p. 110.
 from Venetian Fireworks: "And Here We Are. " GRR (8:3) 77,
   p. 167.
 from Venetian Fireworks: "For These Sights Are Almost Her
   Touch. " GRR (8:3) 77, p. 169.
 from Venetian Fireworks: "In a Pair of Arms. " GRR (8:3) 77,
   p. 171.
 from Venetian Fireworks: "Why Not of You?" GRR (8:3) 77,
   p. 165.

ADONIS (Ali Ahmed Said)
 "Elegy in Exile" (tr. by Samuel Hazo). Mund (10:1) 77, p. 182.

ADY, Endry
 "Psalm of Night" (tr. by Leslie Kelen). QW (3) Spr-Sum 77,
   p. 60.
 "Someone Has Again Remembered" (tr. by Leslie Kelen). QW
   (3) Spr-Sum 77, p. 61.

AGAJANIAN, Shaakeh
 "Existential Humanism Redefined. " LitR (20:3) Spr 77, p. 313.
 "Peacock in a Mirror. " LitR (20:3) Spr 77, p. 312.

AGVENT, Charles
 "Menu. " SmPd (14:1) Wint 77, p. 29.

AHARONI, Ada
 "The Massacre in Kiryat Shmona. " Stonecloud (6) 76, p. 128.
 "On Yom Kippur" (tr. of Yehuda Amichai). WebR (3:4) Aut 77,
   p. 64.
 "To a Captain in Sinai. " Stonecloud (6) 76, p. 129.

AIDOO, Ama Ata
 "As the Dust Begins to Settle. " Nimrod (21:2/22:1) 77, p. 5.
 "Regrets. " Nimrod (21:2/22:1) 77, p. 2.

AIKEN, William
 "To a Greek Astronaut. " NewRena (9) F 77, p. 65.

AIKIN, James Douglas
 "Barnaby Darksteeple Meets the Porn Queen. " CalQ (11/12) Wint-
   Spr 77, p. 154.
 "Flung Down. " Icarus (5:1) Spr 77, p. 18.
 "Light on Pools. " StoneC (77:2) My 77, p. 24.
 "Two Ghost Haiku. " StoneC (77:3) S 77, p. 25.

AJAY, Stephen
 "'Abacadabra. '" PoNow (14/18) 77, p. 3.
 "The Ambush. " CimR (34) Ja 76, p. 52.
 "The Measurers. " PoNow (14/18) 77, p. 3.
 "Winter Delicacies. " Chelsea (36) 77, p. 20.

AKAHITO, Yamabe no
  "At Court" (tr. by Graeme Wilson). DenQ (12:2) Sum 77, p. 374.

AKHMADULINA, Bella
  "I Swear" (tr. by Elaine Feinstein). Stand (18:3) 77, p. 17.

AKHMATOVA, Anna
  "Apology" (tr. by Marianne Bogojavlensky and Sam Bradley).
      WebR (3:4) Aut 77, p. 14.
  "That Evening" (tr. by Marianne Bogojavlensky and Sam Bradley).
      WebR (3:4) Aut 77, p. 13.

AKIKO, Yosano
  "The Flesh" (tr. by Graeme Wilson). WestHR (31:3) Sum 77,
      p. 214.
  "White Bird" (tr. by Graeme Wilson). TexQ (20:4) Wint 77,
      p. 146.

AKMAKJIAN, Alan P.
  "In a Lone Apple Orchard. " Wind (25) 77, p. 1.
  "The Tale of Tom Spears. " Wind (25) 77, p. 1.
  "This Teeming Countryside. " Poem (31) N 77, p. 47.

ALBERTI, Rafael
  "The Angel of Mystery" (tr. by Marty Paul and Jose A. Elgorr-
      iaga). PortR (23) 77, p. 80.
  from Entre el Clavel y la Espada: (29) (tr. by Marty Paul and
      Jose A. Elgorriaga). PortR (23) 77, p. 81.

ALBRECHT, Elizabeth
  "For Mr. Rampal. " Wind (27) 77, p. 1.
  "Something Missing on the Left" (for Lucy Orozco). Wind (27)
      77, p. 1.

ALCALAY, Ammiel W.
  "Blues. " SunM (4) Aut 77, p. 91.
  "Charles River" (for Jack Spicer). SunM (4) Aut 77, p. 90.
  "Old Flame. " SunM (4) Aut 77, p. 92.

ALCOSSER, Sandra
  "The Plant Ladies. " ParisR (71) Aut 77, p. 49.
  "Thief. " ParisR (71) Aut 77, p. 51.

ALDAN, Daisy
  "The Abyss. " LaB (5) Ja 77, p. 5.
  from Break-Through: "to dissipate the darkness of matter. "
      LaB (5) Ja 77, p. 6.
  "In a Frozen Moment. " LaB (5) Ja 77, p. 9.
  "In Seclusion. " LaB (8) Jl-Ag 77, p. 5.
  "mercurial. " LaB (5) Ja 77, p. 8.
  "No Longer Will I Close an Opaque Door. " LaB (5) Ja 77, p. 8.
  "Of Arrows and Vectors. " LaB (5) Ja 77, p. 10.
  "transmutation of glacial ice. " LaB (5) Ja 77, p. 7.

ALDERDICE, Eve
"The Bus Back." Wind (26) 77, p. 1.
"Long Evenings." Wind (26) 77, p. 1.
"Med Student." Wind (26) 77, p. 2.

ALDRIDGE, Richard
"Markings." PoNow (14/18) 77, p. 3.

ALEGRÍA, Claribel
from Flowers from the Volcano: "I Am Root" (tr. by Carolyn
    Forché). Chowder (9) Aut-Wint 77, p. 60.
from Flowers from the Volcano: "Santa Ana in the Dark" (tr.
    by Carolyn Forché). Chowder (9) Aut-Wint 77, p. 56.
from Flowers from the Volcano: "Sorrow" (To Roque Dalton) (tr.
    by Carolyn Forché). Chowder (9) Aut-Wint 77, p. 48.

ALEGRIA, Fernando
"The Fall of the Bishop" (tr. by Stephen Kessler). MontG (6)
    Aut 77, p. 46.

ALEXANDER, L. P.
"Checkmate." CarouselQ (2:2) Aut 77, p. 13.

ALEXANDER, Paul
"Near Summer." SouthernPR (17:1) Spr 77, p. 16.

ALIESAN, Jody
"Among the Malekulans." CalQ (11/12) Wint-Spr 77, p. 122.
"Islanders." CalQ (11/12) Wint-Spr 77, p. 123.

ALIGER, Margarita
"House in Meudon" (tr. by Elaine Feinstein). Stand (18:3) 77,
    p. 14.

ALKES, Joey
"I Hold On to What I Can Touch about Being Alive." PoetL
    (77:2) Sum 77, p. 74.

ALKMAN
Eleven fragments (tr. by Henry R. Davies). DenQ (11:4) Wint 77,
    p. 91.

ALLARDT, Linda
"Baggage." PoetryNW (18:4) Wint 77-78, p. 30.
"Grandpa's Guitar." HiramPoR (22) Aut-Wint 77, p. 5.
"Latecomers." PoetryNW (18:4) Wint 77-78, p. 30.
"Opening Day, Easter Week." PoetryNW (18:1) Spr 77, p. 31.
"Touching the Matter of Seed." PoetryNW (18:1) Spr 77, p. 31.

ALLEN, Dick
"The Adequate Poem." Drag (16) 77.
"At Dusk, Along the Interstate." NoAmR (262:2) Sum 77, p. 6.
"Midlife." WestHR (31:3) Sum 77, p. 243.

"The Mystery" (For Prof. Israel Kapstein). WestHR (31:3) Sum 77, p. 263.
"Variation on a Theme by Ernest Hemingway." ParisR (70) Sum 77, p. 28.

ALLEN, Gilbert
from The Book of Shadows: "The Last Night: II. Dusk." RemR (5) 77, p. 6.
"Friday." KanQ (9:1) Wint 77, p. 103.
"Loss." Shen (28:4) Sum 77, p. 54.
"Winter Dream: The New Suburb." RemR (5) 77, p. 5.

ALLEN, Jackson
"Foreigners." LaB (6) Mr 77, p. 7.
"Garden Varieties." LaB (8) Jl-Ag 77, p. 6.
"Minestrone." LaB (6) Mr 77, p. 6.
"Socrate." LaB (6) Mr 77, p. 6.
"Watermark." LaB (6) Mr 77, p. 5.

ALLEN, James
"Bicycle Rider and Shadows against Stopped Traffic." SouthernPR (18:2) Aut 77, p. 48.
"What Goes Up Must." GRR (8:1/2) 77, p. 131.

ALLEN, Michael
"After Planting" (for Virginia). PraS (51:2) Sum 77, p. 192.
"Rain" (to Anna Cisne). SoDakR (15:2) Sum 77, p. 102.

ALLEN, Robert
"Motor." Rapp (10) 77, p. 45.

ALLEN, Samuel
"In the Temple." Nimrod (21:2/22:1) 77, p. 314.

ALLISON, John
"Gardening." Esq (88:5) N 77, p. 34.
"Night Animal." Poetry (131:2) N 77, p. 88.

ALLISTON, April
"One Lover to Another's Lover." YaleLit (146:4/5) 77, p. 52.

ALLMAN, Eileen Jorge
"Life Tales." Gra (12) 77.

ALLMAN, John
"Her Repertory." KanQ (9:3) Sum 77, p. 83.
"Nana's Visit." PoetryNW (18:2) Sum 77, p. 19.
"You Owe Them Everything." PoetryNW (18:2) Sum 77, p. 20.

ALMON, Bert
"Collisions." CalQ (11/12) Wint-Spr 77, p. 126.
"The Third Symbol" (for Robert Burlingame). DacTerr (14) Spr-Sum 77, p. 27.

ALONSO, Nina Rubinstein
"Letter to Heather." Ploughs (3:3/4) 77, p. 156.

ALPERS, Richard
"Does Anal Intercourse Hurt?" (Poem in 3 parts for Jim Lowe).
Mouth (13) D 77, p. 45.
"My Name Isn't Carl." Mouth (13) D 77, p. 44.

ALPERT, Barry
"Chairs" (via Brecht). LaB (8) Jl-Ag 77, p. 9.
"More Chairs" (homage à George Brecht). LaB (8) Jl-Ag 77,
p. 10.
"Sound Track" (via Ken Jacobs). LaB (8) Jl-Ag 77, p. 11.

ALSUP, Doris Louise
"Touch of Love." LadHJ (94:11) N 77, p. 26.

ALTER, Robert
"By the Waters of Babylon" (tr. of Amir Gilboa). TriQ (39) Spr
77, p. 268.

ALVAREZ, A.
"Closing Time." AmerR (26) N 77, p. 172.

ALVIS, John
"A Brief for Lord Frog." TexQ (20:1) Spr 77, p. 43.
"Esau." TexQ (20:1) Spr 77, p. 44.
"Mustard." TexQ (20:1) Spr 77, p. 45.

ALWAN, Ameen
"Childhood." MassR (18:1) Spr 77, p. 32.
"The Island." TexQ (20:4) Wint 77, p. 143.
"Kelly." MichQR (16:3) Sum 77, p. 305.
"A Mexican Couple in the Park." TexQ (20:4) Wint 77, p. 118.
"Musical Chairs." MichQR (16:3) Sum 77, p. 306.
"Peaches Are Red and Yellow." MassR (18:1) Spr 77, p. 33.
"Winter Afternoons with Children." TexQ (20:4) Wint 77, p. 129.

ALZHEIMER, James
"A Need for Symmetry." DacTerr (14) Spr-Sum 77, p. 70.

AMADEO, Jo Ann
"Empty." CarouselQ (2:3) Wint 77, p. 21.

AMATO, Michael
"Apt. 201." Wind (26) 77, p. 61.

AMER, Sandy
"Interim." Wind (27) 77, p. 1.

AMES, Bernice
"The Flicker Grooms Like All of Us." KanQ (9:1) Wint 77, p.
22.

"In a Cathedral." KanQ (9:1) Wint 77, p. 22.
"Manhattan Exposures." Wind (25) 77, p. 4.
"Never Enough." Wind (25) 77, p. 3.
"On Park Avenue." PoNow (14/18) 77, p. 4.
"One Way to Figure." Wind (25) 77, p. 2.
"Return to Mercer County." PoNow (14/18) 77, p. 4.
"Walking with Amanda (a Chesapeake Retriever)." Wind (25) 77,
    p. 2.

AMICHAI, Yehuda
"All the Generations before Me" (tr. by Robert Friend). TriQ
    (39) Spr 77, p. 250.
"Here" (tr. by Ruth Nevo). TriQ (39) Spr 77, p. 246.
"Lament" (tr. by Ted Hughes). TriQ (39) Spr 77, p. 249.
"My Soul" (tr. by Ted Hughes). TriQ (39) Spr 77, p. 248.
"The old ice factory" (tr. by Bernard Knieger). TriQ (39) Spr
    77, p. 246.
"On Yom Kippur" (tr. by Ada Aharoni). WebR (3:4) Aut 77,
    p. 64.
"Savage Memories" (tr. by Robert Friend). TriQ (39) Spr 77,
    p. 248.
"The Sweet Breakdown of Abigail" (tr. by Ted Hughes). TriQ
    (39) Spr 77, p. 249.
Travels of a Latter-Day Benjamin of Tudela (tr. by Ruth Nevo).
    WebR (3:3) Sum 77. Entire issue.
"We shall live forever" (tr. by Ruth Nevo). TriQ (39) Spr 77,
    p. 244.
"When I was a child" (tr. by Ruth Nevo). TriQ (39) Spr 77,
    p. 245.

AMMONS, A. R.
"By the Boulder Cluster the Wind." Hudson (30:3) Aut 77, p.
    371.
"Continuing." Iowa (8:2) Spr 77, p. 63.
"Hard Lard." CornellR (1) Spr 77, p. 69.
"The Grave Is." ChiR (28:4) Spr 77, p. 12.
"Man's Nature." YaleR (66:3) Spr 77, p. 398.
"My Father, I Hollow for You." Iowa (8:1) Wint 77, p. 86.
"Neighbors." SouthernPR (16:SI) 77, p. 8.
"On Walks I Go a Long Way Along." Madem (83:6) Je 77, p. 54.
"The Perfect Journey Is." Madem (83:6) Je 77, p. 54.
"Significances." Nat (224:11) 19 Mr 77, p. 342.
"Summer Place." Hudson (30:2) Sum 77, p. 173.
"When I Was Young the Silk." Iowa (8:1) Wint 77, p. 85.

AMOROSI, Ray
"Note in a Sanitorium." NewL (43:4) Sum 77, p. 58.
"What I Know." NewL (43:4) Sum 77, p. 59.

AN Chong
"Magic Mountain" (tr. by Graeme Wilson). WestHR (31:3) Sum
    77, p. 211.

ANANIA, Michael
"Aesthetique du Râle." Poetry (129:6) Mr 77, p. 337.
"Tracings." PoNow (14/18) 77, p. 4.

ANDAY, Melih Cevdet
"In Those Small Lakes" (tr. by Talat Halman and Brian Swann).
WebR (3:4) Aut 77, p. 50.
"A Sumerian Tablet" (tr. by Talat Halman and Brian Swann).
WebR (3:4) Aut 77, p. 51.

ANDEREGG, Trudi
"Snowdrops" (tr. of Robert Walser, w. Tom Whalen). ParisR
(71) Aut 77, p. 138.

ANDERS, S.
"Crazy Lady Poem." CimR (39) Ap 77, p. 57.

ANDERSEN, Tim
"The Truck That Brought Soft Water to Our House." PoNow
(14/18) 77, p. 5.

ANDERSON, Carolyn
"Archangel." CalQ (11/12) Wint-Spr 77, p. 46.
"Dead Center." CalQ (11/12) Wint-Spr 77, p. 141.

ANDERSON, David
"About My Body 2." Pig (3) 77, p. 40.

ANDERSON, Forrest
"What Other Realms Await the Adventurer." StoneC (77:1) F 77,
p. 5.

ANDERSON, Jack
"Astounding Tales." PoNow (14/18) 77, p. 199.
"Begins." ThRiPo (10) 77, p. 29.
"The Caller." PoNow (14/18) 77, p. 5.
"Dolls." Ploughs (3:3/4) 77, p. 125.
"Growing Children." PoNow (14/18) 77, p. 6.
"Fetishist." Mouth (11/12) Mr-Je 77, p. 83.
"The Lady with the Glass." Shen (28:3) Spr 77, p. 97.
"Little Poems from Somewhere Else." Falcon (14) 77, p. 34.
"Notes for an Ode to Pubic Hair." Mouth (11/12) Mr-Je 77,
p. 25.
"Second Sight." Some (7/8) 76.
"Toward the Liberation of the Left Hand." Some (7/8) 76.
"Workings of the Mind." Mouth (11/12) Mr-Je 77, p. 84.

ANDERSON, Ken
"Haiku." DeKalb (10:2) Wint 77, p. 4.

ANDERSON, Mai
"Family." GRR (8:3) 77, p. 217.

ANDERSON, Margaret
"The Scarecrows." Drag (16) 77.

ANDERSON, Mary Marta
"Beating a Fast Tattoo." Ploughs (4:1) 77, p. 151.

ANDERSON, Nat
"Fish Wife." SouthernPR (16:SI) 77, p. 9.

ANDERSON, Robert P.
"Reaping." YellowBR (8) 77, p. 11.

ANDERSON, Stanley P.
"Horizontal Identity." KanQ (9:3) Sum 77, p. 43.

ANDERSON, Terryl L.
"Angles and Angels." ChrC (94:41) 14 D 77, p. 1162.
"Ballad of the Church Bazaar." ChrC (94:15) 27 Ap 77, p. 397.

ANDERSON, Wendell
"Why Keep the Dream When You Can Have the Poem."
    CarouselQ (2:2) Aut 77, p. 10.

ANDREWS, Bruce
"Jumpin' Punkins." Hills (4) 77.
"Key Largo." Hills (4) 77.
"Love Songs & Other Poems (A Selection)." LaB (6) Mr 77,
    p. 8.
from Love Songs: (169). LaB (9) N-D 77, p. 7.
from Love Songs: (169B). LaB (9) N-D 77, p. 8.
from Love Songs: (170). LaB (9) N-D 77, p. 9.
from Love Songs: (171). LaB (9) N-D 77, p. 12.
"Narragansett." Hills (4) 77.
"That He Floated." Hills (4) 77.
"Who Where What Why When." Hills (4) 77.

ANDREWS, Michael
"Camp Was Fun." Wind (25) 77, p. 6.
"The Mullah & the Pusher." Stonecloud (6) 76, p. 28.
"The Sunset at the End of the Freeway." Wind (25) 77, p. 6.

ANDREWS, Michael C.
"A Child's Poem." CarouselQ (2:1) Spr 77, p. 10.
"The Fear of Darkness." CarouselQ (2:1) Spr 77, p. 9.
"String." CarouselQ (2:1) Spr 77, p. 10.

ANDREWS, Miriam
"The Mama Doll." PoetL (72:2) Sum 77, p. 55.

ANDREWS, Owen
"Folklore & Mythology." HarvAd (110:5) My 77, p. 17.
"Out on the River, Solace Comes Like Somersaults." HarvAd
    (111:2) D 77, p. 10.

"People in This Valley. " HarvAd (111:2) D 77, p. 17.

ANDRIEKUS, Leonardas
"Night Watch" (tr. by Jonas Zdanys). Rapp (10) 77, p. 13.
"Reed Grass" (tr. by Jonas Zdanys). Rapp (10) 77, p. 11.
"Rivers" (tr. by Jonas Zdanys). Rapp (10) 77, p. 14.
"The Window" (tr. by Jonas Zdanys). Rapp (10) 77, p. 12.

ANGEL, Ralph
"Falling behind, I was trying to hold on. " PartR (44:3) 77, p.
400.

ANGELL, Roger
"Greetings, Friends!" NewYorker (53:45) 26 D 77, p. 25.

ANGLO-SAXON
"The Wanderer" (tr. by Jeffrey Hopkins). VirQR (53:2) Spr 77,
p. 284.

ANGOFF, Charles
"One in Infinity. " KanQ (9:3) Sum 77, p. 42.

ANGUIANO, Carla
"Poetry. " SeC (5:2) 78, p. 37.

ANNAS, Pam
"Rain Dream. " Chomo (4:2) Aut-Wint 77, p. 30.

ANONYMOUS
"Aging" (tr. by Graeme Wilson). DenQ (11:4) Wint 77, p. 173.
"Alba" (tr. by Graeme Wilson). DenQ (12:2) Sum 77, p. 392.
"Apricot Wine" (tr. by Graeme Wilson). DenQ (12:2) Sum 77,
p. 305.
"Assignation" (tr. by Graeme Wilson). DenQ (12:2) Sum 77,
p. 370.
"Autumn Nights" (tr. by Graeme Wilson). DenQ (12:2) Sum 77,
p. 373.
"Bell in the Mountain Mist" (tr. by Graeme Wilson). TexQ
(20:4) Wint 77, p. 145.
"Blest Is the Man Whose Bowels Move. " ChrC (94:43) 28 D 77,
p. 1239.
"Blown" (tr. by Graeme Wilson). DenQ (12:2) Sum 77, p. 370.
from The Book of Poetry: "Gentle Girl" (tr. by Christopher
Howell). PortR (23) 77, p. 77.
"The boy tripped down the steps. " YaleLit (145:4) 77, p. 14.
"Buddhism" (tr. by Graeme Wilson). DenQ (12:2) Sum 77, p.
357.
"Cat" (tr. by Graeme Wilson). DenQ (12:2) Sum 77, p. 300.
"Cat's-Meat Nell. " Playb (24:2) F 77, p. 131.
"A clock dreams of turning to midnight. " AAR (27) 77, p. 116.
"The Condition of Man" (tr. by Graeme Wilson). DenQ (12:2)
Sum 77, p. 299.
"Cow" (tr. by Graeme Wilson). DenQ (12:2) Sum 77, p. 292.

"Cunning Wife." Playb (24:9) S 77, p. 163.
"Curse" (tr. by Graeme Wilson). TexQ (20:4) Wint 77, p. 147.
"Damages" (tr. by Graeme Wilson). DenQ (12:2) Sum 77, p. 373.
"Dan." AAR (27) 77, p. 111.
"(Deja-Vu)." AAR (27) 77, p. 111.
from De planctu naturae: "Alanus de insulis" (tr. by George
     Economou). Hand (1) 77, p. 47.
"Dirge for Heng Chien" (tr. by Graeme Wilson). WestHR (31:3)
     Sum 77, p. 207.
"Doll" (tr. by Graeme Wilson). DenQ (12:2) Sum 77, p. 367.
"Drowned Man" (tr. by Graeme Wilson). DenQ (11:4) Wint 77,
     p. 174.
"Evening darkens until" (tr. by Kenneth Rexroth). Agni (7) 77,
     p. 110.
"Faith Road." YaleLit (145:5) 77, p. 25.
"Fan" (tr. by Graeme Wilson). DenQ (12:2) Sum 77, p. 301.
"Fishing Lanterns" (tr. by Graeme Wilson). DenQ (11:4) Wint 77,
     p. 167.
"The Flea Shooter." Playb (24:2) F 77, p. 131.
"Girl in the Rain" (tr. by Graeme Wilson). VirQR (53:3) Sum 77,
     p. 454.
"Going This Path" (tr. by J. P. Seaton). CarolQ (29:2) Spr-Sum
     77, p. 120.
"Gossip" (tr. by Graeme Wilson). DenQ (11:4) Wint 77, p. 167.
"Habit" (tr. by Graeme Wilson). DenQ (12:2) Sum 77, p. 391.
"Hands" (tr. by Graeme Wilson). DenQ (11:4) Wint 77, p. 164.
"I am a tiger and if anybody." AAR (27) 77, p. 122.
"I once dreamed." AAR (27) 77, p. 124.
"I set off to join the border guards" (tr. by Janine Beichman).
     DenQ (12:2) Sum 77, p. 106.
"I, Will, not go gentle." YaleLit (145:5) 77, p. 27.
"In Case" (tr. by Graeme Wilson). DenQ (12:2) Sum 77, p. 397.
"In the summer, by the river" (tr. by Kenneth Rexroth). Falcon
     (14) 77, p. 92.
"Invitation" (tr. by Graeme Wilson). DenQ (12:2) Sum 77, p. 375.
"It's hard to be a good sport." AAR (27) 77, p. 98.
"Kamunabi" (tr. by Graeme Wilson). DenQ (11:4) Wint 77, p.
     165.
"Karna and Kunti" (tr. by P. Lal). DenQ (12:2) Sum 77, p. 329.
"Kisaeng" (tr. by Graeme Wilson). DenQ (12:2) Sum 77, p. 301.
"Lake" (tr. by Graeme Wilson). DenQ (12:2) Sum 77, p. 58.
"Lament" (tr. by Graeme Wilson). DenQ (11:4) Wint 77, p. 170.
"Last Night" (tr. by Graeme Wilson). DenQ (12:2) Sum 77, p.
     303.
"Last Night's Work" (tr. by Graeme Wilson). DenQ (12:2) Sum
     77, p. 370.
"Letter" (tr. by Graeme Wilson). DenQ (12:2) Sum 77, p. 297.
"A Letter." Playb (24:5) My 77, p. 151.
"Love" (tr. by Graeme Wilson). DenQ (12:2) Sum 77, p. 368.
"Love" (tr. by Graeme Wilson). VirQR (53:3) Sum 77, p. 452.
"Madness on Hershey Highway." YaleLit (145:4) 77, back cover.
"Mister Moon" (tr. by Graeme Wilson). TexQ (20:4) Wint 77,
     p. 144.

"Moonlight" (tr. by Graeme Wilson). DenQ (12:2) Sum 77, p. 373.

"Moss Green Pathway" (tr. by Graeme Wilson). DenQ (12:2) Sum 77, p. 375.

"My lover I have lost" (tr. by Kenneth Rexroth). Falcon (14) 77, p. 91.

"Neighbourliness" (tr. by Graeme Wilson). DenQ (11:4) Wint 77, p. 169.

"Nightmare!" AAR (27) 77, p. 110.

"Nitwit Love" (tr. by Graeme Wilson). DenQ (12:2) Sum 77, p. 377.

"No Hypocrite." Playb (24:5) My 77, p. 151.

"On nights when the evening mist" (tr. by Janine Beichman). DenQ (12:2) Sum 77, p. 106.

"One That Got Away" (tr. by Graeme Wilson). DenQ (12:2) Sum 77, p. 371.

"Orange Tree" (tr. by Graeme Wilson). DenQ (11:4) Wint 77, p. 175.

"The Palace Road" (tr. by Graeme Wilson). DenQ (12:2) Sum 77, p. 371.

"Pony" (tr. by Graeme Wilson). DenQ (12:2) Sum 77, p. 371.

"Prayer at Mitarashi" (tr. by Graeme Wilson). WestHR (31:1) Wint 77, p. 57.

"Prayer for Calling the Eagles" (tr. by Carol Rubenstein). Hand (1) 77, p. 162.

"Priest of the Mountain Temple" (tr. by Graeme Wilson). DenQ (12:2) Sum 77, p. 63.

"Rainbow" (tr. by Graeme Wilson). DenQ (12:2) Sum 77, p. 369.

"Real World" (tr. by Graeme Wilson). DenQ (12:2) Sum 77, p. 60.

"Recall" (tr. by Graeme Wilson). DenQ (11:4) Wint 77, p. 173.

"Red Skirt" (tr. by Graeme Wilson). DenQ (11:4) Wint 77, p. 168.

"Riding for a Fall" (tr. by Graeme Wilson). DenQ (12:2) Sum 77, p. 378.

"Rite of Naming the Child" (tr. by Carol Rubenstein). Hand (1) 77, p. 43.

"Runaway" (tr. by Graeme Wilson). DenQ (12:2) Sum 77, p. 393.

"Self Discovery" (tr. by Graeme Wilson). WestHR (31:3) Sum 77, p. 210.

"Shrimp Sleep" (tr. by Graeme Wilson). DenQ (12:2) Sum 77, p. 295.

"Slander" (tr. by Graeme Wilson). DenQ (12:2) Sum 77, p. 369.

"Some people go through life without ever being touched, without ever." AmerPoR (6:2) Mr-Ap 77, p. 33.

"Song of the Prison." NewYRB (24:19) 24 N 77, p. 57.

"Sparrows" (tr. by Graeme Wilson). DenQ (12:2) Sum 77, p. 396.

"Spell to Speed Childbirth" (tr. by Carol Rubenstein). Hand (1) 77, p. 43.

"Spring Snow" (tr. by Graeme Wilson). DenQ (12:2) Sum 77, p. 374.

"Striving." YaleLit (146:2) 77, p. 16.

"Summer Grass" (tr. by Graeme Wilson). DenQ (12:2) Sum 77,
  p. 375.
"Sundown" (tr. by Graeme Wilson). DenQ (12:2) Sum 77, p. 310.
"Sunrise" (tr. by Graeme Wilson). DenQ (12:2) Sum 77, p. 366.
"Sweets for Sale." Playb (24:5) My 77, p. 151.
"Tamana" (tr. by Graeme Wilson). DenQ (12:2) Sum 77, p. 376.
"There's Somebody Coming." Playb (24:5) My 77, p. 151.
"Troth" (tr. by Graeme Wilson). DenQ (12:2) Sum 77, p. 369.
"Truth Is a Mountain" (tr. by Graeme Wilson). DenQ (12:2) Sum
  77, p. 48.
"Waiting" (tr. by Graeme Wilson). DenQ (11:4) Wint 77, p. 166.
"What wattage is the lightbulb? A bald head." YaleLit (145:4)
  77, p. 12.
"Wildest Dream" (tr. by Graeme Wilson). DenQ (12:2) Sum 77,
  p. 372.
"World Enough" (tr. by Graeme Wilson). TexQ (20:4) Wint 77,
  p. 148.
"Zen Teaching" (tr. by Graeme Wilson). DenQ (12:2) Sum 77,
  p. 58.

ANSON, John S.
"Clouds." Poetry (130:3) D 77, p. 145.
"Early Frost." Poetry (130:3) D 77, p. 146.
"I Know the Star." Poetry (130:3) D 77, p. 145.
"Mothwings." Poetry (130:3) D 77, p. 146.

ANTHONY, Donald B.
"The Transfer." CarouselQ (2:3) Wint 77, p. 1.
"Virginia Yes and No." CarouselQ (2:3) Wint 77, p. 1.

ANTHONY, Steven
"Eagle to Eagle." Mouth (13) D 77, p. 85.

ANTLER
"The Dark Inside a Life." Chelsea (36) 77, p. 64.
"Grace." Chelsea (36) 77, p. 60.
"Rexroth as He Appeared to Exist March 24, 1968, 5:15-9:00
  P. M." Chelsea (36) 77, p. 63.

ANTONICELLI, Theresa
"Genesis." HangL (30) Sum 77, p. 3.

ANTONYCH, Bohdan
"The House Beyond the Star" (tr. by Mark Rudman). Bound
  (5:2) Wint 77, p. 601.
"Houses" (tr. by Mark Rudman). Bound (5:2) Wint 77, p. 600.
"Monumental Landscape" (tr. by Paul Nemser). Bound (5:2)
  Wint 77, p. 604.
"Polaria" (tr. by Paul Nemser). Bound (5:2) Wint 77, p. 603.
"Ritual Dance" (tr. by Paul Nemser). Bound (5:2) Wint 77,
  p. 604.
"Sunset" (tr. by Mark Rudman). Bound (5:2) Wint 77, p. 602.
"To Those Who Have Been Executed" (tr. by Paul Nemser).
  Bound (5:2) Wint 77, p. 603.

"A Village" (tr. by Mark Rudman). Bound (5:2) Wint 77, p. 600.
"Winter" (tr. by Mark Rudman). Bound (5:2) Wint 77, p. 602.

ANYIDOHO, Kofi
"Mythmaker." Nimrod (21:2/22:1) 77, p. 10.

APPEL, Allan
"The Ticket." SoDakR (15:4) Wint 77-78, p. 81.

APPEL, Dori
"Spring Saturday." YellowBR (9) 77, p. 28.

APPELBAUM, Anita
"Ending." LadHJ (94:8) Ag 77, p. 120.

APPELTON, Sarah
"never separate again the poem." Hand (1) 77, p. 24.
"Propitiation to the Creation Dance--Offered to the Dancer."
    Hand (1) 77, p. 24.

APPLEWHITE, James
"Eastern N.C. October." PoNow (14/18) 77, p. 6.
"An Erased Window." PoNow (14/18) 77, p. 6.
"The River, Later." SouthernPR (16:SI) 77, p. 10.
"This Years Models." PoNow (14/18) 77, p. 7.
"Tobacco Men." Atl (240:4) O 77, p. 69.

ARBUCKLE, Chris
"As the wind makes whispering whistle." AmerPoR (6:2) Mr-Ap
    77, p. 34.
"Poetry is like inner peace to people. To let people." AmerPoR
    (6:2) Mr-Ap 77, p. 33.

ARDAYNE, Julia Collins
"Stranger in a Crowd." LadHJ (94:4) Ap 77, p. 78.

ARGÜELLES, Ivan
"Celestina." Kayak (46) O 77, p. 42.
"Eurydice." LaB (7) My 77, p. 5.
"In Search of Dido." Wind (27) 77, p. 2.
"'Lavorare Stanco.'" Mouth (13) D 77, p. 16.
"Lune de miel." LaB (7) My 77, p. 6.
"Para el soldado desconocido." Kayak (46) O 77, p. 39.
"Twenty Calibre Angel." LaB (7) My 77, p. 7.
"Ya Muhammad." Kayak (46) O 77, p. 40.

ARIDJIS, Homero
"7 poemas." Montra (3) Spr 77, p. 132.

ARMSTRONG, Cherryl
"Walk to the Clearing" (for Alice). Wind (25) 77, p. 61.

ARMSTRONG, Kathleen McCullen
"Prairie Fire." MontG (5) Wint 77, p. 32.

"The Sorceress." MontG (5) Wint 77, p. 33.

ARNAUT, Abdel-Kader
"Three Poems" (tr. by Mirene Ghossein). Mund (10:1) 77, p. 188.

ARNERICH, Steven
"Frozen Manifester." Aieee (5/6) 77, p. 6.

ARNOLD, Jean
"Restoration." TexQ (20:4) Wint 77, p. 113.

ARRANGA, Irene
"Changing Cages." StoneC (77:3) S 77, p. 21.

ARTECHE, Miguel
"Bicycle Abandoned in the Rain" (tr. by Carolyne Wright). EnPas
    (4) 76, p. 36.
"Rain" (tr. by Carolyne Wright). EnPas (4) 76, p. 35.

ARTMANN, H. C.
"Craft and Industry" (tr. by Harriett Watts). BosUJ (25:3) 77,
    p. 3.
from Green-Sealed Messages: (88) (tr. by Derk Wynand). WebR
    (3:1) Wint 77, p. 60.

ASANTE, Molefi K.
"The Eagle Was Loose." Obs (3:1) Spr 77, p. 56.
"The Sun Walked on Me." Obs (3:1) Spr 77, p. 54.
"A View from Here." Obs (3:1) Spr 77, p. 55.
"Witchcraft." Obs (3:1) Spr 77, p. 54.

ASH, Sarah Leeds
"Frozen in Time." PoetL (72:1) Spr 77, p. 14.
"Garage Sale." PoetL (72:1) Spr 77, p. 18.
"Love Poem." PoetL (72:1) Spr 77, p. 18.

ASHANTI, Asa
"At Clara's Farm" (for CPG). Obs (3:3) Wint 77, p. 60.
"Elegy for Robeson." Obs (3:3) Wint 77, p. 59.
"Morningside Drive." Obs (3:3) Wint 77, p. 61.
"New York 1976." Obs (3:3) Wint 77, p. 58.
"Sara." Obs (3:3) Wint 77, p. 61.

ASHBERY, John
"And Ut Pictura Poesis Is Her Name." Madem (83:9) S 77,
    p. 96.
"Bird's-Eye View of the Tool and Die Co." Antaeus (27) Aut 77,
    p. 50.
"Blue Sonata." Poetry (130:1) Ap 77, p. 7.
"Business Personals." AmerPoR (6:4) Jl-Ag 77, p. 48.
"Collective Dawns." NewYorker (53:1) 21 F 77, p. 34.
"The Couple in the Next Room." AmerPoR (6:4) Jl-Ag 77, p. 47.
"Crazy Weather." Antaeus (27) Aut 77, p. 49.

"The Explanation. " UnmOx (15) 77, p. 101.
"Fantasia on 'The Nut Brown Maid. '" Poetry (130:5) Ag 77, p.
   260.
"Friends. " NewYRB (24:5) 31 Mr 77, p. 19.
"The Gazing Grain. " NewYRB (24:5) 31 Mr 77, p. 19.
"The Ice-Cream Wars. " Poetry (130:1) Ap 77, p. 9.
"'Kannst du die alten Lieder noch Spielen?'" Ploughs (4:1) 77,
   pp. 60-70.
"The Lament upon the Waters. " NewYorker (53:16) 6 Je 77, p.
   42.
"Lost and Found and Lost Again. " AmerPoR (6:4) Jl-Ag 77, p.
   47.
"Loving Mad Tom. " GeoR (31:1) Spr 77, p. 42.
"Saying It to Keep It from Happening. " AmerPoR (6:4) Jl-Ag 77,
   p. 47.
"Syringa. " Poetry (130:1) Ap 77, p. 4.
"Two Deaths. " Madem (83:9) S 77, p. 96.
"Variant. " AmerPoR (6:4) Jl-Ag 77, p. 47.
"Whether It Exists. " GeoR (31:1) Spr 77, p. 43.
"The Wrong Kind of Insurance. " NewYorker (53:19) 27 Je 77, p. 31.

ASHLEY, Franklin
   from Zarma: "The American Sportsman. " SouthernPR (16:SI)
      77, p. 11.

ASHLEY, Nova Trimble
   "After Sale of the Estate. " KanQ (9:3) Sum 77, p. 49.
   "'How Do I Love Thee?'" LadHJ (94:12) D 77, p. 170.

ASPENBERG, Gary
   "Bruises. " Bits (6) Jl 77.

ATKINS, Russell
   "Dunham Tavern: 1976. " PoNow (14/18) 77, p. 7.
   "New Day. " PoNow (14/18) 77, p. 7.
   "The Silence. " PoNow (14/18) 77, p. 7.

ATKINSON, Alan
   "In Love. " Mouth (11/12) Mr-Je 77, p. 65.
   "Laws of State. " Mouth (13) D 77, p. 40.
   "Searching. " Mouth (11/12) Mr-Je 77, p. 68.

ATWOOD, Calvin
   "Instead of Searching for Gifts. " TexQ (20:3) Aut 77, p. 41.

ATWOOD, Margaret
   "Night Poem. " Field (17) Aut 77, p. 38.
   "Once I could move. " Madem (83:7) Jl 77, p. 142.
   "Threes. " MalR (41) Ja 77, p. 152.
   "Two-Headed Poem. " UnmOx (15) 77, p. 67.
   "We walk in the cedar grove" (worksheets included). MalR (41)
      Ja 77, p. 121.   Entire issue devoted to Margaret Atwood.

AUBERT, Alvin
"As Tongues of Fire" (for Charles H. Rowell). Nimrod (21:2/
    22:1) 77, p. 12.
"Balls and Chain." SouthernPR (17:2) Aut 77, p. 36.
"Charm." Nimrod (21:2/22:1) 77, p. 14.
"Doloroso." Nimrod (21:2/22:1) 77, p. 14.
"Feeling Through." AmerPoR (6:1) Ja-F 77, p. 20.
"'Fo Day Creeper." AmerPoR (6:1) Ja-F 77, p. 20.
"For Alex Haley/author of Roots." Obs (3:1) Spr 77, cover.
"The Housemovers." Nimrod (21:2/22:1) 77, p. 13.
"Jean Toomer." AmerPoR (6:1) Ja-F 77, p. 20.
"The Opposite of Green." AmerPoR (6:1) Ja-F 77, p. 20.
"Or Not at All." Nimrod (21:2/22:1) 77, p. 12.
"South Louisiana." Bits (6) Jl 77.
"The Voice." Obs (3:2) Sum 77, cover.
"Western Haiku." Obs (3:3) Wint 77, p. 54.

AUBERT, J. R.
"An Empty Pillow." SouthernPR (16:SI) 77, p. 12.
"Reunion after Ten." SouthernPR (17:1) Spr 77, p. 21.

AUDAS, Christina
"When I woke up this morning, I." AAR (27) 77, p. 104.

AUGUSTINE, Jane
"Gentians." Pequod (2:3) Sum 77, p. 62.
"On Loss: Five Meditations" (for A. J. M.). Montra (3) Spr 77,
    p. 89.
"The Stars." Montra (3) Spr 77, p. 87.
from The Woman's Guide to Mountain Climbing: (I, IV). PoNow
    (14/18) 77, p. 8.

AUKEMA, Charles
"Oedipal Decomposition." Pequod (2:3) Sum 77, p. 36.

AUSTER, Paul
"Northern Lights." PartR (44:3) 77, p. 411.

AVERILL, Diane
"after school." PortR (23) 77, p. 109.

AVICOLLI, Tommi
"changeling." Mouth (11/12) Mr-Je 77, p. 62.

AVIDAN, David
from Cool Filmscripts: "An elderly lonely woman glances" (tr.
    by the author). TriQ (39) Spr 77, p. 251.
from Vegetative Love: "The Theoretical Offer" (tr. by Richard
    Flantz). TriQ (39) Spr 77, p. 251.

AVSHALOMOV, Doris
"The Gardeners." PortR (23) 77, p. 36.

AWAD, Joseph
"The Catch." Poem (29) Mr 77, p. 25.
"Rivets." Poem (29) Mr 77, p. 26.

AWOONOR, Kofi
from The House by the Sea: "for Henoga Vinoko Akpalu who
    passed away November 1974 (to be read to snatches of his
    dirges)." Nimrod (21:2/22:1) 77, p. 20.
from The House by the Sea: "Poem: I dance in the square be-
    fore." Nimrod (21:2/22:1) 77, p. 16.
from The House by the Sea: "Poem: So he comes now tne
    clown." Nimrod (21:2/22:1) 77, p. 15.
from The House by the Sea: "Sequences." Nimrod (21:2/22:1)
    77, p. 18.

AYRES, Noreen
"Weighing the Scales of a Snake." DacTerr (14) Spr-Sum 77, p. 17.

AXELROD, David
"Why You Should Get a Nose Job." SmPd (14:1) Wint 77, p. 20.

AXELROD, Roberta
"the thin girl." Stonecloud (6) 76, p. 106.

AZTEC
"I cut emerald stones" (tr. by Jeff Burnham). QW (3) Spr-Sum
    77, p. 57.
"My flowers have no end" (tr. by Jeff Burnham). QW (3) Spr-
    Sum 77, p. 57.
"O! I was born with no purpose" (tr. by Jeff Burnham). QW
    (3) Spr-Sum 77, p. 57.

BBB
"Later in a Many-Windowed Room." Wind (24) 77, p. 4.
"Shard-Rites." Wind (24) 77, p. 5.

BABER, Robert
"all in all." Wind (27) 77, p. 4.
"Notice." Wind (27) 77, p. 4.
"war and peace." Wind (27) 77, p. 4.

BACA, Jimmy Santiago
"My Child." YellowBR (8) 77, p. 14.
"The Poets." YellowBR (8) 77, p. 13.

BACHE, William B.
"At the Academy: Michaelangelo." Sparrow (33) Ja 77, p. 19.
"December." Sparrow (33) Ja 77, p. 19.
"May." Sparrow (33) Ja 77, p. 19.
"October." Sparrow (33) Ja 77, p. 19.

BAILEY, Angela
"The Prisoners." ChrC (94:36) 9 N 77, p. 1031.

BAILEY, Jane
"Castaway." MontG (5) Wint 77, p. 51.
"In Missouri Country." CutB (8) Spr 77, p. 68.
"The Silence Up Ambrose Creek." MontG (5) Wint 77, p. 50.

BAILIN, George
"past, present, counterpoint." Confr (15) Aut 77-Wint 78, p. 73.

BAIME, Susan
"Wolf Dream." HiramPoR (23) Wint 77, p. 12.

BAIRD, Andrew
"At a Confederate Cemetery near Resaca, Georgia." NewRep
    (177:10) 3 S 77, p. 27.

BAKALIS, John
"Cowboy Story." Kayak (44) F 77, p. 46.
"The Gunman." Kayak (44) F 77, p. 47.
"Mask and Beast." Kayak (44) F 77, p. 46.
"When I Knock on a Door I Think of Kubla Khan." Kayak (44) F
    77, p. 47.

BAKER, Corrinne
"Rabbit Hunting." QW (2) Wint 77, p. 62.

BAKER, Houston A., Jr.
"'Because I Do Not Hope to Know Again.'" Obs (3:2) Sum 77,
    p. 51.
"The Humble Black/Helpful White." Obs (3:2) Sum 77, p. 52.
"Renewal" (for Alvin Aubert). Obs (3:2) Sum 77, p. 51.

BAKER, Jackson
"The Flat Earth Man Gives Out His Cure." SouthernPR (17:1)
    Spr 77, p. 12.

BALABAN, John
"Opening Le Ba Khon's Dictionary." AmerS (46:2) Spr 77,
    p. 212.

BALAKIAN, Peter
"At the Grave of William Carlos Williams." PoNow (14/18) 77,
    p. 8.
"Facing the Water." Wind (24) 77, p. 8.
"Poem to Comfort Helen." Wind (24) 77, p. 9.
"Portrait before Water." Agni (7) 77, p. 85.
"Reading the Thermometer." Wind (24) 77, p. 6.

BALAZS, Mary
"Among Thistles." GRR (8:1/2) 77, p. 140.
"And the Redbud." Icarus (5:1) Spr 77, p. 20.
"Elegy." GRR (8:1/2) 77, p. 141.
"Parable." StoneC (77:3) S 77, p. 7.

BALDERSTON, Jean
   "A Remorse for Benjamin Gourd on the 300th Anniversary of His
      Hanging." PoNow (14/18) 77, p. 9.

BALDWIN, Neil
   "Cape." Glass (2:2/3) Wint-Spr 77, p. 86.
   "Seal Rock" (for John Logan). Glass (2:2/3) Wint-Spr 77, p. 87.
   from Vergers: (16, 35, 55) (tr. of Rainer Maria Rilke). SunM
      (4) Aut 77, p. 70.

BALDWIN, Robert
   "Leelanua." SmPd (14:3) Aut 77, p. 35.
   "Letter from the Deadstream." SmPd (14:3) Aut 77, p. 36.

BALEST, Alice
   "Middle Age." CarouselQ (2:2) Aut 77, p. 27.

BALL, Alan
   "just because the world stinks." Xa (4) 77, p. 3.

BALL, Angela
   "On the Surface of Your Skin." Rapp (10) 77, p. 57.
   "To My Brother, Hardly Born." Madem (83:10) O 77, p. 144.

BALL, Gordon
   "Yr 20th Birthday." CarolQ (29:1) Wint 77, p. 72.

BALLARD, Virginia
   "in chowdery autumn." HangL (31) Aut 77, p. 71.

BAN Tinh
   "Quintessence" (tr. by Graeme Wilson). DenQ (12:2) Sum 77,
      p. 52.

BANANI, Amin
   "The Singing Reed" (tr. of Rumi, w. Jascha Kessler). CentR
      (21:1) Wint 77, p. 72.

BANDEIRA, Manuel
   "Belém of Pará" (tr. by Jean R. Longland). LitR (21:2) Wint
      78, p. 216.
   "Death in the Absolute" (tr. by Jack Tomlins). LitR (21:2) Wint
      78, p. 218.
   "Deeply" (tr. by Jean R. Longland). LitR (21:2) Wint 78, p. 215.
   "I'm Off at Last for Passargadae" (tr. by Jack Tomlins). LitR
      (21:2) Wint 78, p. 214.
   "The Last Poem" (tr. by Jack Tomlins). LitR (21:2) Wint 78,
      p. 218.
   "Preparation for Death" (tr. by Jack Tomlins). LitR (21:2) Wint
      78, p. 219.

BANGS, Carol Jane
   "Divorce." MontG (5) Wint 77, p. 46.

BANKS, Heather
"Xantippe." SunM (4) Aut 77, p. 147.

BARAKA, Amiri
"An American Oppress Story!" YaleLit (145:5) 77, p. 19.
"Postcard." Montra (3) Spr 77, p. 130.

BARALE, Michele
"Picture Making." HiramPoR (22) Aut-Wint 77, p. 6.
"We Can Read the Barometer Like Shakespearean Drama." KanQ
   (9:2) Spr 77, p. 80.
"The Window Cat." MichQR (16:3) Sum 77, p. 302.

BARASOVSKA, Joan
"The Thin Man." Bits (6) Jl 77.

BARBA, Sharon
"Contemporary Sappho" (for Kris). 13thM (3:2) 77, p. 22.
"Nude." 13thM (3:2) 77, p. 21.

BARBER, April
"The Man in the Moon." QW (3) Spr-Sum 77, p. 29.

BARBERNITZ, Anne
"After the Storm." Ploughs (4:1) 77, p. 168.

BARCIA, José Rubia
   from Payroll of Bones: "Alphonso, you keep looking at me, I
      see" (tr. of César Vallejo, w. Clayton Eshleman). Bound
      (5:3) Spr 77, p. 748.
   from Payroll of Bones: "Chances are, I am another; walking, at
      dawn, another who moves" (tr. of César Vallejo, w. Clayton
      Eshleman). Bound (5:3) Spr 77, p. 751.
   from Payroll of Bones: "Farewell Remembering a Goodbye" (tr.
      of César Vallejo, w. Clayton Eshleman). Bound (5:3) Spr 77,
      p. 750.
   from Payroll of Bones: "I stayed on to warm up the ink in
      which I drown" (tr. of César Vallejo, w. Clayton Eshleman).
      Bound (5:3) Spr 77, p. 747.
   from Payroll of Bones: "Oh bottle without wine! Oh wine the
      widower of this bottle!" (tr. of César Vallejo, w. Clayton
      Eshleman). Bound (5:3) Spr 77, p. 745.
   from Payroll of Bones: "This" (tr. of César Vallejo, w. Clayton
      Eshleman). Bound (5:3) Spr 77, p. 746.
   from Payroll of Bones: "Upon reflecting on life, upon reflecting"
      (tr. of César Vallejo, w. Clayton Eshleman). Bound (5:3)
      Spr 77, p. 744.

BARFOOT, James
"Picasso's Pose." FourQt (26:4) Sum 77, p. 27.

BARGAD, Warren
"The House Is Empty" (tr. of Yona Wallach). TriQ (39) Spr 77,
   p. 310.

BARGEN, Walter
"American History (The Railroads)." SoDakR (15:2) Sum 77,
    p. 24.
"Beirut." NewL (44:1) Aut 77, p. 23.
"Emergency Room." SoDakR (15:2) Sum 77, p. 22.

BARKMAN, Bruce
"The New Physics." RemR (5) 77, p. 41.

BARKS, Coleman
"We Let Each Other Go." SouthernPR (16:SI) 77, p. 12.

BARLOW, George
"Badassed Brothers Isley." AmerPoR (6:1) Ja-F 77, p. 21.
"Little Half-Brother, Little Black Star" (for Mark). AmerPoR
    (6:1) Ja-F 77, p. 20.
"The Place Where He Arose" (for Quincy Troupe). Nimrod
    (21:2/22:1) 77, p. 22.
"Salt" (for August Merrell Richards). Nimrod (21:2/22:1) 77,
    p. 24.

BARNARD, Jane
"In the Whites of Eyes" (tr. of Benjamin Peret, w. A. F. Moritz
    and Margaret Schaus). Aieee (5/6) 77, p. 19.
"My Last Misfortunes" (To Yves Tanguy) (tr. of Benjamin Peret,
    w. A. F. Moritz and Margaret Schaus). Aieee (5/6) 77,
    p. 17.
"Portrait of Andre Breton" (tr. of Benjamin Peret, w. A. F.
    Moritz and Margaret Schaus). Aieee (5/6) 77, p. 18.
"Under a Beating Rain" (tr. of Benjamin Peret, w. A. F. Moritz
    and Margaret Schaus). Aieee (5/6) 77, p. 20.

BARNES, C. C.
"My Hands." Mouth (13) D 77, p. 58.
"?What if the World Were Forced to." Mouth (13) D 77, p. 59.

BARNES, Jim
"Autobiography, Chapter IV: The Mirage." CutB (8) Spr 77,
    p. 70.
"Autobiography, Chapter IX: Leaving, Again." CutB (8) Spr 77,
    p. 71.
"Autobiography, Chapter XI: Prelude to Writing." CutB (8) Spr
    77, p. 72.
"Autobiography, Chapter XIV: Tombstone at Petit Bay, Near
    Tahlequah." QW (4) Aut 77, p. 82.
"The Body Falters." ChiR (28:4) Spr 77, p. 57.
"Elegy for the Girl Who Drowned at Goats Bluff." Nat (224:19)
    14 My 77, p. 600.
"Goshen Tavern." PoNow (14/18) 77, p. 9.
"The Last Trip Somewhere East." Wind (25) 77, p. 10.
"Legacy." Wind (25) 77, p. 9.
"Letter to a Poet." Nat (225:20) 10 D 77, p. 630.

"Looking for Le Bosquet, Oklahoma." Wind (25) 77, p. 9.
"Midwinter." Nat (224:23) 11 Je 77, p. 728.
"Morning at the Sanitarium." Confr (14) Spr-Sum 77, p. 189.
"Morning at Sea" (tr. of Dagmar Nick). ChiR (29:3) Wint 78, p. 87.
"Notes for a Love Letter from Mid-America." ChiR (28:4) Spr 77, p. 58.
"Postcard to James Welch in Missoula." ChiR (28:4) Spr 77, p. 60.
"Prayer of the Little Black Manchild" (tr. of Guy Tirolien). Nimrod (21:2/22:1) 77, p. 291.
"Pyramid Lake, Late Summer." ChiR (28:4) Spr 77, p. 56.
"Return to La Plata, Missouri." Nat (225:17) 19 N 77, p. 534.
"San Miguel de Allende." QW (4) Aut 77, p. 82.
"Under Buffalo Mountain." PoNow (14/18) 77, p. 9.

BARNES, Susan
from Hands and Dreams: (I, IV). PortR (23) 77, p. 110.

BARNES, Tim
"Evening Rain." PortR (23) 77, p. 145.
"Right Now...." PortR (23) 77, p. 143.

BARNES, W. D.
"Nursing Home." Vaga (26) 77, p. 7.

BARNSTONE, Aliki
"Dear friend." Bleb (12) 77, p. 44.
"Hallways" (w. Willis Barnstone). NewL (44:2) Wint 77, p. 26.
"A Letter from the Hotel" (for Marti, Riqui, and Jack). NewL (44:2) Wint 77, p. 23.
"To a Friend's Child." NewL (44:2) Wint 77, p. 25.
"The Star and the Fencer." NewL (44:2) Wint 77, p. 24.

BARNSTONE, Willis
"All Day It Is Dark, and Only My Friend Carmen Sees a Plotin- ian Circle Where Objectively There Is Little to See." Bleb (12) 77, p. 20.
Eleven poems. NewL (44:2) Wint 77, pp. 16-22.
"Hallways" (w. Aliki Barnstone). NewL (44:2) Wint 77, p. 26.
"He Notes the Brevity of Whatever Is Alive and How What Was Alive Now Seems to Be Nothing" (tr. of Francisco de Que- vedo). Bleb (12) 77, p. 19.
"He Shows How All Things Warn of Death" (tr. of Francisco de Quevedo). Bleb (12) 77, p. 18.
"A Revery." Northeast (3:4) Aut-Wint 77-78, p. 3.
"The Suicide" (tr. of Jorge Luis Borges). AmerPoR (6:3) My-Je 77, p. 44.

BARR, Sister Mary Anthony
"The Enchanted Pond--Monet at Giverny." SewanR (85:3) Sum 77, p. 430.

BARRAX, Gerald W.
"Barriers 6." Nimrod (21:2/22:1) 77, p. 25.
"Narrative of a Surprising Conversion." Nimrod (21:2/22:1) 77,
    p. 29.
"Shani." Nimrod (21:2/22:1) 77, p. 26.
"Something I Know about Her." SouthernPR (16:SI) 77, p. 14.

BARRICKLOW, Roland
"Erotic Song II." Mouth (13) D 77, p. 39.

BARROW, Geoffrey R.
"Let everyone bring what he knows" (tr. of Blas de Otero).
    Stand (18:2) 77, p. 43.
"World" (tr. of Blas de Otero). Stand (18:2) 77, p. 42.

BARROWS, Anita
"Salt and Lemon" (for Eleni Vakalo). Nat (224:18) 7 My 77,
    p. 565.

BARRY, Josephine
"Fantasy." LitR (20:3) Spr 77, p. 353.

BARRY, Paul
"With You in the Fields This Morning." KanQ (9:3) Sum 77,
    p. 29.

BARTELS, Susan
"Surviving the Music." DeKalb (10:2) Wint 77, p. 5.

BARTH, R. L.
"A Verbal Love Song" (to Susan). Wind (27) 77, p. 26.
"Winter Song." Wind (27) 77, p. 26.

BARTKOWECH, R.
"A Moment of Freedom." DeKalb (10:2) Wint 77, p. 6.

BARTLETT, Elizabeth
"At the Byoda-In Temple." Icarus (5:2) Aut 77, p. 17.
"Forgotten Language." ModernPS (8:2) Aut 77, p. 136.
"The House of Sleep." VirQR (53:3) Sum 77, p. 509.
"Maybe Others Elsewhere." ModernPS (8:2) Aut 77,
    p. 137.
"An Old Love Story." CarouselQ (2:2) Aut 77, p. 20.
"The Succuba." GRR (8:1/2) 77, p. 139.
"Theme for a Painting." CimR (40) Jl 77, p. 15.
"Theme for a Painting." ModernPS (8:2) Aut 77, p. 136.

BARTLETT, Lee
"Gacela: The Dead Baby" (tr. of Garcia Lorca). CalQ (11/12)
    Wint-Spr 77, p. 81.
"The Old Maid at Mass" (tr. of Garcia Lorca). CalQ (11/12)
    Wint-Spr 77, p. 79.

BARTON, David
"Demeter." ColEng (39:4) D 77, p. 462.
"An Essay on Criticism" (for Mike Bowen). ColEng (38:7) Mr
    77, p. 718.
"House-Sitting with a Friend." ColEng (39:4) D 77, p. 466.
"Jasper Ridge." ColEng (39:4) D 77, p. 464.
"The Wind" (for Kathryn). ColEng (39:4) D 77, p. 463.

BARTON, Fred
"The Old Men in the Park." HiramPoR (23) Wint 77, p. 13.

BARTON, Jill
"The Canal below Richmond Street." QW (4) Aut 77, p. 59.
"The Changes That Come after Midnight." QW (4) Aut 77,
    p. 61.
"The Concert." QW (4) Aut 77, p. 60.

BARTON, Paulé
"The Bee Dice Game" (tr. by Howard Norman). ParisR (70) Sum
    77, p. 96.
"The Bowl Seller" (tr. by Howard Norman). ParisR (70) Sum 77,
    p. 95.
"The Honey Seller" (tr. by Howard A. Norman). Nat (225:22) 24
    D 77, p. 700.
"The Sleep Bus" (tr. by Howard Norman). ParisR (70) Sum 77,
    p. 97.

BARWELL, Jay
"Picking for a Living." Icarus (5:1) Spr 77, p. 13.

BASKFIELD, Jerry
"Disposition of a Father." PoetL (72:2) Sum 77, p. 49.

BASQUETTEBAAL, Bill E.
"Thoroughly Thorough Thoreau." YaleLit (145:5) 77, p. 27.

BASS, Madeline Tiger
Keeping House in This Forest. JnlONJP (1:3, part 2) 76. En-
    tire issue.
"Mady's Blues." Gra (12) 77, p. 24.

BASSETT, Lee
"Getting Married in Smelterville" (for Wendy). CutB (9) Aut-
    Wint 77, p. 88.
"Spruce" (for Maret). CutB (9) Aut-Wint 77, p. 86.
"Up the Beach." PortR (23) 77, p. 105.

BASTIAN, Richard
"Overtrues." Stonecloud (6) 76, p. 26.
"Requiescat." CarouselQ (2:1) Spr 77, p. 20.

BATES, Scott
"Hyena Song." SouthernPR (16:SI) 77, p. 15.

BATKI, John
"Crossing the Sea of Cortez." Hand (1) 77, p. 185.
"Diamond" (tr. of Attila Jozsef). Hand (1) 77, p. 196.
"Down the Block." Spirit (2:2/3) 77, p. 70.
"The Invention of the Gun" (Memoirs of an Assassin). Spirit
    (2:2/3) 77, p. 73.
"Love Poem." Spirit (2:2/3) 77, p. 72.
"Mallarme on July 14, 1889." Spirit (2:2/3) 77, p. 71.
"My Tibet." Hand (1) 77, p. 184.
"Night and Day" (for Frank O'Hara). Spirit (2:2/3) 77, p. 71.
"Nothing" (tr. of Attila Jozsef). Hand (1) 77, p. 194.
"Numbers" (tr. of Attila Jozsef). Hand (1) 77, p. 195.
"Sabine." Spirit (2:2/3) 77, p. 69.
"Touristicism." Spirit (2:2/3) 77, p. 69.
"A Transparent Lion" (tr. of Attila Jozsef). Hand (1) 77, p. 195.

BATSON, Rex
"Rhoda." NewL (43:4) Sum 77, p. 61.

BATTIN, Wendy
"The Greeting." Rapp (10) 77, p. 52.

BAUCHWITZ, Kurt
"Zwischenhändler." GRR (8:3) 77, p. 218.

BAUDELAIRE
Nine poems (tr. by Jonathan Griffin). GRR (8:3) 77, p. 206.

BAUER, Steven
"5th Grade." DacTerr (14) Spr-Sum 77, p. 56.
"In Canaan." ChiR (29:2) Aut 77, p. 118.
"Stars in Maine." Nat (225:14) 29 O 77, p. 438.

BAUER, Tricia
"August 29, 1976 N.Y.C." Epoch (27:1) Aut 77, p. 81.
"Driving to Lomala." Epoch (27:1) Aut 77, p. 80.

BAUMAN, Dana
"Mackalack Lake." PortR (23) 77, p. 132.
"The small white house with the green roof." PortR (23) 77, p.
    133.

BAUMANN, Susan
"Admission of Two." Nat (224:25) 25 Je 77, p. 794.

BAUMEL, Judith
"Letter." HarvAd (110:3) Mr 77, p. 13.
"Message from the Interior." HarvAd (110:4) Ap 77, p. 22.
"Natalia Makarova in Swan Lake." HarvAd (110:3) Mr 77, p. 6.

BAUMHARDT, Don
"Ghost Maps of Gila Bend." PortR (23) 77, p. 135.

BAUR, Katie
"Getting A+'s on a school paper." AAR (27) 77, p. 97.

BAXTER, Charles
"Deprivation." PoetryNW (18:2) Sum 77, p. 38.

al-BAYYATI, Abd al-Wahab
"Lorca Elegies" (tr. by Sargon Boulus). Mund (10:1) 77, p. 64.
from The Torment of Al Hallaj: "1. As a Young Man" (tr. by
Ira Cohen and Petra Vogt). MontG (6) Aut 77, p. 30.

BEACHAM, Hans
"Instructions." TexQ (20:4) Wint 77, p. 110.
"The Not-Said." TexQ (20:3) Aut 77, p. 32.
"On Will Descend." TexQ (20:3) Aut 77, p. 31.
"The Present Present." TexQ (20:4) Wint 77, p. 111.
"Sinister Gerund." TexQ (20:3) Aut 77, p. 32.

BEASLEY, Bruce H.
"Snuffed Candle." Wind (25) 77, p. 40.

BEAUSOLEIL, Laura
"Song to My Electricity." Gra (12) 77, p. 47.

BECK, Art
"Evolution Is Arrogant, Human Nature Is Cruel: The Discovery
of Music As We." Vaga (26) 77, p. 27.
"The Fish Cleaners, Mission Rock." Vaga (26) 77, p. 25.
"Musician." Vaga (26) 77, p. 26.

BECK, Peg
"Coyote." OP (23) Spr-Sum 77, p. 23.
"Cuirana." OP (23) Spr-Sum 77, p. 24.
"Evening sets about itself again." OP (23) Spr-Sum 77, p. 28.
"Love Change." OP (23) Spr-Sum 77, p. 21.
"Madness Contained and Our Gestures." OP (23) Spr-Sum 77,
p. 22.
"The Mountains Nothing More." OP (23) Spr-Sum 77, p. 27.
"The People Called Chippewa These Days." OP (23) Spr-Sum 77,
p. 26.

BECKER, Carol
"Memory." US1 (9) Spr 77, p. 3.
"Snow Oranges." US1 (9) Spr 77, p. 3.

BECKER, Robin
"Return." Chomo (4:1) Sum 77, p. 4.

BEDFORD, William
"Childhood." Nat (225:2) 9-16 Jl 77, p. 60.

BEELER, Janet
"Bone Structure." Esq (87:2) F 77, p. 109.

"Waiting Room. " Esq (87:1) Ja 77, p. 149.

BEHRENS, Alfred
   "Western" (tr. by Timothy McIndoo). WebR (3:4) Aut 77, p. 48.

BEICHMAN, Janine
   "Beautifully-named" (tr. of Kakinomoto Hitomaro). DenQ (12:2)
      Sum 77, p. 106.
   "I set off to join the border guards" (tr. of Anonymous). DenQ
      (12:2) Sum 77, p. 106.
   "On nights when the evening mist" (tr. of Anonymous). DenQ
      (12:2) Sum 77, p. 106.
   "Plovers skimming over the waves" (tr. of Kakinomoto Hitomaro).
      DenQ (12:2) Sum 77, p. 106.
   "Remembrance" (tr. of Tachihara Michizo). DenQ (12:2) Sum 77,
      p. 197.
   "To the First One" (tr. of Tachihara Michizo). DenQ (12:2) Sum
      77, p. 196.

BEINING, Guy
   "the carriage. " Stonecloud (6) 76, p. 68.
   "Chasing the Voice of Forty Odd Years. " EnPas (4) 76, p. 30.
   "Hourglass" (for Larry Eigner) (revised version). LaB (6) Mr
      77, p. 44.
   "The List. " RemR (5) 77, p. 70.
   "ogden measures regression. " WindO (30) Aut 77, p. 18.
   "ogden speaks to his id. " Gra (12) 77, p. 54.
   "Ruins. " Stonecloud (6) 76, p. 106.
   "Smoked. " WindO (30) Aut 77.
   "sunday morning. " Stonecloud (6) 76, p. 27.
   "Sweet Miss Misery. " Stonecloud (6) 76, p. 105.

BELITT, Ben
   "The Double-Goer. " VirQR (53:3) Sum 77, p. 498.

BELL, Marvin
   "Dew at the Edge of a Leaf. " Nat (224:3) 22 Ja 77, p. 88.
   "Three Parts Mud. " MissR (6:1) 77, p. 27.
   "To No One in Particular. " AmerPoR (6:1) Ja-F 77, p. 41.

BELL, Robyn
   "1958. " YaleLit (147:1) 77, p. 26.

BELL, Roni
   "Skoal to a Saturday Afternoon. " CarouselQ (2:2) Aut 77,
      p. 7.

BELLAMY, Joe David
   "The End of the Marathon. " PraS (51:1) Spr 77, p. 88.
   "A Talking Dog Is No Circus. " ParisR (71) Aut 77, p. 57.
   "The Track at Weeks Field. " PraS (51:1) Spr 77, p. 88.
   "The Weather Is Never the Same. " QW (2) Wint 77, p. 59.

BELLCOURT, Susie
"So many dead Indians on the kitchen floor. " AmerPoR (6:2) Mr-
Ap 77, p. 32.

BELLG, Albert
"Raincoats for the Dead. " NewL (43:4) Sum 77, p. 62.
"Watertower. " NewL (43:4) Sum 77, p. 62.

BELLI, Giuseppe Gioachino
"Back to the Roots" (tr. by Anthony Burgess). MalR (44) O 77,
p. 20.
"The Creation of the World" (tr. by Anthony Burgess). MalR
(44) O 77, p. 17.
"The Earthly Paradise of the Beasts" (tr. by Anthony Burgess).
MalR (44) O 77, p. 18.
"The End of the Conclave" (tr. by Desmond O'Grady). MalR (43)
Jl 77, p. 99.
"The Explanation of the Conclave" (tr. by Desmond O'Grady).
MalR (43) Jl 77, p. 97.
"The Limp College (of Cardinals)" (tr. by Desmond O'Grady).
MalR (43) Jl 77, p. 96.
"Man" (tr. by Anthony Burgess). MalR (44) O 77, p. 21.
"The New Election" (tr. by Desmond O'Grady). MalR (43) Jl 77,
p. 98.
"Pride before a Fall" (tr. by Anthony Burgess). MalR (44) O
77, p. 19.
"The Sacred College of Cardinals" (tr. by Desmond O'Grady).
MalR (43) Jl 77, p. 95.

BELLIPANNI, Sylvia
"Providence. " Northeast (3:3) Sum 77, p. 7.
"Touching. " Northeast (3:3) Sum 77, p. 6.

BENAVIDEZ, Max
"Instead, Consider Time Passing. " Sam (56) Sum 77, p. 52.

BENEDIKT, Michael
"Am I Unhappy" (for S. B.). Falcon (14) 77, p. 76.
"Arena. " Gra (12) 77, p. 49.
"Attempt to Convince Somebody of Something. " Ploughs (3:3/4)
77, p. 129.
"The Badminton at Great Barrington. " ParisR (71) Aut 77, p.
134.
"Box. " Some (7/8) 76.
"Enough. " Falcon (14) 77, p. 73.
"Letter to an Old Poet" (tr. of Leonardo Froes). LitR (21:2)
Wint 78, p. 263.
from Night Cries: "Lurching Lunch. " PoNow (14/18) 77,
p. 10.
from Night Cries: "Tale. " PoNow (14/18) 77, p. 10.
from Night Cries: "The Tiny Sisyphus and the Dung Beetle. "
PoNow (14/18) 77, p. 10.

"Up the Hill. " Falcon (14) 77, p. 74.
"Weeping with Mandy. " Falcon (14) 77, p. 75.
"Zinnias. " Iowa (8:3) Sum 77, p. 65.

BENN, Gottfried
"Black Man's Bride" (tr. by Graeme McD. Wilson). DenQ (11:4)
Wint 77, p. 40.
"Cancer Ward" (tr. by Graeme McD. Wilson). DenQ (11:4) Wint
77, p. 37.
"Cycles" (tr. by Graeme McD. Wilson). DenQ (11:4) Wint 77,
p. 39.
"Happy Childhood" (tr. by Graeme McD. Wilson). DenQ (11:4)
Wint 77, p. 36.
"Mother" (tr. by Graeme McD. Wilson). DenQ (11:4) Wint 77,
p. 38.
"Small Aster" (tr. by Graeme McD. Wilson). DenQ (11:4) Wint
77, p. 35.
"Song" (tr. by Graeme McD. Wilson). DenQ (11:4) Wint 77, p.
36.

BENNANI, B. M.
"Day's Delivery. " Bleb (12) 77, p. 40.
"Down at the Local Pawnshop. " PoNow (14/18) 77, p. 9.
"A Frame without a Portrait. " Wind (24) 77, p. 10.
"A Painting on the Wall" (tr. of Mahmoud Darweesh). Bleb (12)
77, p. 38.
"Soft Rain in Distant Autumn" (tr. of Mahmoud Darweesh). Bleb
(12) 77, p. 36.
"Sorrow Is a Sail" (after Sameeh al-Qassim). Bleb (12) 77, p.
41.

BENNETT, Carolyn Grega
"Art Nouveau. " SouthernHR (11:3) Sum 77, p. 270.

BENNETT, E. M.
"Inside Story. " Drag (16) 77.

BENNETT, John
"Energy and Other Things. " MontG (5) Wint 77, p. 34.
"The Pie Man. " PoNow (14/18) 77, p. 11.
"The Squash Squisher. " PoNow (14/18) 77, p. 11.

BENNETT, John M.
"Nick's Piece. " Aieee (5/6) 77, p. 31.

BENSON, Steve
"Translations. " Hills (4) 77.
"Translations 1A. " Hills (4) 77.
"Translations 2. " Hills (4) 77.

BENTLEY, Sean
"American Dream. " PoetryNW (18:2) Sum 77, p. 21.
"As of 6/9/75. " TexQ (20:4) Wint 77, p. 115.

"1907. " YellowBR (8) 77, p. 17.
"Outtakes of My Life. " TexQ (20:4) Wint 77, p. 121.

BENTZMAN, Bruce Harris
"teardrop. " PoetL (72:2) Sum 77, p. 70.
"To My Towel: About Welfare Checks. " WindO (29) Sum 77,
     p. 13.

BENVENISTE, Rachelle
"Cocoa Beach, Florida. " Stonecloud (6) 76, p. 119.
"The Exorcist. " Stonecloud (6) 76, p. 67.

BENVENUTO, Joyce
"Mother's Day Dream. " SoDakR (15:2) Sum 77, p. 66.

BENVENUTO, Richard
"Incident at the Lake. " SoDakR (15:4) Wint 77-78, p. 49.

BERG, Stephen
"Gratitude. " Hand (1) 77, p. 213.

BERGER, Bruce
Ten poems. Aspen (3) Spr 77, p. 82.

BERGERON, June P.
"Yom Kippur. " CarouselQ (2:3) Wint 77, p. 33.

BERGGREN, Edward
"The Visit of the Magi. " Poem (31) N 77, p. 56.
"Winter Hangs in My Hair. " Poem (31) N 77, p. 55.

BERGIN, Thomas G.
"First Love. " SewanR (85:2) Spr 77, p. 206.

BERGMAN, David
"Actors' Equity. " AmerS (46:4) Aut 77, p. 440.
"The Book Lover. " CentR (21:3) Sum 77, p. 279.
"The Dancer Denies a Suitor. " ColEng (39:1) S 77, p. 65.
"Greenhouse Blues. " ParisR (70) Sum 77, p. 36.
"Intercepted Courier. " SoCaR (10:1) N 77, p. 87.
"The Miniaturist. " ParisR (70) Sum 77, p. 37.
"The Peter Doyle Poems" (for Bob). Mouth (11/12) Mr-Je 77,
     p. 8.
"Rubenesque. " AmerS (46:2) Spr 77, p. 158.
"Satan in Suburbia. " CentR (21:3) Sum 77, p. 280.

BERKSON, Bill
from Enigma Variations: "From a Childhood. " PoNow (14/18)
     77, p. 10.
from Enigma Variations: "Leave Cancelled. " PoNow (14/18) 77,
     p. 10.
from Enigma Variations: "Pollen. " PoNow (14/18) 77, p. 10.

BERLIND, Bruce
"Lazarus" (tr. of Agnes Nemes Nagy). <u>NewL</u> (44:2) Wint 77, p. 40.

BERMAN, Ruth
"Frozen in Scarlet." <u>DeKalb</u> (10:2) Wint 77, p. 7.
"The Little Green Men Send an Ambassador to Earth." <u>DeKalb</u> (10:2) Wint 77, p. 9.
"Returned Changeling." <u>DeKalb</u> (10:2) Wint 77, p. 8.

BERNARD, April
"House Plant." <u>HarvAd</u> (110:4) Ap 77, p. 32.
"Remembering Nantucket" (for L. C. H.). <u>HarvAd</u> (111:2) D 77, p. 16.
"Say stillness is the Dividend." <u>HarvAd</u> (110:5) My 77, p. 23.

BERNER, Robert
"Mid-Term" (for Ray Goss). <u>DacTerr</u> (14) Spr-Sum 77, p. 73.
"Problems of an Academic" (for John Quinn). <u>DacTerr</u> (14) Spr-Sum 77, p. 74.
"Summer Nights at the Age of Twelve." <u>PoNow</u> (14/18) 77, p. 12.
"To Poets Everywhere." <u>PoNow</u> (14/18) 77, p. 12.
"To Some of My Students in English-12." <u>Sam</u> (56) Sum 77, p. 51.

BERNHARDT, Suzanne
"The Spinsters." <u>13thM</u> (3:2) 77, p. 19.
"Subtropical." <u>SmPd</u> (14:3) Aut 77, p. 15.

BERNHEIMER, Alan
"Before Defoe." <u>Hills</u> (4) 77.
"Low Tide in Sheboygan." <u>Hills</u> (4) 77.

BERNIKOW, Louise
"Looking for One That Does Not Smell Like a Urinal." <u>13thM</u> (3:2) 77, p. 57.

BERNSTEIN, Charles
"The Bean Field." <u>LaB</u> (9) N-D 77, p. 15.
"a deadness to." <u>LaB</u> (7) My 77, p. 12.
"is like a." <u>LaB</u> (9) N-D 77, p. 14.
"noteworthy no doubt for its/exquisite flaws." <u>LaB</u> (9) N-D 77, p. 18.
"of course." <u>LaB</u> (7) My 77, p. 13.
"r--." <u>LaB</u> (7) My 77, p. 9.
from Sentences: "I feel too dependent." <u>LaB</u> (9) N-D 77, p. 19.
from Sentences: "you say to yourself is it me is it my fault is it." <u>LaB</u> (9) N-D 77, p. 20.
from Sentences: "You think of bringing back together all the people you ever knew." <u>LaB</u> (9) N-D 77, p. 22.
from Sentences: "You try to keep from going crazy with bore-

dom." LaB (9) N-D 77, p. 21.
"Take then, these nail & boards." LaB (7) My 77, p. 8.
"was pealing an apricot." LaB (7) My 77, p. 10.

BERRETT, Jean
"Deer Season." Wind (24) 77, p. 45.
"Prosepoem." Wind (24) 77, p. 34.

BERRIGAN, Daniel
"Homecoming." ChrC (94:24) 20-27 Jl 77, p. 655.
"The Russian Prisoner." ChrC (94:24) 20-27 Jl 77, p. 656.

BERRIGAN, Ted
"A Note from Yang-Kuan." UnmOx (15) 77, p. 92.
"Ode to Medicine." UnmOx (15) 77, p. 91.
"Problems, Problems." UnmOx (15) 77, p. 95.
"Saturday Afternoons on the Piazza." UnmOx (15) 77, p. 94.
"Truth as History." UnmOx (15) 77, p. 93.

BERRY, D. C.
"Gary Snyder, Self-Portrait." CarolQ (29:2) Spr-Sum 77, p. 71.
"Mark Strand, Self-Portrait." CarolQ (29:2) Spr-Sum 77, p. 73.
"Robert Bly, Self-Portrait No. 1." CarolQ (29:2) Spr-Sum 77,
   p. 72.
"Robert Creeley, Self-Portrait No. 1." CarolQ (29:2) Spr-Sum
   77, p. 74.
"Upon Driving Over a White Kitty Near McComb, Mississippi."
   PoNow (14/18) 77, p. 12.

BERRY, John
"By the Sewer Outlet." MichQR (16:3) Sum 77, p. 331.
"The Element of No Gamble." WormR (65/66) 77, p. 34.
"The Fall." WormR (65/66) 77, p. 34.
"How They Got Gimpy Stonehacker." DeKalb (10:2) Wint 77,
   p. 10.

BERRY, Kevin
"if she makes me write." SeC (5:2) 78, p. 39.
"That's Entertainment." SeC (5:2) 78, p. 38.

BERRY, Wendell
"Desolation." Hudson (30:1) Spr 77, p. 47.
"Early Morning Dark." Hudson (30:1) Spr 77, p. 50.
Eight Poems. Harp (255:1528) S 77, p. 65.
"From the Distance." Hudson (30:1) Spr 77, p. 51.
"Healing." Antaeus (27) Aut 77, p. 57.
"The Law That Marries All Things." Hudson (30:1) Spr 77,
   p. 49.
"Setting Out" (for Gurney Norman). Hudson (30:1) Spr 77, p. 50.
"Song." Hudson (30:1) Spr 77, p. 51.
"The Strait." Hudson (30:1) Spr 77, p. 47.

BERRYHILL, Lori
"Mark E. Miller. " QW (3) Spr-Sum 77, p. 93.

BERRYHILL, Michael
"The Talker. " NewOR (5:3) 77, p. 200.

BERSSENBRUGGE, Mei-Mei
"The Field for Blue Corn. " Pequod (2:3) Sum 77, p. 47.

BERTOLINO, James
"December Thirteen. " Waters (5) 77, p. 4.
"Mom & Sally. " ParisR (70) Sum 77, p. 170.
"Not a Normal Tongue. " Waters (5) 77, p. 5.

BERTRAM, James
"Is It Well-Lighted, Papa?" MissR (6:1) 77, p. 74.

BERY, Rohit
"I ate the light bulb in my house. " AAR (27) 77, p. 115.

BETHEL, Gar
"Combing. " PoetryNW (18:2) Sum 77, p. 14.
"Dressing. " PoetryNW (18:2) Sum 77, p. 13.
"Drinking. " PoetryNW (18:2) Sum 77, p. 14.
"Rising. " PoetryNW (18:2) Sum 77, p. 12.

BEUM, Robert
"In Gardens. " LittleR (12) 77, p. 3.

BEVINGTON, Helen
"The Traveler Who Went. " SouthernPR (16:SI) 77, p. 17.

BEYER, William
"The Meeting. " Wind (24) 77, p. 12.
"Question in Autumn. " Wind (24) 77, p. 12.

BIENEK, Horst
"Flüchtige. " ChiR (29:3) Wint 78, p. 72.

BIGBEAR, Joe
"Time is now. " AmerPoR (6:2) Mr-Ap 77, p. 32.
"Up in the North woods. " AmerPoR (6:2) Mr-Ap 77, p. 31.

BIGELOW, Laura
"once I was a bird and. " AAR (27) 77, p. 126.

BIGUENET, John
"After the Shipwreck. " NewOR (5:3) 77, p. 240.
"The Door. " LittleR (12) 77, p. 17.
"The Wall behind the Mirror. " NewOR (5:3) 77, p. 241.

BIHLER, Penny
"I Know What I Know. " Madrona (4:13/14) 77, p. 43.

BILAC, Olavo
"Virgens mortas." TexQ (19:4) Wint 76, p. 96.

BINGEN-KUMIN, Judith
"A Pair of Old Bathing Trunks" (tr. of William Cliff, w. Maxine
   Kumin). Columbia (1) Aut 77, p. 29.

BIRMAN, Abraham
from Against Parting: "Sergeant Weiss" (tr. of Natan Zach, w.
   Jon Silkin). TriQ (39) Spr 77, p. 317.

BIRMINGHAM, Darci
"Making Breasts." YaleLit (146:4/5) 77, p. 39.

BIRNBAUM, Marlene
"The Monument." Stonecloud (6) 76, p. 33.

BISHOP, Guy R., Jr.
"'How Do You Mean "Sensual"?'" Mouth (11/12) Mr-Je 77, p. 60.
"My cock." Mouth (11/12) Mr-Je 77, p. 60.
"Wave cleaned." Mouth (11/12) Mr-Je 77, p. 59.

BISHOP, Helen
"Cruel Assortments" (tr. of René Char, w. Dale Ponikvar and
   Reiner Schürmann). Bound (5:3) Spr 77, p. 755.

BISHOP, Wendy
"Aid-el-Kebir." CutB (9) Aut-Wint 77, p. 136.
"People from Your Jaw." CutB (9) Aut-Wint 77, p. 140.
"1225 B.C." CutB (9) Aut-Wint 77, p. 138.

BISSERT, Ellen Marie
"monday insomnia." Gra (12) 77, p. 22.

BIZZARO, Patrick A.
"The Boy Who Burns Forests." YellowBR (8) 77, p. 8.
"Morning Song." YellowBR (8) 77, p. 9.

BLACK, Charles
"Gauguin Alive and Dead." SewanR (85:3) Sum 77, p. 431.
"The Throathearted Blues." SouthwR (62:1) Wint 77, p. 21.

BLACK, Isaac J.
Eleven poems. Obs (3:2) Sum 77, pp. 39-47.

BLACKBURN, Paul
"Upon Hanging a European Work of Art in a Brazilian House" (tr.
   of Leonardo Froes). LitR (21:2) Wint 78, p. 264.

BLACKETTER, Brian
"What This Poem Can Do." AmerPoR (6:2) Mr-Ap 77, p. 34.

BLACKFORD, Anne
"Journals." TransR (58/59) F 77, p. 132.

BLACKMAN, Gary A.
"Laundromat Haikus." YellowBR (9) 77, p. 35.
"Sketches of Mexico XV." YellowBR (8) 77, p. 30.

BLADE, Tina
"Eating a Pomegranate." CalQ (11/12) Wint-Spr 77, p. 54.
"A Meal, A Spell." CalQ (11/12) Wint-Spr 77, p. 53.

BLAIS, W. A.
"Lost Gatsby and the Great Horizon: a Review." Drag (16) 77.

BLAISDELL, Harold W.
"Rage." Mouth (13) D 77, p. 63.
"The Seventh Month." Mouth (13) D 77, p. 63.

BLAKE, Robert W.
"The Centaur." EngJ (66:5) My 77, p. 52.

BLANTON, Frederick D.
"All This for Love" (tr. of Luis Cernuda, w. Susan C. Blanton).
    Mouth (13) D 77, p. 19.
"The Blackbird, the Seagull" (tr. of Luis Cernuda, w. Susan C.
    Blanton). Mouth (13) D 77, p. 8.
"I Want You" (tr. of Luis Cernuda, w. Susan C. Blanton). Mouth
    (13) D 77, p. 6.
"Sailors Are the Wings of Love" (tr. of Luis Cernuda, w. Susan
    C. Blanton). Mouth (13) D 77, p. 7.
"Unfinished Statue" (tr. of Luis Cernuda, w. Susan C. Blanton).
    Mouth (13) D 77, p. 9.

BLANTON, Susan C.
"All This for Love" (tr. of Luis Cernuda, w. Frederick D.
    Blanton). Mouth (13) D 77, p. 19.
"The Blackbird, the Seagull" (tr. of Luis Cernuda, w. Frederick
    D. Blanton). Mouth (13) D 77, p. 8.
"I Want You" (tr. of Luis Cernuda, w. Frederick D. Blanton).
    Mouth (13) D 77, p. 6.
"Sailors Are the Wings of Love" (tr. of Luis Cernuda, w.
    Frederick D. Blanton). Mouth (13) D 77, p. 7.
"Unfinished Statue" (tr. of Luis Cernuda, w. Frederick D.
    Blanton). Mouth (13) D 77, p. 9.

BLASER, Robin
"An Exercise" (arr. of Jack Spicer, w. John Granger). Bound
    (6:1) Aut 77, p. 3.

BLASING, Randy
"All Present." Poetry (130:1) Ap 77, p. 3.
"Bees" (tr. of Nazim Hikmet, w. Mutlu Konuk). DenQ (12:2)
    Sum 77, p. 237.
"Bor Hotel" (tr. of Nazim Hikmet, w. Mutlu Konuk). AmerPoR
    (6:6) N-D 77, p. 39.
"Disney." PoNow (14/18) 77, p. 12.

"Hymn to Life" (tr. of Nazim Hikmet, w. Mutlu Konuk).   AmerPoR
    (6:6) N-D 77, p. 38.
"In Memory." PoNow (14/18) 77, p. 12.
"Letters from Chankiri Prison" (tr. of Nazim Hikmet, w. Mutlu
    Konuk). DenQ (12:2) Sum 77, p. 231.
"Morning in Prague" (tr. of Nazim Hikmet, w. Mutlu Konuk).
    AmerPoR (6:6) N-D 77, p. 38.
"My Funeral" (tr. of Nazim Hikmet, w. Mutlu Konuk).   AmerPoR
    (6:6) N-D 77, p. 39.
"Optimistic Prague" (tr. of Nazim Hikmet, w. Mutlu Konuk).
    AmerPoR (6:6) N-D 77, p. 39.
"Poem: I'm inside the advancing light" (tr. of Nazim Hikmet, w.
    Mutlu Konuk). DenQ (12:2) Sum 77, p. 236.
"Poem: In this sadness I feel" (tr. of Nazim Hikmet, w. Mutlu
    Konuk). DenQ (12:2) Sum 77, p. 236.
"Poem: My woman came with me as far as Brest" (tr. of Nazim
    Hikmet, w. Mutlu Konuk). AmerPoR (6:6) N-D 77, p. 39.
"Statements." PoNow (14/18) 77, p. 12.

BLAZEK, Douglas
    "Frontier Ballad" (for W. S. Merwin). Drag (16) 77.
    "Impotence." Gra (12) 77, p. 17.
    "A Life Raw with Absence." SunM (4) Aut 77, p. 25.
    "Lovers Entering the Years." PoNow (14/18) 77, p. 13.
    "The Marvelous Meteorites." SunM (4) Aut 77, p. 24.
    "The Mural." Drag (16) 77.
    "Primer in Optics." NewC (7:3) 75-76, p. 25.
    "The Stripper." MontG (5) Wint 77, p. 4.
    "Theory of Economics." Gra (12) 77, p. 4.
    "To a Lady Gazing into the Heavens." MontG (5) Wint 77, p. 3.
    "To Love You in the Style of the Leaves." PoNow (14/18) 77,
        p. 13.
    "Trampled Moon, Bored and Had." PoNow (14/18) 77, p. 13.

BLEIBERG, Germán
    "Origin" (tr. by Nancy Willard). Salm (38/39) Sum-Aut 77,
        p. 104.

BLESSING, Richard
    "Calling Home." PoetryNW (18:3) Aut 77, p. 54.
    "What I Know by Heart." GeoR (31:4) Wint 77, p. 851.
    "Winter Constellations." PoetryNW (18:3) Aut 77, p. 55.

BLEVINS, Steve
    "Full Moons." Ploughs (4:1) 77, p. 161.

BLOCH, Chana
    "Burial." SouthernPR (17:2) Aut 77, p. 12.
    "Hard Winter" (tr. of Dahlia Ravikovitch). TriQ (39) Spr 77,
        p. 296.
    "Hills of Salt" (tr. of Dahlia Ravikovitch). TriQ (39) Spr 77,
        p. 296.
    "How Hong Kong Was Destroyed" (tr. of Dahlia Ravikovitch).
        TriQ (39) Spr 77, p. 299.

"Memory" (tr. of Dahlia Ravikovitch).   Chowder (8) Spr-Sum 77,
    p. 45.

BLOCK, Allan
"Harry Whitney. " AndR (3:2) Aut 76, p. 65.

BLOCKLYN, Paul
"In the Supermarket: A Parable. " HiramPoR (22) Aut-Wint 77,
    p. 7.
"The Scarecrow. " SmPd (14:1) Wint 77, p. 30.

BLOMFIELD, Adelaide
"The Rush. " SouthernPR (17:1) Spr 77, p. 14.

BLOOMFIELD, Maureen
"Ghosts. " Poetry (129:5) F 77, p. 258.
"Isuprel. " Poetry (129:5) F 77, p. 262.
"The Long Ton. " Poetry (129:5) F 77, p. 261.
"Morning. " Poetry (129:5) F 77, p. 257.
"Near the End of June. " Poetry (129:5) F 77, p. 259.

BLOOMINGDALE, Judith
"Country Funeral. " ModernPS (8:1) Spr 77, p. 47.
"To My Unborn Child. " ModernPS (8:1) Spr 77, p. 46.

BLOSSOM, Laurel
"Friggins Division. " Columbia (1) Aut 77, p. 28.

BLOSSOM, Lavina
"That painter. " KanQ (9:1) Wint 77, p. 120.

BLOUNT, Roy, Jr.
"Gryll's State. " BosUJ (25:3) 77, p. 16.
"Light Verse. " BosUJ (25:1) 77, p. 29.
Ten songs. Esq (87:4) Ap 77, p. 105.

BLUM, Etta
"As Though Existence. " Nat (225:15) 5 N 77, p. 478.
"The Dream Re-Dreamed. " Nat (224:1) 1-8 Ja 77, p. 30.
"Olive Tree, First Pilgrim. " NewRep (176:6) 5 F 77, p. 26.

BLUM, Lynda
"125 Paintings. " Glass (2:2/3) Wint-Spr 77, p. 99.
"The Perfume of Old Things. " Glass (2:2/3) Wint-Spr 77, p. 98.

BLUMBERG, Bonnie Birtwistle
"Rocker. " ChrC (94:3) 26 Ja 77, p. 60.

BLUME, Burt
"For Palinurus, Hart Crane, & You. " WebR (3:1) Wint 77,
    p. 26.
"Sea Story. " WebR (3:1) Wint 77, p. 25.

BLY, Robert
"The Blue Raft. " Kayak (45) My 77, p. 7.
"The Crow's Head. " OhioR (18:3) Aut 77, p. 21.
"Driving. " Some (7/8) 76.
"18" (tr. of Kabir). MoonsLT (2:3) 77, inside front cover.
"11" (tr. of Kabir). MoonsLT (2:3) 77, inside front cover.
"The Farallone Islands. " Kayak (45) My 77, p. 9.
"Four Poems after Basho. " Kayak (45) My 77, p. 8.
"A Fragment Written Out of Admiration for James Wright's Po-
    ems. " OhioR (18:2) Spr-Sum 77, p. 58.
"Frost Still in the Ground. " Kayak (45) My 77, p. 9.
"Near Kabekona Lake. " Bits (6) Jl 77.
"Out Picking Up Corn. " Kayak (45) My 77, p. 6.
"Rejoicing When Alone. " CornellR (1) Spr 77, p. 73.
"Standing in a Willow Grove at Dusk. " Some (7/8) 76.
"Tiny Spinning Wheel Concerto. " NewRep (177:10) 3 S 77, p. 28.
"Two Years after the War. " Nat (224:20) 21 My 77, p. 636.
"Watching a Big Shadow Move across the Lake. " Kayak (45) My
    77, p. 7.

BLY, William
"Just Something to Be Said. " Wind (24) 77, p. 13.

BOBROWSKI, Johannes
"Return" (tr. by Don Bogen). Chowder (9) Aut-Wint 77, p. 45.

BOE, Deborah
"Grief. " US1 (9) Spr 77, p. 5.
"Lazarus. " US1 (10) Wint 77-78, p. 2.

BOGAN, Louise
"The Dream. " NewYRB (24:8) 12 My 77, p. 13.

BOGEN, Don
"First Morning at Boulder Creek. " TexQ (20:4) Wint 77, p. 89.
"Hearing the News of a Great Statesman's Illness" (tr. of Bertolt
    Brecht). Chowder (8) Spr-Sum 77, p. 46.
"Reading the Paper and Making Tea" (tr. of Bertolt Brecht).
    Chowder (8) Spr-Sum 77, p. 46.

BOGGIS, Jay
"The Children's Hour. " Some (7/8) 76.
"Dear Snake. " Some (7/8) 76.
"Dear Turk. " Some (7/8) 76.
"Rosa's Cantina. " Some (7/8) 76.
"Selected Death Warrants. " Some (7/8) 76.

BOGGS, Mildred Williams
"Waterskippers. " Wind (25) 77, p. 18.

BOGIN, Meg
"Ballad of the Moon, the Moon" (to Conchita García Lorca) (tr.
    of Federico García Lorca). MassR (18:4) Wint 77, p. 821.

"The Unfaithful Wife" (to Lydia Cabrera and to her friend).
MassR (18:4) Wint 77, p. 822.

BOGOJAVLENSKY, Marianne
"Apology" (tr. of Anna Akhmatova, w. Sam Bradley). WebR (3:4)
Aut 77, p. 14.
"That Evening" (tr. of Anna Akhmatova, w. Sam Bradley). WebR
(3:4) Aut 77, p. 13.

BOIARSKI, Phil
"The Hilarious Beating." ParisR (69) Spr 77, p. 35.
"Landscape." CalQ (11/12) Wint-Spr 77, p. 119.
"Tree Prayers." Hand (1) 77, p. 152.
"Wood Poem." Hand (1) 77, p. 153.

BOLICK, Robert
"Bloodsea." PoetL (72:1) Spr 77, p. 34.

BOLLIER, E. P.
"Notes for an Unwritten Elegy" (for Richard Perrill Adams
August 17, 1917-March 25, 1977). AAUP (63:3) Ag 77,
p. 139.

BOLOTIN, S.
"Ancestors, Please Return to Sanity!" (tr. by Nan Braymer).
NewWR (45:2) Mr-Ap 77, p. 19.

BOLTON, Charles E.
"Waking Up Blind" (for James Merrill). AmerR (26) N 77,
p. 158.

BOMBA, Bernard
"Closing Time." SmPd (14:2) Spr 77, p. 20.

BONAZZI, Robert
"Da Capo/Al Fine." RemR (5) 77, p. 89.

BOND, Harold
"The Fall." Ploughs (4:1) 77, p. 91.
"To the Welcome Wagon Lady." Ploughs (4:1) 77, p. 90.

BONNER, Wendy
"And after All These Years." QW (2) Wint 77, p. 63.

BONOMO, Jacquelyn
"A Tarot Reading for Dianne--Nine of Swords." StoneC (77:3) S
77, p. 14.

BONTEMPI, Art
"Fishing with Ruble in the Wrangell Narrows." Juice (4) 77.
"San José." Sam (52) Ap 77, p. 2.

BOOTH, Martin
"At Scorhill." MalR (44) O 77, p. 122.

BOOTH, Philip
  "Building Her. " Atl (239:5) My 77, p. 85.
  "A Clear Solstice." OhioR (18:1) Wint 77, p. 13.
  "Cycle. " PoetryNW (18:2) Sum 77, p. 54.
  "Here. " Hudson (30:2) Sum 77, p. 227.
  "Not to Tell Lies. " PoetryNW (18:2) Sum 77, p. 55.
  "Rates. " Field (17) Aut 77, p. 87.
  "Round. " Bits (6) Jl 77.
  "She" (For M. K. H.). PoetryNW (18:2) Sum 77, p. 54.
  "Stammerings: 1937. " PoNow (14/18) 77, p. 14.

BORAWSKI, Walta
  "All in white but loveless & without music. " Mouth (13) D 77,
    p. 74.
  "For those who arrived too early or too late. " Mouth (11/12)
    Mr-Je 77, p. 95.
  "Harvard has no class these days; nothing does. " Mouth (13) D
    77, p. 60.
  "Thanksgiving Weekend, 1976. " Mouth (11/12) Mr-Je 77, p. 96.

BORENSTEIN, Emily
  "Because. " Glass (2:2/3) Wint-Spr 77, p. 27.

BORGES, Jorge Luis
  "A Blind Man" (tr. by Alastair Reid). NewYRB (24:19) 24 N 77,
    p. 47.
  "The Blind Man" (tr. by Alastair Reid). NewYRB (24:19) 24 N
    77, p. 47.
  "Browning Resolves to Be a Poet" (tr. by Alastair Reid). NewYRB
    (24:19) 24 N 77, p. 47.
  "Brunanburh, A. D. 937" (tr. by Alastair Reid). NewYorker
    (53:9) 18 Ap 77, p. 42.
  "Hengist Wants Men" (tr. by Alastair Reid). NewYorker (53:18)
    20 Je 77, p. 34.
  "I Am" (tr. by Alastair Reid). AmerPoR (6:6) N-D 77, p. 40.
  "Inventory" (tr. by Alastair Reid). AmerPoR (6:6) N-D 77,
    p. 40.
  "The Keeper" (tr. by Alastair Reid). NewYorker (53:29) 5 S 77,
    p. 26.
  "My Books" (tr. by Alastair Reid). AmerPoR (6:6) N-D 77,
    p. 40.
  "The Palace" (tr. by Alastair Reid). NewYorker (53:32) 26 S 77,
    p. 38.
  "The Suicide" (tr. by Willis Barnstone). AmerPoR (6:3) My-Je
    77, p. 44.
  "Talismans" (tr. by Alastair Reid). NewYorker (53:25) 8 Ag 77,
    p. 26.
  "To the German Language" (tr. by Alastair Reid). NewYRB
    (24:19) 24 N 77, p. 47.
  "To the Nightingale" (tr. by Alastair Reid). NewYorker (53:12)
    9 My 77, p. 42.
  Twenty poems (tr. by Alastair Reid). NewRep (177:21) 19 N 77,
    p. 26.
  "You" (tr. by Alastair Reid). AmerPoR (6:6) N-D 77, p. 40.

BORGZINNER, Yadira
"Dark Love." SeC (5:2) 78, p. 12.
"What Is Poetry?" SeC (5:2) 78, p. 11.

BORROFF, Marie
"Floating." NewRep (177:10) 3 S 77, p. 26.
"The Waves." YaleR (66:3) Spr 77, p. 403.

BORUCH, Marianne
"Chicago Poultry." Some (7/8) 76.

BOSCH, C. William, III
"Untitled." CarouselQ (2:2) Aut 77, p. 8.

BOSLEY, Keith
"Drought." Nat (224:24) 18 Je 77, p. 763.
"Icons." Nat (224:20) 21 My 77, p. 634.

BOSQUÉ, Gloria
"Chantsong: The Two Women" (for Doris Lessing). NewYRB
   (24:6) 14 Ap 77, p. 7.

BOSSERMAN, Lorelei
"Villanelle." HangL (30) Sum 77, p. 75.

BOSTRON, M. A.
"Larry, #1." CarouselQ (2:3) Wint 77, p. 3.

BOTTOMS, David
"The Drunk Hunter." Harp (254:1525) Je 77, p. 85.
"The Faithless Heart." Poem (29) Mr 77, p. 17.
"The Hard Bargain." PraS (51:4) Wint 77-78, p. 413.
"Rediscovering the Good Old Boys" (for Rosemary Daniell).
   SouthernPR (16:SI) 77, p. 18.
"Rubbing the Faces of Angels" (for Lynn). SoCaR (9:2) Ap 77,
   p. 20.
"Shooting Rats at the Bibb County Dump." Harp (254:1525) Je 77,
   p. 85.
"The Shot Hunter." SouthernPR (17:2) Aut 77, p. 9.

BOUDREAU, Jean
"Garden." SmPd (14:1) Wint 77, p. 13.
"In the Hands." CarouselQ (2:2) Aut 77, p. 20.

BOULUS, Sargon
"And Then" (tr. of Sameeh al-Qasim). Mund (10:1) 77, p. 60.
"And Who Are You" (tr. of Fou'ad Rifqah). Mund (10:1) 77,
   p. 70.
"Depths" (tr. of Buland al-Haidari). Mund (10:1) 77, p. 56.
"The Deserted Well" (tr. of Yusuf al-Khal). Mund (10:1) 77,
   p. 50.
"Dream" (tr. of Buland al-Haidari). Mund (10:1) 77, p. 57.
"Exodus" (tr. of Salah Abd al-Sabour). Mund (10:1) 77, p. 58.

"Feast" (tr. of Sameeh al-Qasim). Mund (10:1) 77, p. 60.
"The Five Crosses" (tr. of Sa'di Yusif). Mund (10:1) 77, p. 67.
"Glory to the Three" (tr. of Yusuf al-Khal). Mund (10:1) 77,
    p. 52.
"I Hear Everything" (tr. of Yusuf al-Khal). Mund (10:1) 77,
    p. 51.
"Is This You or the Tale?" (tr. of Unsi al-Haj). Mund (10:1) 77,
    p. 74.
"The Last Line in the Poem" (tr. of Sameeh al-Qasim). Mund
    (10:1) 77, p. 59.
"Lorca Elegies" (tr. of Abd al-Wahab al-Bayyati). Mund (10:1)
    77, p. 64.
"The Mailman's Fear" (tr. of Muhammad al-Maghut). Mund
    (10:1) 77, p. 61.
"Mirage City" (tr. of Badr Shakir al-Sayyab). Mund (10:1) 77,
    p. 62.
"No, and Why" (tr. of Tawfiq Sayegh). Mund (10:1) 77, p. 71.
from Poetry Sequence: (2-3) (tr. of Jabra Ibrahim Jabra). Mund
    (10:1) 77, p. 63.
"Retaliation" (tr. of Yusuf al-Khal). Mund (10:1) 77, p. 52.
"The Siege" (tr. of Muhammad al-Maghut). Mund (10:1) 77,
    p. 61.
"A Stone" (tr. of Sa'di Yusif). Mund (10:1) 77, p. 68.
"Weariness in the Evening of January the Thirty-Second" (tr. of
    Isam Mahfoudh). Mund (10:1) 77, p. 53.
"The Whole of Night" (tr. of Sa'di Yusif). Mund (10:1) 77, p. 68.
"You Want" (tr. of Nazar Qabbani). Mund (10:1) 77, p. 72.

BOURNE, Louis
    "The Coins against the Counter" (tr. of Carlos Bousoño). Stand
        (18:2) 77, p. 44.

BOUSOÑO, Carlos
    "The Coins against the Counter" (tr. by Louis Bourne). Stand
        (18:2) 77, p. 44.

BOUVARD, Guita
    "Plumbing the Silence." Ploughs (3:3/4) 77, p. 95.

BOUVARD, Marguerite Guzman
    "On the Edge of Departure." SouthwR (62:1) Wint 77, p. 63.
    "White Nights." LitR (21:1) Aut 77, p. 101.

BOWEN, James K.
    "Challenge." KanQ (9:1) Wint 77, p. 66.
    "Rain Country." Confr (14) Spr-Sum 77, p. 55.

BOWERING, Marilyn
    "Animals Are Surplus." MalR (43) Jl 77, p. 92.
    "North Coast Lament." MalR (43) Jl 77, p. 90.
    "The Shaman." Waters (6) 77, p. 8.
    "Winter Harbour" (for Cam La Bossière). MalR (43) Jl 77,
        p. 86.

BOWIE, John
"A Night at the Opera." SenR (8:1) My 77, p. 67.
"Ode to Bela Lugosi." SenR (8:2) D 77, p. 8.
"Ode to Dan Blocker." SenR (8:2) D 77, p. 11.
"Ode to Fatty Arbuckle." SenR (8:2) D 77, p. 10.
"Ode to John Wayne." SenR (8:2) D 77, p. 7.

BOWIE, Robert B.
"The Answer." SunM (4) Aut 77, p. 19.
"The Baiting." HolCrit (14:1) F 77, p. 13.
"Changed." DenQ (12:1) Spr 77, p. 144.
"Crow: A Special Kind of Blackness." SunM (4) Aut 77, p. 18.
"El Natural." DenQ (12:1) Spr 77, p. 143.
"Expectant Angels." SunM (4) Aut 77, p. 17.
"Split Personality." SouthernHR (11:1) Wint 77, p. 48.
"Style." DenQ (12:1) Spr 77, p. 144.
"Summer House." DenQ (12:1) Spr 77, p. 145.
"The Visitor." MalR (44) O 77, p. 120.

BOWMAN, P. C.
"Christ and Lord Kitchener." LitR (21:1) Aut 77, p. 126.

BOYCHUK, Bohdan
"To Love, to Go in Endless Thunder" (tr. of Boris Pasternak,
    w. Mark Rudman). Some (7/8) 76.

BOYNTON, Dick
"Stars Fall Don't They?" KanQ (9:1) Wint 77, p. 86.

BRACCHITTA, Vincent F.
"Eastern Holymen." Icarus (5:2) Aut 77, p. 17.

BRACKETT, Kate
"Evening Swimmer." PoetL (72:1) Spr 77, p. 34.
"January Thaw." MichQR (16:1) Wint 77, p. 49.

BRADFIELD, Keith
"Women Born from Trees" (tr. of Lars Gyllensten). WebR (3:1)
    Wint 77, p. 59.

BRADLEY, George
"Expecting an Angel." Shen (28:4) Sum 77, p. 36.

BRADLEY, Marion Minthorn
"Flight-Shy." EngJ (66:5) My 77, p. 50.

BRADLEY, Sam
"And After Embrace." TexQ (20:4) Wint 77, p. 116.
"Apology" (tr. of Anna Akhmatova, w. Marianne Bogojavlensky).
    WebR (3:4) Aut 77, p. 14.
"Base Service." KanQ (9:1) Wint 77, p. 25.
"I Do Not Speak Your Shibboleth." LitR (20:3) Spr 77, p. 270.
"Invitation to Far Space." KanQ (9:1) Wint 77, p. 26.

"A Lonely American. "   SouthwR (62:1) Wint 77, p. 46.
"That Evening" (tr. of Anna Akhmatova, w. Marianne Bogojavlen-
    sky).   WebR (3:4) Aut 77, p. 13.

BRADY, Charles
"Flies in the Surgery Tent. "   Stonecloud (6) 76, p. 142.

BRAGG, Mary Ellen
"Fugue in Burnt Toast Major. "   HangL (31) Aut 77, p. 71.

BRAND, Daniel
"April 18th. "   TransR (58/59) F 77, p. 168.
"Bright Eyed Mole Cleans Up. "   TransR (58/59) F 77, p. 171.
"Give Some Story. "   TransR (58/59) F 77, p. 170.

BRAND, Helena
"Shore Lines, Surf Side. "   ChrC (94:27) 31 Ag-7 S 77, p. 752.

BRANDI, John
"Good Friday Poem. "   Hand (1) 77, p. 197.

BRANDTS, Robert
"Go Directly.... "   OhioR (18:3) Aut 77, p. 23.

BRANSTETTER, Kathy
"Story of the Ants and Grasshoppers" (tr. of Tzeltal, w. W. S.
    Merwin and Santiago Mendez Zapata).   Nat (225:14) 29 O 77,
    p. 444.

BRASIL, Emanuel
"Drifting. "   LitR (21:2) Wint 78, p. 268.
"Just a Note. "   LitR (21:2) Wint 78, p. 269.

BRAUN, Richard Emil
"Text. "   ModernPS (8:1) Spr 77, p. 47.
"Toward Comedy. "   GeoR (31:1) Spr 77, p. 160.

BRAXTON, Jodi
from Sometimes I Think of Maryland: "big old houses have
    passed away. "   Nimrod (21:2/22:1) 77, p. 30.

BRAYMER, Nan
"Ancestors, Please Return to Sanity!" (tr. of S. Bolotin).   NewWR
    (45:2) Mr-Ap 77, p. 19.

BRECHT, Bertolt
"Hearing the News of a Great Statesman's Illness" (tr. by Don
    Bogen).   Chowder (8) Spr-Sum 77, p. 46.
"Reading the Paper and Making Tea" (tr. by Don Bogen).
    Chowder (8) Spr-Sum 77, p. 46.

BRESLIN, Paul
"Shaving. "   GeoR (31:3) Aut 77, p. 616.

BRESSI, Betty
  "Aura." LittleR (12) 77, p. 3.
  "Mars Is Red." Glass (2:2/3) Wint-Spr 77, p. 104.

BRETT, Peter
  "Bone." RemR (5) 77, p. 24.
  "Corn Mush." Juice (5) 77.
  "Rites of Passage." DacTerr (14) Spr-Sum 77, p. 13.
  "The Rush of Being." SenR (8:2) D 77, p. 32.
  "Thomas Wolfe." SenR (8:2) D 77, p. 33.
  "Tonight at the World." RemR (5) 77, p. 25.
  "Words about the Profession." Vaga (26) 77, p. 76.

BREWSTER, David
  "Four Poems" (tr. of Miklos Radnoti). Madrona (4:13/14) 77,
      p. 30.
  "The Grateful Dead." Drag (16) 77.
  "Scarecrow's Tale." NowestR (16:3) 77, p. 69.
  "Song of the Camel." AndR (4:1) Spr 77, p. 24.

BRIDGE, Josiah
  "Blues." StoneC (77:1) F 77, p. 7.

BRIDGES, Lee
  "We'll Go On." NegroHB (40:2) Mr-Ap 77, p. 684.

BRIDGES, William
  "Venice: Sunday Morning in the Gesuati." BelPoJ (27:4) Sum 77,
      p. 35.

BRIGGS, John
  "The Day He Didn't Write." WindO (29) Sum 77, p. 21.

BRINGHURST, Robert
  "The Better Man." Kayak (45) My 77, p. 50.

BRINKMANN, Rolf Dieter
  "Poem: 'The sea' is an entertaining excuse" (tr. by Hartmut
      Schnell). NewL (43:3) Spr 77, p. 22.
  "Red Tomatoes" (tr. by Hartmut Schnell). NewL (43:3) Spr 77,
      p. 20.
  "Tarzan" (tr. by Hartmut Schnell). NewL (43:3) Spr 77, p. 20.
  "To hear one of those" (tr. by Hartmut Schnell). NewL (43:3)
      Spr 77, p. 22.
  "Well, somehow" (tr. by Hartmut Schnell). NewL (43:3) Spr 77,
      p. 19.

BRITT, Alan
  "The Afternoon of the Light." Agni (7) 77, p. 102.
  I Suppose the Darkness Is Ours (for my mother). UTR (5:2) 77.
      Entire issue.
  "I Was Building." Drag (16) 77.
  "Late Nocturne" (for Tomas Tranströmer). AAR (27) 77, p. 90.

"Tiny Lizard." KanQ (9:3) Sum 77, p. 49.
"Together." BallSUF (18:4) Aut 77, p. 19.
"William Matthews Reads to a Sparse Audience at American Uni-
   versity." AAR (27) 77, p. 89.

BRIZENDINE, Nancy
"Bar as Confessional." Madrona (4:13/14) 77, p. 18.

BROCK, Randall
"anchor." Juice (5) 77.
"a-shark." Juice (5) 77.
"the cosmos." Glass (2:2/3) Wint-Spr 77, p. 30.
"darkly." Wind (24) 77, p. 29.
"the death." Glass (2:2/3) Wint-Spr 77, p. 31.
"the death." Juice (5) 77.
"the deep." Juice (5) 77.
"i find." Glass (2:2/3) Wint-Spr 77, p. 30.
"in the foil." Juice (5) 77.
"inside." Glass (2:2/3) Wint-Spr 77, p. 31.
"out of love." Juice (5) 77.
"Poem: the great." Wind (24) 77, p. 29.
"reflection." Wind (24) 77, p. 29.
"seize." Juice (5) 77.
"slowly." Wind (24) 77, p. 29.
"the stone image." Glass (2:2/3) Wint-Spr 77, p. 31.
"tight." Glass (2:2/3) Wint-Spr 77, p. 30.

BROCK, Van K.
"The Deathbirth." SouthernPR (16:SI) 77, p. 20.
Twenty-two poems. Poets (1:1) 77, p. 3-24.

BROCKMEIER, Maureen
"Immigration." CalQ (11/12) Wint-Spr 77, p. 82.

BRODA, Ina Jun
"The Pauper" (tr. of Edvard Kocbek, w. Herbert Kuhner).
   WebR (3:4) Aut 77, p. 17.

BRODINE, Karen
"Cable Vision." Montra (3) Spr 77, p. 140.
"Gardening at Night." Montra (3) Spr 77, p. 138.
"Jigsaw Riddle." Montra (3) Spr 77, p. 141.
"Launder." YellowBR (9) 77, p. 32.
"Repairing the Old Road." Montra (3) Spr 77, p. 139.

BRODKEY, Harold
"Anti-Hymn." TransR (58/59) F 77, p. 91.

BRODOFF, Ami
"Dorianna." Gra (12) 77.
"Folding." Gra (12) 77.

BRODSKY, Joseph
"Elegy: For Robert Lowell." NewYorker (53:37) 31 O 77, p. 38.

"The Thames at Chelsea" (tr. by David Rigsbee). NewYorker
(53:41) 28 N 77, p. 56.

BRODSKY, Louis Daniel
"Trip to Tipton, 7/22/72: The Returning." Sparrow (33) Ja 77,
p. 8.

BRODY, Eliott
"Copper 7." MontG (5) Wint 77, p. 68.

BROMWICH, David
"Kickapoo War Dance." PartR (44:3) 77, p. 409.

BRONK, William
"For Any Speakers." Hand (1) 77, p. 66.
"For Evil and Destruction." Hand (1) 77, p. 65.
"In Verdi, the silly stories may have been true." Montra (3)
Spr 77, p. 34.
"Look for fulfillment if you will, even ask." Montra (3) Spr 77,
p. 35.
"Oh God, I can as little be said to be." Hand (1) 77, p. 66.
"The Random." Hand (1) 77, p. 65.
"The way that we exist as physical." Montra (3) Spr 77, p. 32.
"Your beauty is not your beauty." Montra (3) Spr 77, p. 33.

BROOK, Donna
"Creating Fiction." HangL (30) Sum 77, p. 10.
"Europe for You in Two Parts." HangL (30) Sum 77, p. 4.
"Suicide Attempts." HangL (30) Sum 77, p. 6.
"Why I Am a Whore." HangL (30) Sum 77, p. 9.
"Why Teach Creative Writing." Kayak (44) F 77, p. 41.

BROOKHOUSE, Christopher
"An Old Irish Woman Dead by Falling Glass from a High Rise in
Boston, Massachusetts." CarolQ (29:1) Wint 77, p. 60.

BROOKS, Cora
"The Short Flight." Ploughs (3:3/4) 77, p. 140.

BROOKS, Phyllis
"The Camera Gives and Takes Away." OP (24) Aut-Wint 77,
p. 39.
"Exercise." OP (24) Aut-Wint 77, p. 39.
"Your Legacy." OP (24) Aut-Wint 77, p. 36.

BROOKS, Randy
"Three Prescription Poems." WindO (27) Aut 76.

BROSMAN, Catherine Savage
"Father." NoAmR (262:1) Spr 77, p. 23.
"Notes from a Reconstruction." TexQ (20:3) Aut 77, p. 48.
"Wires." SouthernPR (16:SI) 77, p. 21.

BROUGHTON, T. Alan
"Beyond the Woods." Poem (31) N 77, p. 30.
"Hunt." DeKalb (10:2) Wint 77, p. 11.
"Laces." PoNow (14/18) 77, p. 14.
"Roman Bus." Poem (31) N 77, p. 35.
"A Setting for Motion." Poem (31) N 77, p. 32.
"Seven Lyrics for Absence." BelPoJ (27:3) Spr 77, p. 33.
"Shut Out." Poem (31) N 77, p. 29.
"Thanksgiving." Confr (14) Spr-Sum 77, p. 54.
"Winter Dance." Sparrow (33) Ja 77, p. 12.

BROUMAS, Olga
"Artemis." Madem (83:4) Ap 77, p. 107.
"Sabbath." PortR (23) 77, p. 106.

BROWN, Al
"Young Now Old." BlackF (2:1) Wint 77-78, p. 24.

BROWN, Barbara
"The Island." Paunch (46/47) Ap 77, p. 53.
"Truth Is a Simple Thing." Paunch (46/47) Ap 77, p. 54.

BROWN, Dorothy M.
"The Tree." ConcPo (10:1) Spr 77, p. 50.

BROWN, Elizabeth
"Alexandra after a Freezing Rain--1918." NewRivR (2:1) 77,
    p. 24.
"Father, Returned from Hunting." NewRivR (2:1) 77, p. 23.
"In His Absence." NewRivR (2:1) 77, p. 23.
"Kamala." NewRivR (2:1) 77, p. 22.
"The Man Who Wore Too Many Clothes." Epoch (26:2) Wint 77,
    p. 187.
"Snapshot of Elsie, 1920." HolCrit (14:4) O 77, p. 15.

BROWN, Harry
"The Greatest Wile." KanQ (9:1) Wint 77, p. 56.
"Not About to Burn." KanQ (9:1) Wint 77, p. 57.

BROWN, Judy
"What We See/How We See It." NewL (43:4) Sum 77, p. 99.

BROWN, Kevin
"Chiaroscuro." Mouth (11/12) Mr-Je 77, p. 92.
"Inquiries." Mouth (13) D 77, p. 80.

BROWN, Kurt
Eight poems. Aspen (3) Spr 77, p. 42.

BROWN, Matthew
"Insinuation." GRR (8:1/2) 77, p. 124.
"Mirrors of Gethsemane." GRR (8:1/2) 77, p. 125.

BROWN, Milly
"no use pretending." Chomo (3:3) Spr 77, p. 46.

BROWN, Paul
"Between Harlequin & Columbine." MontG (6) Aut 77, p. 38.
"Between Solstice & Soluble." MontG (6) Aut 77, p. 39.

BROWN, Russell M.
"A New Bird Call." PoetL (72:1) Spr 77, p. 28.
"A Story Told Me, Inside, After I Fled the Beehive, Abandoning
the Mower to Its Fate." ConcPo (10:1) Spr 77, p. 16.

BROWN, Steven Ford
from The City of Light: "Light (1-3)." QW (2) Wint 77, p. 32.
from Eating Autographs: "'Just Like That Old Soap Opera Where
the Dumb Kid Falls in Love with the Moon.'" DeKalb (10:2)
Wint 77, p. 13.
from Eating Autographs: "'Living on the Street of Heartache.'"
DeKalb (10:2) Wint 77, p. 13.
from Eating Autographs: "'She Is in Love with the Sailor.'"
DeKalb (10:2) Wint 77, p. 12.
"Light 4." QW (3) Spr-Sum 77, p. 43.

BROWN, Steven W.
"Bits of Him." Mouth (11/12) Mr-Je 77, p. 61.
"A Thousand Men." Mouth (11/12) Mr-Je 77, p. 61.

BROWN, Terry W.
"Goodbye." MontG (5) Wint 77, p. 70.
"Leap Frog." MontG (5) Wint 77, p. 70.
"The Mortician." MontG (5) Wint 77, p. 70.

BROWNE, Michael Dennis
"Morley, Winter, Maiden Rock." ChiR (28:4) Spr 77, p. 118.
"Morley's Root Song." ChiR (28:4) Spr 77, p. 115.
"'Talk to Me, Baby.'" Iowa (8:2) Spr 77, p. 9.

BROWNING, Ann Hut
"The Legacy." CarolQ (29:1) Wint 77, p. 94.

BROWNING, Stephen
"Across the Moon's White Body." MichQR (16:2) Spr 77, p. 197.
"In Floodtime." MichQR (16:2) Spr 77, p. 198.

BROWNSTEIN, Michael
from Second Apart: "One thing is certain." PartR (44:4) 77,
p. 553.

BRUCE, Debra
"Blue Mountain" (for my father). PoNow (14/18) 77, p. 15.
"For Bad Grandmother and Betty Bumhead." Field (17) Aut 77,
p. 23.
"Perspective." CutB (8) Spr 77, p. 96.

BRUCE, Lennart
"Cloud Marauder." PoNow (14/18) 77, p. 15.

BRUCHAC, Joseph
"Bill Greenfield and the Devil." CutB (9) Aut-Wint 77, p. 104.
"Clear Cut." PoetryNW (18:1) Spr 77, p. 35.
"Commencement." Wind (24) 77, p. 15.
"Evening." Xa (4) 77, p. 59.
"First Moon." Agni (7) 77, p. 34.
"First Snow." Agni (7) 77, p. 33.
"Invocation for a Storm." Bleb (12) 77, p. 2.
"Invocations." Hand (1) 77, p. 173.
"The Killer." CalQ (11/12) Wint-Spr 77, p. 115.
"Lich Gate." Bleb (12) 77, p. 4.
"Listening, with Friends, to Neruda's Poems." Rapp (10) 77,
     p. 26.
"The Magistrate." CalQ (11/12) Wint-Spr 77, p. 114.
"Medicine Song." Xa (4) 77, p. 60.
"Midwinter at Onondaga." SoDakR (15:4) Wint 77-78, p. 57.
"Mountain and River" (for Mike Hogan and Jimmy Lewisohn).
     Bleb (12) 77, p. 1.
"The Old Skin." SoDakR (15:4) Wint 77-78, p. 56.
"Pages." Wind (24) 77, p. 15.
"The Planes." Bleb (12) 77, p. 3.
"Pines Near a Stream." PoNow (14/18) 77, p. 15.
"The Prison Rodeo" (for Paul Foreman). Bleb (12) 77, p. 5.
"Trumpet Fish." Xa (4) 77, p. 58.
"The Victims." CalQ (11/12) Wint-Spr 77, p. 114.
"Walking through Rogner's Woods." Wind (24) 77, p. 16.

BRUSH, Thomas
"Letter from the Street." PoetryNW (18:3) Aut 77, p. 29.

BRUTUS, Dennis
"A Tribute for Steve Biko." Nimrod (21:2/22:1) 77, p. 32.
"What I Need." Nimrod (21:2/22:1) 77, p. 31.

BRYAN, Sharon
"Making Conversation." Nat (225:18) 26 N 77, p. 569.
"New Kitchen." Nat (225:16) 12 N 77, p. 502.
"Sleeping with the Light On." Nat (224:17) 30 Ap 77,
     p. 535.
"What to Answer." Nat (225:10) 1 O 77, p. 316.

BRYANT, Mike
"A huge freighter leaves a harbor with a." QW (2) Wint 77,
     p. 61.

BRYANT, Philip
"Boogie Woogie Afternoon." Nimrod (21:2/22:1) 77, p. 34.
"The Book of the Dead" (for Mongane & Keorapetse). Nimrod
     (21:2/22:1) 77, p. 35.
"The Chicago River." Nimrod (21:2/22:1) 77, p. 37.

"Lorca's Last Request." Nimrod (21:2/22:1) 77, p. 36.
"Raindrop" (to R. L. R.). Nimrod (21:2/22:1) 77, p. 36.
"Remnants." AmerPoR (6:1) Ja-F 77, p. 21.
"Señor Garcia Imitating the Birds." Nimrod (21:2/22:1) 77,
    p. 33.

BUCCIERO, Patricia
"Primitive Settlers." WebR (3:4) Aut 77, p. 52.

BUCHMAN, Ruth
"Basil, What Germans Call 'Brainweed'" (tr. of Jörg Steiner).
    ChiR (29:3) Wint 78, p. 99.

BUCK, Randy
"For Robert, Returning." Mouth (11/12) Mr-Je 77, p. 72.

BUCKAWAY, C. M.
"Sky Blossoms." CarouselQ (2:2) Aut 77, p. 9.

BUCKLEY, Christopher
"Brandenburg, Kentucky." CalQ (11/12) Wint-Spr 77, p. 100.
"Holding You" (for Danielle). CutB (9) Aut-Wint 77, p. 5.
"Lines from Myself at New Year's." Wind (26) 77, p. 3.
"Nevertheless." Wind (26) 77, p. 3.
"Nostalgia." Chowder (9) Aut-Wint 77, p. 16.
"San Cristobel de las Casas, Chiapas, Mexico" (on a photograph
    by Lin Romero). CutB (9) Aut-Wint 77, p. 6.

BUDBILL, David
"The Bottle." Drag (16) 77.
"Tom." PoNow (14/18) 77, p. 16.

BUDENZ, Julia
"No One." PoetL (72:1) Spr 77, p. 7.

BUDIN, Sue
"Poems to My Mother." AAR (27) 77, p. 65.

BUDREAU, Kim
"Crazy Dog Days." AmerPoR (6:2) Mr-Ap 77, p. 34.

BUELL, Frederick
"Lesser Lights." CornellR (2) Aut 77, p. 35.
"Snowgathering." CornellR (2) Aut 77, p. 31.
"XMas." CornellR (2) Aut 77, p. 33.

BUGDEN, Roger
"Winged." Stand (18:2) 77, p. 19.

BUGGS, George
"Moving Beside Myself." AmerPoR (6:1) Ja-F 77, p. 21.

BUISSON, Justine Krug
"Twilight." HiramPoR (22) Aut-Wint 77, p. 8.

BUKOWSKI, Charles
"Blinks a Little Spot of Senseless Yellow in the Middle of It All."
    WormR (65/66) 77, p. 44.
"462-0614." NowestR (16:3) 77, p. 24.
Twenty-five poems. SeC (5:1) 77, pp. 1-46.

BULLIS, Jerald
"The Buckowl." Wind (25) 77, p. 11.
"Continuing Winter." Epoch (26:3) Spr 77, p. 251.
"Entry." PoNow (14/18) 77, p. 16.
"Fishing." Wind (25) 77, p. 11.
"Homestead Act." CornellR (2) Aut 77, p. 112.
"If We Couldn't Go." Wind (25) 77, p. 12.

BULLOCK, Michael
"Fleeting Trail" (tr. of Horst Bienek). ChiR (29:3) Wint 78,
    p. 73.

BUNDALIAN, Maribeth
"No One Cares." SeC (5:2) 78, p. 40.

BUNN, Scott
"Downstream." StoneC (77:1) F 77, p. 23.

BURCH, Edward
"Seasonal." Poem (29) Mr 77, p. 69.

BURDEN, Jean
"Autograph Party." MichQR (16:4) Aut 77, p. 382.
"The Dance." GeoR (31:3) Aut 77, p. 670.
"Insomnia." AmerS (46:4) Aut 77, p. 458.
"Limits." PoetL (72:1) Spr 77, p. 24.
"Piggy Bank." Sparrow (33) Ja 77, p. 16.
"Return to an Island." Ploughs (4:1) 77, p. 93.
"Signs, Cardinal and Mutable." Kayak (44) F 77, p. 37.
"Telephone Jack." PoetL (72:1) Spr 77, p. 23.
"You Ask." Kayak (44) F 77, p. 36.

BURFORD, William
"Guale." SouthwR (62:4) Aut 77, p. 369.

BURGESS, Anthony
"Back to the Roots" (tr. of Giuseppe Gioachino Belli). MalR (44)
    O 77, p. 20.
"The Creation of the World" (tr. of Giuseppe Gioachino Belli).
    MalR (44) O 77, p. 17.
"The Earthly Paradise of the Beasts" (tr. of Giuseppe Gioachino
    Belli). MalR (44) O 77, p. 18.
"Man" (tr. of Giuseppe Gioachino Belli). MalR (44) O 77, p. 21.
"Pride before a Fall" (tr. of Giuseppe Gioachino Belli). MalR
    (44) O 77, p. 19.

BURKE, Carol
"Waking." Rapp (10) 77, p. 49.

BURKE, France
"Double Boxed." Icarus (5:2) Aut 77, p. 23.
"Say Yes to Progress." Icarus (5:1) Spr 77, p. 11.
"The Sea Cucumber." Rapp (10) 77, p. 92.
"The Snake." Confr (14) Spr-Sum 77, p. 86.

BURKHARD, Michael
"The Case of the Sulky Girl." MissR (6:1) 77, p. 141.
"The Literalness of the Penal Colony." MissR (6:1) 77, p. 142.

BURNES, Carol
"Watching." 13thM (3:2) 77, p. 26.

BURNHAM, Jeff
"I cut emerald stones" (tr. of Aztec). QW (3) Spr-Sum 77,
    p. 57.
"My flowers have no end" (tr. of Aztec). QW (3) Spr-Sum 77,
    p. 57.
"O! I was born with no purpose" (tr. of Aztec). QW (3) Spr-
    Sum 77, p. 57.

BURNS, G. F.
"On the Back of a Prayer." WindO (28) Spr 77, p. 24.

BURNS, Ralph
"Caesar, You Knew All About the Ides but Morning Came Cere-
    bral." CutB (8) Spr 77, p. 5.
"Viol." CutB (8) Spr 77, p. 4.

BURNS, William
"Alcoholic: The Morning Beckon." DacTerr (14) Spr-Sum 77,
    p. 60.
"M. D." DacTerr (14) Spr-Sum 77, p. 60.
"Miler" (for Steve Prefontaine). PraS (51:3) Aut 77, p. 306.

BURNSHAW, Stanley
"The Talmudist." NewYRB (24:8) 12 My 77, p. 13.

BURR, Gray
"Claws and Mouths." PoNow (14/18) 77, p. 16.
"John P. Bickerly." NewYorker (53:18) 20 Je 77,
    p. 116.
"Kite-Flying." PoNow (14/18) 77, p. 16.

BURR, Lonnie
"Nuance." KanQ (9:2) Spr 77, p. 85.

BURRITT, Mary
"Ballast Point." SenR (8:1) My 77, p. 48.
"In Touraine." SenR (8:1) My 77, p. 47.
"Ligurian Upland." SenR (8:1) My 77, p. 52.
"Pesar." SenR (8:1) My 77, p. 51.

"Tuscany." SenR (8:1) My 77, p. 49.
"Venice." SenR (8:1) My 77, p. 50.

BURROWS, E. G.
  "Dear Cousin." PoNow (14/18) 77, p. 17.
  "The Jungfrau Hotel." AAR (27) 77, p. 48.
  "Midsummer." PoNow (14/18) 77, p. 17.
  "The Reapers." PoNow (14/18) 77, p. 17.

BURSK, Christopher
  "April 9, 1945/Bewahrung." BelPoJ (28:2) Wint 77-78, p. 10.
  "Bedtime." HiramPoR (22) Aut-Wint 77, p. 10.
  "Knowing I Would Lose Her Again." HiramPoR (22) Aut-Wint 77,
    p. 9.
  "Pests." BelPoJ (28:2) Wint 77-78, p. 9.
  "Town Beach." BelPoJ (28:2) Wint 77-78, p. 13.
  "When Are You Going to Grow Up?" BelPoJ (28:2) Wint 77-78,
    p. 12.

BURT, Lucille
  "Winter Revelation." Aspect (70) Ja-Mr 77, p. 31.

BURTIS, William
  "Why You Have Never Heard of Me Before." SenR (8:2) D 77,
    p. 69.

BURWELL, Rex
  "Alcohol and Death." ChiR (28:4) Spr 77, p. 30.
  "The Soul-Bird." ChiR (28:4) Spr 77, p. 30.
  "Sunday" (for Gordon Preston). ChiR (28:4) Spr 77, p. 31.
  "There's You." CutB (8) Spr 77, p. 55.
  "Trouble." Shen (28:4) Sum 77, p. 93.

BUSCH, C. Trent
  "The Alleghenies." CalQ (11/12) Wint-Spr 77, p. 48.
  "Eulogy: An Old West Piece." SoCaR (9:2) Ap 77, p. 41.
  "The Vanishing of Luther Hull." HiramPoR (22) Aut-Wint 77,
    p. 11.
  "The Wake." NewOR (5:3) 77, p. 247.

BUTCHER, Grace
  "As I Think About It." PoNow (14/18) 77, p. 17.

BUTKIE, J. D.
  "She Made Potato Pierohi for Meatless Fridays." PoNow (14/18)
    77, p. 18.

BUTKIE, Joseph D.
  "Halfway There And." Mouth (13) D 77, p. 23.

BUTLER, Ann
  "Departure." Wind (24) 77, p. 17.
  "A Natural Wedding Day." Wind (24) 77, p. 17.

BUTLER, Jack
"Beefeaters Make Better Lovers of God, or See! See Where
    Christ's Blood Streams in the Cheeseburger?" PoetryNW
    (18:1) Spr 77, p. 42.
"A Fit against Form." MissR (6:1) 77, p. 38.
"Homage to the First Geometer." NewYorker (53:31) 19 S 77,
    p. 40.
"A Prayer for Jehovah's Witnesses." PoetryNW (18:3) Aut 77,
    p. 42.
"What the Grinning Stranger with the Sad Eyes Wrote on a Napkin
    to the Truck-Stop Waitress before Riding Off into the Grenada,
    Mississippi Sunset." MissR (6:1) 77, p. 39.

BUTLER, Jan
"Safari in Ulster" (tr. of Yevgeny Yevtushenko). TransR (60)
    Je 77, p. 154.

BUTRICK, L. H.
"Digging a Can of Worms." PoNow (14/18) 77, p. 18.
"Feeling the Space." PoNow (14/18) 77, p. 18.
"Fool's Gold." KanQ (9:1) Wint 77, p. 111.
"For the Dodo." Wind (24) 77, p. 18.
"Listen I." Wind (24) 77, p. 18.
"Lunar Orbit." KanQ (9:1) Wint 77, p. 112.
"The Shadow Knows." Wind (24) 77, p. 19.
"Tooling Up." PoNow (14/18) 77, p. 18.
"The Tree House." Wind (24) 77, p. 19.
"With Contented Cows." PoNow (14/18) 77, p. 18.

BUTTERFIELD, Stephen T.
"Subway Driver." BelPoJ (27:4) Sum 77, p. 7.
"Unsolicited Manuscripts." BelPoJ (27:4) Sum 77, p. 4.

BUTTERICK, Brian
"I found your gold Dunhill lighter." Mouth (11/12) Mr-Je 77, p. 106.

BYNNER, Witter
"A Boatman." AmerPoR (6:6) N-D 77, p. 9.
"D. H. Lawrence." AmerPoR (6:6) N-D 77, p. 8.
"The Dead Loon." AmerPoR (6:6) N-D 77, p. 8.
"Episode of Decay." AmerPoR (6:6) N-D 77, p. 9.
"In Kamakura." AmerPoR (6:6) N-D 77, p. 8.
"The Two Windows." AmerPoR (6:6) N-D 77, p. 9.

BYNUM, Edward
"Poem in Four Parts." WindO (29) Sum 77, p. 45.
"Portrait." WindO (29) Sum 77, p. 45.

BYRNES, James M., Jr.
"Personality Profile in S." Mouth (13) D 77, p. 73.

CABALQUINTO, Luis
"Figure." Mouth (13) D 77, p. 50.

CABRAL, Olga
"The All-Night Laundromat." PoNow (14/18) 77, p. 20.
"The Arrest." PoNow (14/18) 77, p. 20.
from The Darkness in My Pockets: "(Help!)" PoNow (14/18) 77,
    p. 19.
from The Darkness in My Pockets: "Occupation: Spinster."
    PoNow (14/18) 77, p. 19.

CADUM, Michael
"Cancer." MinnR (NS8) Spr 77, p. 28.
"Frozen Mammoth." CalQ (11/12) Wint-Spr 77, p. 54.
"The Morning of the Massacre." MinnR (NS8) Spr 77, p. 28.

CAGE, John
"If There Isn't Any, Why Do You Wear Them?" UnmOx (15) 77,
    p. 11.
"7 out of 23." TriQ (38) Wint 77, p. 174.

CAIN, Cristy
"Old Age." SeC (5:2) 78, p. 41.

CAIN, John
"At the Nursing Home." NewL (44:2) Wint 77, p. 94.
"Kachina." NewL (44:2) Wint 77, p. 93.
"Potomac." NewL (44:2) Wint 77, p. 91.
"Upon the Bible Belt." NewL (43:4) Sum 77, p. 80.

CAIN, Seymour
"East Tawas." ChrC (94:5) 16 F 77, p. 144.

CALDEIRA, Steve
"In a Foreign City." CarouselQ (2:2) Aut 77, p. 12.
"Jealousy." CarouselQ (2:2) Aut 77, p. 11.
"Pusher." CarouselQ (2:3) Wint 77, p. 30.

CALHOUN, Thomas O.
"Design." MidwQ (18:4) Sum 77, p. 433.
"Leaving Washington." MidwQ (18:4) Sum 77, p. 432.

CALK, Heather
"america the beautiful." SeC (5:2) 78, p. 42.
"Maybe he had one too many." SeC (5:2) 78, p. 44.
"Through My Eyes." SeC (5:2) 78, p. 43.

CAMERON, Beatrice
Nine poems (tr. of Paul Celan). ChiR (29:3) Wint 78, p. 43.

CAMILLO, Victor
"Lament for Selma Asch." PoetL (72:1) Spr 77, p. 16.

CAMPBELL, Dowling G.
"Lapses." StoneC (77:1) F 77, p. 24.

CAMPBELL, Tim
"The Telephone." SeC (5:2) 78, p. 13.

CAMPBELL, Virginia
"Good Morning." PartR (44:3) 77, p. 399.

CAMPION, Daniel
"Bouillabaisse" (for the Cousteau Society). YellowBR (9) 77,
    p. 10.
"camping." NewC (7:2) 75-76, back cover.
"Tom Sawyer's Dream." YellowBR (8) 77, p. 26.

CAMPOS, Augusto de
"Poem." TriQ (38) Wint 77, p. 63.

CAMPOS, Haroldo de
"se len cio" (tr. by Mary Ellen Solt and Jon M. Tolman). LitR
    (21:2) Wint 78, p. 208.

CANNON, Maureen
"For Kathy, Remembered." LadHJ (94:10) O 77, p. P. S. 30.
"Wedding Words." LadHJ (94:8) Ag 77, p. 116.
"Winter Beach." LadHJ (94:9) S 77, p. 78.

CANNON, Melissa
"March." RemR (5) 77, p. 31.
"Metaphor" (for Darcy and Mimi Cummings). RemR (5) 77,
    p. 33.

CANNON, Thomas
"The Backdoor Man." SouthernPR (17:2) Aut 77, p. 23.

CANON, Carolyn
"Matching Nude Statues." LaB (8) Jl-Ag 77, p. 12.

CANTRELL, Charles
"Caribbean Sabbatical." Chowder (9) Aut-Wint 77, p. 98.

CAPPS, Kathleen
"Full Moon." DeKalb (10:3) Spr 77, p. 1.

CARDONA-HINE, Alvaro
"The Aging Process." MoonsLT (2:3) 77, p. 72.
"The Elixir of Solitude." MoonsLT (2:3) 77, p. 74.
"Playing the Piano at Noon on a Cloudy Day." MoonsLT (2:3) 77,
    p. 73.

CAREW, Jan
from Requiem for My Sister: "I sent no flowers for her dying."
    Nimrod (21:2/22:1) 77, p. 40.

CARLILE, Henry
"The Cardinal." NewYorker (53:20) 4 Jl 77, p. 83.

"Grace. " Chowder (8) Spr-Sum 77, p. 33.
"Stalking Morels. " AntR (35:4) Aut 77, p. 404.

CARLISLE, Thomas John
    "The Flight They Took. " ChrC (94:41) 14 D 77, p. 1164.
    "Job's Answer Over Again. " ChrC (94:34) 26 O 77, p. 972.
    "The New House. " LadHJ (94:11) N 77, p. P. S. 11.
    "Shrinkage. " ChrC (94:7) 2 Mr 77, p. 196.

CARLOS, Susan Varvaro
    "lilies are for funerals. " SmPd (14:3) Aut 77, p. 34.

CARLSON, Bobby
    "The Wizard in the Night. " QW (3) Spr-Sum 77, p. 30.

CARLSON, Catherine Anne
    "The Temperance River Madness. " Focus (12:74) F-Mr 77,
        p. 29.

CARLSON, Cathy
    "Je t'aime. " YaleLit (145:4) 77, p. 16.

CARMEN, Marilyn
    "Imaginative Thinking. " CarouselQ (2:3) Wint 77, p. 12.

CARMI, T.
    "Closing Prayer: Yom Kippur" (tr. by Marcia Falk). Hand (1)
        77, p. 214.
    "From There On" (tr. by Marcia Falk). TriQ (39) Spr 77,
        p. 253.
    "Order of the Day" (tr. by Marcia Falk). TriQ (39) Spr 77,
        p. 253.
    "Perspectives" (tr. by Marcia Falk). TriQ (39) Spr 77, p. 254.

CARPENTER, Bill
    "The Man Who Built a Car. " HiramPoR (23) Wint 77, p. 15.
    "Sailing to Damariscove" (for J. T. Plunkett & Kathleen Palm).
        HiramPoR (23) Wint 77, p. 14.

CARPENTER, John R.
    "Water: Yan, Alaska. " SouthwR (62:3) Sum 77, p. 256.

CARPENTER, Lucas
    "Long Island Lights. " PoetL (72:1) Spr 77, p. 14.
    "Passage Suggested. " CarouselQ (2:2) Aut 77, p. 14.
    "Poem Not to Be Read Aloud. " DeKalb (10:3) Spr 77, p. 3.
    "Railroad Yard in a Winter Sunset. " DeKalb (10:3) Spr 77, p. 4.

CARR, John
    "Proofreading at the Picayune: I. " VirQR (53:1) Wint 77, p. 105.
    "Proofreading at the Picayune: II. " VirQR (53:1) Wint 77,
        p. 105.

CARROLL, John
"I Almost Missed Him." HolCrit (14:1) F 77, p. 13.

CARROLL, Paulette
"Life Circle." Aspect (69) O-D 76, p. 32.

CARRUTH, Hayden
"Correspondences." NewL (44:1) Aut 77, p. 105.
"My Meadow." PoNow (14/18) 77, p. 20.
"Transcendence." NewL (44:1) Aut 77, p. 104.
"Two Romantic Pieces." Hudson (30:3) Aut 77, p. 353.

CARTER, Jared
"Gathering Fireflies" (for Selene). Ascent (3:2) 77, p. 24.
"Reprise." WindO (29) Sum 77, p. 34.

CARTER, Lee M.
"Babel." KanQ (9:1) Wint 77, p. 55.
"Question without an Answer." KanQ (9:1) Wint 77,
    p. 56.

CARTER, Rick
"I used to hunt pigeons." Mouth (11/12) Mr-Je 77, p. 108.
"Southern edges." Mouth (11/12) Mr-Je 77, p. 109.

CARTER, Ron
"To My Stepfather." Shen (29:1) Aut 77, p. 111.

CARVER, Raymond
    from At Night the Salmon Move: "At Night the Salmon Move."
        PoNow (14/18) 77, p. 19.
    from At Night the Salmon Move: "Bobber." PoNow (14/18) 77,
        p. 19.
    from At Night the Salmon Move: "Spring, 480 B.C." PoNow
        (14/18) 77, p. 19.

CASHMAN, David
"Friend." WindO (30) Aut 77, p. 15.
"The Soft Underbelly of the Kingdom Is Not One Place." WindO
    (30) Sum 77.

CASS, Michael
"At Home in the Dark." SouthernR (13:2) Spr 77, p. 355.
"The Fairest Lass in All Christendom." SouthernR (13:2) Spr 77,
    p. 356.
"The Lonesome End." SouthernR (13:2) Spr 77, p. 357.

CASSCELLS, R. E. Anne
"Chanson de l'Orpheline." YaleLit (146:2) 77, p. 10.

CASSEL, Mary
"Island." PoetL (72:2) Sum 77, p. 71.

CASSIAN, Nina
  "Capital Punishment" (tr. by Laura Schiff and Virgil Nemoianu).
    AmerPoR (6:6) N-D 77, p. 29.
  "The Doors" (tr. by Laura Schiff and Virgil Nemoianu). AmerPoR
    (6:6) N-D 77, p. 29.
  "Lady of Miracles" (tr. by Laura Schiff and Virgil Nemoianu).
    AmerPoR (6:6) N-D 77, p. 29.
  "Thanks" (tr. by Laura Schiff and Virgil Nemoianu). AmerPoR
    (6:6) N-D 77, p. 29.

CASSITY, Turner
  "Adding Rattles." SouthernPR (16:SI) 77, p. 22.
  "The Space between the Andirons." Poetry (130:3) D 77, p. 137.
  "The Strange Case of Dr. Jekyll and Dr. Jekyll." Poetry (130:3)
    D 77, p. 136.
  "Two Are Four." Poetry (130:3) D 77, p. 137.

CASTINE, J.
  "Phone Message." EngJ (66:5) My 77, p. 55.

CASTLE, Terry
  "Heading Up Like Bricks." Qt (57/58) Wint-Spr 77, p. 49.

CATENACCI, Edward N.
  "Etched Indelibly." Wind (27) 77, p. 8.

CATTAFI, Bartolo
  from L'Aria secca del fuoco: "Like a Trickle of Watered Blood"
    (tr. by Ruth Feldman and Brian Swann). Some (7/8) 76.
  "The Autumn Countryside" (tr. by Ruth Feldman and Brian Swann).
    WebR (3:1) Wint 77, p. 8.
  "The Descent to the Throne" (tr. by Ruth Feldman and Brian
    Swann). WebR (3:1) Wint 77, p. 9.
  "My Mistakes" (tr. by Ruth Feldman and Brian Swann). Confr
    (14) Spr-Sum 77, p. 141.
  "These Myths" (tr. by Ruth Feldman and Brian Swann). WebR
    (3:1) Wint 77, p. 7.
  "Visit" (tr. by Ruth Feldman and Brian Swann). Some (7/8) 76.
  "With the War Over" (tr. by Ruth Feldman and Brian Swann).
    WebR (3:1) Wint 77, p. 8.

CATTONAR, Joanna
  "Miscarriage." Aspen (4) Aut 77, p. 59.
  "La Sierra." Hand (1) 77, p. 171.
  "Vengeance." Aspen (4) Aut 77, p. 58.

CAVAFY, Constantine
  "The Bandaged Shoulder" (tr. by Edmund Keeley and Philip
    Sherrard). NewYRB (24:2) 17 F 77, p. 33.
  "Ionic" (tr. by Edmund Keeley and Philip Sherrard). NewYRB
    (24:2) 17 F 77, p. 33.
  "Kaisarion" (tr. by Edmund Keeley and Philip Sherrard).
    NewYRB (24:2) 17 F 77, p. 33.

CAZALAS, James K.
"Grandfather." SouthwR (62:1) Wint 77, p. 64.

CECIL, Richard
"Dagwood." PoNow (14/18) 77, p. 21.
"Dialogue." Ploughs (3:3/4) 77, p. 63.
"Diminuendo for Creation." AmerPoR (6:6) N-D 77, p. 30.
"The Friends." CalQ (11/12) Wint-Spr 77, p. 99.
"Uncle Scrooge Rejects Daisy Duck." PoNow (14/18) 77, p. 21.
"Woodcraft." AmerPoR (6:6) N-D 77, p. 30.

CEDRINS, Inara
"Room." KanQ (9:2) Spr 77, p. 19.

CELAN, Paul
"Chanson of a Lady in Shadow" (tr. by Alice MacMullen). PortR
(23) 77, p. 91.
"Memory of France" (tr. by Alice MacMullen). PortR (23) 77,
p. 90.
"On the High Seas" (tr. by Alice MacMullen). PortR (23) 77,
p. 90.
Twenty-three poems. ChiR (29:3) Wint 78, p. 42.

CELUM, F. Richard
"The Old Lady Lay Babbling." NewC (7:3) 75-76, p. 30.

CERNUDA, Luis
"All This for Love" (tr. by Frederick D. Blanton and Susan C.
Blanton). Mouth (13) D 77, p. 19.
"The Blackbird, the Seagull" (tr. by Frederick D. Blanton and
Susan C. Blanton). Mouth (13) D 77, p. 8.
"I Want You" (tr. by Frederick D. Blanton and Susan C. Blanton).
Mouth (13) D 77, p. 6.
"Sailors Are the Wings of Love" (tr. by Frederick D. Blanton
and Susan C. Blanton). Mouth (13) D 77, p. 7.
"Unfinished Statue" (tr. by Frederick D. Blanton and Susan C.
Blanton). Mouth (13) D 77, p. 9.

CERVANTES, James V.
"On The Therapeutist, A Sculpture by René Magritte" (for Norman
Dubie). CutB (8) Spr 77, p. 36.

CERVO, Nathan
Fourteen poems. EnPas (6) 77, p. 5.
"The Glass Blower." EnPas (4) 76, p. 18.
"The Man in the Public Garden." EnPas (4) 76, p. 20.

CHACE, Joel
"Advice for Nervous People." PoNow (14/18) 77, p. 21.

CHADWICK, Jerry
"Bearing and Being." Mouth (11/12) Mr-Je 77, p. 15.
"Cult of the Body." Mouth (11/12) Mr-Je 77, p. 13.

"The Dream Horse." <u>Mouth</u> (13) D 77, p. 17.
"Instead of Eros Avenged." <u>Mouth</u> (11/12) Mr-Je 77, p. 16.
"Maintenance." <u>Mouth</u> (13) D 77, p. 17.
"Old Men." <u>Mouth</u> (11/12) Mr-Je 77, p. 12.

CHALFI, Raquel
  "I, the Barracuda" (tr. by E. A. Levenston). <u>TriQ</u> (39) Spr 77,
      p. 256.
  "Porcupine Fish" (tr. by Robert Friend). <u>TriQ</u> (39) Spr 77,
      p. 255.

CHALPIN, Lila
  "Pair." <u>KanQ</u> (9:1) Wint 77, p. 51.

CHAMBERS, Leland H.
  "The Epic of a Day: Rural Meditations" (tr. of Antonio Machado).
      <u>DenQ</u> (11:1) Wint 77, p. 157.
  "The Miracle" (tr. of Antonio Machado). <u>DenQ</u> (11:4) Wint 77,
      p. 156.

CHAMBERS, Thomas
  "The First Snow." <u>Wind</u> (27) 77, p. 36.

CHAMISH, Barry
  "The State of Poetry--America 1970's." <u>Sam</u> (56) Sum 77, p. 19.

CHANDRA, G. S. Sharat
  "At the Burning Ghats." <u>AmerPoR</u> (6:4) Jl-Ag 77, p. 46.
  "Boots." <u>AmerPoR</u> (6:4) Jl-Ag 77, p. 46.
  "Harvest Song." <u>AmerPoR</u> (6:4) Jl-Ag 77, p. 47.
  "Sunday Afternoon." <u>NewL</u> (43:4) Sum 77, p. 66.

CHANG, Diana
  "Counting Neighbors." <u>Confr</u> (14) Spr-Sum 77, p. 94.

CHAO Shih-hsu
  "In the Season of Yellow Plums" (tr. by Graeme Wilson). <u>DenQ</u>
      (12:2) Sum 77, p. 395.

CHAPMAN, Diane
  "Four Love Poems." <u>Gra</u> (12) 77.
  "Honeymoon." <u>YellowBR</u> (9) 77, p. 15.
  "The Message." <u>Gra</u> (12) 77.

CHAPPELL, Fred
  "Beerdrinking in America." <u>SouthernPR</u> (17:1) Spr 77, p. 30.
  "Bucket Stop." <u>SouthernPR</u> (16:SI) 77, p. 23.
  "Child in the Fog." <u>SewanR</u> (85:3) Sum 77, p. 454.
  "Dawn Wind Unlocks the River Sky." <u>SouthernPR</u> (17:2) Aut 77,
      p. 49.
  "The Highest Wind That Ever Blew: Homage to Louis." <u>QW</u> (4)
      Aut 77, p. 42.
  "Humility." <u>SewanR</u> (85:3) Sum 77, p. 453.

"My Father Burns Washington." LittleR (12) 77, p. 21.
"Transmogrification of the Diva." SewanR (85:3) Sum 77, p. 455.

CHAR, René
"Cruels Assortiments." Bound (5:3) Spr 77, p. 754.
Eight poems (tr. by Charles Guenther). WebR (3:1) Wint 77,
    p. 10.

CHASE, Rafe
"At Polk & Post." Mouth (13) D 77, p. 43.
"Cockring." Mouth (11/12) Mr-Je 77, p. 105.
"Poem or a Sigh." Mouth (13) D 77, p. 43.

CHATFIELD, Hale
"Chapter I & Chapter II." ThRiPo (10) 77, p. 42.
"Going to Work for Horace Sondergard." DacTerr (14) Spr-Sum
    77, p. 35.
"I Have Internalized My Fingers." DacTerr (14) Spr-Sum 77,
    p. 34.
"The Life Lovers." PoNow (14/18) 77, p. 21.
"The Passionate Shepherd to His Love." Pig (3) 77, p. 57.
"Tears." PoNow (14/18) 77, p. 22.

CHAVES, Jonathan
"My Late Father's Favorite Horse Fell Ill and Was Sent to a
    Separate Stable--Now It Has Died" (tr. of Su Shun-ch'in).
    DenQ (12:2) Sum 77, p. 68.
"That year we got drunk together" (tr. of Su Shun-ch'in). DenQ
    (12:2) Sum 77, p. 68.

CHEATWOOD, Kiarri T-H.
"Deep Nights' Meditation" (for Sister Mari Evans). Nimrod
    (21:2/22:1) 77, p. 52.
"A Sad Sad Song ... A Little Joy." Nimrod (21:2/22:1) 77, p.
    53.

CHEN Tzu-ang
"At Yu-Chou Terrace" (tr. by Graeme Wilson). DenQ (12:2) Sum
    77, p. 49.
"Men of Affairs" (tr. by Graeme Wilson). DenQ (12:2) Sum 77,
    p. 49.

CHEN Yu-yi
"Coming Clear" (tr. by Graeme Wilson). DenQ (12:2) Sum 77,
    p. 55.
"Spring" (tr. by Graeme Wilson). DenQ (12:2) Sum 77, p. 56.

CHENEVARE, Karen J.
"Thinking of You." AAR (27) 77, p. 103.

CHERNER, Anne
"Reply to My Uncle Joseph." Ploughs (3:3/4) 77, p. 109.

CHERNOFF, Maxine
"For Daily Use." PartR (44:4) 77, p. 560.
"Fred Astaire." Chelsea (36) 77, p. 45.
"His Pastime." Chelsea (36) 77, p. 45.
"Rehearsal." Gra (12) 77.

CHERRY, Kelly
"A Book." NewL (44:1) Aut 77, p. 91.
"Interstate." RemR (5) 77, p. 43.
"Ithaca." RemR (5) 77, p. 42.
"Songs for a Soviet Composer." FourQt (26:4) Sum 77, p. 30.

CHESNEY, Tom
"Primeval Response." CarouselQ (2:2) Aut 77, p. 18.
"Souvenir." CarouselQ (2:2) Aut 77, p. 18.
"Supermarket Whimsy." CarouselQ (2:2) Aut 77, p. 18.

CHESS, Rick
"At Luria's Grave." SmPd (14:1) Wint 77, p. 13.
"Farewell America." SmPd (14:1) Wint 77, p. 12.

CHIA Tao
"Visiting the Master" (tr. by Graeme Wilson). TexQ (20:4)
    Wint 77, p. 149.

CHIECO, Michael
"Max." Wind (27) 77, p. 5.

CHIGAMI, Sany
"Who?" (tr. by Graeme Wilson). DenQ (11:4) Wint 77, p. 167.

CHILDERS, David C.
"And Then." GRR (8:1/2) 77, p. 108.
"A Romance." GRR (8:1/2) 77, p. 107.
"To Start with There Is This." GRR (8:1/2) 77, p. 108.

CHILDERS, Joanne
"Period Piece." PoetL (72:2) Sum 77, p. 78.
"The Visit." PoetL (72:2) Sum 77, p. 57.

CHILDRESS, William
"Butch Cassidy's Last Letter from Etta Place." PoNow (14/18)
    77, p. 23.
"Harry Longbaugh Tries His Hand at Verse." PoNow (14/18) 77,
    p. 22.
"Midwest Legion Bar." PoNow (14/18) 77, p. 23.

CHIN, Wai Wah
"(a fragment)." YaleLit (145:3) 77, p. 5.
"old folks." YaleLit (145:4) 77, p. 19.
"Still Life." YaleLit (145:3) 77, p. 27.

CH'IN Kuan
   "Poem Written Dream Side" (tr. by Angela Elston).   DenQ (12:2)
      Sum 77, p. 1.

CHINMOY, Sri
   "Between Nothingness and Eternity. " DeKalb (10:2) Wint 77,
      p. 14.

CHO Chon-song
   "Fishing" (tr. by Graeme Wilson).   DenQ (12:2) Sum 77, p. 299.

CHOCK, Eric
   "Poem for My Father. " Wind (27) 77, p. 6.

CHOE Chi-won
   "The Mirror of the Heart" (tr. by Graeme Wilson).   TexQ (20:4)
      Wint 77, p. 148.

CHOE Chung
   "When China Was a Child" (tr. by Graeme Wilson).   DenQ (12:2)
      Sum 77, p. 298.

CHONG Chol
   "The Great Bell of Silla" (tr. by Graeme Wilson).   DenQ (12:2)
      Sum 77, p. 396.
   "House by the Highway" (tr. by Graeme Wilson).   DenQ (12:2)
      Sum 77, p. 300.
   "Two Stone Buddhas" (tr. by Graeme Wilson).   VirQR (53:3) Sum
      77, p. 451.
   "Widow" (tr. by Graeme Wilson).   DenQ (12:2) Sum 77, p. 294.

CHONG Min-gyo
   "Fallen Petals" (tr. by Graeme Wilson).   VirQR (53:3) Sum 77,
      p. 453.

CHONG Mong-ju
   "Loyalty" (tr. by Graeme Wilson).   DenQ (12:2) Sum 77, p. 298.

CHON Gum
   "Barking at the Moon" (tr. by Graeme Wilson).   DenQ (12:2) Sum
      77, p. 306.

CHOU Pang-yen
   "Vigil" (tr. by Graeme Wilson).   DenQ (12:2) Sum 77, p. 395.

CHRISTENSEN, Nancy
   "Far Off Reaches. " CarouselQ (2:1) Spr 77, p. 16.
   "The Feast. " CarouselQ (2:1) Spr 77, p. 15.

CHRISTENSEN, Paul
   "The Drawer. " Shen (28:4) Sum 77, p. 70.
   Fifteen poems. Peb (16) Wint 76-77, pp. 41-56.

CHRISTENSON, Kathryn
"Clues to the Second Coming." ChrC (94:9) 16 Mr 77, p. 254.

CHRISTIANSEN, Nadia
"At the Border, With Hippocrates Looking Over My Shoulder."
KanQ (9:3) Sum 77, p. 42.

CHRISTOPHER, Nicholas
"Skirting the Calm." NewYorker (53:45) 26 D 77, p. 65.

CHUANG Tzu
"Butterfly" (tr. by Graeme Wilson). WestHR (31:3) Sum 77,
p. 207.
"Song of the Madman of Ch'u" (tr. by A. C. Graham). Montra
(3) Spr 77, p. 5.

CHURA, David
"Louisiana Christmas Rain." Mouth (13) D 77, p. 18.
"Zion's Hanging Gardens." Mouth (13) D 77, p. 18.

CHURRY, Craig
"Seeing with the First Eye." MontG (5) Wint 77, p. 9.

CHU Ui-sik
"New Year" (tr. by Graeme Wilson). DenQ (12:2) Sum 77,
p. 296.
"Talk" (tr. by Graeme Wilson). DenQ (12:2) Sum 77, p. 310.

CHYET, S. F.
"Cycle" (tr. of Haim Gouri). TriQ (39) Spr 77, p. 274.
"Holiday's End" (tr. of Haim Gouri). TriQ (39) Spr 77, p. 273.
"Lookout on a Rock on the Heights of Mount Hermon" (tr. of Abba
Kovner). TriQ (39) Spr 77, p. 280.
"My Samsons" (tr. of Haim Gouri). TriQ (39) Spr 77, p. 272.
"On Your Heart, Open" (tr. of Ya'ir Hurvitz, w. Leonore Gor-
don). TriQ (39) Spr 77, p. 278.
"Samson's Hair" (tr. of Natan Zach). TriQ (39) Spr 77, p. 316.
"Sun Watchers" (tr. of Abba Kovner). TriQ (39) Spr 77, p. 282.
"Waking Up" (tr. of Tuvia Ruebner). TriQ (39) Spr 77, p. 303.
"Whispering in Me" (tr. of Ya'ir Hurvitz, w. Leonore Gordon).
TriQ (39) Spr 77, p. 277.

CICCARELLI, Sharon
"The Play." YaleLit (147:1) 77, p. 25.
"Sunset." YaleLit (147:2) 77, p. 26.
"Tanner and the Dandylion." YaleLit (147:1) 77, p. 24.
"Tanner on Parade." YaleLit (147:2) 77, p. 27.

CIRINO, Leonard
"All the Fields." Vaga (25) 77, p. 11.
"Pond." NewC (7:2) 75-76, p. 22.

CISNEROS, Sandra
"Poem: To startle yourself' (tr. of Dario Ruiz Gomez).   DenQ
(12:1) Spr 77, p. 153.

CITINO, David
"Art Museum." HiramPoR (22) Aut-Wint 77, p. 12.
"The Bed." Wind (26) 77, p. 5.
"The Death of Mungo Park." SouthernPR (17:2) Aut 77, p. 38.
"The Drum." Wind (26) 77, p. 6.
"Evening Prayer." WindO (29) Sum 77, p. 29.
"Hazel." PoetC (10:1) 77, p. 20.
"Imagine Being Buried." Confr (15) Aut 77-Wint 78, p. 16.
"In a Gallery." StoneC (77:3) S 77, p. 6.
"The Last Poem." HiramPoR (22) Aut-Wint 77, p. 12.
"The Laws of Hospitality." PoetC (10:1) 77, p. 20.
"The Magician." WindO (29) Sum 77, p. 28.
"The Process." Pig (3) 77, p. 93.
"Spring Frost/Anniversary." WindO (29) Sum 77, p. 27.
"Warnings." WindO (29) Sum 77, p. 29.

CLAFLIN, Lola White
"Pearl Harbor Revisited." Aspect (70) Ja-Mr 77, p. 29.
"Schoodic Point, June 1975." Aspect (70) Ja-Mr 77, p. 30.
"You don't give me any time to myself." Aspect (70) Ja-Mr 77,
p. 57.

CLAIRE, William
"Letter to My Son, Number One." CarlMis (16:1/2) Aut-Wint
76-77, p. 94.
"Stopping for Directions: Greetings to Charles Olson, Dead."
LaB (7) My 77, p. 17.
"Unloading." Waters (6) 77, p. 19.

CLAMURRO, William
"The Drunk Tank." QW (4) Aut 77, p. 81.

CLARK, Colette
"Am I Mad!!!" AAR (27) 77, p. 119.

CLARK, Dennis Marden
"Knifing a Piggy Bank." PoetryNW (18:2) Sum 77, p. 48.

CLARK, Gerald
"Still Life." AAR (27) 77, p. 62.
"you hung curtains." AAR (27) 77, p. 61.

CLARK, Jim
"Maps." Stonecloud (6) 76, p. 16.
"Night in Autumn." Stonecloud (6) 76, p. 16.

CLARK, Martha
"When Fire Meets Water." Iowa (8:3) Sum 77, p. 61.

CLARK, Sylvia
"Changing Your Name" (for Teri). Chomo (4:1) Sum 77, p. 43.
"Nine Parts of These Days. " CutB (9) Aut-Wint 77, p. 39.

CLARK, Tom
"Amo. " PoNow (14/18) 77, p. 24.
"Autobiography. " PoNow (14/18) 77, p. 24.
"The Death of Vuillard. " SunM (4) Aut 77, p. 50.
"Hot Agate. " PoNow (14/18) 77, p. 24.
"No sooner have. " PoNow (14/18) 77, p. 24.
"35. " PoNow (14/18) 77, p. 24.
"To Reverdy, Again. " SunM (4) Aut 77, p. 58.
"To Ungaretti. " SunM (4) Aut 77, p. 54.

CLARKE, Reed
"After Looking at Chinese Painting. " MalR (44) O 77, p. 115.
"'The Limit, The Agony'" (In Memory of Arshile Gorky [1905-
   1948]). MalR (44) O 77, p. 118.

CLARY, Killarney
"Someone else. " PartR (44:4) 77, p. 551.

CLAUDEL, Alice Moser
"Et Tu, Brute. " Glass (2:2/3) Wint-Spr 77, p. 100.
"Mirages. " Poem (31) N 77, p. 19.
"The Rip Off of Silver Bowls. " Poem (31) N 77, p. 21.
"You Can't Tell. " Poem (31) N 77, p. 20.

CLAYTON, Candyce
"The Ballet. " MoonsLT (2:3) 77, p. 22.
"The Man's Hands. " MoonsLT (2:3) 77, p. 21.

CLEMENTE, Vince
"Saturday Morning at Home. " KanQ (9:1) Wint 77, p. 118.

CLENDENIN, Chris
"A Raker. " SouthernR (13:2) Spr 77, p. 360.

CLEWELL, David
"Daylight: Another Showdown. " MidwQ (18:4) Sum 77, p. 436.
"My Father's Secret. " MidwQ (18:4) Sum 77, p. 435.
"Pleistocene Wisconsin. " Chowder (8) Spr-Sum 77, p. 28.
"Prayer for the New Year. " MidwQ (18:4) Sum 77, p. 434.
"Returning: Early March. " Chowder (8) Spr-Sum 77, p. 30.

CLIFF, William
"A Pair of Old Bathing Trunks" (tr. by Maxine Kumin and Judith
   Bingen-Kumin). Columbia (1) Aut 77, p. 29.

CLIFTON, Lucille
"For the Blind. " Nimrod (21:2/22:1) 77, p. 54.
"One Village. " Nimrod (21:2/22:1) 77, p. 55.
"THERE IS A GIRL INSIDE. " AmerPoR (6:1) Ja-F 77, p. 21.

"What I Want to Do" (for Alice Smith who will understand completely). Nimrod (21:2/22:1) 77, p. 54.

CLIFTON, Merritt
"Lost Generation." Sam (55) 77, p. 44.
"The Specimen." Sam (59) 77, p. 79.
Vindictment. Sam (61) 77. Entire issue.

CLIFTON, Nicole
"Beach, Early Morning, February." Sam (56) Sum 77, p. 48.

CLIMENHAGA, Joel
"After Surgery." KanQ (9:1) Wint 77, p. 46.

CLIPPARD, Dave
"Baths." Mouth (13) D 77, p. 15.
"Words to the Grass." Mouth (13) D 77, p. 21.

CLOUTIER, David
"Chuckchee Riddles." Agni (7) 77, p. 112.

COCCIMIGLIO, Vic
"Moon Child." ParisR (69) Spr 77, p. 31.

COCHRANE, Shirley G.
"Inheritance." PoetL (72:2) Sum 77, p. 56.
"Medea Mourns Apsyrtus." GRR (8:1/2) 77, p. 51.

COCKRELL, Douglas
"The First Time." PoNow (14/18) 77, p. 24.

COCTEAU, Jean
"The Angel Heurtebise" (tr. by Perry Oldham). WebR (3:1) Wint 77, p. 37.

CODRESCU, Andrei
"The Gambling Phoenix." Gra (12) 77, p. 51.
"Lipstick Bicycles." Gra (12) 77, p. 15.
"The New Gazette." Gra (12) 77, p. 3.
"Pastoral." Gra (12) 77, p. 40.
"Testimonial." ChiR (28:4) Spr 77, p. 32.

COGGESHALL, Rosanne
"Contemplative." Epoch (26:2) Wint 77, p. 191.
"Last Night I Told Them." CarolQ (29:1) Wint 77, p. 64.
"Reading Mammy's Will" (for CHC). CarolQ (29:1) Wint 77, p. 63.

COHEN, Barbara
"The Descant." YaleLit (146:4/5) 77, p. 31.

COHEN, Gerald
"Bring On Uriburu" (for Pete Seeger). LitR (20:3) Spr 77, p. 316.

"Untitled Dance." LitR (20:3) Spr 77, p. 315.

COHEN, Ira
"Night Song." MontG (6) Aut 77, p. 31.
from The Torment of Al Hallaj: "1. As a Young Man" (tr. of
    Abd al-Wahab al-Bayyati, w. Petra Vogt). MontG (6) Aut 77,
    p. 30.

COHEN, Marc
"A Blood Canzone." Shen (29:1) Aut 77, p. 104.

COHEN, Marcia
"Promise." LadHJ (94:1) Ja 77, p. 132.
"Song for a Friend." LadHJ (94:6) Je 77, p. 146.

COHEN, Marty
"After Emerson." GRR (8:1/2) 77, p. 64.

COHEN, Marvin
"A Capsule Affair." WormR (65/66) 77, p. 7.
"Emancipation by Depreciation." WormR (65/66) 77, p. 5.
"A Gradually Dwindling Play." WormR (65/66) 77, p. 8.
"Increased Unemployment That Finally Reaches the Philosophical
    Stage." WormR (65/66) 77, p. 6.

COHEN, Rosetta
"Lament of the Swan Prince." YaleLit (146:4/5) 77, p. 13.
"The Poet Studies Herself in the Mirror." Madem (83:8) Ag 77,
    p. 139.

COHRS, Timothy
"An Acute Crevice." Agni (7) 77, p. 74.
"Motion." Agni (7) 77, p. 68.

COLBY, Joan
"Auto-Immune Diseases." HolCrit (14:3) Je 77, p. 15.
"Crocodile." Icarus (5:1) Spr 77, p. 2.
"Dawn Snow." Aspect (70) Ja-Mr 77, p. 3.
"Eclipse." Aspect (70) Ja-Mr 77, p. 4.
"Elm and Willow." StoneC (77:2) My 77, p. 5.
"Red Lodge." NewRivR (2:1) 77, p. 46.
"Rings." Ascent (3:1) 77, p. 18.
"Rituals." EnPas (5) 77, p. 25.
"Simonetta Vespucci." WindO (29) Sum 77, p. 23.
"Unroofed." Chowder (9) Aut-Wint 77, p. 22.
"When the Great Depression Hits." EnPas (5) 77, p. 24.

COLDIRON, Carla
"Headquarters." Xa (4) 77, p. 40.

COLE, Charles C., Jr.
"Waiting One Evening." CarouselQ (2:2) Aut 77, p. 21.

COLE, E. R.
"hole in his trousers." WindO (30) Aut 77.
"this late snowfall." WindO (30) Aut 77.
"2 a. m." WindO (30) Aut 77.

COLE, James
"College Town." PraS (51:2) Sum 77, p. 184.
"The Island Graveyard." PraS (51:2) Sum 77, p. 183.
"The Quiet Dump." KanQ (9:1) Wint 77, p. 78.

COLE, Michael
"Sewing Scissors." HiramPoR (23) Wint 77, p. 16.

COLE, Richard
"The Pale Fish in Limestone Caves." ChiR (29:2) Aut 77, p. 22.

COLEMAN, Horace
"the fear of 'niggers.'" AmerPoR (6:1) Ja-F 77, p. 22.
"Out." Nimrod (21:2/22:1) 77, p. 56.
"poem for a 'divorced' daughter." NewL (43:3) Spr 77, p. 50.
"Rainy Day List." Nimrod (21:2/22:1) 77, p. 56.
"there is much music in this room." NewL (43:3) Spr 77, p. 49.

COLEMAN, Mary Ann Braunlin
"The Laundry Man Drives Up While We're Making Love." KanQ
(9:1) Wint 77, p. 94.

COLEMAN, Mary Joan
"Afternoon in a Blind Alley." Wind (26) 77, p. 7.
"Humpty Dumpty." Wind (26) 77, p. 8.
"Three Years on Pierpoint Mountain." Wind (26) 77, p. 7.

COLEMAN, Wanda
"My Years." Chomo (4:1) Sum 77, p. 24.

COLINAS, Antonio
"Giacomo Casanova Accepts the Office of Librarian Offered Him
in Bohemia by Count Waldstein" (tr. by Anthony Kerrigan).
Confr (14) Spr-Sum 77, p. 28.
"To Encounter Ezra Pound--Posthumous Instructions" (ad. by
Anthony Kerrigan). Confr (14) Spr-Sum 77, p. 29.

COLLINGWOOD, Harris
"Seepage" (for J. G.). HarvAd (111:1) N 77, p. 26.

COLLINS, Billy
"For Bartleby the Scrivener." Ploughs (3:3/4) 77, p. 135.
"Instructions to the Artist." ParisR (71) Aut 77, p. 133.

COLLINS, Dana
"For Lisa." US1 (10) Wint 77-78, p. 9.

COLLINS, Martha
"Friend." CarolQ (29:3) Aut 77, p. 64.

"Having to Do with Yourself. " DenQ (12:2) Sum 77, p. 215.
"Having to Do with Yourself. " DenQ (12:4) Wint 78, p. 68.
"Meeting. " DenQ (12:2) Sum 77, p. 214.
"You Go to a Party. " DenQ (12:2) Sum 77, p. 215.

COLLINS, Stephen
"A Message. " Ploughs (4:1) 77, p. 172.

COLOMBO, John Robert
from Los placeres de Edipo: "XIV. Everything in That Sphere"
   (tr. of Ludwig Zeller, w. Susana Wald). MontG (6) Aut 77,
   p. 33.
from The Rules of the Game: "Guess or I Get You" (tr. of Lud-
   wig Zeller, w. Susana Wald). MontG (6) Aut 77, p. 34.
from The Rules of the Game: "Landscape for the Blind" (tr. of
   Ludwig Zeller, w. Susana Wald). MontG (6) Aut 77, p. 37.
from The Rules of the Game: "Riches to Register" (tr. of Lud-
   wig Zeller w. Susana Wald). MontG (6) Aut 77, p. 36.
from The Rules of the Game: "The Smugglers' Laws" (tr. of
   Ludwig Zeller, w. Susana Wald). MontG (6) Aut 77, p. 35.

COLONY, Joyce
"Old Woman Dreaming. " Chelsea (36) 77, p. 22.
"Three O'Clock on the Solstice. " Shen (29:1) Aut 77, p. 46.

COLQUITT, Betsy
"The Terrible Peaceable Kingdom. " ChrC (94:18) 18 My 77,
   p. 476.

COLT, George
"The Skywriter. " Ploughs (3:3/4) 77, p. 145.

COLVER, Russell
"Salvation. " Shen (29:1) Aut 77, p. 109.

COMPTON, Gayle
"Hunchback. " CarouselQ (2:3) Wint 77, p. 4.

CONANT, Louise
"Maine Headstone. " VirQR (53:2) Spr 77, p. 331.
"Mending. " VirQR (53:2) Spr 77, p. 330.

CONANT-BISSELL, Jane
"Tree. " CalQ (11/12) Wint-Spr 77, p. 55.

CONGDON, Constance
"I Remember Grade School. " Qt (57/58) Wint-Spr 77, p. 37.

CONKLE, D. Steven
"june 21 down here noone goes into the woods without his claws. "
   MissR (6:1) 77, p. 44.

CONLEY, Robert J.
"Spirits. " Waters (6) 77, p. 16.

CONNELL, Kim
"Last Red Cent." NewC (8:1) 76-77, p. 19.
"Loss." NewC (7:3) 75-76, p. 6.
"Potato." Agni (7) 77, p. 103.

CONNELLAN, Leo
"Penobscot Raccoons." Kayak (44) F 77, p. 28.
"Scott Huff." Ploughs (4:1) 77, p. 95.

CONNER, Randolph
"bathe with me." Mouth (11/12) Mr-Je 77, p. 53.

CONNOLLY, James F.
"Elegy for the 'Painter Man.'" Wind (27) 77, p. 7.
"First Pick Up." KanQ (9:1) Wint 77, p. 87.

CONNOR, Tony
"Squared by Walls" (tr. of László Nagy). AmerPoR (6:3) My-Je
    77, p. 24.
"Squared by Walls" (tr. of László Nagy). ModernPS (8:2) Aut 77,
    p. 112.

CONTOSKI, Victor
"The Dream of John" (tr. of Tadeusz Rozewicz). Chowder (9)
    Aut-Wint 77, p. 44.
"Fugue in D Minor for Girl, Torturer, and Broken Machine"
    (Dedicated to Johann Sebastian Bach). Epoch (27:1) Aut 77,
    p. 21.
"Journey West." ArkRiv (3:4/4:1) 77, p. 26.
"Santa Fe Trail." PoNow (14/18) 77, p. 25.

CONWAY, Jack
"Routines." PoetL (72:1) Spr 77, p. 21.
"Trumps." Wind (27) 77, p. 65.

COOK, Beverly
"April." EngJ (66:5) My 77, p. 52.

COOK, Paul
"Business as Usual." Madrona (4:13/14) 77, p. 32.

COOK, R. L.
"Sanctuary." ArizQ (33:4) Wint 77, p. 292.
"Sing No More." ArizQ (33:2) Sum 77, p. 132.

COOK, William T.
"An Edge on Boredom." TexQ (20:4) Wint 77, p. 176.
"Behind the Fog." Drag (16) 77.
"Northern Stasis in Late Fall." TexQ (20:4) Wint 77, p. 96.

COOKE, Michael G.
"Jazz Man." Nimrod (21:2/22:1) 77, p. 59.
"To Miles Davis." Nimrod (21:2/22:1) 77, p. 57.

COOKE, Robert
"Giving Up Gym Class, Physics, and Teaching." DeKalb (10:2)
Wint 77, p. 15.
"Holding Things Together." DeKalb (10:2) Wint 77, p. 15.

COOLEY, Peter
"An Aftermath." NewOR (5:3) 77, p. 198.
"The Descent Into Heaven." MidwQ (19:1) Aut 77, p. 51.
"For James Hearst." TexQ (20:4) Wint 77, p. 172.
"Inventing Peter." MidwQ (19:1) Aut 77, p. 55.
"Moving South, He Hears This Colloquy Inside Himself." MidwQ
(19:1) Aut 77, p. 54.
"The Rainmaker." MidwQ (19:1) Aut 77, p. 53.

COON, Betty
"Daddy." SouthernPR (17:1) Spr 77, p. 18.

COOPER, Jane
"Life under the Sun, Life under the Moon: Two Drawings."
TransR (60) Je 77, p. 94.
"A Mission with the Night." TransR (60) Je 77, p. 93.
"Praise." TransR (60) Je 77, p. 95.
"S. Eliason 66: Double Portrait of Emily Dickinson and the Rev.
Charles Wadsworth." Iowa (8:2) Spr 77, p. 13.
"Scattered Words for Emily Dickinson." TransR (60) Je 77,
p. 95.

COOPERMAN, Robert
"Prothalamion." DenQ (12:2) Sum 77, p. 324.
"You Seemed Too Old to Have a Father." DenQ (12:2) Sum 77,
p. 323.
"You Seemed Too Old to Have a Father." DenQ (12:4) Wint 78,
p. 70.

COPE, Steven R.
"Going Home." Wind (24) 77, p. 21.
"Town Square Statue." Wind (24) 77, p. 22.

COPELAND, Beth
"A Woman Without Lips." Ascent (3:2) 77, p. 16.

COPELAND, Helen
"Toward 1984." SouthernPR (17:1) Spr 77, p. 36.

CORBETT, Sarah Anne
"Reversals." ChrC (94:36) 9 N 77, p. 1033.

CORDING, Robert
"Circles." KanQ (9:3) Sum 77, p. 43.
"Dowser." SouthernHR (11:4) Aut 77, p. 383.
"Perspectives." PraS (51:2) Sum 77, p. 132.

CORKERY, Christopher Jane
"Bestiary." SouthernPR (17:2) Aut 77, p. 18.

CORLEY, Florrie
"After the Flight." HarvAd (110:5) My 77, p. 18.

CORMAN, Cid
"January." Montra (3) Spr 77, p. 104.
"Not posthumous yet." Montra (3) Spr 77, p. 103.
"The Shadow." Montra (3) Spr 77, p. 105.
"There was something I." Montra (3) Spr 77, p. 105.
"What's the point." Montra (3) Spr 77, p. 104.

CORN, Alfred
"April." Shen (28:3) Spr 77, p. 64.
"Declaration, July 4." YaleR (66:4) Sum 77, p. 576.
"Earth, Stone, Brick, Metal: 'Mannahatta.'" FourQt (26:4) Sum
    77, p. 10.
Eight poems. Poetry (130:4) Jl 77, p. 187.
"Impression." Poetry (129:4) Ja 77, p. 193.
"January." Poetry (129:4) Ja 77, p. 187.
"Nine to Five." Poetry (129:4) Ja 77, p. 189.
"Return" (for Edmund White). GeoR (31:2) Sum 77, p. 365.
"Some New Ruins." Poetry (129:4) Ja 77, p. 193.
"Spring and Summer." Poetry (129:4) Ja 77, p. 190.
"To A Muse." NewRep (177:10) 3 S 77, p. 25.
"Visits to Other Cities." GeoR (31:2) Sum 77, p. 366.

CORNETT, Fran
"The Poetess." Wind (25) 77, p. 45.

CORNFORD, Adam
"Blues for Coleridge." MontG (6) Aut 77, p. 51.
"A Brief Vacation." Kayak (45) My 77, p. 41.
"Chamber." MontG (6) Aut 77, p. 50.
"The Cold Room." Kayak (45) My 77, p. 40.
"History." MontG (6) Aut 77, p. 49.
"Our Sorcerers." MontG (6) Aut 77, p. 52.
"So You Want To They Said." Kayak (45) My 77, p. 39.

CORPMAN, Izora
"Wells." ModernPS (8:2) Aut 77, p. 138.

CORRIGAN, Paul
"Puckerbush." PoNow (14/18) 77, p. 25.

CORRIGAN, Sheila
"Old Woman." Gra (12) 77.

CORRINGTON, John William
"Archaic Torso of Apollo." NewOR (5:3) 77, p. 234.
"The Beloved." SewanR (85:2) Spr 77, p. 207.
"I Know a Girl Whose Heart." SouthernR (13:2) Spr 77, p. 336.
"Joe Tolliver Who Mowed Our Lawn." SouthernR (13:2) Spr 77,
    p. 334.
"On the Flesh of Christ." SouthernR (13:2) Spr 77, p. 337.

CORTÉS, Margaret
"Variations on Poems by Ezra Pound." Poetry (131:2) N 77,
    p. 63.

CORTEZ, Jayne
"For the Brave Young Students in Soweto." Nimrod (21:2/22:1)
    77, p. 60.

CORWIN, Phillip
"Child World." Icarus (5:1) Spr 77, p. 21.
"Dream." KanQ (9:2) Spr 77, p. 59.
"High Leaves." Icarus (5:2) Aut 77, p. 21.
"Integrity." Northeast (3:3) Sum 77, p. 8.
"Rhododendrons." WindO (29) Sum 77, p. 41.

COSCA, Laurie
"Doves." DenQ (12:2) Sum 77, p. 254.
"Emerald Bay." DenQ (12:2) Sum 77, p. 255.
"In the Mirror." DenQ (12:2) Sum 77, p. 253.
"Kite." DenQ (12:2) Sum 77, p. 255.
"Letter from My Mother." DenQ (12:2) Sum 77, p. 254.

COSSEBOOM, Ray
"Our Town Hall." Xa (4) 77, p. 7.

COSTAKIS, Tony
"Crazy John died." SeC (5:2) 78, p. 45.
"Duane." SeC (5:2) 78, p. 46.

COSTANZO, Gerald
"Crime Stopper's Notebook." MidwQ (18:4) Sum 77, p. 438.
"In the Blood." MidwQ (18:4) Sum 77, p. 437.
"The Sacred Cows of Los Angeles." NoAmR (262:3) Aut 77,
    p. 34.
"Vesuvius Crucible" (for Thomas Johnson). MidwQ (18:4) Sum 77,
    p. 439.
"Welfare." PoNow (14/18) 77, p. 25.

COSTELLO, James A.
"No Roses, I Remember." EnPas (4) 76, p. 34.
"Roots." EnPas (5) 77, p. 34.

COTTER, James Finn
"Along King's Highway." Comm (104:26) 23 D 77, p. 818.
"Spring Walks, Mountain Vistas." Thought (52:207) D 77, p. 439.
"Trailways to Jersey Shore." Comm (104:18) 2 S 77, p. 555.

COUNCILMAN, Emily Sargent
"As Wind Will Prod." ArizQ (33:3) Aut 77, p. 240.

COURSEN, H. R.
"Practice" (In Memory of Joe Abeyounis [1933-1956]). Sam (55)
    77, p. 43.

"Sister. " PoNow (14/18) 77, p. 25.
Walking Away. Sam (60) 77. Entire issue.

COWEN, Sonia
"Vivid and Dark, I Come at Last. " DacTerr (14) Spr-Sum 77,
p. 68.

COX, C. B.
"An Interview with God. " BelPoJ (28:2) Wint 77-78, p. 21.
"Mr. Parker. " BelPoJ (28:2) Wint 77-78, p. 23.

COX, Dorothy
"She Was Afraid of Light. " CutB (9) Aut-Wint 77, p. 12.

COX, Kathleen
"Labour. " Poem (29) Mr 77, p. 46.

COX, Vicki
"Shall We Gas the Dog?" KanQ (9:1) Wint 77, p. 132.

COYNE, Bill
"Prayer for You Sleeping in My Arms. " Mouth (11/12) Mr-Je
77, p. 115.

CRAFT, David
"Gravestones or Immortality. " Wind (26) 77, p. 36.

CRAMER, Steven
"Poem for Chicago. " AntR (35:1) Wint 77, p. 67.
"Riddle. " Agni (7) 77, p. 115.

CRASE, Douglas
"Color-Peak Weekend. " NewYorker (53:36) 24 O 77, p. 50.
"Covenant. " PoetryNW (18:1) Spr 77, p. 17.
"Experience and What to Make of It. " Poetry (129:4) Ja 77,
p. 204.
"The Lake Effect. " Poetry (129:4) Ja 77, p. 202.
"Replevin. " PoetryNW (18:1) Spr 77, p. 17.
"Trover. " PoetryNW (18:1) Spr 77, p. 18.

CRAWFORD, Jack, Jr.
"Always the Dolphins Leaping Before. " PoetryNW (18:2) Sum 77,
p. 3.
"Blue-Green Lids. " PoetryNW (18:2) Sum 77, p. 8.
"Brushing Away Gnats. " PoetryNW (18:4) Wint 77-78, p. 36.
"Pauline. " PoetryNW (18:2) Sum 77, p. 5.
"Setting Down a Friday Foot. " PoetryNW (18:2) Sum 77, p. 7.

CREASY, Kenda
"Running Barefoot: not to be taken literally. " EngJ (66:5) My 77,
p. 59.

CREEDON, Michael
"Confusions. " LaB (6) Mr 77, p. 23.

"I Think We Kiss Off the Night." <u>LaB</u> (8) Jl-Ag 77, p. 16.
"In Our New York Marriage, You Were the One." <u>LaB</u> (6) Mr 77, p. 21.
"Meat Crisis." <u>LaB</u> (6) Mr 77, p. 22.
"Seance." <u>LaB</u> (8) Jl-Ag 77, p. 14.
"Too Much Freud." <u>LaB</u> (8) Jl-Ag 77, p. 15.

CRESSANI, Cheryl A.
from A Seasonal Process: "What Prevails." <u>Wind</u> (26) 77, p. 49.

CREWS, Judson
"Now Song" (transcription of Charley John Greasybear). <u>PraS</u> (51:1) 77, p. 84.
"Song of Half Dying" (transcription of Charley John Greasybear). <u>PraS</u> (51:1) Spr 77, p. 85.

CRIBBEN, Carol
"Buckaroo." <u>Madem</u> (83:3) Mr 77, p. 108.

CRIPE, Clyde Edward
"The Porpoises." <u>DeKalb</u> (10:3) Spr 77, p. 6.

CROBAUGH, Emma
"Dream Falls on Frozen Hours." <u>CarouselQ</u> (2:1) Spr 77, p. 17.
"Shouts of Golden Roosters." <u>DeKalb</u> (10:2) Wint 77, p. 16.

CROCKER, Jack
"Running in a Certain Scent." <u>SouthernPR</u> (17:2) Aut 77, p. 33.

CROLAND, Carol
"Miriam." <u>BerksR</u> (12:1) Spr 77.
"On Henri Matisse's Portrait of Madame Matisse." <u>BerksR</u> (12:1) Spr 77.
"Thomas." <u>BerksR</u> (12:1) Spr 77.

CROOKER, Barbara
"Thanksgiving." <u>Chomo</u> (3:3) Spr 77, p. 47.

CROWLEY, Melvin
"In God We Trust." <u>NegroHB</u> (40:3) My-Je 77, p. 704.

CRUM, Shutta
Twelve poems. <u>AAR</u> (27) 77, p. 20.

CSOÓRI, Sándor
"The Dreamers of My Dream" (tr. by Daniel Hoffman). <u>NewRep</u> (176:13) 26 Mr 77, p. 29.
"I Stole Your Face" (tr. by Daniel Hoffman). <u>NewRep</u> (176:13) 26 Mr 77, p. 29.
"I Would Rather Run Back" (tr. by Alan Dixon). <u>AmerPoR</u> (6:3) My-Je 77, p. 25.
"Whispers, for Two Voices" (tr. by Alan Dixon). <u>AmerPoR</u> (6:3) My-Je 77, p. 24.

CSUKÁS, Istrán
"The Macadam Road Remembers" (tr. by Barbara Howes).
AmerPoR (6:3) My-Je 77, p. 26.

CUBEIRO, Emilio
"you think your ass is so fucking important." Mouth (11/12) Mr-
Je 77, p. 34.

CUDDIHY, Michael
"Anesthesia." Rapp (10) 77, p. 4.

CULBERT, Steven
"Night Bus to Key West." LittleR (12) 77, p. 3.
"Spooking Two Black Horses at Feeding Time." LittleR (12) 77,
p. 10.

CULBERTSON, Nancy
"More Than Clean." PoetL (72:2) Sum 77, p. 75.
"This One I Owe." StoneC (77:2) My 77, p. 11.

CULLEN, John T.
"Entreaty to a Munchkin." DeKalb (10:3) Spr 77, p. 7.

CUNNINGHAM, Edward
"The Hour before Evening." LadHJ (94:4) Ap 77, p. P. S. 8.

CURLEY, Daniel
"The Sleeping Woman." BelPoJ (27:4) Sum 77, p. 22.
"The Woman Who Lives on the Corner." BelPoJ (27:4) Sum 77,
p. 24.

CURRAN, Mary Doyle
"To Norman Silverstein a Flashback from Nantucket." Salm (36)
Wint 77, p. 43.

CURRIER, Vinny
"Cello." HarvAd (110:4) Ap 77, p. 17.

CURRY, David
"Gibberish." NoAmR (262:4) Wint 77.

CURTIS, David
"Rainbow" (for Charles, who is older now). ChrC (94:16) 4 My
77, p. 425.

CURTIS, Walt
"The Cockroach God." Vaga (25) 77, supplement.

CUSACK, A.
"As fish in shale, remember the seabed drift." Wind (27) 77,
p. 9.
"No One Photographs the Concrete Tree." Wind (27) 77, p. 10.
"Stone Beach." Wind (27) 77, p. 9.

CUSACK, Cyril
"Confiteor." Comm (104:2) 21 Ja 77, p. 39.

CUSHMAN, Don
"Morning." YellowBR (8) 77, p. 35.

CUSUMANO, Michele
"Soft Limbed Boy." RemR (5) 77, p. 71.

CUTLER, Bruce
"Bahnhof Bern." ArkRiv (3:4/4:1) 77, p. 39.
"Big Sky, Switzerland." YaleR (66:3) Spr 77, p. 399.
"A Little Sensitivity Training." KanQ (9:1) Wint 77, p. 35.
"Roman Tomb." KanQ (9:1) Wint 77, p. 34.
"Your Number." ArkRiv (3:4/4:1) 77, p. 38.

CUTLER, Jill
"Picnic in the Rain." Icarus (5:1) Spr 77, p. 8.

CYNDIAN, Charles London
"Cards." Wind (26) 77, p. 9.
"A Cloud the Color of a Man." YellowBR (8) 77, p. 32.
"You Looking Into It." Wind (26) 77, p. 9.

DACEY, Florence
"A Letter from the Asylum." MoonsLT (2:3) 77, p. 31.
"Wife to Poet." MoonsLT (2:3) 77, p. 32.

DACEY, Philip
"The Body." Epoch (27:1) Aut 77, p. 34.
"Elegy: A January Walk in Cottonwood, Minnesota." HiramPoR
    (22) Aut-Wint 77, p. 13.
"Emptying Your Pockets." QW (4) Aut 77, p. 94.
"Fall Back a Moment." FourQt (26:3) Spr 77, p. 39.
"From the Clearing." Poetry (129:5) F 77, p. 252.
"Frost Warnings." Thought (52:204) Mr 77, p. 103.
"He Writes an Old Girlfriend and Asks Her to Have an Affair
    with Him." GeoR (31:2) Sum 77, p. 362.
"Hopkins to Bridges: From the Lost Correspondence." NowestR
    (16:3) 77, p. 47.
"Hopkins to Bridges: From the Secret Correspondence." AmerR
    (26) N 77, p. 286.
"Hopkins to His Jesuit Superior." CarlMis (17:1) Wint 77-78,
    p. 93.
"The Ingrown Tiger." CarlMis (17:1) Wint 77-78, p. 98.
"Inspired Iron." BelPoJ (27:3) Spr 77, p. 6.
"Knowing How Easily." CarlMis (17:1) Wint 77-78, p. 97.
"Lies." SouthernPR (17:2) Aut 77, p. 59.
"Manual." Sparrow (33) Ja 77, p. 5.
"Mater Investida." CarlMis (17:1) Wint 77-78, p. 94.
"Mystery Football." PoNow (14/18) 77, p. 26.
"Prisms (Altea, Spain)." CarlMis (16:1/2) Aut-Wint 76-77, p.
    130.

"Skin." MichQR (16:3) Sum 77, p. 280.
"Sleeping Parents, Wakeful Children." PoetryNW (18:2) Sum 77,
    p. 45.
"Study." Confr (14) Spr-Sum 77, p. 95.
"The Three Graces." KanQ (9:2) Spr 77, p. 30.
"A Used Car Lot at Night." PoetryNW (18:2) Sum 77, p. 44.
"Where We Were." PartR (44:3) 77, p. 412.

DAGENAIS, John
    "Coyotes." HiramPoR (22) Aut-Wint 77, p. 14.

DAGHER, Jeanice
    "coq au vin." PortR (23) 77, p. 27.
    "new rooms." HangL (31) Aut 77, p. 6.
    "note from a column on modern living." HangL (31) Aut 77, p. 3.
    "one poem/in the n. y. painter series." HangL (31) Aut 77, p. 4.
    "sunday evening in mid-march." Wind (25) 77, p. 13.
    "Unnamed Water Poem." StoneC (77:2) My 77, p. 26.

DAIGON, Ruth
    "For the First Time." Wind (27) 77, p. 12.

DAILEY, Joel
    "The Mad Poet's Bio." Drag (16) 77.
    "Rosemary Drawing." HolCrit (14:3) Je 77, p. 8.
    "Saturday Night." Juice (5) 77.

DALE, Kathleen
    "Kiva Woman." 13thM (3:2) 77, p. 32.

D'ALORNA, Marquesa
    "Como está sereno o Céu." TexQ (19:4) Wint 76, p. 108.

DALTON, Dorothy
    "Classic View." PoetL (72:1) Spr 77, p. 4.
    "The Enduring." PoetL (72:1) Spr 77, p. 4.
    "The Map." PoetL (72:1) Spr 77, p. 4.
    "The Substitution." PoetL (72:1) Spr 77, p. 3.

DALY, William F.
    "Navajo Woman." Nat (225:22) 24 D 77, p. 697.
    "Old Ladies at the Slots: Vegas." WindO (29) Sum 77, p. 33.

DAMERON, Chip
    "A Picasso Montage." TexQ (20:4) Wint 77, p. 178.

DANA, James L.
    "The Courtesan" (tr. of Rainer Maria Rilke). DenQ (11:4) Wint
        77, p. 47.
    "The Panther" (tr. of Rainer Maria Rilke). DenQ (11:4) Wint 77,
        p. 42.
    "Spanish Dancer" (tr. of Rainer Maria Rilke). DenQ (11:4) Wint
        77, p. 46.

"A Woman's Fate" (tr. of Rainer Maria Rilke). DenQ (11:4)
    Wint 77, p. 41.

DANA, Robert
    "Astronomies. " NewYorker (53:24) 1 Ag 77, p. 60.
    "Burning the Steaks in the Rain. " NoAmR (262:1) Spr 77, p. 60.
    "Dream Works. " Kayak (46) O 77, p. 57.
    "Mineral Point. " NewL (44:1) Aut 77, p. 109.
    "Mnemosyne. " NewYorker (53:32) 26 S 77, p. 34.
    from Natural Odes/American Elegies: "38: In Memoriam, MSH,
        1929-1974. " Bleb (12) 77, p. 56.
    "Running Falling Standing. " Bleb (12) 77, p. 55.
    "Your Own. " Bleb (12) 77, p. 57.

DANGAI
    "Earth, river, mountain" (tr. by Lucien Stryk). ChiR (29:2) Aut
        77, p. 89.

DANIEL, Marky
    "Bestiary for the Rancher's Daughter. " PoetryNW (18:2) Sum 77,
        p. 42.
    "Naked Ladies. " PoetryNW (18:2) Sum 77, p. 41.

DANIELL, Rosemary
    "Of Jayne Mansfield, Flannery O'Connor, My Mother & Me" (for
        Alice Walker, whose blackness made the enemy visible).
        SouthernPR (16:SI) 77, p. 25.

DANIELS, Guy
    "Monologue of the World's Last Poetry Reader (Poetry Day,
        1999)" (tr. of Andrei Voznesensky). AmerR (26) N 77,
        p. 389.

DANKLEFF, Richard
    "Funeral. " KanQ (9:1) Wint 77, p. 47.
    "Sifting Our Responses. " KanQ (9:3) Sum 77, p. 78.

DANNER, Richard
    "grammaire de la vie. " WestHR (31:1) Wint 77, p. 30.
    "Sonnerie de villes. " WestHR (31:3) Sum 77, p. 248.

DANTE, Robert
    "You Should Have Stuck to Stamp Collecting. " EnPas (4) 76,
        p. 23.

DARDEN, Douglas
    "Coffee Break. " StoneC (77:1) F 77, p. 9.

DARIO, Rubén
    "Autumn Poem" (tr. by Chris Dunn). DenQ (11:4) Wint 77,
        p. 154.
    "Campoamor" (tr. by Chris Dunn). DenQ (11:4) Wint 77, p. 155.
    "Metempsychosis" (tr. by Chris Dunn). DenQ (11:4) Wint 77, p. 153.

"Nocturne" (tr. by Chris Dunn). DenQ (11:4) Wint 77, p. 155.
"Vesper" (tr. by Chris Dunn). DenQ (11:4) Wint 77, p. 154.

DARLINGTON, Andrew
"Bracken Edge Dawn." WindO (29) Sum 77, p. 32.
"Val." Sam (52) Ap 77, p. 19.

DARR, Ann
"A Day in the Life Of" (for Samuel Allen). Hand (1) 77, p. 101.
"Dear James Wright." CarlMis (16:1/2) Aut-Wint 76-77, p. 62.
"Everything in the Kitchen." ParisR (71) Aut 77, p. 52.
"I Gave My Love a." PoNow (14/18) 77, p. 197.
"I Will Have No Idols Before Me." CarlMis (16:1/2) Aut-Wint
   76-77, p. 63.
"Lines for W. H. Auden Who Said We Took Him Too Seriously."
   Box (5) Spr 77, p. 22.
"The Pot-Bellied Anachronism." PoNow (14/18) 77, p. 26.
"The Reply." ParisR (71) Aut 77, p. 52.

DARRING, Walter
"The Stanza Form." MissR (6:1) 77, p. 102.

DARWEESH, Mahmoud
"A Painting on the Wall" (tr. by B. M. Bennani). Bleb (12) 77,
   p. 38.
"Soft Rain in Distant Autumn" (tr. by B. M. Bennani). Bleb (12)
   77, p. 36.

DARWISH, Joe
"Ten O'Clock Break, Door Eight." Waters (5) 77, p. 7.

DARYUSH, Elizabeth
"Song of a Pentecostal Summer." SouthernR (13:4) Aut 77, p. 739.
"Two Poems." SouthernR (13:3) Sum 77, p. 570.

DAS GUPTA, Kolyan
"I wish I could change myself invisible." AAR (27) 77, p. 96.

DASH, Jon
Thirteen poems. DenQ (12:2) Sum 77, p. 379.

DAUER, Rosamond
"Trained Chickens." Glass (2:2/3) Wint-Spr 77, p. 67.

DAUFFENBACH, D. W.
"matins." PoetL (72:1) Spr 77, p. 21.

DAUGHTER of the GOVERNOR of KAZURA
"Dialogue of Wind and Rose" (tr. by Graeme Wilson). DenQ
   (12:2) Sum 77, p. 358.

DAUMAL, René
"The Four Cardinal Times" (tr. by Louise Landes-Levi). MontG
   (6) Aut 77, p. 63.

"The Shadow's Skin" (tr. by Kelton W. Knight). WebR (3:4) Aut
   77, p. 45.
"Yellow Laughter" (tr. by Kelton W. Knight). WebR (3:4) Aut 77,
   p. 44.
"Yellow Laughter" (tr. by Louise Landes-Levi). MontG (6) Aut
   77, p. 62.

DAUNT, Jon
"Light Bulb." Xa (4) 77, p. 52.
"The Shy Hours." Xa (4) 77, p. 50.
"Statue Without a Face." Aspect (69) O-D 76, p. 40.

D'AURIA, Gemma
"Down to the Candid Glory" (For Martyrs without Compass).
   PraS (51:1) Spr 77, p. 94.

DAVIDSON, Ann Beggs
"Amanda Practices." WindO (27) Aut 76.
"Mall." Wind (27) 77, p. 13.
"Pastoral" (For Norm). Wind (27) 77, p. 13.

DAVIDSON, Matthew
"Love." QW (3) Spr-Sum 77, p. 31.

DAVIDSON, Michael
"At Last." SunM (4) Aut 77, p. 38.
"The Big Thomson Flood." LaB (9) N-D 77, p. 23.
"Love Me, Love My Dog." LaB (9) N-D 77, p. 24.
"Mixed Days, The Mindless Years." LaB (7) My 77, p. 21.
from The News: "A late quartet late at night." LaB (7) My 77,
   p. 20.
from The News: "I wanted the present tense." LaB (7) My 77,
   p. 19.
from The News: "Not much else to know." LaB (7) My 77,
   p. 19.

DAVIDSON, Richard
"Nostalgia for an Old Bike." NewOR (5:3) 77, p. 59.

DAVIE, Donald
Eleven poems. NewRep (177:17) 22 O 77, p. 21.

DAVIES, Henry R.
Eleven fragments (tr. of Alkman). DenQ (11:4) Wint 77, p. 91.

DAVIES, Nancy
"October First." BallSUF (18:4) Aut 77, p. 2.

DAVIS, Fred S.
"Ice Skating, Midnight." CarouselQ (2:2) Aut 77, p. 19.

DAVIS, Glover
"The Clouds." PoNow (14/18) 77, p. 26.

DAVIS, Helene
"The Interior." Ploughs (3:3/4) 77, p. 152.

DAVIS, Joyce
"Wild Geese." EngJ (66:5) My 77, p. 57.

DAVIS, Kay
"Repair." QW (2) Wint 77, p. 46.

DAVIS, Ki
Eighteen poems. Aspen (3) Spr 77, p. 140.

DAVIS, Lloyd
"Late in the Evening." OhioR (18:1) Wint 77, p. 98.

DAVIS, Melody
"Nightmare of the Realist." WindO (28) Spr 77, p. 35.

DAVIS, Stanley
"Academic." Wind (24) 77, p. 31.
"Dream." Wind (24) 77, p. 31.
"a face I couldn't name." Wind (24) 77, p. 31.

DAVIS, Vernon J., Jr.
"Beautiful Black Woman." BlackF (2:1) Wint 77-78, p. 39.

DAVIS, Wallace Spencer
"'Anthanon.'" DeKalb (10:2) Wint 77, p. 18.
"'Papa Finally Came Home.'" DeKalb (10:2) Wint 77, p. 17.

DAVIS, William Virgil
"An Animal in the Room." PoNow (14/18) 77, p. 28.
"The Blessing." DenQ (12:4) Wint 78, p. 57.
"The Bones at Rest." Poem (30) Jl 77, p. 18.
"Confrontation in a Rented Cabin." Poem (30) Jl 77, p. 16.
Eight poems. Wind (26) 77, p. 11.
"The Field Left Alone." PoNow (14/18) 77, p. 28.
"In Lieu of a Letter." PoNow (14/18) 77, p. 28.
"Snow." ChrC (94:43) 28 D 77, p. 1215.
"That House, This Room." DenQ (12:4) Wint 78, p. 58.
"The Time of Year, the Hour." DenQ (12:4) Wint 78, p. 56.
"Twilight." SouthernHR (11:2) Spr 77, p. 194.
"Two Days before the Beginning of Summer." PoNow (14/18) 77,
    p. 28.

DAVISON, Peter
"La Bocca Della Verità." Atl (240:3) S 77, p. 42.
"Circolo Della Caccia." Iowa (8:2) Spr 77, p. 40.
"Cross Cut." Atl (240:1) Jl 77, p. 75.
"Day of Wrath." NewRep (177:10) 3 S 77, p. 27.
"The Hanging Man." Atl (239:1) Ja 77, p. 71.
"Skiing by Moonlight." PoetryNW (18:2) Sum 77, p. 52.
"Thanksgiving." PoetryNW (18:2) Sum 77, p. 53.

"Zenith: Walker Creek." NewYorker (53:18) 20 Je 77, p. 38.

DAWSON, David
"To Touch You Must Reach Out." CarouselQ (2:3) Wint 77,
     p. 25.

DAWSON, Gene
"For 'Jaggers' (Stock Response)." Paunch (46/47) Ap 77, p. 47.

DAWSON, Richard G.
"Vulture Spring." Wind (26) 77, p. 15.

DAWSON, Thomas
"Junaluska's Grave." Waters (6) 77, p. 34.
"What the Land Sings." Waters (6) 77, p. 23.

DAY, Jean Trelease
"Au Bord de la Mer Or After the Bath." AntR (35:1) Wint 77,
     p. 60.
"Had a Horse." AntR (35:1) Wint 77, p. 61.

DAYAN, Joan
Eight poems (tr. of Rene Depestre). AmerPoR (6:4) Jl-Ag 77,
     p. 38.

DAYTON, David
"Family." Kayak (45) My 77, p. 54.
"The Hole in My Head." Madrona (4:13/14) 77, p. 34.

DEAGON, Ann
"Lo Sposalizio." NewC (8:1) 76-77, p. 9.
Nineteen poems. Poets (1:1) 77, pp. 45-66.
"There are names for everything we do." SouthernPR (16:SI) 77,
     p. 28.
"Women and Children First." SouthernPR (17:1) Spr 77, p. 13.

DEAL, Borden
"Fellowship with Men." Confr (15) Aut 77-Wint 78, p. 101.
"Increase." Confr (15) Aut 77-Wint 78, p. 101.

DEAL, Susan Strayer
"On the Plains." EnPas (6) 77, p. 37.

DEAN, John
"To Jacob, on His Leaving." NewOR (5:3) 77, p. 245.

DeANDRADE, Carlos Drummond
"Ceramics" (tr. by Jack Tomlins). LitR (21:2) Wint 78, p. 168.
"Confession" (tr. by Jack Tomlins). LitR (21:2) Wint 78, p. 166.
"Dead Men in Their Frock Coats" (tr. by Jack Tomlins). LitR
     (21:2) Wint 78, p. 169.
"The Dirty Hand" (tr. by Jean R. Longland). LitR (21:2) Wint
     78, p. 164.

"Discovery" (tr. by Jack Tomlins). LitR (21:2) Wint 78, p. 168.
"Double Dentures" (tr. by Jean R. Longland). LitR (21:2) Wint
     78, p. 161.
"Heptagonal Poem" (tr. by Jack Tomlins). LitR (21:2) Wint 78,
     p. 166.
"International Congress of Fear" (tr. by Jack Tomlins). LitR
     (21:2) Wint 78, p. 167.
"The Man from Itabira Tells His Secret" (tr. by Jack Tomlins).
     LitR (21:2) Wint 78, p. 169.
"News from Spain" (tr. by Jean R. Longland). LitR (21:2) Wint
     78, p. 160.
"Science Fiction" (tr. by Ricardo Sternberg). Drag (16) 77.

DEANE, Gladys Verville
"Whatever Container." PoetL (72:1) Spr 77, p. 19.

DeARAUJO, Virginia
"Carlos." BelPoJ (27:3) Spr 77, p. 24.
"Intervene." BelPoJ (27:3) Spr 77, p. 21.
"Rim Trail." BelPoJ (27:3) Spr 77, p. 19.

DeBEVOISE, Arlene
"Meditations of an Errant Pilgrim." ChrC (94:39) 30 N 77,
     p. 1116.

DeBOLT, William Walter
"Arithmetic." BallSUF (18:1) Wint 77, p. 64.
"Athiest." ChrC (94:5) 16 F 77, p. 140.
"Contrast." ChrC (94:33) 19 O 77, p. 939.
"Exegesis for a New Year." ChrC (94:43) 28 D 77, p. 1218.
"Intersection." ChrC (94:10) 23 Mr 77, p. 275.
"Intruders." ChrC (94:1) 5-12 Ja 77, p. 16.
"Out of His Youth." ChrC (94:29) 21 S 77, p. 812.
"Primal Wedding." ChrC (94:25) 3-10 Ag 77, p. 684.
"Reincarnation Explained." ChrC (94:27) 31 Ag-7 S 77, p. 753.

DeCAMPOS, Augusto
"Poem" (tr. by Mary Ellen Solt, Heitor Martins, and Jon M.
     Tolman). LitR (21:2) Wint 78, p. 276.

DeCASTRO, Rosalía
"Nubes." TexQ (19:4) Wint 76, p. 106.

DEDRICK, Eleanore
"The Monthly Faculty Meeting on Grading." EngJ (66:5) My 77,
     p. 44.

DeFOE, Mark
"The Artificial Swan." MissR (6:1) 77, p. 55.
"Daughters with Toad." CarolQ (29:2) Spr-Sum 77, p. 75.
"I-70--Crossing Kansas in August." KanQ (9:3) Sum 77, p. 120.
"Ogallala, Nebraska." WebR (3:1) Wint 77, p. 61.
"Okla wildweed junk car fender." MissR (6:1) 77, p. 146.

"Wichita Bop--1956." WebR (3:4) Aut 77, p. 62.

DeFREES, Madeline
 "The Chow, a Dog of Ancient Origin, Has a Blue-Black Tongue."
     Columbia (1) Aut 77, p. 22.
 "For Ed Harkness Lost in a Contributor's Note in the Quarterly
     West." CutB (9) Aut-Wint 77, p. 82.
 "Imaginary Ancestors: Grandmother Grant." QW (4) Aut 77,
     p. 54.
 "Sanding the Chairs." Columbia (1) Aut 77, p. 21.

DeGRAVELLES, Charles N.
 "Amnesia." SouthernR (13:2) Spr 77, p. 329.
 "The Legitimacy of Strangers." NewL (43:4) Sum 77, p. 60.
 "Pieta." SouthernPR (17:2) Aut 77, p. 47.
 "The Pilgrims." HolCrit (14:5) D 77, p. 14.

DEINES, Mike
 "Once More." Sparrow (33) Ja 77, p. 15.

DEITERING, Cindi
 "River Poem." WindO (28) Spr 77, p. 17.

DELANEY, John
 "A Lullaby in Rigamarole." DeKalb (10:3) Spr 77, p. 9.
 "Sun and Moon." Wind (24) 77, p. 23.
 "To a Previous Occupant." Wind (24) 77, p. 23.
 "Typographical Signs." PoetryNW (18:1) Spr 77, p. 40.

DELGADO, Holly
 "Conga Rap." CarouselQ (2:3) Wint 77, p. 19.

DeLONGCHAMPS, Joanne
 "Bottle." PoNow (14/18) 77, p. 29.

DELP, Michael
 "Going North." GRR (8:1/2) 77, p. 16.
 "Letter from Monet." Agni (7) 77, p. 39.
 "Love Poem." GRR (8:1/2) 77, p. 96.
 "Old Loneliness." GRR (8:1/2) 77, p. 92.
 "Photograph." GRR (8:1/2) 77, p. 94.
 "Poem of the Inner Ghost" (for James Tipton). GRR (8:1/2) 77,
     p. 85.
 "Praises." GRR (8:1/2) 77, p. 89.

DelVECCHIO, Gloria
 "The Dog." US1 (10) Wint 77-78, p. 9.
 "In a Museum." US1 (10) Wint 77-78, p. 9.
 "Venus." US1 (9) Spr 77, p. 10.

DeMELLO, Agustin
 "Surrealists." CarouselQ (2:2) Aut 77, p. 22.
 "Triangle." CarouselQ (2:2) Aut 77, p. 22.

DeMELO NETO, João Cabral
  "Childhood" (tr. by Jean R. Longland). LitR (21:2) Wint 78,
    p. 237.
  "Poem: My eyes have telescopes" (tr. by Jean R. Longland).
    LitR (21:2) Wint 78, p. 238.
  "Psychology of Composition" (tr. by Jack Tomlins). LitR (21:2)
    Wint 78, p. 240.
  "Seated Woman" (tr. by Jack Tomlins). LitR (21:2) Wint 78,
    p. 240.
  "The Table" (tr. by Jack Tomlins). LitR (21:2) Wint 78, p. 239.
  "To Carlos Drummond de Andrade" (tr. by Jean R. Longland).
    LitR (21:2) Wint 78, p. 237.

DEMPSTER, Barry
  "Accordion Notes." HiramPoR (23) Wint 77, p. 17.
  "A Fable for Isolated Men." EnPas (6) 77, p. 28.
  "The Man Who Loves Statistics." Mouth (13) D 77, p. 61.
  "Observing the Performance." Poem (30) Jl 77, p. 49.
  "Offerings." Poem (30) Jl 77, p. 48.
  "Quipu." Mouth (11/12) Mr-Je 77, p. 18.

DENBERG, Kenneth
  "The Great Star Bear in Pursuit of Game Shows." StoneC (77:3)
    S 77, p. 17.

Den BOER, David C.
  "Animal Songs." WindO (28) Spr 77, p. 14.
  "First Returns of Spring." SmPd (14:3) Aut 77, p. 11.
  "March Impasse." WindO (28) Spr 77, p. 13.
  "Riddles, Answers." WindO (28) Spr 77, p. 13.

DENIS, Nelson
  "In Snow." YaleLit (145:5) 77, p. 13.
  "morning." YaleLit (145:5) 77, p. 13.

DENNIS, Carl
  "Grandmother and I." Salm (38/39) Sum-Aut 77, p. 105.
  "Margaret's Answer." Epoch (27:1) Aut 77, p. 79.
  "The Trip." ConcPo (10:2) Aut 77, p. 70.

DENT, Tom
  "Running & Dipping Poem No. 1." Nimrod (21:2/22:1) 77, p. 63.
  "St. Thomas Island." Nimrod (21:2/22:1) 77, p. 66.

DENTINGER, Philip
  "You." Epoch (26:3) Spr 77, p. 271.

DENTON, Toni
  "To Dawn:" CimR (38) Ja 77, p. 43.

DENZER, Peter W.
  "The Orchard." BelPoJ (27:4) Sum 77, p. 30.

DEPESTRE, Rene
    Eight poems (tr. by Joan Dayan).   AmerPoR (6:4) Jl-Ag 77,
        p. 38.

DEPTA, Victor M.
    "The Eerie Light." ConcPo (10:1) Spr 77, p. 78.
    "I'm Sitting Down in the Field like an Idiot." CutB (9) Aut-Wint
        77, p. 110.
    "The Paradisiacal Cake." ConcPo (10:1) Spr 77, p. 78.
    "When I Read Statements." PoNow (14/18) 77, p. 29.

DeQUEVEDO, Francisco
    "He Notes the Brevity of Whatever Is Alive and How What Was
        Alive Now Seems To Be Nothing" (tr. by Willis Barnstone).
        Bleb (12) 77, p. 19.
    "He Shows How All Things Warn of Death" (tr. by Willis Barn-
        stone). Bleb (12) 77, p. 18.
    "Quevedo Speaks of His Sores" (tr. by Carolyne Wright). EnPas
        (4) 76, p. 37.

Der HOVANESSIAN, Diana
    "Chauvinism (Female)." LadHJ (94:12) D 77, p. 168b.
    "Fisherman's Mother." Nat (224:18) 7 My 77, p. 566.
    "From a Nerja Hotel Window." AmerS (46:1) Wint 76-77, p. 93.
    "Rain." Nat (224:2) 15 Ja 77, p. 56.
    "Two Armenians Walking on Sunday." AmerPoR (6:2) Mr-Ap 77,
        p. 29.

DERR, Mark B.
    "A Moment's Confusion" (for Wyatt Prunty). KanQ (9:4) Aut 77,
        p. 68.

DERRICOTTE, Toi
    "Couplets." US1 (9) Spr 77, p. 6.
    "Intimations of Mortality." US1 (9) Spr 77, p. 6.
    "last will of one who lived alone." Gra (12) 77, p. 55.
    "morning ride." HangL (29) Wint 76-77, p. 3.

DERRINGER, Sally Lipton
    "Poem: I would enter the seed you were born as." DenQ (12:1)
        Spr 77, p. 47.

DESJARDINS, Lorel
    "Old Oraibi." ArizQ (33:3) Aut 77, p. 275.

DESMOND, Larry
    from Algebraic Hills: (III). NewC (7:2) 75-76, p. 14.

DESSNER, Lawrence Jay
    "Hungaria." PoetC (10:1) 77, p. 14.

DEUTSCH, Babette
    "A Nursery Rhyme Recalled." Nat (224:23) 11 Je 77, p. 730.

"A Pot of Crocuses." <u>Nat</u> (225:21) 17 D 77, p. 664.
"Remembering the Animals." <u>NewRep</u> (177:6/7) 6-13 Ag 77,
   p. 34.

DEVECSERI, Gábor
"The Bath in Pylos" (tr. by Robert Graves). <u>AmerPoR</u> (6:3) My-
   Je 77, p. 24.

DeVOTI, William
"Where They Lived." <u>Nat</u> (224:21) 28 My 77, p. 668.

deVRIES, Rachel
"Changes." <u>Chomo</u> (3:3) Spr 77, p. 13.
"The Chef" (for my father). <u>Gra</u> (12) 77.

DeWICK, Edmund LeRoy
"Passing." <u>CarouselQ</u> (2:3) Wint 77, p. 27.

DeWITT, Theo
"I did not like myself or Dody." <u>YaleLit</u> (145:3) 77, p. 16.

DeYOUNG, Robert
"Passing." <u>SouthernHR</u> (11:1) Wint 77, p. 47.
"Return Voyage." <u>SouthernHR</u> (11:3) Sum 77, p. 242.

DIAO, Edward
"Tarzan of the Sestina." <u>Ploughs</u> (3:3/4) 77, p. 78.

DIBBLE, Brian
"Maine." <u>BelPoJ</u> (27:4) Sum 77, p. 28.

DiCICCO, Pier Giorgio
"A*M*E*R*I*C*A." <u>SenR</u> (8:2) D 77, p. 67.
"L'Artiste." <u>Kayak</u> (44) F 77, p. 32.
"Basta!" <u>ConcPo</u> (10:1) Spr 77, p. 71.
"Birthday Poem for Myself." <u>DacTerr</u> (14) Spr-Sum 77, p. 15.
"Conscience." <u>DacTerr</u> (14) Spr-Sum 77, p. 14.
"Credo." <u>SenR</u> (8:2) D 77, p. 66.
"Errore." <u>Kayak</u> (44) F 77, p. 32.
"How to Get Ahead in this World." <u>DenQ</u> (12:1) Spr 77, p. 248.
"The Idea of Places." <u>DacTerr</u> (14) Spr-Sum 77, p. 14.
"In the Cup of His Hands." <u>Stonecloud</u> (6) 76, p. 67.
"Lines Written from the Wrong Side of the Bed." <u>DacTerr</u> (14)
   Spr-Sum 77, p. 15.
"The Literary Man." <u>DenQ</u> (12:1) Spr 77, p. 247.
"Love Using Many Words." <u>DacTerr</u> (14) Spr-Sum 77, p. 16.
"Maledetto." <u>Kayak</u> (44) F 77, p. 33.
"Mezza-Notte." <u>DenQ</u> (12:1) Spr 77, p. 248.
"Song." <u>Kayak</u> (44) F 77, p. 31.

DICKEY, R. P.
"America." <u>PoNow</u> (14/18) 77, p. 29.
"Charm." <u>PoNow</u> (14/18) 77, p. 29.

"Riddle." <u>Agni</u> (7) 77, p. 117.

DICKEY, William
"First Take: Hawaii." <u>PoNow</u> (14/18) 77, p. 29.

DICKINSON, Emily
"As from the earth the light Balloon." <u>AmerPoR</u> (6:1) Ja-F 77,
    p. 48.
"By homely gift and hindered Words." <u>AmerPoR</u> (6:1) Ja-F 77,
    p. 48.
"A House upon the Height--" <u>AmerPoR</u> (6:1) Ja-F 77, p. 48.
"The Life that tied too tight escapes." <u>AmerPoR</u> (6:1) Ja-F 77,
    p. 48.
"Rearrange a 'Wife's' affection!" <u>AmerPoR</u> (6:1) Ja-F 77, p. 48.

DICKINSON, Helen
"A Large Fog." <u>PortR</u> (23) 77, p. 28.
"Sleeping Alone." <u>PoetryNW</u> (18:3) Aut 77, p. 14.
"Through the Screen" (for John Petke, who liked "Throne of
    Blood"). <u>PortR</u> (23) 77, p. 29.

DICKINSON-BROWN, Roger
"Asparagus Pickers." <u>SouthernR</u> (13:4) Aut 77, p. 765.
"Epitaph." <u>SouthernR</u> (13:4) Aut 77, p. 766.
"holofernes." <u>NewC</u> (7:3) 75-76, p. 8.
"Marcus Aurelius Antoninus c. 178 A.D." <u>SouthernR</u> (13:4) Aut
    77, p. 764.

DICKSON, Alan
"The Frosts Are Coming" (tr. of László Nagy). <u>ModernPS</u> (8:2)
    Aut 77, p. 109.
"Upon the Grindstone" (tr. of László Nagy). <u>ModernPS</u> (8:2) Aut
    77, p. 110.

DICKSON, John
"Ariana" (tr. of Giovanni Francesco Straparola). <u>Playb</u> (24:10)
    O 77, p. 175.
"Ashland School." <u>StoneC</u> (77:1) F 77, p. 12.
"Clara" (tr. of Giovanni Francesco Straparola). <u>Playb</u> (24:10) O
    77, p. 175.
"Collector's Item." <u>KanQ</u> (9:2) Spr 77, p. 100.
"Floriana" (tr. of Giovanni Francesco Straparola). <u>Playb</u> (24:10)
    O 77, p. 175.
"Four Snapshots of Aunt Claire." <u>AmerS</u> (46:3) Sum 77, p. 348.
"Leonora" (tr. of Giovanni Francesco Straparola). <u>Playb</u> (24:10)
    O 77, p. 175.
"Love Song." <u>StoneC</u> (77:1) F 77, p. 11.
"Lucrezia" (tr. of Giovanni Francesco Straparola). <u>Playb</u> (24:10)
    O 77, p. 175.
"The Ravenswood 'L.'" <u>SmPd</u> (14:3) Aut 77, p. 14.

DIGBY, John
"Before Day Appears." <u>Kayak</u> (44) F 77, p. 49.

"Daughter of the Lightning. " Kayak (46) O 77, p. 19.
"Legend of the Lost Woman. " MontG (6) Aut 77, p. 64.
"Nine Day's Wonder. " Kayak (44) F 77, p. 48.
"Riding Out. " Kayak (46) O 77, p. 18.

DIGGORY, Terence
"The Cyclists. " WindO (28) Spr 77, p. 31.

DILLARD, Annie
"Ethiopian Monastery. " HolCrit (14:3) Je 77, p. 11.
"God. " Drag (16) 77.

DILSAVER, Paul
"General Motors and Sex. " Wind (24) 77, p. 26.
"Veteran in the Quagmire. " Paunch (48/49) S 77, p. 158.

DINE, Carol
"Estranged. " 13thM (3:2) 77, p. 62.

DIOMEDE, Matthew
"A Patient of the Night. " DeKalb (10:3) Spr 77, p. 10.

DIORIO, Margaret
"Night Drivers: The End of Time. " Icarus (5:2) Aut 77, p. 19.

DiPALMA, Ray
"Chalk. " SunM (4) Aut 77, p. 37.
"Dominocus. " SunM (4) Aut 77, p. 36.
"Porch. " Hills (4) 77.
Ten poems. LaB (7) My 77, p. 22.

DiPASQUALE, Emanuel
"Albert Is Dead. " PoNow (14/18) 77, p. 30.
"John Winthrop Saves Himself When, Caught in the Woods in a
    Rain Storm, He Finds a Hut and Shuts an Indian Girl Out. "
    PoNow (14/18) 77, p. 30.
"The Lumberjack. " PoNow (14/18) 77, p. 30.
"Nude Not Going Anywhere. " StoneC (77:2) My 77, p. 28.

DiPIERO, W. S.
"Dear and Formal Dido. " SouthernPR (13:3) Sum 77, p. 586.
"Four Mad Studies. " GRR (8:1/2) 77, p. 103.
"The Music of the Space. " SouthernR (13:1) Wint 77, p. 170.
"On Mt. Philo in November. " SouthernR (13:3) Sum 77, p. 587.
"Presuppositions" (tr. of Leonardo Sinisgalli). GRR (8:1/2) 77,
    p. 19.
"Scrimshaw. " Hudson (30:3) Aut 77, p. 395.
"Two Poets in the Park" (tr. of Leonardo Sinisgalli). GRR
    (8:1/2) 77, p. 23.
"Vantage between Two Planes. " SouthernR (13:3) Sum 77, p. 585.
"Walt, the Wounded. " Bound (5:3) Spr 77, p. 887.
"Warlord. " SouthernR (13:3) Sum 77, p. 585.

DiPRISCO, Joseph
"Escape." RemR (5) 77, p. 57.
"The Restaurant." PoetryNW (18:1) Spr 77, p. 32.

DISCH, Donna
"Bathers" (for T. C.). Aspen (3) Spr 77, p. 24.
"Bosch." Aspen (3) Spr 77, p. 26.
"Comparative Religions." Aspen (3) Spr 77, p. 25.
"Live Oak." Aspen (3) Spr 77, p. 27.
"Monday." Aspen (3) Spr 77, p. 24.
"The Prince of Liquid Storage." Aspen (3) Spr 77, p. 23.
"September Forest Fire." Aspen (3) Spr 77, p. 25.

DISCH, Thomas M.
"Descriptions of the Wilderness." Poetry (129:5) F 77, p. 249.
"A Note to Romeo." TransR (60) Je 77, p. 118.
"Song to Venus." TransR (60) Je 77, p. 116.
"Song to Venus II." TransR (60) Je 77, p. 117.

DISCHELL, Stuart
"Salt Country." AntR (35:1) Wint 77, p. 63.

DISEND, David
"The Butcher." NewC (7:2) 75-76, p. 21.

DiSUVERO, Victor M.
"Fire and Rhythm" (tr. of Agostinho Neto). Kayak (46) O 77,
     p. 4.
"The Path of the Stars" (tr. of Agostinho Neto). Kayak (46) O
     77, p. 5.
"Western Civilization" (tr. of Agostinho Neto). Kayak (46) O 77,
     p. 3.

DITSKY, John
"Dispatch." Gra (12) 77.
"The Greening of Detroit." DenQ (11:4) Wint 77, p. 138.
"I Am Reading." WindO (27) Aut 76, p. 5.
"In the End." AndR (3:2) Aut 76, p. 88.
"Juice." Juice (4) 77.
"Leavings." SouthwR (62:2) Spr 77, p. 148.
"Locket." CutB (9) Aut-Wint 77, p. 142.
"Martyrs' Memorial, Oxford." WindO (27) Aut 76, p. 6.
"The Mistakes of a Night." SouthernHR (11:4) Aut 77, p. 383.
"Municipal Lighting." Shen (28:4) Sum 77, p. 76.
"Oxford Market." WindO (27) Aut 76, p. 5.
"Pax." CentR (21:2) Spr 77, p. 155.
"The Rookie, Retiring." Focus (12:76) Jl-Ag 77, p. 26.

DITTA, Joseph M.
"In Another City." Poetry (130:2) My 77, p. 89.
"Winter Poem." Poetry (130:2) My 77, p. 88.

DIXON, Alan
"Whispers, for Two Voices" (tr. of Sándor Csoóri).   AmerPoR
(6:3) My-Je 77, p. 25.

DIXON, Darryl
"sometimes with a shell."   AAR (27) 77, p. 117.
"The world spins like a rock rolling slowly down."   AAR (27) 77,
p. 117.

DIXON, Melvin
"Man Holding Boy."   Focus (12:77) S-O 77, p. 29.

DiZAZZO, Raymond
"Excavation."   PoNow (14/18) 77, p. 30.

DJANIKIAN, Gregory
"After Planting."   Nat (224:21) 28 My 77, p. 663.
"Excerpts from Noah's Log."   FourQt (26:2) Wint 77, p. 27.
"Paul Gauguin: Vision after the Sermon (Jacob Wrestling the
Angels)."   SoDakR (15:2) Sum 77, p. 25.

DOBB, Edwin Charles
"Limes Peel" (for Susan).   MontG (6) Aut 77, p. 27.

DOBBS, Jeannine
"Mabel: 1918-1960."   Aspect (69) O-D 76, p. 38.
"Pocketbook Poem."   Glass (2:2/3) Wint-Spr 77, p. 32.

DoBELL, Stephen
"Release."   PoetL (72:1) Spr 77, p. 28.
"Still Life, 10 P.M."   PoetL (72:2) Sum 77, p. 74.

DOBRIN, Arthur
"Portrait in a Dutch Home."   Xa (4) 77, p. 10.
"Summer Lessons."   Xa (4) 77, p. 11.

DOBYNS, Stephen
"Rain Song."   NewYorker (53:11) 2 My 77, p. 36.

DODD, Wayne
"Again, This Elegy."   Chowder (8) Spr-Sum 77, p. 8.
"And Yet."   GeoR (31:4) Wint 77, p. 872.
"With the Absent."   NewRivR (2:1) 77, p. 48.

DOHENY, John
"December 31, 1974."   Paunch (46/47) Ap 77, p. 66.

DOLAN, John D.
"Cruising."   Mouth (11/12) Mr-Je 77, p. 90.
"Fever."   Mouth (13) D 77, p. 29.
"He just sits."   Mouth (13) D 77, p. 31.
"Of an Obsidian Shadow."   Mouth (13) D 77, p. 32.
"While the others bite."   Mouth (13) D 77, p. 31.

DOLEGA, Christine Lahey
"I Return to My Father" (for Thomas Ignatius Lahey, d. 1951).
CarouselQ (2:1) Spr 77, p. 18.

DOLLARHIDE, Louis
"October Poem for One Who Sleeps." DeKalb (10:2) Wint 77,
p. 19.
"On an Indian Exposed to Public View." DeKalb (10:2) Wint 77,
p. 20.
"On an Indian Exposed to Public View." TexQ (20:4) Wint 77,
p. 158.
"On This Downward Slope." DeKalb (10:2) Wint 77, p. 20.

DOLPHIN
"Toward a Houston of Inner Space." NewL (44:2) Wint 77, p. 85.

DOMINA, Lynn
"autobiography." GRR (8:3) 77, p. 237.
"poet poem." GRR (8:3) 77, p. 238.

DOMINGO, Sandy
"crazy john wanted." SeC (5:2) 78, p. 47.

DONAGHY, Michael
"The Executioner's Account of the Martyrdom of St. Catherine of
Alexandria." NewC (7:3) 75-76, p. 28.
"Exhortation of the Bones." DeKalb (10:2) Wint 77, p. 21.
"Khalypso Allegory of Birth." KanQ (9:3) Sum 77, p. 59.

DONAHUE, George Michael
"Having One at Twenty-Five." StoneC (77:1) F 77, p. 32.

DONAVEL, David F.
"Love Poem." Wind (26) 77, p. 22.

DONOVAN, Brad
"Marshland" (for Linda). SenR (8:2) D 77, p. 82.

DONOVAN-SMITH, Clyde Wendell
"Tornado." KanQ (9:4) Aut 77, p. 22.

DONZELLA, D. W.
"Deadfall into Night." DacTerr (14) Spr-Sum 77, p. 50.
"These Spring Girls." DacTerr (14) Spr-Sum 77, p. 49.

DOOLEY, Dennis M.
"The Simple Angler." Icarus (5:1) Spr 77, p. 15.

DOOLEY, Edward
"The Perfect Crime." Ploughs (3:3/4) 77, p. 123.

DOOLITTLE, James A.
"A Bookstore Burns in Iowa City." SouthwR (62:1) Wint 77, p. 20.

DOR, Moshe
"The Dwelling" (tr. by the author and Denis Johnson).   TriQ (39)
    Spr 77, p. 257.
"Progression" (tr. by the author and Denis Johnson).   TriQ (39)
    Spr 77, p. 258.

DORÉ, Donn T.
"Silvered in Sunset." Icarus (5:1) Spr 77, p. 20.
"A Strange Loneliness on Galveston Island." KanQ (9:1) Wint 77,
    p. 79.

DORESKI, William
"The Fat Man Plants a Rose." Agni (7) 77, p. 63.
"May Day, My Thirty-Third." Ploughs (4:1) 77, p. 58.
"Sleeping Near Glastonbury Peak." Agni (7) 77, p. 64.
"Somerville Junction." Aspect (69) O-D 76, p. 31.
"Trolling at Dawn on Crystal Lake, Stafford, Connecticut." RemR
    (5) 77, p. 8.

DORMAN, Sonya
"Apples." OP (24) Aut-Wint 77, p. 24.
"Between Us." Drag (16) 77.
"A Child for All Seasons." OP (24) Aut-Wint 77, p. 22.
"Dear Constance." OP (24) Aut-Wint 77, p. 20.
"February's End." OP (24) Aut-Wint 77, p. 19.
"Flying Home." PoNow (14/18) 77, p. 30.
"I Sing Adapted Man." Drag (16) 77.
"Making Flowers without a Garden." PoNow (14/18) 77, p. 31.
"The Myth of the Far Traveller" (for A. Bertram Chandler).
    SouthernPR (17:1) Spr 77, p. 20.
from Stretching Fence: "Campers." PoNow (14/18) 77, p. 31.
from Stretching Fence: "New Roof on My Neighbor's House."
    PoNow (14/18) 77, p. 31.
from Stretching Fence: "Pigs and All." PoNow (14/18) 77,
    p. 31.
"Tale of Departure" (for Constance and Robert Hunting). OP (24)
    Aut-Wint 77, p. 18.

DORSAM, Hester E.
"Three Haiku." PoetL (72:2) Sum 77, p. 61.

DORSET, Gerald
"Grandmother of Us All." Paunch (48/49) S 77, p. 140.

DORSETT, Robert
"Interval." DeKalb (10:2) Wint 77, p. 23.
"Moon Light." DeKalb (10:2) Wint 77, p. 22.
"On the Use of the Cliché: Flower." PoetL (72:1) Spr 77,
    p. 10.
"The Page Prints." PoetL (72:1) Spr 77, p. 10.
"Snakeman, Kowloon Market." PoetL (72:1) Spr 77, p. 10.
"Water People, Hong Kong." CimR (39) Ap 77, p. 25.

DORSETT, Thomas
"Idyll: The Ages of Man." WebR (3:4) Aut 77, p. 55.
"Two Ways to Look at the Zoo." NewC (7:3) 75-76, p. 7.

DOTY, M. R.
"Aunt India." Kayak (45) My 77, p. 48.
"Daphne." Chelsea (36) 77, p. 28.
"The Deaths of the Months." Kayak (45) My 77, p. 46.
"Infamy." Chelsea (36) 77, p. 29.
"Poem for Bertha Cudd, Boice, Louisiana." Kayak (45) My 77,
    p. 45.

DOUCET, Calvin
"Border Crossing." Mouth (13) D 77, p. 57.
"a boy on the edge." Mouth (13) D 77, p. 49.
"Fan Mail." Mouth (13) D 77, p. 27.
"He found me in the quarry." Mouth (13) D 77, p. 48.
"Summer Solstice/Padre Island." Mouth (13) D 77, p. 51.
"Yesterday, drunk on champagne and fresh pineapple and." Mouth
    (13) D 77, p. 47.

DOUGHERTY, Beatrice G.
"The Broom." Wind (24) 77, p. 28.

DOUGHERTY, Sister Mary Ellen
"In Search of a Poem." SouthernHR (11:1) Wint 77, p. 66.

DOULIS, Thomas
"Lazarina" (tr. of George Ioannou). PortR (23) 77, p. 96.

DOUSKEY, Franz
"Dying Young." Madrona (4:13/14) 77, p. 17.
"Grandmotherless Child." PoNow (14/18) 77, p. 31.
"Night Swim." EnPas (4) 76, p. 21.
"Sheets." YellowBR (9) 77, p. 16.

DOW, Philip
"Mouth of the Tillamook." PoNow (14/18) 77, p. 32.
"Snail." PoNow (14/18) 77, p. 32.

DOWD, John
"Some Say Crazy Lonely, Some Say Not." DeKalb (10:2) Wint 77,
    p. 24.

DOWNS, Stuart
"Hazel Mary and Jesus in 1923." HiramPoR (23) Wint 77, p. 18.
"Of an Autumn Afternoon." EnPas (4) 76, p. 7.

DOXEY, W. S.
"At the Nudist Camp." Esq (87:5) My 77, p. 30.
"Flannery's Peacocks." SouthwR (62:4) Aut 77, p. 347.

"Heitse-Ebib. " LitR (20:4) Sum 77, p. 460.
"The Meeting. " TexQ (20:3) Aut 77, p. 30.
"Snowbound. " Esq (88:3) S 77, p. 54.

DOYLE, James
"The Bestowal. " Confr (15) Aut 77-Wint 78, p. 15.
"Birthdays. " RemR (5) 77, p. 56.
"The Bravado of Spring. " ConcPo (10:2) Aut 77, p. 4.
"Civil Service. " DeKalb (10:2) Wint 77, p. 25.
"Estragon to the Writers' Association. " SmPd (14:1) Wint 77,
    p. 18.
"Guard. " Aspen (4) Aut 77, p. 60.
"Ritual of the Mask. " Icarus (5:1) Spr 77, p. 10.
"Sincerity Should Be Played Pianissimo. " ConcPo (10:2) Aut 77,
    p. 4.
"Tar. " Aspen (4) Aut 77, p. 61.
"Views from an Airplane. " RemR (5) 77, p. 56.

DRACHLER, Rose
"As I Am My Father's. " Hand (1) 77, p. 126.
"In the fifth month. " Hand (1) 77, p. 123.
"North. " Hand (1) 77, p. 125.
"The Wives of Hillel and Isaiah. " Hand (1) 77, p. 124.

DRAKE, Barbara
"The Mouse. " GRR (8:1/2) 77, p. 24.

DRESSEL, Jon
"Handyman. " PraS (51:4) Wint 77-78, p. 414.
"The Whore of Babylon Meets the Press. " WebR (3:2) Spr 77,
    p. 5.

DREW, George
"Falling in Love with Aunt Joyce. " Wind (25) 77, p. 15.
"Just Around the Corner from School 10. " SmPd (14:1) Wint 77,
    p. 8.

DRISCOLL, Jack
"Being Dropped Off a Couple Miles from Home. " ArkRiv (3:4/4:1)
    77, p. 20.
"The Creation. " Chelsea (36) 77, p. 10.
"Heart Attack in the Snow. " ConcPo (10:2) Aut 77, p. 83.
"The Language of Bone. " ConcPo (10:2) Aut 77, p. 83.

DRURY, Michael
"First Born. " LadHJ (94:9) S 77, p. P. S. 8.

DUBAY, Leona
"Seeing Myself on TV. " EngJ (66:5) My 77, p. 49.

DUBIE, Norman
"The Ambassador Diaries of Jean de Bosschère and Edgar Poe"
    (For Michael Burkard). Poetry (129:6) Mr 77, p. 324.

"Ars Poetica. " MissR (6:1) 77, p. 160.

"Comes Winter, the Sea Hunting" (For Hannah). SenR (8:2) D 77, p. 62.

"The Duchess' Red Shoes" (after Proust). Antaeus (27) Aut 77, p. 69.

Eight poems. AmerPoR (6:4) Jl-Ag 77, p. 3.

"Elizabeth's War with the Christmas Bear: 1601. " NewYorker (53:45) 26 D 77, p. 30.

"The Hours" (For Ingrid Erhardt, 1951-71). NewYorker (52:51) 7 F 77, p. 38.

"The Infant. " Field (16) Spr 77, p. 79.

"The Lake Utopia of Soren Kierkegaard" (For Jon Anderson). Ploughs (3:3/4) 77, p. 92.

"Norway. " NewYorker (53:13) 16 My 77, p. 42.

"A Widow Speaks to the Auroras of a February Night. " YellowBR (8) 77, p. 11.

DUDD, Mike
    "I here creks and craks. " AAR (27) 77, p. 121.

DUDDY, Patrick
    "Headwater: Salmon in the Skin. " Wind (27) 77, p. 14.
    "Moosehorn. " Wind (27) 77, p. 14.

DUDERSTADT, Susan
    "I wish I could go back and forth in time. " AAR (27) 77, p. 95.

DUDIS, Ellen Kirvin
    "Composition. " SmPd (14:2) Spr 77, p. 4.
    "Tomato Stakes. " WebR (3:1) Wint 77, p. 28.

DUEMER, Joseph
    "Falling" (for Billy Felix Ayac, 1953-1975). PoetryNW (18:2) Sum 77, p. 35.

DUFF, Gerald
    "Cerne Abbas: Joining the Giant. " BosUJ (25:1) 77, p. 46.
    "History. " SouthernPR (17:1) Spr 77, p. 3.
    "Privileged Looks. " BosUJ (25:1) 77, p. 45.
    "Welding" (for Terry Bradshaw, Quarterback and Welder). GRR (8:1/2) 77, p. 50.

DUFFANY, Brett
    "When the Visigoths Have Come and Gone. " Wind (26) 77, p. 51.

DUFFIN, Kathryn
    "The Skull of the Coyote Still Cries at Night. " EngJ (66:5) My 77, p. 44.

DUFRENY, Susie
    "In a Chateau Greenhouse. " YaleLit (146:2) 77, p. 15.

DUKES, Norman
    "Barbershop Quartets. " LittleR (12) 77, p. 4.

DUNCAN, Judith
"Another Lamentation." PoetL (72:2) Sum 77, p. 52.

DUNCAN, Robert
"Circulations of the Song/After Jalāl al-Dīn Rūmī." PartR (44:1)
    77, p. 87.

DUNN, Chris
"Autumn Poem" (tr. of Rubén Darío). DenQ (11:4) Wint 77,
    p. 154.
"Campoamor" (tr. of Rubén Darío). DenQ (11:4) Wint 77, p. 155.
"Metempsychosis" (tr. of Rubén Darío). DenQ (11:4) Wint 77,
    p. 153.
"Nocturne" (tr. of Rubén Darío). DenQ (11:4) Wint 77, p. 155.
"Vesper" (tr. of Rubén Darío). DenQ (11:4) Wint 77, p. 154.

DUNN, Robert
"The Idea of Community in Los Angeles." CarolQ (29:3) Aut 77,
    p. 100.
"Memory." NewYorker (53:40) 21 N 77, p. 174.

DUNN, Stephen
"At the Atlantic City Hospital Emergency Room." QW (4) Aut 77,
    p. 6.
"Beached Whales off Margate." Nat (224:4) 29 Ja 77, p. 119.
"Being Pleased." NewL (43:4) Sum 77, p. 40.
"Belongings." Aspen (4) Aut 77, p. 64.
"Confession." PoetryNW (18:2) Sum 77, p. 16.
"Contact" (For Ron Banner). QW (4) Aut 77, p. 5.
"Notes Toward a 20th Century Newsreel." DenQ (12:1) Spr 77,
    p. 78.
"The Obsession." PoetryNW (18:2) Sum 77, p. 17.
"The Problems." Iowa (8:4) Aut 77, p. 66.
"Split: 1962." Iowa (8:4) Aut 77, p. 67.
"The Truth" (for Jeanne-Andree). PoetryNW (18:2) Sum 77,
    p. 18.
"The Way an Angel Might." Aspen (4) Aut 77, p. 65.

DUNNE, Carol A.
"The Outing." DeKalb (10:2) Wint 77, p. 26.
"Yesterday." Wind (24) 77, p. 58.

DUNNING, Stephen
"Bones." Wind (26) 77, p. 16.
"Dreams of Ducks." PoetryNW (18:2) Sum 77, p. 30.
"How Dabney Found the Golden Girl." ConcPo (10:2) Aut 77,
    p. 65.
"My Self." ConcPo (10:2) Aut 77, p. 66.
"Not for Publication." EngJ (66:5) My 77, p. 56.
"St. Clair Street." Wind (26) 77, p. 18.
"Sledding." Wind (26) 77, p. 17.

DuPLESSIS, Rachel Blau
"Voyaging" (for George Oppen). Montra (3) Spr 77, p. 99.

"'Whirr Shrill Crickets.'" Montra (3) Spr 76, p. 101.

DuPRIEST, Travis
  "Domain." Wind (24) 77, p. 11.
  "A Painting." Wind (24) 77, p. 11.

DURBIN, Reed
  "Greaser's Speech." LittleR (12) 77, p. 10.
  "Hymnal." LittleR (12) 77, p. 10.

DUREN, Francis
  "Fever." Focus (12:76) Jl-Ag 77, p. 25.
  "How It Happens." MissR (6:1) 77, p. 145.

DUVAL, Quinton
  "The Eyes of Mullet." NewRivR (2:1) 77, p. 57.
  "Guerilla Letter." NewRivR (2:1) 77, p. 56.
  "In Port." QW (4) Aut 77, p. 9.
  "The River of Birds." QW (4) Aut 77, p. 7.
  "Song of Paraguay." QW (4) Aut 77, p. 7.
  "Thinking Too Much." NewL (44:1) Aut 77, p. 21.

DWYER, Frank
  "According to Luke." (27:4) Sum 77, p. 1.

DYBEK, Stuart
  "Canvas." NewOR (5:3) 77, p. 234.
  "Dead Trees." PoetryNW (18:2) Sum 77, p. 39.
  "December." GRR (8:3) 77, p. 229.
  "Dirigible Dawn." Drag (16) 77.
  "Dirigibles." Drag (16) 77.
  "Franciscan Daydreams." DacTerr (14) Spr-Sum 77, p. 47.
  "Infrared" (for Miss Eva). MassR (18:1) Spr 77, p. 177.
  "Inside the Turtle." Bits (6) Jl 77.
  "Jack." Drag (16) 77.
  "My Neighborhood." SenR (8:2) D 77, p. 25.
  "Rain." MissR (6:1) 77, p. 77.
  "Stickball/Iowa City." HiramPoR (23) Wint 77, p. 19.
  "Sunlight." PoNow (14/18) 77, p. 33.

DYC, Gloria
  "driving." 13thM (3:2) 77, p. 41.

EADES, Joan
  "Escape on Highway 2." DacTerr (14) Spr-Sum 77, p. 42.
  "Landscape." DacTerr (14) Spr-Sum 77, p. 43.
  "Pieces." Northeast (3:4) Aut-Wint 77-78, p. 56.
  "Waking." DacTerr (14) Spr-Sum 77, p. 42.

EAKINS, Patricia
  "Crushed bay laurel." StoneC (77:3) S 77, p. 25.
  "Into Holes between Steps of Dances, Falling Away from Our-
    selves--Oh." StoneC (77:3) S 77, p. 25.

"The Old Animal Floating in Bandages." MassR (18:2) Sum 77,
    p. 271.

EARLE, Ralph
    "Kidnapped Vasectomy." Gra (12) 77, p. 20.

EASTERLING, Kellie
    "Do not make Anglo-Saxon square." EngJ (66:5) My 77, p. 56.

EASTMAN, Jon
    "The Landscape Near a Resthome." CutB (9) Aut-Wint 77,
    p. 79.
    "Memory of a Skeleton." CutB (9) Aut-Wint 77, p. 80.

EASTWOOD, David R.
    "Lapses at Parting." StoneC (77:2) My 77, p. 18.

EATON, Barton Denis
    "Happy Birthday Catullus." Madrona (4:13/14) 77, p. 15.

EATON, Charles Edward
    "Blue Bedspread." Shen (28:3) Spr 77, p. 71.
    "The Canoe." SouthernHR (11:1) Wint 77, p. 46.
    "Collector's Items." Poem (30) Jl 77, p. 42.
    "Colophon of the Rover." ArizQ (33:1) Spr 77, p. 26.
    "The Exhibitionist." Confr (14) Spr-Sum 77, p. 107.
    "Five O'Clock Shadow." ColEng (39:1) S 77, p. 64.
    "The Lip-Reader." Poem (30) Jl 77, p. 43.
    "Pomegranate." HolCrit (14:3) Je 77, p. 14.
    "The Prime Minister's World View." Icarus (5:2) Aut 77, p. 14.
    "The Senile Rooster." Poem (30) Jl 77, p. 41.
    "The Spendthrift." Icarus (5:1) Spr 77, p. 1.
    "Squatter's Rights to the Marine Lands." GeoR (31:3) Aut 77,
    p. 636.
    "Traumerei for a Touch Group." PoNow (14/18) 77, p. 33.

EBERHART, Richard
    "The Flag." PoNow (14/18) 77, p. 34.
    "Jeffers." PoNow (14/18) 77, p. 34.
    "Lilac Feeling." NewL (43:4) Sum 77, p. 39.
    "Waiting for Something to Happen." MissR (6:1) 77, p. 29.

EBERLY, David
    "Ghosts." HangL (31) Aut 77, p. 8.

EBNER, Jeannie
    "Poetic Renown" (tr. by Derk Wynand). ChiR (29:3) Wint 78,
    p. 116.

ECKHAUS, Steve
    "I Am Slowly Killing My Room." Rapp (10) 77, p. 54.

ECONOMOU, George
    from 'Amepikh: (VII and VIII). Bound (5:2) Wint 77, p. 529.

from De planctu naturae: "Alanus de insulis" (tr. of Anonymous).
<u>Hand</u> (1) 77, p. 47.

EDDINGS, Ann
"The Doll." <u>DeKalb</u> (10:3) Spr 77, p. 11.

EDDY, Darlene Mathis
"Coming to Terms." <u>GRR</u> (8:3) 77, p. 195.
"Sketches: Seasons in Shadow." <u>GRR</u> (8:1/2) 77, p. 112.
"Tending Switches" (In Memoriam). <u>BallSUF</u> (18:2) Spr 77,
   p. 78.

EDDY, Gary
from Waking Up, Late: "Driving South on Peter Smith Road."
   <u>Rapp</u> (10) 77, p. 103.

EDELSTEIN, Scott
"Comic Book Tale." <u>Drag</u> (16) 77.
"Mold Is All We Buffalo Have to Look Forward To." <u>Drag</u> (16)
   77.
"switches." <u>Drag</u> (16) 77.

EDER, Mari K.
"Track." <u>EngJ</u> (66:5) My 77, p. 51.

EDGERTON, David
"For a Friend Jailed in Mexico." <u>Shen</u> (28:3) Spr 77, p. 98.

EDMOND, Murray
"A House by the Sea" (An Open Letter to Russell Haley). <u>Stand</u>
   (18:3) 77, p. 19.

EDSON, Russell
"The Anxious Room." <u>AmerPoR</u> (6:5) S-O 77, p. 13.
"The Best Mercy." <u>Drag</u> (16) 77.
"The Biting Contest." <u>AmerPoR</u> (6:5) S-O 77, p. 14.
"The Candy Situation." <u>AmerPoR</u> (6:5) S-O 77, p. 13.
"The Closet Dwarf." <u>Iowa</u> (8:1) Wint 77, p. 39.
"The Falling King." <u>Drag</u> (16) 77.
"From a Clam's Diary." <u>AmerPoR</u> (6:5) S-O 77, p. 13.
"The Hobbling Mixture Full of Noodles and Squeals." <u>MoonsLT</u>
   (2:3) 77, p. 19.
"The Inconvenienced Farmer." <u>AmerPoR</u> (6:5) S-O 77, p. 13.
"The King's Mirror." <u>Drag</u> (16) 77.
"An Old Man Reading a Newspaper." <u>PoNow</u> (14/18) 77, p. 34.
"Oyster Stuffing." <u>PoNow</u> (14/18) 77, p. 34.
"The Package." <u>PoNow</u> (14/18) 77, p. 35.
"Song of the Rattled Pot." <u>PoNow</u> (14/18) 77, p. 34.
"The Undressing of the Bride." <u>MoonsLT</u> (2:3) 77, p. 20.
"Visiting the Midget." <u>MoonsLT</u> (2:3) 77, p. 17.
"The Whittler's Baby." <u>MoonsLT</u> (2:3) 77, p. 18.

EDWARDS, George D.
"Hands." <u>DeKalb</u> (10:2) Wint 77, p. 27.

"Time Is." DeKalb (10:2) Wint 77, p. 27.

EDWARDS, Robert
"Living Upstairs." DacTerr (14) Spr-Sum 77, p. 78.
"The Sleeper" (for Michael Milner). DacTerr (14) Spr-Sum 77, p. 78.

EFIRD, Susan
"Nebuchadnezzar's Robes." Poetry (130:2) My 77, p. 98.

EGGELING, Jim
"A Farmboy's Recollection of John Henry." PoNow (14/18) 77, p. 35.

EHRHART, W. D.
"Cast Out." Sam (56) Sum 77, p. 34.
"Colorado." Sam (55) 77, p. 16.
"The Flying Gypsy." Wind (25) 77, p. 16.
A Generation of Peace (for Dorrit Von Haven). Sam (54) 77. Entire issue.
"Granddad." Sam (52) Ap 77, p. 20.
Rootless. Sam (53) 77. Entire issue.
"The Trial." Sam (56) Sum 77, p. 50.

EHRLICH, Shelley
"Deciding to Turn Off the Porch Light." Chowder (8) Spr-Sum 77, p. 27.
"Making Soup." Chowder (8) Spr-Sum 77, p. 26.

EHRLICHER, Edward
"Reaching to Unknown Freedom." CarouselQ (2:3) Wint 77, p. 34.

EIAN
"Joshu's 'Oak in the courtyard'" (tr. by Lucien Stryk). ChiR (29:2) Aut 77, p. 85.

EICHHORN, Douglas
"Linda" (for Leo). PoNow (14/18) 77, p. 35.

EICHWALD, Richard
"Andrew Wyeth." SewanR (85:3) Sum 77, p. 432.

EIGNER, Larry
"Africans." SunM (4) Aut 77, p. 33.
"Air" (For Sam Borash). LaB (9) N-D 77, p. 26.
"any" (for Bob and Bobbie). Hills (4) 77.
"(as you go into Seir or Ives)." Hills (4) 77.
"Aug 9, 1976." LaB (9) N-D 77, p. 25.
"Aug 18, 1976." LaB (9) N-D 77, p. 25.
"Aug 19, 1976." LaB (9) N-D 77, p. 26.
"A-Z." SunM (4) Aut 77, p. 35.

"Doorknobs about. " Hills (4) 77.
"the forest. " PoNow (14/18) 77, p. 35.
"Head nor tail. " SunM (4) 77, p. 34.
"If he cut the. " Hills (4) 77.
"a life. " LaB (9) N-D 77, p. 26.
"my mother is Jewish. " SunM (4) Aut 77, p. 34.
"round red. " SunM (4) Aut 77, p. 35.
"so Goya went mad in the end something like. " Hills (4) 77.
"stars and starlight. " WebR (3:1) Wint 77, p. 30.
"up Chagall. " Hills (4) 77.
"Whoppers Whoppers Whoppers!" Hills (4) 77.

EISELEY, Loren
"The Buzzards. " Harp (254:1525) Je 77, p. 56.
"Dreamed in a Dark Millennium. " Harp (254:1525) Je 77, p. 57.
"Mars. " Harp (254:1525) Je 77, p. 56.
"The Shore Haunters. " Harp (254:1525) Je 77, p. 57.
"Two Hours from Now. " Poetry (130:1) Ap 77, p. 33.

EISENSTEIN, Sam
"One Year Dead. " Xa (4) 77, p. 46.

EISIMINGER, Skip
"After the Shock. " GRR (8:1/2) 77, p. 76.

EKELOF, Gunnar
from Guide to the Underworld: Six segments (tr. by Rika Lesser).
     Pequod (2:3) Sum 77, p. 55.

ELAINE, Marsha
"Desire & the Slow, Cold Death. " Juice (5) 77.

ELDAN, Anadad
"Samson Rends His Clothes" (tr. by Ruth Nevo). TriQ (39) Spr
     77, p. 259.
"When the Waves Fell Silent" (tr. by Ruth Nevo). TriQ (39) Spr
     77, p. 259.
"When You Gave Light" (tr. by Bat-Sheva Sheriff and Jon Silkin).
     TriQ (39) Spr 77, p. 260.

ELDER EDDA
"The Spaewife's Speech" (tr. by Daniel B. Marin). CarolQ (29:1)
     Wint 77, p. 115.

ELDER, Karl
"Crow's Feet" (for Thomas James). Sparrow (33) Ja 77, p. 6.
"Glove. " Poem (31) N 77, p. 58.
"Jade Plant. " Madrona (4:13/14) 77, p. 19.
"Late November Afternoon, Hazman's Field. " Poem (31) N 77,
     p. 59.
"The Laying-On of the Poem. " ArkRiv (3:4/4:1) 77, p. 54.
"The Poem Grows or To Help Build Strong Lines One Way. "
     KanQ (9:2) Spr 77, p. 60.

"Poem: In love with the porch swing." Poem (31) N 77, p. 57.

ELDRIDGE, Robert
"The Luxury of Language." Box (5) Spr 77, p. 7.

ELDRIDGE, Stanley
"If It Weren't So Cold Outside." Obs (3:1) Spr 77, p. 67.
"Morning, chains unleashed, Sun." Obs (3:1) Spr 77, p. 67.
"uir bwana couko m'cuumba." Obs (3:1) Spr 77, p. 68.

ELGORRIAGA, Jose A.
"The Angel of Death" (tr. of Rafael Alberti, w. Marty Paul).
    PortR (23) 77, p. 80.
from Entre el Clavel y la Espada: (29) (tr. of Rafael Alberti,
    w. Marty Paul). PortR (23) 77, p. 81.

ELIOT, Eileen
"alter-ego." HangL (31) Aut 77, p. 9.

ELIZONDO, Salvador
"History According to Pao Cheng" (tr. by Earl Rees). PortR
    (23) 77, p. 82.
"The Man Who Cries" (tr. by Earl Rees). PortR (23) 77, p. 82.

ELKIND, Sue Saniel
"Old Man Sitting." DeKalb (10:2) Wint 77, p. 28.

ELKINGTON, William C.
"Helen." ConcPo (10:1) Spr 77, p. 12.
"Prisoners." Wind (24) 77, p. 12.
"Winter Beast." DenQ (12:1) Spr 77, p. 125.
"Winter Golf." ConcPo (10:1) Spr 77, p. 12.

ELLEDGE, Jim
"Tamer." Mouth (11/12) Mr-Je 77, p. 100.

ELLIOTT, Harley
"At the Lindsborg, Kansas Museum." ArkRiv (3:4/4:1) 77,
    p. 47.
"Blues for the Secret Lover." HangL (30) Sum 77, p. 14.
"Dick Makes an Omelet." PoNow (14/18) 77, p. 37.
"For the Man Who Stole a Rose." NewL (44:2) Wint 77, p. 89.
"The Men Who Loved Everything." NewL (44:2) Wint 77, p. 91.
"A Murder in Town." YellowBR (9) 77, p. 5.
"My Brother in Lake Wilson." ArkRiv (3:4/4:1) 77, p. 46.
"Older." HiramPoR (23) Wint 77, p. 20.
"On the Trail of the Secret Lover." HangL (30) Sum 77, p. 15.
"The One Who Tilts Her Head." HiramPoR (22) Aut-Wint 77,
    p. 16.
"The Poet's Primer." Drag (16) 77.
"The Secret Lover Deals a Hand." HangL (30) Sum 77, p. 12.
"Self Portrait As Crazy Horse." Focus (12:76) Jl-Ag 77, p. 26.
"Self Portrait As Custer." Focus (12:76) Jl-Ag 77, p. 26.

from Sky Heart: "Changing a Tire by the Missouri River."
  PoNow (14/18) 77, p. 36.
from Sky Heart: "Rest Stop." PoNow (14/18) 77, p. 36.
from Sky Heart: "Three Histories of the Prairie." PoNow
  (14/18) 77, p. 36.
"Starting the World." NewL (44:2) Wint 77, p. 88.
"The Thing to Do." NewL (44:2) Wint 77, p. 90.
"Two Men See into the World" (for Dick). HiramPoR (22) Aut-
  Wint 77, p. 15.

ELLIOTT, John J.
"View from the Inside." ParisR (69) Spr 77, p. 166.

ELLIOTT, William
"The Barns and Churches from Bemidji to Benson." StoneC
  (77:1) F 77, p. 26.
"Living at Boot Hill, Nebraska." CimR (38) Ja 77, p. 55.
"Softly, and Softly Freeze." DeKalb (10:2) Wint 77, p. 29.

ELLIOTT, William D.
"Bird." BallSUF (18:4) Aut 77, p. 77.

ELLIS, Gordon
"Lone Frank Pass." Wind (24) 77, p. 30.
"The Osborn Ranch." Wind (24) 77, p. 31.

ELLIS, Keith
from Los placeres de Edipo: (XVI) (tr. of Ludwig Zeller).
  MontG (6) Aut 77, p. 33.

ELLISON, Jessie T.
"The Golden Reign of King Craterus." WindO (27) Aut 76.
"The Marble Nursemaids." WindO (28) Spr 77, p. 32.
"The Widow's Broom." HangL (30) Sum 77, p. 16.

ELMAN, Richard
"Contextualization." PartR (44:4) 77, p. 552.
"For a Young Woman." TransR (58/59) F 77, p. 100.

ELMORE, Jeff
"Poet." SeC (5:2) 78, p. 14.

ELON, Florence
"Epithalamium for a Second Marriage." LitR (20:4) Sum 77,
  p. 435.
"Pain Killer." Atl (240:1) Jl 77, p. 62.
"'Tipsy Parson.'" LitR (20:4) Sum 77, p. 436.
"The Transformation of Father." NewYorker (53:40) 21 N 77,
  p. 66.

ELSON, Virginia
"The Cutting." PoNow (14/18) 77, p. 37.
"Mother's Helper." HiramPoR (22) Aut-Wint 77, p. 17.

"Suddenly During the Night." HiramPoR (22) Aut-Wint 77, p. 18.
"Wet Season." HiramPoR (23) Wint 77, p. 21.

ELSTON, Angela
"Poem Written Dream Side" (tr. of Ch'in Kuan). DenQ (12:2)
Sum 77, p. 1.

EMANS, Elaine V.
"For Mary Shelley." KanQ (9:2) Spr 77, p. 67.

EMANUEL, J. A.
from Panther Man: "Black Poet on the Firing Range." Nimrod
(21:2/22:1) 77, p. 78.
from Panther Man: "For the 4th Grade, Prospect School: How
I Became a Poet." Nimrod (21:2/22:1) 77, p. 79.

EMERSON, Ralph Waldo
"Concord Hymn." PoNow (14/18) 77, p. 92.

EMERY, Stuart
"The Apartment Hunters." Wind (27) 77, p. 16.

EMMONS, David
"Espresso." PortR (23) 77, p. 141.
"Horses." PortR (23) 77, p. 142.
"Oil." PortR (23) 77, p. 141.
"Sunflower." PortR (23) 77, p. 142.

EMMONS, Jean
"Creatures of Light and Darkness." Chomo (4:1) Sum 77, p. 29.

ENGELS, John
"Bad Weather on Blood Mountain." CarlMis (16:1/2) Aut-Wint
76-77, p. 14.
"Dawn on Blood Mountain." CarlMis (16:1/2) Aut-Wint 76-77,
p. 16.
"The Lake." PoNow (14/18) 77, p. 38.
"Love Poem, Describing the Austere Comfort of the Dream in
Which Nothing Is Named." Ploughs (3:3/4) 77, p. 154.
"On Top of Blood Mountain." CarlMis (16:1/2) Aut-Wint 76-77,
p. 14.
"Photograph When You Are Not Looking." PoNow (14/18) 77,
p. 38.
"Prince Mahasattva on Blood Mountain." CarlMis (16:1/2) Aut-
Wint 76-77, p. 15.
"Searching for You on Blood Mountain." CarlMis (16:1/2) Aut-
Wint 76-77, p. 16.
from Signals from the Safety Coffin: "The Bedroom." PoNow
(14/18) 77, p. 36.
from Signals from the Safety Coffin: "The Fish Dream." PoNow
(14/18) 77, p. 36.
"Vivaldi in Early Fall." Iowa (8:4) Aut 77, p. 88.

ENGLE, John D., Jr.
   "Be with Me." Poem (30) Jl 77, p. 2.
   "Thanks at Evening." Poem (30) Jl 77, p. 1.

ENGONOPOULOS, Nikos
   "Dance Stately and Sentimental" (tr. by Martin McKinsey).
      ParisR (69) Spr 77, p. 127.
   "The Final Appearance of Judas Iscariot" (tr. by Martin McKin-
      sey). ParisR (69) Spr 77, p. 125.
   "Four and Ten Subjects for a Painting" (to Raymond Roussel) (tr.
      by Martin McKinsey). ParisR (69) Spr 77, p. 124.
   "Mercurios Bouas" (tr. by Martin McKinsey). ParisR (69) Spr
      77, p. 126.

ENRIGHT, D. J.
   "Concerning the Future of Britain." MassR (18:1) Spr 77,
      p. 104.
   "Lives of the Gaolers." NewYRB (24:18) 10 N 77, p. 4.
   "Oyster Lament." MassR (18:1) Spr 77, p. 105.

ENSLIN, Theodore
   "River: Still Shot." Harp (255:1531) D 77, p. 16.
   "A well-worn piece of wood." PoNow (14/18) 77, p. 38.

ENTREKIN, Charles
   "The Artist" (for John Mullen). US1 (10) Wint 77-78, p. 4.
   "This Stillness." US1 (9) Spr 77, p. 3.
   "Thoughts from a Plane over Birmingham." US1 (9) Spr 77,
      p. 3.

EPLING, Kathy
   "The Burning Fields." PraS (51:4) Wint 77-78, p. 395.
   "In This Lace Orchard." Kayak (44) F 77, p. 55.
   "Learning Gaelic" (for S. C.). Kayak (46) O 77, p. 22.
   "Solstice." PraS (51:4) Wint 77-78, p. 394.
   "Summer Vacation." Kayak (44) F 77, p. 54.
   "Walking Night's Ridge." Kayak (46) O 77, p. 23.
   "Your Daughter Draws Owls." Kayak (46) O 77, p. 23.

EPSTEIN, Elaine
   "Crossing Water." OP (24) Aut-Wint 77, p. 42.
   "Late Night Talk with My Muse." OP (24) Aut-Wint 77, p. 43.
   "Portage." OP (24) Aut-Wint 77, p. 43.
   "Religion." OP (24) Aut-Wint 77, p. 40.

EPSTEIN, Susan
   "To My Friends on the Surface." Aspect (70) Ja-Mr 77, p. 25.

ERCEGOVIC, Mark
   "Keys." PoetryNW (18:2) Sum 77, p. 46.
   "Running War Movies Backwards." PoetryNW (18:2) Sum 77,
      p. 47.

ERDRICH, Louise
"All the Comforts of Home." DacTerr (14) Spr-Sum 77, p. 52.
"Certain Fields." DacTerr (14) Spr-Sum 77, p. 53.
"His Deathmap." DacTerr (14) Spr-Sum 77, p. 54.

ERFORD, Esther
"On a Girl Who Refused a Trip to Europe for Her Fifteenth Birth-
    day." PoetL (72:2) Sum 77, p. 51.

ERICKSON, Catherine
"Delivery Lullaby." CimR (39) Ap 77, p. 20.
"Salt Soup." Poem (29) Mr 77, p. 64.

ERNST, Ruth Shaw
"Cat on the Breakfast Table." LadHJ (94:9) S 77, p. 80.

ESHLEMAN, Clayton
"The Dragon Rat Tail" (for Norm Weinstein). Pequod (2:3) Sum
    77, p. 30.
"The English Department of the Spirit." Montra (3) Spr 77,
    p. 42.
"'for your father' she said." Pequod (2:3) Sum 77, p. 26.
from Payroll of Bones: "Alphonso, you keep looking at me, I
    see" (tr. of César Vallejo, w. José Rubia Barcia). Bound
    (5:3) Spr 77, p. 748.
from Payroll of Bones: "Chances are, I am another; walking,
    at dawn, another who moves" (tr. of César Vallejo, w. José
    Rubia Barcia). Bound (5:3) Spr 77, p. 751.
from Payroll of Bones: "Farewell Remembering a Goodbye" (tr.
    of César Vallejo, w. José Rubia Barcia). Bound (5:3) Spr
    77, p. 750.
from Payroll of Bones: "I stayed on to warm up the ink in
    which I drown" (tr. of César Vallejo, w. José Rubia Barcia).
    Bound (5:3) Spr 77, p. 747.
from Payroll of Bones: "Oh bottle without wine! Oh wine the
    widower of this bottle!" (tr. of César Vallejo, w. José Rubia
    Barcia). Bound (5:3) Spr 77, p. 745.
from Payroll of Bones: "This" (tr. of César Vallejo, w. José
    Rubia Barcia). Bound (5:3) Spr 77, p. 746.
from Payroll of Bones: "Upon reflecting on Life, upon reflecting"
    (tr. of César Vallejo, w. José Rubia Barcia). Bound (5:3)
    Spr 77, p. 744.
"Study for a Portrait of Norman Glass." Bound (5:2) Wint 77,
    p. 552.
"Study of a Shadow." Bound (5:2) Wint 77, p. 554.
"36 Variations on Shiki's 'furukabe no sumi ni ugokazu harami
    gumo.'" Montra (3) Spr 77, p. 41.
"The Wood of Isis." Montra (3) Spr 77, p. 44.

ESKOW, John
"The Coat" (tr. of Rumi Jalaluddin). Some (7/8) 76.
"The Fight." Some (7/8) 76.
"The Stoning." PoNow (14/18) 77, p. 38.

"Words for the Doorman (At the Tavern of the Void)" (tr. of Rumi Jalaluddin). Some (7/8) 76.

ESPELAND, Pamela
"From All Sides. " CarlMis (17:1) Wint 77-78, p. 62.

ESRIG, Mark
"Inside the Light. " ConcPo (10:2) Aut 77, p. 10.
"Prayer. " ConcPo (10:2) Aut 77, p. 9.

ESTAVER, Paul
"Three Widows. " StoneC (77:2) My 77, p. 20.

ESTRIN, Jerry
"Garden of the Spaceship. " MontG (6) Aut 77, p. 25.
"Gerard de Nerval. " MontG (6) Aut 77, p. 24.

ESTROFF, Nadine F.
"Apex. " TexQ (20:4) Wint 77, p. 138.
"Bodies. " Pig (3) 77, p. 87.
"Closet Class. " SouthernHR (11:3) Sum 77, p. 267.
"Crosspieces. " SouthernHR (11:3) Sum 77, p. 252.
"Crosspieces. " TexQ (20:4) Wint 77, p. 126.
"Dichotomy. " SouthernHR (11:3) Sum 77, p. 251.
"Magic. " TexQ (20:4) Wint 77, p. 128.
"Navigations. " Pig (3) 77, p. 22.
"Navigations. " TexQ (20:4) Wint 77, p. 127.
"Renegade. " Pig (3) 77, p. 50.

ETCHETO, John
"Love is a gorgeous. " SeC (5:2) 78, p. 15.

ETTER, Dave
"After Showing Grant Wood's 'American Gothic' to My Children. " PoNow (14/18) 77, p. 40.
"Drummers. " PoNow (14/18) 77, p. 39.
"Green-Eyed Boy after Reading Whitman and Sandburg. " PoNow (14/18) 77, p. 39.
"Hotel Tall Corn. " MidwQ (18:2) Wint 77, p. 200.
"The Morning Ride of Joni LeFevre. " PoNow (14/18) 77, p. 39.
"Omaha. " MidwQ (18:2) Wint 77, p. 202.
"Requiem. " KanQ (9:3) Sum 77, p. 13.
"Scarecrow Watching a Snowstorm. " MidwQ (18:2) Wint 77, p. 201.
"The Smell of Lilacs. " MidwQ (18:2) Wint 77, p. 201.
"Spring Snow. " PoNow (14/18) 77, p. 40.
"Why I Don't Go to Parties Anymore. " PoNow (14/18) 77, p. 39.

EULERT, Don
"In Here. " DenQ (11:4) Wint 77, p. 113.
"The Rocket. " DenQ (11:4) Wint 77, p. 114.
"Second Thursday, November. " StoneC (77:1) F 77, p. 32.

EVANS, Dave
"Cryptic Life." LaB (8) Jl-Ag 77, p. 18.
"Phoebus: Apollo as the Sun God." LaB (8) Jl-Ag 77, p. 19.
"Playing a Conga." LaB (8) Jl-Ag 77, p. 17.
"Waiting for 2 O'Clock." LaB (8) Jl-Ag 77, p. 17.

EVANS, David Allan
"The Kranz Brothers." Chowder (8) Spr-Sum 77, p. 17.

EVANS, Deborah
"It smashed us again." PartR (44:2) 77, p. 246.
"Sometimes it seems that he's coming in in bounds." PartR
    (44:2) 77, p. 247.
"Whoever is sucked in; blown out." PartR (44:2) 77, p. 245.

EVANS, Elisabeth Murawski
"For Alun Lewis (1915-44)." NewRep (176:6) 5 F 77, p. 25.
"Tinder." ChrC (94:32) 12 O 77, p. 902.

EVANS, George
"Laughter: A Warning above My Door." MontG (6) Aut 77,
    p. 28.

EVANS, Jay
"In Vegas." PoetL (72:2) Sum 77, p. 68.
"Pilot." PoetL (72:2) Sum 77, p. 68.
"Reunion." PoetL (72:2) Sum 77, p. 69.
"Roadblock." PoetL (72:2) Sum 77, p. 69.
"Turbulence." PoetL (72:2) Sum 77, p. 69.

EVANS, Mari
"Curving Stonesteps in the Sun." Nimrod (21:2/22:1) 77, p. 80.
"Nicodemus (1879-1970)." AmerPoR (6:1) Ja-F 77, p. 22.
"Remembering Willie." Nimrod (21:2/22:1) 77, p. 81.

EVANS, Michael
"The Ecstasy Game." EnPas (4) 76, p. 12.
"Her." EnPas (4) 76, p. 13.
"Taking Stock in California." EnPas (4) 76, p. 15.
"Through My Own Eyes the City Dreams Itself." EnPas (4) 76,
    p. 14.

EVANS, R. Daniel
"From the Diary of Master Pontormo" (#1 to #5). HangL (30)
    Sum 77, p. 17.
"Relationship." PoNow (14/18) 77, p. 40.

EVE, Barbara
Eight poems. Agni (7) 77, p. 41.
"Last Night I Remembered You, Penelope Alderdice." AndR (3:1)
    Spr 76, p. 12.
"Man Reading Newspaper, 1952." PoNow (14/18) 77, p. 40.

EVERHARD, James
"The Invisible Brother" (-for J.).   HangL (31) Aut 77, p. 10.

EVERHARD, Jim
"Cruising. "   Mouth (13) D 77, p. 62.
"'What Captures Light Belongs to What It Captures. '--Thom Gunn."
   Mouth (13) D 77, p. 72.

EVERWINE, Peter
"Counting. "   Rapp (10) 77, p. 61.
"The Story of the Fiesta. "   PoNow (14/18) 77, p. 41.

FAHEY, W. A.
"Hair. "   Confr (14) Spr-Sum 77, p. 188.

FAINLIGHT, Harry
"The Bayswater. "   PartR (44:4) 77, p. 558.
"You Have Wasted Your Life. "   PartR (44:4) 77, p. 558.

FAINLIGHT, Ruth
"Evening and Dawn. "   Hudson (30:3) Aut 77, p. 355.
"The Route Napoleon. "   Hudson (30:3) Aut 77, p. 355.

FALIT, Judy
"I wish the world was made of candy. "   AAR (27) 77, p. 96.

FALK, Marcia
"Closing Prayer: Yom Kippur" (tr. of T. Carmi).   Hand (1) 77,
   p. 214.
"From There On" (tr. of T. Carmi).   TriQ (39) Spr 77, p. 253.
"Home for Winter. "   Hand (1) 77, p. 7.
"Order of the Day" (tr. of T. Carmi).   TriQ (39) Spr 77,
   p. 253.
"Perspectives" (tr. of T. Carmi).   TriQ (39) Spr 77, p. 254.
"Pride" (tr. of Dahlia Ravikovitch).   TriQ (39) Spr 77, p. 297.
"Songs of the Priestess" (tr. of Malka Heifetz Tussman).   Hand
   (1) 77, p. 54.

FALLON, T.
"Bud Powell. "   Xa (4) 77, p. 2.

FANALE, James
"Vineyard. "   EngJ (66:5) My 77, p. 58.

FANDEL, John
"Damselfly. "   Comm (104:21) 14 O 77, p. 660.
"Highway Birdwatcher. "   Hudson (30:4) Wint 77-78, p. 545.
Out of Our Blue.   Sparrow (34) 77.   Entire issue.
"Powdered Sky. "   Comm (104:23) 11 N 77, p. 719.

FANNING, Patrick
"Flea Market Day. "   Stonecloud (6) 76, p. 119.
"Found under a Rock. "   Vaga (26) 77, p. 87.

"My Father's Hands. " Pig (3) 77, p. 65.
"Small Lives Gone. " DeKalb (10:2) Wint 77, p. 30.

FAN Yen-long
"Partings" (tr. by Graeme Wilson). DenQ (12:2) Sum 77, p. 391.

FARBER, Norma
"Anguish of the Snail" (Malcolm de Chazal). Wind (26) 77, p. 19.
"Carol of the Porcupine. " ChrC (94:42) 21 D 77, p. 1192.
"Dead Man. " Wind (26) 77, p. 19.
"The Forger. " Wind (26) 77, p. 21.
"High Balcony, High Resolve with Binoculars. " PoNow (14/18)
      77, p. 41.
"High Rise. " PoNow (14/18) 77, p. 41.
"In the Anemone Capital of the World. " PoNow (14/18) 77, p. 41.
"Ponder of Learning. " AndR (3:2) Aut 76, p. 97.
"Taking. " Wind (26) 77, p. 20.
"Tempest in a Willow. " Wind (26) 77, p. 20.
"To Sea for Pearls" (Christopher Smart). Wind (26) 77, p. 21.

FAREWELL, Patricia
"Mrs. Fitt Views a Sculpture Called Harbor in the Bayville Gal-
      lery. " Gra (12) 77.

FARINELLA, Salvatore
"Abacus" (for charlie shively). Mouth (11/12) Mr-Je 77, p. 51.
"Beach Day. " Mouth (11/12) Mr-Je 77, p. 89.
"Delight. " Mouth (11/12) Mr-Je 77, p. 27.
"Each Day. " Aspect (70) Ja-Mr 77, p. 57.
"Love Song of the Dispossessed. " GRR (8:1/2) 77, p. 70.
"News. " PoNow (14/18) 77, p. 41.

FAROOGI, Ijaz
"Shahryar" (tr. by Muhammad Umar Memon). DenQ (12:2) Sum
      77, p. 242.

FAROOGI, Sagi
"Poster" (tr. by Muhammad Umar Memon). DenQ (12:2) Sum 77,
      p. 241.

FATISHA
"Sayings of the Indoors People. " AmerPoR (6:2) Mr-Ap 77,
      p. 41.

FAUCHER, Real
"A Dying Hero. " Wind (24) 77, p. 32.

FAUDE, Jeff
"Monologue of a Dwarf. " AntR (35:1) Wint 77, p. 64.

FAULKNER, Margherita Woods
"The Attic. " Wind (27) 77, p. 17.
"I Give Up the Thought of Owning Things. " FourQT (26:4) Sum
      77, p. 9.

"Suicide. "   Chomo (4:1) Sum 77, p. 5.

FAULWELL, Dean
"Alone. " Chelsea (36) 77, p. 23.
"Dreamboat. " ParisR (71) Aut 77, p. 43.
"The Ecstatic Moron. " Chelsea (36) 77, p. 23.
"The Funeral. " Chelsea (36) 77, p. 25.
"Relapse. " Chelsea (36) 77, p. 24.

FAUTEUX, Bob
"Postcard from Tripoli, Wisconson. " Wind (24) 77, p. 37.

FAWCETT, Susan
"The Creation. " SenR (8:2) D 77, p. 76.
"The Fisherman. " Nat (224:1) 1-8 Ja 77, p. 26.
"Optics. " SenR (8:2) D 77, p. 75.
"The Woman in Bed. " SouthernPR (17:2) Aut 77, p. 46.

FEE, Dan
"Im Grünen Klee. " KanQ (9:4) Aut 77, p. 48.
"Threnody. " Mouth (13) D 77, p. 84.

FEGAN, Kris
"My Dream. " AAR (27) 77, p. 106.

FEHER, Tom
"Gunner in the Belfry. " RemR (5) 77, p. 98.

FEHLER, Gene
"Collection. " Wind (26) 77, p. 10.
"Smoke Kissed Me. " Wind (26) 77, p. 10.
"Voices. " Wind (26) 77, p. 33.

FEIN, Cheri
"#16 for December. " PartR (44:3) 77, p. 406.

FEIN, Debby
"The Demands. " US1 (9) Spr 77, p. 12.
"The Familiar Stranger. " US1 (9) Spr 77, p. 12.
"The Marker. " US1 (9) Spr 77, p. 12.

FEINSTEIN, Elaine
"House in Meudon" (tr. of Margarita Aliger). Stand (18:3) 77,
    p. 14.
"I Swear" (tr. of Bella Akhmadulina). Stand (18:3) 77, p. 17.
"Poem: Do you think of her, geranium Yelabuga?" (tr. of
    Yevgeny Yevtushenko). Stand (18:3) 77, p. 16.

FEIRSTEIN, Frederick
"Big Lady Lullaby. " DenQ (12:2) Sum 77, p. 325.
"For Sheba, My Student. " Hand (1) 77, p. 6.

FELD, Martha Headley
"Because You Love Her. " Poem (29) Mr 77, p. 49.

FELDMAN, Ruth
from L'Aria secca del fuoco: "Like a Trickle of Watered Blood"
(tr. of Bartolo Cattafi, w. Brian Swann). Some (7/8) 76.
"The Autumn Countryside" (tr. of Bartolo Cattafi, w. Brian
Swann). WebR (3:1) Wint 77, p. 8.
"The Descent to the Throne" (tr. of Bartolo Cattafi, w. Brian
Swann). WebR (3:1) Wint 77, p. 7.
from Foglio Di Via: "Advice to the Dead Man" (tr. of Franco
Fortini). Glass (2:2/3) Wint-Spr 77, p. 19.
from Foglio Di Via: "Song for a Small Girl" (tr. of Franco
Fortini). Glass (2:2/3) Wint-Spr 77, p. 21.
"The Gift." SouthwR (62:2) Spr 77, p. 115.
"Letter" (tr. of Franco Fortini). Glass (2:2/3) Wint-Spr 77,
p. 7.
"Letter to Isaac Bashevis-Singer." Chowder (8) Spr-Sum 77,
p. 37.
"My Mistakes" (tr. of Bartolo Cattafi, w. Brian Swann). Confr
(14) Spr-Sum 77, p. 141.
"Paestum." SouthernPR (17:1) Spr 77, p. 17.
from Questo Muro: "For Three Moments" (tr. of Franco For-
tini). Glass (2:2/3) Wint-Spr 77, p. 11.
from Questo Muro: "From the Hill" (tr. of Franco Fortini).
Glass (2:2/3) Wint-Spr 77, p. 15.
"Reflection." Aspect (69) O-D 76, p. 17.
"Stranglehold." Aspect (69) O-D 76, p. 17.
"These Myths" (tr. of Bartolo Cattafi, w. Brian Swann). WebR
(3:1) Wint 77, p. 7.
from Una Volta Per Sempre: "Translating Brecht" (tr. of Franco
Fortini). Glass (2:2/3) Wint-Spr 77, p. 9.
"Visit" (tr. of Bartolo Cattafi, w. Brian Swann). Some (7/8)
76.
"With the War Over" (tr. of Bartolo Cattafi, w. Brian Swann).
WebR (3:1) Wint 77, p. 8.

FELIKS, Pat
"Four score and three months ago." AAR (27) 77, p. 123.

FELIX, Leesa
"Beyond the Lace (Guapalo, Ecuador, 1976)." HangL (30) Sum 77,
p. 77.
"Friend (1975)." HangL (30) Sum 77, p. 76.

FELLOWES, Peter
"Fable." PoNow (14/18) 77, p. 42.
"The Prophecy." PoNow (14/18) 77, p. 42.

FELSTINER, John
"Archaic Torso of Apollo" (tr. of Rainer Maria Rilke). DenQ
(11:4) Wint 77, p. 44.
"The Carousel" (tr. of Rainer Maria Rilke). DenQ (11:4) Wint
77, p. 45.
"The Panther" (tr. of Rainer Maria Rilke). DenQ (11:4) Wint 77,
p. 43.

FELT, Tom
"An Investigation of Angels" (For R. , and all the others, who
    died too young). Mouth (13) D 77, p. 37.
"The Letter. " Mouth (13) D 77, p. 70.
"The Philosophers. " Mouth (13) D 77, p. 13.

FERACA, Jean
"South Paradise Hotel. " Nat (224:6) 12 F 77, p. 184.

FERGUSON, Lynne
"To the Friend I Broke Up With. " EngJ (66:5) My 77, p. 53.

FERICANO, Paul F.
"At Her Funeral. " Vaga (25) 77, p. 89.
"At Her Funeral. " Vaga (26) 77, p. 84. Corrected version.
"Sperm Count. " StoneC (77:1) F 77, p. 30.
"Then/Party" (for Karl Shapiro). Xa (4) 77, p. 23.
"Twenty-Five Years after Conception. " Vaga (26) 77, p. 85.

FERRA, Lorraine
"Light. " QW (3) Spr-Sum 77, p. 83.
"Poverty. " QW (3) Spr-Sum 77, p. 83.

FERRARI, Mary
"The Seine. " Glass (2:2/3) Wint-Spr 77, p. 72.

FERRARY, Jeannette
"Second Nature. " MoonsLT (2:3) 77, p. 69.

FERRIS, Lucy
"Aftermath. " Pequod (2:3) Sum 77, p. 74.

FIALKOWSKI, Barbara
"What You Feared. " NewL (43:3) Spr 77, p. 24.

FICKERT, Kurt J.
"Long Beach Revisited. " DeKalb (10:3) Spr 77, p. 13.
"Specimens. " WindO (29) Sum 77, p. 19.
"Walt Whitman in West Hills (Long Island). " PoetL (72:1) Spr
    77, p. 5.

FICOCIELLO, John
"The Domestic's Retirement. " PortR (23) 77, p. 63.
"Poems" (for Sally Robinson). PortR (23) 77, p. 64.

FIEDLER, Michael
"Host and Prince, Jewel of Flanders. " MontG (6) Aut 77, p. 16.

FIELD, Matt
"Edinburgh. " CEACritic (39:4) My 77, p. 48.

FIELDER, William
"Your lips are pink" (tr. of Cahit Kulebi, w. Ozcan Yal'm and
    Dionis Coffin Riggs). DenQ (12:2) Sum 77, p. 230.

FIELDS, Ed, Jr.
"Poltergeist." Bits (6) Jl 77.

FIELDS, JoAnn
"I like to jump." Nimrod (21:2/22:1) 77, p. 82.
"Lean Baby Lean." Nimrod (21:2/22:1) 77, p. 82.

FIFER, Ken
"Bifurcation." WebR (3:4) Aut 77, p. 29.
"F." HangL (31) Aut 77, p. 12.
"A Short Story" (w. Ricardo Viera). Juice (4) 77.

FIGGINS, Ross
Five Haiku. ColEng (38:6) F 77, p. 590.
"Haiku #388." SmPd (14:1) Wint 77, p. 28.
"Haiku #767." SmPd (14:3) Aut 77, p. 18.
"Senryu #771." SmPd (14:3) Aut 77, p. 16.

FINALE, Frank
"Duke." Wind (27) 77, p. 18.
"For Sale." Wind (27) 77, p. 18.
"In Texas." DeKalb (10:3) Spr 77, p. 15.

FINCH, Annie R. C.
"The August Porch." YaleLit (147:2) 77, p. 25.

FINCH, J. F.
"Missal-thrush Memories." Stand (18:3) 77, p. 37.

FINE, Philip
"Birds of Winter" (for Sophia B. Fine). PoetryNW (18:2) Sum
    77, p. 32.

FINK, Jon-Stephen
"Abraham/Sarah." ChiR (29:2) Aut 77, p. 64.

FINKEL, Donald
"Grandma Is Playing the Moonlight Sonata." PoNow (14/18) 77,
    p. 42.
"Resources." PoNow (14/18) 77, p. 42.

FINKELSTEIN, Caroline
"Ride." Columbia (1) Aut 77, p. 31.

FINLAY, Ian Hamilton
"waterwheels in." AmerPoR (6:4) Jl-Ag 77, p. 20.

FINLAY, John
"The Bog Sacrifice." SouthernR (13:1) Wint 77, p. 168.

FINLAY, Michael
"Frankenstein in the Cemetery." Bits (6) Jl 77.

FINLEY, C. Stephen
    "The Dwelling Place." VirQR (53:3) Sum 77, p. 513.
    "In Virginia." SouthernPR (17:2) Aut 77, p. 53.

FINLEY, Mike
    "Bloodletters." HangL (31) Aut 77, p. 13.
    "Greetings." Northeast (3:3) Sum 77, p. 17.
    "Hard Times Come to Li Po." HangL (31) Aut 77, p. 17.
    "In Praise of Granite." Northeast (3:3) Sum 77, p. 16.
    "Noise Interrupting Minestrone." HangL (31) Aut 77, p. 16.

FINNE, Diderik
    "Chanterelles." Kayak (46) O 77, p. 33.
    "Cri du Chat." Shen (28:4) Sum 77, p. 71.

FINNEY, Jim
    "Ghosting down the supermarket aisles." TransR (58/59) F 77,
        p. 140.
    "I counted all over again." TransR (58/59) F 77, p. 139.

FINUCANE, Martin Louis
    "Hallways and their stairwells are always." HarvAd (111:1) N
        77, p. 9.

FIORE, Paul
    "Pressure Cooker." DeKalb (10:2) Wint 77, p. 31.

FISHER, David
    "The House." CarlMis (17:1) Wint 77-78, p. 68.
    "The Keepsake Corporation." Kayak (44) F 77, p. 44.

FISHER, George William
    "Parents' Attic." Sam (56) Sum 77, p. 55.

FISHER, Grant
    "1836 (Eighteen Thirty-six)." LaB (8) Jl-Ag 77, p. 20.
    "Holst" (for John Herbert McDowell). LaB (8) Jl-Ag 77, p. 20.
    "Salt." LaB (8) Jl-Ag 77, p. 20.

FISHER, Harrison
    "On the Pedestrian." SenR (8:2) D 77, p. 48.
    "The Posthumous Poems of Arnold Harold Thenkin." Falcon (14)
        77, p. 52.
    "Things Not Coming True." SenR (8:2) D 77, p. 49.
    "A Young Pipefitter Wondereth How Long His Life Will Live
        Without Him, Especially as it Sitteth Before Him at Break-
        fast and Complaineth." Falcon (14) 77, p. 54.

FISHER, Roy
    "Diversions." Montra (3) Spr 77, p. 157.

FISHER, Sally
    "Daylight Ghazal." Shen (28:2) Wint 77, p. 91.

FISHER, Tony
"In the Middle of the Night." AAR (27) 77, p. 109.
"I was born a human bean." AAR (27) 77, p. 114.
"Red." AAR (27) 77, p. 127.
"Worms are little and slimy. They don't have any feet." AAR
(27) 77, p. 99.

FISHMAN, Charles
"Adagio for Bagpipe and Fiddle." Gra (12) 77, p. 12.
"For the Tough Guys." PoNow (14/18) 77, p. 43.
"Going Toward but Holding Back." Northeast (3:3) Sum 77, p. 4.
"Origin of the Law." Hand (1) 77, p. 88.
"Remembering the Dream." HolCrit (14:3) Je 77, p. 9.
"To Amy on Ward 10W." Juice (4) 77.
"The Werewolf's Polonaise." KanQ (9:1) Wint 77, p. 76.

FITZPATRICK, Vincent
"'Richard.'" Mouth (11/12) Mr-Je 77, p. 91.

FITZPATRICK, W. P.
"One Thousand and Two." CimR (40) Jl 77, p. 36.

FLAGG, John S.
"Plot to Restore Reason to the Chair." PoetryNW (18:2) Sum 77,
p. 15.

FLAHERTY, Doug
"Approaching the Nativity" (for Anick). CalQ (11/12) Wint-Spr
77, p. 118.
"First Hunt." PoNow (14/18) 77, p. 43.

FLANAGAN, Robert
"Harlem Childing." SmPd (14:3) Aut 77, p. 13.
"Winter Evening." PoetL (72:1) Spr 77, p. 25.

FLANDERS, Jane
"Cinderella at Forty." Bits (6) Jl 77.
"Cloisonne." Nat (225:9) 24 S 77, p. 281.
"How We Won the War." HiramPoR (22) Aut-Wint 77, p. 19.
"Just Because You're Comfortable." Chomo (3:3) Spr 77, p. 49.
"Kiss Them Goodbye." Chomo (4:2) Aut-Wint 77, p. 37.
"The Real Jane Flanders" (for my sister-in-law, the former Jane
Flanders). LitR (21:1) Aut 77, p. 90.
"Sarah's Song." MassR (18:2) Sum 77, p. 323.

FLANNER, Hildegarde
"Hungers." Salm (36) Wint 77, p. 37.
"A Request." Salm (36) Wint 77, p. 38.

FLANTZ, Richard
from Vegetative Love: "The Theoretical Offer" (tr. of David
Avidan). TriQ (39) Spr 77, p. 251.

FLAVIN, Jack
"Concordat. " MidwQ (18:3) Spr 77, p. 259.
"The Departure for Venusberg. " MidwQ (18:3) Spr 77, p. 258.
"Estivating in Connecticut, or Torpid on the Border. " MidwQ
    (18:3) Spr 77, p. 260.
"May. " MidwQ (18:3) Spr 77, p. 261.

FLEISCHMAN, Ted
"His Nurses Biting It Off. " US1 (10) Wint 77-78, p. 7.
"While I lay in the webbing of my hammock. " US1 (10) Wint 77-
    78, p. 7.

FLEMMING, Ray
"The Pines of Rome. " NewRep (177:10) 3 S 77, p. 27.

FLETCHER, Ralph J. , Jr.
"mense. " Wind (26) 77, p. 23.

FLEU, Richard
"Ankh. " StoneC (77:1) F 77, p. 28.
"Enough for Two. " StoneC (77:1) F 77, p. 27.

FLOCK, Miriam
"Bequest. " RemR (5) 77, p. 60.
"Litany. " RemR (5) 77, p. 59.
"Our God and God of Our Fathers. " HiramPoR (22) Aut-Wint 77,
    p. 20.
"Then You'll Be a True Love of Mine. " RemR (5) 77, p. 58.

FLOTT, Phil, Jr.
"Epithalamion for Kate. " BallSUF (18:1) Wint 77, p. 80.

FOERSTER, Richard A.
"In a Formal Boxwood Garden. " RemR (5) 77, p. 93.

FOGEL, Al
"Hunting Etiquette. " WormR (65/66) 77, p. 17.
"VA Benefit. " Box (5) Spr 77, p. 23.
"VA Benefit. " WormR (65/66) 77, p. 17.

FOLKESTAD, Marilyn
"The Lovers: A Drama. " PortR (23) 77, p. 37.
"Warning. " ConcPo (10:1) Spr 77, p. 62.

FOLLAIN, Jean
"Black Ants" (tr. by Geoffrey Gardner). WebR (3:4) Aut 77,
    p. 46.
"Natural" (tr. by Geoffrey Gardner). WebR (3:4) Aut 77, p. 47.
"Presence" (tr. by Geoffrey Gardner). WebR (3:4) Aut 77, p. 46.
"Seed Dealer" (tr. by Geoffrey Gardner). WebR (3:4) Aut 77, p. 47.

FOLLY, Dennis W.
"a old beard. " Nimrod (21:2/22:1) 77, p. 85.

"Question" (for djanita). Nimrod (21:2/22:1) 77, p. 83.
"sometimes at night." Nimrod (21:2/22:1) 77, p. 84.
"The Voice of a Toad." Nimrod (21:2/22:1) 77, p. 86.

FOLTZ-GRAY, Dorothy
"Alice, Shrink for the Keyhole." SouthwR (62:4) Aut 77, p. 396.

FORBES, Calvin
"Homing." PraS (51:2) Sum 77, p. 130.
"Overcast, Fullmoon" (for Karen). Nimrod (21:2/22:1) 77, p. 87.
"The Plea." PraS (51:2) Sum 77, p. 131.

FORCHÉ, Carolyn
from Flowers from the Volcano: "I Am Root" (tr. of Claribel
    Alegría). Chowder (9) Aut-Wint 77, p. 60.
from Flowers from the Volcano: "Santa Ana in the Dark" (tr. of
    Claribel Alegría). Chowder (9) Aut-Wint 77, p. 56.
from Flowers from the Volcano: "Sorrow" (To Roque Dalton) (tr.
    of Claribel Alegría). Chowder (9) Aut-Wint 77, p. 48.
"Shediac." Chowder (9) Aut-Wint 77, p. 14.

FORD, Charles Henri
"10. ii. 77." SunM (4) Aut 77, p. 26.

FORD, Dan
"Charlie Hyde." TexQ (20:2) Sum 77, p. 42.
"Entrances." TexQ (20:2) Sum 77, p. 42.
"1964 Savage." TexQ (20:2) Sum 77, p. 43.

FORD, Michael C.
"There's Someone Out on the Strand I Think About Sometimes."
    Stonecloud (6) 76, p. 104.

FORD, R. A. D.
"A Gangrenous Year." MalR (42) Ap 77, p. 111.
"Without Horizon." MalR (42) Ap 77, p. 110.

FORD, William
"Becca." PoetC (10:1) 77, p. 16.

FORKER, Greg
"Solving the Waves." Field (16) Spr 77, p. 31.
"Thunder." Field (16) Spr 77, p. 31.

FORTENBAUGH, Laura
"Our Poem." Harp (254:1520) Ja 77, p. 90.

FORTIN, Dede
"Walpi." Chomo (3:3) Spr 77, p. 50.

FORTINI, Franco
from Foglio Di Via: "Canzone Per Bambina." Glass (2:2/3)
    Wint-Spr 77, p. 20.

from Foglio Di Via: "E Tu Pregali." Glass (2:2/3) Wint-Spr 77,
    p. 18.
"Lettera." Glass (2:2/3) Wint-Spr 77, p. 6.
from Questo Muro: "Dalla Collina." Glass (2:2/3) Wint-Spr 77,
    p. 14.
from Questo Muro: "Per Tre Momenti." Glass (2:2/3) Wint-Spr
    77, p. 10.
from Una Volta Per Sempre: "Traducendo Brecht." Glass (2:2/3)
    Wint-Spr 77, p. 8.

FORTNER, Ethel
    "Tahitian Interval." PoetL (72:2) Sum 77, p. 71.

FOSS, Phillip, Jr.
    "Riding the Wheel." StoneC (77:3) S 77, p. 10.

FOSSO, D. R.
    "Chill Factor." Wind (26) 77, p. 25.
    "Early Out." Wind (26) 77, p. 24.
    "Logos." Wind (26) 77, p. 24.
    "Opposing." Poetry (130:1) Ap 77, p. 21.
    "Salute." Poetry (130:1) Ap 77, p. 22.
    "Strategy." Wind (26) 77, p. 25.
    "Volume." Poetry (130:1) Ap 77, p. 22.

FOSTER, Toshi
    "Quiet Night." QW (3) Spr-Sum 77, p. 30.

FOURNIER, Donald N.
    "The Hanging." CarouselQ (2:2) Spr 77, p. 6.
    "The Old Emmet." CimR (39) Ap 77, p. 45.
    "Poem: The way to stand like a monument." CarouselQ (2:2)
        Aut 77, p. 6.

FOX, Hugh
    "COSMEP Transmutation--1975." Juice (4) 77.
    "Fall Cleaning." KanQ (9:4) Aut 77, p. 87.
    "Flight 76--Miami-Dallas-Kansas City." Juice (4) 77.
    "Holy, Roman, Apostolic Pyramid." Juice (5) 77.
    "Lord of Goblins." Juice (4) 77.
    "Ontological Fieldguide for Terrorists and Counter-Insurgents."
        Juice (5) 77.
    "The Pill." Juice (4) 77.
    "To U. S. Citizens Entering the United States (Put U. S. Seal Here)
        Welcome Home...." Juice (4) 77.
    "Universal Baby--The Cat and the Cookie." Juice (5) 77.
    "Vitamin C." Juice (4) 77.

FOX, Ray
    "The Stripper." MichQR (16:2) Spr 77, p. 173.

FOX, Sherre
    "Duchess II." Sam (52) Ap 77, p. 32.

FOX, Siv Cedering
"Letter from Isaac Newton." Hand (1) 77, p. 113.
"Letter to Zakarias and My Friends." Hand (1) 77, p. 112.
"The Lyre" (for Robin). NewRep (177:6/7) 6-13 Ag 77, p. 36.
"Orbium Coelestium." Hand (1) 77, p. 114.
"The Ship Builder." Hand (1) 77, p. 187.
"The Wild Geese." Confr (14) Spr-Sum 77, p. 27.

FOX, Susan
"Sceaux the Day They Turn Off the Fountain." ParisR (71) Aut
    77, p. 178.

FOX, Willard
"Behind Centre Market." WindO (28) Spr 77, p. 30.

FOX, William L.
"Poem: a small disease patiently instructs me in the ways."
    Drag (16) 77.
"Poem: the underground construction co. is at it again." Drag
    (16) 77.
"Poem: we're afraid of waste and teach ourselves to." Drag
    (16) 77.
"Time by Distance." Chelsea (36) 77, p. 32.

FRANCIS, Jan
"frightening lightening struck my tree." Aspect (70) Ja-Mr 77,
    p. 24.

FRANCIS, Pat-Therese
"Fire." PoetryNW (18:3) Aut 77, p. 20.
"Your Shirt." PoetryNW (18:3) Aut 77, p. 21.

FRANCIS, Robert
"Bull." NewL (44:2) Wint 77, p. 87.
"Loan Exhibit." HolCrit (14:4) O 77, p. 7.
"Play Ball!" NewL (44:2) Wint 77, p. 86.

FRANCISCO, Nia
"escaping the turquoise sky." ColEng (39:3) N 77, p. 348.
"i have sat through sunlight." ColEng (39:3) N 77, p. 353.
"men tell and talk." ColEng (39:3) N 77, p. 352.
"ode to a drunk woman." ColEng (39:3) N 77, p. 350.
"sweat house." ColEng (39:3) N 77, p. 347.
"táchééh." ColEng (39:3) N 77, p. 346.

FRANCO, Lorraine
"President Ford." SeC (5:2) 78, p. 16.

FRANK, Jacqueline
"Translating." AndR (4:1) Spr 77, p. 6.

FRANK, Jeanne
"Miner." Bits (6) Jl 77.

FRANK, Peter
   "The Beer Council." LaB (9) N-D 77, p. 27.
   "Guitar." LaB (6) Mr 77, p. 25.
   "Medley" (for David and Lindsay Shapiro). LaB (6) Mr 77,
      p. 26.
   "Nostalgia Elephant." LaB (6) Mr 77, p. 26.
   "Onion Country" (for Juliet Green). LaB (6) Mr 77, p. 28.
   "Paris Feet" (for Stewart Lindh and Beresford Hayward). LaB
      (6) Mr 77, p. 27.
   "Poem: Very strange tears" (for Margaret Nomentana). LaB (9)
      N-D 77, p. 30.
   "Rare Balls." LaB (9) N-D 77, p. 28.
   "Rooms" (for David Ricks and Lynn Coburn). LaB (9) N-D 77,
      p. 30.
   "Special Difficulties" (found poem). LaB (6) Mr 77, p. 25.
   "Where We Mean." LaB (9) N-D 77, p. 27.

FRANKLIN, Phillip B.
   "Fireworks." KanQ (9:3) Sum 77, p. 82.
   "26 Priests." KanQ (9:3) Sum 77, p. 82.

FRATUS, David
   "Things to Teach Your Kids to Be Afraid Of." Northeast (3:4)
      Aut-Wint 77-78, p. 57.

FRAZIER, Eric E.
   "The Four Seasons." BlackF (2:1) Wint 77-78, p. 33.

FREDSON, Michael
   "Perfect." Bits (6) Jl 77.
   "Wind Song." StoneC (77:1) F 77, p. 17.

FREEDMAN, Jonathan
   "Chuck-Will's-Widow." HarvAd (110:5) My 77, p. 4.

FREEK, George A.
   "From Another Perspective." CarouselQ (2:3) Wint 77, p. 16.
   "Harlequinade." TexQ (20:3) Aut 77, p. 19.
   "Like the Book." SmPd (14:1) Wint 77, p. 32.
   "Synopsis." CarouselQ (2:3) Wint 77, p. 17.
   "Zeroing In." Vaga (26) 77, p. 15.

FREEMAN, Peter
   "Two Rivers" (Belatedly, for Richard Tuttle). HarvAd (111:1) N
      77, p. 22.

FREILICH, Kim
   "Who Is This Judi's Jack?" Ploughs (4:1) 77, p. 98.

FREIS, Richard
   "The Beach Motel." Poetry (130:5) Ag 77, p. 257.
   "Life Story." Poetry (130:5) Ag 77, p. 256.

FRENAUD, Andre
  Eight poems (tr. by Evelyn Robson and John Montague). MalR
    (43) Jl 77, p. 77.
  "Who Owns What?" (tr. by William Kulik). AmerPoR (6:2) Mr-
    Ap 77, p. 21.

FRENCH, Donna
  "Answer." CutB (8) Spr 77, p. 95.

FREY, Charles H.
  "The Globe Restored." DenQ (12:3) Aut 77, p. 90.

FREY, Kirk
  "I wish I was a steam engine." AAR (27) 77, p. 96.

FRIAR, Kimon
  "The Earthen Adolescent" (tr. of Yannis Ritsos, w. Kostas
    Myrsiades). Epoch (27:1) Aut 77, p. 82.
  "Hyalography of the Bath" (tr. of Yannis Ritsos, w. Kostas
    Myrsiades). Epoch (27:1) Aut 77, p. 82.
  "On the Television Screen" (tr. of Yannis Ritsos, w. Kostas
    Myrsiades). DenQ (12:2) Sum 77, p. 268.
  "Opposition" (tr. of Yannis Ritsos, w. Kostas Myrsiades). DenQ
    (12:2) Sum 77, p. 268.
  "Surveillance" (tr. of Yannis Ritsos, w. Kostas Myrsiades).
    AntR (35:4) Aut 77, p. 407.
  Twelve poems (for Louis Aragon) (tr. of Yannis Ritsos, w.
    Kostas Myrsiades). Falcon (15) 77, p. 4.

FRIEBERT, Stuart
  "After Which." CutB (8) Spr 77, p. 56.
  "And Give Lessons to Your Son." PoNow (14/18) 77, p. 43.
  "Basta" (tr. of Karl Krolow). ChiR (29:3) Wint 78, p. 93.
  "The Fall." Shen (28:2) Wint 77, p. 87.
  "Fraud." ThRiPo (10) 77, p. 33.
  "I Set the Clock Ahead" (tr. of Karl Krolow). ChiR (29:3) Wint
    78, p. 91.
  "I Want to Go Along the River" (tr. of Karl Krolow). ChiR
    (29:3) Wint 78, p. 89.
  "More on Stealing." Shen (28:2) Wint 77, p. 88.
  "Old Joke for JW." DenQ (11:4) Wint 77, p. 112.
  "Some Things Keep" (tr. of Karl Krolow). ChiR (29:3) Wint 78,
    p. 91.
  "Three Hidden Marbles." MoonsLT (2:3) 77, p. 68.
  "Three Hungarian Pieces." CutB (8) Spr 77, p. 58.
  "Uncertain Health." PoNow (14/18) 77, p. 43.
  "We Should Never Grow Jealous." CutB (8) Spr 77, p. 57.
  "The Worst Yet." Shen (28:2) Wint 77, p. 88.
  "Your Mother, the Alcoholic." PoetryNW (18:1) Spr 77, p. 39.

FRIED, Elliot
  "Amtrak." Aspect (69) O-D 76, p. 39.
  "Barstow Circle K." YellowBR (8) 77, p. 18.

153   FRIED

FRIED, Eric Wolf
   "Daisy, Eighteen Months Old." TexQ (20:4) Wint 77, p. 130.
   "Divers More Characters." TexQ (20:4) Wint 77, p. 183.
   "Opening Day on the Hudson." TexQ (20:4) Wint 77, p. 90.

FRIED, Philip
   "Columbus Hospital: The Trick Knee Poems." Falcon (14) 77,
      p. 62.
   "Johnny Soyuz." Bits (6) Jl 77.
   "The Realistic Library." Falcon (14) 77, p. 65.

FRIEDLANDER, Ginny
   "Yesterday my father died." Glass (2:2/3) Wint-Spr 77, p. 78.

FRIEND, Robert
   "All the Generations before Me" (tr. of Yehuda Amichai). TriQ
      (39) Spr 77, p. 250.
   "Among Iron Fragments" (tr. of Tuvia Ruebner). TriQ (39) Spr
      77, p. 302.
   "Armchairs" (tr. of Dan Pagis). TriQ (39) Spr 77, p. 284.
   "Autobiography" (tr. of Dan Pagis). TriQ (39) Spr 77, p. 285.
   "The Elephant" (tr. of Dan Pagis). TriQ (39) Spr 77, p. 284.
   "Folk Tune" (tr. of Esther Raab, w. Shimon Sandbank). TriQ
      (39) Spr 77, p. 294.
   "Fossils" (tr. of Dan Pagis). TriQ (39) Spr 77, p. 286.
   "From a Late Diary" (tr. of Gabriel Preil). TriQ (39) Spr 77,
      p. 294.
   "I Saw" (tr. of Natan Zach). TriQ (39) Spr 77, p. 316.
   "In the Laboratory" (tr. of Dan Pagis). TriQ (39) Spr 77, p. 288.
   "The Last" (tr. of Dan Pagis). TriQ (39) Spr 77, p. 287.
   "Porcupine Fish" (tr. of Raquel Chalfi). TriQ (39) Spr 77,
      p. 255.
   "The Portrait" (tr. of Dan Pagis). TriQ (39) Spr 77, p. 286.
   "Romantic Reminder" (tr. of Gabriel Preil). TriQ (39) Spr 77,
      p. 293.
   "Savage Memories" (tr. of Yehuda Amichai). TriQ (39) Spr 77,
      p. 248.
   "Some Words in Praise of My Friends" (tr. of Haim Gouri).
      TriQ (39) Spr 77, p. 270.
   "A Somewhat Clouded Study" (tr. of Gabriel Preil). TriQ (39)
      Spr 77, p. 292.
   "Song of the Great Mind" (tr. of Uri Avi Greenberg). TriQ (39)
      Spr 77, p. 275.
   "Sunset Possibilities" (tr. of Gabriel Preil). TriQ (39) Spr 77,
      p. 292.
   from To God in Europe: "III. No other instances" (tr. of Uri
      Zvi Greenberg). TriQ (39) Spr 77, p. 276.
   "Today I Am Modest" (tr. of Esther Raab, w. Shimon Sandbank).
      TriQ (39) Spr 77, p. 295.

FRITZ, Walter Helmut
   "Biem Lesen Der Philosophischen Tagebücher Leonardos." ChiR
      (29:3) Wint 78, p. 104.

"Domenico Di Bartolo. " ChiR (29:3) Wint 78, p. 102.
"Michelangelo. " ChiR (29:3) Wint 78, p. 100.

FROES, Leonardo
"Letter to an Old Poet" (tr. by Michael Benedikt). LitR (21:2)
     Wint 78, p. 263.
"Upon Hanging a European Work of Art in a Brazilian House" (tr.
     by Paul Blackburn). LitR (21:2) Wint 78, p. 264.

FROSCH, Thomas
"Glue. " NewRena (9) F 77, p. 43.
"Town. " NewRena (9) F 77, p. 44.

FROST, Carol
"Apogee. " CutB (8) Spr 77, p. 25.
"The Black and White Photographer. " PraS (51:2) Sum 77,
     p. 167.
"The Blue Chair. " Falcon (14) 77, p. 71.
"Bonfire Makers. " PoetryNW (18:3) Aut 77, p. 23.
"The Coldest Day of the Year. " Agni (7) 77, p. 31.
"Fat Children. " BelPoJ (27:3) Spr 77, p. 14.
"King Midas. " SouthernPR (17:1) Spr 77, p. 5.
"Let Be. " CutB (8) Spr 77, p. 24.
"The Olive Jug. " Falcon (14) 77, p. 70.
"The Owner. " NewRivR (2:1) 77, p. 41.
"Postcard from Greece. " NewRivR (2:1) 77, p. 42.
"A Restaurant on Eighth Street. " DacTerr (14) Spr-Sum 77, p. 2.
"Snow Animal. " Agni (7) 77, p. 30.
"Well. " NewRivR (2:1) 77, p. 40.
"What Is Red and White. " Agni (7) 77, p. 32.

FROST, Celestine
"The Window. " Paunch (48/49) S 77, p. 191.

FROST, Richard
"Animal Graves. " Esq (88:5) N 77, p. 54.
"A Bird of Some Kind. " Confr (14) Spr-Sum 77, p. 93.
"Collecting. " MassR (18:3) Aut 77, p. 607.
"Heart. " PoetryNW (18:4) Wint 77-78, p. 32.
"I Stroke My Sleeping Son. " AmerS (46:4) Aut 77, p. 513.
"In a Film Winding Backwards. " PoetryNW (18:4) Wint 77-78,
     p. 31.
"The Lasting Season. " SouthwR (62:3) Sum 77, p. 255.
"My Friend Told Me. " AmerS (46:1) Wint 76-77, p. 103.
"On Open Forms. " MissR (6:1) 77, p. 54.
"Schoolhouse Lovers. " PoNow (14/18) 77, p. 44.
"Sun in Winter. " NewRivR (2:1) 77, p. 51.
"The Village. " MassR (18:3) Aut 77, p. 607.
"Walking Home at Night, Drunk, through the Woods, Alone" (for
     Sayed and Inge). MichQR (16:1) Wint 77, p. 50.

FRUMKIN, Gene
"American Foreign Policy. " Bound (5:2) Wint 77, p. 607.

"Another Backward Glance." Bound (5:2) Wint 77, p. 609.
"Baird's Sandpiper." PoNow (14/18) 77, p. 44.
"Identity." Bound (5:2) Wint 77, p. 606.
"Terrorism." Bound (5:2) Wint 77, p. 608.
"That One." PoNow (14/18) 77, p. 44.
"White Paper Napkin." PoNow (14/18) 77, p. 44.

FUCHS, Alan
"Nursery Rhyme." PartR (44:2) 77, p. 248.
"With a Pressed Flower." PartR (44:2) 77, p. 248.
"The Wives of the Poets." PartR (44:2) 77, p. 249.

FULLEN, George
"Who Am I?" Wind (27) 77, p. 49.

FULLER, John
Eight poems. NewRep (176:22) 28 My 77, p. 29.

FULLER, Roy
"In His Sixty-Fifth Year." MinnR (NS8) Spr 77, p. 5.
"Musical Offering." SouthernPR (13:1) Wint 77, p. 149.

FUNG, David
"Ching P'ing Lo" (tr. of Li Yu, w. Julie Landau). DenQ (12:2)
    Sum 77, p. 351.
"Coming Down Chungnan Mountain and Staying with Hermit Hussy"
    (tr. of Li Po, w. Julie Landau). DenQ (12:2) Sum 77,
    p. 352.
"Drinking with a Hermit Friend in the Mountains" (tr. of Li Po,
    w. Julie Landau). DenQ (12:2) Sum 77, p. 352.
"Listening to a Flute at the Frontier" (tr. of Li Yi, w. Julie
    Landau). DenQ (12:2) Sum 77, p. 351.
"River Snow" (tr. of Liu Tsung Yuan, w. Julie Landau). DenQ
    (12:2) Sum 77, p. 351.

FUNK, Allison
"The Lake." Columbia (1) Aut 77, p. 23.

FUNKHOUSER, Erica
"The Blue in Beets." ParisR (70) Sum 77, p. 26.
"Fishing for Flounder." ParisR (70) Sum 77, p. 27.
"Teaching English to Gun Owners." AndR (4:1) Spr 77, p. 70.

FURTNEY, Diane
"Everypoet, Everyman" (For C. L. C.). PoetryNW (18:3) Aut 77,
    p. 33.
"North Winter, Crocodile." Iowa (8:4) Aut 77, p. 93.
"Mrs. Renfrow Speaks from Her Garden (A Voice at 52)." Wind
    (25) 77, p. 8.
"Night Raid." PoetryNW (18:3) Aut 77, p. 34.

FURY, Lucinda Turner
"Last Call." CarouselQ (2:2) Aut 77, p. 29.

GABBARD, G. N.
"'R. S. V. P. '" NewL (43:4) Sum 77, p. 26.

GAGE, John
"Eavesdroppers." Shen (28:4) Sum 77, p. 92.
Nine couplets (after Ghalib). Epoch (26:3) Spr 77, p. 230.

GALANG, Deanna
"one day after school." SeC (5:2) 78, p. 18.

GALASSI, Jonathan
from Diario del '71 e del '72: Eight poems (tr. of Eugenio
   Montale). Pequod (2:2) Wint 77, pp. 20-27.
"Harmony" (tr. of Eugenio Montale). Pequod (2:2) Wint 77,
   p. 31.
"Memory" (tr. of Eugenio Montale). Pequod (2:2) Wint 77,
   p. 30.
"Saving Minutes." Pequod (2:3) Sum 77, p. 75.
"Talking Birds" (tr. of Eugenio Montale). Pequod (2:2) Wint 77,
   p. 29.
"To Pio Rajna" (tr. of Eugenio Montale). Pequod (2:2) Wint 77,
   p. 28.

GALLAGHER, Tess
"The Ritual of Memories." AmerPoR (6:3) My-Je 77, p. 48.
"Still Moment at Dun Loaghaire" (for Stevie). QW (3) Spr-Sum
   77, p. 32.

GALLER, David
"From Lotos Island." MichQR (16:1) Wint 77, p. 48.
"The Plague." Humanist (37:3) My-Je 77, p. 55.

GALLO, Louis
"Nostalgia." Bits (6) Jl 77.

GALLOWAY, Betty
"amor seca." Shen (28:4) Sum 77, p. 50.

GALVIN, Brendan
"Bear's Heart with Love Doth Fry with Fear Doth Freeze."
   LittleR (12) 77, p. 6.
"The Birds." Chowder (9) Aut-Wint 77, p. 42.
"Christmas in the Summer Colony." PoNow (14/18) 77,
   p. 45.
"Fear of Gray's Anatomy." ParisR (70) Sum 77, p. 44.
"For the Way Home." ConcPo (10:1) Spr 77, p. 4.
"Glass." NewYorker (53:28) 29 Ag 77, p. 30.
"Goodbye." PoetryNW (18:3) Aut 77, p. 37.
"Jumping the Grave-Sized Hole." PoetryNW (18:3) Aut 77,
   p. 35.
"Listening to the Summer House in Winter." PoNow (14/18) 77,
   p. 45.
"North-Northeast." NewYorker (53:13) 16 My 77, p. 130.

"A Photo of Miners." NewYorker (53:11) 2 My 77, p. 100.
"Running." PoetryNW (18:2) Sum 77, p. 26.
"Them." ParisR (70) Sum 77, p. 43.

GALVIN, James
  "A Discrete Love Poem." AntR (35:1) Wint 77, p. 62.
  "Everyone Knows Whom the Saved Envy." Antaeus (27) Aut 77,
    p. 111.
  "For Remembering How to Live Without You." Antaeus (27) Aut
    77, p. 113.
  "Fugue for a Drowned Girl." OhioR (18:3) Aut 77, p. 25.
  "A Lemon Ode for Neruda." Nat (225:11) 8 O 77, p. 342.
  "Notes for the First Line of a Spanish Poem." Nat (224:20) 21
    My 77, p. 629.
  "Rosary of Conspiracies." Nat (225:16) 12 N 77, p. 502.
  "Something to Save Us." Nat (224:24) 18 Je 77, p. 758.
  "The Stone's Throw." Nat (225:8) 17 S 77, p. 246.
  "That Falling We Fall." Nat (224:17) 30 Ap 77, p. 534.
  "Totem." PoNow (14/18) 77, p. 46.

GAMMILL, William
  "That Was the Clearest Moment of His Life." MontG (6) Aut 77,
    p. 71.

GANTZ, Jeffrey
  "The Ark" (tr. of Eugenio Montale). PraS (51:3) Aut 77, p. 257.
  "If they have likened you" (tr. of Eugenio Montale). PraS (51:3)
    Aut 77, p. 258.
  "In Sleep" (tr. of Eugenio Montale). PraS (51:3) Aut 77, p. 259.
  "Letter" (tr. of Salvatore Quasimodo). MichQR (16:1) Wint 77,
    p. 11.
  "Towers." Icarus (5:1) Spr 77, p. 13.

GARAI, Gábor
  "Vigil at Dawn" (tr. by Daniel Hoffman). NewRep (176:13) 26
    Mr 77, p. 30.

GARCIA, Germán Pardo
  "Os dije: amad primero a la Naturaleza." GRR (8:1/2) 77,
    p. 114.

GARCIA, Lou
  "The Boy." Vaga (25) 77, p. 56.
  "The Musicians." Vaga (25) 77, p. 56.

GARDNER, Geoffrey
  "Alarm" (tr. of Jules Supervielle). VirQR (53:4) Aut 77,
    p. 679.
  "Black Ants" (tr. of Jean Follain). WebR (3:4) Aut 77, p. 46.
  "47 Boulevard Lannes" (tr. of Jules Supervielle). VirQR (53:4)
    Aut 77, p. 677.
  "Natural" (tr. of Jean Follain). WebR (3:4) Aut 77, p. 47.
  "Presence" (tr. of Jean Follain). WebR (3:4) Aut 77, p. 46.

"Projection" (tr. of Jules Supervielle). VirQR (53:4) Aut 77,
   p. 681.
"Seed Dealer" (tr. of Jean Follain). WebR (3:4) Aut 77, p. 47.

GARDNER, Isabella
   "The Telephone." Poetry (130:4) Jl 77, p. 208.

GARDNER, Lewis
   "At the Maytag." US1 (10) Wint 77-78, p. 11.
   "'Could Reinhold Niebuhr love a worm? I doubt it. But I--we--
     can.' Theodore Roethke." US1 (10) Wint 77-78, p. 11.
   "Moxie." Columbia (1) Aut 77, p. 24.

GARDNER, Stephen
   "Going Home." NewOR (5:3) 77, p. 208.
   "Taking Pictures." SouthernPR (16:SI) 77, p. 29.

GARDNER, Thomas
   "Ferry Bluff." Northeast (3:3) Sum 77, p. 40.

GARFINKEL, Patricia
   "Cricket Music." HolCrit (14:5) D 77, p. 7.

GARIN, Marita
   "Blackberry Hill." GRR (8:1/2) 77, p. 66.
   "Nexus." GRR (8:1/2) 77, p. 65.

GARLAND, Max
   "At Six-Thirty." Wind (26) 77, p. 26.
   "The Morning After." SouthernPR (17:1) Spr 77, p. 26.
   "Where They Buried Her Husband." Wind (26) 77, p. 26.

GARMON, John
   "All Day Week Days." SouthernHR (11:2) Spr 77, p. 157.
   "Field Mice." PoetL (72:1) Spr 77, p. 24.
   "Spilling the Sun in Translation." SoDakR (15:2) Sum 77, p. 49.

GARNER, Sky
   "Desperate Acts versus Desperation." MontG (6) Aut 77, p. 3.
   "The Jagged Edge of Eden." MontG (6) Aut 77, p. 4.
   "Ode to the Beast and Shiva." MontG (6) Aut 77, p. 6.
   "the open end of a dream." MontG (6) Aut 77, p. 5.

GARRETT, George
   "York Harbor Morning." SouthernPR (16:SI) 77, p. 30.

GARRISON, Joseph
   "First Sabbatical." Wind (25) 77, p. 17.
   "In the Quiet." Chowder (8) Spr-Sum 77, p. 36.
   "Looking at Beef." Box (5) Spr 77, p. 8.
   "A Psalm." Wind (25) 77, p. 17.

GARRISON, Peggy
   "There Was That Time." PoNow (14/18) 77, p. 46.

GARST, Tom
"Poetry Wanted. " CarlMis (16:1/2) Aut-Wint 76-77, p. 20.

GARTEE, Richard
"Fifteen. " AAR (27) 77, p. 92.
"Ken. " AAR (27) 77, p. 91.
"Unity. " AAR (27) 77, p. 91.

GASS, William
"The Statues. " NewYorker (53:42) 5 D 77, p. 48.

GASSER, Frederick
"Art Lesson. " CarouselQ (2:2) Aut 77, p. 23.
"Insomnia. " CarouselQ (2:3) Wint 77, p. 5.

GAST, David K.
"B-29742-Z. " PoNow (14/18) 77, p. 46.

GATENBY, Greg
"ddoouubbllee. " ArizQ (33:1) Spr 77, p. 60.
"Debra II. " DeKalb (10:2) Wint 77, p. 32.
"Sucker. " DeKalb (10:2) Wint 77, p. 33.
"Terry's Comment. " Aspect (70) Ja-Mr 77, p. 53.
"To Gatenby 2030 A. D. " PoetL (72:1) Spr 77, p. 22.

GATTEN, Tom
"Churning out from the East River. " Shen (28:4) Sum 77, p. 94.
"Rained Out. " PoNow (14/18) 77, p. 46.
"Visiting Walt Whitman's House" (For Sandy). PoNow (14/18) 77,
    p. 46.

GAVIN, Julianne
"Insomnia VIII" [for Pop, my Grandfather (Martin Gavin)].
    Ploughs (4:1) 77, p. 163.

GAY, Harriet
"Creators and Spectators. " NewRena (9) F 77, p. 6.

GEARY, Patricia
"Louisiana Likes Me. " MontG (5) Wint 77, p. 24.
"The Way He Makes Her Feel She Retreats into New Orleans. "
    MontG (5) Wint 77, p. 22.

GELERNTER, David
"Kiddush. " LitR (20:3) Spr 77, p. 318.
"Ode. " LitR (20:3) Spr 77, p. 317.

GELLER, Conrad
"Pastoral. " Wind (24) 77, p. 20.

GELPÍ, José Manuel Cuscó
from El Arquero Proscrito: "Es Mejor Olvidar. " GRR (8:1/2)
    77, p. 74.

GENSLER, Kinereth
"It Happens in a Foreign Country." Shen (28:4) Sum 77, p. 53.

GENTLEMAN, Dorothy Corbett
"The Empty House." Wind (27) 77, p. 19.
"From the Gondola." Wind (27) 77, p. 19.

GEORGE, Emery
"Elegy, or Icon, Nailless" (tr. of Miklós Radnóti). WebR (3:4)
    Aut 77, p. 49.
"Homage to Edward Hopper." ModernPS (8:3) Wint 77, p. 253.
"On a Rhine Excursion." ModernPS (8:3) Wint 77, p. 252.
"Pranksters." ModernPS (8:3) Wint 77, p. 247.
"Solstice." Poetry (130:5) Ag 77, p. 249.

GERBER, Dan
"Being Who I Am." PoNow (14/18) 77, p. 47.
"Meditation on Nothing." PoNow (14/18) 77, p. 47.
"The Story of I." PoNow (14/18) 77, p. 47.
"Sunday Morning." PoNow (14/18) 77, p. 47.

GERGELY, Agnes
"Crazed Man in Concentration Camp" (tr. by Edwin Morgan).
    AmerPoR (6:3) My-Je 77, p. 25.

GERMAN, Brad
"The Sleeve." Bits (6) Jl 77.

GERNER, Ken
"Summer Solstice." MontG (5) Wint 77, p. 49.

GERNERT, David
"Shore Morning." StoneC (77:3) S 77, p. 24.

GERNES, Sonia
"Moon for My Grandmother's Grand'mère." SouthernHR (11:1)
    Wint 77, p. 6.
"Reading Pooh without Parachutes" (for Payson Oberg). KanQ
    (9:1) Wint 77, p. 110.

GERSHATOR, David
"O. D. on the Antidote." Confr (14) Spr-Sum 77, p. 140.

GERSHENSON, Bernard
"Mother Lode." MissR (6:1) 77, p. 138.
"A Note to My Brother on His Way to Jupiter." CalQ (11/12)
    Wint-Spr 77, p. 50.

GERSHGOREN, Sid
"Our Child Is Arriving." CalQ (11/12) Wint-Spr 77, p. 47.

GERTSCHEN, G.
"Difficult Balance." PoetL (72:2) Sum 77, p. 56.

GERY, John
   "Casting the Rear Bumper Guard." ChiR (29:1) Sum 77, p. 126.
   "Charlemagne at Macy's." ChiR (29:1) Sum 77, p. 127.

GESS, D. P.
   "Perspective." CarouselQ (2:3) Wint 77, p. 6.

GHIGNA, Charles
   "Divers." SouthernPR (16:SI) 77, p. 31.
   "Night Wash." YellowBR (9) 77, p. 29.
   "Samuel." EngJ (66:5) My 77, p. 47.
   "The Suicide Poets." Juice (4) 77.

GHISELIN, Brewster
   "Return to the North." WestHR (31:4) Aut 77, p. 330.

GHITELMAN, David
   "Love Song." AntR (35:1) Wint 77, p. 65.

GHOSSEIN, Mirene
   "Three Poems" (tr. of Abdel-Kader Arnaut). Mund (10:1) 77,
     p. 188.

GIBB, Robert
   "The Adorations." DacTerr (14) Spr-Sum 77, p. 64.
   "The Dream Animal." Chowder (8) Spr-Sum 77, p. 34.
   "The Man Whose Leg Was Asleep." MissR (6:1) 77, p. 150.
   "The Minotaur." NewL (43:4) Sum 77, p. 100.
   "New Year's Eve." MissR (6:1) 77, p. 151.
   "Osprey." HolCrit (14:5) D 77, p. 14.
   "Picking Wild Berries Near Stine's Corner, Pennsylvania."
     PoNow (14/18) 77, p. 48.
   "Some Reflections on the Sun." Chowder (9) Aut-Wint 77, p. 24.
   "Spring." EnPas (6) 77, p. 25.
   "Summer Evening, 1954." MissR (6:1) 77, p. 152.

GIBBONS, Reginald
   "The Gods in Virginia." SouthernR (13:4) Aut 77, p. 752.
   "The Homecoming." Iowa (8:4) Aut 77, p. 90.

GIBBS, Sheri
   "Why Paris." WebR (3:1) Wint 77, p. 62.

GIBSON, Margaret
   "August List." Shen (28:4) Sum 77, p. 91.
   "Illness and Idleness." MinnR (NS8) Spr 77, p. 44.

GIBSON, Stephen M.
   "Sestina: Of the Pain." MissR (6:1) 77, p. 72.

GIFFORD, Barry
   "Ahetenrai." Hand (1) 77, p. 181.

GIL
"a chant for breath reproduction in celebration. " Hand (1) 77,
p. 46.

GILBERT, Jack
Eight poems. Esq (88:2) Ag 77, p. 125.
Eleven poems. Esq (87:1) Ja 77, p. 124.

GILBERT, Richard
"Late at Night You Can Hear Them Clicking. " US1 (9) Spr 77,
p. 5.

GILBERT, Sandra M.
"Bright Venus, glowing, wandering in Heaven" (tr. of Louise
Labé). CalQ (11/12) Wint-Spr 77, p. 76.
"Daphne. " PoetryNW (18:2) Sum 77, p. 24.
"Elegy. " Poetry (131:2) N 77, p. 68.
"Evening/Mirror/Poem. " CornellR (2) Aut 77, p. 73.
"Godly Diana, breathing hard, because" (tr. of Louise Labé).
CalQ (11/12) Wint-Spr 77, p. 77.
"Her House. " BelPoJ (27:3) Spr 77, p. 2.
"I live, I'm dead, as though I'm cut in half" (tr. of Louise Labé).
CalQ (11/12) Wint-Spr 77, p. 77.
"Ladies, don't blame me for loving. Please don't scorn" (tr. of
Louise Labé). CalQ (11/12) Wint-Spr 77, p. 78.
"Metastasis. " SouthernPR (17:1) Spr 77, p. 45.
"The minute I fall asleep I dream of you" (tr. of Louise Labé).
CalQ (11/12) Wint-Spr 77, p. 76.
"The Night Grandma Died. " 13thM (3:2) 77, p. 25.
"Not even Ulysses had it as bad as this" (tr. of Louise Labé).
CalQ (11/12) Wint-Spr 77, p. 75.
"On the Third Hand. " PoetryNW (18:2) Sum 77, p. 22.
"Sculpture: Naiad/Fountain. " Poetry (131:2) N 77, p. 67.
"Spinster. " PoetryNW (18:2) Sum 77, p. 23.
"Still Life: Old Woman with Apples. " CornellR (2) Aut 77,
p. 71.
"Still Life: Woman in Frog Mask. " CornellR (2) Aut 77, p. 72.
"What good does it do me sweetheart, that you once" (tr. of
Louise Labé). CalQ (11/12) Wint-Spr 77, p. 78.

GILBERT, Virginia
"The Flights of Otis Wicher. " PoNow (14/18) 77, p. 48.
"The Vision. " DeKalb (10:3) Spr 77, p. 16.

GILBOA, Amir
"By the Waters of Babylon" (tr. by Robert Alter). TriQ (39)
Spr 77, p. 268.
from Gazelle, I'll Send You: "Prologue" and (1-15) (tr. by
Shirley Kaufman and Shlomit Rimmon). TriQ (39) Spr 77,
p. 261.
"Samson" (tr. by Stephen Mitchell). TriQ (39) Spr 77, p. 267.
"To My City Jerusalem, 1967" (tr. by Shirley Kaufman and
Shlomit Rimmon). TriQ (39) Spr 77, p. 266.

GILCHRIST, Ellen
"Dr. Davis Watches His Muscular Dystrophy Daughter Do Her
    Dance." CalQ (11/12) Wint-Spr 77, p. 125.
"Dream Song." CalQ (11/12) Wint-Spr 77, p. 124.

GILDNER, Gary
"The Blue Moth." Chowder (8) Spr-Sum 77, p. 38.
"Ice Shanties." NewL (44:2) Wint 77, p. 65.
"In the Beginning." NewL (44:2) Wint 77, p. 66.
"A Memory." NewL (44:1) Aut 77, p. 76.
"My Father after Work." NewL (44:2) Wint 77, p. 64.
"The Page Turner." AmerR (26) N 77, p. 135.
"Scraping the Front Porch." PoNow (14/18) 77, p. 48.
"Toads in the Greenhouse." PoetryNW (18:2) Sum 77, p. 28.

GILDZEN, Alex
"& Such." Mouth (13) D 77, p. 20.
"Nothin' Could Be Finer" (for Jonathan & Tom). Mouth (13) D
    77, p. 20.

GILEAD, Zerubavel
"Chosen Land" (tr. by Dorothea Krook). TriQ (39) Spr 77, p. 268.
"Ibn Gvirol" (tr. by Dorothea Krook). TriQ (39) Spr 77, p. 269.

GILL, John
"The Mercury Poems." PoNow (14/18) 77, p. 50.

GILL, Kathy
"At Night I hear a creaking sound from my." AAR (27) 77, p. 109.

GILLESPIE, Jonathan
"Complaint against Sensual Dreams." SouthernPR (16:SI) 77,
    p. 32.
"Survivor." Poetry (130:2) My 77, p. 80.

GILLESPIE, Robert
"Floundering for Firewood in Deep Snow in Maine, I Flash on
    Dorothy Molter's Life and Then on Three Times in My Own."
    PoetryNW (18:3) Aut 77, p. 43.
"Liberation." NewL (43:3) Spr 77, p. 51.

GILLESPIE, Tim
"End of the Season." EngJ (66:5) My 77, p. 53.

GILLEY, Leonard
"Malfi." DenQ (12:3) Aut 77, p. 20.
"Ritual." SouthwR (62:2) Spr 77, p. 147.

GILMAN, Dugan
"Field Days." PoNow (14/18) 77, p. 51.

GILMAN, Milton
"Bertholt Brecht." ArizQ (33:2) Sum 77, p. 120.

GILMAN, Roger
"The Plains around Rainy Mountain." PoetryNW (18:1) Spr 77,
    p. 51.
"Words of a Dying Chief." PoetryNW (18:1) Spr 77, p. 51.

GILSDORF, Gordon
"Another Letter to Henry David Thoreau." BallSUF (18:2) Spr
    77, p. 65.

GILSON, Saul
"Lyric from Earth." NewRena (9) F 77, p. 39.

GIMELSON, Deborah
"Derain." AntR (35:1) Wint 77, p. 66.

GINGERICH, Willard
"Hymn of Teotihuacan." Rapp (10) 77, p. 81.
"Jaina Statuette." Rapp (10) 77, p. 84.
"Xochipilli, His Song." Rapp (10) 77, p. 82.

GINSBERG, Louis
"Letter to My Two Sons." PoNow (14/18) 77, p. 52.
from Lines Before I Fall Asleep: "Sometimes, I lie in darkness,
    musing how." MidwQ (18:2) Wint 77, p. 203.
"Somewhere." PoNow (14/18) 77, p. 52.
"Two on Porch." MidwQ (18:2) Wint 77, p. 203.

GINTER, Laurel
"Another Nightmare Visit by Elizabeth." CimR (39) Ap 77,
    p. 54.

GIPE, Ann
"Killer Fog." Wind (24) 77, p. 53.

GITIN, David
"Another Song for Maria." LaB (8) Jl-Ag 77, p. 21.
"Horizon (#2)" (for Michael Palmer). LaB (8) Jl-Ag 77, p. 21.
"Letter (#2)." Hills (4) 77.
"Love You." LaB (8) Jl-Ag 77, p. 22.
"The Measure." Hills (4) 77.
"Miles Beyond." LaB (8) Jl-Ag 77, p. 21.
"Pacific Grove." LaB (8) Jl-Ag 77, p. 22.

GITLIN, Todd
"Screws Loose." PoNow (14/18) 77, p. 51.

GLASER, Elton
"Delta Blues." PoNow (14/18) 77, p. 53.
"The Gift." ChiR (29:2) Aut 77, p. 117.
"The Middle Way." PoNow (14/18) 77, p. 52.
"Night Letter." PoetryNW (18:3) Aut 77, p. 13.

GLASER, Michael S.
"Voices." Poem (29) Mr 77, p. 6.

GLASGOW, Mary
"Rock Road Farm, A Visit." Xa (4) 77, p. 56.

GLASS, Adam
"Kite." HarvAd (110:3) Mr 77, p. 7.

GLASS, Jesse, Jr.
"Never Too Old." SmPd (14:1) Wint 77, p. 11.

GLASS, Malcolm
"Braille." NewOR (5:3) 77, p. 197.
"Drowning." NewOR (5:3) 77, p. 198.
"Hunting Spiders" (for Oather Van Hyning). BallSUF (18:4) Aut
    77, p. 78.
"Jar." Drag (16) 77.
"Seeing." SewanR (85:3) Sum 77, p. 456.

GLASSER, Barry
"Everything I hated about you." PoNow (14/18) 77, p. 53.

GLAZE, Andrew
"Address." SouthernPR (17:2) Aut 77, p. 29.
"Back Lot." SouthernPR (17:2) Aut 77, p. 28.
"Banquet." Iowa (8:1) Wint 77, p. 56.
"A Child." Iowa (8:1) Wint 77, p. 57.
"Dr. Freud." Atl (239:6) Je 77, p. 81.
"Elevation." Iowa (8:4) Aut 77, p. 68.
"Eyes of the Heart." NewYorker (53:4) 14 Mr 77, p. 40.
"Fantasy Street." NewYorker (53:8) 11 Ap 77, p. 40.
"A Guide." PoNow (14/18) 77, p. 53.
"An Honorary Hapsburg." CalQ (11/12) Wint-Spr 77, p. 56.
"The People of My Head." PoNow (14/18) 77, p. 53.
"Separation Is Best." PoNow (14/18) 77, p. 53.
"September." NewYorker (53:29) 5 S 77, p. 32.

GLAZIER, Lyle
"Pilgrim from New England." Paunch (48/49) S 77, p. 181.

GLEN, Emilie
"Best Skirt." Juice (5) 77.
"Dark Steep in the Sun." Juice (5) 77.
"Do See." Juice (5) 77.
"Have." Juice (5) 77.
"Just Before." StoneC (77:3) S 77, p. 20.
"Looka." Juice (5) 77.
"The Way." Juice (5) 77.
"Whoople Lane." Juice (5) 77.

GLENN, Karen
"Poem: At the cannery." DenQ (11:4) Wint 77, p. 23.

GLÜCK, Louise
"The Blind Girl." NewYorker (53:6) 28 Mr 77, p. 111.

"The Dream of Mourning." Salm (38/39) Sum-Aut 77, p. 101.
"Epithalamium." Salm (38/39) Sum-Aut 77, p. 101.
"Illuminations." NewYorker (52:46) 3 Ja 77, p. 34.
"Three for Tom Absher." Salm (38/39) Sum-Aut 77, p. 100.

GOAD, Craig M.
"Two Moons." KanQ (9:1) Wint 77, p. 104.

GOEBEL, Ulf
"Not for Provocation." Paunch (48/49) S 77, p. 83.

GOEDICKE, Patricia
"Al's Underground Market." DacTerr (14) Spr-Sum 77, p. 6.
"The Beautiful Building of the Present." AmerPoR (6:2) Mr-Ap
    77, p. 41.
"Crossing the Same River." NewL (44:2) Wint 77, p. 96.
"The Enemy Within." SouthernPR (17:1) Spr 77, p. 10.
"Fish Story." Chowder (9) Aut-Wint 77, p. 27.
from For the Four Corners: "In the Hospital." PoNow (14/18)
    77, p. 56.
from For the Four Corners: "My Mother's/My/Death/Birthday."
    PoNow (14/18) 77, p. 56.
"For the Path She Must Follow." Harp (255:1526) Jl 77, p. 72.
"How Central It Is." NewL (44:1) Aut 77, p. 93.
"I Said I Would Not be Choked." SouthernPR (17:2) Aut 77,
    p. 71.
"In the Body Shop." DacTerr (14) Spr-Sum 77, p. 7.
"In the Market." Confr (14) Spr-Sum 77, p. 108.
"In the Sinai." Wind (27) 77, p. 22.
"In Spite of the Danger of Forest Fires." PoNow (14/18) 77,
    p. 54.
"Inside Every Machine There's a Human." QW (2) Wint 77,
    p. 10.
"Knock on Any Door." ParisR (70) Sum 77, p. 29.
"Landscape." Ascent (3:1) 77, p. 41.
"Letter to King Love." Wind (27) 77, p. 21.
"The Line." Wind (27) 77, p. 22.
"The Mailman." PoNow (14/18) 77, p. 54.
"Miss America, Sounding Off." PoNow (14/18) 77, p. 54.
"The Prayer Against Sickness." Ascent (3:1) 77, p. 42.
"Shredded Wheat." PoNow (14/18) 77, p. 54.
"Though It Looks Clever It Is Not." NewL (44:1) Aut 77, p. 94.
"Towards Delphi." AmerPoR (6:2) Mr-Ap 77, p. 40.
"Two Weeks." Shen (28:3) Spr 77, p. 100.
"The White Horses." Chowder (9) Aut-Wint 77, p. 26.

GOGOL, John M.
"In Haste" (tr. of Tadeusz Różewicz). WebR (3:4) Aut 77, p. 37.
"Lyric" (tr. of Harij Skuja). WebR (3:4) Aut 77, p. 36.
"Night Mood" (tr. of Robert Weber). WebR (3:4) Aut 77, p. 35.
"On Perseverance" (tr. of Robert Weber). WebR (3:4) Aut 77,
    p. 34.

GOLD, Sid
  "I slowly." RemR (5) 77, p. 97.

GOLDBARTH, Albert
  "Against Disaster." MinnR (NS9) Aut 77, p. 18.
  "Alternate Versions." Drag (16) 77.
  "The Always." Drag (16) 77.
  "Balance/Mullion." MidwQ (18:4) Sum 77, p. 441.
  "Bar Darkened." Chowder (9) Aut-Wint 77, p. 39.
  "Beneath the K. A." (toward homilies for Ginnie). CutB (8) Spr
      77, p. 20.
  "Bin" (for KSD). BelPoJ (28:2) Wint 77-78, p. 28.
  "Centuries." Kayak (46) O 77, p. 59.
  "Contract." PoetryNW (18:3) Aut 77, p. 50.
  "Crawl." KanQ (9:4) Aut 77, p. 47.
  "The Depth We Reach in Some Paper." Falcon (15) 77, p. 23.
  "The Errors--Central YMCA Community College, 1971-73." Shen
      (28:2) Wint 77, p. 92.
  "Evolution: A Song." MidwQ (18:4) Sum 77, p. 443.
  "The Evolution of Equus." AmerPoR (6:2) Mr-Ap 77, p. 42.
  "The Family Business." CarolQ (29:3) Aut 77, p. 19.
  "Getting Out the Album." MidwQ (19:1) Aut 77, p. 56.
  "The Gland Upstate." DacTerr (14) Spr-Sum 77, p. 59.
  "Hate." SouthernPR (17:1) Spr 77, p. 49.
  "A Journal of Cope." Shen (28:4) Sum 77, p. 87.
  "A Little Whet." MidwQ (18:4) Sum 77, p. 440.
  "My Covenant with Old Thundermug." ConcPo (10:2) Aut 77,
      p. 35.
  "Nostalgia." Drag (16) 77.
  "The Origin of Porno." NewYRB (24:6) 14 Ap 77, p. 7.
  "Other." CutB (9) Aut-Wint 77, p. 35.
  "The Paean: One Cent." Confr (14) Spr-Sum 77, p. 52.
  "Painter." Bits (6) Jl 77.
  "Phylacteries." Shen (28:4) Sum 77, p. 90.
  "Poem Again: Of Duplication." PoetryNW (18:3) Aut 77, p. 51.
  "Read." MidwQ (18:4) Sum 77, p. 444.
  "Recipe." PraS (51:2) Sum 77, p. 194.
  from The Saint of Beef: "An Animal Works." PraS (51:2) Sum
      77, p. 193.
  from The Saint of Beef: "The Tale of Piety." PraS (51:2) Sum
      77, p. 195.
  "Silence." MidwQ (18:4) Sum 77, p. 442.
  "Silk." AmerPoR (6:2) Mr-Ap 77, p. 42.
  "Sleepsong." CutB (9) Aut-Wint 77, p. 38.
  "Song: Goodbye." MidwQ (18:4) Sum 77, p. 445.
  "Theory of Entropy." AmerPoR (6:2) Mr-Ap 77, p. 43.
  "Venom." PoNow (14/18) 77, p. 55.
  "The Way of All Flash." ConcPo (10:2) Aut 77, p. 36.
  "What We Know of Evolution." AmerPoR (6:2) Mr-Ap 77, p. 43.
  "What They Don't Say in the High School Text on Spontaneous
      Combustion." PoetryNW (18:1) Spr 77, p. 38.
  "Wichita" (-KSD). CutB (9) Aut-Wint 77, p. 36.

GOLDENSOHN, Barry
"Our Other Mind Problem. " Ploughs (3:3/4) 77, p. 160.
"To the Author of a Single Poem. " MissR (6:1) 77, p. 148.

GOLDENSOHN, Lorrie
"Letter for a Daughter. " Ploughs (3:3/4) 77, p. 102.

GOLDMAN, Beate
"Towards an Organized Universe. " Chelsea (36) 77, p. 19.

GOLDMAN, Dona Lu
"Home Town. " Aspect (69) O-D 76, p. 30.
"Italy. " Aspect (69) O-D 76, p. 29.
"This Rose Petal. " Aspect (69) O-D 76, p. 29.

GOLDMAN, Maximilian
"Mother's Day, 1976. " SouthernPR (17:1) Spr 77, p. 47.

GOLDSBERRY, Steven
"Witch Teeth. " PoetryNW (18:3) Aut 77, p. 48.

GOLDSTEIN, Henry
"Day of Atonement" (To Dorothy). Salm (38/39) Sum-Aut 77,
    p. 110.
"Listening to Kunitz Read Voznesensky. " CarolQ (29:3) Aut 77,
    p. 118.

GOLDSTEIN, Laurence
"Amazon River Solitaries. " AAR (27) 77, p. 15.

GOLDSTEIN, Sanford
"Six Tanka. " Sparrow (33) Ja 77, p. 24.

GOLDWIN, Seth
"Birth Copulation Death. " NewC (7:3) 75-76, p. 12.
"Oil. " NewC (8:1) 76-77, p. 5.

GOLFFING, Francis
"The Question. " NewYorker (53:38) 7 N 77, p. 58.

GOLLUB, Christian-Albrecht
"Ode on an Asparagus Spear. " DeKalb (10:2) Wint 77, p. 34.
"Rose Hips' Tea Time. " DeKalb (10:2) Wint 77, p. 34.
"Tale. " DeKalb (10:2) Wint 77, p. 34.

GOMEZ, Dario Ruiz
"Poem: To startle yourself" (tr. by Sandra Cisneros). DenQ
    (12:1) Spr 77, p. 153.

GONZALEZ, Angel
Thirteen poems. TexQ (20:1) Spr 77, pp. 6-35.

GONZALEZ, N. V. M.
"Memo to a Survivor. " GreenR (6:1/2) Spr 77, p. 56.

GONZALEZ-GERTH, Miguel
"Dead Virgins" (tr. of Olavo Bilac). TexQ (19:4) Wint 76, p. 97.
"The Musicians and Other Poems." TexQ (20:3) Aut 77, pp. 85-
    130.
"My Death Was Born Along with Me" (tr. of Marío de Miranda
    Quintana). TexQ (19:4) Wint 76, p. 99.
Thirteen poems (tr. of Angel Gonzalez). TexQ (20:1) Spr 77,
    pp. 6-35.
"Twenty Centuries of Revolt" (tr. of Jorge de Lima). TexQ
    (19:4) Wint 76, p. 99.

GOOD, Ruth
"Censoring Children's Books." PoNow (14/18) 77, p. 55.
"The Safari." PoNow (14/18) 77, p. 55.

GOODE, James B.
"Filling a Gully." Wind (24) 77, p. 34.
"Song of Sorrow." Wind (24) 77, p. 33.
"The University of Life." NewC (7:3) 75-76, p. 29.

GOODING, Cynthia
"Ariadne and Cora Walking in the Garden." US1 (9) Spr 77,
    p. 8.
"The Easy Way." US1 (9) Spr 77, p. 2.

GOODISON, Lorna
"For the Poet at Fort Augusta." Nimrod (21:2/22:1) 77, p. 90.
"Ocho Rios." Nimrod (21:2/22:1) 77, p. 88.

GOODMAN, Alice
"Elegy on a Seventeenth-century Gentleman" (after Aubrey).
    HarvAd (110:5) My 77, p. 21.
"To Peter, who is painting a map of the world." HarvAd (111:2)
    D 77, p. 17.

GOODMAN, Judith
"On Hunting Words at Night." PoetL (72:2) Sum 77, p. 70.
"Sampler." PoetL (72:2) Sum 77, p. 70.

GOODMAN, Ryah Tumarkin
"Ancestors." Poem (29) Mr 77, p. 54.
"The Business of Living." NewRep (177:6/7) 6-13 Ag 77, p. 36.
"Loving Is Losing." Poem (29) Mr 77, p. 55.
"The Others." Poem (29) Mr 77, p. 53.

GOODPASTER, H. K.
"Under My Eyelids." CarouselQ (2:3) Wint 77, p. 20.

GOODWYN, Frank
"To Nancy Hanks Lincoln." JnlOPC (11:2) Aut 77, p. 358.

GORBANEVSKAYA, Natalya
"Not in an airplane's wing" (tr. by Daniel Weissbort). DenQ
    (11:4) Wint 77, p. 24.

GORDETT, Marea
"Grandmother." DenQ (12:2) Sum 77, p. 228.
"In the Shoe Factory." DenQ (12:2) Sum 77, p. 229.

GORDON, Coco
"I am the waves resounding in." Xa (4) 77, p. 42.
"To Get Off a Theme: Beyond the Last Pier." Xa (4) 77, p. 44.
"The Visit." Confr (14) Spr-Sum 77, p. 109.

GORDON, Dane R.
"The Fire of Christ's Nearness." ChrC (94:42) 21 D 77, p. 1189.

GORDON, Don
"Ancestors." StoneC (77:2) My 77, p. 9.
"Days." Icarus (5:2) Aut 77, p. 18.
"The Fourth World." Harp (255:1526) Jl 77, p. 82.

GORDON, Donna
"Streetwalker." SmPd (14:3) Aut 77, p. 5.
"Visitor in the Cadaver Room." Ploughs (4:1) 77, p. 159.

GORDON, Leonore
"Cradle Song" (tr. of Yona Wallach). TriQ (39) Spr 77, p. 310.
"On Your Heart, Open" (tr. of Ya'ir Hurvitz, w. S. F. Chyet).
    TriQ (39) Spr 77, p. 278.
"When the Angels Are Exhausted" (tr. of Yona Wallach). TriQ
    (39) Spr 77, p. 309.
"Whispering in Me" (tr. of Ya'ir Hurvitz, w. S. F. Cheyet).
    TriQ (39) Spr 77, p. 277.
"Yonatan" (tr. of Yona Wallach). TriQ (39) Spr 77, p. 309.

GORDON, Robert
"One of Those Things." CEACritic (39:2) Ja 77, p. 27.
"Scène Pinteresque." CEACritic (39:2) Ja 77, p. 8.
"Upper-Class Clerihew." CEACritic (39:2) Ja 77, p. 24.

GÖRGEY, Gábor
"Anatomy of a Supper" (tr. by Jascha Kessler). AmerR (26) N
    77, p. 110.

GORHAM, Sarah
"Avenue des Bois: Armistice Day." AntR (35:1) Wint 77, p. 70.
"Northern Refuge." AntR (35:1) Wint 77, p. 69.

GORLIN, Debra
"Man River." QW (4) Aut 77, p. 110.

GORMAN, Michael
"Single-Shot B-B Rifle." PoNow (14/18) 77, p. 57.

GOULBOURNE, Jean L.
"Vida and Ant." Nimrod (21:2/22:1) 77, p. 91.

GOURI, Haim
"Cycle" (tr. by S. F. Chyet). TriQ (39) Spr 77, p. 274.
"Holiday's End" (tr. by S. F. Chyet). TriQ (39) Spr 77, p. 273.
"My Samsons" (tr. by S. F. Chyet). TriQ (39) Spr 77, p. 272.
"Some Words in Praise of My Friends" (tr. by Robert Friend).
    TriQ (39) Spr 77, p. 270.
"Tree Bone #18: The Dance of the Trees." PoetL (72:1) Spr
    77, p. 6.

GRABILL, James
"Goat Night." PoetryNW (18:3) Aut 77, p. 4.
"Guessing Song." PoetryNW (18:3) Aut 77, p. 3.
"Red Leaves." PortR (23) 77, p. 138.
"Sonata." Drag (16) 77.

GRABILL, Paul
"God's Lights." ChrC (94:23) 6-13 Jl 77, p. 623.

GRADY, Jack
"Dream of Tibet" (for Jeffrey Hopkins). LaB (8) Jl-Ag 77,
    p. 23.

GRADY, Naomi
"Aqua Vitae." Stonecloud (6) 76, p. 25.

GRAFFLIN, Marjorie
"I Remember Summer." WindO (28) Spr 77, p. 18.

GRAHAM, A. C.
"Song of the Madman of Ch'u" (tr. of Chuang-tzu). Montra (3)
    Spr 77, p. 5.

GRAHAM, Jorie
"How Morning Glories Could Bloom at Dusk." Nat (225:7) 10 S
    77, p. 214.

GRAHAM, Philip
"A Great Moment in Sports." Some (7/8) 76.
"Ronald McDonald." Madrona (4:13/14) 77, p. 20.
"Weather." Juice (5) 77.

GRAHAM, Taylor
"Breaking Point." SouthwR (62:3) Sum 77, p. 268.
"The Family Smith." Stonecloud (6) 76, p. 30.
"Reflections in Ice." PortR (23) 77, p. 128.
"Walking across Turnagain." PortR (23) 77, p. 129.

GRANATO, Carole Anne
"Again at Dawn." CarouselQ (2:3) Wint 77, p. 28.

GRANGER, John
"An Exercise" (arr. of Jack Spicer, w. Robin Blaser). Bound
    (6:1) Aut 77, p. 3.

GRANT, J. B.
"3 Ages Loving." Stonecloud (6) 76, p. 25.

GRAPES, Marcus J.
"Break-Down." NewOR (5:3) 77, p. 275.
"Break-Down." Stonecloud (6) 76, p. 132.
"Emily's Dance." NewOR (5:3) 77, p. 274.
"Feeding Time." Vaga (25) 77, p. 10.
"going home To Watch My Brother." Stonecloud (6) 76, p. 29.
"I Can't Go On." Vaga (25) 77, p. 80.
"She Fucks and I Fuck." Vaga (25) 77, p. 81.
"That Place My Father Flew From." Stonecould (6) 76, p. 14.

GRASS, Günter
"Dein Ohr." ChiR (29:3) Wint 78, p. 110.
"Mein Schuh." ChiR (29:3) Wint 78, p. 112.

GRAVES, Robert
"The Bath in Pylos" (tr. of Gábor Devecseri). AmerPoR (6:3)
    My-Je 77, p. 24.

GRAVES, Steven
"Early Invitations." YaleR (66:3) Spr 77, p. 401.
"Small Anthem." Poetry (131:1) O 77, p. 19.

GRAY, Alice Wirth
"Sign Language." BelPoJ (27:3) Spr 77, p. 29.
"Victorian Diary: Fragment with Anachronisms." Chelsea (36)
    77, p. 47.

GRAY, Allan
"Aubade." Poetry (129:6) Mr 77, p. 335.
"A Family Argument." Poetry (129:6) Mr 77, p. 336.
"Two Theories for the Muses' Mother." Poetry (130:3) Je 77,
    p. 140.

GRAY, Darrell
"The Art of Poetry." Spirit (2:2/3) 77, p. 85.
"For George Oppen." Spirit (2:2/3) 77, p. 77.
"In June." Spirit (2:2/3) 77, p. 80.
"The Musical Ape." Spirit (2:2/3) 77, p. 79.
"Ode to Jibberish." Spirit (2:2/3) 77, p. 80.
"An Old Southern Critic Takes a Look at My Poems." Spirit
    (2:2/3) 77, p. 76.
"Sonnet for All Greeks Living Now." Spirit (2:2/3) 77, p. 78.

GRAY, Janet
"Mt. Rainier." HangL (31) Aut 77, p. 18.
"So You Won't Miscarry." HangL (31) Aut 77, p. 19.

GRAY, Nigel
"On Art." MinnR (NS9) Aut 77, p. 19.
"The Promise." MinnR (NS9) Aut 77, p. 20.

GRAY, Pat
"Old Seeds." 13thM (3:2) 77, p. 63.

GRAY, Patrick Worth
"Above My Head." LittleR (12) 77, p. 16.
"Beyond the Firehouse." LittleR (12) 77, p. 16.
"But Yesterday Is Now." Icarus (5:2) Aut 77, p. 5.
"Disappearances." CalQ (11/12) Wint-Spr 77, p. 57.
"Even Her Virtues Are Bad:" ColEng (38:8) Ap 77, p. 812.
"Final Draft 1984 Plan [Para 13b2.16-68]." GRR (8:1/2) 77,
    p. 73.
"Four for Debbie." Poem (30) Jl 77, p. 46.
"From the Deeps." Wind (26) 77, p. 27.
"Hearing Loss." ColEng (38:8) Ap 77, p. 812.
"House above the Sea." Poem (30) Jl 77, p. 44.
"Huh?" HiramPoR (22) Aut-Wint 77, p. 21.
"I Do Not Know the City." ChrC (94:8) 9 Mr 77, p. 225.
"I Have the One Suit." Poem (30) Jl 77, p. 45.
"Laughter." SouthernHR (11:1) Wint 77, p. 20.
"Marion." DenQ (12:3) Aut 77, p. 81.
"Martial's Epigrams" (tr.). PoetL (72:1) Spr 77, p. 26.
"Near Roe, Arkansas." Wind (26) 77, p. 27.
"Quatrina." AndR (3:2) Aut 76, p. 72.
"Ramirez." CEACritic (39:3) Mr 77, p. 34.
"The Room above Barber's Drug." Icarus (5:1) Spr 77, p. 3.
"A Story of a State." Sam (52) Ap 77, p. 19.
"Student Conferences." CarolQ (29:2) Spr-Sum 77, p. 76.
"Then and Now." DenQ (12:3) Aut 77, p. 80.
"Wild Geese." ChrC (94:36) 9 N 77, p. 1033.

GRAYDON, Ruth
"Reflections of a Minor Character." KanQ (9:1) Wint 77, p. 39.

GRAYSON, Richard
"Scenes from a Mirage: Atlantic City, March 1972." HangL
    (29) Wint 76-77, p. 4.

GRAYSTON, Joan Byers
"The Road." HiramPoR (22) Aut-Wint 77, p. 22.

GRAZIANO, Frank
"Basualto." BelPoJ (28:1) Aut 77, p. 12.
"Cuernavaca: Dia de los Muertos." CutB (8) Spr 77, p. 99.
"A Mission to Ch'u" (-for Laura). Falcon (14) 77, p. 93.

GREASYBEAR, Charley John
"Now Song" (transcribed by Judson Crews). PraS (51:1) Spr 77,
    p. 84.
"Song of Half Dying" (transcribed by Judson Crews). PraS (51:1)
    Spr 77, p. 85.

GREEN, Galen
"Along the Back Fence." PoNow (14/18) 77, p. 57.

"Love in the Woods." PoNow (14/18) 77, p. 57.

GREEN, Olivia
"Living." NegroHB (40:2) Mr-Ap 77, p. 684.
"Unsung Melody." NegroHB (40:5) S-O 77, p. 750.

GREEN, Samuel
"At My In-Laws' on Christmas Eve I Listen to my Son Celebrate the Christ." SouthernPR (17:1) Spr 77, p. 44.
"Comment/Exchange with a Student on the Last Day." PoetryNW (18:3) Aut 77, p. 30.
"Poem for the Weekend I read 35 Western Novels." FourQt (26:4) Sum 77, p. 28.
"Warming Up at Cape Alava." CutB (9) Aut-Wint 77, p. 32.
"Where the Lines Cross." CutB (9) Aut-Wint 77, p. 33.

GREENBERG, Alvin
"poem beginning with 'beginning' and ending with 'ending.'"
PoetryNW (18:4) Wint 77-78, p. 17.
"political poem." MinnR (NS9) Aut 77, p. 21.
"the world of apples." Ploughs (3:3/4) 77, p. 163.

GREENBERG, Barbara L.
"Sib." Qt (57/58) Wint-Spr 77, p. 36.
"Sometimes Her Dog Reminds Her of Her Dreams." Shen (28:2)
Wint 77, p. 103.
"Spindrift." Bits (6) Jl 77.
"A Young Mother, to Her Husband." Shen (28:2) Wint 77, p. 104.

GREENBERG, Harry
"Threatening the Lives of the Famous." PoNow (14/18) 77,
p. 57.

GREENBERG, Uri Zvi
"Song of the Great Mind" (tr. by Robert Friend). TriQ (39) Spr
77, p. 275.
from To God in Europe: "III. No other instances" (tr. by Robert Friend). TriQ (39) Spr 77, p. 276.

GREENE, Frances M.
"To My Cat Who Keeps Staring at Things." PoetL (72:2) Sum
77, p. 54.

GREENE, Jeffrey
"At Dusk." OhioR (18:3) Aut 77, p. 109.
"Block Island." Nat (224:17) 30 Ap 77, p. 534.
"Charleston R.I." Nat (225:16) 12 N 77, p. 508.
"Winter in Plainfield N.H." Nat (225:5) 20-27 Ag 77, p. 156.

GREENE, Richard L.
"On the 'Personal' Advertisements in the New York Review of
Books." CEACritic (39:3) Mr 77, p. 20.

GREENWALD, Ted
　"A Cloud Light." SunM (4) Aut 77, p. 89.
　"Collected Works." LaB (8) Jl-Ag 77, p. 25.
　"Dark Near Green." SunM (4) Aut 77, p. 87.
　"A Picture Pushes You." Hills (4) 77.
　"She Wore." LaB (8) Jl-Ag 77, p. 29.
　"String." Hills (4) 77.
　"The Table." LaB (8) Jl-Ag 77, p. 27.

GREENWOOD, Robert
　"Myth and History." KanQ (9:1) Wint 77, p. 58.
　"On a Painting by Vermeer." KanQ (9:1) Wint 77, p. 58.

GREGER, Debora
　"After Iceland, William Morris Dreams of Panama." NewYorker
　　(53:42) 5 D 77, p. 129.
　"The Amorer's Daughter." NewYorker (53:3) 7 Mr 77, p. 107.
　"Any Story." AntR (35:2/3) Spr-Sum 77, p. 253.
　"At the Winter Palace." PraS (51:4) Wint 77-78, p. 399.
　"Bed." MissR (6:1) 77, p. 131.
　"Body of Work." Nat (225:20) 10 D 77, p. 629.
　"Closing." Nat (224:17) 30 Ap 77, p. 534.
　"Harboring the Angel of Solitude." PraS (51:4) Wint 77-78,
　　p. 398.
　"Hugging the Ground." SenR (8:1) My 77, p. 55.
　"Inventing the Third Person." NewYorker (53:8) 11 Ap 77,
　　p. 128.
　"Knowing." SenR (8:1) My 77, p. 53.
　"The Last Resort." MissR (6:1) 77, p. 132.
　"Not Working." Iowa (8:4) Aut 77, p. 85.
　"Not You." Nat (225:20) 10 D 77, p. 629.
　"The Seduction of Solitude." Nat (225:20) 10 D 77, p. 629.
　"Sleeping Beauty." Ploughs (3:3/4) 77, p. 104.
　"Thinking of Failure." PoetryNW (18:1) Spr 77, p. 30.
　"Two Rooms." PoetryNW (18:1) Spr 77, p. 30.
　"What Dances." SenR (8:1) My 77, p. 54.
　"A Woman of My Description." Nat (225:18) 26 N 77, p. 573.

GREGERSON, Linda
　"Alone." Shen (28:4) Sum 77, p. 51.
　"Each Day." Shen (28:3) Sum 77, p. 51.
　"Rain." Field (17) Aut 77, p. 19.

GREGG, Linda
　"As When the Blowfish Perishing." Nat (225:7) 10 S 77, p. 217.

GREGOR, Arthur
　"Cul-de-Sac." NewYorker (53:10) 25 Ap 77, p. 38.
　"Markings." Nat (224:16) 23 Ap 77, p. 509.
　"Not This Departure." PoNow (14/18) 77, p. 57.
　"Songs of Belonging" (A Sequence for Hanna Axmann-Rezzori).
　　Hudson (30:1) Spr 77, p. 16.
　"Two-Sided." Nat (224:22) 4 Je 77, p. 700.

"A Visit." PoNow (14/18) 77, p. 57.

GREGORY, Carolyn Holmes
"About Flowers." AAR (27) 77, p. 45.
"The Suit." AAR (27) 77, p. 46.

GREGORY, Mary
"Kostes Palamas: Patrides." Poetry (130:4) Jl 77, p. 211.

GREGORY, R. D.
"Men & Angels." KanQ (9:4) Aut 77, p. 86.

GREGORY, Thomas M.
"Far Louder Than Goliath Would." StoneC (77:1) F 77, p. 10.

GRENANDER, M. E.
"Low Desert." PoetL (72:1) Spr 77, p. 13.

GRIERSON, Patricia
"Logic Survives." StoneC (77:2) My 77, p. 11.
"Plots." Poem (29) Mr 77, p. 65.
"Self-Consciousness." KanQ (9:1) Wint 77, p. 35.
"The Spain That Never Came." Poem (29) Mr 77, p. 66.
"To an Olympics Winner." NewC (8:1) 76-77, p. 17.

GRIFFIN, Jonathan
"Houses" (tr. of Jutta Schutting). ChiR (29:3) Wint 78, p. 109.
Nine poems (tr. of Baudelaire). GRR (8:3) 77, p. 206.
"Ophelia" (tr. of Rimbaud). GRR (8:3) 77, p. 224.
"The Spell-Bound" (tr. of Rimbaud). GRR (8:3) 77, p. 225.
Twenty-five poems. Montra (3) Spr 77, pp. 9-31.

GRIFFIN, Walter
"The Blue Trajectory." SouthernPR (16:SI) 77, p. 33.
"Old Allen." TexQ (20:4) Wint 77, p. 142.
"Paper Dolls." TexQ (20:4) Wint 77, p. 125.
"That Semester." TexQ (20:4) Wint 77, p. 124.

GRIGSON, Geoffrey
"Death for the Undying." Poetry (130:3) D 77, p. 147.

GRILLO, Paul
"Everyone Is Waiting on the Wrong Side of Invisibility" (Journal
Poem for Sotere Torregian). Aieee (5/6) 77, p. 28.

GRINDLAY, J. R.
"Steal the Dawn." Hudson (30:3) Aut 77, p. 399.

GRINNELL, Jeff
"Widow" (for W. C. W. and L. N.). PortR (23) 77, p. 114.

GRINYER, Mark
"Fishing for Corvina in the Salton Sea." LitR (20:4) Sum 77,
p. 464.

"Poem in a Pig's Ass" (for Merritt Clifton). <u>Sam</u> (52) Ap 77, inside back cover.

GROSSBARDT, Andrew
"Always a Place. " <u>NewRivR</u> (2:1) 77, p. 25.
"The Death of Poetry. " <u>Columbia</u> (1) Aut 77, p. 17.
"I am looking for last year's snow. " <u>QW</u> (3) Spr-Sum 77, p. 82.
"It Is Nearly Autumn. " <u>PoNow</u> (14/18) 77, p. 58.
"Learning to Fly" (for Connie). <u>Confr</u> (15) Aut 77-Wint 78, p. 43.
"Montana, again. " <u>NewL</u> (43:3) Spr 77, p. 98.
"The moonlight has turned sour, lover. " <u>Madrona</u> (4:13/14) 77, p. 26.
"Poem after some lines by Paul Eluard. " <u>QW</u> (3) Spr-Sum 77, p. 82.
"The Secret Sea" (tr. of Jules Supervielle). <u>QW</u> (2) Wint 77, p. 45.
"Sorrow to Sorrow" (for Quinton Duval). <u>Columbia</u> (1) Aut 77, p. 15.
"To Live Again" (tr. of Jules Supervielle). <u>QW</u> (2) Wint 77, p. 45.
"An Unnatural Weight. " <u>SouthernPR</u> (17:1) Spr 77, p. 22.
"Winter in Mid-Country. " <u>Nat</u> (224:11) 19 Mr 77, p. 344.

GROSSMAN, Allen
"The Children's Houses. " <u>GeoR</u> (31:1) Spr 77, p. 211.
"Nightmare. " <u>Poetry</u> (129:6) Mr 77, p. 323.
Nine poems. <u>Peb</u> (16) Wint 76-77, pp. 7-20.
"O Great O North Cloud. " <u>Poetry</u> (129:6) Mr 77, p. 321.
"The Runner. " <u>Poetry</u> (129:6) Mr 77, p. 322.

GROSSMAN, Arnold
"Je Prefère. " <u>Mouth</u> (11/12) Mr-Je 77, p. 28.

GROSSMAN, Elizabeth
"Colorless Sunday morning, joyful because the. " <u>YaleLit</u> (146:4/5) 77, p. 19.
"Visiting Cathedrals. " <u>YaleLit</u> (146:4/5) 77, p. 50.

GROSSMAN, Jill
"Completing the Puzzle. " <u>AmerR</u> (26) N 77, p. 75.
"Participating Anthropology. " <u>AmerR</u> (26) N 77, p. 77.

GROSSMAN, Martin
"The Arable Mind. " <u>Agni</u> (7) 77, p. 29.
from M. 's Adventures on the Earth of Ideas: "12. The Space Needle. " <u>Drag</u> (16) 77.
"The Way the World Will End. " <u>Agni</u> (7) 77, p. 28.

GROSSMAN, Richard
"Amoeba. " <u>ParisR</u> (69) Spr 77, p. 30.
"Anaconda. " <u>SoDakR</u> (15:2) Sum 77, p. 68.
"Butterfly. " <u>CarolQ</u> (29:3) Aut 77, p. 14.

"Clarity." PoetryNW (18:4) Wint 77-78, p. 26.
"Dead Beauty." SenR (8:2) D 77, p. 28.
"The Farm Bar." PoNow (14/18) 77, p. 58.
"Hog." NoAmR (262:1) Spr 77, p. 59.
"Loss." Icarus (5:2) Aut 77, p. 13.
"Mole." CarolQ (29:3) Aut 77, p. 13.
"Ode to Apollinaire." SenR (8:2) D 77, p. 30.
"Regret." Icarus (5:2) Aut 77, p. 12.
"Roach." ParisR (69) Spr 77, p. 29.
"Sea Urchin." SoDakR (15:2) Sum 77, p. 66.
"The Shepherd and His Animals." Kayak (46) O 77, p. 43.
"Toads." SenR (8:2) D 77, p. 29.
"Torture." PoetryNW (18:4) Wint 77-78, p. 26.
"Wolf." SoDakR (15:2) Sum 77, p. 67.

GROVE, Thomas N.
   from Hrsil: Eight poems (tr. of Ragnhildur Ófeigsdóttir). GRR
   (8:1/2) 77, p. 57.

GROVER, Laura
   "Calls from a Booth in Time's Square." PoetryNW (18:2) Sum
   77, p. 36.
   "Room Enough." KanQ (9:1) Wint 77, p. 129.

GRUND, M. T.
   "Description of the Dreamer." PoetL (72:1) Spr 77, p. 9.

GRYNIEWICZ, Eugene R.
   "In Chicago's Grant Park." Mouth (13) D 77, p. 66.

GRZESIAK, Rich
   "418." Mouth (11/12) Mr-Je 77, p. 99.

GUAY, Cheri
   "crazy john used to sell comic books." SeC (5:2) 78, p. 19.

GUENTHER, Charles
   Eight poems (tr. of Renê Char). WebR (3:1) Wint 77, p. 10.
   from Penelope: (XII-XVIII) (tr. of Monique Laederach). WebR
   (3:2) Spr 77, p. 50.

GUERNSEY, Bruce
   "A Certain Providence." Atl (239:5) My 77, p. 60.

GUERRARD, Philip
   "The Silence." NewYorker (53:44) 19 D 77, p. 130.

GUEST, Barbara
   "After Horace." SunM (4) Aut 77, p. 47.
   "All That." SunM (4) Aut 77, p. 48.
   "Door Bells." SunM (4) Aut 77, p. 49.

GUGGENHEIM, Herbert S.
   "Close to Fog." NewC (7:2) 75-76, p. 26.

"In Our Nakedness. " NewC (8:1) 76-77, p. 13.

GUIDO, Ann
"The Farm. " HangL (30) Sum 77, p. 22.

GUILFORD, Chuck
"The Vacation. " KanQ (9:4) Aut 77, p. 56.

GUILLÉN, Jorge
"Arte Rupestre, 1939-1969, 1" (tr. by Edmund L. King).
    NewRep (176:15) 9 Ap 77, p. 29.

GULLBERG, Hjalmar
"Balloons" (tr. by Judith Moffett). NewYorker (53:43) 12 D 77,
    p. 188.

GUNN, Thom
"Elegy. " SouthernR (13:3) Sum 77, p. 583.
"Hide and Seek. " SouthernR (13:3) Sum 77, p. 582.

GUREN, Clifford
"A Brief Meditation on Cats Growing on Trees" (tr. of Miroslav
    Holub). Field (16) Spr 77, p. 69.
"A Brief Meditation on Cows" (tr. of Miroslav Holub). Field
    (16) Spr 77, p. 71.
"A Brief Meditation on Gargoyles" (tr. of Miroslav Holub). Field
    (16) Spr 77, p. 74.
"A Brief Meditation on Laughter" (tr. of Miroslav Holub). Field
    (16) Spr 77, p. 72.
"A Brief Meditation on Logic" (tr. of Miroslav Holub). Field
    (16) Spr 77, p. 70.
"A Brief Meditation on the Insect" (tr. of Miroslav Holub).
    Field (16) Spr 77, p. 73.

GURLEY, George H. , Jr.
"Estate Planning. " RemR (5) 77, p. 68.
"Sacraments. " WebR (3:4) Aut 77, p. 61.

GUSACK. Nancy C.
"Museum of Natural History. " Juice (5) 77.

GUSTAFSON, Jim
from Bright Eyes Talks Crazy to Rembrandt: "House Tour. "
    PoNow (14/18) 77, p. 56.
from Bright Eyes Talks Crazy to Rembrandt: "Mother Cupcake
    and the Oblivion Boys. " PoNow (14/18) 77, p. 56.
from Bright Eyes Talks Crazy to Rembrandt: "Wild Dogs. "
    PoNow (14/18) 77, p. 56.
"The Heroes. " ChiR (29:1) Sum 77, p. 109.
from Shameless: "Dirge. " HangL (29) Wint 76-77, p. 6.

GUSTAFSON, Ralph
"In Time of the Comet. " MalR (41) Ja 77, p. 29.

"Sermon for the Day." <u>MalR</u> (41) Ja 77, p. 28.

GUSTAFSON, Richard
Ten poems. <u>PoetC</u> (10:1) 77, pp. 3-13.

GUSTAVSON, J.
"Song, If I Sing." <u>HarvAd</u> (110:3) Mr 77, p. 19.

GUTHRIE, Jeri
"Julien Gracq or The Illumined Interior" (tr. of Joyce Mansour,
w. Peter Koch). <u>MontG</u> (6) Aut 77, p. 19.
from Rapaces Cris: "I like your stockings that strengthen your
legs" (tr. of Joyce Mansour, w. Peter Koch). <u>MontG</u> (6)
Aut 77, p. 20.

ap GWILYM, Dafydd
"The Girl of Eithinfynydd" (tr. by Bill McCann and Philip
Holmes). <u>Stand</u> (18:2) 77, p. 35.

GWYNN, R. S.
"Ars Poetica." <u>MissR</u> (6:1) 77, p. 9.
"The Hunchback with the Withered Arm." <u>MissR</u> (6:1) 77, p. 14.
"Scenes from the Playroom." <u>MissR</u> (6:1) 77, p. 13.

GYLLENSTEN, Lars
"Women Born from Trees" (tr. by Keith Bradfield). <u>WebR</u> (3:1)
Wint 77, p. 59.

HAAGENSEN, Jane
"Chicken Wings." <u>Field</u> (17) Aut 77, p. 91.
"Flock." <u>Field</u> (17) Aut 77, p. 89.
"Runt." <u>SouthernPR</u> (17:1) Spr 77, p. 31.

HAAS, Scott
"The Lovers" (for the French sea and Cezanne). <u>Box</u> (5) Spr 77,
p. 30.

HADAS, Pamela
"Circle." <u>WebR</u> (3:2) Spr 77, p. 13.
"Excavation on the Kolyma." <u>WebR</u> (3:2) Spr 77, p. 16.
"Post-Thalamion" (for Dr. & Mrs. Stephen Post, married 8
November 1975). <u>WebR</u> (3:2) Spr 77, p. 8.

HADAS, Rachel
"For My Lady" (tr. of Stephanos Xenos). <u>EnPas</u> (6) 77, p. 36.
"International Sculpture Exhibit, Philopappos Hill" (tr. of
Stephanos Xenos). <u>EnPas</u> (6) 77, p. 33.
"Kalamita" (tr. of Stephanos Xenos). <u>EnPas</u> (6) 77, p. 35.
"Old Men of Democracy" (tr. of Stephanos Xenos). <u>EnPas</u> (6) 77,
p. 34.
"September Song." <u>NewRep</u> (177:10) 3 S 77, p. 25.

HADDIX, Winnie
"Grade School Principal." <u>Wind</u> (27) 77, p. 2.

HAESSLER, Mike
"Once I was leaning on air and eating. " AAR (27) 77, p. 124.

HAGEDORN, Jessica
"Ming the Merciless." GreenR (6:1/2) Spr 77, p. 16.
"Seven Songs for an Elegant Hoodlum. " GreenR (6:1/2) Spr 77,
    p. 18.
"Smokey's Getting Old" (for Smokey Robinson). GreenR (6:1/2)
    Spr 77, p. 14.

HAGEN, Cecilia
"The Coat. " LittleR (12) 77, p. 3.

HAGER, Charles
"Why do people wear clothes?" AAR (27) 77, p. 98.

HAGIWARA, Sakutaro
"Chairs" (tr. by Graeme Wilson). WestHR (31:2) Spr 77, p. 156.
"Death" (tr. by Graeme Wilson). WestHR (31:2) Spr 77, p. 110.
"Idealism" (tr. by Graeme Wilson). WestHR (31:2) Spr 77,
    p. 156.
"Skylark Nest" (tr. by Hiroaki Sato). Montra (3) Spr 77, p. 37.

HAHN, Robert
"The Pilgrim's Way. " Chowder (9) Aut-Wint 77, p. 32.

al-HAIDARI, Buland
"Depths" (tr. by Sargon Boulus). Mund (10:1) 77, p. 56.
"Dream" (tr. by Sargon Boulus). Mund (10:1) 77, p. 57.

HAINES, John
from Forest Without Leaves: (VII, XI, XV). QW (3) Spr-Sum
    77, p. 12.
"The Head on the Table. " Kayak (44) F 77, p. 56.
"The Head on the Table. " Stand (18:3) 77, p. 56.
"The Sun on Your Shoulder. " MichQR (16:3) Sum 77, p. 256.
"Tale of the Clock. " Kayak (44) F 77, p. 57.
"Victoria. " NowestR (16:3) 77, p. 37.

HAISLIP, John
"On the First Cosmic Comfort Station. " Drag (16) 77.

al-HAJ, Unsi
"Is This You or the Tale?" (tr. by Sargon Boulus). Mund (10:1)
    77, p. 74.

HAJNAL, Anna
"The Deserted Angel" (tr. by Jeanette Nichols). ModernPS (8:2)
    Aut 77, p. 103.
"Fear" (tr. by Daniel Hoffman). AmerPoR (6:3) My-Je 77,
    p. 22.
"Seals" (tr. by Jeanette Nichols). ModernPS (8:2) Aut 77,
    p. 103.

"To the Creator of My Bones" (tr. by Jeanette Nichols).
ModernPS (8:2) Aut 77, p. 102.

HAKUSHU, Kitahara
"Lao Tzu" (tr. by Graeme Wilson).   TexQ (20:4) Wint 77,
p. 145.

HALE, Oliver
"Appraisal."   Sparrow (33) Ja 77, p. 8.

HALL, Donald
"Names of Horses."   NewYorker (53:39) 14 N 77, p. 207.
"Ox Cart Man."   NewYorker (53:33) 3 O 77, p. 44.

HALL, James Baker
"Birthday Poem."   AntR (35:2/3) Spr-Sum 77, p. 258.
"Cliff Hagan's Rib Eye Steak House."   PoNow (14/18) 77,
p. 58.
"The Field Hand's Dream."   SewanR (85:2) Spr 77, p. 208.
Fifteen poems.   DenQ (12:1) Spr 77, p. 97.
"Flying."   SouthernPR (16:SI) 77, p. 34.
"In the Meadow."   AmerS (46:4) Aut 77, p. 503.
"Love's Terrain."   Kayak (46) O 77, p. 37.
"Sunday Morning, Fall, 1973, Second Floor of the Courthouse."
PoNow (14/18) 77, p. 58.
"Trakyl, At War."   Epoch (26:2) Wint 77, p. 109.
"Transmigrations."   Kayak (46) O 77, p. 36.
"Witnessing the Full Moon."   Hudson (30:1) Spr 77, p. 79.

HALL, Jim
"For My Mother: Finally a Poem with No Mention of Sex."
SouthernPR (17:2) Aut 77, p. 14.

HALL, John
"Klee."   SouthernPR (17:2) Aut 77, p. 39.

HALL, Nellie
"Fisherman."   Comm (104:11) 27 My 77, p. 336.

HALLIDAY, Mark
"Secret Symphony."   CalQ (11/12) Wint-Spr 77, p. 84.
"Some of the Existers."   CalQ (11/12) Wint-Spr 77, p. 82.

HALMAN, Talat Sait
"Ghazal" (tr. of Rumi, w. W. S. Merwin).   Nat (224:6) 12 F 77,
p. 190.
"In Those Small Lakes" (tr. of Melih Cevdet Anday, w. Brian
Swann).   WebR (3:4) Aut 77, p. 50.
"A Sumerian Tablet" (tr. of Melih Cevdet Anday, w. Brian
Swann).   WebR (3:4) Aut 77, p. 51.

HALPERIN, Mark
"Holding Him."   NoAmR (262:3) Aut 77, p. 58.

"Polestar." NoAmR (262:3) Aut 77, p. 58.

HALPERN, Daniel
"Above the Port." GeoR (31:2) Sum 77, p. 472.
"Aubade." Atl (240:2) Ag 77, p. 75.
"Beggar." MissR (6:1) 77, p. 69.
"The Beginning." PoNow (14/18) 77, p. 59.
"Blue Suspension." Harp (254:1525) Je 77, p. 12.
"Distant Faces." Iowa (8:4) Aut 77, p. 70.
"Family Likeness." NoAmR (262:3) Aut 77, p. 43.
"Final Scene." PoNow (14/18) 77, p. 59.
"Five Riddles by Symphosius." Agni (7) 77, p. 118.
"Green." PoetryNW (18:3) Aut 77, p. 15.
"The Hero at Midnight." GeoR (31:2) Sum 77, p. 471.
"I Am a Dancer." AmerR (26) N 77, p. 278.
"I Hear Nothing." Atl (240:2) Ag 77, p. 75.
"In My House of Others." AmerPoR (6:6) N-D 77, p. 34.
"Landmarks." Ploughs (3:3/4) 77, p. 149.
"Let Me Tell You." Nat (225:6) 3 S 77, p. 189.
"Letter to the Midwest." NoAmR (262:4) Wint 77, p. 51.
"Person Smoking." Iowa (8:4) Aut 77, p. 69.
"Status Quo." PoNow (14/18) 77, p. 59.
"Still." NewYorker (53:21) 11 Jl 77, p. 28.
"Summer House" (for M. S.). AmerPoR (6:6) N-D 77, p. 34.
"Take for Example." Harp (254:1525) Je 77, p. 12.

HALPERN, Nick
"The German Painter." YaleLit (145:5) 77, p. 10.

HAMBURGER, Michael
"asleep" (tr. of Ernst Jandl). BosUJ (25:3) 77, p. 51.
"Before Dinner." Stand (18:2) 77, p. 18.
Fourteen poems (tr. of Paul Celan). ChiR (29:3) Wint 78, p. 43.
"Mornings." Stand (18:2) 77, p. 18.
"My Shoe" (tr. of Günter Grass). ChiR (29:3) Wint 78, p. 113.
"then and now" (tr. of Ernst Jandl). BosUJ (25:3) 77, p. 51.
"thingsure" (tr. of Ernst Jandl). BosUJ (25:3) 77, p. 52.
"to remember" (tr. of Ernst Jandl). BosUJ (25:3) 77, p. 52.
"two in one" (tr. of Ernst Jandl). BosUJ (25:3) 77, p. 52.
"Your Ear" (tr. of Günter Grass). ChiR (29:3) Wint 78, p. 111.

HAMBY, Dick
"Dream Man" (for Thomas Brush). PoetryNW (18:1) Spr 77,
    p. 36.
"Going Home with the Drowned Man." PoetryNW (18:4) Wint 77-
    78, p. 39.
"The Pond Floyd Made in a Raku Kiln." PoetryNW (18:1) Spr 77,
    p. 37.
"Running Back." PoetryNW (18:4) Wint 77-78, p. 40.

HAMBY, James
"Healing." Poem (31) N 77, p. 41.
"Outside the Medicine Lodge." Poem (31) N 77, p. 42.

"A Poem of the Blood." Waters (6) 77, p. 18.

HAMILL, Sam
"Duwamish Blue." PoNow (14/18) 77, p. 60.
"Letter to Nancy Steele from Alaska." CutB (9) Aut-Wint 77,
   p. 30.
"Saphrophyte" (for Jo). PortR (23) 77, p. 152.
"Sometime." MontG (5) Wint 77, p. 63.
"To Davia, Alone." Gra (12) 77, p. 52.
"The Widow." PortR (23) 77, p. 153.

HAMILTON, Alfred Starr
"Broom Factory." PoNow (14/18) 77, p. 60.
"Card Factory." Bleb (12) 77, p. 42.
"Dark Continent." Glass (2:2/3) Wint-Spr 77, p. 69.
"Holy Water." Bleb (12) 77, p. 43.
"Iron Tooth." Bleb (12) 77, p. 42.
"Little Candle." Bleb (12) 77, p. 43.
"Our Flag." PoNow (14/18) 77, p. 60.
"The Pool." PoNow (14/18) 77, p. 60.
"Poor White." NewL (43:3) Spr 77, p. 79.
"Rome, N.Y." Glass (2:2/3) Wint-Spr 77, p. 69.
"Visitations." PoNow (14/18) 77, p. 60.
"War." PoNow (14/18) 77, p. 61.
"Wilkes Barre, Pa." PoNow (14/18) 77, p. 60.

HAMILTON, Carol S.
"Fog." RemR (5) 77, p. 13.
"In Snow." EnPas (4) 76, p. 24.
"The Season of Old Men." RemR (5) 77, p. 13.
"True North." Kayak (46) O 77, p. 27.

HAMLIN, Gary
"For My Grandfather in November" (-after Robert Bly). GRR
   (8:1/2) 77, p. 133.
"Surprised by Autumn." GRR (8:1/2) 77, p. 132.

HAMMER, Langdon
"Bel Ami" (for N.C.C.). YaleLit (147:2) 77, p. 30.
"Chenega Island." YaleLit (147:1) 77, p. 12.
"Three Seascapes." YaleLit (147:2) 77, p. 28.

HAMMOND, Anthony
"Your breast is forever beyond me." Stand (18:3) 77, p. 58.

HAMMOND, John G.
"The Green Place." Wind (24) 77, p. 14.

HAMMOND, Karla M.
"Cento (2)." Chomo (4:2) Aut-Wint 77, p. 32.
"Cento (3)." Chomo (4:2) Aut-Wint 77, p. 33.
"Immortality." AAR (27) 77, p. 11.
"Love Sentence" (after Creeley). AAR (27) 77, p. 11.

"Martha's Vineyard." Confr (14) Spr-Sum 77, p. 154.
"Metaphor." AAR (27) 77, p. 12.
"Racing Season." SmPd (14:2) Spr 77, p. 18.
"The Tenth Muse." Chomo (4:2) Aut-Wint 77, p. 34.

HAMOD, Sam
"After the Funeral of Assam Hamady" (for my mother, David and
   Laura). US1 (10) Wint 77-78, p. 6.
"The Famous Hot Pepper Eating Contest." US1 (10) Spr 77,
   p. 6.
"Here" (in memory of Joan Scholes). US1 (10) Wint 77-78,
   p. 7.
"Moving." CentR (21:2) Spr 77, p. 150.

HANEY, Marilyn Plowman
"James and John Revisited." ChrC (94:10) 23 Mr 77, p. 274.
"To a Young Christian Friend in Rhodesia." ChrC (94:21) 8-15
   Je 77, p. 563.

HANSEN, Carol
"Turning." MinnR (NS8) Spr 77, p. 58.

HANSEN, Gunnar
"Accidents." PoetL (72:1) Spr 77, p. 12.
"Crow." PoetL (72:1) Spr 77, p. 6.

HANSEN, Tom
"From 18,000 Feet." Gra (12) 77.
"The History of Music." Wind (26) 77, p. 28.

HAN Shan
"Cold Mountain" (tr. by Graeme Wilson). WestHR (31:1) Wint 77,
   p. 56.
"Holy Man" (tr. by Graeme Wilson). DenQ (12:2) Sum 77,
   p. 51.

HANSON, Dereck
"Death." SeC (5:2) 78, p. 20.
"200 years ago." SeC (5:2) 78, p. 21.

HANSON, Howard G.
"Not Thel but Lucifers." ArizQ (33:3) Aut 77, p. 215.
"To Apollo." ArizQ (33:4) Wint 77, p. 366.
"The Unaccustomed View." BallSUF (18:3) Sum 77, p. 78.
"You Were Right, Heraclitus!" ArizQ (33:2) Sum 77, p. 100.

HANSON, Karen
"Redolence of Death." Epoch (27:1) Aut 77, p. 52.

HAN Wo
"Letter to a Ch'an Master" (tr. by Graeme Wilson). DenQ (12:2)
   Sum 77, p. 53.

HANZLICEK, C. G.
"Eclipse." PoNow (14/18) 77, p. 61.

HARDEMAN, Louise
"A Composition of Negatives and Developments." SouthernPR
(16:SI) 77, p. 37.

HARDING, Cory
"Lines." GRR (8:1/2) 77, p. 113.

HARDING, Donald E.
"Fourth of July." WindO (30) Aut 77.

HARDING, Jeff
"I wish I was an adult." AAR (27) 77, p. 113.

HARDISON, O. B., Jr.
"Flora." SouthernPR (17:2) Aut 77, p. 21.
"In the Palazzo of Pellucid." NewRep (177:6/7) 6-13 Ag 77,
p. 35.

HARGREAVES, Anne
"Chuang Tsu." AAR (27) 77, p. 19.
"Youngest love." AAR (27) 77, p. 18.

HARKNESS, Edward
"Forrest." PortR (23) 77, p. 146.
"A High School Girl, Smiling, Advocates the Death Penalty on
National TV." PortR (23) 77, p. 147.

HARLOW, Michael
"Devotion to the Small." Nat (224:9) 5 Mr 77, p. 282.

HARMON, Paul
"At the Library." Waters (5) 77, p. 2.
"The Dolphin." Waters (5) 77, p. 1.

HARMON, William
"En Route to the Purchase of a Cummerbund." CarolQ (29:1)
Wint 77, p. 79.
"Iron Water: A Letter to Albert Goldbarth." SouthernPR (17:1)
Spr 77, p. 50.
"Welcome to Your Plural Dungeons." SouthernPR (16:SI) 77,
p. 38.
"World I." Kayak (44) F 77, p. 16.
"World II." Kayak (44) F 77, p. 17.

HARPER, Michael S.
"Bristol: Bicentenary Remembrances of Trade." MassR (18:3)
Aut 77, p. 467.
"Crossing Lake Michigan." MassR (18:3) Aut 77, p. 470.
"Driving the Big Chrysler across the Country of My Birth."
MassR (18:4) Wint 77, p. 671.

"Going to the Territory: Icons of Geography of the Word: A
   Meditation on the Life and Times of Ralph Waldo Emerson."
   MassR (18:4) Wint 77, p. 668.
"Going to the Territory: Icons of Geography of the Word: A
   Meditation on the Life and Times of Ralph Waldo Emerson."
   Nimrod (21:2/22:1) 77, p. 92.
"The Hawk Tradition: Embrochures of a Photo Not Taken of
   Coleman Hawkins." MassR (18:4) Wint 77, p. 669.
"Healing Song for Robert Hayden." PoNow (14/18) 77, p. 63.
"Landfill" (for Shirl). AmerPoR (6:1) Ja-F 77, p. 23.
"Made Connections." AmerPoR (6:5) S-O 77, p. 40.
"Made Connections." MassR (18:3) Aut 77, p. 469.
"Major Price." MissR (6:1) 77, p. 21.
"Major Price." PoNow (14/18) 77, p. 63.
"A Narrative of the Life and Times of John Coltrane: Played by
   Himself." MassR (18:4) Wint 77, p. 670.
"Smoke." MassR (18:3) Aut 77, p. 471.
"Uplift from a Dark Tower." MassR (18:4) Wint 77, p. 660.

HARRAL, Warren
   "I Have Come Again to the Sea." Xa (4) 77, p. 1.
   "Passing Love." HangL (30) Sum 77, p. 24.
   "Peonies." HangL (30) Sum 77, p. 23.

HARRIGAN, Stephen
   "Letter from the Desert." NewL (44:2) Wint 77, p. 43.
   "Over to God." NewL (44:2) Wint 77, p. 42.
   "Rescue Party." NewL (44:2) Wint 77, p. 45.
   "River Proposal." NewL (44:2) Wint 77, p. 44.

HARRINGTON, Janet R.
   "The Face in the Window." Chelsea (36) 77, p. 71.

HARRIS, Jana
   "The Clackamas." Nat (225:16) 12 N 77, p. 504.

HARRIS, Joseph
   "The Jain." Icarus (5:1) Spr 77, p. 19.
   "A Lady of Amherst." KanQ (9:2) Spr 77, p. 74.
   "On Enjoying a Bach Suite with a Whiskey Sour." Wind (27) 77,
      p. 24.
   "The Vessel and the Fire." Wind (27) 77, p. 24.

HARRIS, Lester Lee, Jr.
   "dawn to dawning." Wind (25) 77, p. 14.

HARRIS, Marguerite
   "Decoration Day." PoNow (14/18) 77, p. 63.
   "'The Good Life.'" PoNow (14/18) 77, p. 64.

HARRIS, Marie
   from Interstate: "cargo goes north." PoNow (14/18) 77, p. 64.
   from Interstate: "I kissed Mike Donahue in the ivy." Hand (1)
      77, p. 106.

from Interstate: "I occupy this winter." PoNow (14/18) 77,
  p. 64.
from Interstate: "it's not too late to begin again." Epoch (27:1)
  Aut 77, p. 58.
from Interstate: "out of habit I preserve nothing." Epoch (27:1)
  Aut 77, p. 58.
from Interstate: "out of habit I preserve nothing." Hand (1) 77,
  p. 106.
from Interstate: "stay" (for Basil). Hand (1) 77, p. 105.
from Interstate: "the hurricane." PoNow (14/18) 77, p. 64.
from Interstate: "the unmistakable noise of migrating geese."
  PoNow (14/18) 77, p. 64.
from Interstate: "you moved" (for Susan). Hand (1) 77, p. 104.
from Raw Honey: "The Bullfighter's Wife." PoNow (14/18) 77,
  p. 65.
from Raw Honey: "Early Frost." PoNow (14/18) 77, p. 65.
from Raw Honey: "Visitors." PoNow (14/18) 77, p. 65.

HARRIS, Nancy
  "Ape Woman Finds a Charm for Invisibility." Pig (3) 77, p. 44.
  "Ape Woman Takes Witch Lessons." Pig (3) 77, p. 42.

HARRIS, Steve
  "Meditation, Overlooking Creve Coeur on Trash Day Morning."
    WebR (3:2) Spr 77, p. 75.

HARRIS, Van
  "A Result of Love." DeKalb (10:3) Spr 77, p. 17.

HARRIS, William J.
  "Mouths." Wind (25) 77, p. 19.
  "The Only Thing" (for Madelon). Wind (25) 77, p. 19.
  "Rainy Day." Wind (25) 77, p. 20.
  "Speed Demon." PoNow (14/18) 77, p. 66.
  "You Say." PoNow (14/18) 77, p. 66.
  "Your House" (for my students). Wind (25) 77, p. 20.

HARRISON, Jim
  "Gathering April" (for Simic). PoNow (14/18) 77, p. 66.
  from Returning to Earth. Ploughs (4:1) 77, p. 43.
  "The Woman from Spiritwood" (for Guy). PoNow (14/18) 77,
    p. 66.

HARRISON, Keith
  "Basho Beside the Mountain." CarlMis (16:1/2) Aut-Wint 76-77,
    p. 96.
  "Basho Rejects Hinduism or Marshall McLuhan in India."
    CarlMis (16:1/2) Aut-Wint 76-77, p. 100.
  from Basho's Poems on the Moods and Modes of the Pigeon: "I
    have been thinking about dogs." CarlMis (16:1/2) Aut-Wint
    76-77, p. 101.
  from Basho's Poems on the Moods and Modes of the Pigeon:
    "pigeons flying." CarlMis (16:1/2) Aut-Wint 76-77, p. 100.

from Basho's Poems on the Moods and Modes of the Pigeon:
"These days of wind. " <u>CarlMis</u> (16:1/2) Aut-Wint 76-77,
p. 101.
from Basho's Poems on the Moods and Modes of the Pigeon:
"They're packing horse dung in a pile. " <u>CarlMis</u> (16:1/2)
Aut-Wint 76-77, p. 101.
"Travelling toward the Vache Qui Pue River or Basho Attempts
to Translate Robert Bly. " <u>CarlMis</u> (16:1/2) Aut-Wint 76-77,
p. 99.

HARRISON, Sam G.
"Bonegift. " <u>SouthernHR</u> (11:4) Aut 77, p. 403.
"Sunset Polaroid. " <u>SouthernHR</u> (11:4) Aut 77, p. 336.

HARRISON, Tony
"The Ballad of Babelabour. " <u>Stand</u> (18:2) 77, p. 17.
"Cremation. " <u>Stand</u> (18:2) 77, p. 16.
"Social Mobility. " <u>Stand</u> (18:2) 77, p. 16.

HARROD, Lois Marie
"Vélo-Douche. " <u>PoetL</u> (71:1) Spr 77, p. 23.

HARROLD, D. C.
"Glass of Water in the Storm. " <u>Aieee</u> (5/6) 77, p. 25.
"Meditation Pump. " <u>Aieee</u> (5/6) 77, p. 26.
"Of Sky in Storms. " <u>Icarus</u> (5:1) Spr 77, p. 12.

HARROLD, William
"Postmark. " <u>PoNow</u> (14/18) 77, p. 67.

HARROW, Elizabeth
"The River Sink. " <u>CarouselQ</u> (2:3) Wint 77, p. 18.

HARRUFF, Greg
"Butterflies. " <u>OhioR</u> (18:1) Wint 77, p. 26.
"Everything in Its Place. " <u>OhioR</u> (18:1) Wint 77, p. 25.

HARTMAN, Charles O.
"The Essayist" (for John N. Morris). <u>Poetry</u> (131:2) N 77,
p. 99.
"Stars: Flat, Blue, Large Stars. Nothing. " <u>Poetry</u> (131:2) N
77, p. 100.

HARTMAN, Geoffrey
"Genius Loci. " <u>Poetry</u> (130:3) D 77, p. 138.

HARTMAN, Susan
"Troubles. " <u>KanQ</u> (9:3) Sum 77, p. 34.

HARVEY, Gayle Elen
"the flamingo eater. " <u>CarouselQ</u> (2:2) Aut 77, p. 9.
"it's easier, sometimes. " <u>Pig</u> (3) 77, p. 98.
"Moon-Song. " <u>WindO</u> (27) Aut 76.

"Night Heron. " SmPd (14:3) Aut 77, p. 17.
"Now. " StoneC (77:3) S 77, p. 20.
"Pastoral. " DeKalb (10:2) Wint 77, p. 35.

HARVEY, Steven
    "The Inheritance: A Broken Elegy for My Mother. " HangL (31)
        Aut 77, p. 20.
    "The Tenth Month. " BelPoJ (27:4) Sum 77, p. 38.

HARWOOD, Lee
    "Machines. " PartR (44:2) 77, p. 259.

HASHMI, Alamgir
    "The Final Draft for To His Coy Mistress. " SenR (8:2) D 77,
        p. 55.
    "My Second in Kentucky. " DeKalb (10:2) Wint 77, p. 36.
    "On Seeing an Ad about Teaching Vacancy in Wabash College. "
        SenR (8:2) D 77, p. 56.
    "Whorehouse. " DeKalb (10:2) Wint 77, p. 37.

HASKINS, Lola
    "From the Top of the Hill. " BelPoJ (28:1) Aut 77, p. 20.

HASLEY, Louis
    "Could Be Verse. " ColEng (38:5) Ja 77, p. 515.

HASS, Robert
    "The Feast. " Iowa (8:3) Sum 77, p. 27.
    "Like Three Fayre Branches from One Root Deriv'd. " Iowa
        (8:3) Sum 77, p. 26.
    "Weed. " Iowa (8:3) Sum 77, p. 26.

HASWELL, Richard H.
    "Earth Poems" (tr. of Janvier Heraud). MalR (44) O 77, p. 47.

HATFIELD, Barbara
    "Stained Windows. " Poem (30) Jl 77, p. 13.

HATHAWAY, Dev
    "Herringbone. " PoNow (14/18) 77, p. 67.

HATHAWAY, James
    "Foraging. " Rapp (10) 77, p. 50.

HATHAWAY, Jeanine
    "Egyptian Bride Vanishes When Sidewalk Opens Up. " ArkRiv
        (3:4/4:1) 77, p. 22.
    "Even in the Better Families. " ArkRiv (3:4/4:1) 77, p. 23.

HATHAWAY, Lodene Brown
    "For My Mother. " ChrC (94:6) 23 F 77, p. 170.

HATHAWAY, William
    "The New Earth Poem. " MissR (6:1) 77, p. 98.

"The Orphan Maker." NewL (44:2) Wint 77, p. 68.
"Several Estates in North Carolina." PoNow (14/18) 77, p. 67.
"When I Was Dying." PoNow (14/18) 77, p. 68.
from A Wilderness of Monkeys: "Coonass." PoNow (14/18) 77,
    p. 65.
from A Wilderness of Monkeys: "Finding the Lost Child."
    PoNow (14/18) 77, p. 65.
from A Wilderness of Monkeys: "High Distance Dive." PoNow
    (14/18) 77, p. 65.

HAUCK, Richard
"A Lost Poem by E. Dickinson?" ColEng (39:1) S 77, p. 67.

HAUG, James
"On T. V." Sam (59) 77, p. 67.

HAUK, Barbara
"Night Driving on the Freeway." Wind (24) 77, p. 25.

HAVLIK, Helen
"This Process of Moving." RemR (5) 77, p. 66.

HAWKES, John E.
"Masked Door." WindO (29) Sum 77, p. 16.

HAWKINS, Hunt
"Allende, Allende." Kayak (45) My 77, p. 44.
"The Revolution in Oakland." Kayak (45) My 77, p. 43.

HAWKINS, Tom
"At the Majestic." Juice (4) 77.
"Civility in Love." KanQ (9:3) Sum 77, p. 34.

HAWKSWORTH, Marjorie
"Black Hour." Chowder (8) Spr-Sum 77, p. 35.
"Dim Caboret." Chowder (9) Aut-Wint 77, p. 29.
"I Never Clean It." PoetryNW (18:4) Wint 77-78, p. 22.
"New to Me." Gra (12) 77.
"A Reminder." SouthwR (62:3) Sum 77, p. 279.
"Under the Future Lizard." MontG (5) Wint 77, p. 62.
"Urban Renewal." ParisR (70) Sum 77, p. 173.
"Water Witch." Chowder (9) Aut-Wint 77, p. 29.
"The Windows of Euthina." Chelsea (36) 77, p. 62.

HAWLEY, Beatrice
"Hibernation." LittleR (12) 77, p. 17.
"The Lovers." LittleR (12) 77, p. 9.
"The Marsh." Ploughs (3:3/4) 77, p. 101.

HAWLEY, J. D.
"Cold Storage." KanQ (9:3) Sum 77, p. 73.

HAWLEY, Richard A.
"The Idiot-Child." BerksR (12:1) Sum 76, p. 19.

"My Father Eating an Ice Cream Cone." BerksR (12:1) Sum 76, p. 17.

HAXTON, Brooks
"Easter Mass for Little John." SouthernR (13:2) Spr 77, p. 317.

HAYDEN, Robert
"Astronauts." MassR (18:4) Wint 77, p. 643.
"Elegies for Paradise Valley." MassR (18:3) Aut 77, p. 436.
"A Letter from Phillis Wheatley." MassR (18:4) Wint 77, p. 645.
"Names." MassR (18:4) Wint 77, p. 643.
"The Peacock Room" (in memory of Betsy Graves Reyneau). WorldO (11:3) Spr 77, p. 43.
from The Snow Lamp: "it is beginning oh." MassR (18:4) Wint 77, p. 647.
"Zinnias" (for Mildred Harter). MassR (18:4) Wint 77, p. 645.

HAYMAN, Jane
"Kate, 10 Days Old." Nat (224:3) 22 Ja 77, p. 90.

HAYMES, G. C.
"Coney Island Photo." Some (7/8) 76.

HAYNA, Lois
"Veneers." Gra (12) 77, p. 14.

HAYNES, John
"Thief." Stand (18:2) 77, p. 27.

HAYS, H. R.
"The Past Recaptured." PoNow (14/18) 77, p. 68.

HAZARD, James
"From Our Tub, to My Wife." MinnR (NS8) Spr 77, p. 35.

HAZEL, Robert
"The Hunter, the Catch." SouthernPR (16:SI) 77, p. 40.

HAZO, Samuel
"Cowardice" (tr. of Fouad Gabriel Naffah). Mund (10:1) 77, p. 187.
"Elegy in Exile" (tr. of Adonis). Mund (10:1) 77, p. 182.
"Flying Down the Dream." Hudson (30:4) Wint 77-78, p. 547.
"In the Future" (tr. of Fouad Gabriel Naffah). Mund (10:1) 77, p. 186.
"Long Distance Isn't." Hudson (30:4) Wint 77-78, p. 546.
"Prayer" (tr. of Fouad Gabriel Naffah). Mund (10:1) 77, p. 187.
"Statues from a January River." Nat (224:22) 4 Je 77, p. 695.
"A Sunset" (tr. of Fouad Gabriel Naffah). Mund (10:1) 77, p. 186.
"The Voyage" (tr. of Fouad Gabriel Naffah). Mund (10:1) 77, p. 185.

HEAD, Gwen
"After Appalachian Spring." PraS (51:1) Spr 77, p. 51.
"The Bicentennial Circus." PoNow (14/18) 77, p. 69.
"Edith Ascending." PoNow (14/18) 77, p. 68.
"Edith Cast Down." PoNow (14/18) 77, p. 68.
"The Facts of Life" (for Lee). PoetryNW (18:1) Spr 77, p. 9.
"A Musical Offering" (for Marvin McGee). PoetryNW (18:1) Spr
     77, p. 6.
"Not Sleeping." Poetry (129:5) F 77, p. 263.
"The Price of Admission." PraS (51:1) Spr 77, p. 53.
"Proteus." PoetryNW (18:1) Spr 77, p. 4.
"Rain." PraS (51:1) Spr 77, p. 52.
"The Ten Thousandth Night." PoetryNW (18:1) Spr 77, p. 3.

HEANEY, Seamus
"The Pigeon Shoot." NewYorker (52:50) 31 Ja 77, p. 34.

HEARST, James
"Growing Up." Chowder (8) Spr-Sum 77, p. 24.
"It Never Went Away." NewRivR (2:1) 77, p. 58.
"No News Is Good News." PoNow (14/18) 77, p. 69.
"The Promise Seems True." NewRivR (2:1) 77, p. 60.
"The Snapshot." PoNow (14/18) 77, p. 70.
"The Will to Possess." Chowder (8) Spr-Sum 77, p. 25.
"Words That Smell Bad." NewRivR (2:1) 77, p. 59.

HEATH, William
"A Vision of Helen." PoNow (14/18) 77, p. 70.

HEBALD, Carol
"Echo: From Leaf to Flower." TexQ (20:4) Wint 77, p. 161.

HEBERT, Sue
"Night Journey to Oruro." Wind (24) 77, p. 35.

HECHT, Anthony
"Dichtung und Wahrheit" (for Cyrus Hoy). AmerS (46:1) Wint
     76-77, p. 56.
"Sestina d'Inverno." Madem (83:2) F 77, p. 51.

HEDIN, Robert
"Due North." MoonsLT (2:3) 77, p. 33.
"On Williams Street." CutB (9) Aut-Wint 77, p. 44.
"Transcanadian." MoonsLT (2:3) 77, p. 34.

HEFFERNAN, Michael
"Another Part of the Field." Shen (28:2) Wint 77, p. 89.
"The Life of the Mind." ArkRiv (3:4/4:1) 77, p. 21.
"Listen Here." US1 (10) Wint 77-78, p. 8.
"Nineteenth of April." AmerPoR (6:3) My-Je 77, p. 39.
"The Plight of the Old Apostle." Chowder (8) Spr-Sum 77, p. 22.
"The Unexpurgated Version." US1 (10) Wint 77-78, p. 8.

HEFFERNAN, Thomas
"On Mount Mitchell between Stone and Sky at Dusk." StoneC
(77:1) F 77, p. 18.
"The Story Old Woman Considine Told." SouthernPR (17:2) Aut
77, p. 30.

HEGURI, Lady
"Love Token" (tr. by Graeme Wilson). DenQ (12:2) Sum 77,
p. 376.

HEILBRUNN, Evi
"We start building empires." Confr (14) Spr-Sum 77, p. 108.

HEILIGER, William
"Death" (tr. of Srečko Kosovel). PoetL (72:2) Sum 77, p. 72.
"Impression" (tr. of Srečko Kosovel). PoetL (72:2) Sum 77,
p. 72.
"Poem from Chaos" (tr. of Srečko Kosovel). PoetL (72:2) Sum
77, p. 72.
"Red Rocket" (tr. of Srečko Kosovel). PoetL (72:2) Sum 77,
p. 72.

HEINZELMAN, Kurt
"The Carthaginians' Letter to the Vandals." GeoR (31:3) Aut 77,
p. 575.

HEJINIAN, Lyn
"An Adjustment for Winter." LaB (6) Mr 77, p. 29.

HEKIGODO, Kawahigashi
"Hand" (tr. by Graeme Wilson). DenQ (12:2) Sum 77, p. 62.

HELDENBRAND, Sheila
Eight poems. Spirit (2:2/3) 77, pp. 104-09.

HELLDORFER, Mary Claire
"The Sand Sculptor." Wind (25) 77, p. 22.
"While Writing a Review." PoNow (14/18) 77, p. 70.

HELLER, Michael
"After Montale." Montra (3) Spr 77, p. 156.
"Dressed Stone." Montra (3) Spr 77, p. 153.
"Florida Letter." PoNow (14/18) 77, p. 70.
"For Paul Blackburn." Montra (3) Spr 77, p. 155.
"On the Beach." Pequod (2:3) Sum 77, p. 9.
"Seeing the Pain Again." Pequod (2:3) Sum 77, p. 7.
"Speculum Mortis." Pequod (2:3) Sum 77, p. 8.
"Stele" (for J.). Montra (3) Spr 77, p. 154.

HEMAN, Bob
"The Drama" (for Harry G.). WormR (65/66) 77, p. 39.
"News Brief." WormR (65/66) 77, p. 39.
"Passing the Blame." WormR (65/66) 77, p. 39.

"The Terminal. " WormR (65/66) 77, p. 39.
"The Whistle. " WormR (65/66) 77, p. 39.
"you suck. " Some (7/8) 76.

HEMPHILL, Essex C.
    from Diary of a Suicide: "Sunday Sept. 19. " Obs (3:3) Wint 77,
        p. 69.
    "Essex. " Obs (3:3) Wint 77, p. 69.
    "Holiday. " Obs (3:3) Wint 77, p. 69.
    "'U. S. Drawing Up Plans to Wage War in Space. '" Obs (3:3)
        Wint 77, p. 68.

HEMSCHEMEYER, Judith
    "The Back Hall Was All Wrong. " QW (3) Spr-Sum 77, p. 16.
    "Evening and Mother and I. " QW (3) Spr-Sum 77, p. 17.
    "Penelope. " ThRiPo (10) 77, p. 19.
    "To My Next Poem. " KanQ (9:2) Spr 77, p. 67.
    "Turning the Earth, the Earth Turning. " NowestR (16:3) 77,
        p. 68.

HENLEY, Mark
    "like love. " CarolQ (29:3) Aut 77, p. 75.

HENLEY, Patricia
    "Becoming" (for Thistle). Xa (4) 77, p. 49.

HENN, Mary Ann
    "Ashes. " ChrC (94:34) 26 O 77, p. 978.

HENN, Sister Mary Ann
    "Fresh Snow Field. " StoneC (77:3) S 77, p. 27.
    "Satire. " Wind (26) 77, p. 29.
    "Window Shopping. " Wind (26) 77, p. 29.

HENNING, C. J.
    "Enochian Key Two. " LitR (20:3) Spr 77, p. 344.
    "Enochian Key Three. " LitR (20:3) Spr 77, p. 345.

HERAUD, Janvier
    "Earth Poems" (tr. by Richard H. Haswell). MalR (44) O 77,
        p. 47.

HERBERT, Erynn
    "When it rained. " AAR (27) 77, p. 125.

HERBERT, Joyce
    "The Workers of Stalingrad. " Stand (18:2) 77, p. 45.

HERBERT, Zbigniew
    "The Ardennes Forest" (tr. by John Pijewski). Field (17) Aut
        77, p. 5.
    "A Little Box Called Imagination" (tr. by John Pijewski). Field
        (17) Aut 77, p. 7.

HERMAN, Ira
"Just Like Charles Bukowski. " Vaga (25) 77, p. 92.
"Sparrow. " Sam (52) Ap 77, p. 51.

HERMSEN, Terry
"Finding My Way Back. " SoDakR (15:2) Sum 77, p. 87.
"Late News (Summer, 1976). " HiramPoR (22) Aut-Wint 77,
     p. 23.
"Winter Decision. " SoDakR (15:2) Sum 77, p. 88.

HERNAN, Owen
Eight poems. Northeast (3:3) Sum 77, p. 21.

HERRON, Bill
"Culture Shock in Venezuela. " Northeast (3:4) Aut-Wint 77-78,
     p. 32.
"Day in the City Denver 1976. " Wind (27) 77, p. 64.
"Day in the City II. " Wind (27) 77, p. 64.
"Icarus. " Northeast (3:4) Aut-Wint 77-78, p. 29.
"Mitosis. " Northeast (3:4) Aut-Wint 77-78, p. 33.
"Most Common Object. " Northeast (3:4) Aut-Wint 77-78, p. 30.
"What You Were Fell Away" (for Kim Wood). Northeast (3:4)
     Aut-Wint 77-78, p. 31.

HERRSTROM, David
"To Strike North. " US1 (9) Spr 77, p. 7.
"What Thomas Said. " US1 (10) Wint 77-78, p. 4.

HERSHON, Robert
"Calling in Sick. " HangL (30) Sum 77, p. 25.
"For Lizzie, on Her Discovery of 1936. " PoNow (14/18) 77,
     p. 71.
"Friends of Friends. " Some (7/8) 76.
"Gentleman James Watt Takes the Local. " HangL (30) Sum 77,
     p. 28.
"The History Machine/Ninth Inning. " PoNow (14/18) 77, p. 71.
"The Public Hug. " HangL (30) Sum 77, p. 29.
"The Real New Yorkers. " Some (7/8) 76.
from Rocks and Chairs: "The Big-Leafed Vine. " PoNow (14/18)
     77, p. 71.
from Rocks and Chairs: "Pulling Hats out of Rabbits. " PoNow
     (14/18) 77, p. 71.
from Rocks and Chairs: "Visit to a Brooklyn Zoo. " PoNow
     (14/18) 77, p. 71.
"Sleeping in a Room with Friends. " HangL (30) Sum 77, p. 26.
"To a Turn. " HangL (30) Sum 77, p. 27.
"We Never Ask Them Questions. " PoetryNW (18:1) Spr 77,
     p. 23.

HERTLE, Frank
"Tom Lee Is Dead. " Gra (12) 77.

HERZBERG, Judith
"Father" (tr. of Huub Oosterhuis, rendered into poetry by Jean
    Valentine). AmerPoR (6:2) Mr-Ap 77, p. 21.
"Orpheus" (tr. of Huub Oosterhuis, rendered into poetry by Jean
    Valentine). AmerPoR (6:2) Mr-Ap 77, p. 21.

HESKETH, Phoebe
"The Horses." Stand (18:3) 77, p. 8.
"Ivy." Stand (18:3) 77, p. 8.

HESTER, M. L., Jr.
"Alone with Storm." SoDakR (15:2) Sum 77, p. 20.
"Cleek." NewC (8:1) 76-77, p. 22.
"Cosmopolitan Montage." KanQ (9:1) Wint 77, p. 84.
"Coyotes and Does." DeKalb (10:3) Spr 77, p. 18.
"The Day of Rest Manchurian Radioactive Rain." WindO (29)
    Sum 77, p. 37.
"If Not the Real Thing." Wind (27) 77, p. 25.
"Looking for Mr. Blue." SouthernHR (11:4) Aut 77, p. 354.
"Night Blindness." Wind (27) 77, p. 25.
"Noon Wine." KanQ (9:1) Wint 77, p. 85.
"The Second Night." WebR (3:4) Aut 77, p. 54.
"Sometimes." Focus (12:74) F-Mr 77, p. 29.
"Stone." ConcPo (10:2) Aut 77, p. 60.
"Two Kinds of Revenge." HiramPoR (22) Aut-Wint 77, p. 24.
"220 North." GRR (8:3) 77, p. 239.
"Watching Locusts." GRR (8:3) 77, p. 240.
"Watching Star Die." GRR (8:1/2) 77, p. 69.
"Words." GRR (8:1/2) 77, p. 68.

HESTER, Michele
"Bietz-Begietan" (tr. of Blas de Otero). PortR (23) 77, p. 79.
"Child Saint." QW (3) Spr-Sum 77, p. 14.
"Far Away" (tr. of Blas de Otero). PortR (23) 77, p. 78.
"The Hand." QW (3) Spr-Sum 77, p. 15.

HEWITT, Christopher
"The Blacksmiths." EnPas (5) 77, p. 21.
"Evesham Station 9/9/74." CalQ (11/12) Wint-Spr 77, p. 142.
"On Listening to Josquin Des Prez." CalQ (11/12) Wint-Spr 77,
    p. 141.

HEWITT, Geof
"At One with the Blue Night." Drag (16) 77.
"Eagle Rock." PoNow (14/18) 77, p. 72.
"The Frozen Man." Drag (16) 77.
"In Like a Lion." PoNow (14/18) 77, p. 72.
"Missing Now 5 Days." NewL (44:1) Aut 77, p. 48.
"Murdering the New Neighbor's Kid." ParisR (69) Spr 77, p. 33.
"Nov 8." NewL (44:1) Aut 77, p. 49.
"Sunday Outing." PoNow (14/18) 77, p. 72.
"Vermont." NewL (44:1) Aut 77, p. 48.

HEY, Phillip
"This Reminds You of Fishing with Uncle Harry. " PoNow (14/18)
   77, p. 72.

HEYEN, William
"The Jewish Children. " AmerPoR (6:6) N-D 77, p. 33.
"Mushrooms. " NewYorker (53:33) 3 O 77, p. 48.
"Wenzel. " OhioR (18:1) Wint 77, p. 99.

HEYMANN, John
"The Bears. " OP (24) Aut-Wint 77, p. 46.
"The Engine. " OP (24) Aut-Wint 77, p. 44.
"The Ice Poem. " OP (24) Aut-Wint 77, p. 48.
"Somedays. " OP (24) Aut-Wint 77, p. 45.
"Spring Cat. " OP (24) Aut-Wint 77, p. 50.
"The Towel Poem. " Aspect (69) O-D 76, p. 15.
"Visit to a Geisha House. " OP (24) Aut-Wint 77, p. 47.

HEYNEN, Jim
"Crib Death. " PortR (23) 77, p. 60.
"Executive Suite. " PoNow (14/18) 77, p. 73.
"Farewell, Oregon. " CarlMis (16:1/2) Aut-Wint 76-77, p. 148.
"Fewer Cats Now. " Kayak (46) O 77, p. 25.
"How the Sow Became a Goddess. " MontG (5) Wint 77, p. 30.
"The Man Who Kept Cigars in His Cap. " Kayak (46) O 77,
   p. 24.
"Sometimes a Sow. " CarlMis (16:1/2) Aut-Wint 76-77, p. 147.
"Teasing the Steers. " Kayak (46) O 77, p. 25.
"Tornado Alert. " NowestR (16:3) 77, p. 71.
"What Started Walking Home from School. " Kayak (46) O 77,
   p. 26.
"When You Move to a New Town. " PoNow (14/18) 77, p. 198.
"Widow. " PoNow (14/18) 77, p. 73.

HICKS, John V.
"Up from the River. " KanQ (9:1) Wint 77, p. 79.

HIGGINS, Anne
"Raisins. " Icarus (5:1) Spr 77, p. 22.

HIGGINS, Frank
"Historic Marker Ahead. " Wind (25) 77, p. 21.
"An Irrelevant Poem. " Wind (25) 77, p. 21.
"John Spizziri. " CutB (8) Spr 77, p. 19.
"O O" (A Love Poem to All the Women in the World Named
   Nancy Fuller). RemR (5) 77, p. 36.
"Social. " KanQ (9:1) Wint 77, p. 36.
"Summer Night: KC. " KanQ (9:1) Wint 77, p. 36.
"Tire Selection of the State Street Junkyard. " RemR (5) 77,
   p. 35.
"When Basketball Season Rolls Around. " RemR (5) 77,
   p. 34.

HIGGINS, Susan
"I Remember." AAR (27) 77, p. 105.
"I remember staying at a friend's house to play." AAR (27) 77,
   p. 105.
"The third eye can see china." AAR (27) 77, p. 118.

HIGGINSON, William J.
"Christmas 1972: No Flight into Egypt." Sparrow (33) Ja 77,
   p. 26.
"New York City Enlightenment." Sparrow (33) Ja 77, p. 26.

HIKMET, Nazim
"Bees" (tr. by Randy Blasing and Mutlu Konuk). DenQ (12:2)
   Sum 77, p. 237.
"Bor Hotel" (tr. by Randy Blasing and Mutlu Konuk). AmerPoR
   (6:6) N-D 77, p. 39.
"Hymn to Life" (tr. by Randy Blasing and Mutlu Konuk).
   AmerPoR (6:6) N-D 77, p. 38.
"Letters from Chankiri Prison" (tr. by Randy Blasing and Mutlu
   Konuk). DenQ (12:2) Sum 77, p. 231.
"Morning in Prague" (tr. by Randy Blasing and Mutlu Konuk).
   AmerPoR (6:6) N-D 77, p. 38.
"My Funeral" (tr. by Randy Blasing and Mutlu Konuk). AmerPoR
   (6:6) N-D 77, p. 39.
"Optimistic Prague" (tr. by Randy Blasing and Mutlu Konuk).
   AmerPoR (6:6) N-D 77, p. 39.
"Poem: I'm inside the advancing light" (tr. by Randy Blasing
   and Mutlu Konuk). DenQ (12:2) Sum 77, p. 236.
"Poem: In this sadness I feel" (tr. by Randy Blasing and Mutlu
   Konuk). DenQ (12:2) Sum 77, p. 236.
"Poem: My woman came with me as far as Brest" (tr. by Randy
   Blasing and Mutlu Konuk). AmerPoR (6:6) N-D 77, p. 39.

HILBERRY, Conrad
"Body and Mind." PoNow (14/18) 77, p. 73.
"Script for a Cold Christmas." PoetryNW (18:4) Wint 77-78,
   p. 9.

HILDEBIDLE, John
"Love Poems in Memory of William Henry Pratt." Agni (7) 77,
   p. 77.

HILDUM, Leah
"Once a bee kissed me." AAR (27) 77, p. 125.

HILL, Ethan
"Grey Lady." YaleLit (145:3) 77, p. 17.
"Through the Prism Rock." YaleLit (145:3) 77, p. 28.

HILL, Jim
"A Lady Who Visits." Chelsea (36) 77, p. 39.

HILL, Nellie
"Bachelor's Bedroom." CarlMis (16:1/2) Aut-Wint 76-77, p. 75.

"Bareback Rider." PoNow (14/18) 77, p. 73.
"Broken Cook." CarlMis (16:1/2) Aut-Wint 76-77, p. 76.
"First Lesson." Aspect (70) Ja-Mr 77, p. 17.
"Large White Flowers." AmerPoR (6:2) Mr-Ap 77, p. 36.
"Leftovers." AmerPoR (6:2) Mr-Ap 77, p. 36.
"Little Garden Family." PoNow (14/18) 77, p. 73.
"Lone Man on Vacation." Chelsea (36) 77, p. 21.
"Making the Poet Angry." AmerPoR (6:2) Mr-Ap 77, p. 36.
"Morning." TexQ (21:4) Wint 77, p. 168.
"On the Mountain." CalQ (11/12) Wint-Spr 77, p. 51.
"The Myth." TexQ (20:4) Wint 77, p. 166.
"The Poet." TexQ (20:4) Wint 77, p. 167.
"The Poet's Origins." AmerPoR (6:2) Mr-Ap 77, p. 36.
"Routine." Aspect (70) Ja-Mr 77, p. 18.
"Their Marriage." KanQ (9:3) Sum 77, p. 62.

HILL, Robert
"Rivers Running." NegroHB (40:2) Mr-Ap 77, p. 684.

HILL, Robert W.
"How Are You Far Away?" SouthernPR (17:1) Spr 77, p. 42.

HILL, Roberta
"Patterns." NoAmR (262:3) Aut 77, p. 33.

HILL, Rowland M.
"The Cloak upon a Stick." WebR (3:4) Aut 77, p. 30.

HILLBERRY, Conrad
"The Letter." CarlMis (17:1) Wint 77-78, p. 64.
"Watch." CarlMis (17:1) Wint 77-78, p. 63.

HILLEBRAND, Robert
"And Then I Was Too Old." EnPas (4) 76, p. 6.
"The Coming of the Cold Season." Wind (25) 77, p. 24.
"Counting." Wind (25) 77, p. 23.

HILLMAN, Brenda
"An Effort to Enter into Morning." Poetry (130:2) My 77, p. 84.
"On the Pier." Poetry (130:2) My 77, p. 84.
"Song" (tr. of Cecilia Meireles, w. Helen Hillman). PortR (23)
    77, p. 76.
"Walking the Dunes." Poetry (130:2) My 77, p. 83.

HILLMAN, Helen
"Song" (tr. of Cecilia Meireles, w. Brenda Hillman). PortR
    (23) 77, p. 76.

HILTON, David
from Huladance: "Bathrobe." PoNow (14/18) 77, p. 74.
from Huladance: "Huladance." PoNow (14/18) 77, p. 74.
from Huladance: "I Try to Turn In My Jock." PoNow (14/18)
    77, p. 74.

from Huladance: "Poem: I want to be one of those poets."
   PoNow (14/18) 77, p. 74.
"Iowa unto Morning." PoNow (14/18) 77, p. 75.
Ten poems. Spirit (2:2/3) 77, pp. 93-103.

HINCKLEBURRY, C. P.
"Reflections on a Magazine Called Samisdat." Sam (59) 77,
   p. 28.

HIND, Steven
"Arrowhead Hunting, A Guide." Focus (12:74) F-Mr 77, p. 29.
"Collision." Focus (12:74) F-Mr 77, p. 29.
"More Silent Than Trees." KanQ (9:3) Sum 77, p. 32.
"The Poet's Wife." KanQ (9:3) Sum 77, p. 33.
"Sam's Nephew Hunting." ArkRiv (3:4/4:1) 77, p. 70.

HINDEN, M. Charles
"Byrd Thou Never Wert--The Collected Poems and Post Cards of
   Emmett Byrd (a Sampler)." Northeast (3:3) Sum 77, p. 10.
"Emmett and the Duck." Northeast (3:3) Sum 77, p. 11.
"The Poet Speaks." Northeast (3:3) Sum 77, p. 12.

HINER, Jim
"Cigarette." DenQ (12:1) Spr 77, p. 202.
"My Plot." DenQ (12:1) Spr 77, p. 200.
"Real Ice." DenQ (12:1) Spr 77, p. 201.
"Two Poems on Living Forever 1.) Death." DenQ (12:1) Spr 77,
   p. 203.
"Two Poems on Living Forever 2.) Let's Hope So." DenQ (12:1)
   Spr 77, p. 204.
"Where Robert Bly." BelPoJ (27:4) Sum 77, p. 15.

HINRICHSEN, Dennis
"And over here, the prairie...." Rapp (10) 77, p. 65.
"The Farm: 1939." Rapp (10) 77, p. 64.

HIROKAWA, Princess
"The Harvest of the Heart" (tr. by Graeme Wilson). DenQ (11:4)
   Wint 77, p. 166.

HIRSCH, Edward
"Apologia for Buzzards." PoetryNW (18:1) Spr 77, p. 50.
"Dance of the Moon." ConcPo (10:1) Spr 77, p. 72.
"Interlude During War: Paul Klee." CarlMis (17:1) Wint 77-78,
   p. 116.
"A Letter." PoetryNW (18:4) Wint 77-78, p. 45.
"Song Against Natural Selection." PoNow (14/18) 77, p. 76.
"Visitation." MidwQ (18:2) Wint 77, p. 204.
"A Walk with Vallejo in Paris." BelPoJ (27:4) Sum 77, p. 12.

HIRSCHMAN, Jack
"The Illumination." LaB (6) Mr 77, p. 31.
"Longly I sit" (tr. of Nat Scammacca). LaB (7) My 77, p. 36.

"RBR." PoNow (14/18) 77, p. 76.

HIRSHMAN, Rose
"Nursery School Outing." StoneC (77:3) S 77, p. 29.

HISSHO, Ryojin
"Things That Comply with the Wind" (tr. by Graeme Wilson).
    DenQ (12:2) Sum 77, p. 359.

HITCHCOCK, George
"All That Can Be Profitably Said About the Mosquito." SenR
    (8:2) D 77, p. 23.
"Exordium." NewL (44:1) Aut 77, p. 71.
"Mirror on Horseback." SenR (8:2) D 77, p. 24.
"Ultima Thule Hotel." NewL (44:1) Aut 77, p. 70.
"Variations on a Line from Hans Arp." MontG (6) Aut 77, p. 14.
"The Years." SenR (8:2) D 77, p. 22.

HITOMARO, Kakinomoto
"At Karu" (tr. by Graeme Wilson). DenQ (11:4) Wint 77, p. 171.
"Beautifully-named" (tr. by Janine Beichman). DenQ (12:2) Sum
    77, p. 106.
"Plovers skimming over the waves" (tr. by Janine Beichman).
    DenQ (12:2) Sum 77, p. 106.
"The Road of Love" (tr. by Graeme Wilson). DenQ (11:4) Wint
    77, p. 168.

HIXON, Jeff
"Dialogue." ArkRiv (3:4/4:1) 77, p. 49.

HOAGLAND, Everett
"American Flyer" (for two school masters, Michael S. Harper
    and Albert Murray). AmerPoR (6:5) S-O 77, p. 34.
"Blue You (a pieta in which the two figures hold one another)."
    AmerPoR (6:5) S-O 77, p. 34.
"Celebration" (for Alex Haley and for Alice Trimiew). Nimrod
    (21:2/22:1) 77, p. 93.
"Indian Blood." AmerPoR (6:1) Ja-F 77, p. 23.
from the suite: "Scrimshaw: Black Bones." AmerPoR (6:1)
    Ja-F 77, p. 23.

HOBBS, Suzanne Marie
"Lake Whetstone." PoetL (72:1) Spr 77, p. 14.

HOBSON, Laura
"Shemiaka's Judgement." Waters (5) 77, p. 3.

HO Chi Minh
"Prison Poems" (fourteen poems) (tr. by Ian McLachlan). MalR
    (43) Jl 77, p. 123.

HOEFER, Jacqueline
"Knots and Dry Places." CarlMis (17:1) Wint 77-78, p. 11.

. "Small Claims." CarlMis (17:1) Wint 77-78, p. 11.

HOEFT, Robert D.
"And I Didn't Even Get My Dime Back." MalR (44) O 77, p. 66.
"My Fear." Wind (25) 77, p. 38.
"Planting Potatoes." KanQ (9:1) Wint 77, p. 106.
"The Roomless Door." PoetL (72:1) Spr 77, p. 19.

HOEY, Allen
"Evening in the Antipodes." EnPas (4) 76, p. 4.
"The Garden." Wind (25) 77, p. 50.

HOFFMAN, Chana
"From the Songs of Childhood" (tr. of Zelda). TriQ (39) Spr 77,
    p. 324.

HOFFMAN, Daniel
"Alone" (tr. of Zoltán Zelk). NewRep (176:13) 26 Mr 77, p. 30.
"The Dreamers of My Dream" (tr. of Sandor Csoóri). NewRep
    (176:13) 26 Mr 77, p. 29.
"Fairy Tale of the Cosmos" (tr. of György Somlyó). NewRep
    (176:13) 26 Mr 77, p. 30.
"Fear" (tr. of Anna Hajnal). AmerPoR (6:3) My-Je 77, p. 22.
"I Stole Your Face" (tr. of Sandor Csoóri). NewRep (176:13) 26
    Mr 77, p. 29.
"Moment" (tr. of Zoltán Zelk). NewRep (176:13) 26 Mr 77,
    p. 30.
"Tale of the Double Helix" (tr. of György Somlyó). NewRep
    (176:13) 26 Mr 77, p. 30.
"Vigil at Dawn" (tr. of Gábor Garai). NewRep (176:13) 26 Mr
    77, p. 30.
"Voyeurs." AmerS (46:2) Spr 77, p. 190.

HOFFMAN, Jill
"Late August." PartR (44:3) 77, p. 404.
"Nudists." PartR (44:3) 77, p. 404.

HOFFMAN, Richard
"A Visitor." Shen (28:2) Wint 77, p. 105.

HOGAN, Ed
"He Is Looking for Something Other Than I Have to Give." Vaga
    (26) 77, p. 11.
"Waiting for the Bus in Ball Square." Vaga (26) 77, p. 12.

HOGAN, Linda
"Body." PraS (51:3) Aut 77, p. 236.
"Tightrope Walker." PraS (51:3) Aut 77, p. 237.

HOGAN, Mia
"One day I stayed to make a world record and on the fourth day."
    AAR (27) 77, p. 125.

HOGAN, Michael
"Apostate." NewL (43:3) Spr 77, p. 78.
"Great-Grandmother's Eyes." NewL (43:3) Spr 77, p. 77.
"A Green Pass." Iowa (8:1) Wint 77, p. 66.
"The Message of Onan." Epoch (26:2) Wint 77, p. 112.
"An Old Place." Hand (1) 77, p. 151.
"Refunding for a Therapeutic Community." NewL (43:3) Spr 77,
    p. 77.
"Water, Water." Madrona (4:13/14) 77, p. 9.
"Wedlock." WebR (3:4) Aut 77, p. 31.

HOGE, Phyllis [see also THOMPSON]
"Letters" (for Caroline Garrett, for Rene Tillich). PoetryNW
    (18:3) Aut 77, p. 24.

HOHEISEL, Peter
"Limestone and Iron." Nat (224:4) 29 Ja 77, p. 124.

HOLBROOK, John
"Starting with What I Have at Home." PoetryNW (18:1) Spr 77,
    p. 19.

HOLDEN, Jonathan
"Before Sunrise." DacTerr (14) Spr-Sum 77, p. 44.
"The Death of Jessie Wrench." Aspen (4) Aut 77, p. 22.
"The '50 Storm." Aspen (4) Aut 77, p. 17.
"Golf." PoNow (14/18) 77, p. 77.
"Harding Township School." PoNow (14/18) 77, p. 77.
"Home from Work." OhioR (18:2) Spr-Sum 77, p. 95.
"Peter Rabbit." Iowa (8:3) Sum 77, p. 63.
"Saturday Afternoon, October (Home Game)." DacTerr (14) Spr-
    Sum 77, p. 44.
"The Store." Aspen (4) Aut 77, p. 23.
"A Tale of Two Cities." Aspen (4) Aut 77, p. 21.
"Tornado Symptoms." Aspen (4) Aut 77, p. 19.
"The Wisdom Tooth." Aspen (4) Aut 77, p. 20.

HOLENDER, Barbara D.
"October Thoughts on a Campus Walk." AndR (3:1) Spr 76,
    p. 89.
"Success (after the poetry reading)." ArizQ (33:2) Sum 77,
    p. 115.

HOLLAMAN, Keith
"A Bunch of Carrots" (tr. of Benjamin Péret). Field (16) Spr
    77, p. 35.
"Gone without Leaving an Address" (tr. of Benjamin Péret).
    Field (16) Spr 77, p. 32.
"Stale Bread" (tr. of Benjamin Péret). Field (16) Spr 77, p. 34.
"To Sleep Standing Up" (tr. of Benjamin Péret). Field (16) Spr
    77, p. 36.
"To Wash Your Hands" (tr. of Benjamin Péret). Field (16) Spr
    77, p. 33.

HOLLAND, Barbara A.
"End of an Era" (To the figure of Victory, torn by wind from
her chariot on the arch in Grand Army Plaza, Brooklyn).
Icarus (5:2) Aut 77, p. 16.
"Guess Who Crashed This Party." Hand (1) 77, p. 75.

HOLLAND, Robert
"The Elizabethan Zoo." NowestR (16:3) 77, p. 39.
"Of the Ass." NowestR (16:3) 77, p. 42.
"Of the Camel." NowestR (16:3) 77, p. 43.
"Of the Cockatrice." NowestR (16:3) 77, p. 42.
"Of the Hart and Hind." NowestR (16:3) 77, p. 40.
"Of the Phoenix." NowestR (16:3) 77, p. 39.
"Of the Unicorn." NowestR (16:3) 77, p. 41.

HOLLANDER, Jean
"Cornelia." Qt (57/58) Wint-Spr 77, p. 49.
"Cristo Morto." CimR (38) Ja 77, p. 64.
"Lazarus, My Cat." GRR (8:1/2) 77, p. 154.
"Lilith." LitR (20:3) Spr 77, p. 292.
"Painting on Wood." PoetL (72:2) Sum 77, p. 63.
"Ulysses to America." LitR (20:3) Spr 77, p. 293.

HOLLANDER, John
"Deja Vu." NewYRB (24:8) 12 My 77, p. 35.
"Indian Summer, 1975." NewYorker (53:39) 14 N 77, p. 46.
"Some of the Parts." PartR (44:3) 77, p. 410.
from Spectral Emanations. Poetry (129:4) Ja 77, p. 214.
"A Statue of Something." PartR (44:3) 77, p. 410.
"Stone Carving: August." GeoR (31:2) Sum 77, p. 343.
"What Was Happening Later at Night." GeoR (31:2) Sum 77,
p. 343.

HOLLANDER, Martha
"Telling Tales." YaleLit (147:1) 77, p. 13.

HOLLO, Anselm
"the beautiful days of franz innerhofer." Hills (4) 77.
from heavy jars: "slowly." Hills (4) 77.
from lingering tangoes: "a bunch of gods." Hills (4) 77.
Ten poems. Spirit (2:2/3) 77, pp. 35-44.

HOLMES, Charlotte Amalie
"The Impossible Man" (For Paul Gaugin). Madem (83:8) Ag 77,
p. 139.

HOLMES, James S.
"Conversation Piece." Mouth (11/12) Mr-Je 77, p. 73.
"The Sodom and Gomorrah Bit." Mouth (11/12) Mr-Je 77,
p. 76.

HOLMES, John Clellon
"Death Drag (The Elegist)." SouthernR (13:2) Spr 77, p. 342.

"Fayetteville Dawn." NewL (43:4) Sum 77, p. 81.
"North Cove Revenant." SouthernR (13:2) Spr 77, p. 338.

HOLMES, Oliver Wendell
"Old Ironsides." PoNow (14/18) 77, p. 95.

HOLMES, Olivia
"Souvenirs." YaleLit (146:2) 77, p. 26.

HOLMES, Philip
"The Girl of Eithinfynydd" (tr. of Dafydd ap Gwilym, w. Bill
    McCann). Stand (18:2) 77, p. 35.

HOLOP, Betty
"Remembrance." Poem (29) Mr 77, p. 50.

HOLSHOUSER, W. L.
"Silence." Shen (29:1) Aut 77, p. 77.

HOLST, Spencer
"Good Friday Meditation" (tr. of Vera Lachmann, w. the author).
    Hand (1) 77, p. 202.

HOLUB, Miroslav
"A Brief Meditation on Brief Meditations" (tr. by Liza Tucker,
    w. Michael Kraus). Field (16) Spr 77, p. 77.
"A Brief Meditation on Cats Growing on Trees" (tr. by Clifford
    Guren). Field (16) Spr 77, p. 69.
"A Brief Meditation on Cows" (tr. by Clifford Guren). Field
    (16) Spr 77, p. 71.
"A Brief Meditation on Gargoyles" (tr. by Clifford Guren). Field
    (16) Spr 77, p. 74.
"A Brief Meditation on Laughter" (tr. by Clifford Guren). Field
    (16) Spr 77, p. 72.
"A Brief Meditation on Logic" (tr. by Clifford Guren). Field
    (16) Spr 77, p. 70.
"A Brief Meditation on an Old Woman and a Pushcart" (tr. by
    Liza Tucker, w. Michael Kraus). Field (16) Spr 77, p. 76.
"A Brief Meditation on the Insect" (tr. by Clifford Guren).
    Field (16) Spr 77, p. 73.

HONEN
"Radiance" (tr. by Graeme Wilson). WestHR (31:3) Sum 77,
    p. 211.

HONG-NANG
"Willow Cuttings" (tr. by Graeme Wilson). DenQ (12:2) Sum 77,
    p. 295.

HONGO, Garrett Kaoru
"Gardena, Los Angeles" (for Eldon Hongo). GreenR (6:1/2) Spr
    77, p. 70.
"Ho-Tei Hongo." GreenR (6:1/2) Spr 77, p. 76.

"In Search of the Silent Zero" (for Frank Chin).   GreenR (6:1/2)
    Spr 77, p. 74.

HONG So-bong
    "Delivering the Hostages" (tr. by Graeme Wilson).   DenQ (12:2)
    Sum 77, p. 293.

HONIG, Edwin
    "An Art of Summer."   MichQR (16:2) Spr 77, p. 145.
    "The House."   MichQR (16:2) Spr 77, p. 142.
    "In the Cellarway."   PoNow (14/18) 77, p. 77.
    "Letting Go."   NewL (43:3) Spr 77, p. 76.

HOOPER, Patricia
    "Deer Park."   Epoch (26:2) Wint 77, p. 135.
    "Departures/Arrivals."   ChiR (29:2) Aut 77, p. 23.
    "Psalm."   OhioR (18:1) Wint 77, p. 76.

HOOVER, Gayle Marie
    "Balm."   WorldO (11:4) Sum 77.
    "Poem: Your Hands."   WorldO (11:4) Sum 77, p. 29.

HOOVER, Paul
    "Fortune."   PartR (44:4) 77, p. 557.
    "Lesson of the Billboard Dogs."   OhioR (18:3) Aut 77, p. 60.

HOPES, David B.
    "The Basswood Tree."   PortR (23) 77, p. 13.
    "Calving."   CarouselQ (2:3) Wint 77, p. 23.
    "Dormitory."   BallSUF (18:3) Sum 77, p. 16.
    "Flutter."   StoneC (77:3) My 77, p. 8.
    "Hands."   PortR (23) 77, p. 11.
    "Lawn Concert."   Mouth (13) D 77, p. 35.
    "Lunch Hour."   Mouth (13) D 77, p. 35.
    "Rou Hill."   NewC (7:2) 75-76, p. 16.
    "The Runner."   Mouth (13) D 77, p. 35.
    "Zack."   PortR (23) 77, p. 12.

HOPKINS, Jeffrey
    "The Wanderer" (tr. of Anglo-Saxon).   VirQR (53:2) Spr 77,
        p. 284.

HOPPER, Paul T.
    "Clouds" (tr. of Rosalía De Castro).   TexQ (19:4) Wint 76,
        p. 107.
    "How Calm and Bright Is the Sky."   TexQ (19:4) Wint 76, p. 109.

HOPPER, Virginia Shearer
    "Delphian Oracle."   PoetL (72:1) Spr 77, p. 9.

HORNE, Lewis B.
    "A Car Goes By."   Rapp (10) 77, p. 15.
    "The Sour Man."   SouthernHR (11:1) Wint 77, p. 46.

HORNER, Joyce
"Words for Music." Comm (104:9) 29 Ap 77, p. 272.

HOROVITZ, Frances
"The Woman's Dream." Stand (18:3) 77, p. 66.

HORSTING, Eric
"Without You." DenQ (11:4) Wint 77, p. 90.

HORVATH, Attila
"Family Tree" (tr. by Jeanette Nichols). ModernPS (8:2) Aut 77,
    p. 100.

HORVATH, Lou
"Blue Drums." LaB (9) N-D 77, p. 33.
"By the End of the 19th Century." LaB (5) Ja 77, p. 12.
"Catholic Ice Cream." LaB (5) Ja 77, p. 13.
"Cat's Eye Camera." LaB (9) N-D 77, p. 31.
"Credo in Unam" (for Rimbaud). LaB (5) Ja 77, p. 14.
"Describe the Dark." LaB (9) N-D 77, p. 32.
"I Thought You." LaB (9) N-D 77, p. 33.
"My Poem." LaB (9) N-D 77, p. 31.
"Painterly Coil." LaB (9) N-D 77, p. 34.
"Question to the Mystic Bridge [ ] 1967." LaB (5) Ja 77, p. 13.
"Robot Portrait." LaB (5) Ja 77, p. 14.
"Silver Eye Setting Fire." LaB (5) Ja 77, p. 12.
"Slaughter Beach." LaB (5) Ja 77, p. 11.

HOTHAM, Gary
Eight poems. EnPas (4) 76, p. 16.
"Haiku." WindO (27) Aut 76.

HOUCHIN, Ronald Edmond
"Beside Me Like a Banana." Poem (29) Mr 77, p. 62.
"Epitaph." Poem (29) Mr 77, p. 63.
"Handful of Flies." Poem (29) Mr 77, p. 61.
"Picasso Dying." CalQ (11/12) Wint-Spr 77, p. 147.

HOUGHTON, Elgar
"Air Lift." Poem (29) Mr 77, p. 42.

HOUSEMAN, Rick
"Gettin' High." Sam (56) Sum 77, p. 33.
"Winter Lady." Sam (56) Sum 77, p. 38.

HOUSLEY, Dave
"The Astronaut and the Radio Dial." Drag (16) 77.

HOUY, Julie
"Stuffed Husband." PoNow (14/18) 77, p. 78.

HOVDE, A. J.
"Epiphany." HolCrit (14:3) Je 77, p. 12.

HOWARD, Ben
"Distances." CarolQ (29:1) Wint 77, p. 21.
"Penelope." MidwQ (18:2) Wint 77, p. 207.
"Sortition." MidwQ (18:2) Wint 77, p. 206.
"Two Deer" (For L. E.). Poetry (130:5) Ag 77, p. 258.
"Use." MidwQ (18:2) Wint 77, p. 206.

HOWARD, Richard
"Charles Garnier." Poetry (131:2) N 77, p. 101.
"Codes." GeoR (31:1) Spr 77, p. 61.
"A Letter from the Sorcerer's Apprentice." Shen (28:2) Wint 77,
    p. 23.
"With the Remover to Remove." GeoR (31:2) Sum 77, p. 378.

HOWARD, Roger
"Spring Sequence." Stand (18:3) 77, p. 66.

HOWE, Fanny
"San Francisco" (for Frank MacShane). Columbia (1) Aut 77,
    p. 32.

HOWELL, Anthony
"Narratives." PartR (44:2) 77, p. 251.

HOWELL, Christopher
from The Book of Poetry: "Gentle Girl" (tr. of Anonymous).
    PortR (23) 77, p. 77.
"Dear Mrs. Terry." PoetryNW (18:4) Wint 77-78, p. 34.
"Initiation: Song for a New Life" (for Bette & Jessica Johnsrud).
    PortR (23) 77, p. 55.
"Memories of Mess Duty and the War." PoetryNW (18:4) Wint
    77, p. 34.
"On Reading the Shan Hai Ching" (tr. of Tao Ch'ien). PortR
    (23) 77, p. 99.
"The Plum Snow Blossom" (tr. of Lu Mei-P'O). PortR (23) 77,
    p. 98.
"Sadness Is Not Beautiful" (for Rod). CarlMis (17:1) Wint 77-78,
    p. 100.
"Spring Storm." CarlMis (17:1) Wint 77-78, p. 99.
"Thrushes on the Eve of Parting." MidwQ (18:2) Wint 77,
    p. 209.
"To My Unicorn." MidwQ (18:2) Wint 77, p. 208.
"The Twin of Hearts" (for William Budzack, 1945-1974). PortR
    (23) 77, p. 56.
"Water Sculpture" (for Patricia White, 1944 to 1968). PoetryNW
    (18:4) Wint 77-78, p. 35.
"Western." Falcon (14) 77, p. 38.
"The Wu General Writes from Far Away." NowestR (16:3) 77,
    p. 49.

HOWELL, Mark
"An All-Night Drive." DacTerr (14) Spr-Sum 77, p. 40.

HOWES, Barbara
"The Macadam Road Remembers" (tr. of Istrán Csukás).
AmerPoR (6:3) My-Je 77, p. 26.
"The Way" (tr. of Zoltán Zelk). AmerPoR (6:3) My-Je 77,
p. 22.

HO Xuan Hong
"Buddhist Priest" (tr. by Graeme Wilson). DenQ (12:2) Sum 77,
p. 59.

HOZUMI, Prince
"Party Song" (tr. by Graeme Wilson). DenQ (11:4) Wint 77,
p. 169.

HSIAO Yen
"Principle" (tr. by Graeme Wilson). WestHR (31:3) Sum 77,
p. 208.

HSUAN-CHIEN
"Ch'an Sermon" (tr. by Graeme Wilson). DenQ (12:2) Sum 77,
p. 53.

HUANG, Parker Po-fei
"Yale Campus in Riot." YaleLit (146:4/5) 77, p. 51.

HUANG Ting-chien
"River Parting" (tr. by Graeme Wilson). DenQ (12:2) Sum 77,
p. 394.

HUBENTHAL, Mahlon
"Anthole Branches." MontG (5) Wint 77, p. 73.
"Selections from Conductor Gulch." MontG (5) Wint 77, p. 72.

HUBERT, Karen
"My Sponge." ParisR (71) Aut 77, p. 46.

HUCHEL, Peter
"The Boy's Pond" (tr. by Rich Ives). CutB (8) Spr 77, p. 52.
"Die Niederlage." ChiR (29:3) Wint 78, p. 82.
"Hahnenkämme." ChiR (29:3) Wint 78, p. 76.
"Schnee" (Dem Gedächtnis Hans Henny Jahns). ChiR (29:3) Wint
78, p. 74.
"Vor Nîmes 1452." ChiR (29:3) Wint 78, p. 78.

HUDDLE, David
"Bac Ha." SouthernPR (17:2) Aut 77, p. 48.
"Girl on an Overpass." PoNow (14/18) 77, p. 78.
"The Syntax Agonies." SouthernPR (16:SI) 77, p. 41.
"Them." Field (17) Aut 77, p. 28.
"Theory." Field (17) Aut 77, p. 26.
"Words." Field (17) Aut 77, p. 27.
"Vermont." Field (17) Aut 77, p. 29.

HUDDLE, Louise
"A Lazy Afternoon's Refrain." CarouselQ (2:3) Wint 77, p. 29.

HUDDLESTON, Sheri
"If I had a kid." SeC (5:2) 78, p. 22.

HUDGINS, Andrew
"All My Friends Live in 'Genesis.'" CarolQ (29:2) Spr-Sum 77,
    p. 26.
"An Angel at Absolute Zero." Epoch (27:1) Aut 77, p. 78.
"Five Ways to Sunday." SoCaR (9:2) Ap 77, p. 56.
"The Hindmost and the Devil." SoCaR (9:2) Ap 77, p. 56.
"Holofernes Reminisces after Three Thousand Years." GeoR
    (31:4) Wint 77, p. 904.
"Shallow Grave." SouthernPR (17:1) Spr 77, p. 48.
"Shopping with Franz Liszt." SoCaR (9:2) Ap 77, p. 57.

HUDSON, Marc
"Painter at Dusk." CalQ (11/12) Wint-Spr 77, p. 127.

HUDZIK, Robert
"The Cost of Living." Waters (5) 77, p. 8.

HUE Minh
"The Law" (tr. by Graeme Wilson). DenQ (12:2) Sum 77, p. 55.

HUETER, Diane
"Josies Poem." MoonsLT (2:3) 77, p. 66.
"Wind Poem." MoonsLT (2:3) 77, p. 67.

HUEY, Mark
"Itinerary on the River Lethe" (for W. L. H.). Shen (29:1) Aut
    77, p. 78.

HUFFSTICKLER, Albert
"Karen." PoetL (72:1) Spr 77, p. 29.

HUGHES, Glenn Arthur
"Advice to an American." PoetryNW (18:1) Spr 77, p. 41.

HUGHES, Kenneth
"Names" (tr. of Jutta Schutting). ChiR (29:3) Wint 78, p. 107.

HUGHES, Laurena
"The Visitor." PortR (23) 77, p. 71.

HUGHES, Ted
"The Baptist." TransR (58/59) F 77, p. 55.
from Caprichos: "Dead, she became space-earth." BosUJ
    (25:2) 77, p. 23.
"The Desert of Love" (tr. of János Pilinszky). AmerPoR (6:3)
    My-Je 77, p. 24.
"The Judge." TransR (58/59) F 77, p. 57.

"Lament" (tr. of Yehuda Amichai). TriQ (39) Spr 77, p. 249.
"My Soul" (tr. of Yehuda Amichai). TriQ (39) Spr 77, p. 248.
"A Riddle. " TransR (58/59) F 77, p. 55.
"The Scapegoat Culprit. " TransR (58/59) F 77, p. 56.
"The Sweet Breakdown of Abigail" (tr. of Yehuda Amichai). TriQ
    (39) Spr 77, p. 249.
"Under the Winter Sky" (tr. of János Pilinszky). AmerPoR (6:3)
    My-Je 77, p. 23.

HUGO, Richard
"Doing the House" (for Philip Levine). Shen (29:1) Aut 77, p. 82.
"1805 Gratiot. " Ploughs (3:3/4) 77, p. 71.
"From Altitude, the Diamonds. " Shen (29:1) Aut 77, p. 81.
"Getty. " Iowa (8:2) Spr 77, p. 42.
"Houses. " Atl (239:1) Ja 77, p. 39.
"How to Use a Storm. " SouthwR (62:2) Spr 77, p. 116.
"Letter to Mantsch from Havre. " SouthwR (62:1) Wint 77, p. 45.
"Medicine Bow. " PoNow (14/18) 77, p. 197.
"To Women. " Shen (29:1) Aut 77, p. 80.
"With Ripley at the Grave of Albert Parenteau. " Iowa (8:2) Spr
    77, p. 41.

HUHN, Luci
"At Midnight. " Rapp (10) 77, p. 34.
"Mother, These Fragments. " Chowder (9) Aut-Wint 77, p. 18.
"Thaw. " Rapp (10) 77, p. 33.

HUI-Chi
"Shan-shan" (tr. by Graeme Wilson). WestHR (31:1) Wint 77,
    p. 56.

HUIZENGA, Laura
"When I woke up this morning I. " AAR (27) 77, p. 103.

HUMES, Harry
"Departure. " Wind (25) 77, p. 26.
"Fishhead. " Wind (25) 77, p. 25.
"Hunters Keep Out. " Wind (25) 77, p. 25.
"The Man Who Carves Whales. " Kayak (45) My 77, p. 49.
"My Neighbor's Daughter at Dawn. " Falcon (14) 77, p. 57.

HUMMER, T. R.
"Space. " SmPd (14:3) Aut 77, p. 34.

HUMPHREY, Jennifer
"The New World. " CarlMis (16:1/2) Aut-Wint 76-77, p. 60.
"On Awaking. " CarlMis (16:1/2) Aut-Wint 76-77, p. 61.
"The Supernumerary. " CarlMis (16:1/2) Aut-Wint 76-77, p. 61.

HUNDLEY, Robert
"The ligaments were torn indiscriminately. " EngJ (66:5) My 77,
    p. 53.

HUNT, Evelyn Tooley
"A Haiku Sampler" (four poems).   StoneC (77:2) My 77, p. 13.

HUNT, Ralph
"Her Apron Strings."   PoetL (72:2) Sum 77, p. 57.
"The Revolving Doors at Gimbels."   PoetL (72:2) Sum 77, p. 75.

HUNT, Tim
"F. S. A. Documentary Photos of the Thirties."   CutB (9) Aut-Wint
    77, p. 10.
"Lake County Elegy."   CutB (9) Aut-Wint 77, p. 8.

HUNTER, Terryl
"The Boating Party."   Pig (3) 77, p. 11.
"The Caring of Birds."   Pig (3) 77, p. 19.

HUNTINGTON, Cynthia
"The House by the Tracks."   Columbia (1) Aut 77, p. 34.

HURST, Ardath Frances
"The Earth Spoke."   TexQ (20:4) Wint 77, p. 93.

HURVITZ, Ya'ir
"On Your Heart, Open" (tr. by S. F. Chyet and Leonore Gordon).
    TriQ (39) Spr 77, p. 278.
"Whispering in Me" (tr. by S. F. Chyet and Leonore Gordon).
    TriQ (39) Spr 77, p. 277.

HUTCHINSON, Robert
"Mahler at Seventeen."   SoDakR (15:4) Wint 77-78, p. 82.
"Wild Ices."   PoNow (14/18) 77, p. 78.

HUTCHISON, Joe
"At Sunset."   LittleR (12) 77, p. 8.
"From a Tour Boat on Crater Lake."   Nat (224:15) 16 Ap 77,
    p. 477.
"The Gift."   Agni (7) 77, p. 27.
"Grandma."   Northeast (3:3) Sum 77, p. 14.
"The Map" (for William Stafford).   LittleR (12) 77, p. 8.
"The Refuge."   Rapp (10) 77, p. 89.
"Sportsmen."   LittleR (12) 77, p. 8.
"Suburban Housewife Eating a Plum."   Northeast (3:3) Sum 77,
    p. 15.
"A Transformation."   Agni (7) 77, p. 26.

HUTTO, Henry Hubert
"The Rabid Dog."   ChrC (94:29) 21 S 77, p. 808.

HWANG Chi-ni
"Crazy Crazy Crazy Love" (tr. by Graeme Wilson).   DenQ (12:2)
    Sum 77, p. 399.
"Long November Night" (tr. by Graeme Wilson).   DenQ (12:2)
    Sum 77, p. 303.

HWANG Hwi
"Autumn" (tr. by Graeme Wilson). DenQ (12:2) Sum 77, p. 305.
"Spring" (tr. by Graeme Wilson). DenQ (12:2) Sum 77, p. 302.

IBANEZ, Egardo
"Grandpa is a. " SeC (5:2) 78, p. 23.

IBSEN, Henrik
"Brente Skibe. " PortR (23) 77, p. 85.
"Burnt Ships" (tr. by Sam Oakland). PortR (23) 77, p. 85.

ICHIJITSU, Ōkuro
"The snow falls and falls" (tr. by Kenneth Rexroth). Falcon (14)
    77, p. 91.

IDRISSA
"Co-Ed. " Obs (3:3) Wint 77, p. 64.
"In a Circle. " Obs (3:3) Wint 77, p. 64.
"The Passing. " Obs (3:3) Wint 77, p. 65.
"Poem: mothers. " Obs (3:3) Wint 77, p. 63.
"Shared Solitude. " Obs (3:3) Wint 77, p. 63.

IGNATOW, David
"As We Walk Our Lives. " ModernPS (8:2) Aut 77, p. 175.
"A Closet Named Love. " QW (2) Wint 77, p. 43.
"Confusion is what I know best. " QW (2) Wint 77, p. 42.
"Examine me, I am continuous. " Rapp (10) 77, p. 97.
"Poem: My parents are two skeletons under the lid. " SenR
    (8:1) My 77, p. 40.
"A Prayer in Part. " ParisR (71) Aut 77, p. 179.
"Scenario. " Paunch (48/49) S 77, p. 141.
"So many people are dead. " Rapp (10) 77, p. 96.
"Subway Scene. " PoNow (14/18) 77, p. 79.
"The Suicide. " ModernPS (8:2) Aut 77, p. 174.
"Suicide in Two Voices. " PoNow (14/18) 77, p. 79.
"Two Poems. " OhioR (18:1) Wint 77, p. 78.
"The Two Selves. " Rapp (10) 77, p. 98.

IKEDA, Patricia
"Lines. " Epoch (26:2) Wint 77, p. 160.

IKEMOTO, Takashi
Eight Haiku (tr. of Japanese Masters, w. Lucien Stryk). NewL
    (43:3) Spr 77, p. 56.
"Haiku of the Japanese Masters" (tr. , w. Lucien Stryk).
    NowestR (16:3) 77, p. 98.
"Lap Dog" (tr. of Skinkichi Takahashi, w. Lucien Stryk). Bleb
    (12) 77, p. 9.

IKER, Gladys McKee
"Conversation for Two. " LadHJ (94:5) My 77, p. 152.
"Of Bread ... and Love. " LadHJ (94:4) Ap 77, p. 200.
"Small Lesson in Love. " LadHJ (94:9) S 77, p. P.S. 12.

IKKYU
  "Common Humanity" (tr. by Graeme Wilson).   DenQ (12:2) Sum
    77, p. 359.
  "Extraordinary World" (tr. by Graeme Wilson).   DenQ (12:2)
    Sum 77, p. 59.
  "Modalities of Dream" (tr. by Graeme Wilson).   WestHR (31:3)
    Sum 77, p. 211.

ILLYÉS, Gyula
  "While the Record Plays" (tr. by William Jay Smith).   AmerPoR
    (6:3) My-Je 77, p. 21.

INADA, Lawson Fusao
  "From Left to Right."   GreenR (6:1/2) Spr 77, p. 110.
  "The Island, the People, and the River."   GreenR (6:1/2) Spr 77,
    p. 105.
  "Kap-pa Song" (for my sons).   GreenR (6:1/2) Spr 77, p. 101.
  "Making Miso" (for Noboru Muramoto).   GreenR (6:1/2) Spr 77,
    p. 99.
  "My Father and Myself Facing the Sun."   GreenR (6:1/2) Spr 77,
    p. 108.

INEZ, Colette
  "Balloon Sleeves and Velvet, the Century Turned."   Glass (2:2/3)
    Wint-Spr 77, p. 24.
  "Caliph of Iberia."   Glass (2:2/3) Wint-Spr 77, p. 25.
  "Deskset Humidor Hatrack Piece."   Agni (7) 77, p. 108.
  "Farmboy Whipped for Fidgeting in Church."   Xa (4) 77, p. 13.
  "Monday's Children."   PoNow (14/18) 77, p. 79.
  "The Moon's Fa So, the Mind's Closed Song."   Glass (2:2/3)
    Wint-Spr 77, p. 26.
  "Mother's Song for an Elizabethan Daughter."   HolCrit (14:4) O
    77, p. 12.
  "Selling Harvesters."   PoNow (14/18) 77, p. 79.
  "Twenty Song."   Confr (14) Spr-Sum 77, p. 70.

INGRAM, A. M.
  "The Rooster."   SmPd (14:1) Wint 77, p. 14.

INGRAM, Forrest
  "Bodied."   DacTerr (14) Spr-Sum 77, p. 62.
  "Confession."   DacTerr (14) Spr-Sum 77, p. 62.
  "Expedition."   DacTerr (14) Spr-Sum 77, p. 63.
  "Final Message."   DacTerr (14) Spr-Sum 77, p. 63.

INGRAM, Nida E. Jones
  "Morning breezes."   Wind (27) 77, p. 47.

INMAN, P.
  "Islip."   LaB (7) My 77, p. 31.
  "TPD."   LaB (7) My 77, p. 33.

INNES, Rob
  "Barcelona."   StoneC (77:2) My 77, p. 6.

"The Poet as Lover." StoneC (77:2) My 77, p. 6.

IN-PYONG, Prince
"Politician" (tr. by Graeme Wilson). DenQ (12:2) Sum 77,
p. 293.

IOANNOU, George
"Lazarina" (tr. by Thomas Doulis). PortR (23) 77, p. 96.

IORIO, G.
"Love." Pig (3) 77, p. 8.

IRA
"Expo." TexQ (19:4) Wint 76, p. 148.
"Fugato." TexQ (19:4) Wint 76, p. 148.

IRION, Mary Jean
"The Dry Arrangers." SouthernHR (11:4) Aut 77, p. 382.
"The Hippopotamuses." DeKalb (10:2) Wint 77, p. 40.
"House, Woman, Rock, Sea." ChrC (94:37) 16 N 77, p. 1060.
"The Madonna of the Navel" (To My Daughter). ChrC (94:31) 5
O 77, p. 875.
"Note Scribbled in Stinsford Churchyard." SouthernHR (11:2) Spr
77, p. 183.
"The Puddle-Wader." DeKalb (10:2) Wint 77, p. 39.

IRWIN, Mark
"Frog's Advice to a Young Girl in Love." Comm (104:7) 1 Ap
77, p. 210.

ISAACS, Jay B.
"Alabaster Balustrades." CarouselQ (2:2) Aut 77.
"Moth." CarouselQ (2:3) Wint 77.

ISE, Lady
"As the first spring mists appear" (tr. by Kenneth Rexroth).
ParisR (69) Spr 77, p. 119.
"Shall I come to see" (tr. by Kenneth Rexroth). ParisR (69) Spr
77, p. 119.

ISHIKAWA, Lady
"Old Woman" (tr. by Graeme Wilson). DenQ (12:2) Sum 77,
p. 368.

ISSA, Kobayashi
"Within the Dewdrop" (tr. by Graeme Wilson). DenQ (12:2) Sum
77, p. 59.

ITZIN, C.
"Stone Soup." MassR (18:1) Spr 77, p. 187.

IVES, Rich
"The Boy's Pond" (tr. of Peter Huchel). CutB (8) Spr 77, p. 52.

"Promise for a Dark Child" (for Anita Endrezze).   CutB (8) Spr
   77, p. 53.
"Shingles, an Open Notebook."   CutB (9) Aut-Wint 77, p. 15.

JABRA, Jabra Ibrahim
   from Poetry Sequence: (2-3) (tr. by Sargon Boulus).   Mund
   (10:1) 77, p. 63.

JACKSON, Daniel
"Fantacist."   CarouselQ (2:2) Aut 77, p. 2.

JACKSON, Haywood
"At Dooney Park, County Sligo."   DenQ (11:4) Wint 77, p. 122.
"Dog Day at Stonehenge."   DenQ (11:4) Wint 77, p. 122.
"A Double Life."   DenQ (12:2) Sum 77, p. 286.
"The Killing of the Python."   DenQ (11:4) Wint 77, p. 121.
"Maybe: On the Moor Again."   Sam (59) 77, p. 39.
"The Moving Picture."   DenQ (12:2) Sum 77, p. 287.
"Two Letters from Troy."   DenQ (11:4) Wint 77, p. 119.

JACKSON, Mae
"On Learning."   Nimrod (21:2/22:1) 77, p. 96.

JACKSON, Richard
"Stump Burning" (for Michael Cooke).   Chowder (9) Aut-Wint 77,
   p. 40.

JACOB, John
"Area."   Poetry (130:2) My 77, p. 86.
"Kingsrider."   Poetry (130:2) My 77, p. 85.

JACOBS, A. C.
"Distant Land" (tr. of Dahlia Ravikovitch).   TriQ (39) Spr 77,
   p. 298.

JACOBS, Daniel
"Ride."   NewYorker (53:35) 17 O 77, p. 50.

JACOBS, Lucky
"After Bartleby."   Epoch (26:3) Spr 77, p. 229.
"After 6 Months in a Cottage Called 'God's Country.'"   RemR (5)
   77, p. 22.
"Along for the Ride."   Wind (25) 77, p. 28.
"The Creature."   Wind (25) 77, p. 28.
"For Heidegger."   SoCaR (9:2) Ap 77, p. 59.
"For Heidegger."   Xa (4) 77, p. 53.
"The Hope."   Confr (14) Spr-Sum 77, p. 16.
"Only Gift for My Brother."   Xa (4) 77, p. 54.
"Preparations for Spring."   DacTerr (14) Spr-Sum 77, p. 4.
"Psyched."   SoCaR (9:2) Ap 77, p. 58.
"Squash after Wine."   WindO (28) Spr 77, p. 16.
"Worm Persuader."   DacTerr (14) Spr-Sum 77, p. 5.

JACOBS, M. G.
"Consolation." KanQ (9:3) Sum 77, p. 12.
"Forever Momentarily." BallSUF (18:3) Sum 77, p. 9.
"Tackle Box." KanQ (9:3) Sum 77, p. 11.

JACOBS, Tim
"The Slinger Coming to It." YellowBR (8) 77, p. 36.

JACOBSEN, George
"Memento Mori." Glass (2:2/3) Wint-Spr 77, p. 65.

JACOBSEN, Josephine
"Daughter to Archeologist." SouthernPR (16:SI) 77, p. 42.
"Forest Dialogue." SouthernPR (17:1) Spr 77, p. 40.
"The Gulf." PoNow (14/18) 77, p. 80.
"Spread of Mrs. Mobey's Lawn." PoNow (14/18) 77, p. 80.

JACOBSEN, Rolf
"An Old Woman Night" (tr. by William Mishler). DenQ (11:4)
    Wint 77, p. 48.
"A Path in the Grass" (tr. by William Mishler). DenQ (11:4)
    Wint 77, p. 47.
"Right behind Your Foot" (tr. by William Mishler). DenQ (11:4)
    Wint 77, p. 48.

JACOBSON, Dale
"You, A. E. Housman." Sam (55) 77, p. 25.

JACQUES, Ben
"San Onefre." KanQ (9:1) Wint 77, p. 119.

JAFFE, Ellen S.
"The Octopus." Stand (18:3) 77, p. 55.

JAFFE, Susan
"Hunger Season." HangL (31) Aut 77, p. 24.

JAGENDORF, Zvi
"I Stood in Jerusalem" (tr. of Zelda). TriQ (39) Spr 77, p. 322.
"The Seamstress" (tr. of Zelda). TriQ (39) Spr 77, p. 323.
"When you were here" (tr. of Zelda). TriQ (39) Spr 77, p. 324.

JAHNS, T. R.
"The Deed which Clings." LitR (20:4) Sum 77, p. 399.
"Excavation in Recent History." KanQ (9:3) Sum 77, p. 110.
"The Gift." PoetryNW (18:1) Spr 77, p. 29.
"How to Change the World." DenQ (12:4) Wint 78, p. 34.
"If This Keeps Up." DenQ (12:4) Wint 78, p. 32.
"The Malcontent." TexQ (20:2) Sum 77, p. 32.
"Retreat." Rapp (10) 77, p. 90.
"Spider." DenQ (12:4) Wint 78, p. 33.
"Supine in a Tailored Ditch." Stonecloud (6) 76, p. 129.
"Surrender." LitR (20:4) Sum 77, p. 399.

"Wishing." Rapp (10) 77, p. 91.

JAMES, Billie Jean
   "Capacity for Escape in Nineteen Minutes Together." Poem (29)
       Mr 77, p. 21.
   "Into an Envelope." Poem (29) Mr 77, p. 18.

JAMES, David
   "Blind Infatuation." Some (7/8) 76.
   "Child Collecting." PoNow (14/18) 77, p. 80.
   "Revelations." PoNow (14/18) 77, p. 80.
   "Songs for an Old Woman." CutB (9) Aut-Wint 77, p. 143.

JAMES, David L.
   "The Dream of Ancestors." Vaga (25) 77, p. 8.
   "Taking the Shortest Way Home." QW (4) Aut 77, p. 85.
   "Those Lovely Years before the Invention of Music." QW (4) Aut
       77, p. 84.
   "You Are Made of Glass." ParisR (71) Aut 77, p. 42.
   "You Can't Teach Your Grandmother to Suck Eggs." Vaga (25)
       77, p. 9.

JAMES, Nancy Esther
   "Cameo: An Old Man's Face." ChrC (94:36) 9 N 77, p. 1029.
   "Elect." StoneC (77:3) S 77, p. 28.
   "Jayne Henley Davis, Expecting." 13thM (3:2) 77, p. 9.

JAMES, Sibyl
   "An Imperfect Gesture." Paunch (48/49) S 77, p. 19.

JAMES, Synthia
   "Untitled." CarouselQ (2:3) Wint 77, p. 13.

JAMISON, Stephen
   "The Hotel" (to Big Sur Lodge). AmerPoR (6:2) Mr-Ap 77,
       p. 30.
   "The Sea Which Is Always Bringing Us Brides." NewYorker
       (52:47) 10 Ja 77, p. 28.
   "A Star of His Sleep." NewYorker (52:52) 14 F 77, p. 34.

JANDL, Ernst
   "asleep" (tr. by Michael Hamburger). BosUJ (25:3) 77, p. 51.
   "suchen wissen." ChiR (29:3) Wint 78, p. 130.
   "then and now" (tr. by Michael Hamburger). BosUJ (25:3) 77,
       p. 51.
   "thingsure" (tr. by Michael Hamburger). BosUJ (25:3) 77,
       p. 52.
   "to remember" (tr. by Michael Hamburger). BosUJ (25:3) 77,
       p. 52.
   "two in one" (tr. by Michael Hamburger). BosUJ (25:3) 77,
       p. 52.

JANES, Kelly
   "To St. Mary of Magdala." ChrC (94:12) 6 Ap 77, p. 326.

JANEY, Peggy
"The Piney Forest." Ploughs (4:1) 77, p. 155.
"The Young Girl's Dream" (for Eve). Ploughs (4:1) 77, p. 156.

JANNETTA, Thomas P.
"A Moving Day." StoneC (77:2) My 77, p. 25.

JANOWITZ, Phyllis
"Coming of Age." PraS (51:3) Aut 77, p. 308.
"Facing It." Shen (29:1) Aut 77, p. 108.
"The Ground Is Hardest in the Middle of Winter." AndR (3:1)
    Spr 76, p. 21.
"Harmony: Four Rites." LitR (20:4) Sum 77, p. 457.
"Madeleine." Esq (88:1) Jl 77, p. 126.
"Pepper Young Ends the War." Stonecloud (6) 76, p. 31.
"The Professor." AndR (3:2) Aut 76, p. 12.
"Soon the Final Decree." Esq (87:6) Je 77, p. 10.
"You." DeKalb (10:2) Wint 77, p. 41.

JAOUDI, Maria
"Azalea." Wind (27) 77, p. 11.
"lying on the beach." Wind (27) 77, p. 11.

JARLSSON, Rolf Tor
"Driving around Oceanside California with Donny." Mouth (13) D
    77, p. 36.

JARMAN, Mark
"Goodbye to a Poltergeist." Poetry (130:3) Je 77, p. 146.
"My Parents Have Come Home Laughing." Field (17) Aut 77,
    p. 22.
"Planting." Iowa (8:3) Sum 77, p. 36.
"Required Mysteries." Field (17) Aut 77, p. 20.
"Writing for Nora." PoetryNW (18:4) Wint 77-78, p. 18.

JARRATT, Kent
"Listening to the Radio." HangL (31) Aut 77, p. 25.
"Sunbathing." HangL (31) Aut 77, p. 26.

JARRETT, Emmett
"Hew-Fly, Deep-Lie, Mary-Fish." HangL (29) Wint 76-77,
    p. 10.
"Those Walker Girls." PoNow (14/18) 77, p. 81.

JARZOMBEK, Anthony P.
"Dysfunction." NewC (7:2) 75-76, p. 25.

JASON, Philip K.
"Definition." Comm (104:9) 29 Ap 77, p. 278.
"The Sun Is Setting." MidwQ (18:3) Spr 77, p. 262.
"Too Quick Upon Me." FourQt (26:2) Wint 77, p. 16.

JASPERSEN, Barbara
"Elegiac Verse for Violence." Rapp (10) 77, p. 53.

JASTERMSKY, Karen
"It is right before me. " SmPd (14:3) Aut 77, p. 36.

JAUSS, David
"The Ghost Dance. " Waters (6) 77, p. 38.

JAY, T. E.
"Snow. " MontG (5) Wint 77, p. 20.

JEFFERS, Lance
"Adulterous Betrayal Lay in Her Father's Penis. " Obs (3:1) Spr
    77, p. 50.
"Chronicle. " Obs (3:1) Spr 77, p. 48.
"For when that eager oath is taken. " Obs (3:1) Spr 77, p. 49.
"Sleep catches me in the nape. " Obs (3:1) Spr 77, p. 49.

JEFFREY, D. L.
"Adam. " GRR (8:3) 77, p. 228.
"Eve. " GRR (8:3) 77, p. 227.

JEN, Gish
"To Catullan Poets. " HarvAd (110:3) Mr 77, p. 29.

JENKINS, Patricia
"An Afterthought. " Poem (29) Mr 77, p. 56.

JENKINS, Peter
"Woman Wanted. " WindO (28) Spr 77, p. 20.

JENNINGS, Elizabeth
"Rhodes. " Poetry (130:2) My 77, p. 87.

JENNINGS, Kate
"Deep sea diver. " Xa (4) 77, p. 39.
"Fable 1. " TexQ (20:2) Sum 77, p. 34.
"Getting Up Early. " Sparrow (33) Ja 77, p. 13.
"Lab/October 15-30. " Sparrow (33) Ja 77, p. 13.
"Poem on the Cover Picture 'Freewheelin' Bob Dylan. '" Sparrow
    (33) Ja 77, p. 14.
"Stock Pot. " AmerS (46:3) Sum 77, p. 376.
"Thanksgiving Day NYC. " CarolQ (29:3) Aut 77, p. 97.
"Transformation. " CarolQ (29:3) Aut 77, p. 98.

JENNINGS, Michael
"Fatima's Wedding Dance. " FourQt (27:1) Aut 77, p. 21.

JENSEN, Dana Christian
"Blood's Last Visit. " KanQ (9:3) Sum 77, p. 14.

JENSEN, Laura
"As the Window Darkens. " Field (16) Spr 77, p. 5.
Eight poems. Antaeus (27) Aut 77, p. 7.
"Heavy Snowfall in a Year Gone Past. " NewYorker (52:50) 31 Ja
    77, p. 38.

"Kite." NewYorker (53:24) 1 Ag 77, p. 34.
"Night Typewriter Sounds." Field (16) Spr 77, p. 6.
Nine poems. OP (23) Spr-Sum 77, pp. 4-13.
"Patience Is a Leveling Thing." Field (16) Spr 77, p. 8.
"Weather." Columbia (1) Aut 77, p. 12.
"Winter Evening Poem." Field (16) Spr 77, p. 7.

JEREMY
"Jesu Kristê." PoetL (72:1) Spr 77, p. 25.
"Judas." PoetL (72:1) Spr 77, p. 25.

JIEN, Archbishop
"Tenure" (tr. by Graeme Wilson). DenQ (12:2) Sum 77, p. 358.

JIMENEZ, Juan Ramón
"Nocturne" (tr. by Mark Leviton). WebR (3:4) Aut 77, p. 32.
"Restlessness" (tr. by Mark Leviton). WebR (3:4) Aut 77,
    p. 32.
"Winter Scene (Snow)" (tr. by Mark Leviton). WebR (3:4) Aut 77,
    p. 33.

JITO, Empress
"Stories" (w. Granny Shihi) (tr. by Graeme Wilson). DenQ (12:2)
    Sum 77, p. 372.

JOAN, Polly
"She Asked Herself about Creativity." Chomo (3:3) Spr 77,
    p. 22.

JOHNS, Don
"A Post Script." CarouselQ (2:3) Wint 77, p. 32.

JOHNSON, Abby Arthur
"A Fierce Woman of the North." Gra (12) 77.

JOHNSON, Connie Sue
"In Explanation." Obs (3:2) Sum 77, p. 54.
"Soledad." Obs (3:2) Sum 77, p. 53.
"Something in the Wind." Obs (3:2) Sum 77, p. 53.

JOHNSON, David
"Firstling." NewOR (5:3) 77, p. 254.

JOHNSON, David Owen
"Father." GRR (8:3) 77, p. 204.
"Hester Contemplates Winter." PraS (51:3) Aut 77, p. 293.
"Hester Thinks of Her Pregnancy." PraS (51:3) Aut 77, p. 293.
"Hester Thinks of Meeting Dimmesdale: Thoughts of Love."
    PraS (51:3) Aut 77, p. 292.
"Hester Thinks on Chillingworth." PraS (51:3) Aut 77, p. 291.
"Hester's Thoughts on Fetching Water from the Spring." PraS
    (51:3) Aut 77, p. 295.
"Without Cluck or Crow." GRR (8:3) 77, p. 234.

JOHNSON, Denis
"The Dwelling" (tr. of Moshe Dor, w. the author).   TriQ (39)
    Spr 77, p. 257.
"Progression" (tr. of Moshe Dor, w. the author).   TriQ (39) Spr
    77, p. 258.
"The Song." Iowa (8:3) Sum 77, p. 33.

JOHNSON, Don
"Snake Doctors." LittleR (12) 77, p. 15.
"Tick Picking in the Quetico." LittleR (12) 77, p. 15.

JOHNSON, Halvard
"Improvisation, IV." HangL (30) Sum 77, p. 39.
"The Incalculable Perfection of Heaven." PoNow (14/18) 77,
    p. 81.
"Oil." DacTerr (14) Spr-Sum 77, p. 41.
"Stamping." DacTerr (14) Spr-Sum 77, p. 41.
"Utrecht, 1287." Pig (3) 77, p. 94.
"Wild Horses." Juice (4) 77.
"Winter Journey." HangL (30) Sum 77, p. 30.

JOHNSON, Jean
"Seer." StoneC (77:3) S 77, p. 31.

JOHNSON, Judy
"A Letter to a Potter." BlackF (2:1) Wint 77-78, p. 25.

JOHNSON, Larry
"Cavafy Poem." TexQ (20:4) Wint 77, p. 112.
"Tanous." TexQ (20:4) Wint 77, p. 159.

JOHNSON, Manly
"Closed Circuit" (for two friends departed).   Qt (57/58) Wint-Spr
    77, p. 46.
"A Penny." Qt (57/58) Wint-Spr 77, p. 36.

JOHNSON, Marilyn
"Our Mothers Were Sisters." PartR (44:4) 77, p. 563.

JOHNSON, Michael L.
"Buffalo." StoneC (77:3) S 77, p. 19.
"A Coyote's Death in Winter." Sam (55) 77, p. 60.
"History Lesson." BallSUF (18:1) Wint 77, p. 11.
"Meditation on Madame Bovary." StoneC (77:3) S 77, p. 19.
"Memento Mori." Poem (29) Mr 77, p. 14.
"The Nazca Lines." Poem (29) Mr 77, p. 12.
"Nocturne: The Fourth of July." KanQ (9:3) Sum 77, p. 33.
"Summer Heat." Poem (29) Mr 77, p. 11.

JOHNSON, Nan C.
"Suspect in the Scarlet Hour." Vaga (25) 77, p. 11.

JOHNSON, Nate
"Mendicancy." Obs (3:1) Spr 77, p. 65.

"night's. " Obs (3:1) Spr 77, p. 65.
"Train Rhythm: a Constellation on Africa's Freedom. " Epoch
    (26:2) Wint 77, p. 105.
"two. " Obs (3:1) Spr 77, p. 64.

JOHNSON, Nick
    "Laundrymat Blues. " YellowBR (9) 77, p. 33.

JOHNSON, Rita Lavon
    "But It's Such a Nice Aquarium. " KanQ (9:3) Sum 77, p. 121.
    "The Witches of Spring. " Wind (27) 77, p. 27.

JOHNSON, Thomas
    "After a Death Two Doors East. " PoNow (14/18) 77, p. 81.
    "Amherst County Log. " Falcon (14) 77, p. 80.
    "Ark. " YaleR (67:1) Aut 77, p. 68.
    "Catechism. " Nat (224:14) 9 Ap 77, p. 443.
    "December Rain. " SouthernPR (17:2) Aut 77, p. 13.
    "Drawing Too Near a Lover's Face. " Falcon (14) 77, p. 78.
    "Each Day. " Agni (7) 77, p. 22.
    "Each Evening. " CarolQ (29:3) Aut 77, p. 40.
    "From Day to Day. " Northeast (3:3) Sum 77, p. 46.
    "The Lag. " Some (7/8) 76.
    "Letter to Myself in Late August. " Rapp (10) 77, p. 44.
    "The Lie of Solidness. " CarolQ (29:3) Aut 77, p. 39.
    "Listening to the Earth's Spin. " OhioR (18:3) Aut 77, p. 26.
    "Lines Emptied Toward a Hundred-Branched Bolt of Lightning in
        North Georgia. " Falcon (14) 77, p. 79.
    "New Grass on the Edge of a Rockslide. " Drag (16) 77.
    "Persimmon. " LittleR (12) 77, p. 17.
    "Reunion. " YaleR (67:1) Aut 77, p. 69.
    "Sandstorm. " PoNow (14/18) 77, p. 82.
    "Toward Our Use. " CarolQ (29:3) Aut 77, p. 38.
    "Wrung Through a Mile of Honeysuckle. " Agni (7) 77, p. 21.

JOHNSON, Tom
    "A Civil War Photograph. " SewanR (85:4) Aut 77, p. 604.
    "George C. Marshall. " SewanR (85:4) Aut 77, p. 605.
    "Supper on the Terrace. " NewRep (177:10) 3 S 77, p. 28.

JOHNSTON, Kelly
    "First Hunt. " ArkRiv (3:4/4:1) 77, p. 71.

JOHNSTON, Pauline
    "Monuments. " KanQ (9:3) Sum 77, p. 85.

JOKL, Vivian
    "Paper Kite. " SoDakR (15:4) Wint 77-78, p. 53.
    "The Temperature of Need Is the Same in Desert or Sea. "
        SoDakR (15:4) Wint 77-78, p. 51.

JOLAS, Eugene
    "The Tramp's Sin and Charlie Chaplin. " WebR (3:1) Wint 77,
        p. 54.

JOLLY, John
"Being Prepared to Die." Rapp (10) 77, p. 51.

JONAS, George
"Atwood: A Miniature." MalR (41) Ja 77, p. 190.

JONES, Charles T., Jr.
"There Is a Fire." NewC (8:1) 76-77, p. 6.

JONES, David W.
"Untitled." CarouselQ (2:3) Wint 77, p. 22.

JONES, Don
Medical Aid. Sam (62) 77. Entire issue.

JONES, Mark
from Oak Hills: (1-5). PortR (23) 77, p. 30.

JONES, Patricia
"Anoche." Nimrod (21:2/22:1) 77, p. 127.
"Sonnet/For Pedro Pietri." Nimrod (21:2/22:1) 77, p. 127.

JONES, Rodney
Eight poems. SmF (6) Aut 77, p. 10.

JONES, Seaborn
"Bed Time Story." Xa (4) 77, p. 15.
"The Golden Gate Bridge." YellowBR (8) 77, p. 29.
"Name." Xa (4) 77, p. 14.

JONES, Tammy
"Spring Banquet." Wind (27) 77, p. 17.

JONES, Tiger
"When I Die." AmerPoR (6:2) Mr-Ap 77, p. 33.

JONES, Tom
"Moloch's Place." NewRep (176:6) 5 F 77, p. 25.
"Nearing Palenque." YaleR (66:3) Spr 77, p. 406.

JONG, Erica
"Depression in Early Spring." ParisR (71) Aut 77, p. 137.
"His Tuning of the Night." NewYorker (53:41) 28 N 77, p. 47.
"Jubilate Canis." ParisR (71) Aut 77, p. 136.

JONKE, G. F.
"Lethargic Apperception I-II" (tr. by John Michel). ParisR (69)
    Spr 77, p. 129.
"The Town" (tr. by John Michel). ParisR (69) Spr 77, p. 130.
"The Town of Torsaric Acriby: Construction Site (I-II)" (tr. by
    John Michel). ParisR (69) Spr 77, p. 130.

JOOSSE, Barbara M.
"Sisters." Vaga (25) 77, p. 48.

JORDAN, June
"The Name of the Poem Is." TransR (58/59) F 77, p. 98.
"1977: Poem for Mrs. Fannie Lou Hamer." Nimrod (21:2/22:1)
77, p. 128.
"no more the chicken and the egg come." AmerPoR (6:1) Ja-F
77, p. 25.
"Poem for Nana." Nimrod (21:2/22:1) 77, p. 130.

JORDAN, Suzanne Britt
"Backroads." Poem (31) N 77, p. 23.
"A Clean Thing." Poem (31) N 77, p. 24.

JORDAN, Tari
"How Many Days in a Week?" YaleLit (145:3) 77, p. 4.

JORGENSON, Kregg P. J.
"The Waistland ... Sort Of." DeKalb (10:3) Spr 77, p. 19.

JOSEPH, David
"Dad Wakes Up to the Bad News." Sam (56) Sum 77, p. 40.

JOSHI, Vasant B.
"(Addressing Krishna)" (tr. of Surdas). DenQ (12:2) Sum 77,
p. 91.
"The beloved of Krishna" (tr. of Surdas). DenQ (12:2) Sum 77,
p. 93.
"God is the dyer" (tr. of Kabir). DenQ (12:2) Sum 77, p. 89.
"The holy places" (tr. of Kabir). DenQ (12:2) Sum 77, p. 88.
"O sparrow" (tr. of Mirabai). DenQ (12:2) Sum 77, p. 94.
"Where else could my mind" (tr. of Surdas). DenQ (12:2) Sum
77, p. 92.
"You've spent your life" (tr. of Kabir). DenQ (12:2) Sum 77,
p. 90.

JOY, Debra
"I would write: I want to know." StoneC (77:2) My 77, p. 16.

JOYCE, William
"Eyes for the Fish Cutter." Madem (83:11) N 77, p. 192.
"The Voice of the Poem You Never Hear." KanQ (9:1) Wint 77,
p. 120.

JOZSEF, Attila
"Diamond" (tr. by John Batki). Hand (1) 77, p. 196.
"Nothing" (tr. by John Batki). Hand (1) 77, p. 194.
"Numbers" (tr. by John Batki). Hand (1) 77, p. 195.
"A Transparent Lion" (tr. by John Batki). Hand (1) 77, p. 195.

JUAN Chi
"Learning" (tr. by Graeme Wilson). DenQ (12:2) Sum 77, p. 45.
"Nocturne" (tr. by Graeme Wilson). DenQ (12:2) Sum 77, p. 392.

JUDSON, John
"Compass and Bearing." HiramPoR (22) Aut-Wint 77, p. 25.

"Coon Creek. " SmF (6) Aut 77, p. 20.
"East/West. " SmF (6) Aut 77, p. 18.
"Fisherman: Below Genoa" (for Felix).   SmF (6) Aut 77,
    p. 19.
"I Am Thick with Another's Noise. " SmF (6) Aut 77, p. 22.
"Morning Song. " SmF (6) Aut 77, p. 23.
"*. " SmF (6) Aut 77, p. 21.
"22 October. " NoAmR (262:1) Spr 77, p. 48.

JUERGENSEN, Hans
"'Frisco. '" NewC (8:1) 76-77, p. 20.

JUNKINS, Donald
"Approaches to Blue Hill Bay: Chart No. 13313. " NewYorker
    (53:19) 27 Je 77, p. 38.

JURADO, James
"The Brute. " Juice (5) 77.

JUSTICE, Donald
"The Contentment of Tremayne. " NewYorker (53:20) 4 Jl 77,
    p. 30.
"The Mild Despair of Tremayne. " NewYorker (53:20) 4 Jl 77,
    p. 30.

KABDEBO, Thomas
"Insult" (tr. of Istvan Vas).   ModernPS (8:2) Aut 77, p. 115.

KABIR
"11" (tr. by Robert Bly).   MoonsLT (2:3) 77, inside front cover.
"18" (tr. by Robert Bly).   MoonsLT (2:3) 77, inside front cover.
"God is the dyer" (tr. by Vasant B. Joshi).   DenQ (12:2) Sum 77,
    p. 89.
"The holy places" (tr. by Vasant B. Joshi).   DenQ (12:2) Sum 77,
    p. 88.
"You've spent your life" (tr. by Vasant B. Joshi).   DenQ (12:2)
    Sum 77, p. 90.

KAEBITZSCH, Reinhold Johannes
"We sit as vegetables. " NewRena (9) F 77, p. 24.

KAHN, Hannah
"Carla (Two Years Old). " LadHJ (94:9) S 77, p. 116.
"To a Young Bride. " LadHJ (94:6) Je 77, p. P. S. 22.

KAITZ, Merrill
"Maybe a Bird. " Ploughs (3:3/4) 77, p. 131.

KAKOOK, Daniel
"Crystal Gazing. " YellowBR (8) 77, p. 12.

KALÁSZ, Márton
"Legacy" (tr. by Jascha Kessler).   AmerPoR (6:3) My-Je 77,
    p. 25.

"Legacy" (tr. by Jascha Kessler). CentR (21:1) Wint 77, p. 71.
"Legacy" (tr. by Jascha Kessler). ParisR (69) Spr 77, p. 134.
"Maiden" (tr. by Jascha Kessler). NewL (44:1) Aut 77, p. 95.

KALLAS, Anthony C.
"The Bushwhacker." StoneC (77:3) S 77, p. 11.
"Progress." Aspect (70) Ja-Mr 77, p. 35.

KALLAS, Julianne
"Tower of Mothers." Aspect (69) O-D 76, p. 42.

KALLSEN, T. J.
"To My Elder Daughter." Qt (57/58) Wint-Spr 77, p. 36.

KALTOVICH, Edith Rusconi
"God" (tr. of Enriquillo Rojas Abreu). WebR (3:4) Aut 77, p. 15.

KAMATARI, Fujiwara no
"Yasumiko" (tr. by Graeme Wilson). DenQ (12:2) Sum 77,
    p. 374.

KAMENETZ, Rodger
"Garden of Eden." PoetL (72:1) Spr 77, p. 21.

KAMINSKY, Daniel
"Son of the Stone Man." SmPd (14:2) Spr 77, p. 3.

KAMINSKY, Marc
"Erev Shabbos" (for Esther Schwartzman). Hand (1) 77, p. 8.
"Pig Market." Hand (1) 77, p. 9.

KAMM, Nancy P.
"Blacktide." PoetL (72:1) Spr 77, p. 28.

KANE, Emily
"Firstly" (after Paul Eluard's Premièrement). HarvAd (111:1) N
    77, p. 10.

KANE, Julie
"Prayer to Chaos." Epoch (26:2) Wint 77, p. 113.
"Reasons for Loving the Harmonica Above All Other Instruments."
    Epoch (26:2) Wint 77, p. 115.
"Sunbeam Blues." Epoch (26:2) Wint 77, p. 114.

KANE, Katherine
"At the Mirror in the Woodmere Hotel." PortR (23) 77, p. 9.
"Elegy." PortR (23) 77, p. 8.
"The Wheelwright's Son." PortR (23) 77, p. 10.

KANE, Mary Eileen
"The Balance of Things Breathing." TexQ (20:2) Sum 77, p. 58.
"Dog Dilemma." TexQ (20:2) Sum 77, p. 58.
"On Her Husband's Inattentiveness." CimR (39) Ap 77, p. 53.

KANE, Paul
"Canada." AmerR (26) N 77, p. 331.

KANEKO, Lonny
"Issei." GreenR (6:1/2) Spr 77, p. 20.
"Lee Siu Long: Little Dragon Lee." GreenR (6:1/2) Spr 77,
    p. 22.
"Renewal: Algona, Washington." GreenR (6:1/2) Spr 77, p. 21.
"View from an Office Building." KanQ (9:3) Sum 77, p. 60.

KANEKO, Norm
"Luck, Himself." GreenR (6:1/2) Spr 77, p. 59.

KANES, Evelyn
"Corkscombs" (tr. of Peter Huchel). ChiR (29:3) Wint 78, p. 77.
"Defeat" (tr. of Peter Huchel). ChiR (29:3) Wint 78, p. 83.
"Outside Nîmes 1452" (tr. of Peter Huchel). ChiR (29:3) Wint
    78, p. 79.
"Snow" (In memory of Hans Henny Jahnn) (tr. of Peter Huchel).
    ChiR (29:3) Wint 78, p. 75.

KANFER, Allen
"Emerson Went Home." DenQ (12:1) Spr 77, p. 218.

KAO Chi
"Whetstone Mountain" (tr. by Graeme Wilson). DenQ (12:2) Sum
    77, p. 57.

KAPLAN, Bob
"Looking Back." CarouselQ (2:2) Aut 77, p. 17.

KAPLAN, Edward
"The Internal Temper Koan." Sam (52) Ap 77, p. 52.
"Letter to Allen Ginsberg on the Death of His Father." StoneC
    (77:3) S 77, p. 16.
"Sheridan Square Poem." Mouth (13) D 77, p. 67.

KAPLAN, Rhoda
"I Had Him Removed from the Room." Paunch (48/49) S 77,
    p. 4.
"I Wanted to Bring My Father Back." Paunch (48/49) S 77,
    p. 5.

KAPLAN, Robin
"Last Friday." 13thM (3:2) 77, p. 18.

KARLAGE, Rocky
"South Road Tavern" (for Tom & Joe). Waters (5) 77, p. 17.

KASCHNITZ, Maria Luise
"Threatening Letter" (tr. by Derk Wynand). WebR (3:1) Wint 77,
    p. 51.

KASHNER, Samuel
"captain of bad memories." HangL (29) Wint 76-77, p. 24.
"the ham of sleep." HangL (31) Aut 77, p. 28.
"a hero to the earth." HangL (29) Wint 76-77, p. 28.
"hot flashes in an empty bed." HangL (29) Wint 76-77, p. 23.
"message from the plain of jars." HangL (31) Aut 77, p. 30.
"the mushroom chronicles." HangL (31) Aut 77, p. 34.
"the slow god." HangL (29) Wint 76-77, p. 26.
"a woman crying into her sculpture." HangL (31) Aut 77, p. 32.

KASPER, M.
"Radiation from a Hot Body." WormR (65/66) 77, p. 40.
"Standard Clauses or Riders." WormR (65/66) 77, p. 41.

KATES, J.
"Nothing in Art." Chowder (9) Aut-Wint 1977, p. 99.

KATZ, Arlene
"The Pond." Shen (28:4) Sum 77, p. 34.

KATZ, Steve
"On Taking the Cure." Rapp (10) 77, p. 55.

KATZ-LEVINE, Judy
"At the last ballgame." Some (7/8) 76.

KAUFFMAN, Janet
"Ghost of a Second Shift Mother." NewL (44:1) Aut 77, p. 90.
"Off-Loom Weaving." Nat (224:11) 19 Mr 77, p. 346.

KAUFMAN, Elizabeth
"The Glass House." SouthernPR (17:1) Spr 77, p. 41.

KAUFMAN, Shirley
"Divorce." MassR (18:1) Spr 77, p. 120.
"Friends" (tr. of Meir Wieseltier, w. Shlomit Rimmon). TriQ
    (39) Spr 77, p. 315.
from Gazelle, I'll Send You: "Prologue" and (1-15) (tr. of Amir
    Gilboa, w. Shlomit Rimmon). TriQ (39) Spr 77, p. 261.
"I didn't know if Mount Zion would recognize itself" (tr. of Abba
    Kovner). TriQ (39) Spr 77, p. 279.
"March" (tr. of Meir Wieseltier, w. Shlomit Rimmon). TriQ
    (39) Spr 77, p. 315.
"Meeting." Kayak (45) My 77, p. 37.
"Niagara Falls" (tr. of Avner Treinin, w. Shlomit Rimmon).
    TriQ (39) Spr 77, p. 304.
"Observation at Dawn" (tr. of Abba Kovner, w. Shlomit Rimmon).
    TriQ (39) Spr 77, p. 283.
"Observation on Jerusalem at Twilight and a Dialogue" (tr. of
    Abba Kovner). TriQ (39) Spr 77, p. 281.
"A Request" (tr. of Meir Wieseltier, w. Shlomit Rimmon). TriQ
    (39) Spr 77, p. 313.
"Reruns." Kayak (45) My 77, p. 36.

"The Secret of Authority" (tr. of Meir Wieseltier, w. Shlomit
    Rimmon). TriQ (39) Spr 77, p. 311.
from Songs of Leonardo: (1-7) (tr. of Avner Treinin, w. Judy
    Levy). TriQ (39) Spr 77, p. 306.
"To My City Jerusalem, 1967" (tr. of Amir Gilboa, w. Shlomit
    Rimmon). TriQ (39) Spr 77, p. 266.
"The Words. " MassR (18:1) Spr 77, p. 120.

KAUFMAN, Stuart
    "Politico. " LaB (8) Jl-Ag 77, p. 30.
    "Proem. " LaB (8) Jl-Ag 77, p. 32.
    "Rockaway Beach" (for my father). LaB (8) Jl 77, p. 35.
    "Searchlight. " LaB (8) Jl-Ag 77, p. 33.

KAUFMAN, Wallace
    "Distance. " SouthernPR (16:SI) 77, p. 43.

KAUN Han-ching
    "Lover" (tr. by Graeme Wilson). DenQ (12:2) Sum 77, p. 395.

KAVEN, Bob
    "Locating Sleep. " NewYorker (53:10) 25 Ap 77, p. 135.

KAWSON, Patty
    "In the Land of Aob. " QW (2) Wint 77, p. 60.

KAZUKO, Shiraishi
    "I Fire at the Face of the Country Where I Was Born" (tr. by
        Kenneth Rexroth). PortR (23) 77, p. 92.
    "The Man Root" (tr. by Kenneth Rexroth). PortR (23) 77, p. 94.
    "Winter" (tr. by Kenneth Rexroth). Epoch (26:2) Wint 77, p. 164.

KEANE, Patrick J.
    "A Word for Wordsworth. " Salm (38/39) Sum-Aut 77, p. 108.

KEEFER, Monique
    "I'd like my 3rd eye. " AAR (27) 77, p. 118.

KEELEY, Edmund
    "The Bandaged Shoulder" (tr. of Constantine Cavafy, w. Philip
        Sherrard). NewYRB (24:2) 17 F 77, p. 33.
    "In the Ruins of an Ancient Temple" (tr. of Yannis Ritsos).
        BosUJ (25:3) 77, p. 63.
    "Incense" (tr. of Yannis Ritsos). BosUJ (25:3) 77, p. 64.
    "Ionic" (tr. of Constantine Cavafy, w. Philip Sherrard). NewYRB
        (24:2) 17 F 77, p. 33.
    "Kaisarion" (tr. of Constantine Cavafy, w. Philip Sherrard).
        NewYRB (24:2) 17 F 77, p. 33.
    "The Meaning of Simplicity" (tr. of Yannis Ritsos). BosUJ
        (25:3) 77, p. 62.
    "Miniature" (tr. of Yannis Ritsos). BosUJ (25:3) 77, p. 62.
    "Reconstruction" (tr. of Yannis Ritsos). BosUJ (25:3) 77, p. 64.
    "Women" (tr. of Yannis Ritsos). BosUJ (25:3) 77, p. 63.

KEELY, Stephen
"Anonymous Heroes." KanQ (9:3) Sum 77, p. 28.

KEENAN, Deborah
"losses and the colors of snow." Wind (24) 77, p. 36.

KEENAN, Terrance
"In the Bright Blue There Were Stars." DacTerr (14) Spr-Sum
     77, p. 74.
"Light the Fish." DacTerr (14) Spr-Sum 77, p. 75.

KEENEY, William E.
"You Can Can Parenthetics." NewC (7:3) 75-76, p. 10.

KEENS, William
"How It Feels to Walk on the Moon." Poetry (129:5) F 77,
     p. 277.
"Skull House, Heart Flower." Poetry (129:5) F 77, p. 276.

KEITHLEY, George
"Dread of Darkness." PoNow (14/18) 77, p. 82.
"Fr. Tein Resigns Rock Lake Parish." PoNow (14/18) 77,
     p. 82.
"Only Imperiled People See the Sun." PoNow (14/18) 77, p. 82.

KELEN, Leslie
"Listening." QW (3) Spr-Sum 77, p. 4.
"Psalm of Night" (tr. of Endry Ady). QW (3) Spr-Sum 77, p. 60.
"Someone Has Again Remembered" (tr. of Endry Ady). QW (3)
     Spr-Sum 77, p. 61.

KELLEHER, Ann
"'Bee-Wolves.'" Iowa (8:4) Aut 77, p. 86.
"Divorce." Iowa (8:4) Aut 77, p. 87.
"Frogs." Iowa (8:4) Aut 77, p. 86.
"Rape." AmerPoR (6:6) N-D 77, p. 43.

KELLER, David
"Beauty, She Supposes." US1 (10) Wint 77-78, p. 4.
"Ceremony." US1 (9) Spr 77, p. 2.
"Giving Them Names." US1 (10) Wint 77-78, p. 4.
"Not Speaking." MinnR (NS8) Spr 77, p. 56.
"The Plants Started the Hunger Strike." DenQ (12:3) Aut 77,
     p. 44.
"The Plants Started the Hunger Strike." US1 (9) Spr 77, p. 2.

KELLER, Joseph John
"The Farm." PoetL (72:1) Spr 77, p. 13.

KELLER, Pat
"The Breaking." SouthernHR (11:4) Aut 77, p. 384.
"Lecture." Stonecloud (6) 76, p. 71.
"Phases." Stonecloud (6) 76, p. 143.

"The Relic Hunter" (for Oxford Stroud).   TexQ (20:4) Wint 77,
     p. 157.
"Winter Flight. "   Stonecloud (6) 76, p. 66.

KELLER, Ray
"To a Departed Lady. "   SmPd (14:3) Aut 77, p. 6.

KELLEY, James L.
"Lakeland. "   PoetL (72:1) Spr 77, p. 14.

KELLEY, Shannon Keith
"Review of a Children's Classic for the 70's. "   KanQ (9:1) Wint
     77, p. 113.

KELLEY, Tim
"The Word Is Like a Cold Beer. "   StoneC (77:3) S 77, p. 8.

KELLNHAUSER, John T.
"Footnotes on Empire. "   SmPd (14:2) Spr 77, p. 12.

KELLY, Dave
"Plot Outline. "   PoNow (14/18) 77, p. 84.

KELSEY, Laura
"Daughter to Mother. "   HangL (31) Aut 77, p. 72.

KEMP, June
"1977. "   Sam (59) 77, p. 26.
"El Valle. "   Sam (52) Ap 77, p. 2.
"Yearbook. "   Sam (56) Sum 77, p. 55.

KEMPHER, Ruth Moon
"Hilda Halfheart's Notes to the Milkman: # 69. "   HiramPoR (23)
     Wint 77, p. 22.
"The Letters from Prattsburg ... The Tenth Letter, Another
     P. S. "   WindO (28) Spr 77, p. 27.
"On the Way Back to Jacksonville and the Beaches Sylvia Savage
     Formulates a List of Things with Which to Empathize. "
     WindO (30) Aut 77, p. 11.
"Picture #36" (At the Asylum).   DeKalb (10:2) Wint 77, p. 43.

KENNEDY, Stephen
"Freedom Poem. "   SouthernPR (17:1) Spr 77, p. 16.
"John's Metamorphoses. "   NowestR (16:3) 77, p. 87.
"My New Prayer. "   PoetL (72:1) Spr 77, p. 27.
"Rimbaud in Parenthesis. "   PoetL (72:1) Spr 77, p. 17.

KENNEDY, Terry
"dear jack. "   Bound (5:3) Spr 77, p. 889.
"for the woman who says she is my mother. "   Chelsea (36) 77,
     p. 17.

KENNEY, Joseph
"to look for to know" (tr. of Ernst Jandl).   ChiR (29:3) Wint 78,
     p. 131.

KENNEY, Richard
"Desperados." YaleR (66:3) Spr 77, p. 401.
"Grotesques." YaleR (66:3) Spr 77, p. 400.
"Notes from Greece." NewYorker (53:36) 24 O 77, p. 41.

KENNY, John
"Heat." CalQ (11/12) Wint-Spr 77, p. 107.

KENNY, Maurice
"Cyclist." Glass (2:2/3) Wint-Spr 77, p. 96.
"In Baja Mexico." Waters (6) 77, p. 14.
"Mole." Glass (2:2/3) Wint-Spr 77, p. 97.

KENT, Rolly
"The Woman They Stole Away." AmerPoR (6:2) Mr-Ap 77, p. 27.
"World War II." AmerPoR (6:2) Mr-Ap 77, p. 28.

KENYON, Jane
"From Room to Room." AmerPoR (6:2) Mr-Ap 77, p. 21.
"Hanging Pictures in Nanny's Room." MichQR (16:3) Sum 77,
     p. 301.

KÉPES, Géza
"Letter to My Mother" (tr. by Paul Tabori). ModernPS (8:2) Aut
     77, p. 104.

KERLEY, Gary
"The Chameleon's Nightmare." KanQ (9:1) Wint 77, p. 117.
"Kept Balance." GRR (8:3) 77, p. 233.
"Preparing a Room for Love." Poem (30) Jl 77, p. 21.
"They Have Ways." Poem (30) Jl 77, p. 22.

KERMAN, Judith
"Daughters (II) A False Sestina." HangL (30) Sum 77, p. 40.
from Mothering: "rocking, rocking, rocking, rocking, the tide
     coming slowly into." HangL (30) Sum 77, p. 45.
from Mothering: "she goes to her father's funeral it's awful, as
     she expected." HangL (30) Sum 77, p. 44.
"Red Lollipop." HangL (30) Sum 77, p. 46.
"Upstream." HangL (30) Sum 77, p. 42.

KEROACK, Elizabeth Carros
"Night Tremors." EngJ (66:5) My 77, p. 44.

KERRIGAN, Anthony
"Giacomo Casanova Accepts the Office of Librarian Offered Him
     in Bohemia by Count Waldstein" (tr. of Antonio Colinas).
     Confr (14) Spr-Sum 77, p. 28.
"To Encounter Ezra Pound--Posthumous Instructions" (ad. of
     Antonio Colinas). Confr (14) Spr-Sum 77, p. 29.

KERRIGAN, Thomas
"Prologos." StoneC (77:1) F 77, p. 6.

KESEY, Ken
  Thirteen poems. NowestR (16:1/2) 77, p. 190. Entire issue de-
    voted to Ken Kesey.

KESSLER, Jascha
  "Anatomy of a Supper" (tr. of Gábor Görgey). AmerR (26) N 77,
    p. 110.
  "The Face of Creation" (tr. of Ottô Orbân). MassR (18:2) Sum
    77, p. 282.
  "Four Literary Encounters. " Kayak (46) O 77, p. 14.
  "Legacy" (tr. of Mârton Kalâsz). AmerPoR (6:3) My-Je 77,
    p. 25.
  "Legacy" (tr. of Mârton Kalâsz). ParisR (69) Spr 77, p. 134.
  "Legacy" (tr. of Mârton Kalâsz). CentR (21:1) Wint 77, p. 71.
  "Maiden" (tr. of Mârton Kalâsz). NewL (44:1) Aut 77, p. 95.
  "The Old Muse. " PoNow (14/18) 77, p. 84.
  "Poetry: I-IV. " Kayak (45) My 77, p. 10.
  "Seine Wharves Southeast" (tr. of Judit Tôth). ParisR (69) Spr
    77, p. 133.
  "The Singing Reed" (tr. of Rumi, w. Amin Banani). CentR (21:1)
    Wint 77, p. 72.
  "A Summer on the Lake" (tr. of Ottô Orbân). MassR (18:2) Sum
    77, p. 284.

KESSLER, Milton
  "'In the House Where We Laugh and Cry'" (for Charles Reznikoff
    [1894-1976]). MoonsLT (2:3) 77, p. 62.
  "Standpoing. " Nat (225:12) 15 O 77, p. 380.
  "Winter Windows. " Iowa (8:3) Sum 77, p. 28.

KESSLER, Stephen
  "Death" (tr. of Pablo Neruda). Chowder (8) Spr-Sum 77, p. 44.
  "The Fall of the Bishop" (tr. of Fernando Alegria). MontG (6)
    Aut 77, p. 46.
  "Ode to the Birds of Chile" (tr. of Pablo Neruda). Bleb (12) 77,
    p. 28.
  "Two Drink Minimum. " Madrona (4:13/14) 77, p. 39.

KESZTHELYI, Zoltán
  "After the Flood" (tr. by Paul Tabori). ModernPS (8:2) Aut 77,
    p. 106.

KETCHUM, K. D.
  "Lulu. " CarolQ (29:1) Wint 77, p. 39.

KEVORKIAN, Karen
  "Cleaning Doves. " EnPas (4) 76, p. 17.
  "Holiday. " EnPas (5) 77, p. 22.

KEYISHIAN, M. D.
  "Delphi. " Sparrow (33) Ja 77, p. 7.

KEYS, Kerry Shawn
  "Brazil, Some Parts. " Kayak (45) My 77, p. 24.

"Narcissus of His Shadow. " Icarus (5:1) Spr 77, p. 16.
"These Things I Can't Say. " Kayak (45) My 77, p. 23.

KEYSER, Grant
"Reading Mary Margaret. " Drag (16) 77.

al-KHAL, Yusuf
"The Deserted Well" (tr. by Sargon Boulus). Mund (10:1) 77,
    p. 51.
"Glory to the Three" (tr. by Sargon Boulus). Mund (10:1) 77,
    p. 52.
"I Hear Everything" (tr. by Sargon Boulus). Mund (10:1) 77,
    p. 51.
"Retaliation" (tr. by Sargon Boulus). Mund (10:1) 77, p. 52.

KHERDIAN, David
"Chuck. " Wind (26) 77, p. 31.
"The First Time" (for Donny Hansen and Sam Margosian). Wind
    (26) 77, p. 31.
"Junior Rognerud. " Wind (26) 77, p. 32.
"Letter to H. K. " Wind (26) 77, p. 32.
"Little Sis. " NewL (44:2) Wint 77, p. 95.
"Melkon. " NewL (44:2) Wint 77, p. 96.
"Root River. " NewL (43:3) Spr 77, p. 96.
"Rosemary. " Wind (26) 77, p. 30.
"That Day. " Wind (26) 77, p. 30.
"Uncle Jack. " NewL (43:3) Spr 77, p. 96.

KICKNOSWAY, Faye
"and what shall you be today, fair maid, and what. " Bleb (12)
    77, p. 24.
"the condoms keep catching at the rivers. " Bleb (12) 77, p. 23.
"Pieta. " PoNow (14/18) 77, p. 84.
"the pig in the dark sty sings. " Bleb (12) 77, p. 22.
"roaches in the toilet. " Bleb (12) 77, p. 23.
from 2nd Chance Man: The Cigarette Poem: "make no sexual
    energy. " Hand (1) 77, p. 38.
from 2nd Chance Man: The Cigarette Poem: "you are a memory
    i have. " Hand (1) 77, p. 39.
from 2nd Chance Man: The Cigarette Poem: "you walk off the
    calendar, out of the old. " Hand (1) 77, p. 37.
"Spitting Backward. " Bleb (12) 77, p. 21.

KIKO
"Mount Sumeru--my fist!" (tr. by Lucien Stryk). ChiR (29:2)
    Aut 77, p. 87.

KILDARE, D.
"The Gar. " KanQ (9:1) Wint 77, p. 106.
"Timor Mortis. " Wind (26) 77, p. 34.
"Why I Believe God Is a Trochee. " CalQ (11/12) Wint-Spr 77,
    p. 143.
"Xenophobia. " Wind (26) 77, p. 34.

KILGORE, James C.
  "It's Thundering Again." Nimrod (21:2/22:1) 77, p. 134.

KIMBALL, Jack
  "Song for Division of Cortex." LaB (6) Mr 77, p. 33.
  "Vampire Poem." LaB (6) Mr 77, p. 34.
  "Xylophone." LaB (6) Mr 77, p. 35.

KIM Chang-op
  "Falcon" (tr. by Graeme Wilson). VirQR (53:3) Sum 77, p. 453.
  "Realist" (tr. by Graeme Wilson). DenQ (12:2) Sum 77, p. 300.

KIM Chang-so
  "Fame" (tr. by Graeme Wilson). DenQ (12:2) Sum 77, p. 297.

KIM Chin-tae
  "Sword" (tr. by Graeme Wilson). DenQ (12:2) Sum 77, p. 299.

KIM Chon-taek
  "Such Cold Case" (tr. by Graeme Wilson). DenQ (12:2) Sum 77,
    p. 398.

KIM Kwang-uk
  "Property" (tr. by Graeme Wilson). DenQ (12:2) Sum 77,
    p. 306.

KIM Sam-hyon
  "Out of Office" (tr. by Graeme Wilson). DenQ (12:2) Sum 77,
    p. 296.

KIM Sang-yong
  "Lies" (tr. by Graeme Wilson). DenQ (12:2) Sum 77, p. 310.
  "Marriage" (tr. by Graeme Wilson). VirQR (53:3) Sum 77,
    p. 451.
  "The Tree of Happiness" (tr. by Graeme Wilson). DenQ (12:2)
    Sum 77, p. 298.

KIM Su-jang
  "Capital" (tr. by Graeme Wilson). DenQ (12:2) Sum 77, p. 308.
  "Girls" (tr. by Graeme Wilson). DenQ (12:2) Sum 77, p. 297.
  "The Mind of Man" (tr. by Graeme Wilson). DenQ (12:2) Sum 77,
    p. 304.
  "Per Incuriam" (tr. by Graeme Wilson). DenQ (12:2) Sum 77,
    p. 301.
  "Time to Be Writing Songs" (tr. by Graeme Wilson). DenQ (12:2)
    Sum 77, p. 293.

KING, Dave
  "Brekhage Fragment." YaleLit (146:4/5) 77, p. 38.

KING, Edmund L.
  "Arte Rupestre, 1939-1969, 1" (tr. of Jorge Guillén). NewRep
    (176:15) 9 Ap 77, p. 29.

KING, Francis
"Dawn." Poetry (130:5) Ag 77, p. 255.
"Down by the Lake, Up at the Villa." Poetry (130:5) Ag 77,
    p. 253.
"Intruders." Poetry (130:5) Ag 77, p. 254.
"Lago di Como." Poetry (130:5) Ag 77, p. 255.
"Villa Serbelloni." Poetry (130:5) Ag 77, p. 251.

KING, Jeffrey W.
"I Saw a Woman Sit Alone." CimR (34) Ja 76, p. 64.

KING, Jenny
"A different city." Stand (18:3) 77, p. 7.
"Restaurant." Stand (18:3) 77, p. 7.

KING, Linda
"Daddy and the Birds." WormR (65/66) 77, p. 31.

KING, Pat
"The Old House." Wind (24) 77, p. 16.
"When You Went Away." Wind (24) 77, p. 16.

KING, Robert S.
"Communion." Xa (4) 77, p. 36.
"Ice-Sparkles." Xa (4) 77, p. 37.
"Prophets Climbing to Machu Picchu." SmPd (14:3) Aut 77,
    p. 16.
"Well Water and Mother's Makeup." DeKalb (10:3) Spr 77, p. 21.

KINGBIRD, Bonnie
"Worms and storms." AmerPoR (6:2) Mr-Ap 77, p. 32.

KINGMA, Daphne Rose
"The Death of Uncle Frank." KanQ (9:3) Sum 77, p. 76.
"Meeting Again the Photographer I Once Loved." Chelsea (36)
    77, p. 14.

KINNELL, Galway
"Ballade I" (tr. of François Villon). ParisR (70) Sum 77, p. 102.
"Ballade II" (tr. of François Villon). ParisR (70) Sum 77,
    p. 103.
from The Testament: "In the thirtieth year of my time" (tr. of
    François Villon). AmerPoR (6:5) S-O 77, p. 23.

KINNICK, B. Jo
"To a Black American Soldier in Frankfort, Germany." EngJ
    (66:5) My 77, p. 47.

KINSELLA, Thomas
"Anniversaries." Chowder (9) Aut-Wint 77, p. 36.

KINTO, Fujiwara no
"Face" (tr. by Graeme Wilson). DenQ (12:2) Sum 77, p. 367.

KINZIE, Mary
"Accidie." Poetry (131:2) N 77, p. 95.
"The Bamberger Reiter." Poetry (129:6) Mr 77, p. 333.
"Chagall in His Sickness." Poetry (131:2) N 77, p. 96.
"Consummate." Salm (36) Wint 77, p. 36.
"The Human Face." Poetry (129:6) Mr 77, p. 331.
"In a Political Year/Which Began with the Fall of Prague." Shen
    (28:2) Wint 77, p. 99.
"Midnight Mass." SouthernR (13:2) Spr 77, p. 358.
"Nature Morte." Poetry (131:2) N 77, p. 98.
"Olympiad." Poetry (131:2) N 77, p. 93.
"A Renaissance Canticle." Salm (36) Wint 77, p. 36.

KIPLINGER, Janet
"Coming To in Another City." PoNow (14/18) 77, p. 84.

KIPP, Allan F.
"Here's Looking at You, Kid!" ChrC (94:22) 22-29 Je 77,
    p. 587.

KIRBY, David
"The Briefing." SouthernPR (17:1) Spr 77, p. 4.
"The Car." SouthernPR (17:2) Aut 77, p. 37.
"Dr. Warren and Mr. O'Connor." KanQ (9:4) Aut 77, p. 126.
"The Schloss." SouthernPR (16:SI) 77, p. 44.

KIRKPATRICK, Stephen
"Mr. Harvey." Chelsea (36) 77, p. 43.

KIRSCHEN, Mark
"Entering the City." Montra (3) Spr 77, p. 83.
"Invitation." Montra (3) Spr 77, p. 85.
"The Song." Montra (3) Spr 77, p. 82.
"The Third Window." Montra (3) Spr 77, p. 84.
"A Wall of Substance." Montra (3) Spr 77, p. 81.

KIRSCHNER, Sandra
"Straw Flowers." NewC (7:2) 75-76, p. 12.

KISER, Thelma
"Ante." Wind (24) 77, p. 39.
"Return to Kentucky." Wind (24) 77, p. 38.
"Weeding." Wind (24) 77, p. 38.

KISKEN, Nathan
"I." AAR (27) 77, p. 94.

KITCHEN, Judith
"Elegy." Gra (12) 77.

KIZER, Gary Allan
"Sky Hook." Gra (12) 77, p. 42.
"Tree Poem." CalQ (11/12) Wint-Spr 77, p. 146.

KLAPPERT, Peter
"Boy Walking Back to Find His Father's Cattle." Agni (7) 77,
    p. 5.
"Estienne." Antaeus (27) Aut 77, p. 65.
"Laughter in the Peroration." Falcon (14) 77, p. 32.
from The Subjects of Discontent: "The Flower Cart and the
    Butcher." Falcon (14) 77, p. 28.
from The Subjects of Discontent: "The Mole's Eye." Falcon
    (14) 77, p. 30.

KLEIN, Elizabeth
"Dialogue" (for Robert Creeley). KanQ (9:3) Sum 77, p. 40.

KLEIN, Marlis
"Hole in the Heart of the Country." ArkRiv (3:4/4:1) 77, p. 66.
"The Truth of It." ArkRiv (3:4/4:1) 77, p. 67.

KLEIN, Mary
"To the Intruder." ArkRiv (3:4/4:1) 77, p. 25.

KLEIN, Peter
"Judge Jenk." Atl (239:5) My 77, p. 60.

KLEINPOPPEN, Paul
"Anniversary." Poetry (130:3) Je 77, p. 147.
"Domination of Yellow." Poetry (130:3) Je 77, p. 148.

KLINGER, Mary
"California Autumn." BallSUF (18:4) Aut 77, p. 69.

KLOEFKORN, William
"Adam Fenton." Northeast (3:4) Aut-Wint 77-78, p. 21.
from Alvin Turner as Farmer: (3, 7, 14, 18, 20, 26, 43, 52,
    55). PoNow (14/18) 77, p. 83.
"at certain times ludi jr holds his breath, expecting something."
    NewOR (5:3) 77, p. 218.
"Dollard." NewOR (5:3) 77, p. 215.
"Legerdemain." ArkRiv (3:4/4:1) 77, p. 50.
"ludi jr goes to bed with the chickens." NewOR (5:3) 77, p. 217.
"ludi jr practices the sermon that so far he has not been invited
    to deliver." NewOR (5:3) 77, p. 216.
"ludi jr runs all the way around his paper route without stopping."
    PraS (51:1) Spr 77, p. 68.
"ludi jr walks barefooted through a stickerpatch without saying
    ouch." NewOR (5:3) 77, p. 219.
"Prock." ArkRiv (3:4/4:1) 77, p. 52.
"This Is a Poem, and Posted." Northeast (3:4) Aut-Wint 77-78,
    p. 18.
"Why the Stone Remains Silent." PraS (51:4) Wint 77-78, p. 412.

KNAUTH, Stephen
"On the Midway." Pig (3) 77, p. 6.

KNEUPFEL, George M.
"Night Owl. " Mouth (11/12) Mr-Je 77, p. 2.

KNIEGER, Bernard
"The old ice factory" (tr. of Yehuda Amichai).   TriQ (39) Spr
77, p. 246.

KNIFFEL, Leonard
"The Soul Stations. " GRR (8:1/2) 77, p. 122.

KNIGHT, Arthur Winfield
"Naked Angels. " Wind (25) 77, p. 29.
"Puzzles. " Wind (25) 77, p. 29.
"Reconciliation. " ArkRiv (3:4/4:1) 77, p. 30.

KNIGHT, Etheridge
"Con/Tin/U/Way/Shun-Blues (Part II). " AmerPoR (6:5) S-O 77,
p. 4.
Eleven poems. NewL (43:4) Sum 77, p. 34.
"A Fable" (for Etheridge Bambata and Mary Tandiwe). AmerPoR
(6:5) S-O 77, p. 4.
"From the Moment (or, Right/at-The Time). " AmerPoR (6:5)
S-O 77, p. 3.
"I and Your Eyes. " AmerPoR (6:5) S-O 77, p. 4.
"Poem for the Liberation of Southern Africa. " AmerPoR (6:5)
S-O 77, p. 3.
"To Keep On Keeping On. " Nimrod (21:2/22:1) 77, p. 135.

KNIGHT, John
"Elegy After Mourning. " MalR (42) Ap 77, p. 103.
"Elegy Before Mourning. " MalR (42) Ap 77, p. 100.
"Elegy Between Solstices. " MalR (42) Ap 77, p. 108.
"Elegy for the Drowned. " MalR (42) Ap 77, p. 98.
"Elegy for the Trouser Gods. " MalR (42) 77, p. 106.
"Make Light. " MalR (42) 77, p. 102.
"Spare a Yesterday" (for my mother). MalR (42) Ap 77, p. 95.

KNIGHT, Kelton W.
"The Shadow's Skin" (tr. of René Daumal). WebR (3:4) Aut 77,
p. 45.
"Yellow Laughter" (tr. of René Daumal). WebR (3:4) Aut 77,
p. 44.

KNIGHT, Thomas J.
"Insomnia. " PoetL (72:1) Spr 77, p. 11.
"Salamander" (tr. of Octavio Paz). PoetL (72:1) Spr 77, p. 32.

KNISLEY, Phyllis
"Ohio I-75. " EngJ (66:5) My 77, p. 51.

KNOPF, Helen
"Memories. " Atl (240:2) Ag 77, p. 54.

KNOTT, Bill
"Absubtraction." SenR (8:1) My 77, p. 44.
"The Dumbfounding." AmerPoR (6:5) S-O 77, p. 11.
"For Anne." Ploughs (4:1) 77, p. 42.
"Missing." AmerPoR (6:5) S-O 77, p. 11.
"Modifiers." AmerPoR (6:5) S-O 77, p. 11.
"Poem: Even now, when I patrol my thoughts of you." AmerPoR
    (6:5) S-O 77, p. 11.
"Poem: Our eyes unlash slowly one." Ploughs (4:1) 77, p. 38.
"Poem: when we're always alone." SenR (8:1) My 77, p. 45.
"Song." Ploughs (4:1) 77, p. 41.
"The Stillborn (Domesticity #3)." Ploughs (4:1) 77, p. 40.
"Where." Ploughs (4:1) 77, p. 39.
"Yeah." SenR (8:1) My 77, p. 46.

KNOWLES, Christopher
"Everything Is Beautiful." NewYorker (53:3) 7 Mr 77, p. 30.
"A Horse with No Name." NewYorker (53:3) 7 Mr 77, p. 30.
"Loof and Let Dime." UnmOx (15) 77, p. 96.

KNUEPFEL, George M.
"For Orion." Nat (224:2) 15 Ja 77, p. 56.

KOCBEK, Edvard
"The Pauper" (tr. by Herbert Kuhner and Ina Jun Broda). WebR
    (3:4) Aut 77, p. 17.

KOCH, Claude
"The Gallery" (M. P. K.). FourQt (27:1) Aut 77, p. 2.

KOCH, Kenneth
"Our Hearts." NewYRB (24:7) 28 Ap 77, p. 23.
"The Problem of Anxiety." AmerR (26) N 77, p. 1.

KOCH, Peter
"Julien Gracq or The Illumined Interior" (tr. of Joyce Mansour,
    w. Jeri Guthrie). MontG (6) Aut 77, p. 18.
"Memory." MontG (6) Aut 77, p. 22.
from Rapaces Cris: "I like your stockings that strengthen your
    legs" (tr. of Joyce Mansour, w. Jeri Guthrie). MontG (6)
    Aut 77, p. 20.

KOCH, Sumner
"The Cockfights." YaleLit (146:4/5) 77, p. 10.
"Dusk Curves." YaleLit (145:3) 77, p. 3.
"On the Days." YaleLit (145:3) 77, p. 4.
"Walking at Night." YaleLit (145:3) 77, p. 2.
"You Joseph Conrad." YaleLit (145:4) 77, p. 9.

KOERTGE, Ronald
"Adults Only!" PoNow (14/18) 77, p. 86.
"Answered Prayers." PoNow (14/18) 77, p. 86.
"Dry." YellowBR (9) 77, p. 3.

"The First Time I Ever Saw A Naked Woman. " PoNow (14/18)
     77, p. 85.
"George & Emil. " KanQ (9:1) Wint 77, p. 48.
"Gerry and I. " Vaga (26) 77, p. 62.
"Giant Tubes. " Falcon (14) 77, p. 56.
"'Jesus Is a Personal Friend of Mine. '" Madrona (4:13/14) 77,
     p. 8.
"Light on My Feet. " Juice (5) 77.
"The Manager of the Drive In Dairy. " PoNow (14/18) 77, p. 85.
"The Other Man. " Juice (5) 77.
"Signs of the Times. " PoNow (14/18) 77, p. 85.
"Solo. " PoNow (14/18) 77, p. 86.
"The Student Poetry Reading. " Madrona (4:13/14) 77, p. 6.
"When She Comes. " Madrona (4:13/14) 77, p. 7.

KO Hung
     from Lives of the Taoists: "Uncle Shan-fu" (tr. by William
          McNaughton). DenQ (12:2) Sum 77, p. 67.
     from Lives of the Taoists: "Wang Yao" (tr. by William
          McNaughton). DenQ (12:2) Sum 77, p. 64.

KOLUMBAN, Nicholas
     "For a Dead Poet. " Wind (25) 77, p. 30.
     "For Miklos Yoo. " Wind (25) 77, p. 30.

KOMA, Ono no
     "Love" (tr. by Graeme Wilson). WestHR (31:3) Sum 77,
          p. 209.

KOMACHI, Ono no
     "Following the Roads" (tr. by Kenneth Rexroth). Agni (7) 77,
          p. 110.
     "Love" (tr. by Graeme Wilson). WestHR (31:3) Sum 77, p. 209.

KOMISHANE, Robert
     "Old Shoes Are Better than New Ones. " Icarus (5:2) Aut 77,
          p. 24.
     "On my Morning's Break. " Icarus (5:1) Spr 77, p. 5.

KOMUNYAKAA, Yusef
     "Annabelle. " Nimrod (21:2/22:1) 77, p. 138.
     from Family Tree: (III-IV). PortR (23) 77, p. 42.
     "Instructions for Building Straw Huts. " Nimrod (21:2/22:1) 77,
          p. 136.
     "Letter to Bob Kaufman. " Nimrod (21:2/22:1) 77, p. 137.
     "The Month That Begins Black. " Obs (3:1) Spr 77, p. 51.
     "Oakframed Dreams. " Obs (3:1) Spr 77, p. 51.
     "Optimism. " Obs (3:1) Spr 77, p. 53.
     "Privileged Information. " Obs (3:1) Spr 77, p. 52.
     "Punchdrunk. " ColEng (38:5) Ja 77, p. 512.
     "Pyromania. " Nimrod (21:2/22:1) 77, p. 139.
     "Thalidomide. " Obs (3:1) Spr 77, p. 53.

KONUK, Mutlu
    "Bees" (tr. of Nazim Hikmet, w. Randy Blasing).   DenQ (12:2)
       Sum 77, p. 237.
    "Bor Hotel" (tr. of Nazim Hikmet, w. Randy Blasing).   AmerPoR
       (6:6) N-D 77, p. 39.
    "Hymn to Life" (tr. of Nazim Hikmet, w. Randy Blasing).
       AmerPoR (6:6) N-D 77, p. 38.
    "Letters from Chankiri Prison" (tr. of Nazim Hikmet, w. Randy
       Blasing).   DenQ (12:2) Sum 77, p. 231.
    "Morning in Prague" (tr. of Nazim Hikmet, w. Randy Blasing).
       AmerPoR (6:6) N-D 77, p. 38.
    "My Funeral" (tr. of Nazim Hikmet, w. Randy Blasing).
       AmerPoR (6:6) N-D 77, p. 39.
    "Optimistic Prague" (tr. of Nazim Hikmet, w. Randy Blasing).
       AmerPoR (6:6) N-D 77, p. 39.
    "Poem: I'm inside the advancing light" (tr. of Nazim Hikmet,
       w. Randy Blasing).   DenQ (12:2) Sum 77, p. 236.
    "Poem: In this sadness I feel" (tr. of Nazim Hikmet, w. Randy
       Blasing).   DenQ (12:2) Sum 77, p. 236.
    "Poem: My woman came with me as far as Brest" (tr. of
       Nazim Hikmet, w. Randy Blasing).   AmerPoR (6:6) N-D 77,
       p. 39.

KOONS, Bill
    "Notes to a Friend, a Suicide."   Wind (25) 77, p. 31.

KOOSER, Ted
    "For Kathy."   Vaga (26) 77, p. 86.
    "Hard Frost Warnings."   Vaga (26) 77, p. 86.
    "New Year's Day."   Drag (16) 77.
    "Uncle Adler."   PoNow (14/18) 77, p. 87.

KOPLAND, Rutger
    "Above the hay the farmer is hanging among" (tr. by Ria Leigh-
       Loohuizen).   Field (16) Spr 77, p. 10.
    "Johnson Brothers Ltd." (tr. by Ria Leigh-Loohuizen).   Field
       (16) Spr 77, p. 9.
    "Spring, now everything comes back to me" (tr. by Ria Leigh-
       Loohuizen).   Field (16) Spr 77, p. 11.

KOPP, Karl
    "'Deputies Find Boat, Trash.'"   PoNow (14/18) 77, p. 87.

KORNBLUM, Allan
    Nine poems.   Spirit (2:2/3) 77, pp. 14-24.
    "Varoom: A Sonnet!"   PoNow (14/18) 77, p. 87.

KORNBLUM, Cinda
    Ten poems.   Spirit (2:2/3) 77, pp. 45-54.

KOSMICKI, Greg
    "... And Then, Suddenly, Apropos of Nothing...."   ParisR (69)
       Spr 77, p. 163.

"Lester Pyrtle Gets Snared by Sin and Caught in the Act by God
  in Old Man Mooney's Barn, Summer, 1956" (for Bill
  Kloefkorn). ParisR (69) Spr 77, p. 162.
"Today. " ParisR (69) Spr 77, p. 164.
"Waiting at Night Outside an Elementary School. " DacTerr (14)
  Spr-Sum 77, p. 21.
"Walking Down to Get the Mail on Veteran's Day. " DacTerr (14)
  Spr-Sum 77, p. 20.

KOSOVEL, Srečko
"Death" (tr. by William Heiliger). PoetL (72:2) Sum 77, p. 72.
"Impression" (tr. by William Heiliger). PoetL (72:2) Sum 77,
  p. 72.
"Poem from Chaos" (tr. by William Heiliger). PoetL (72:2) Sum
  77, p. 72.
"Red Rocket" (tr. by William Heiliger). PoetL (72:2) Sum 77,
  p. 72.

KOSTAKIS, Peter
"The Anteater. " PoNow (14/18) 77, p. 87.

KOSTELANETZ, Richard
"Asphyxiation. " AmerPoR (6:4) Jl-Ag 77, p. 21.
"A Constructivist Fiction. " NewL (44:2) Wint 77, p. 69.
"Emancipation Proclamation. " MissR (6:1) 77, p. 80.
"Genesis. " MontG (6) Aut 77, p. 61.

KOTOMICHI, Okuma
"Mind" (tr. by Graeme Wilson). DenQ (12:2) Sum 77, p. 61.

KOVNER, Abba
"I didn't know if Mount Zion would recognize itself' (tr. by
  Shirley Kaufman). TriQ (39) Spr 77, p. 280.
"Lookout on a Rock on the Heights of Mount Hermon" (tr. by S.
  F. Chyet). TriQ (39) Spr 77, p. 280.
"Observation at Dawn" (tr. by Shirley Kaufman and Shlomit
  Rimmon). TriQ (39) Spr 77, p. 283.
"Observations on Jerusalem at Twilight and a Dialogue" (tr. by
  Shirley Kaufman). TriQ (39) Spr 77, p. 281.
"Sun Watchers" (tr. by S. F. Chyet). TriQ (39) Spr 77, p. 282.

KOWIT, Steve
"The Apology. " Vaga (25) 77, p. 78.
"Claudia. " Vaga (25) 77, p. 78.
"Harper's Ferry. " PoNow (14/18) 77, p. 87.
"A Swell Idea. " Vaga (25) 77, p. 79.

KRAILLER, Jim
"Dreaming of Friends. " HangL (29) Wint 76-77, p. 13.
"Note to Two Loves. " HangL (29) Wint 77, p. 12.

KRAMER, Aaron
"And You Depart. " CarlMis (16:1/2) Aut-Wint 76-77, p. 42.

"Athens: Through Wide Open Shutters. " Xa (4) 77, p. 32.
"Bay Parkway. " CarlMis (16:1/2) Aut-Wint 76-77, p. 42.
"Bluejays. " Icarus (5:2) Aut 77, p. 2.
"The Florida Succulents. " Icarus (5:2) Aut 77, p. 3.
"Nafplion: Snapshot. " Xa (4) 77, p. 28.
"New Ghosts. " ModernPS (8:3) Wint 77, p. 254.
"Thessaloniki: Three Sleeps. " Xa (4) 77, p. 26.

KRAPF, Norbert
"Butchering: After a Family Photograph" (For my grandmother,
     Mary Hoffmann Schmidt). PoNow (14/18) 77, p. 88.
"In Lohr Am Main. " DacTerr (14) Spr-Sum 77, p. 72.

KRAUS, Michael
"A Brief Meditation on Brief Meditations" (tr. of Miroslav Holub,
     w. Liza Tucker). Field (16) Spr 77, p. 77.
"A Brief Meditation on an Old Woman and a Pushcart" (tr. of
     Miroslav Holub, w. Liza Tucker). Field (16) Spr 77, p. 76.

KRAUSE, Barbara
"dreaming. " Paunch (48/49) S 77, p. 125.

KRAUSS, Janet
"A Dark Girl from Minsk. " 13thM (3:2) 77, p. 28.

KRAUSS, Ruth
"Poem-Strip. " PoNow (14/18) 77, p. 88.
"Strange Boy. " LaB (5) Ja 77, p. 15.

KREITZBERG, D. B.
"An Enounter at the Tubs; A Brief Correspondence; and a Bad
     Case of Mid-Summer Madness" (Sewing words upon the south-
     west wind for Mr. Fletcher). Mouth (11/12) Mr-Je 77,
     p. 30.
"How Did You Know to Send Me a Post Card Warning of Valentine
     Visitors?" (for Dr. Theo List). Mouth (13) D 77, p. 69.
"Sarah Orne Jewett Never Wrote This Post Card to Jim in Los
     Angeles. " Mouth (11/12) Mr-Je 77, p. 29.

KRESH, David
"Blake. " WindO (30) Aut 77, p. 16.
"Blue Montana Blues # 5: Observations of the Geology of Eastern
     Montana. " Wind (25) 77, p. 56.
"Leaving Indiana. " RemR (5) 77, p. 7.
"The Song of Old Song and Dance. " WindO (28) Spr 77, p. 47.
"You Who Always Counted. " RemR (5) 77, p. 7.

KRIEGER, Ian
"Boundary. " Wind (24) 77, p. 40.
"Curators. " Rapp (10) 77, p. 24.
"December Fog. " Rapp (10) 77, p. 23.
"For Carol. " Wind (24) 77, p. 41.
"L. A. Night. " Wind (24) 77, p. 40.

"Limits." DeKalb (10:3) Spr 77, p. 22.
"Mime" (for Jan). Wind (24) 77, p. 40.
"The Night I Call This Funky Neighborhood Home." DeKalb
  (10:3) Spr 77, p. 22.

KRIEGER, Ted
"Fell Asleep." Wind (27) 77, p. 28.
"Funeral Song." Wind (27) 77, p. 28.
"On Awakening." WebR (3:2) Spr 77, p. 70.
"On Going Crazy." CarouselQ (2:2) Aut 77, p. 24.

KRIEGSMAN, Betsey
from Beowulf: "The Comfortless Grief of the King." StoneC
  (77:2) My 77, p. 23.
"Erosion (L'Affouillement)." StoneC (77:2) My 77, p. 23.

KROGFUS, Miles
"Comes the Harvest." CutB (8) Spr 77, p. 35.
"Fame and the Empire." Epoch (27:1) Aut 77, p. 32.
"Lulu in London." Epoch (27:1) Aut 77, p. 31.
"My Desert Camp-Out Is Over." Epoch (27:1) Aut 77, p. 33.
"The Night of December 31st." CutB (8) Spr 77, p. 34.
"Stopover in Reykjavik: Visiting the Viking Relics." Epoch (27:1)
  Aut 77, p. 30.

KROHN, Herbert
"Georgia Island Turtles" (for my mother). Chelsea (36) 77, p.
  77.

KROLL, Ernest
"Autopsy." Icarus (5:1) Spr 77, p. 3.
"Comes In Like a Lion." Wind (26) 77, p. 36.
"Constitution." MinnR (NS8) Spr 77, p. 43.
"D. H. Lawrence." WebR (3:4) Aut 77, p. 60.
"Dawn (Ohio)." PoNow (14/18) 77, p. 88.
"Disc Jockey." KanQ (9:3) Sum 77, p. 62.
"Edith Wharton." WestHR (31:2) Spr 77, p. 143.
"Full Moon at Idaho Springs." WebR (3:4) Aut 77, p. 60.
"Greenbrier Winter." Wind (26) 77, p. 35.
"Guitar in the Rush Hour." KanQ (9:3) Sum 77, p. 61.
"High Life." HiramPoR (22) Aut-Wint 77, p. 26.
"Lower East Side." Wind (26) 77, p. 35.
"Midwinter Spring." TexQ (20:4) Wint 77, p. 174.
"Muna Lee (1895-1965)." TexQ (20:4) Wint 77, p. 152.
"Mutual Admiration." Chowder (9) Aut-Wint 77, p. 100.
"My Father at Bull Run." FourQt (27:1) Aut 77, p. 12.
"Not Rose of Sharon." TexQ (20:4) Wint 77, p. 181.
"Poe and the Ladies." KanQ (9:3) Sum 77, p. 61.
"The Praying Mantis." PoetL (72:2) Sum 77, p. 76.
"Ruminant." CarlMis (16:1/2) Aut-Wint 76-77, p. 32.
"A Shanty in Alabama." PoNow (14/18) 77, p. 88.
"The Story in a Nutshell." CarlMis (16:1/2) Aut-Wint 76-77,
  p. 44.

"The Strike." PoNow (14/18) 77, p. 88.
"Three Mountains to Marion." Icarus (5:2) Aut 77, p. 1.
"Time Table." Focus (12:75) My-Je 77, p. 9.
"To a Firefly." PoetL (72:1) Spr 77, p. 24.
"Yankee Homecoming." HiramPoR (23) Wint 77, p. 23.

KROLOW, Karl
"Basta." ChiR (29:3) Wint 78, p. 92.
"Einiges Bleibt." ChiR (29:3) Wint 78, p. 90.
"Goldfish on the Prowl" (tr. by Silvia Scheibli). Agni (7) 77,
    p. 109.
"Ich Stelle Die Uhr Vor." ChiR (29:3) Wint 78, p. 90.
"Ich Will Den Fluss Entanggehn." ChiR (29:3) Wint 78, p. 88.

KROOK, Dorothea
"Chosen Land" (tr. of Zerubavel Gilead). TriQ (39) Spr 77,
    p. 268.
"Ibn Gvirol" (tr. of Zerubavel Gilead). TriQ (39) Spr 77,
    p. 269.

KRYNSKI, Magnus
"Méliès" (tr. of Tadeusz Rózewicz, w. Robert Maguire). NewRep
    (176:12) 19 Mr 77, p. 34.

KRYSS, T. L.
"Ballerina by the Sea." Vaga (25) 77, p. 46.
"More Beautiful Than the Stars." Vaga (25) 77, p. 47.
"Praying Mantis." Vaga (25) 77, p. 46.

KUBO, Leonard
"America." Drag (16) 77.
"The Cat." Drag (16) 77.
"The Cricket." Drag (16) 77.

KUCHU
"Joshu's word--Nothingness" (tr. by Lucien Stryk). ChiR (29:2)
    Aut 77, p. 83.

KUHNER, Herbert
"The Pauper" (tr. of Edvard Kocbek, w. Ina Jun Broda). WebR
    (3:4) Aut 77, p. 17.

KUKAI
"Ignorance" (tr. by Graeme Wilson). DenQ (12:2) Sum 77, p. 52.

KULEBI, Cahit
"Your lips are pink" (tr. by Ozcar Yal'm, William Fielder, and
    Dionis Coffin Riggs). DenQ (12:2) Sum 77, p. 230.

KULIK, William
"Who Owns What?" (tr. of Andre Frenaud). AmerPoR (6:2) Mr-
    Ap 77, p. 21.

KULKA, Jan
"I John the Almoner ..." (tr. by Reuel Wilson). NewYRB (24:7)
28 Ap 77, p. 37.
"Patients Take a Walk on a Sunday Afternoon" (tr. by Reuel Wil-
son). NewYRB (24:7) 28 Ap 77, p. 37.

KULKARNI, Venkatesh Srinivas
"The Iguanas of Yesterday." DeKalb (10:3) Spr 77, p. 23.
"Thomas Hart Benton" (to Ernest Philip Bollier). KanQ (9:4)
Aut 77, p. 24.

KULYCKY, Michael
"The Bass." SouthwR (62:3) Sum 77, p. 278.

KUMIN, Maxine
"Address to the Angels." PoNow (14/18) 77, p. 89.
"July, Against Hunger." NewYorker (53:21) 11 Jl 77, p. 34.
"A Pair of Old Bathing Trunks" (tr. of William Cliff, w. Judith
Bingen-Kumin). Columbia (1) Aut 77, p. 29.
"Remembering Pearl Harbor at the Tutankhamun Exhibit."
NewRep (176:21) 21 My 77, p. 48.
"Tonight." ConcPo (10:2) Aut 77, p. 46.
"Waiting Inland." ChiR (29:1) Sum 77, p. 32.

KUNDERT, Gregory
"Bananas." ParisR (71) Aut 77, p. 168.

KUNEC, Kristy
"I feel mad." AAR (27) 77, p. 119.

KUO Pu
"Vision" (tr. by Graeme Wilson). DenQ (12:2) Sum 77, p. 46.

KUSINITZ, Kevin
"Translation of a German Zeppelin Poster." Ploughs (4:1) 77,
p. 172.

KUZMA, Greg
"After Long Deliberation." CalQ (11/12) Wint-Spr 77, p. 98.
"The Dead." NewYorker (53:42) 5 D 77, p. 228.
"Gray Day." DenQ (12:1) Spr 77, p. 50.
"In Death." NowestR (16:3) 77, p. 83.
"A Long Rain." CalQ (11/12) Wint-Spr 77, p. 97.
"The Mulberry Trees." PoNow (14/18) 77, p. 198.
"Poet to Poet." MichQR (16:4) Aut 77, p. 374.
"The Presence." DenQ (12:1) Spr 77, p. 49.
"Telling the Children." DenQ (12:1) Spr 77, p. 50.
"The Tree." DenQ (12:1) Spr 77, p. 49.

KUZMIN, Mikhail
from Molested Oafs: "Fuses in a Little Blood" (tr. by Rod
Tulloss). Some (7/8) 76.

KVAM, Wayne
"Sunflower Fall." WindO (30) Aut 77.

KYCKELHAHN, Christy
"The Builder." Northeast (3:3) Sum 77, p. 43.
"For Myra, My Grandmother." Northeast (3:3) Sum 77, p. 42.

KYLE, Frank
"The Buoy." CarouselQ (2:2) Aut 77, p. 1.

KYNELL, Kermit S.
"For C. S. Lewis." ArizQ (33:3) Aut 77, p. 196.

LABÉ, Louise
"Bright Venus, glowing, wandering in Heaven" (tr. by Sandra M.
    Gilbert). CalQ (11/12) Wint-Spr 76, p. 76.
"Godly Diana, breathing hard because" (tr. by Sandra M. Gilbert).
    CalQ (11/12) Wint-Spr 77, p. 77.
"I live, I'm dead, as though I'm cut in half" (tr. by Sandra M.
    Gilbert). CalQ (11/12) Wint-Spr 77, p. 77.
"Ladies, don't blame me for loving. Please don't scorn" (tr. by
    Sandra M. Gilbert). CalQ (11/12) Wint-Spr 77, p. 78.
"The minute I fall asleep I dream of you" (tr. by Sandra M.
    Gilbert). CalQ (11/12) Wint-Spr 77, p. 76.
"Not even Ulysses had it as bad as this" (tr. by Sandra M.
    Gilbert). CalQ (11/12) Wint-Spr 77, p. 75.
"What good does it do me, sweetheart, that you once" (tr. by
    Sandra M. Gilbert). CalQ (11/12) Wint-Spr 77, p. 78.

LaBOMBARD, Joan
"Marbles." PoetryNW (18:4) Wint 77-78, p. 29.

LACHMANN, Vera
"Karfreitagsfeier." Hand (1) 77, p. 202.

LACKOW, Stephen
"Antique." AmerPoR (6:6) N-D 77, p. 42.
"Marine." AmerPoR (6:6) N-D 77, p. 42.
"Veil." AmerPoR (6:6) N-D 77, p. 42.

LAEDERACH, Monique
from Penelope: (XII-XVIII) (tr. by Charles Guenther). WebR
    (3:2) Spr 77, p. 50.

LaFARGE, A. D.
"The Death Monologues III: Basilica Erotica." HarvAd (111:2)
    D 77, p. 9.

LaFLEUR, William R.
"Deep in the mountains" (tr. of Saigyo). DenQ (12:2) Sum 77,
    p. 128.
"Patter of pathos--" (tr. of Saigyo). DenQ (12:2) Sum 77,
    p. 127.

"Propped up by my cane" (tr. of Saigyo).   DenQ (12:2) Sum 77,
  p. 128.
"Pushed along by wind" (tr. of Saigyo).   DenQ (12:2) Sum 77,
  p. 127.
"The Sound of water" (tr. of Saigyo).   DenQ (12:2) Sum 77,
  p. 127.
"That night when we met" (tr. of Saigyo).   DenQ (12:2) Sum 77,
  p. 128.
"The wisps of smoke from Fuji" (tr. of Saigyo).   DenQ (12:2)
  Sum 77, p. 128.

LAHIKAINEN, Linda
  "Expectancy. " HangL (29) Wint 76-77, p. 14.
  "Finns in North America. " HangL (29) Wint 76-77, p. 15.

LAKE, Paul
  "Light. " Icarus (5:2) Aut 77, p. 8.
  "Nirvana. " MissR (6:1) 77, p. 106.

LAKIN, R. D.
  "Common Inheritances. " Qt (57/58) Wint-Spr 77, p. 33.
  "Down at the Paint and Hardware Store. " RemR (5) 77, p. 29.
  "For a Master Paper-Ruler. " Wind (27) 77, p. 30.
  "The Fox. " RemR (5) 77, p. 30.
  "The Library at MacDowell. " Wind (27) 77, p. 30.
  "On an Early Love of F. Scott Fitzgerald. " Wind (27) 77, p. 31.
  "Sleeping Out on the Miss. " Sam (52) Ap 77, p. 64.
  "Strip Mining at Night Near Pittsburg, Kansas. " RemR (5) 77,
    p. 30.
  "What Kind of a Bug. " KanQ (9:1) Wint 77, p. 129.

LAL, P.
  "Karna and Kunti" (tr. of Anonymous).   DenQ (12:2) Sum 77,
    p. 329.

LALEAU, Leon
  "Atavism" (tr. by Norman R. Shapiro).   DenQ (11:4) Wint 77,
    p. 131.
  "Cannibal" (tr. by Norman R. Shapiro).   DenQ (11:4) Wint 77,
    p. 130.
  "Heredities" (tr. by Norman R. Shapiro).   DenQ (11:4) Wint 77,
    p. 131.
  "Voodoo" (tr. by Norman R. Shapiro).   DenQ (11:4) Wint 77,
    p. 130.

LALLO
  "Harvester. " Nat (224:14) 9 Ap 77, p. 444.

LALLY, Michael
  "DC. " SunM (4) Aut 77, p. 103.
  "Fortune. " PoNow (14/18) 77, p. 89.
  from Rocky Dies Yellow: "Dreaming of the Potato. " PoNow
    (14/18) 77, p. 90.

from Rocky Dies Yellow: "Now." PoNow (14/18) 77, p. 90.
from Rocky Dies Yellow: "Poem to 1956." PoNow (14/18) 77,
p. 90.
from Rocky Dies Yellow: "We were always afraid of." PoNow
(14/18) 77, p. 90.
"This Pace." PoNow (14/18) 77, p. 89.
"Untitled." AmerR (26) N 77, p. 147.

LALLY, P. T.
"Twins." Wind (24) 77, p. 42.

LAMORTE, Pat
"Back Streets of Beirut." KanQ (9:1) Wint 77, p. 39.
"Cairo at Twilight." KanQ (9:1) Wint 77, p. 38.
"Jerusalem." KanQ (9:1) Wint 77, p. 38.

LAMPORT, Felicia
"It Takes a Heap of Compost to Make a House a Mess." Atl
(240:5) N 77, p. 102.

LANDAU, Julie
"Ching P'ing Lo" (tr. of Li Yu, w. David Fung). DenQ (12:2)
Sum 77, p. 351.
"Coming Down Chungnan Mountain and Staying with Hermit Hussu"
(tr. of Li Po, w. David Fung). DenQ (12:2) Sum 77,
p. 352.
"Drinking with a Hermit Friend in the Mountains" (tr. of Li Po,
w. David Fung). DenQ (12:2) Sum 77, p. 352.
"Listening to a Flute at the Frontier" (tr. of Li Yi, w. David
Fung). DenQ (12:2) Sum 77, p. 351.
"River Snow" (tr. of Liu Tsung Yuan, w. David Fung). DenQ
(12:2) Sum 77, p. 351.

LANDES-LEVI, Louise
"The Four Cardinal Times" (tr. of Rene Daumal). MontG (6)
Aut 77, p. 63.
"Yellow Laughter" (tr. of Rene Daumal). MontG (6) Aut 77,
p. 62.

LANDGRAF, Susan
"Semi-Annual Mailing to Hungary." NewRivR (2:1) 77, p. 43.

LANDOR, R. A.
"The Kittens." NewRep (177:6/7) 6-13 Ag 77, p. 35.

LANDRY, John
"Charles River Frozen." Wind (26) 77, p. 2.

LANDSTROM, Elsie H.
"Evening Is a Time of Waking." Poem (31) N 77, p. 22.

LANE, Erskine
"Ascetic." Mouth (11/12) Mr-Je 77, p. 24.

Five Waka (tr. of Fujiwara no Sadaie). Bleb (12) 77, p. 50.
"Notes for Luis, toward the End of His Nineteenth Year." Mouth
   (11/12) Mr-Je 77, p. 23.

LANE, John
   "Viewing the Body." Icarus (5:2) Aut 77, p. 10.

LANE, Mary
   "Moon." Bits (6) Jl 77.

LANE, Mervin
   "The Carp." LaB (8) Jl-Ag 77, p. 37.
   "Coming to Meet." ColEng (38:7) Mr 77, p. 722.
   "Dissolution." ColEng (38:7) Mr 77, p. 723.
   "Increase." Stonecloud (6) 76, p. 143.
   "Work on What Has Been Spoiled." LaB (8) Jl-Ag 77, p. 36.

LANE, Pinkie Gordon
   "Baton Rouge #2." SouthernR (13:2) Spr 77, p. 352.
   "Kaleidoscope: Leaving Baton Rouge." Nimrod (21:2/22:1) 77,
      p. 140.
   "Lake Murry." SouthernR (13:2) Spr 77, p. 351.
   "Leaves." Obs (3:3) Sum 77, p. 54.
   "Listenings." Obs (3:3) Wint 77, p. 56.
   "Opossum." Obs (3:3) Sum 77, p. 55.
   "Sexual Privacy of Women on Welfare." Nimrod (21:2/22:1) 77,
      p. 141.
   "Southern University." SouthernR (13:2) Spr 77, p. 353.

LANE, William
   "Driving to Work." PoNow (14/18) 77, p. 111.
   "Perfect sunlight. What an instrument is able to do." Hand (1)
      77, p. 207.
   "Sitting in McDonald's." PoNow (14/18) 77, p. 111.
   "Two Winds." Hand (1) 77, p. 206.
   "Woman Speaking at a Rally." PoNow (14/18) 77, p. 111.
   "You who would look deeply into faces, listen." Hand (1) 77,
      p. 207.

LANG, Jon
   "Good News" (for Julia Alvarez). StoneC (77:2) My 77, p. 17.
   "Ode to the Artist on His Birthday" (for James Little). Wind
      (26) 77, p. 37.
   "Snow at the Solstice." Wind (26) 77, p. 37.
   "Winter Landscape." Poetry (130:1) Ap 77, p. 24.
   "Winter Music." Poetry (130:1) Ap 77, p. 24.
   "Winter Night." Poetry (130:1) Ap 77, p. 23.
   "Winter Tree." Poetry (130:1) Ap 77, p. 23.

LANG, Susanna
   "The Cour Carré of the Louvre." BerksR (12:1) Spr 77.
   "The Gift." BerksR (12:1) Spr 77.
   "St. Francis under the Arch." BerksR (12:1) Spr 77.

LANGE, Gerald
"The Women on the Bus." PoNow (14/18) 77, p. 111.

LANGFORD, Gary
"The House." Drag (16) 77.

LANGLAND, Joseph
"In the Shell of the Ear and Other Poems" (ten poems). MassR
(18:2) Sum 77, p. 333.
"Intimations of the Ordinary Truth." NewYorker (53:3) 7 Mr 77,
p. 36.

LANGTON, Daniel J.
"For William Dickey." PoNow (14/18) 77, p. 111.
"The Heroes of My Youth Are Dying." PoNow (14/18) 77,
p. 111.
"To Ford Madox Ford in Deauville." DacTerr (14) Spr-Sum 77,
p. 61.

LANIER, Larry
"Moving Sale." PoNow (14/18) 77, p. 112.

LAO Tzu
"The Use of Nothingness" (tr. by Graeme Wilson). WestHR
(31:1) Wint 77, p. 55.
"Yin" (tr. by Graeme Wilson). DenQ (12:2) Sum 77, p. 45.

LAPE, Sue
"The Bombardier." Gra (12) 77, p. 7.

LAPIDUS, Jacqueline
"When I Was Queen Elizabeth II." 13thM (3:2) 77, p. 55.

LAPPIN, Linda
"Arriving." Kayak (44) F 77, p. 52.
"Between Us There Are All Those Years." Kayak (44) F 77,
p. 50.
"Grievances: Looking at Your Wedding Picture." Kayak (46) O
77, p. 32.
"Letter from the Village." Kayak (44) F 77, p. 51.

LARBAUD, Valery
"Ode to the Orient Express." MoonsLT (2:3) 77, p. 23.
"Postscript." MoonsLT (2:3) 77, p. 24.

LARDAS, Konstantinos
"How Sharp the Jawbone, Love." TexQ (20:4) Wint 77, p. 117.

LaRICHE, William
"Ramon Guthrie, American, Returns to Montparnasse." BerksR
(12:1) Sum 76, p. 24.

LARSEN, Carl
"The Sands of Sorrow." WormR (65/66) 77, p. 11.

"The Sands of Sorrow." YellowBR (8) 77, p. 21.

LARSEN, Jim
  "I'm indian because the wolf howls my name in the night when."
  AmerPoR (6:2) Mr-Ap 77, p. 34.

LARSEN, M. Deen
  "He who now brings me the steely bread" (tr. of Christine
  Lavant, w. Soraya Wimmer). ChiR (29:3) Wint 78, p. 9.
  "It smells much less like fruit and grain" (tr. of Christine
  Lavant, w. Soraya Wimmer). ChiR (29:3) Wint 78, p. 13.
  "Keep twisting the heart-spindle for me" (tr. of Christine
  Lavant, w. Soraya Wimmer). ChiR (29:3) Wint 78, p. 15.
  "The moon leapt up and a toad fell" (tr. of Christine Lavant, w.
  Soraya Wimmer). ChiR (29:3) Wint 78, p. 11.

LARSEN, Rich
  "Brainwaves." Poem (29) Mr 77, p. 67.
  "Nel Mezzo del Cammin in the Suburbs." Poem (29) Mr 77,
  p. 68.

LARSEN, Stephen
  "Again and Again." Pig (3) 77, p. 99.

LARSON, Kathryn
  "Lament for Muted Strings." Chomo (4:1) Sum 77, p. 44.
  "Ward C." Chomo (4:1) Sum 77, p. 46.

LaSALLE, Peter
  "Saturday." Esq (87:5) My 77, p. 12.

LASKER-SCHÜLER, Else
  "Georg Trakl" (tr. by Felix de Villiers). TransR (58/59) F 77,
  p. 166.
  "Homesickness" (tr. by Felix de Villiers). TransR (58/59) F 77,
  p. 167.
  "Homesickness" (tr. by Joachim Neugroschel). Hand (1) 77,
  p. 186.
  "My People" (tr. by Felix de Villiers). TransR (58/59) F 77,
  p. 168.
  "Styx" (tr. by Felix de Villiers). TransR (58/59) F 77, p. 168.

LATTA, John
  "Poem Beginning with a Line by John Latta." Epoch (26:3) Spr
  77, p. 274.

LATTIMORE, Richmond
  "Gehenna." NewYorker (53:16) 6 Je 77, p. 129.
  "Rondel" (from the French of Charles, Duke of Orleans). BosUJ
  (25:2) 77, p. 18.
  "To Charles, Duke of Orleans." BosUJ (25:2) 77, p. 18.

LAU, Alan Chong
  "calling out the nameless ones." GreenR (6:1/2) Spr 77, p. 9.

"driving home." GreenR (6:1/2) Spr 77, p. 7.
"(garrett, forget the radishes)." GreenR (6:1/2) Spr 77, p. 10.
"if I visited china." GreenR (6:1/2) Spr 77, p. 6.
"'tiniest giant of all stands tall'" (for toshio mori, almost short-
    stop for the cubs and the pinoy who played for the seattle
    rainers). GreenR (6:1/2) Spr 77, p. 12.

LAU, Craig
"in the night when." SeC (5:2) 78, p. 24.

LAUTERBACH, Ann
"Window." Nat (224:13) 2 Ap 77, p. 409.

LAUTERMILCH, Steven J.
"In the End." TexQ (20:4) Wint 77, p. 150.
"Old Man Fisher." TexQ (20:4) Wint 77, p. 155.
"The Spider and the Little Spider." TexQ (20:4) Wint 77, p. 154.

LAVANT, Christine
"Der jetzt das stählerne Brot mir bringt." ChiR (29:3) Wint 78,
    p. 8.
"Der Mond sprang auf und eine Kröte fiel." ChiR (29:3) Wint
    78, p. 10.
"Drehe die Herzspindel weiter für mich." ChiR (29:3) Wint 78,
    p. 14.
"Es riecht nach Weltenuntergang." ChiR (29:3) Wint 78, p. 12.

LAVIN, S. R.
"The Bombay Sleeper." Chelsea (36) 77, p. 46.
"He restores the balance of the world." Chelsea (36) 77, p. 46.
"Too many in the cages, too many." Chelsea (36) 77, p. 46.

LAWERY, Evelyn Wood
"Patchwork Poems." EngJ (66:5) My 77, p. 43.

LAWLER, Al
"Marketing the Poem." SmPd (14:1) Wint 77, p. 10.
"Response to a Criticism Found in One of My Student Evaluations
    ('He Mumbles.')" SmPd (14:1) Wint 77, p. 9.

LAWRENCE, D. T.
"War." BlackF (2:1) Wint 77-78, p. 25.

LAWSON, Tamzin
"Suicide Plan." EngJ (66:5) My 77, p. 50.

LAX, Robert
"One Is Land." HangL (29) Wint 76-77, p. 53.

LAYTON, Irving
"Aetna." ChiR (28:4) Spr 77, p. 142.
"The Arcade." ChiR (28:4) Spr 77, p. 143.
"El Diablo" (for Nicholas Haines). ChiR (28:4) Spr 77, p. 141.

"King Kong." ChiR (28:4) Spr 77, p. 143.

LAZARD, Naomi
"The High Water Mark." AmerPoR (6:4) Jl-Ag 77, p. 17.

LAZER, Hank
"Early American History." ThRiPo (10) 77, p. 41.
"Instead of Waiting." VirQR (53:2) Spr 77, p. 332.
"Letting the Fence Fall." VirQR (53:2) Spr 77, p. 331.
"Sunday Drive." PoNow (14/18) 77, p. 112.
"Vulture." VirQR (53:4) Aut 77, p. 727.

LAZERSON, Arlyne
"Dreams of Drowning." GeoR (31:4) Wint 77, p. 814.

LEA, Sydney
"First Blood." PoetL (72:2) Sum 77, p. 76.
"Holiday Ramble." BelPoJ (27:4) Sum 77, p. 20.
"To the Summer Sweethearts." Hudson (30:2) Sum 77, p. 229.

LEARD, Lonnie
"Barbara LaFurge." Mouth (13) D 77, p. 28.
"Rex's 'Going to the Moon' Party." Mouth (13) D 77, p. 28.

LEARY, Denis
"He weeds the clouds." Ploughs (4:1) 77, p. 170.
"the rabbits." Ploughs (4:1) 77, p. 171.

LEAVITT, Jean
"Rhythms." Chomo (4:2) Aut-Wint 77, p. 56.

LEBECK, Michael
"Admission." Mouth (13) D 77, p. 12.
"Insolence." Mouth (13) D 77, p. 12.

LEBOVITZ, Richard
"Childhood." Drag (16) 77.
"Fossil." Drag (16) 77.
"Night Poem." Drag (16) 77.
"Poem: Something comes out of the woods while I sleep." Drag
   (16) 77.

LECARD, Marc
"L'Arriviste." MontG (6) Aut 77, p. 80.

LEDBETTER, J. T.
"run on sentences." Stonecloud (6) 76, p. 142.
"The Sentence." Bits (6) Jl 77.

LEDES, Richard C.
"A Lost Fragment of Sappho, Containing the Soul of a Woman,
   Speaks to Its Memories." ModernPS (8:1) Spr 77, p. 91.

"Saint Peter in Kansas Boarding with Woman and Child. "
  ModernPS (8:1) Spr 77, p. 92.
"Watched by a Small Dog, I Stand in Leverett, Mass. "
  ModernPS (8:1) Spr 77, p. 93.

LEE, David
"A Day of Mourning, 24 June 75. " Peb (16) Wint 76-77, p. 115.
"For Jan, with Love. " Peb (16) Wint 76-77, p. 107.
"Jan's Birthday. " Peb (16) Wint 76-77, p. 110.
"Jubilate Agno, 1975" (Christopher Smart, 1722-1771, in memori-
  am). Peb (16) Wint 76-77, p. 112.
"Poem: I watched it. " Drag (16) 77.

LEE, Dorothy
"Readymade. " EnPas (6) 77, p. 31.

LEE, John
"Abbott and Costello. " SeC (5:2) 78, p. 48.

LEE, Lance
"Quiet Time. " Poem (29) Mr 77, p. 7.
"Solitary, in Stony Fields. " Poem (29) Mr 77, p. 8.
"Wrenching. " Poem (29) Mr 77, p. 10.

LEE, Lauri S.
"Thursdays, Usually. " KanQ (9:3) Sum 77, p. 48.

LEE, M. E.
"Elegy for Igor Stravinsky. " PoetL (72:1) Spr 77, p. 16.
"To Anne Sexton and Sylvia Plath. " PoetL (72:1) Spr 77, p. 16.

LEE, Maria Berl
"The Eleventh of March. " PoetL (72:2) Sum 77, p. 63.
"My One Small Light. " PoetL (72:1) Spr 77, p. 7.

LEE, Tom
"Only a Chipmunk. " CarouselQ (2:3) Wint 77, p. 14.

LEET, Judith
"An Apology. " MichQR (16:2) Spr 77, p. 169.
"Chapter 2. Bettina. " Ploughs (3:3/4) 77, p. 65.

LEFCOWITZ, Barbara F.
"Envy: For Nadia Comaneci. " WindO (27) Aut 76, p. 4.
"The Late Blooming Poet. " WindO (27) Aut 76.

LEFFLER, Merrill
"A Dream. " PoNow (14/18) 77, p. 112.

LeFORGE, P. V.
"The Rapist as Jolson. " NewC (8:1) 76-77, p. 14.

LEGLER, Philip
"How to Keep Warm. " MidwQ (19:1) Aut 77, p. 60.

"I Talk to Myself. " SouthwR (62:2) Spr 77, p. 117.
"Mirage. " MidwQ (19:1) Aut 77, p. 62.
"A Rising" (for Julanne). Bits (6) Jl 77.
"Wishes for Karen: View from Presque Isle at Sunset Point. "
    MidwQ (19:1) Aut 77, p. 59.

LEHMAN, David
"Les Enfants Terribles. " Agni (7) 77, p. 53.
"The Heroic Couple" (for Stefanie Green). Poetry (130:4) Jl 77,
    p. 209.
"Of Self and Soul. " PartR (44:4) 77, p. 556.
"Twenty Questions. " PraS (51:2) Sum 77, p. 168.

LEHMAN, Paul
"A. C. Don't See" (to Albert Camus). Nimrod (21:2/22:1) 77,
    p. 142.
"Travel. " Nimrod (21:2/22:1) 77, p. 143.

LEICHNER, Greg
"Childhood Documentary: Two Weeks in Nashville-1955. " CutB
    (9) Aut-Wint 77, p. 146.

LEIGH-LOODHUIZEN, Ria
"Above the hay the farmer is hanging among" (tr. of Rutger
    Kopland). Field (16) Spr 77, p. 10.
"Johnson Brothers Ltd. " (tr. of Rutger Kopland). Field (16) Spr
    77, p. 9.
"Spring, now everything comes back to me" (tr. of Rutger
    Kopland). Field (16) Spr 77, p. 11.

LEIPER, Esther
"Mad Willie and Pegasus. " Aspect (70) Ja-Mr 77, p. 52.

LEISER, Dorothy
"The Merciful. " ChrC (94:12) Ap 77, p. 327.

LEISER, Wayne
"In Order to Be Born Again" (To a New President). ChrC (94:16)
    4 My 77, p. 426.

LEITHAUSER, Brad
"The Life-Giving. " Ploughs (3:3/4) 77, p. 141.

LeMIEUX, Dotty
"Experience. " HangL (30) Sum 77, p. 47.
"The Scrimshaw Man. " HangL (30) Sum 77, p. 50.

LENOWITZ, Harris
"In the Forest" (tr. of Pinhas Sadeh). QW (3) Spr-Sum 77,
    p. 58.
"In the Garden of the Turkish Consulate" (tr. of Pinhas Sadeh).
    QW (3) Spr-Sum 77, p. 59.

LEONARD, Byron
"The Names. " StoneC (77:1) F 77, p. 4.

LEPSON, Ruth
"Jerusalem. " Ploughs (4:1) 77, p. 86.
"Someone was Cezanne. " Bits (6) Jl 77.

LERNER, Linda
"Digging. " Rapp (10) 77, p. 74.
"A Girl from Vermont. " PoNow (14/18) 77, p. 112.
"Lady of the Four Seasons. " TexQ (20:4) Wint 77, p. 103.
"The Magi. " CentR (21:1) Wint 77, p. 68.
"A Silver Ring. " Rapp (10) 77, p. 72.
"Snow White, Years Later. " CalQ (11/12) Wint-Spr 77, p. 116.
"Target Practice. " TexQ (20:4) Wint 77, p. 105.
"Verdict. " Epoch (26:3) Spr 77, p. 249.

LESNIAK, Rose
"The Oak Tree. " PartR (44:3) 77, p. 408.
"Only in October. " UnmOx (15) 77, p. 102.

LESSER, Rika
"Growing Back" (for Judith Hoberman Kinsley). PraS (51:2) Sum
     77, p. 169.
from Guide to the Underworld: Six segments (tr. of Gunnar
     Ekelof). Pequod (2:3) Sum 77, p. 55.
"Vaeröy. " PraS (51:2) Sum 77, p. 171.

LEVANT, Howard
"Old Time Biography. " PoNow (14/18) 77, p. 113.

LEVENDOSKY, Charles
"collecting precious and semi-precious things (for the new year). "
     Hand (1) 77, p. 14.
"long swollen river. " Hand (1) 77, p. 15.

LEVENSTON, E. A.
"I, the Barracuda" (tr. of Raquel Chalfi). TriQ (39) Spr 77,
     p. 256.
"Really" (tr. of Avner Treinin). TriQ (39) Spr 77, p. 306.

LEVERING, Donald
"Planting in December. " WindO (29) Sum 77, p. 5.
"Twenty-First Day of Rain. " Aspen (4) Aut 77, p. 16.

LEVERTOV, Denise
"On the 32nd Anniversary of the Bombing of Hiroshima and
     Nagasaki. " Harp (255:1531) D 77, p. 83.
"The Poet Li Po Admiring a Waterfall. " BosUJ (25:1) 77,
     p. 44.
"Split Second. " BosUJ (25:1) 77, p. 43.

LEVIN, David
"Enlightenment. " SouthernR (13:4) Aut 77, p. 781.

LEVIN, James
"Cleveland Remembered." Agni (7) 77, p. 98.

LEVIN, M. H.
"A Vision." LitR (20:3) Spr 77, p. 348.

LEVINE, Miriam
"Blue Angel." Ploughs (4:1) 77, p. 81.
"Miracle." PoNow (14/18) 77, p. 113.

LEVINE, Philip
"Coming Down." MoonsLT (2:3) 77, p. 11.
"Dark Head." Field (16) Spr 77, p. 58.
"Don't Look Back." MoonsLT (2:3) 77, p. 9.
"The Gift." NewYorker (53:36) 24 O 77, p. 154.
"Here and Now." Poetry (130:6) S 77, p. 319.
"I Could Believe." Field (16) Spr 77, p. 60.
"The Journey into America" (for Michael Joseph). QW (4) Aut
    77, p. 33.
"The Last Step." NewYorker (53:31) 19 S 77, p. 123.
"Left on the Shore." Field (16) Spr 77, p. 63.
"The Life Ahead." NewYorker (53:41) 28 N 77, p. 188.
"Little by Little." Field (17) Aut 77, p. 94.
"Making Pop." MoonsLT (2:3) 77, p. 7.
"Milk Weed." Field (16) Spr 77, p. 57.
"The Miracle." NewYorker (53:5) 21 Mr 77, p. 44.
"Montjuich." Antaeus (27) Aut 77, p. 51.
"Peace." QW (4) Aut 77, p. 32.
"Planting." Field (16) Spr 77, p. 65.
"7 Years from Somewhere." Antaeus (27) Aut 77, p. 54.
"Travelling Music" (for my brother). Field (16) Spr 77, p. 64.
"We Came Back." NewYorker (53:33) 3 O 77, p. 133.
"Why I'm Not Making My Last Trip Now." Field (17) Aut 77,
    p. 93.
"Words." AntR (35:2/3) Spr-Sum 77, p. 249.

LEVINE, R. S.
"The All-Time Greatest Hit Is...." ParisR (69) Spr 77, p. 168.
"'Plastic.'" ParisR (69) Spr 77, p. 167.

LEVINSON, Margaret
"Joey's Night." AmerPoR (6:5) S-O 77, p. 17.
"The Moon-Watchers." AmerPoR (6:5) S-O 77, p. 16.

LEVIS, Larry
"For Zbigniew Herbert, Summer, 1971, Los Angeles." Field
    (17) Aut 77, p. 8.
"The Future of Hands." Field (17) Aut 77, p. 10.
"Road, Hog, Assassin, Mirror." Ploughs (4:1) 77, p. 50.
"Signs." OhioR (18:2) Spr-Sum 77, p. 80.
"Soon." Ploughs (4:1) 77, p. 49.
"Wasps." Ploughs (4:1) 77, p. 48.
"Weldon Kees." NewL (44:1) Aut 77, p. 102.

"Words for the Axe." <u>Field</u> (17) Aut 77, p. 9.

LEVITEN, David
"The Earth Swept Clean." <u>Ploughs</u> (4:1) 77, p. 102.

LEVITIN, Alexis
"Bird" (tr. of Cecília Meireles). <u>LitR</u> (21:2) Wint 78, p. 206.

LEVITON, Mark
"Nocturne" (tr. of Juan Ramón Jiménez). <u>WebR</u> (3:4) Aut 77, p. 32.
"Restlessness" (tr. of Juan Ramón Jiménez). <u>WebR</u> (3:4) Aut 77, p. 32.
"Winter Scene (snow)" (tr. of Juan Ramón Jiménez). <u>WebR</u> (3:4) Aut 77, p. 33.

LEVOY, Gregg
"Always in Passing." <u>Wind</u> (27) 77, p. 62.

LEVY, John
"Father." <u>Madrona</u> (4:13/14) 77, p. 78.
"La Cucaracha." <u>Madrona</u> (4:13/14) 77, p. 77.
"Moving through the Desert." <u>Sparrow</u> (33) Ja 77, p. 18.
"November on a Bus." <u>Madrona</u> (4:13/14) 77, p. 82.
"Your grave, Grandpa." <u>Sparrow</u> (33) Ja 77, p. 18.

LEVY, Judy
from Songs of Leonardo: (1-7) (tr. of Avner Treinin, w. Shirley Kaufman). <u>TriQ</u> (39) Spr 77, p. 306.

LEVY, Larry
"Good Lord John." <u>PoetL</u> (72:1) Spr 77, p. 20.
"Little People." <u>PoetL</u> (72:1) Spr 77, p. 20.
"Winter Dreams." <u>PoetL</u> (72:1) Spr 77, p. 20.

LEWANDOWSKI, Stephen
"Arbor Vitae." <u>Falcon</u> (15) 77, p. 22.
"November 17th." <u>PoNow</u> (14/18) 77, p. 113.
"Useful Blossoms." <u>Glass</u> (2:2/3) Wint-Spr 77, p. 46.

LEWIS, Harry
"The Ant." <u>Hand</u> (1) 77, p. 87.
"Love Poem" (for Nana). <u>Hand</u> (1) 77, p. 16.
"A Photograph of a Revolutionary Frank Sinatra Singing a Love Song to Lenin as a Broken-Hearted Child." <u>Falcon</u> (14) 77, p. 60.

LEWIS, Janet
"Easter Laudate." <u>SouthernR</u> (13:3) Sum 77, p. 567.

LEWIS, Tom
"Part of My Life in Late August 1975 in the Literal River of Words." <u>Harp</u> (254:1522) Mr 77, p. 79.

LEWTER, John
"Little Love Poems." Wind (25) 77, p. 32.

LIBBEY, Elizabeth
"Da Vinci's Flying Machine" (for Richard Hugo). ThRiPo (10)
   77, p. 25.
"Forcing the End." ThRiPo (10) 77, p. 24.
"An Impossible Couch to Rest On." SenR (8:1) My 77, p. 65.
"Keeper." ThRiPo (10) 77, p. 26.
"Not Words." SenR (8:1) My 77, p. 63.
"On Making His Bed One Morning." NewYorker (53:26) 15 Ag
   77, p. 63.

LICHTER, Alan
"Script for a Poem in Context." KanQ (9:2) Spr 77, p. 10.

LIEBERMAN, David
"Middling." Poem (30) Jl 77, p. 5.
"Moving." KanQ (9:1) Wint 77, p. 28.

LIEBERMAN, Laurence
"Joren: The Volcanic Falls." Hudson (30:4) Wint 77-78, p. 489.
"Shimoda: The Lava Shores." YaleR (67:2) Wint 78, p. 247.

LIETZ, Robert
"Father: Second Thoughts." PoetryNW (18:1) Spr 77, p. 45.
"Report from the Athlete Who Cradled the Head of the Epileptic
   Child." Confr (14) Spr-Sum 77, p. 30.
"Taking Stock." SenR (8:2) D 77, p. 72.
"Trying to Second Guess the Gypsy." PoetryNW (18:3) Aut 77,
   p. 17.

LIFSHIN, Lyn
"Another Woman Who Marries Her House Poem." Ploughs (4:1)
   77, p. 87.
"Blue Woman Blues." HangL (29) Wint 76-77, p. 19.
"Cape Cod." Falcon (15) 77, p. 21.
"Cape Cod 1970." Ploughs (4:1) 77, p. 88.
"Christmas Dance 1954." CalQ (11/12) Wint-Spr 77, p. 72.
"The Dream of Right Here, of Pleasing." Stonecloud (6) 76,
   p. 105.
"The Family Was Last Seen Together Friday Night." PoNow
   (14/18) 77, p. 114.
"He Said I Took the." PoNow (14/18) 77, p. 114.
"In a Room with the Stained Glass after Five Years." 13thM
   (3:2) 77, p. 34.
"Inside Out Madonna." HangL (29) Wint 76-77, p. 17.
"It's Like a Woman." HolCrit (14:1) F 77, p. 12.
The January Poems. Waters (Supplement #1) 77. Entire issue.
"Lately I'm Not Writing Many Love Poems." Falcon (14) 77,
   p. 49.
"Like My Father Who." WindO (27) Aut 76.
"Lyn He Says Comes from the Word River." Stonecloud (6) 76,
   p. 123.

"The Man Being Questioned After the Blood the Branches."
PoNow (14/18) 77, p. 114.
"Monet's Les Nympheas." Stonecloud (6) 76, p. 123.
"More Things You Can't Do with a Lover." HangL (29) Wint 76-
77, p. 16.
"1945." HangL (29) Wint 76-77, p. 18.
"1945 1/2." CalQ (11/12) Wint-Spr 77, p. 74.
"1952." CalQ (11/12) Wint-Spr 77, p. 71.
"1955." Bleb (12) 77, p. 34.
"On the Morning before the Divorce." Bleb (12) 77, p. 33.
Patagonia (Thirty poems). WormR (65/66) 77, pp. 19-30.
"People We Don't Know in Photos in the Old House." Bleb (12)
77, p. 35.
"Pieces of Eight Pieces of the Moon." Bleb (12) 77, p. 32.
"Plymouth." Falcon (15) 77, p. 20.
"Poems: like the Kind of." Bleb (12) 77, p. 32.
"She said the Poems in the House are Old Smell." Falcon (14)
77, p. 51.
"Sunday Driving Home." Falcon (14) 77, p. 50.
"Testimony." PoNow (14/18) 77, p. 114.
"Testimony after the Blood in the Leaves." PoNow (14/18) 77,
p. 114.
"The Woman Who Married Her House." WindO (27) Aut 76.
"The Woman Who Married Her House, II." WindO (27) Aut 76.
"Women with Eyes Like Glazed Stones." YellowBR (9) 77, p. 4.
"You Must Know." CalQ (11/12) Wint-Spr 77, p. 73.

LIFSHITZ, Leatrice
"Names & Voices." StoneC (77:2) My 77, p. 15.

LIGHTFOOT, Susan
"Dragon Valley." 13thM (3:2) 77, p. 60.

LIGI, Gary E.
"Blackberries." DacTerr (14) Spr-Sum 77, p. 36.
"If You Elected Me President." YellowBR (8) 77, p. 5.
"In the Mornings." DeKalb (10:3) Spr 77, p. 26.
"I've Written So Many Letters." DacTerr (14) Spr-Sum 77,
p. 36.
"The Latest Germ." Agni (7) 77, p. 89.
"Love Song: A Separation." Agni (7) 77, p. 96.
"Now You Have Gone." DeKalb (10:3) Spr 77, p. 27.
"On Your Fifty-Fifth Birthday." Agni (7) 77, p. 91.
"20 Century Soliloquy." Aspect (70) Ja-Mr 77, p. 10.
"What It's Like." Aspect (70) Ja-Mr 77, p. 9.
"Your Finger." Agni (7) 77, p. 87.

LIGNELL, Kathleen
"Calamity Jane and Buffalo Bill's Wild West Show." Chomo (3:3)
Spr 77, p. 3.
"Calamity Jane Faces Herself." Icarus (5:2) Aut 77, p. 6.
"Myth #1." Wind (24) 77, p. 43.

"Tule Fog." Wind (24) 77, p. 43.

LILLY, Othelia
"Bells and Bells Ago." ChrC (94:13) 13 Ap 77, p. 355.

LILLY, Paul
"Target" (for Jim Kelly). HiramPoR (22) Aut-Wint 77, p. 27.

LIMA, Jorge de
"Vinte séculos de revolução." TexQ (19:4) Wint 76, p. 98.

LIMAN, Claude
"The Cancer Dream." ConcPo (10:1) Spr 77, p. 44.
"There in That Winter." Drag (16) 77.

LIND, Jakov
"The Story of Lilith and Eve." WebR (3:1) Wint 77, p. 48.

LINDEMAN, Jack
"Self-Portrait." SouthernPR (17:2) Aut 77, p. 67.
"Timeless." DeKalb (10:3) Spr 77, p. 28.

LINDNER, Carl
"Angela's Garden." SouthwR (62:2) Spr 77, p. 159.
"Dancer." SouthernPR (17:1) Spr 77, p. 4.
"One Shaft of Sunlight." Vaga (25) 77, p. 14.
"To Keep What Cargo." KanQ (9:1) Wint 77, p. 131.

LINDSAY, Frannie
"Gethsemane." Pig (3) 77, p. 24.

LINDSEY, Jim
"Pictures Out of Doors." LittleR (12) 77, p. 12.

LINDSTRAND, Gordon
"Fantasy of a Sleeping Compass." KanQ (9:1) Wint 77, p. 130.

LINK, Gordden
"My Failing Student." AndR (3:2) Aut 76, p. 88.

LINTON, Joan Pong
"The mind fishes." StoneC (77:2) My 77, p. 14.

LI Pang-ling
"Letter" (tr. by Graeme Wilson). DenQ (12:2) Sum 77, p. 400.

LI P'in
"Fording the Han" (tr. by J. P. Seaton). CarolQ (29:2) Spr-Sum
    77, p. 120.

LIPMAN, Ed "Foots"
Twenty-seven poems. SeC (5:1) 77, pp. 77-118.

LI Po
"Coming Down Chungnan Mountain and Staying with Hermit Hussu"
(tr. by David Fung and Julie Landau). DenQ (12:2) Sum 77,
p. 352.
"Drinking with a Hermit Friend in the Mountains" (tr. by David
Fung and Julie Landau). DenQ (12:2) Sum 77, p. 352.
"A Letter" (tr. by Lenore Mayhew and William McNaughton).
DenQ (12:2) Sum 77, p. 327.
"The Old Dust" (tr. by Lenore Mayhew and William McNaughton).
DenQ (12:2) Sum 77, p. 327.
"The Temple of the Peak" (tr. by Graeme Wilson). DenQ (12:2)
Sum 77, p. 50.
"Visiting a Taoist" (tr. by Graeme Wilson). DenQ (12:2) Sum
77, p. 50.

LIPSITZ, Louis
"Incomplete Developments." SouthernPR (16:SI) 77, p. 45.
"The Neurotic Woman." CarolQ (29:1) Wint 77, p. 61.

LISK, Thomas
"A Diminished Thing." KanQ (9:1) Wint 77, p. 28.
"Pillar." KanQ (9:4) Aut 77, p. 9.
"Vague Bird." KanQ (9:1) Wint 77, p. 27.

LITTAUER, Andrew
"Belatedly for Norman Douglas." SewanR (85:2) Spr 77, p. 212.
"Cold Spring Harbor--A Decade After." SewanR (85:2) Spr 77,
p. 210.
"Palladian Pastoral." SewanR (85:2) Spr 77, p. 211.

LITTLE, Geraldine C.
"Lion Approaching the Stable." ColEng (39:1) S 77, p. 66.
"Poem for Murakami Kijo, 1865-1938, A Poet Deafened by Ill-
ness." BelPoJ (27:4) Sum 77, p. 16.
"Stepping Stones." StoneC (77:3) S 77, p. 9.

LITWACK, Susan
"Prayer." Hand (1) 77, p. 147.
"The Synagogue." Hand (1) 77, p. 148.

LITZ, Robert
"Downriver, for Jonah." BelPoJ (27:4) Sum 77, p. 2.
"Land and Seascape." DeKalb (10:2) Wint 77, p. 44.
"Montana." DeKalb (10:2) Wint 77, p. 45.

LIU Chang-chui
"Leaving the Temple" (tr. by Graeme Wilson). DenQ (12:2) Sum
77, p. 392.

LIU, Stephen Shu Ning
"Adultery at a Las Vegas Bookstore." Shen (29:1) Aut 77, p. 75.
"A Comparative Study." SenR (8:2) D 77, p. 34.
"How Abundant Was the Spring." Shen (29:1) Aut 77, p. 76.

"I'm Entering Your Shadow." SenR (8:2) D 77, p. 35.
"Night Conversation." PortR (23) 77, p. 117.

LIU Tsung Yuan
   "River Snow" (tr. by David Fung and Julie Landau). DenQ (12:2)
      Sum 77, p. 351.

LIVINGSTON, James
   "Self, That Old Whore, Dreams of Eating." YellowBR (8) 77,
      p. 34.

LIVINGSTON, John
   "Fly slow for your heart guides you. See through your eyes."
      AmerPoR (6:2) Mr-Ap 77, p. 32.
   "Once when I was walking in the woods with my 22, I felt like
      shooting at." AmerPoR (6:2) Mr-Ap 77, p. 32.

LI Yi
   "Listening to a Flute at the Frontier" (tr. by David Fung and
      Julie Landau). DenQ (12:2) Sum 77, p. 351.

LI Yu
   "Ching P'ing Lo" (tr. by David Fung and Julie Landau). DenQ
      (12:2) Sum 77, p. 351.
   "I Remember Them" (tr. by Lenore Mayhew and William
      McNaughton). DenQ (12:2) Sum 77, p. 328.
   "Poem: Autumn" (tr. by Lenore Mayhew and William
      McNaughton). DenQ (12:2) Sum 77, p. 326.

LLOYD, Roseann
   "Dreaming the Cabbage Patch." CutB (8) Spr 77, p. 74.

LOCK, Norman G.
   "Tom Swift and the Cap of Invisibility." CalQ (11/12) Wint-Spr
      77, p. 155.

LOCKE, Duane
   "The middle aged man drove past the plowed peanut field."
      PoNow (14/18) 77, p. 115.
   "Walking Down an Old Street and Turning a Corner in Arezzo."
      SouthernPR (16:SI) 77, p. 46.

LOCKE, Edward
   "On the Death of James Thurber." ChiR (29:1) Sum 77, p. 127.
   "The Wing and the Talon." YaleR (67:1) Aut 77, p. 69.

LOCKE, Karen
   "Cooking Soup." SmPd (14:3) Aut 77, p. 7.

LOCKLIN, Gerald
   "The Great War." Madrona (4:13/14) 77, p. 42.
   "Her Endearing Young Charms." Madrona (4:13/14) 77, p. 41.
   "Illumination." YellowBR (9) 77, p. 14.

"An Indelible Impression." Madrona (4:13/14) 77, p. 41.
"Inscape." PoNow (14/18) 77, p. 116.
"The Late, Late, Late Show." PoNow (14/18) 77, p. 115.
"A Light Afternoon." PoNow (14/18) 77, p. 198.
"Marilyn Powell." PoNow (14/18) 77, p. 115.
"Obligatory Bicentennial Poem." PoNow (14/18) 77, p. 115.
"Paleontology." WindO (28) Spr 77, p. 22.
"A Reprieve." PoNow (14/18) 77, p. 117.
"A Thousand Years This Side of the Millenium." WindO (28)
    Spr 77, p. 22.
"The Wife of the Ex-Filmmaker." PoNow (14/18) 77, p. 115.

LOEB, Joan H.
"About Thomas Wolfe and My Father." DeKalb (10:4) Sum 77,
    p. 72.
"Sisters." DeKalb (10:4) Sum 77, p. 73.

LOEBELL, Larry
"Chili and Eggs" (for Bob McNamara). Wind (24) 77, p. 44.
"Home in the Heart." Wind (24) 77, p. 44.
"Home Movies" (for Diane). DacTerr (14) Spr-Sum 77, p. 48.
"Letter to Bob McNamara from Mount Airy." Wind (26) 77,
    p. 39.
"Presidential Debates." QW (2) Wint 77, p. 72.

LOFTIS, N. J.
"Lucifer." AmerPoR (6:6) N-D 77, p. 12.
"The Obsession." AmerPoR (6:6) N-D 77, p. 12.
"Vesuvius." AmerPoR (6:6) N-D 77, p. 10.

LOGAN, John
"The Bridge of Change" (For Roger Aplon). ParisR (69) Spr 77,
    p. 50.

LOGAN, Thean
"Obsession." NewL (44:1) Aut 77, p. 72.

LOGAN, William
"Anamnesis." Poetry (131:3) D 77, p. 127.
"The Children Who Guard Us." Shen (29:1) Aut 77, p. 84.
"The Desert of Reminiscence." Poetry (131:3) D 77, p. 126.
"Fever." Nat (225:23) 31 D 77, p. 730.
"In December, Thirty-One Moons." Poetry (131:3) D 77, p. 125.
"Lighting the Lantern." SenR (8:2) D 77, p. 52.
"The Lizard in His Medium." NewYorker (53:33) 3 O 77, p. 111.
"Monocular." Poetry (130:3) D 77, p. 128.
"The Moth Disturbs the Night." Poetry (130:4) Jl 77, p. 206.
"My Friend Who Has Become a Quick-Sketch Man." PraS (51:3)
    Aut 77, p. 278.
"The Object." Poetry (130:4) Jl 77, p. 202.
"Passage." SenR (8:2) D 77, p. 54.
"Three Lives." Poetry (130:4) Jl 77, p. 204.
"Totenlieder." Poetry (130:4) Jl 77, p. 201.

LONEY, Estil
"Dream of an Interview with Joyce Carol Oates." Some (7/8)
    76.

LONG, D. S.
"from an idling truck." Drag (16) 77.
from The Winter Fisherman: "96." CutB (9) Aut-Wint 77,
    p. 111.

LONG, David
"A Father & Son Shoot Horseshoes beside the Floodstage
    Missouri." PortR (23) 77, p. 6.
"Irene." PortR (23) 77, p. 7.
"Why We Do Not Cook Eggs in Our House." PortR (23) 77, p.
    7.
"You Don't Know Who to Thank." MontG (5) Wint 77, p. 47.

LONG, Doc
"Time-Focus." Nimrod (21:2/22:1) 77, p. 144.

LONG, Mike
"Prodigal Doldrums/A Meal of Fish." AAR (27) 77, p. 64.

LONG, Robert
"The Death of Montovani." HangL (29) Wint 76-77, p. 20.
"Rome Adventure." MontG (5) Wint 77, p. 59.
from The Sonnets: (22). PartR (44:3) 77, p. 403.

LONGFELLOW, Henry Wadsworth
"The Arrow and the Song." PoNow (14/18) 77, p. 93.

LONGLAND, Jean R.
"Belém of Pará" (tr. of Manuel Bandeira). LitR (21:2) Wint 78,
    p. 216.
"The Cactus" (tr. of Cassiano Ricardo). LitR (21:2) Wint 78,
    p. 222.
"Childhood" (tr. of João Cabral de Melo Neto). LitR (21:2) Wint
    78, p. 237.
"Deeply" (tr. of Manuel Bandeira). LitR (21:2) Wint 78, p. 214.
"The Dirty Hand" (tr. of Carlos Drummond de Andrade). LitR
    (21:2) Wint 78, p. 164.
"Double Dentures" (tr. of Carlos Drummond de Andrade). LitR
    (21:2) Wint 78, p. 160.
"Letter from the Boy I Was at That Time" (tr. of Marcos
    Konder Reis). LitR (22:1) Wint 78, p. 259.
"News from Spain" (tr. of Carlos Drummond de Andrade). LitR
    (21:2) Wint 78, p. 160.
"Poem: My eyes have telescopes" (tr. of João Cabral de Melo
    Neto). LitR (21:2) Wint 78, p. 238.
"Solitude" (tr. of Marcos Konder Reis). LitR (21:2) Wint 78,
    p. 260.
"Sun and Showers" (tr. of Cassiano Ricardo). LitR (21:2) Wint
    78, p. 223.

"The Taste of Your Kiss" (tr. of Cassiano Ricardo). LitR
(21:2) Wint 78, p. 221.
"To Carlos Drummond de Andrade" (tr. of João Cabral de Melo
Neto). LitR (21:2) Wint 78, p. 237.

LOOBY, Georgette
"Four Young Cowboys." SeC (5:2) 78, p. 49.

LOOTS, Barbara Kunz
"Chins on a Window." LadHJ (94:7) Jl 77, p. 20.
"The Six Million Dollar Cat." LadHJ (94:9) S 77, p. P.S. 28.

LOPES, Michael
"Sketch from a Small Town." PoNow (14/18) 77, p. 116.

LORCA, Federico García
"Ballad of the Moon, the Moon" (to Conchita García Lorca) (tr.
by Meg Bogin). MassR (18:4) Wint 77, p. 821.
"Gacela: Del niño muerto." CalQ (11/12) Wint-Spr 77, p. 80.
"The Guitar" (tr. by Edward Stanton). AntR (35:2/3) Spr-Sum 77,
p. 248.
"La soltera en misa." CalQ (11/12) Wint-Spr 77, p. 79.
"The Unfaithful Wife" (to Lydia Cabrera and to her friend) (tr.
by Meg Bogin). MassR (18:4) Wint 77, p. 822.

LORD, Linda
"The burning afternoon thirsts for shade" (after the Spanish
Nuevos Cantos by Federico García Lorca). HarvAd (111:1)
N 77, p. 9.

LORDE, Audre
"The Black Unicorn." AmerPoR (6:6) N-D 77, p. 35.
"Coniagui Women." NewYorker (53:41) 28 N 77, p. 84.
"From the House of Yemanja." AmerPoR (6:6) N-D 77, p. 35.
"Outside." AmerPoR (6:1) Ja-F 77, p. 26.
"Scar." Epoch (26:3) Spr 77, p. 256.
"Sister Outsider." Nimrod (21:2/22:1) 77, p. 145.

LOSCH, Rita S.
"On Wanting to Be an Egg." StoneC (77:2) My 77, p. 14.

LOSPALLUTO, Frank
"Behavior 95." Waters (5) 77, p. 6.

LOUGHLIN, Richard L.
"Musée des Faux Arts." CEACritic (39:3) Mr 77, p. 25.

LOURIE, Dick
"In the Revolution." HangL (31) Aut 77, p. 43.
"Invocation to My Muse" (for Jim Tippett, for Jim Moore).
HangL (31) Aut 77, p. 46.
"Living in the Present." HangL (31) Aut 77, p. 44.

"What It's Like Living in Ithaca New York." HangL (31) Aut 77,
     p. 42.

LOURIE, Richard
     "Antithin" (tr. of Sándor Weöres). AmerPoR (6:3) My-Je 77,
     p. 23.
     "A Day without Poetry." Ploughs (4:1) 77, p. 57.

LOUTHAN, Robert
     "I've Always Been a Matador." SenR (8:1) My 77, p. 73.
     "The Suicide." SenR (8:1) My 77, p. 73.

LOUVIERE, Matthew
     "Ancestral Moments." Wind (24) 77, p. 46.

LOVE, John
     "A Death that Interests Me." Some (7/8) 76.
     "Fall Down." Some (7/8) 76.
     "Moving Account." Some (7/8) 76.

LOVELL, Barbara
     "The Life Pouring Out." SouthernPR (17:1) Spr 77, p. 15.

LOVETT, Herbert
     "How to Abandon Ship." ParisR (69) Spr 77, p. 38.

LOW, Terry Allen
     "Coincidental Murders." Mouth (11/12) Mr-Je 77, p. 117.

LOWE, Ralph
     "Settlement." QW (2) Wint 77, p. 11.

LOWELL, Robert
     "Arethusa to Lycotas." Shen (28:4) Sum 77, p. 3.
     "Christmas Eve Under Hooker's Statue." Comm (104:25) 9 D 77,
     p. 786.
     "The Dead in Europe." Comm (104:25) 9 D 77, p. 786.
     "Domesday Book." Salm (37) Spr 77, p. 14.
     "Epilogue." Harp (255:1531) D 77, p. 112.
     "Epilogue." Salm (37) Spr 77, p. 115.
     "Executions." NewYRB (24:12) 14 Jl 77, p. 22.
     "The Flaw." Harp (255:1531) D 77, p. 111.
     "For John Berryman." NewYRB (24:11) 23 Je 77, p. 14.
     "Our Afterlife" (For Peter Taylor). Shen (28:2) Wint 77, p. 5.
     "Ylysses and Circe." Salm (37) Spr 77, p. 7.
     "You Knocked Yourself Out." HarvAd (111:1) N 77, p. 27.

LOWENKRON, David
     "Marriage." PoetL (72:1) Spr 77, p. 8.
     "On Changing Professions" (For fellow teachers). PoetL (72:1)
     Spr 77, p. 8.
     "Subway." DeKalb (10:3) Spr 77, p. 29.

LOWENKRON, Lauren
"Autumn Portraiture." PoetL (72:1) Spr 77, p. 7.
"Odysseus." KanQ (9:1) Wint 77, p. 65.

LOWERY, Mike
"As I Huddle among My Bones." Wind (25) 77, p. 33.
"Changes." Wind (25) 77, p. 33.
"Now Is Forever." Wind (25) 77, p. 34.
"Susan Sparrow, 1963 Graduate, Bryan Business School." WindO
   (27) Aut 76.
"Uptown." BlackF (2:1) Wint 77-78, p. 24.

LOWRY, Robert
"Extraordinary Living." Wind (24) 77, p. 47.
"My Name." Wind (24) 77, p. 47.

LOWTHER, Vicki
"The Circus Is about to Begin." Juice (4) 77.
"He Doesn't Touch." Juice (4) 77.

LOY, Mina
"Love Songs." Aspen (3) Spr 77, p. 18.
"Lunar Baedeker." Aspen (3) Spr 77, p. 16.

LOYD, Marianne
"Equinox." StoneC (77:3) S 77, p. 32.
"November Murders." StoneC (77:3) S 77, p. 33.

LU Chi
"Self Seeking" (tr. by Graeme Wilson). DenQ (12:2) Sum 77,
   p. 46.

LUCINA, Sister Mary
"Memorial Day." ChrC (94:19) 25 My 77, p. 506.
"My Sixth Grade Teacher." ChrC (94:4) 2-9 F 77, p. 84.
"Storm." Icarus (5:1) Spr 77, p. 6.

LUDVIGSON, Susan
"Myths." TexQ (20:4) Wint 77, p. 122.
"Prodigy." RemR (5) 77, p. 88.
"Sonnet for My Father." TexQ (20:4) Wint 77, p. 132.
"Trying to Change the Subject." Nat (224:25) 25 Je 77, p. 791.

LUDWIG, Tina
"Gary Gilmore." SeC (5:2) 78, p. 51.
"Madness." SeC (5:2) 78, p. 50.

LUHN, David
"Winter Ceremony." NewC (7:3) 75-76, p. 4.

LUHRMANN, Tom
"Eschatological Hermeneutic." TransR (58/59) F 77, p. 140.
"Hope." OhioR (18:2) Spr-Sum 77, p. 35.

"Wednesday. "   OhioR (18:2) Spr-Sum 77, p. 36.

LU Hsing-che
    "The Scullion's Reply" (tr. by Graeme Wilson).   WestHR (31:3)
        Sum 77, p. 209.

LULL, Janis
    "Dodge Center, Minnesota, 1977. " Epoch (27:1) Aut 77, p. 61.
    "Dream Man. " PoetryNW (18:4) Wint 77-78, p. 4.
    "Sestina for Old Love and Faulty Recollection. " Epoch (27:1)
        Aut 77, p. 60.
    "There Are Five Great Themes. " PoetryNW (18:4) Wint 77-78,
        p. 3.
    "To Herself Reflected. " PoetryNW (18:4) Wint 77-78, p. 3.

LU Mei-P'O
    "The Plum Snow Blossom" (tr. by Christopher Howell).   PortR
        (23) 77, p. 98.

LUMSDEN, Phil
    "He Lived Near McGill, Near the Water. " NewC (8:1) 76-77,
        p. 16.

LUND, Morten
    "I feel like a piece of gum in a. " AAR (27) 77, p. 115.

LUNDE, David
    "For Pioneers. " PoNow (14/18) 77, p. 116.
    "The Gunfighter. " PoNow (14/18) 77, p. 116.
    "Moonwalk. " Drag (16) 77.

LUNDGREN, Sandy
    "Cockroach. " YellowBR (8) 77, p. 33.

LUSCHEI, Glenna
    "Are You Losing Your Grip?" Drag (16) 77.
    "The New American Grain. " Drag (16) 77.

LUSK, Daniel
    "A Dream of Montana, Naked. " MontG (5) Wint 77, p. 11.
    "If I Were You. " MontG (5) Wint 77, p. 12.
    "Where Ravens Sleep. " MontG (5) Wint 77, p. 10.

LUTTINGER, Abigail
    "How to Prevent Bad Things. " Madrona (4:13/14) 77, p. 14.
    "Mother's Day. " HangL (30) Sum 77, p. 51.
    "poem protesting this sort of poem. " Gra (12) 77, p. 57.
    "Poem to Myself. " Gra (12) 77.
    "self indulgent poem. " Gra (12) 77, p. 48.
    "Slide Show. " Kayak (44) F 77, p. 7.
    "Surgery. " Gra (12) 77.
    "To Whom It May Concern. " Gra (12) 77.
    "yesterday. " 13thM (3:2) 77, p. 40.

LUX, Thomas
  "Barn Fire." Iowa (8:2) Spr 77, p. 64.
  "The Enemy of the Wind." VirQR (53:4) Aut 77, p. 724.
  from The Glassblower's Breath: "History and Abstraction."
      PoNow (14/18) 77, p. 90.
  from The Glassblower's Breath: "Lament City." PoNow (14/18)
      77, p. 90.
  from The Glassblower's Breath: "Longitude and Latitude: Hart
      Crane." PoNow (14/18) 77, p. 90.
  "The Hunting." Ploughs (4:1) 77, p. 53.
  "Lament for the Friend Who Lost His Brother" (for Gary Wilson
      & in memoriam: Kenneth Wilson, 1943-1977). Ploughs (4:1)
      77, p. 52.
  "Madrigal on the Way Home." Some (7/8) 76.
  "Portrait of the Man Who Drowned Wearing His Best Suit and
      Shoes." Ploughs (4:1) 77, p. 51.
  "Spiders Wanting." VirQR (53:4) Aut 77, p. 725.

LU Yu
  "The Gateway of the Sword" (tr. by Graeme Wilson). DenQ
      (12:2) Sum 77, p. 398.

LYLE, K. Curtiss
  "Curtis Spiritual Sunwolf: or The Conversation of Death."
      Epoch (26:3) Spr 77, p. 224.
  "Ritual: Dance at the End of Rage." Epoch (26:3) Spr 77,
      p. 222.

LYLES, Peggy Willis
  "First autumn evening." WindO (30) Aut 77.
  "Funeral." PoetL (72:1) Spr 77, p. 22.
  "Love's Phases." Wind (27) 77, p. 27.
  "Measuring the Relics." HiramPoR (23) Wint 77, p. 24.

LYMAN, Stephany
  "Incomplete." DeKalb (10:3) Spr 77, p. 30.

LYNCH, Kathleen
  "Double Exposure." CutB (8) Spr 77, p. 9.

LYNE, Sandford
  "Armadillo." VirQR (53:4) Aut 77, p. 725.

LYNN, Sandra
  "A Leaf from the Book of Trees." TexQ (20:4) Wint 77, p. 85.
  "Replies by Wind." TexQ (20:4) Aut 77, p. 87.

LYONS, Arla
  "Puerto Angel, Oaxaca." EngJ (66:5) My 77, p. 48.

LYONS, Deborah
  "Leopard Census Encouraging." ColEng (38:7) Mr 77, p. 724.

LYSOHORSKY, Ondra
"At the Forge" (tr. by Hugh McKinley).   MalR (43) Jl 77,
     p. 118.
"Shadows" (tr. by Hugh McKinley).   MalR (43) Jl 77, p. 119.
"'Who Will Take Me in His Hands?'" (tr. by Olive and Hugh
     McKinley).   MalR (43) Jl 77, p. 119.

M. , E.
"lacking the imposition to breathe. "   Pig (3) 77, p. 51.

MacADAMS, Lewis
"Autumn in Bolinas. "   Chelsea (36) 77, p. 68.

McAFEE, Thomas
"At Home, Far Away Inside. "   Ploughs (4:1) 77, p. 89.
"Brothers Meeting. "   NewL (43:4) Sum 77, p. 53.
"A Gentleman Not to Worry About. "   Poem (30) Jl 77, p. 52.
"Janis Joplin: The Road Taken. "   LittleR (12) 77, p. 5.
"Letter from North Carolina to Alabama. " LittleR (12) 77, p. 11.
"The Perfect Murder. "   LittleR (12) 77, p. 3.
"Uncle Ezra on Rainy Days. "   NoAmR (262:1) Spr 77, p. 17.
"When the Wind Comes Through. "   Poem (30) Jl 77, p. 51.

McALEAVEY, David
"After Dinner with Mark Spitz. "   SenR (8:1) My 77, p. 83.
"Lighting Out for the Territory. "   SenR (8:1) My 77, p. 82.
"Plainly Spoken. "   Chowder (9) Aut-Wint 77, p. 100.
"Recession, 1974. "   Icarus (5:1) Spr 77, p. 4.

McALLISTER, Bruce
"First and Last Contact. "   Drag (16) 77.
"The Last Man and Supper. "   ColEng (38:6) F 77, p. 589.

McALLISTER, Byron Leon
"Fringes of Ratiocination. "   Poem (31) N 77, p. 3.
"Skeptical Essay. "   Poem (31) N 77, p. 4.
"The Stars Replace Themselves. "   Poem (29) Mr 77, p. 16.
"The Way. "   Poem (29) Mr 77, p. 15.

MACALUSO, Timothy L.
"Epitaph for Hart Crane. "   Mouth (13) D 77, p. 46.

MACARI, Anne Marie
"After the Rain. "   Field (17) Aut 77, p. 35.
"Burial Mound. "   Field (17) Aut 77, p. 33.
"Counting the Years. "   Field (17) Aut 77, p. 34.

MacBETH, George
"The Break-Up" (tr. of László Nagy).   AmerPoR (6:3) My-Je 77,
     p. 24.

McBRIDE, Mekeel
"Asking for Help at a Late Hour. "   Agni (7) 77, p. 19.

"Breaking Surface" (for D. K. W.)." <u>AntR</u> (35:2/3) Spr-Sum 77,
  p. 260.
"The Keeper of the Sea." <u>Kayak</u> (45) My 77, p. 3.
"Love Poem." <u>Kayak</u> (45) <u>My 77</u>, p. 4.
"Mangoes and Clean Water" (for Barbara). <u>PoetryNW</u> (18:1) Spr
  77, p. 48.
"Marlon Brando and I Attend Several Japanese Films." <u>Agni</u> (7)
  77, p. 18.
"The Names We Were Born With." <u>Kayak</u> (45) My 77, p. 4.
"No Child of Earthly Kitchens." <u>Chowder</u> (8) Spr-Sum 77, p. 4.
"The Source of Light." <u>Agni</u> (7) <u>77</u>, p. 14.
"To Prepare for This." <u>Kayak</u> (45) My 77, p. 5.
"What Cannot Be Tasted." <u>Chowder</u> (8) Spr-Sum 77, p. 5.
"What Light There Is." <u>Agni</u> <u>(7)</u> 77, p. 17.

McCABE, Victoria
"Acquaintance." <u>DeKalb</u> (10:3) Spr 77, p. 31.
"Divorce." <u>PoNow</u> <u>(14/18)</u> 77, p. 122.

McCAFFREY, Phillip
"Apprehension." <u>BelPoJ</u> (27:4) Sum 77, p. 29.
"Family Reunion." <u>PoNow</u> (14/18) 77, p. 122.
"Germination." <u>Wind</u> <u>(25)</u> 77, p. 36.
"Signature." <u>YellowBR</u> (9) 77, p. 17.

McCANN, Bill
"The Girl of Eithinfynydd" (tr. of Dafydd ap Gwilym, w. Philip
  Holmes). <u>Stand</u> (18:2) 77, p. 35.

McCANN, David
"David." <u>Poetry</u> (130:1) Ap 77, p. 1.
"Dying on a Seldom-Travelled Road." <u>Ploughs</u> (3:3/4) 77, p. 151.
"Morning Light." <u>Poetry</u> (130:1) Ap 77, p. 2.

McCANN, Janet
"Another Dream Poem." <u>LitR</u> (20:3) Spr 77, p. 358.
"Cookies." <u>Wind</u> (25) 77, p. 37.
"Explanation." <u>FourQt</u> (27:1) Aut 77, p. 23.
"For My Blind Friend." <u>Wind</u> (25) 77, p. 37.
"In the Library." <u>HolCrit</u> (14:2) Ap 77, p. 10.
"The Jump-Rope Poem." <u>FourQt</u> (27:1) Aut 77, p. 22.
"Magritte." <u>ConcPo</u> (10:1) Spr 77, p. 74.
"The Woman Who Loved a Vampire." <u>WebR</u> (3:1) Wint 77,
  p. 27.

McCANN, Richard
"Dreams of Absence, Men." <u>HangL</u> (31) Aut 77, p. 54.

McCARTHY, Gerald
"The Warriors" (for Dave Kelly). <u>Rapp</u> (10) 77, p. 76.

McCLANE, Ken
"The Child." <u>NowestR</u> (16:3) 77, p. 35.

"Gainsaying." Nimrod (21:2/22:1) 77, p. 152.
"Grandfather." Nimrod (21:2/22:1) 77, p. 151.
"In Sow's Thistle." Wind (26) 77, p. 41.
"The Old." CornellR (2) Aut 77, p. 76.
"Sloane's Woods." Wind (26) 77, p. 40.

McCLATCHY, J. D.
"Breakfast Table." Nat (225:20) 10 D 77, p. 636.
"A Capriccio of Roman Ruins and Sculpture with Figures." GeoR
    (31:3) Aut 77, p. 700.
"Scenes from Another Life." Poetry (130:1) Ap 77, p. 30.
"Suffering the Cut." Poetry (130:1) Ap 77, p. 28.
"Variations on a Line." YaleR (67:1) Aut 77, p. 70.

McCLAURIN, Irma
"Africa." Nimrod (21:2/22:1) 77, p. 155.
"Children's Cycle II" (A response to the Vietnam baby airlift--
    1975, dedicated to The Democratic People's Republic of
    Vietnam). Nimrod (21:2/22:1) 77, p. 154.
"I, Woman" (For JoAnn Little and other oppressed women). Obs
    (3:2) Sum 77, p. 55.
"Poem for a Strung-Out Friend" (for J). Nimrod (21:2/22:1) 77,
    p. 153.
"Return." Nimrod (21:2/22:1) 77, p. 155.

McCLEERY, Nancy
"Everything Keeps Me Here, The Swallow." PortR (23) 77,
    p. 35.

McCLOSKEY, Mark
"The Fear of Death." QW (3) Spr-Sum 77, p. 18.
"Her Departure." PoetryNW (18:1) Spr 77, p. 21.
"Her Pictures." PoetryNW (18:4) Wint 77-78, p. 46.
"How to Keep Your Lover." PoetryNW (18:1) Spr 77, p. 20.
"My Daughter Enters High School." PoetryNW (18:4) Wint 77-78,
    p. 47.

McCLURE, Michael
"Echoing." UnmOx (15) 77, p. 103.
"The Energy and Consciousness Conference." UnmOx (15) 77,
    p. 105.
from Jaguar Skies: "At Night on the River." PoNow (14/18) 77,
    p. 121.
from Jaguar Skies: "The Glow" (for Imamu Amiri Baraka).
    PoNow (14/18) 77, p. 121.
from Jaguar Skies: "July Morning." PoNow (14/18) 77, p. 121.
"Poem with a Gift." Atl (239:3) Mr 77, p. 97.

McCLUSKEY, Sally
"Family Snapshot, Edges Trimmed." HiramPoR (23) Wint 77,
    p. 25.
"Red-Haired Woman at the Ouija Board." HiramPoR (23) Wint
    77, p. 26.

McCOLL, Mike
"We Sleep without Dreaming." HolCrit (14:4) O 77, p. 15.

McCOLLUM, Malcolm Stiles
"Moth." ColEng (38:8) Ap 77, p. 811.
"Winter, 1944." CarlMis (17:1) Wint 77-78, p. 117.

McCOMAS, Marilyn
"The Force That Conquers." Poem (29) Mr 77, p. 27.
"The Fortress." Poem (29) Mr 77, p. 28.

McCOMBS, Judith
"The Heavy One." GRR (8:3) 77, p. 220.
"How It Is." ModernPS (8:2) Aut 77, p. 139.
"Travelling Alone." GRR (8:3) 77, p. 222.

McCONEGHEY, Nelljean
"The Bat." BelPoJ (27:4) Sum 77, p. 19.
"The Fat Woman Addresses Herself to The Ladies' Home Journal
    'How America Lives.'" LittleR (12) 77, p. 14.
"For My Library Lover I Leave This Poem Pressed between
    Pages 9 & 10 of My Secret Life." CutB (8) Spr 77, p. 31.
"Joe Makes a Mistake and the Fat Woman Meets Molly Bloom."
    BelPoJ (27:4) Sum 77, p. 18.
"She Raced a Coyote up a Howard County Hill." LittleR (12) 77,
    p. 14.

McCORD, Howard
"Catalogue Raisonne." PoNow (14/18) 77, p. 123.
"For Someone Far South." PoNow (14/18) 77, p. 122.
"Three Admissions." Iowa (8:2) Spr 77, p. 65.
"Tonight." QW (2) Wint 77, p. 13.
"What's Happening Right Now." QW (2) Wint 77, p. 12.

MacCORMICK, Chris
"All the Pretty Little Horses." Iowa (8:4) Aut 77, p. 83.

McCORMMACH, Carol
"Rough Drafts." PoetryNW (18:4) Wint 77-78, p. 16.

McCORQUODALE, Robin
"You Told Me That You Loved the Pine Trees." TexQ (20:4)
    Wint 77, p. 109.
"Your Apartment." TexQ (20:4) Wint 77, p. 108.

McCOWN, Clint
"Real Life Romances." PoNow (14/18) 77, p. 123.

McCOY, Jane
"The Hidden Handicap--Shadow Child." StoneC (77:3) S 77,
    p. 30.

McCULLAGH, James C.
"For the Child Who Said." StoneC (77:3) S 77, p. 23.

McCULLOUGH, Ken
"Fruits from the Outside World." NewL (43:4) Sum 77, p. 68.

McCUNE, Catherine
"The Elephant Man" (for D. L. G.). BerksR (12:1) Spr 77.
"Saeth" (for Pat). BerksR (12:1) Spr 77.

McCURRY, Jim
"Job Cut-Up." Aspect (69) O-D 76, p. 16.
"Three Days at Home." QW (2) Wint 77, p. 14.

MacDIARMID, Hugh
"Diamond Body (In a Cave of the Sea)." Montra (3) Spr 77, p. 95.

McDONAGH, Michael
"diary entry." Mouth (13) D 77, p. 65.

McDONALD, Anne
"From Flat to Blowup." Wind (27) 77, p. 32.

MACDONALD, Bernell
"Old Photograph." WindO (30) Aut 77.

McDONALD, Bray
"10th Song of Thace of the Old Country." DeKalb (10:3) Spr 77, p. 32.

MACDONALD, Cynthia
"Burying the Babies." NoAmR (262:2) Sum 77, p. 21.
"It Is Dangerous to Be the Conductor." GeoR (31:2) Sum 77, p. 453.
"The World's Fattest Dancer." NewYorker (53:38) 7 N 77, p. 52.

McDONALD, Susan Schwartz
"The Restoration." Humanist (37:5) S-O 77, p. 33.

McDONOUGH, George E.
"The Wanderer." ChrC (94:43) 28 D 77, p. 1223.

McDONOUGH, Robert E.
"My Wife's Elbow." CalQ (11/12) Wint-Spr 77, p. 152.

MacDOUGALL, Richi
"My I Remember Poem." Mouth (11/12) Mr-Je 77, p. 55.
"Titled:: Talking about:: Liberal Standpoints." Mouth (11/12) Mr-Je 77, p. 104.

McELROY, Colleen J.
"Breaking the Kula Ring." Chowder (9) Aut-Wint 77, p. 34.
"A Poem for My Old Age." Nimrod (21:2/22:1) 77, p. 156.
"Speech: I." Xa (4) 77, p. 18.

"There Are No Absolutes." Xa (4) 77, p. 16.
"Why Tu Fu Does Not Speak of the Nubian." Nimrod (21:2/22:1)
    77, p. 159.

McELROY, David
"Big Dumb." PoNow (14/18) 77, p. 124.
from Making It Simple: "Ode to a Dead Dodge." PoNow (14/18)
    77, p. 125.
from Making It Simple: "Spawning in Northern Minnesota."
    PoNow (14/18) 77, p. 125.
from Making It Simple: "State of Siege." PoNow (14/18) 77, p. 125.
"Young, You Thought of How It Would Be." PoNow (14/18) 77,
    p. 123.

MACEWEN, Gwendolyn
"Roots" (For Margaret Atwood). MalR (41) Ja 77, p. 189.

McFARLAND, Myra
"Umbra." WindO (30) Aut 77.

McFARLAND, Ron
"Going Mad in Winter." PoetL (72:2) Sum 77, p. 60.

McGARTY, Ray
"Davey's Portuguese Grandmother." Madrona (4:13/14) 77,
    p. 26.

McGINNIS, Ronald L.
"An Educational Funeral." NegroHB (40:4) Jl-Ag 77, p. 721.

McGOVERN, Robert
"To Old Soldier Allen on His 77th Birthday." HolCrit (14:3) Je
    77, p. 13.

McGRATH, Kristina
"The Dream, the Tool." Ploughs (3:3/4) 77, p. 97.
"The Family at Their Meal of Snow." Epoch (26:3) Spr 77,
    p. 254.
"Under the Eyelid" (for Karen). MassR (18:2) Sum 77, p. 293.

McGUINN, Rex
"Malone Riechard." CarolQ (29:1) Wint 77, p. 75.

McGUIRE, Daniel
"Unconditional Hesitation." SoDakR (15:2) Sum 77, p. 84.

McGUIRE, Michael
"Lent." PortR (23) 77, p. 72.
"Room." PortR (23) 77, p. 73.

MACHADO, Antonio
"The Epic of a Day: Rural Meditations" (tr. by Leland H.
    Chambers). DenQ (11:4) Wint 77, p. 157.

"The Miracle" (tr. by Leland H. Chambers). DenQ (11:4) Wint
    77, p. 156.
"To the Great Zero" (two versions) (tr. by Justin Vitiello).
    PoetL (72:2) Sum 77, p. 62.

McHARG, Alistair
"After the Portrait Painter Was Gone. " Poem (29) Mr 77, p. 5.

MACHUGA, Cindy
"Edna is my freer self. " YaleLit (145:4) 77, p. 10.

McHUGH, Heather
"Cool. " SouthernPR (17:1) Spr 77, p. 8.
"Hag. " AmerPoR (6:2) Mr-Ap 77, p. 35.
"Having Read Books. " NewYRB (24:8) 12 My 77, p. 13.
"High Jinx" (for the rat who survives me). AmerPoR (6:2) Mr-
    Ap 77, p. 35.
"How We Live. " Bound (5:3) Spr 77, p. 776.
"Latitude. " Madem (83:12) D 77, p. 86.
"Left Hemisphere. " AmerPoR (6:2) Mr-Ap 77, p. 35.
"A Living. " SouthernPR (16:SI) 77, p. 48.
"Mirrors Are Water Specified. " AmerPoR (6:2) Mr-Ap 77,
    p. 35.
"Moment. " Bound (5:3) Spr 77, p. 778.
"A Moral Season. " Bound (5:3) Spr 77, p. 777.
"On Time. " NewYorker (53:35) 17 O 77, p. 179.
"Promise. " Bound (5:3) Spr 77, p. 780.
"Sense. " Bound (5:3) Spr 77, p. 779.
"Tendencies. " SouthernPR (16:SI) 77, p. 47.
"Voyeur. " Bound (5:3) Spr 77, p. 782.

McINDOO, Timothy
"Western" (tr. of Alfred Behrens). WebR (3:4) Aut 77, p. 48.

McINTOSH, Joan
"The Fence Stringer. " SmPd (14:1) Wint 77, p. 6.

McINTYRE, Alice T.
"That Nag. " Agni (7) 77, p. 114.

McKAY, Matthew
"Anima. " DeKalb (10:3) Spr 77, p. 33.
"Island. " CutB (9) Aut-Wint 77, p. 85.

McKEE, Louis
"After the Beating. " Poem (31) N 77, p. 26.
"The Hero's Duty. " Poem (31) N 77, p. 25.
"Reading My Work. " Icarus (5:1) Spr 77, p. 23.
"Writer's Bloc. " Icarus (5:1) Spr 77, p. 23.

MACKENDRICK, John
"The Last Empress of China. " Stand (18:3) 77, p. 57.

MacKENZIE, Ginny
"At the Movies." MissR (6:1) 77, p. 137.
"An Invitation." MissR (6:1) 77, p. 137.

McKEOWN, Tom
"Advice from the Glacier." Kayak (44) F 77, p. 14.
"The Black Roads." Bleb (12) 77, p. 14.
"The Florida Sea." Bleb (12) 77, p. 12.
"In Squaw Winter." Bleb (12) 77, p. 11.
"The Lady on Black Oak Road." PoNow (14/18) 77, p. 124.
"Other Lives." Comm (104:18) 2 S 77, p. 555.
"Pictures from Winter." Kayak (44) F 77, p. 14.
"Whatever the Hour." Bleb (12) 77, p. 13.
"The White Dogs." Bleb (12) 77, p. 10.

McKERNAN, John
"The Gift." Wind (26) 77, p. 8.
"A Hand Mirror Covered with Silk." Shen (29:1) Aut 77, p. 45.
"Poem in the Shape of a Balloon." Shen (29:1) Aut 77, p. 44.
"To My Father." Focus (12:75) My-Je 77, p. 22.

McKERNAN, Llewellyn
"All Hallows Eve." Wind (27) 77, p. 33.
"The Guest is God. Emily." Wind (27) 77, p. 33.

MACKIE, J.
from Passages: (IV and IX). DacTerr (14) Spr-Sum 77, p. 77.

McKINLEY, Hugh
"At the Forge" (tr. of Ondra Lysohorsky). MalR (43) Jl 77, p. 118.
"Shadows" (tr. of Ondra Lysohorsky). MalR (43) Jl 77, p. 119.
"'Who Will Take Me in His Hands?'" (tr. of Ondra Lysohorsky,
    w. Olive McKinley). MalR (43) Jl 77, p. 119.

McKINLEY, Olive
"'Who Will Take Me in His Hands?'" (tr. of Ondra Lysohorsky,
    w. Hugh McKinley). MalR (43) Jl 77, p. 119.

MacKINNON, Brian
"At Sea Again." GRR (8:1/2) 77, p. 28.

McKINSEY, Martin
"Dance Stately and Sentimental" (tr. of Nikos Engonopoulos).
    ParisR (69) Spr 77, p. 127.
"The Final Appearance of Judas Iscariot" (tr. of Nikos
    Engonopoulos). ParisR (69) Spr 77, p. 125.
"Four and Ten Subjects for a Painting" (to Raymond Roussel) (tr.
    of Nikos Engonopoulos). ParisR (69) Spr 77, p. 124.
"Mercurios Bouas" (tr. of Nikos Engonopoulos). ParisR (69) Spr
    77, p. 126.

MACKLIN, Elizabeth
"Three Views of a Woman Inhaling." NewYorker (53:27) 22 Ag
    77, p. 36.

McLACHLAN, Ian
"Prison Poems" (fourteen poems) (tr. of Ho Chih Minh). MalR
   (43) Jl 77, p. 123.

McLAUGHLIN, Emma S.
"Decision. " PoetL (72:1) Spr 77, p. 23.

McLAUGHLIN, Joseph
"Discovering a Snowfall at 5 A. M. " StoneC (77:1) F 77, p. 26.

McLAUGHLIN, William
"In the Kansas Landscape. " PoNow (14/18) 77, p. 126.

MacLEAN, Crystal
"John Isley, 85. " Focus (12:74) F-Mr 77, p. 29.

McLELLAND, Chris
"A Woman After Rain. " AAR (27) 77, p. 4.

MacLENNAN, Ian
"The Hind of Artemis. " KanQ (9:3) Sum 77, p. 74.

McMAHON, Michael
"The Circus, Bradford, New Hampshire. " SmPd (14:3) Aut 77,
   p. 8.
"The Etruscan Tooth. " YellowBR (8) 77, p. 25.
"From the Corner of My Eye. " StoneC (77:3) S 77, p. 30.
"Going Out to Work on a Sunday Morning. " RemR (5) 77,
   p. 10.
"Little Empty Spaces. " RemR (5) 77, p. 10.
"A Low Place. " RemR (5) 77, p. 9.
"My Bones. " RemR (5) 77, p. 12.
"One or Two Men See a Crow or Something. " EnPas (5) 77,
   p. 38.
"A Sense of Place. " RemR (5) 77, p. 11.
"The Wish. " Wind (25) 77, p. 39.
"Working on Ragged Mountain. " EnPas (5) 77, p. 39.

McMANUS, J. L.
"Jazz Portrait of My Imagination. " KanQ (9:1) Wint 77, p. 74.

McMILLAN, Sam
"If. " NewC (7:2) 75-76, p. 5.
"Without Maps, Without Compass. " NewC (7:2) 75-76, p. 27.

MacMULLEN, Alice
"Chanson of a Lady in Shadow" (tr. of Paul Celan). PortR (23)
   77, p. 91.
"Memory of France" (tr. of Paul Celan). PortR (23) 77, p. 90.
"On the High Seas" (tr. of Paul Celan). PortR (23) 77, p. 90.

McMULLEN, Mark T.
"Whatever Happened to the President. " Pig (3) 77, p. 52.

McMULLEN, Richard E.
"The Deep Woods." CalQ (11/12) Wint-Spr 77, p. 49.
"Three Leaves." Comm (104:13) 24 Je 77, p. 397.
"Trying to Sleep." Comm (104:6) 18 Mr 77, p. 168.

McNAIR, Wesley
"The Little Louey Comic." PoNow (14/18) 77, p. 126.

McNALLY, Marilyn
"Hans." Wind (26) 77, p. 65.

McNAMARA, Bob
"Breaking New Ground" (for Bill Tremblay). PortR (23) 77,
    p. 54.
"To Danny." Wind (24) 77, p. 48.

McNAMARA, Eugene
"Strange Comfort Afforded by the Profession." TexQ (20:4) Wint
    77, p. 170.
"Strange Comfort Number Two." TexQ (20:4) Wint 77, p. 171.

McNATT, Robert
"with the doubt of young virgins." YaleLit (146:4/5) 77, p. 20.

McNAUGHTON, William
"Goodbye" (tr. of Wang Wei, w. Lenore Mayhew). DenQ (12:2)
    Sum 77, p. 326.
"I Remember Them" (tr. of Li Yu, w. Lenore Mayhew). DenQ
    (12:2) Sum 77, p. 328.
"A Letter" (tr. of Li Po, w. Lenore Mayhew). DenQ (12:2) Sum
    77, p. 327.
from Lives of the Taoists: "Uncle Shan-fu" (tr. of Ko Hung).
    DenQ (12:2) Sum 77, p. 67.
from Lives of the Taoists: "Wang Yao" (tr. of Ko Hung). DenQ
    (12:2) Sum 77, p. 64.
"The Old Dust" (tr. of Li Po, w. Lenore Mayhew). DenQ (12:2)
    Sum 77, p. 327.
"Poem: Autumn" (tr. of Li Yu, w. Lenore Mayhew). DenQ
    (12:2) Sum 77, p. 326.

McNEILL, Anthony
"Hello Ungod." Nimrod (21:2/22:1) 77, p. 160.
"write through the night." Nimrod (21:2/22:1) 77, p. 161.
"un God." Nimrod (21:2/22:1) 77, p. 162.

McNEILL, Patricia
"Old Age." SeC (5:2) 78, p. 53.

MACON, E. L.
"Bell Jar Jive." Vaga (25) 77, p. 13.
"Chrome Fever." Vaga (25) 77, p. 12.
"Covered with Fur." Vaga (25) 77, p. 12.

McPHERSON, James L.
"What It Would. " BelPoJ (28:2) Wint 77-78, p. 6.

McPHERSON, Sandra
"The Blue Sky. " PoetryNW (18:4) Wint 77-78, p. 25.
"Centerfold Reflected in a Jet Window. " Iowa (8:2) Spr 77,
    p. 64.
"His Rhythm. " Aspen (4) Aut 77, p. 37.
"The Mouse. " Field (16) Spr 77, p. 68.
"Senility. " Field (16) Spr 77, p. 67.
"To My Mother. " PoetryNW (18:4) Wint 77-78, p. 24.
"Untitled: Preoccupied as last year's matted nests. " Iowa (8:4)
    Aut 77, p. 62.
"Untitled: Storms side to side. " Iowa (8:4) Aut 77, p. 61.

MADDEN, David
"As the Other Sees Me. " GeoR (31:3) Aut 77, p. 669.
from Cherokee Lyrics: (IV, V, IX-XIII). PoNow (14/18) 77,
    p. 118.

MADDOX, Everette
"Armistice Day. " SouthernPR (17:1) Spr 77, p. 37.
"Rutledge Youngblood Refuses to Lie under the Banyan Tree Any-
    more. " NoAmR (262:1) Spr 77, p. 66.
"2900 Prytania. " SouthernPR (16:SI) 77, p. 49.

MADHUBUTI, Haki R.
"Abortion. " Nimrod (21:2/22:1) 77, p. 148.
"Future. " Nimrod (21:2/22:1) 77, p. 147.
"We Do Not Love Our Own. " Nimrod (21:2/22:1) 77, p. 146.

MADIGAN, Michael
"A Hundred Miles from Athens. " LittleR (12) 77, p. 16.

MADRICK, Robert
"Breaking New Earth. " Rapp (10) 77, p. 48.

MAGEE, Michael
"Choosing Myself. " PoetryNW (18:3) Aut 77, p. 46.
"Last Words. " PoetryNW (18:3) Aut 77, p. 47.

MAGEE, Wes
"The Dead Poets. " SoDakR (15:2) Sum 77, p. 47.
"Visiting a Remote Valley. " SoDakR (15:2) Sum 77, p. 48.

MAGGIO, Mike
"Pig. " QW (2) Wint 77, p. 47.

al-MAGHUT, Muhammad
"The Mailman's Fear" (tr. by Sargon Boulus). Mund (10:1) 77,
    p. 61.
"The Siege" (tr. by Sargon Boulus). Mund (10:1) 77, p. 61.

MAGORIAN, James
"Letter." MontG (5) Wint 77, p. 69.
"The Night Shift at the Poetry Factory." Sam (59) 77, p. 58.
"Old Men Raking Leaves." StoneC (77:3) S 77, p. 5.
"The Tomb of the Unknown Poet." Sam (52) Ap 77, p. 19.

MAGUIRE, Francis
"Sleeping Among the Animals." ChrC (94:15) 27 Ap 77, p. 404.

MAGUIRE, Robert
"Méliès" (tr. of Tadeusz Rózewicz, w. Magnus Krynski). NewRep
    (176:12) 19 Mr 77, p. 34.

MAHAN, Robert
"Maternal Poem." Aspect (69) O-D 76, p. 34.
"Midnight." Aspect (69) O-D 76, p. 34.

MAHAPATRA, Jayanta
"Ash." Poetry (130:1) Ap 77, p. 19.
"Shadows." Poetry (130:1) Ap 77, p. 18.

MAHER, Barry
"Oil for the Slicks." Sam (56) Sum 77, p. 42.

MAHER, James
"St. Thomas." SmPd (14:1) Wint 77, p. 11.

MAHFOUDH, Isam
"Weariness in the Evening of January the Thirty-Second" (tr. by
    Sargon Boulus). Mund (10:1) 77, p. 53.

MAHNKE, John
"To the Savage Child." Ploughs (4:1) 77, p. 153.
"Win a Vigil." Ploughs (4:1) 77, p. 154.

MAILMAN, Leo
"The First Time." PoNow (14/18) 77, p. 118.

MAINO, Jeannette
"It Was Finally the Dirt." SouthwR (62:4) Aut 77, p. 395.
"Mavericks of Spring." Poem (29) Mr 77, p. 51.
"The Tolling Bell." PoetL (72:1) Spr 77, p. 26.
"Verily, Verily." Poem (29) Mr 77, p. 52.

MAISHA
"The Junkie/When Death Became the Reality and Life Became the
    Dream." Obs (3:1) Spr 77, p. 60.
"Pasteles." Obs (3:1) Spr 77, p. 59.

MAKKAI, Adam
"Twentieth-Century Fresco" (tr. of Sándor Weöres). ModernPS
    (8:2) Aut 77, p. 116.

MAKUCK, Peter
"Above Challes-les-Eaux." Hudson (30:3) Aut 77, p. 351.
"Photo Exhibit in Pittsburgh." KanQ (9:4) Aut 77, p. 67.
"Sleds on the Rue de l'Eglise." Hudson (30:3) Aut 77, p. 350.
"Street Lamps." Nat (224:23) 11 Je 77, p. 733.

MALANGA, Gerard
"After Reading Anne Sexton's The Death Notebooks." PoNow
    (14/18) 77, p. 119.
"Benedetta Does Not Remember." SunM (4) Aut 77, p. 77.
"An Hour and a Day." SunM (4) Aut 77, p. 73.
"in memory of willard maas." PoNow (14/18) 77, p. 119.
"Sitting in the Woodberry Poetry Room at Lamont." PoNow
    (14/18) 77, p. 119.
"V-E Day." SunM (4) Aut 77, p. 76.
"World Without Men." SunM (4) Aut 77, p. 74.

MALINOWITZ, Michael
"Lover:" SunM (4) Aut 77, p. 149.
"The Reception of a Sonnet as Autobiography." SunM (4) Aut 77,
    p. 150.

MALLALIEU, H. B.
"Voyage to Naxos" (A sonnet cycle for Ariadne). Poetry (130:6)
    S 77, p. 321.

MALLORY, Lee
"The Rest Home." StoneC (77:1) F 77, p. 30.

MALONEY, John
"Words." Ploughs (3:3/4) 77, p. 159.

MALRAISON, Bobbie
"How to Write a Poem." CarlMis (16:1/2) Aut-Wint 76-77,
    p. 21.

MAMPALAM, Thomas
"The evening comes, passionless." YaleLit (146:4/5) 77, p. 29.
"How the old men squat, insects." YaleLit (146:4/5) 77, p. 29.

MANDEL, Peter
"My One." Harp (255:1531) D 77, p. 16.

MANDELBAUM, Allen
from Ossi di seppia: "Mediterranean" (tr. of Eugenio Montale).
    Pequod (2:2) Wint 77, pp. 1-9.

MANDELSTAM, Osip
"Stalin Ode Sequence: Five Poems from the Second Voronezh
    Notebook" (tr. by John Riley). Stand (18:2) 77, p. 28.

MANFRED, Freya
"The Death in Small Things." Stonecloud (6) 76, p. 69.

"Male Poets. " Stonecloud (6) 76, p. 143.
"A New Way of Walking. " PoNow (14/18) 77, p. 119.
"Unidentified Flying Object. " StoneC (77:2) My 77, p. 8.

MANGAN, Kathy
"Acts of Kindness on Uncle Henry's Farm. " SouthernPR (17:1)
    Aut 77, p. 32.

MAN Jang
"Sailor" (tr. by Graeme Wilson). DenQ (12:2) Sum 77, p. 294.

MANKER, Don
"The Single Leaf. " LadHJ (94:10) O 77, p. 157.
"Translation. " LadHJ (94:9) S 77, p. 139.

MANLEY, Frank
"Retardation Center. " AmerS (46:2) Spr 77, p. 180.

MANLEY, Gail
"Exhortation to Artemis. " KanQ (9:2) Spr 77, p. 73.

MANN, Paul
"Chicago. " Bleb (12) 77, p. 17.
"The Parasites. " Bleb (12) 77, p. 15.

MANSEI, Shami
"This world of ours" (tr. by Kenneth Rexroth). Falcon (14) 77,
    p. 92.

MANSOUR, Joyce
"Julien Gracq or The Illumined Interior" (tr. by Peter Koch &
    Jeri Guthrie). MontG (6) Aut 77, p. 19.
from Rapaces Cris: "I like your stockings that strengthen your
    legs" (tr. by Jeri Guthrie and Peter Koch). MontG (6) Aut
    77, p. 20.

MANZAN
"Beginnings" (tr. by Graeme Wilson). WestHR (31:3) Sum 77,
    p. 212.

MAPLE, John
"The Man with the Flashlight. " ArkRiv (3:4/4:1) 77, p. 6.
"Redemption. " ArkRiv (3:4/4:1) 77, p. 7.

MAR, Laureen
"Chinatown #1. " GreenR (6:1/2) Spr 77, p. 25.
"Chinatown #2" (for my father, Ling Kim). GreenR (6:1/2) Spr
    77, p. 26.
"I'll Take My Place. " GreenR (6:1/2) Spr 77, p. 29.
"Slugs, China, Fire. " Madem (83:5) My 77, p. 34.
"To My Brother, Who Is Working on His Doctorate in Psychology. "
    GreenR (6:1/2) Spr 77, p. 27.

MARABLE, Manning
"Discovering God." SoDakR (15:2) Sum 77, p. 52.
"Original Sin." SoDakR (15:2) Sum 77, p. 50.

MARANO, Russell
"I Am." CimR (41) O 77, p. 55.

MARCAS, Sahar
"At night I hear me walking." AAR (27) 77, p. 109.

MARCOTTI, Diane
"Arcane Processional." Ploughs (4:1) 77, p. 169.

MARCUS, Adrianne
"The Frigid Wife." SouthernPR (17:2) Aut 77, p. 60.
"A New Year's Wish." Nat (224:22) 4 Je 77, p. 696.
"Reading Auden before Sleep." SouthernPR (16:SI) 77, p. 50.
"Red: Weathering the House." Confr (14) Spr-Sum 77, p. 84.
"Reruns: Twenty Years Later." Drag (16) 77.
"Science/Fiction." Drag (16) 77.
"What I Wish You." PoNow (14/18) 77, p. 119.

MARCUS, Marne
"Love in the Laundromat." PoetL (72:2) Sum 77, p. 74.

MARCUS, Mordecai
"Cactus." Sparrow (33) Ja 77, p. 9.
"Conversational Basketball." Sparrow (33) Ja 77, p. 10.
"Matters of Taste." Icarus (5:2) Aut 77, p. 5.
"Suburban Dairy Queen Restaurant." Rapp (10) 77, p. 95.
"Summer Shadows." Agni (7) 77, p. 106.

MARCUS, Morton
"The Armies Encamped in the Fields beyond Unfinished Avenues."
    Kayak (45) My 77, p. 15.

MARGOLIS, Gary
"The Carver." VirQR (53:1) Wint 77, p. 103.
"The Doctor's Quarantine." AntR (35:4) Aut 77, p. 406.
"Notes Toward an Almanac." ColEng (38:6) F 77, p. 591.
"A Portrait or a Box of Matches." PoetryNW (18:3) Aut 77, p. 53.

MARIAH, Paul
"We've all been waiting too long." Bleb (12) 77, p. 25.

MARIANI, Paul L.
"Classic Lines." DenQ (11:4) Wint 77, p. 132.
"Emely." DenQ (11:4) Wint 77, p. 133.
"Golden Oldie." DenQ (11:4) Wint 77, p. 136.

MARIN, Daniel B.
"The Spaewife's Speech" (tr. of Elder Edda). CarolQ (29:1) Wint
    77, p. 115.

MARINO, Gigi
"Mother's Pains." CarouselQ (2:3) Wint 77, p. 9.

MARION, Jeff Daniel
"Riving." SouthernPR (16:SI) 77, p. 51.
"Transparency." SouthernPR (17:1) Spr 77, p. 9.

MARK, Steven
"Lying on his stomach." Mouth (11/12) Mr-Je 77, p. 69.

MARKHAM, Robert
"Blizzard." Aspen (3) Spr 77, p. 78.
"Coyotes." Aspen (3) Spr 77, p. 80.
"Heat Waves." Aspen (3) Spr 77, p. 81.
"In the Night Now." Aspen (3) Spr 77, p. 79.

MARKO, Jim
"hand." Mouth (13) D 77, p. 11.

MARKS, Steven
"A Birth." CarouselQ (2:2) Aut 77, p. 17.

MARLIS, Stephanie
"Laid Down around Everything Is Something Else." Paunch
     (48/49) S 77, p. 192.

MARRAFFINO, Elizabeth
"Apology for Being Virgo." Hand (1) 77, p. 110.
"It should have been wine." Hand (1) 77, p. 109.
"May 12, 1975." Hand (1) 77, p. 110.
"Night after night light after light." Hand (1) 77, p. 111.
"Photo Album." Hand (1) 77, p. 111.

MARSH, Daniel J.
"Moves." PoetL (72:2) Sum 77, p. 59.
"Naming Stars." PoetL (72:1) Spr 77, p. 27.
"Waiting." PoetL (72:1) Spr 77, p. 27.

MARSH, Richard
"Caution: In Case of Eye Contact, Flush with Water. Call a
     Physician. Keep Out of the Reach of Children." YellowBR
     (9) 77, p. 31.

MARSHALL, Jack
"In Place of a Rain Dance." Pequod (2:3) Sum 77, p. 63.
"Sickbed Poems." PoNow (14/18) 77, p. 120.

MARSHALL, Kathy
"one man's song is another man's poetry." SeC (5:2) 78, p. 52.

MARSHALL, Robert
"Reflections in a V.W. Wonder Window." SmPd (14:1) Wint 77,
     p. 5.

MARSHALL, Teresa
"The Cleaning Women's Workday." ArkRiv (3:4/4:1) 77, p. 24.

MARSHALL, Tom
"Barnyard and Garden Sonnet" (for Margaret Atwood). MalR (41)
    Ja 77, p. 145.

MARTIAL
"Epigrams" (tr. by Richard O'Connell). Playb (24:7) Jl 77,
    p. 151.

MARTIN, Brenda "A-life"
"Poetry for the Soul." BlackF (2:1) Wint 77-78, p. 24.

MARTIN, Clarence L., Jr.
"By a Name I Know, She Sings for Me." EngJ (66:5) My 77,
    p. 43.

MARTIN, Herbert Woodward
from The Log of the Vigilante: "Blues Piece." Nimrod
    (21:2/22:1) 77, p. 149.
"Monday." Nimrod (21:2/22:1) 77, p. 150.

MARTIN, Jeanne Iacono
"Untitled on Sunday." CarouselQ (2:3) Wint 77, p. 15.

MARTIN, Richard
"Doctors." Sam (56) Sum 77, p. 39.

MARTIN, Stephen
"Central Park." SoDakR (15:2) Sum 77, p. 19.
"Morning Thaw." SoDakR (15:2) Sum 77, p. 19.

MARTINI, Galen
"Ogden at Night." StoneC (77:2) My 77, p. 7.

MARTINS, Heitor
"Poem" (tr. of Augusto De Campos, w. Mary Ellen Solt and Jon
    M. Tolman). LitR (21:2) Wint 78, p. 276.

MARTONE, Mike
"City of Restaurants--City of Churches." WindO (30) Aut 77,
    p. 3.
"Fort Wayne Is Seventh on Hitler's List." WindO (30) Aut 77,
    p. 5.
"Racing the Sun from Ohio." WindO (30) Aut 77, p. 4.

MARTY, Martin E.
"Auld Mainline Acquaintances." ChrC (94:42) 21 D 77, p. 1207.
"A Garland for Pentefundelicals." ChrC (94:41) 14 D 77, p. 1175.

MARX, Douglas
"Song." ConcPo (10:2) Aut 77, p. 76.

MASARIK, Al
"After Midnight Music." Vaga (25) 77, p. 82.
"Burlesque." Vaga (25) 77, p. 83.
"cormorant." Vaga (26) 77, p. 43.
"Coup." Vaga (25) 77, p. 85.
"in the garden fists." Vaga (26) 77, p. 44.
"lately I've been thinking." Vaga (26) 77, p. 45.
"October Again." Vaga (25) 77, p. 84.
"This Is As Far." Vaga (25) 77, p. 82.

MA-SHIB-A-SHANZ
"I stood still as a rock watching." AmerPoR (6:2) Mr-Ap 77,
    p. 34.

MASON, Madeline
"Rhapsody" (tr. of László Nagy). ModernPS (8:2) Aut 77, p. 111.

MASON, Rosemary
"Amnesia." ChrC (94:15) 27 Ap 77, p. 404.

MASSARO, S. A.
"children." Icarus (5:2) Aut 77, p. 15.

MASSMAN, Gordon
"And." SouthwR (62:2) Spr 77, p. 134.
"Clearing Land." TexQ (20:4) Wint 77, p. 95.
"Halloween Pumpkins." Esq (87:3) Mr 77, p. 24.
"Ice, Wind and Rock." PoNow (14/18) 77, p. 121.
"Remembering." TexQ (20:4) Wint 77, p. 131.

MASSON, Jeff
from the Amarusataka: "Lush clouds in" (tr. , w. W. S.
    Merwin). Nat (224:16) 23 Ap 77, p. 506.
from the Amarusataka: "When hundreds of prayers at last" (tr. ,
    w. W. S. Merwin). Nat (224:16) 23 Ap 77, p. 506.
from the Siddhahemasabdanusasana: "My husband" (tr. , w. W.
    S. Merwin). Nat (224:16) 23 Ap 77, p. 506.

MASTERSON, Dan
"The Lawn." Poetry (130:1) Ap 77, p. 35.
"The Outing." Poetry (130:1) Ap 77, p. 34.
"The Survivors." GeoR (31:1) Spr 77, p. 117.

MATCHETT, William H.
"Fireweed." NewYorker (53:13) 16 My 77, p. 46.

MATHESON, Frank
"Cathedral at Santiago de Compostela." QW (4) Aut 77, p. 99.
"Night Drive from Madrid to Teruel." QW (4) Aut 77, p. 99.

MATHEWS, Gordon
"Arabian Nights read by candlelight." YaleLit (146:4/5) 77,
    p. 15.

"I used to climb mountains." YaleLit (145:5) 77, p. 21.

MATHEWS, Harry
"A Homecoming" (for David Kalstone on his birthday). PartR
    (44:4) 77, p. 561.

MATHEWS, Mark
"Intimate Poem No. 6." YaleLit (145:5) 77, p. 28.

MATHIS, Cleopatra
"Aerial View of Louisiana." QW (4) Aut 77, p. 46.
"Los Americanos-" AmerPoR (6:5) S-O 77, p. 77.
"Grandmother (1895-1928)." AmerPoR (6:5) S-O 77, p. 44.
"Learning to Live with Friends." US1 (10) Wint 77-78, p. 1.
"Maria." AmerPoR (6:5) S-O 77, p. 44.
"On a Twenty-First Birthday." QW (4) Aut 77, p. 45.
"Rearranging My Body." US1 (10) Wint 77-78, p. 1.
"Three Meetings." US1 (9) Spr 77, p. 5.
"The Traveler." Ploughs (4:1) 77, p. 97.

MATSUO-ALLARD, R. Clarence
"Sequence: Manchester." Sparrow (33) Ja 77, p. 21.

MATTE, Robert, Jr.
"Off the Beaten Track." YellowBR (8) 77, p. 28.
"Plugging In." Madrona (4:13/14) 77, p. 22.
"Pursuit." YellowBR (9) 77, p. 36.
"Supermarket." Vaga (25) 77, p. 15.
"Thrust and Parry." Vaga (25) 77, p. 15.
"The Wonder Exterminators." Gra (12) 77, p. 46.

MATTESON, Fredric
"Beanstalk." NewL (44:1) Aut 77, p. 107.
"Groom." NewL (44:1) Aut 77, p. 107.
"Season's End." DenQ (12:1) Spr 77, p. 128.
"A Small Accuracy." DenQ (12:1) Spr 77, p. 130.
"Summer Father (Man in a Hammock)." DenQ (12:1) Spr 77,
    p. 126.

MATTHEWS, Amy
"The Shell Collector." EnPas (5) 77, p. 20.

MATTHEWS, Jack
"The Aging Visiting Poet Reads." Confr (14) Spr-Sum 77,
    p. 125.
"The Bears." PoetryNW (18:3) Aut 77, p. 31.
"The Prophet." SouthwR (62:1) Wint 77, p. 44.

MATTHEWS, William
"The Blue Nap." Chowder (8) Spr-Sum 77, p. 13.
"Flood." CornellR (1) Spr 77, p. 74.
"Her Hands." Aspen (4) Aut 77, p. 15.
"The High Jump." PoNow (14/18) 77, p. 122.

"Snow Leopards at the Denver Zoo." Aspen (4) Aut 77, p. 14.

MATTINGLY, George
"The Best Thing Going." Spirit (2:2/3) 77, p. 112.
"Cruising for Burgers." Spirit (2:2/3) 77, p. 113.
"God's Words to the Last Ape." Spirit (2:2/3) 77, p. 112.
"Goodbye Sonnet." Spirit (2:2/3) 77, p. 115.
from The Lives of the Poets: "After a long evening waiting for
     John Wayne." Spirit (2:2/3) 77, p. 115.
"Patience, No Speed." Spirit (2:2/3) 77, p. 116.
"Tide." Spirit (2:2/3) 77, p. 117.

MATTISON, Alice
"Germchild." Aspect (70) Ja-Mr 77, p. 33.
"The Guidebook." MassR (18:1) Spr 77, p. 79.
"Totalled Cat." Aspect (70) Ja-Mr 77, p. 32.

MAURA, Sister
"After the Abortion." SouthernHR (11:3) Sum 77, p. 270.
"Christmas: The Reason." ChrC (94:42) 21 D 77, p. 1189.
"Notes for an Autobiography." SouthernHR (11:1) Wint 77, p. 36.

MAUREN, Steven
"A Question." Wind (25) 77, p. 35.

MAUTNER, Jorge
"Dionysus in Brazil" (tr. by Romney Meyran). LitR (21:2) Wint
     78, p. 132.

MAXFIELD, John E.
"Dinosaur Morning Song." KanQ (9:3) Sum 77, p. 29.

MAXFIELD, Margaret W.
"Education." KanQ (9:3) Sum 77, p. 60.
"The Pupil." KanQ (9:3) Sum 77, p. 59.

MAXSON, Gloria
"Brute." PoetL (72:2) Sum 77, p. 54.
"Complacent." ChrC (94:40) 7 D 77, p. 1140.
"Green Wilderness." ChrC (94:32) 12 O 77, p. 911.
"The Last Census." ChrC (94:37) 16 N 77, p. 1054.
"Outspoken." ChrC (94:33) 19 O 77, p. 946.
"Quarry." PoetL (72:2) Sum 77, p. 54.

MAXSON, H. A.
"Cicadas" (after Bashō). CimR (39) Ap 77, p. 32.
"The Fishermen Arrive Again." QW (4) Aut 77, p. 24.
"A Letter from the Desert." QW (4) Aut 77, p. 23.
"A New Economy." MissR (6:1) 77, p. 139.
"Pond Cleaning/Opening Day." QW (4) Aut 77, p. 23.
"Riverwalking." QW (2) Wint 77, p. 73.

MAY, Connie
"Crowded Closets." AAR (27) 77, p. 70.

"A Soliloquy of a Seven Year Old." AAR (27) 77, p. 69.

MAY, Todd
"The Word." WestHR (31:4) Aut 77, p. 329.

MAYER, Bernadette
"Antarctica." 13thM (3:2) 77, p. 37.

MAYER, Bill
"Among the Others." MontG (5) Wint 77, p. 29.

MAYES, Frances
"At Chartres." TexQ (20:4) Wint 77, p. 189.
"Lovers at Noon." TexQ (20:4) Wint 77, p. 119.
"Lullaby." TexQ (20:4) Wint 77, p. 156.
"The Memory." Epoch (26:2) Wint 77, p. 138.

MAYFIELD, Carl
"Notation from the Journey." KanQ (9:1) Wint 77, p. 49.

MAYHALL, Jane
"Welcome Break." PoNow (14/18) 77, p. 122.

MAYHEW, Lenore
"Goodbuy" (tr. of Wang Wei, w. William McNaughton). DenQ
     (12:2) Sum 77, p. 326.
"I Remember Them" (tr. of Li Yu, w. William McNaughton).
     DenQ (12:2) Sum 77, p. 328.
"A Letter" (tr. of Li Po, w. William McNaughton). DenQ (12:2)
     Sum 77, p. 327.
"The Old Dust" (tr. of Li Po, w. William McNaughton). DenQ
     (12:2) Sum 77, p. 327.
"Poem: Autumn" (tr. of Li Yu, w. William McNaughton). DenQ
     (12:2) Sum 77, p. 326.

MAYO, E. L.
"The Let Go." NewL (43:4) Sum 77, p. 22.
"The Soul." NewL (43:4) Sum 77, p. 23.
"The Way." NewL (43:4) Sum 77, p. 22.
"Why People Avoid Poetry." NewL (43:4) Sum 77, p. 23.

MAYRÖCKER, Friederike
"odysseus variations" (tr. by Derk Wynand). ChiR (29:3) Wint
     78, p. 132.
"on a sea of air" (tr. by Derk Wynand). ChiR (29:3) Wint 78,
     p. 134.

MAYS, Adele
"The Nest Has No Doors. No Brass Fastenings." EnPas (4) 76,
     p. 28.

MAZUR, Gail
"Baseball" (for John Limon). Ploughs (4:1) 77, p. 83.

MAZZARO, Jerome
 "Accounts. " Humanist (37:1) Ja-F 77, p. 53.
 "Autumn Landscape. " Poetry (131:2) N 77, p. 70.
 "The Dardanelles. " Humanist (37:6) N-D 77, p. 39.
 "Entering Matlacha. " Salm (38/39) Sum-Aut 77, p. 102.
 "The Lesson. " Poetry (131:2) N 77, p. 69.
 "Quadrille. " Poetry (131:2) N 77, p. 72.
 "Ripples. " ModernPS (8:1) Spr 77, p. 48.
 "The Visit. " Poetry (131:2) N 77, p. 71.

MAZZOCCO, Robert
 "Brothers. " NewYRB (24:12) 14 Jl 77, p. 27.
 "Doors. " Antaeus (27) Aut 77, p. 106.
 "Fame. " Antaeus (27) Aut 77, p. 105.
 "Houses. " NewYorker (53:1) 21 F 77, p. 40.

MBEMBE (Milton Smith)
 "Dying with Political Prisoners in the Sixties. " Obs (3:3) Wint 77,
  p. 67.
 "The Measured Rage: A Poetic Statement for the Printer. "
  Nimrod (21:2/22:1) 77, p. 261.
 "Nostalgia of the Mud" (for Etheridge Knight). Obs (3:3) Wint
  77, p. 67.
 "The Old Woman in the Green House on the Corner. " Obs (3:3)
  Wint 77, p. 66.

MEAD, Matthew
 "Abdath" (tr. of David Rokeah, w. Ruth Mead). TriQ (39) Spr
  77, p. 301.
 "You Know" (tr. of David Rokeah, w. Ruth Mead). TriQ (39)
  Spr 77, p. 301.
 "You Let Me Go" (tr. of David Rokeah, w. Ruth Mead). TriQ
  (39) Spr 77, p. 302.

MEAD, Ruth
 "Abdath" (tr. of David Rokeah, w. Matthew Mead). TriQ (39)
  Spr 77, p. 301.
 "You Know" (tr. of David Rokeah, w. Matthew Mead). TriQ (39)
  Spr 77, p. 301.
 "You Let Me Go" (tr. of David Rokeah, w. Matthew Mead).
  TriQ (39) Spr 77, p. 302.

MEADE, Mary Ann
 "The Holocaust. " PoetC (10:1) 77, p. 22.

MECHEM, James
 from Slices: "the breakfast code was broken in two" (w. Ann
  Menebroker). Iowa (8:3) Sum 77, p. 116.
 from Slices: "please send me one telegram" (w. Ann Menebroker).
  Iowa (8:3) Sum 77, p. 116.
 from Slices: "she unbuttoned her white blouse" (w. Ann
  Menebroker). Iowa (8:3) Sum 77, p. 116.

MEDINA, Pablo
"Crossing." US1 (9) Spr 77, p. 2.
"Winter Story." US1 (9) Spr 77, p. 2.

MEE, Suzi
"Brighton Beach Line." Poetry (130:2) My 77, p. 82.

MEEK, Jay
"The Confessor." PoNow (14/18) 77, p. 126.
Eight poems. OP (23) Spr-Sum 77, pp. 29-39.
"The Last Book." YaleR (67:1) Aut 77, p. 66.
"Old Bet." Chowder (8) Spr-Sum 77, p. 18.
"Prelude to Rimsky-Korsakov." PoetryNW (18:1) Spr 77, p. 10.
"Repechages on the Last Morning." YaleR (67:1) Aut 77, p. 65.
"Still Life with Aspirin." PoetryNW (18:1) Spr 77, p. 12.

MEHROTRA, Arvind Krishna
"Halves." DenQ (12:2) Sum 77, p. 365.
"Note Left in a Bottle." DenQ (12:2) Sum 77, p. 365.
"The Principal Characters." DenQ (12:2) Sum 77, p. 364.
"Two Lakes." DenQ (12:2) Sum 77, p. 364.

MEIER, Sandra D.
"Garden Party" (for Sylvia Plath). Wind (26) 77, p. 42.
"Landscapes." Wind (25) 77, p. 48.

MEINERS, R. K.
"Armadillo Turns South." Shen (29:1) Aut 77, p. 110.
"Cat as Light of the World." BelPoJ (27:4) Sum 77, p. 39.
"Eikampf at the Fish House." MichQR (16:4) Aut 77, p. 425.
"Opposition Is True Friendship" (to O. B.). DenQ (12:1) Spr 77,
   p. 270.

MEINKE, Peter
"Charleston." SouthernPR (16:SI) 77, p. 52.
"Cinnabar." SouthernPR (17:1) Spr 77, p. 58.
"Lift a Glass to the Memory." NewC (7:3) 75-76, p. 14.
"Making Love with the One." NewC (8:1) 76-77, p. 12.
"Mendel's Laws." NewOR (5:3) 77, p. 199.
"The Night Train." NewC (8:1) 76-77, p. 18.

MEIRELES, Cecilia
"Bird" (tr. by Alexis Levitin). LitR (21:2) Wint 78, p. 206.
"The Dead Horse" (tr. by Jack Tomlins). LitR (21:2) Wint 78,
   p. 205.
"Song" (tr. by Brenda and Helen Hillman). PortR (23) 77, p. 76.

MEISSNER, William
"Death of the Track Star." PoetryNW (18:1) Spr 77, p. 28.
"Letters from the Madman: 4." PortR (23) 77, p. 113.
"Letters from the Madman: 6." PortR (23) 77, p. 112.
"Letters from the Madman: 9." GRR (8:1/2) 77, p. 67.
"Letters from the Madman: 16." Box (5) Spr 77, p. 29.

"Mutiny of the Animals. " PoNow (14/18) 77, p. 126.

MELANCOM, Yvonne
"Stack of Records; Record Player. " SmPd (14:3) Aut 77, p. 18.

MELHAM, D. H.
   from country: "Baths of a Continent. " Confr (15) Aut 77-Wint
       78, p. 25.
   from Poems for You: "the one time I remember running with
       such joy. " Confr (15) Aut 77-Wint 78, p. 26.

MEMON, Muhammad Umar
   "A Poem: Again the nights" (tr. of Shahryar). DenQ (12:2) Sum
       77, p. 242.
   "Poster" (tr. of Sagi Faroogi). DenQ (12:2) Sum 77, p. 241.
   "Shahryar" (tr. of Ijaz Faroogi). DenQ (12:2) Sum 77, p. 242.

MENDELSON, Chaim
   "G. " SouthernHR (11:1) Wint 77, p. 62.

MENEBROKER, Ann
   "The Girl. " Vaga (26) 77, p. 10.
   "Portrait of a Man Returning to His Life. " Vaga (26) 77, p. 11.
   "Rituals. " PoNow (14/18) 77, p. 127.
   from Slices: "the breakfast code was broken in two" (w. James
       Mechem). Iowa (8:3) Sum 77, p. 116.
   from Slices: "please send me one telegram" (w. James Mechem).
       Iowa (8:3) Sum 77, p. 116.
   from Slices: "she unbuttoned her white blouse" (w. James
       Mechem). Iowa (8:3) Sum 77, p. 116.

MENGER, Paula
   "Picture Postcards" (for C. H.). NewL (43:4) Sum 77, p. 71.

MENKITI
   "The Sons of Revolution. " Nimrod (21:2/22:1) 77, p. 186.
   "You Rat Godwin. " Nimrod (21:2/22:1) 77, p. 185.

MERCADO, Manuel
   "The Angel. " PoetL (72:1) Spr 77, p. 11.

MERCATANTE, John
   "Reflections on a Campaign Speech. " EngJ (66:5) My 77, p. 59.

MEREDITH, Joseph E.
   "The Conductor on the Media Local. " TexQ (20:4) Wint 77,
       p. 140.
   "On the Beach. " TexQ (20:4) Wint 77, p. 139.

MERLE, Susan
   "Reflections in an Early Morning Rain. " AAR (27) 77, p. 83.
   "Wheat Fields. " AAR (27) 77, p. 81.

MERNIT, Susan
   "Before I Sleep, I Dance to the Rose." Hand (1) 77, p. 191.
   "Newsreel." Confr (15) Aut 77-Wint 78, p. 89.
   "Poem: Men come to speak of stars." RemR (5) 77, p. 27.
   "The Scholar's Wife" (for R. R.). Hand (1) 77, p. 25.
   "Teaching the Law of Questions." Hand (1) 77, p. 192.
   "Wood" (for Rose and David). Hand (1) 77, p. 127.
   "Yiddish." Hand (1) 77, p. 41.

MERRIAM, Eve
   "Marriages" (tr. of Jacques Prévert). NewRep (177:2/3) 9-16 Jl
      77, p. 26.
   "My Little Lioness" (tr. of Jacques Prévert). NewRep (177:2/3)
      9-16 Jl 77, p. 26.
   "Prodigal Returns." PoNow (14/18) 77, p. 127.
   "To Laugh in Society" (tr. of Jacques Prévert). NewRep
      (177:2/3) 9-16 Jl 77, p. 26.
   "War" (tr. of Jacques Prévert). NewRep (177:2/3) 9-16 Jl 77,
      p. 26.
   "The Wheelbarrow or Great Inventions" (tr. of Jacques Prévert).
      NewRep (177:2/3) 9-16 Jl 77, p. 26.

MERRILL, James
   "The Help." Shen (28:3) Spr 77, p. 72.
   "Lenses." Nat (225:6) 3 S 77, p. 187.
   "O." Poetry (131:1) O 77, pp. 1-18.
   "Palm Beach with Portuguese Man-of-War." NewYorker (52:48)
      17 Ja 77, p. 34.
   "The School Play." NewYRB (24:19) 24 N 77, p. 18.

MERRIMAN, Patience
   "This Modern House Is My Own Submarine." 13thM (3:2) 77,
      p. 61.

MERWIN, W. S.
   from the Amarusataka: "Lush clouds in" (tr., w. Jeff Masson).
      Nat (224:16) 23 Ap 77, p. 506.
   from the Amarusataka: "When hundreds of prayers at last" (tr.,
      w. Jeff Masson). Nat (224:16) 23 Ap 77, p. 506.
   "The Briefcase." Atl (239:5) My 77, p. 81.
   "By the Mango Trees." Falcon (14) 77, p. 99.
   "The Coin." NewYorker (52:48) 17 Ja 77, p. 38.
   "The Cow." Falcon (14) 77, p. 101.
   "The Fig Tree." OhioR (18:1) Wint 77, p. 75.
   "The Ford." NewYorker (53:6) 28 Mr 77, p. 37.
   "Ghazal" (tr. of Rumi, w. Talat Sait Halman). Nat (224:6) 12 F
      77, p. 190.
   "Green Water Tower." NewYorker (53:42) 5 D 77, p. 44.
   "Happens Every Day." Nat (225:16) 12 N 77, p. 502.
   "Harbor." NewYorker (53:13) 16 My 77, p. 37.
   "Island City." Nat (224:7) 19 F 77, p. 218.
   "Line of Trees." Nat (224:24) 18 Je 77, p. 760.
   "Old Garden." OhioR (18:1) Wint 77, p. 75.

"The Red House." Nat (224:24) 18 Je 77, p. 760.
"The Roof." Kayak (44) F 77, p. 10.
from the Siddhahemasabdanusasana: "My husband" (tr., w. Jeff
    Masson). Nat (224:16) 23 Ap 77, p. 506.
"Story of the Ants and Grasshoppers" (tr. of the Tzeltal, w.
    Santiago Mendez Zapata and Kathy Branstetter). Nat
    (224:14) 29 O 77, p. 445.
"Strawberries." Nat (225:6) 3 S 77, p. 190.
"A Street of Day." NewYorker (52:47) 10 Ja 77, p. 25.
"Tidal Lagoon." Nat (224:24) 18 Je 77, p. 760.
"The Trestle." AntR (35:1) Wint 77, p. 7.
"Visitation." Falcon (14) 77, p. 103.
"Warm Pastures." Nat (225:8) 17 S 77, p. 249.
"The Waving of a Hand." AmerR (26) N 77, p. 213.
"The Windows." Atl (239:1) Ja 77, p. 58.

MESSER, R. E.
"Night Letter." HiramPoR (22) Aut-Wint 77, p. 28.

MESSER, Richard
"Thinking of Brueghel the Elder in Nebraska." NewRivR (2:1)
    77, p. 50.

MESSERLI, Douglas
from Naming: "Eros." LaB (9) N-D 77, p. 35.
from Naming: "Mohawk." LaB (9) N-D 77, p. 35.
from Naming: "The Tides." LaB (9) N-D 77, p. 36.
"The Villainy of Clare Booth Luce." LaB (9) N-D 77, p. 39.
"Why Columbus Left." LaB (9) N-D 77, p. 42.

MESZAROS, Robert
"Spring, Summer, and the Life Cycles of Swans and Middle-Class
    Parents." EnPas (6) 77, p. 26.

METH, David L.
"A fast wind touched a piece of paper." Confr (15) Aut 77-Wint
    78, p. 123.
"An Unending Desert." PoetL (72:1) Spr 77, p. 13.

METRAS, Gary
"Cherokee Winter." Sam (56) Sum 77, p. 36.

METZ, Jerred
"Four Turns." WebR (3:2) Spr 77, p. 53.
"Medicine." WebR (3:2) Spr 77, p. 54.
"The Pond." BallSUF (18:3) Sum 77, p. 39.

METZ, Roberta
"Attic." Glass (2:2/3) Wint-Spr 77, p. 37.
"Daughters." TexQ (20:4) Wint 77, p. 134.
"Friends." Chelsea (36) 77, p. 67.
"Models." Chelsea (36) 77, p. 65.
"Split." Glass (2:2/3) Wint-Spr 77, p. 36.

"Take Candy from Strangers." TexQ (20:4) Wint 77, p. 136.

MEYER, Beatrice
"Two Girls." LadHJ (94:10) O 77, p. 188.
"Yesterday's Sonnet." LadHJ (94:11) N 77, p. 84.

MEYER, Tom
"Another Elegy for Lorca." Mouth (13) D 77, p. 5.
"Platonic Monologue." Mouth (13) D 77, p. 4.

MEYRAN, Romney
"Dionysus in Brazil" (tr. of Jorge Mautner). LitR (21:2) Wint
   78, p. 132.

MEZEY, Robert
"In the Fields of the Dead." Kayak (44) F 77, p. 8.

MEZO, Richard E.
"Job's Daughter." SouthernPR (17:1) Spr 77, p. 7.

MICHAUD, Elizabeth
"Passion by Permit." YaleLit (145:4) 77, p. 18.
"The site of a royal ruin." YaleLit (145:4) 77, p. 18.

MICHEL, John
"Lethargic Apperception I-II" (tr. of G. F. Jonke). ParisR (69)
   Spr 77, p. 129.
"The Town" (tr. of G. F. Jonke). ParisR (69) Spr 77, p. 130.
"The Town of Torsaric Acriby: Construction Site (I-II)" (tr. of
   G. F. Jonke). ParisR (69) Spr 77, p. 130.

MICHELSON, Joan
"Brief Narrative." CutB (9) Aut-Wint 77, p. 106.
"Hunter's Dance." CutB (9) Aut-Wint 77, p. 108.

MICHIE, Robert
"A Dream of Time and No River." Wind (26) 77, p. 43.
"November Potpourri." Wind (26) 77, p. 43.
"Somewhere a Miller Grinding." Poem (30) Jl 77, p. 50.

MICHIZO, Tachihara
"Remembrance" (tr. by Janine Beichman). DenQ (12:2) Sum 77,
   p. 197.
"To the First One" (tr. by Janine Beichman). DenQ (12:2) Sum
   77, p. 196.

MICKELBERRY, William
"After-Hours at the Snake Farm." LitR (21:1) Aut 77, p. 4.

MIDDLETON, Christopher
"Carnal Pleasure (senior) and Carnal Pleasure (junior) are
   rowing" (tr. of Oskar Pastior). ChiR (29:3) Wint 78, p. 95.

"The effect groundlessness has when points of concentration are"
(tr. of Oskar Pastior). ChiR (29:3) Wint 78, p. 94.
"The gourmet is a tormented man" (tr. of Oskar Pastior). ChiR
(29:3) Wint 78, p. 97.

MIECZKOWSKI, Ron
"Too Drunk." RemR (5) 77, p. 99.

MIKHAILUSENKO, Igor
"Peace" (tr. by Miriam Morton). NewWR (45:3) My-Je 77,
p. 23.

MILBURY-STEEN, John
"Liste des fautes frequentes" (found poem). Kayak (44) F 77,
p. 23.

MILES, Josephine
"Figure." PoNow (14/18) 77, p. 127.
"Institution." PoNow (14/18) 77, p. 127.
"Parent." NewYorker (53:12) 9 My 77, p. 126.

MILES, Sandra
"Lust." CarouselQ (2:2) Aut 77, p. 3.

MILES, Sara
"Mesopotamia." AndR (4:1) Spr 77, p. 14.

MILLARD, Bob
"Bury Our Faces." Wind (27) 77, p. 35.
"The Runner" (for Walter Griffin). Wind (27) 77, p. 35.
"Winter Comes and I Am Not Alone." Wind (27) 77, p. 35.

MILLER, A. McA.
"'Eighty Seven, Aftermath.'" Drag (16) 77.
"Epistle on Dr. Anomie: Or, On This Day He Completes His
39th Year: Or, A Message at Last from the Analyst."
DeKalb (10:3) Spr 77, p. 35.
"Monody--Charles Olson." SouthernPR (17:2) Aut 77, p. 16.
"Of Kidney Stones, an Essay." StoneC (77:1) F 77, p. 22.
"Sundown. Chopping Back the Banyan" (spoken for my father, b.
1897). SouthernPR (16:SI) 77, p. 54.
"Thunderclouds with Angles." FourQt (26:3) Spr 77, p. 14.
"Wading in Tequesta's Waters." NewC (7:3) 75-76, p. 11.
"Wringing the Handlebar for Speed" (For W.H., poet & biker,
killed in a car wreck). Juice (4) 77.

MILLER, Adam David
"Maudelle." Nimrod (21:2/22:1) 77, p. 187.

MILLER, Arthur
"How Many Times." SouthernPR (17:1) Spr 77, p. 11.
"Why the Dead Return." PoetryNW (18:4) Wint 77-78, p. 43.

MILLER, Brown
"Flesh Embracing Desolation." Xa (4) 77, p. 21.
"Poem from Prison." Xa (4) 77, p. 20.

MILLER, Carl
"Exekias." KanQ (9:2) Spr 77, p. 68.

MILLER, Carol
"First Person Once Removed." Confr (15) Aut 77-Wint 78, p. 115.

MILLER, Chuck
"The Duke of York (Courage)." Spirit (2:2/3) 77, p. 29.
"For Judy." Spirit (2:2/3) 77, p. 30.
"How in the Morning." Spirit (2:2/3) 77, p. 26.
"I Write for Those Unknown." Spirit (2:2/3) 77, p. 32.
"Requiem: A Surrealist Graveyard." Spirit (2:2/3) 77, p. 33.
"Things Are As They Are." Spirit (2:2/3) 77, p. 31.
"When I Began This Funny Journey." Spirit (2:2/3) 77, p. 27.

MILLER, Dolores
"Renewal." KanQ (9:1) Wint 77, p. 131.

MILLER, Errol
"Backstage Corridor." Aspect (69) O-D 76, p. 23.
"Beyond." WindO (30) Aut 77, p. 8.
"the camp." Stonecloud (6) 76, p. 128.
"The Dahlias." Wind (27) 77, p. 37.
"The Fame of Myth." DeKalb (10:2) Wint 77, p. 46.
"Flying by Night." CarouselQ (2:1) Spr 77, p. 3.
"Fodder." StoneC (77:1) F 77, p. 31.
"If You Must Have Asylum." NewRivR (2:1) 77, p. 33.
"In a Louisiana Jail." NewOR (5:3) 77, p. 271.
"On Empty." CarouselQ (2:1) Spr 77, p. 2.
"Profound Junkie with a Flute." WindO (27) Aut 76.
"ripple." Stonecloud (6) 76, p. 122.
"Saturday." Wind (27) 77, p. 38.
"The Seedy Side." CarouselQ (2:1) Spr 77, p. 1.
"Sonavax." CarouselQ (2:1) Spr 77, p. 4.
"Travertone." CarouselQ (2:1) Spr 77, p. 5.
"What Shall We Gather Now?" Wind (27) 77, p. 37.
"Working on Me." DeKalb (10:2) Wint 77, p. 47.
"You Give Me Divestitude and Vertical Disintegration." EnPas
     (4) 76, p. 8.

MILLER, Frances M.
"Western Union Days." CalQ Wint-Spr 77, p. 145.

MILLER, J. L.
"For a Satirist." CEACritic (39:3) Mr 77, p. 25.
"One Morning." Drag (16) 77.

MILLER, Jane
"Blue Nude." Antaeus (27) Aut 77, p. 95.

"Fragments for My Voyeuristic Biographer." Antaeus (27) Aut
    77, p. 96.
"A Rose for the Audience." MontG (5) Wint 77, p. 71.
"Saudade." Antaeus (27) Aut 77, p. 97.
"September, at Sea." AntR (35:4) Aut 77, p. 403.

MILLER, Jim Wayne
"The Brier Thinking about His Poems." Wind (25) 77, p. 41.
"Brier Weather." Wind (25) 77, p. 42.
"The Brier's Ghost Story." Wind (25) 77, p. 41.
"How America Came to the Mountains." SouthernPR (17:1) Spr
    77, p. 54.
"Jim Worley Fries Trout on South Squalla." SouthernPR (16:SI)
    77, p. 56.

MILLER, John N.
"It Couldn't Happen Here." CarlMis (16:1/2) Aut-Wint 76-77,
    p. 79.
"Snapshots." CarlMis (16:1/2) Aut-Wint 76-77, p. 78.
"The Young Poets." CarlMis (16:1/2) Aut-Wint 76-77, p. 78.

MILLER, Kristin
"The Bir-Ham-Fro." AAR (27) 77, p. 100.

MILLER, Leslie
"Cinderella." BelPoJ (27:3) Spr 77, p. 1.

MILLER, Michael
"Bride of Ashes." CarolQ (29:2) Spr-Sum 77, p. 98.

MILLER, Raeburn
"Paranoia." PoetryNW (18:1) Spr 77, p. 44.

MILLER, Vassar
"Awkward Goodbyes." NewL (43:4) Sum 77, p. 75.
"Bike Ride: For Pat in Passing." NewL (43:4) Sum 77, p. 74.
"Boredom." SouthernPR (17:2) Aut 77, p. 69.
"A Clash with Cliches." NewL (44:1) Aut 77, p. 99.
"Elegy for a Dog." NewL (44:2) Wint 77, p. 51.
"False Alarm." SouthernPR (16:SI) 77, p. 59.
"first love song." Qt (57/58) Wint-Spr 77, p. 47.
"Fugue on the Word 'Stranger.'" PraS (51:4) Wint 77-78, p. 410.
"Obstinate." PoetryNW (18:4) Wint 77-78, p. 23.
"One Minor Death." NewL (44:2) Wint 77, p. 50.
"rain storm." Qt (57/58) Wint-Spr 77, p. 47.
"Relative Amnity." GeoR (31:2) Sum 77, p. 403.
"A Resignation." PoetryNW (18:4) Wint 77-78, p. 23.
"Sleepers." HiramPoR (23) Wint 77, p. 27.
"The Sun Has No History." NewL (44:2) Wint 77, p. 49.
"Tedium." NewL (44:2) Wint 77, p. 51.
"Winter Solstice." Qt (57/58) Wint-Spr 77, p. 48.
"With No Hint of Danger." HiramPoR (22) Aut-Wint 77, p. 29.

MILLIGAN, Estelle
from Quilts: "Whig Rose." BelPoJ (28:2) Wint 77-78, p. 1.

MILLIGAN, Thomas
"This Day." HolCrit (14:2) Ap 77, p. 11.

MILLIKEN, Patrick A.
"Of Peaches and Georgia, 1973." SouthernPR (17:2) Aut 77,
    p. 15.

MILLIS, Christopher
"God Went Crazy." ColEng (39:1) S 77, p. 67.
"Villanelle: Ocean Clay." EngJ (66:5) My 77, p. 51.

MILLS, Ralph J., Jr.
"Across the Cold" (for Arthur Heiserman, 1929-1975). DacTerr
    (14) Spr-Sum 77, p. 76.
"Angel of Death." Poem (30) Jl 77, p. 6.
"The Moon" (for Denise Levertov). DacTerr (14) Spr-Sum 77,
    p. 76.
"A Poem for Louise Glück." QW (3) Spr-Sum 77, p. 81.
"Rise" (for Milton Kessler). Poem (30) Jl 77, p. 12.
"River." Poem (30) Jl 77, p. 10.
"Sun." Poem (30) Jl 77, p. 11.
"Thickets." Poem (30) Jl 77, p. 9.
"Waking." PoNow (14/18) 77, p. 128.
"Where No One Is." Poem (30) Jl 77, p. 8.

MILLS, William
"Equinox." SouthernPR (16:SI) 77, p. 60.

MILOSZ, Czeslaw
"Diary of a Naturalist" (tr. by the author, w. Lillian Vallee).
    Chowder (8) Spr-Sum 77, p. 48.
Fifteen poems (tr. by the author and Lillian Vallee). AmerPoR
    (6:4) Jl-Ag 77, p. 23.

MILTON, Joyce
"The Nursery of Advancing Frost." SouthernPR (17:2) Aut 77,
    p. 65.
"The Overseas Exchange ... Pacific Bell System." BelPoJ
    (27:4) Sum 77, p. 26.

MINARIK, John
"The Champion." SmPd (14:2) Spr 77, p. 13.

MINCZESKI, John
"The Earth Sweetens What It Touches" (for Tony). AAR (27) 77,
    p. 10.

MINER, Virginia Scott
"Question--and One Answer" (For a Young Friend). ArizQ (33:4)
    Wint 77, p. 347.

MINOCK, Daniel
"Driving the Interstate." PoetryNW (18:2) Sum 77, p. 50.
"Remedial Student Reads a Poem about Pheasants." FourQt
    (26:4) Sum 77, p. 22.
"Remedial Student Suffers A Death in the Family." FourQt
    (26:3) Spr 77, p. 11.

MINOR, James
"Vermillion South Dakota." SoDakR (15:2) Sum 77, p. 85.

MINSHALL, Ellen
"Camping." SeC (5:2) 78, p. 25.

MINTY, Judith
"Raven." CarlMis (17:1) Wint 77-78, p. 92.

MINTZER, Yvette
from The Planting Moon: "An Old Woman's Song." Hand (1) 77,
    p. 149.
"This Small Corner." Hand (1) 77, p. 150.

MIRABAI
"O Sparrow" (tr. by Vasant B. Joshi). DenQ (12:2) Sum 77,
    p. 94.

MIRANDA, Gary
"Arrowhead." Atl (239:5) My 77, p. 62.
"Collision." Poetry (130:3) D 77, p. 134.
"Horse Chestnut." Atl (240:3) S 77, p. 48.
"Lines for an Imaginary Son." PoetryNW (18:2) Sum 77, p. 49.
"The Must-Be-Admired Things." Poetry (130:1) Ap 77, p. 14.
"Survivor" (For Conrad Casarjian). Poetry (130:1) Ap 77, p. 15.
"The Thickets of Sleep." Poetry (130:3) D 77, p. 133.
"This Choosing." NewYorker (53:7) 4 Ap 77, p. 83.

MISHKIN, Julie
"For All We Know." PoetryNW (18:1) Spr 77, p. 47.
"Mad River." PoNow (14/18) 77, p. 128.
"Poem: This was a poem for you." Nat (224:1) 1-8 Ja 77,
    p. 22.
"Sick Child." Rapp (10) 77, p. 60.
"Skylight: Living without Windows." Rapp (10) 77, p. 58.
"The Voices You Hear Might Be Your Own." Nat (225:1) 2 Jl 77,
    p. 27.

MISHLER, William
"An Old Woman Night" (tr. of Rolf Jacobsen). DenQ (11:4) Wint
    77, p. 48.
"A Path in the Grass" (tr. of Rolf Jacobsen). DenQ (11:4) Wint
    77, p. 47.
"Right behind Your Foot" (tr. of Rolf Jacobsen). DenQ (11:4)
    Wint 77, p. 48.

MITCHAM, Allison
"inukshuk." GRR (8:1/2) 77, p. 134.
"The Slaughter." GRR (8:1/2) 77, p. 135.

MITCHELL, Homer
"Dance." Wind (24) 77, p. 49.
"River Watch." RemR (5) 77, p. 37.
"Search." Wind (24) 77, p. 49.

MITCHELL, Roger
"Who Needs a Bicycle." MinnR (NS9) Aut 77, p. 38.

MITCHELL, Stephen
"Fragments of an Elegy" (tr. of Dan Pagis). TriQ (39) Spr 77,
    p. 291.
"Samson" (tr. of Amir Gilboa). TriQ (39) Spr 77, p. 267.
from Selected Poems: "A Lesson in Observation" (tr. of Dan
    Pagis). TriQ (39) Spr 77, p. 288.
"Twelve Faces of the Emerald" (tr. of Dan Pagis). TriQ (39)
    Spr 77, p. 289.

MITCHELL, Susan
"Night Tree." NewYorker (52:52) 14 F 77, p. 44.

MITCHELL, Tom
"The View at Cedar Beach 1956." CutB (8) Spr 77, p. 50.

MITSUI, James Masao
"Lines for Fortune Cookies" (after Frank O'Hara). GreenR
    (6:1/2) Spr 77, p. 66.
"Photographer's Shadow in a Picture of Our Dog" (-for my
    sister, Sumiko). GreenR (6:1/2) Spr 77, p. 65.
"Poem for Willow." GreenR (6:1/2) Spr 77, p. 64.
"Samurai" (for Miyamoto Musashi). GreenR (6:1/2) Spr 77,
    p. 64.
"The Spoon Player with the Jug Band at the Pike Place Market"
    (for Garrett Hongo, playwright). GreenR (6:1/2) Spr 77,
    p. 67.
"Surrounded by Autumn." GreenR (6:1/2) Spr 77, p. 69.

MIYORI, Otomo no
"Dear Lady" (tr. by Graeme Wilson). DenQ (12:2) Sum 77, p. 369.

MOE, Mark
"Fall." CarlMis (17:1) Wint 77-78, p. 9.
"First Snow." CarlMis (17:1) Wint 77-78, p. 10.
"Shunned." CarlMis (17:1) Wint 77-78, p. 8.

MOELLER, Jeff
"Girls are Impossible." AAR (27) 77, p. 95.

MOFFEIT, Tony
"Black Cat Bone." Juice (5) 77.

MOFFETT 308

"Hoodoo." Juice (5) 77.
"Lowdown Blues." Juice (4) 77.
"Out on the Long Highway." Juice (4) 77.
"Rhythm." Juice (5) 77.
"Stance." Juice (5) 77.

MOFFETT, Judith
"Balloons" (tr. of Hjalmar Gullberg). NewYorker (53:43) 12 D
77, p. 188.
"Fadeout." Poetry (131:1) O 77, p. 36.
"Family Planning." Shen (28:4) Sum 77, p. 52.
"For Willa Cather." Iowa (8:1) Wint 77, p. 64.
"Moving Parts." Poetry (131:1) O 77, p. 32.
"Passage." Poetry (131:1) O 77, p. 29.
"Relay." Poetry (131:1) O 77, p. 34.
"Twinings Orange Pekoe." Poetry (131:1) O 77, p. 38.

MOFFI, Laurence
"'My Son the Writer Never Writes.'" PortR (23) 77, p. 116.
"Putting an End to the War Stories." PoNow (14/18) 77, p. 128.
"Riding to Work with the Gastarbeiter." PortR (23) 77, p. 115.

MOHLER, Stephen C.
from El Arquero Proscrito: "It's Best to Forget" (tr. of José
Manuel Cuscó Gelpí). GRR (8:1/2) 77, p. 74.
"First Testament of the Hero" (tr. of Germán Pardo García).
GRR (8:1/2) 77, p. 115.

MOLINARI, Chris
"Ode to Elisia Rondeau." EngJ (66:5) My 77, p. 45.

MOLL, Ernest G.
"De Senectute." NowestR (16:3) 77, p. 51.

MONETTE, Paul
"No Witnesses." MassR (18:1) Spr 77, p. 136.
"The Practice of Arrows." MichQR (16:1) Wint 77, p. 23.
"The Wedding Letter." Poetry (129:5) F 77, p. 278.

MONROE, Irene
"Happy Moments." BlackF (2:1) Wint 77-78, p. 26.
"On Todays." BlackF (2:1) Wint 77-78, p. 26.

MONTAG, Tom
from Mapping America: A Narrative of the Expedition, by
Meriwether Lewis, William Clark & Tom Montag: (31-33,
37, 39). MontG (5) Wint 77, p. 14.
from Mapping America: A Narrative of the Expedition: Fourteen
poems. PoNow (14/18) 77, pp. 129-131.

MONTAGUE, John
Eight poems (tr. of Andre Frenaud). MalR (43) Jl 77, p. 77.

MONTALE, Eugenio
"The Ark" (tr. by Jeffrey Gantz).   PraS (51:3) Aut 77, p. 257.
from Diario del '71 e del '72:   Eight poems (tr. by Jonathan
    Galassi).   Pequod (2:2) 77, pp. 20-27.
"The Ghost" (tr. by G. Singh).   NewYRB (24:10) 9 Je 77, p. 36.
"Harmony" (tr. by Jonathan Galassi).   Pequod (2:2) Wint 77,
    p. 31.
"If they have likened you" (tr. by Jeffrey Gantz).   PraS (51:3)
    Aut 77, p. 258.
"In Sleep" (tr. by Jeffrey Gantz).   PraS (51:3) Aut 77, p. 259.
"A Letter" (tr. by G. Singh).   NewYRB (24:10) 9 Je 77, p. 36.
"Lights and Colours" (tr. by G. Singh).   NewYRB (24:10) 9 Je
    77, p. 36.
"Memory" (tr. by Jonathan Galassi).   Pequod (2:2) Wint 77, p. 30.
from Le Occasioni: "Motets" (tr. by Charles Wright).   Pequod
    (2:2) Wint 77, pp. 10-19.
from Ossi di seppia: "Mediterranean" (tr. by Allen Mandelbaum).
    Pequod (2:2) Wint 77, pp. 1-9.
"Talking Birds" (tr. by Jonathan Galassi).   Pequod (2:2) Wint 77,
    p. 29.
"To Pia Rajna" (tr. by Jonathan Galassi).   Pequod (2:2) Wint 77,
    p. 28.

MONTO, Steve
"Before I was born. "   AAR (27) 77, p. 101.
"A gorilla is as noisy as a piece of dust. "   AAR (27) 77, p. 101.
"Tasmanian dodos are found in the Bula" (w. Mark Weymouth).
    AAR (27) 77, p. 101.

MOORE, Gregory S.
"The Tired Logician. "   Esq (88:2) Ag 77, p. 24.
"Under the Hart Bridge. "   Esq (87:3) Mr 77, p. 14.

MOORE, James
"Autumn. "   MoonsLT (2:3) 77, p. 27.
"Beyond the Border. "   MoonsLT (2:3) 77, p. 29.
"The Scarves against Our Flesh. "   MoonsLT (2:3) 77, p. 28.

MOORE, Janice Townley
"'To Love That Well. '"   SouthernHR (11:1) Wint 77, p. 62.

MOORE, Joan
"Grace" (for Grace).   ParisR (70) Sum 77, p. 178.
"My Family Seines the Rivers. "   ParisR (70) Sum 77, p. 181.
"Not Colette" (for Maria T. G.).   Antaeus (27) Aut 77, p. 103.
"On Choosing This Poet's Name. "   ParisR (70) Sum 77, p. 179.
"Poem after not Colette. "   AmerPoR (6:6) N-D 77, p. 33.
"Poem Re: Woman's Vanity #2" (for P).   ParisR (70) Sum 77,
    p. 184.
"Spring #2 (The Wild Geese). "   AmerPoR (6:6) N-D 77, p. 34.

MOORE, Todd
"Geo Rogers Clark Orders. "   Vaga (26) 77, p. 13.

"3 W/Guns." YellowBR (9) 77, p. 11.

MOORE, Tom
"Three Births." BelPoJ (27:3) Spr 77, p. 30.

MOORHEAD, Andrea
"Gravenhurst." DeKalb (10:3) Spr 77, p. 36.
"Synapse." DeKalb (10:3) Spr 77, p. 37.

MOOS, Michael
"Conducting the Silence." GRR (8:1/2) 77, p. 71.
"Painting the Rowboat White." Icarus (5:1) Spr 77, p. 17.
"The Scapular." GRR (8:1/2) 77, p. 72.
"We Cannot Reach the Island." Icarus (5:1) Spr 77, p. 17.

MOOSE, Ruth
"The Snake." PraS (51:2) Sum 77, p. 190.

MORDECAI, Pam
"Protest Poem" (for all the brothers). Nimrod (21:2/22:1) 77,
    p. 191.
"Up Tropic." Nimrod (21:2/22:1) 77, p. 188.
"Walker II." Nimrod (21:2/22:1) 77, p. 189.
"You Listened." Nimrod (21:2/22:1) 77, p. 190.

MOREHEAD, Maureen
"the athlete." Wind (25) 77, p. 44.
"the funeral." Wind (25) 77, p. 44.

MORELAND, Jane P.
"After Halloween." PoetL (72:2) Sum 77, p. 65.

MORELL, Susan
"Chicken." US1 (10) Wint 77-78, p. 7.
"The Father Poem." US1 (9) Spr 77, p. 4.
"Listening to Julie." US1 (10) Wint 77-78, p. 7.
"The Mother Poem." US1 (9) Spr 77, p. 4.
"Pretty." US1 (10) Wint 77-78, p. 7.

MORGAN, Edwin
"Crazed Man in Concentration Camp" (tr. of Agnes Gergely).
    AmerPoR (6:3) My-Je 77, p. 25.

MORGAN, Frederick
"After Shen Chou." Harp (254:1520) Ja 77, p. 90.
"After Su Shih." Harp (254:1520) Ja 77, p. 90.
"After Wen Cheng-ming." Harp (254:1520) Ja 77, p. 90.
"As It Was." Atl (239:4) Ap 77, p. 65.
"Centaurs." PoNow (14/18) 77, p. 131.
"Deborah Poem." PoNow (14/18) 77, p. 132.
"The Further Adventures of." Salm (36) Wint 77, p. 39.
"The Ghost." Nat (225:10) 1 O 77, p. 310.
"Hideyoshi." Nat (224:13) 2 Ap 77, p. 407.

"In the Forest" (tr. of Jules Supervielle). Humanist (37:1) Ja-F
    77, p. 56.
"Music. " VirQR (53:1) Wint 77, p. 98.
"1949. " NewYRB (24:8) 12 My 77, p. 13.
"The Priest. " Ploughs (3:3/4) 77, p. 143.
"Suspiria. " Comm (104:25) 9 D 77, p. 777.

MORGAN, John
"Chekhov Variation. " Iowa (8:4) Aut 77, p. 83.
"The End. " NewYorker (53:2) 28 F 77, p. 81.
"In Which a Total Eclipse of the Moon Is Eclipsed by Clouds,
    and a White-Tailed Deer Bounds off into the Woods. " CarolQ
    (29:2) Spr-Sum 77, p. 25.
"Our 'Civilization. '" NewRep (177:6/7) 6-13 Ag 77, p. 35.

MORGAN, Robert
"Agile. " Rapp (10) 77, p. 46.
"Appalachian Trail. " SmF (6) Aut 77, p. 3.
"Baptism of Fire. " Iowa (8:2) Spr 77, p. 37.
"Bartram's Ixia. " Iowa (8:1) Wint 77, p. 44.
"Bean Money. " Iowa (8:3) Sum 77, p. 52.
"Canning Time. " Iowa (8:1) Wint 77, p. 44.
"Canning Time. " SmF (6) Aut 77, p. 9.
"The Flying Snake. " Iowa (8:3) Sum 77, p. 56.
"Grave House. " SmF (6) Aut 77, p. 8.
"Handicap. " Chowder (8) Spr-Sum 77, p. 16.
"The Hollow. " CornellR (1) Spr 77, p. 75.
"Huckleberry Bald. " YaleR (66:3) Spr 77, p. 405.
"Marked. " SouthernPR (17:2) Aut 77, p. 70.
"Mumps. " SouthernPR (17:1) Spr 77, p. 34.
"Muscling Rocks. " Chowder (8) Spr-Sum 77, p. 14.
"Plankroad. " SouthernPR (16:SI) 77, p. 61.
"Smokehouse Dirt. " SmF (6) Aut 77, p. 5.
"Snowlight. " Iowa (8:3) Sum 77, p. 56.
"Soreshin. " Iowa (8:1) Wint 77, p. 41.
"Spit and Image. " SmF (6) Aut 77, p. 4.
"Splashdam. " PoNow (14/18) 77, p. 132.
"Sport. " CornellR (1) Spr 77, p. 76.
"Thermal Belt. " Chowder (8) Spr-Sum 77, p. 15.
"Three. " PoNow (14/18) 77, p. 132.
"Tying Bean Strings. " Iowa (8:2) Spr 77, p. 39.
"Upstairs at the Country Store. " SmF (6) Aut 77, p. 6.
"Urn. " Iowa (8:1) Wint 77, p. 43.
"Wallowing. " Iowa (8:3) Sum 77, p. 55.
"Walnutry. " Iowa (8:3) Sum 77, p. 53.
"Woodsburn. " Iowa (8:1) Wint 77, p. 45.

MORGAN, Susan
"'S-Gravenhage. '" Box (5) Spr 77, p. 16.

MORICE, Dave
Eighteen poems. Spirit (2:2/3) 77, pp. 135-44.
"Feedback. " Hills (4) 77.

"Honking Geese part II." Hills (4) 77.
"Nearing the Ceiling." Hills (4) 77.
"Yeast in Cloud Dust." Hills (4) 77.

MORITZ, Albert Frank
"Catalogue of Bourgeois Objects." Some (7/8) 76.
"From a Line by Charles Simic." CutB (9) Aut-Wint 77, p. 14.
"In the Whites of Eyes" (tr. of Benjamin Peret, w. Jane Barnard
    and Margaret Schaus). Aieee (5/6) 77, p. 19.
"My Last Misfortunes" (To Yves Tanguy) (tr. of Benjamin Peret,
    w. Jane Barnard and Margaret Schaus). Aieee (5/6) 77,
    p. 17.
"Planting the Winter Wheat in the Ice Box." BallSUF (18:1) Wint
    77, p. 56.
"Portrait of Andre Breton" (tr. of Benjamin Peret, w. Jane
    Barnard and Margaret Schaus). Aieee (5/6) 77, p. 18.
"Since the Wind Went Over Us." Chelsea (36) 77, p. 16.
"Under a Beating Rain" (tr. of Benjamin Peret, w. Jane Barnard
    and Margaret Schaus). Aieee (5/6) 77, p. 20.

MORRIS, Gilbert L.
"Broken Stone." TexQ (20:4) Aut 77, p. 153.

MORRIS, Harry
"Our Old Stock." SouthernPR (16:SI) 77, p. 63.

MORRIS, Herbert
"At the Hotel Where the Long Dark Begins." AmerR (26) N 77,
    p. 304.
"In the Movies." Kayak (46) O 77, p. 20.
"The Search for You." Kayak (45) My 77, p. 16.
"Thinking of Darwin." VirQR (53:1) Wint 77, p. 100.
"Vermeer" (for Robin Fredenthal). VirQR (53:1) Wint 77,
    p. 100.
"What the Nights Are For" (for Edmund White). Shen (28:3) Spr
    77, p. 32.
"The White Gloves, O the Panama." Salm (38/39) Sum-Aut 77,
    p. 111.

MORRIS, John N.
"The Christmas Letter." Poetry (129:5) F 77, p. 269.
"Halloween." Poetry (129:5) F 77, p. 266.
"The Hours You Keep." Poetry (129:5) F 77, p. 265.
"In There." NewYorker (53:32) 26 S 77, p. 133.
"Map Problems." Poetry (129:5) F 77, p. 267.

MORRIS, Mary
"Godzilla Versus the Thing." Agni (7) 77, p. 80.
"In the Arms of the Radiologist." Agni (7) 77, p. 82.

MORRIS, Mervyn
"Programme." Nimrod (21:2/22:1) 77, p. 193.
"Storypoem." Nimrod (21:2/22:1) 77, p. 193.

MORRIS, Patricia Ann
"Saturday in the Cellar." StoneC (77:2) My 77, p. 10.

MORRIS, Peter
"Maximum Security Mood." PraS (51:3) Aut 77, p. 305.

MORRIS, Richard
"The Crazed Frog." WormR (65/66) 77, p. 10.
"The Mysterious Watermelon." WormR (65/66) 77, p. 10.
"The Pigeon." WormR (65/66) 77, p. 9.
"The Tail." WormR (65/66) 77, p. 10.

MORRISON, Terry L.
"She Dreamed Once." SmPd (14:3) Aut 77, p. 10.

MORRISON, Vincent
"The Polish Rider." Stand (18:3) 77, p. 29.

MORROW, Mary
"I am a flower all pretty and sweet." AAR (27) 77, p. 119.
"I had a dream that me and my family." AAR (27) 77, p. 106.

MORSE
"Push to shove." Juice (4) 77.

MORT, Jo-Ann
"To Mandelstam on Riverside Drive." Pequod (2:3) Sum 77,
   p. 24.

MORTON, Miriam
"Peace" (tr. of Igor Mikhailusenko). NewWR (45:3) My-Je 77,
   p. 23.

MOSER, John W.
"Marimba Starlets." NewL (44:1) Aut 77, p. 47.
"Wind." NewL (44:2) Wint 77, p. 27.

MOSES, W. R.
"Drought: I." KanQ (9:3) Sum 77, p. 30.
"Drought: II." KanQ (9:3) Sum 77, p. 30.
from Passage: "Another Winter's Tale." PoNow (14/18) 77,
   p. 125.
from Passage: "Berry Picker." PoNow (14/18) 77, p. 125.
from Passage: "Dream." PoNow (14/18) 77, p. 125.

MOSS, Howard
"Catnip and Dogwood." NewYorker (53:15) 30 My 77, p. 36.
"Clammy Campion." NewYorker (53:15) 30 My 77, p. 37.
"Cowslip." NewYorker (53:15) 30 My 77, p. 36.
"Four Birds." NewYorker (53:6) 28 Mr 77, p. 40.
"Gravel." NewYorker (53:26) 15 Ag 77, p. 29.
"Harebell." NewYorker (53:15) 30 My 77, p. 37.
"Horse-Chestnut Tree." NewYorker (53:15) 30 My 77, p. 37.

"Listening to Jazz on a Summer Terrace." NewYorker (53:23)
    25 Jl 77, p. 34.
"Ostrich Fern." NewYorker (53:15) 30 My 77, p. 36.
"Standards." NewYorker (53:31) 19 S 77, p. 35.
"Viper's Bugloss, Wolfberry, Red-Hot Cattail, Spiderwort."
    NewYorker (53:15) 30 My 77, p. 37.

MOSS, Stanley
"Fact Song." Nat (225:6) 3 S 77, p. 184.
"Potato Song." AmerR (26) N 77, p. 44.

MOTT, Michael
"Crossing the Line." Poetry (129:6) Mr 77, p. 316.
Eight poems. Poem (30) Jl 77, pp. 25-40.
"Juniper." Poetry (129:6) Mr 77, p. 314.
"The Sheep II." MissR (6:1) 77, p. 63.

MOUL, Keith
"The Agitated Edge." MissR (6:1) 77, p. 115.
"Crow God." TexQ (20:2) Sum 77, p. 22.
"Keeping Warm." Chelsea (36) 77, p. 11.
"Waking to the Edge." MissR (6:1) 77, p. 114.
"Winter in the Fields." TexQ (20:2) Sum 77, p. 23.

MOUNTJOY, Jesse
"Grandparents." SmPd (14:1) Wint 77, p. 29.

MUELLER, Lisel
"Drawings by Children." OhioR (18:3) Aut 77, p. 18.
"For a Thirteenth Birthday." PoetryNW (18:3) Aut 77, p. 9.
"Not Only the Eskimos." PoetryNW (18:3) Aut 77, p. 11.
"The Possessive Case." NewYorker (53:35) 17 O 77, p. 45.
"Postcards from All Over." Chowder (9) Aut-Wint 77, p. 15.

MUELLER, Melinda
"Proverbs." CutB (8) Spr 77, p. 78.

MUFSON, Steven
"Puddles." YaleLit (146:2) 77, p. 24.

MUIR, Malcolm, III
"Rituals." Wind (26) 77, p. 44.

MULAC, Jim
Ten poems. Spirit (2:2/3) 77, pp. 86-92.

MULLEN, Harryette
"Anatomy." Nimrod (21:2/22:1) 77, p. 198.
"The Big One." Nimrod (21:2/22:1) 77, p. 194.
"Eyes in the Back of Her Head." Nimrod (21:2/22:1) 77, p. 195.
"Floorwax Mother." Nimrod (21:2/22:1) 77, p. 196.
"Heritage." Obs (3:2) Sum 77, p. 49.
"The Joy." Nimrod (21:2/22:1) 77, p. 199.

"Juke Box Man." Nimrod (21:2/22:1) 77, p. 194.
"Jump City." Obs (3:2) Sum 77, p. 49.
"Stirrings." Nimrod (21:2/22:1) 77, p. 231.

MULLER, Erik S.
"My Parent Eyes." SmPd (14:3) Aut 77, p. 7.

MULLIGAN, J. B.
"the mountain like a fist." Wind (26) 77, p. 59.

MUMFORD, Erika
"Persephone." AndR (4:1) Spr 77, p. 44.

MUNDELL, William
"Miranda" (Elegy for a Young Black Cat). PoetL (72:1) Spr 77,
   p. 12.

MUNDIS, Carl
"At dusk I see." Wind (27) 77, p. 31.

MUNGIN, Horace
"The Poet." BlackF (2:1) Wint 77-78.
"To Steve Biko." BlackF (2:1) Wint 77-78, p. 25.

MUNRO, Deborah
"Generation: Dusk Song." StoneC (77:2) My 77, p. 27.

MUNROE, Kathlyn
"Autumn." Wind (24) 77, p. 41.
"Pumpkin." Wind (24) 77, p. 35.
"The Same Spring." Wind (24) 77, p. 46.

MURATORI, Fred
"Confessional Poem." PoetryNW (18:4) Wint 77-78, p. 12.

MURAWSKI, Elisabeth
"Sunflower." LitR (20:4) Sum 77, p. 430.

MURCKO, Terry
"Peeling and Eating a Grapefruit." Pig (3) 77, p. 6.

MURDOCH, Iris
"Agememnon Class 1939" (In Memoriam Frank Thompson 1920-
   1944). BosUJ (25:2) 77, p. 57.
"The Brown Horse" (for Emma Stone). TransR (60) Je 77,
   p. 32.
"Poem and Egg." TransR (60) Je 77, p. 31.
"The Public Garden in Calimera." TransR (60) Je 77, p. 33.

MURPHEY, Joseph Colin
"An Inconstant Nymph." Qt (57/58) Wint-Spr 77, p. 46.

MURPHY, Joseph Francis
"Locust in the Heart." PoetL (72:2) Sum 77, p. 57.

"Thoughts While Approaching the Park." LitR (20:3) Spr 77,
    p. 320.

MURPHY, Richard
    "Care." NewYRB (24:4) 17 Mr 77, p. 20.
    "Guidance Counselor." LaB (8) Jl-Ag 77, p. 40.
    "Hatrack." LaB (8) Jl-Ag 77, p. 38.
    "Mother Fucker." LaB (8) Jl-Ag 77, p. 39.
    "Sharp Curves." LaB (8) Jl-Ag 77, p. 38.

MURPHY, Romaine
    "malediction." Gra (12) 77, p. 56.

MURPHY, Sister Ellen
    "Lines from a Primitive." Comm (104:5) 4 Mr 77, p. 135.
    "Watching the Olympics." Comm (104:16) 5 Ag 77, p. 504.

MURRAY, Carole
    "Black Magic." Vaga (26) 77, p. 46.
    "Desmond." Vaga (26) 77, p. 50.
    "Somewhere in Melbourne a Man Sleeps On." Vaga (26) 77,
        p. 48.

MURRAY, Catherine
    "From That Desk." Glass (2:2/3) Wint-Spr 77, p. 89.

MURRAY, G. E.
    "Chicago Journal: Turning Thirty." PoetryNW (18:3) Aut 77,
        p. 28.
    "Fancy Machines." SouthernPR (17:2) Aut 77, p. 62.
    "New Liniments." Ascent (3:1) 77, p. 12.
    "Oyster Love." Ascent (3:1) 77, p. 11.
    "The Substitute." SmPd (14:1) Wint 77, p. 21.

MURRAY, Joan
    "The Planting." 13thM (3:2) 77, p. 65.

MURRAY, Philip
    "Hebi-Gami: The Serpent Bridegroom." Poetry (130:1) Ap 77,
        p. 12.
    "The Mugging of Charlie Chan: Or, Interruptions in an 18th
        Century German Romance." ParisR (70) Sum 77, p. 171.

MUSGRAVE, Susan
    "Deadfall." MalR (41) Ja 77, p. 149.
    "Then There Was the Week." MalR (41) Ja 77, p. 148.

MUSKE, Carol
    "The Painter's Daughter." AmerPoR (6:3) My-Je 77, p. 45.
    "Parole." PoNow (14/18) 77, p. 133.

MYERS, Gary
    "Loss of a Satyr." PoetryNW (18:2) Sum 77, p. 52.

MYERS, Hobart
"The Mock Orange." SewanR (85:3) Sum 77, p. 458.

MYERS, Jack
"Day of Rest." Iowa (8:2) Spr 77, p. 44.
"The Immigrant." OhioR (18:3) Aut 77, p. 27.
"Night Inside the Hunter." Esq (87:2) F 77, p. 120.
"Payment." SouthernPR (17:1) Spr 77, p. 6.

MYERS, Neil
"Child in an Orchard." Madem (83:5) My 77, p. 195.
"Friday Nights." Esq (87:1) Ja 77, p. 12.

MYLES, Eileen
"An Attitude about Poetry." PartR (44:4) 77, p. 559.

MYOGUN, Yo
"Lespedezas" (tr. by Graeme Wilson). DenQ (12:2) Sum 77,
    p. 370.

MYRSIADES, Kostas
"The Earthen Adolescent" (tr. of Yannis Ritsos, w. Kimon Friar).
    Epoch (27:1) Aut 77, p. 82.
"Hyalography of the Bath" (tr. of Yannis Ritsos, w. Kimon
    Friar). Epoch (27:1) Aut 77, p. 82.
"On the Television Screen" (tr. of Yannis Ritsos, w. Kimon
    Friar). DenQ (12:2) Sum 77, p. 268.
"Opposition" (tr. of Yannis Ritsos, w. Kimon Friar). DenQ
    (12:2) Sum 77, p. 268.
"Surveillance" (tr. of Yannis Ritsos, w. Kimon Friar). AntR
    (35:4) Aut 77, p. 407.
Twelve poems (for Louis Aragon) (tr. of Yannis Ritsos, w.
    Kimon Friar). Falcon (15) 77, p. 4.

NADLER, Alan
"Entering a Fish Store with Dry Skin." KanQ (9:3) Sum 77,
    p. 75.
"Fancy a Hat for All Seasons." KanQ (9:3) Sum 77, p. 75.

NAFFAH, Fouad Gabriel
"Cowardice" (tr. by Samuel Hazo). Mund (10:1) 77, p. 187.
"In the Future" (tr. by Samuel Hazo). Mund (10:1) 77, p. 186.
"Prayer" (tr. by Samuel Hazo). Mund (10:1) 77, p. 187.
"A Sunset" (tr. by Samuel Hazo). Mund (10:1) 77, p. 186.
"The Voyage" (tr. by Samuel Hazo). Mund (10:1) 77, p. 185.

NAGY, Agnes Nemes
"Lazarus" (tr. by Bruce Berlind). NewL (44:2) Wint 77, p. 40.

NAGY, László
"The Break-Up" (tr. by George MacBeth). AmerPoR (6:3) My-
    Je 77, p. 24.
"The Frosts Are Coming" (tr. by Alan Dickson). ModernPS (8:2)
    Aut 77, p. 109.

"Rhapsody" (tr. by Madeline Mason). ModernPS (8:2) Aut 77,
    p. 111.
"Squared by Walls" (tr. by Tony Connor). AmerPoR (6:3) My-Je
    77, p. 24.
"Squared by Walls" (tr. by Tony Connor). ModernPS (8:2) Aut
    77, p. 112.
"Upon the Grindstone" (tr. by Alan Dickson). ModernPS (8:2)
    Aut 77, p. 110.

NAGY, Sharon
    "Once I wore my brother's socks and I had to. " AAR (27) 77,
    p. 126.

NAIDEN, James
    "Elegy for Franklin Brainard. " PoNow (14/18) 77, p. 133.

NAKELL, Mark
    "A Visit. " Chelsea (36) 77, p. 42.

NALLEY, Richard
    "Backriver Dawn. " HarvAd (110:4) Ap 77, p. 30.
    "Cocytus Riposte. " HarvAd (110:3) Mr 77, p. 28.
    "Sleepless. " HarvAd (110:5) My 77, p. 23.
    "Tate Mountain. " HarvAd (110:4) Ap 77, p. 16.

NAMAIS, June
    "Hijacked at Entebbe--July 4, 1976. " ChrC (94:23) 6-13 Jl 77,
    p. 620.

NANEI
    "Descending Moon" (tr. by Graeme Wilson). DenQ (12:2) Sum 77,
    p. 57.

NANGLE, Julian
    "After the Death. " GRR (8:1/2) 77, p. 154.

NANG-WON, Prince
    "The Last of the Serious Drinkers" (tr. by Graeme Wilson).
    DenQ (12:2) Sum 77, p. 307.

NAONE, Dana
    "Two. " Nat (224:17) 30 Ap 77, p. 539.

NASH, Valery
    "Mamma. " SouthernPR (17:2) Aut 77, p. 63.

NASIO, Brenda
    "at the calexico/mexicali border. " Icarus (5:2) Aut 77, p. 4.

NATHAN, Leonard
    "Closure. " PoNow (14/18) 77, p. 134.
    "Creed. " PoNow (14/18) 77, p. 134.
    "The Difference. " Shen (28:3) Spr 77, p. 99.

"Habakkuk." PoNow (14/18) 77, p. 134.
"The Lover." Shen (28:3) Spr 77, p. 99.
"Recognitions." Chowder (9) Aut-Wint 77, p. 10.
"Release" (tr. of Wang Yang-ming, w. Tu Wei-ming). Chowder
    (8) Spr-Sum 77, p. 47.
"To Transcend the Cat." Chowder (8) Spr-Sum 77, p. 40.
"Vigils." PoNow (14/18) 77, p. 133.

NATHAN, Norman
"Having Infinite Roadways." Sparrow (33) Ja 77, p. 6.
"inside." PoetL (72:1) Spr 77, p. 29.
"Playthings." Qt (57/58) Wint-Spr 77, p. 35.
"the second deluge." DeKalb (10:3) Spr 77, p. 38.
"Still Life." PoetL (72:1) Spr 77, p. 19.
"uniting." DeKalb (10:3) Spr 77, p. 39.

NATHAN, Terry
"Arthur Rimbaud." CutB (8) Spr 77, p. 77.

NATHANIEL, Isabel
"Places." SouthernPR (17:2) Aut 77, p. 51.

NATIONS, Ellen
"A Nice Family" (tr. of Gisèle Prassinos). ParisR (69) Spr 77,
    p. 121.

NATIONS, Opal L.
"Plunging into General Standards." MontG (5) Wint 77, p. 18.
"Try Dr. R. C. Leggins' Dragon-off Antispirit & Night Paste"
    (for Dick and Allison). LaB (8) Jl-Ag 77, p. 41.

NAVARRE, Jane
"Daddy on the Road." PoNow (14/18) 77, p. 134.

NAYDAN, Michael
"The Hall of Animals." PoetL (72:2) Sum 77, p. 75.

NAYLOR, Ruth
"Dealing with Guilt." ChrC (94:20) 1 Je 77, p. 534.

NEELD, Judith Phillips
"Black Ash Woods." NewC (8:1) 76-77, p. 23.
"Drought Forces Water Rationing." PoetL (72:2) Sum 77, p. 73.
"The Sacrist." DeKalb (10:3) Spr 77, p. 42.
"Statue in Ocean Park." KanQ (9:4) Aut 77, p. 54.
"Waking to Heat." Wind (25) 77, p. 46.
"Women's Consciousness-Raising." Wind (25) 77, p. 46.

NEFF, Allen
"Canals Full of Rain." GRR (8:3) 77, p. 232.
"The Dentist's Chair." HiramPoR (23) Wint 77, p. 28.
"The Family Stump." GRR (8:3) 77, p. 230.
"Gift." WindO (28) Spr 77, p. 7.

"Guards Closing the Borghese Museum." SouthernPR (17:1) Spr 77, p. 23.
"In a Train Delayed Three Hours During a Snow Storm between Segovia and Madrid on Christmas Eve." DenQ (11:4) Wint 77, p. 115.
"Range Horses in Wickenburg." Epoch (26:2) Wint 77, p. 189.
"Running Among Horses." SmPd (14:1) Wint 77, p. 7.
"Santa Fe Park." KanQ (9:4) Aut 77, p. 86.
"Shoes." WindO (28) Spr 77, p. 7.
"Starting with Roses." WindO (28) Spr 77, p. 8.
"The Station." LitR (21:1) Aut 77, p. 59.
"Theme and Variations on a Glass." WindO (29) Sum 77, p. 31.

NEIDITZ, Elizabeth
"That I Was Not Insane, or Worse." ParisR (71) Aut 77, p. 41.

NELSON, Leroy
"Song." QW (4) Aut 77, p. 121.

NELSON, Natalie
"Family Tree." HiramPoR (23) Wint 77, p. 29.

NELSON, Nathan
"Finders, Keepers." EngJ (66:5) My 77, p. 54.

NELSON, Nils
"A grandfather clock." Rapp (10) 77, p. 32.
"He loses himself." Rapp (10) 77, p. 32.
"Three Poems Written in October." Rapp (10) 77, p. 28.

NELSON, Paul
"Beasts Belong to Themselves" (for my friend). Ploughs (3:3/4) 77, p. 80.
"Binge." Iowa (8:2) Spr 77, p. 66.
"The Language of Starvation." Iowa (8:2) Spr 77, p. 66.
"Two by Two." Iowa (8:2) Spr 77, p. 67.
"Wintering the Animals." Iowa (8:2) Spr 77, p. 68.

NELSON, Ralph
"Marriage Flute." LaB (5) Ja 77, p. 16.

NEMARICH, Patricia
"A Happening in Lancaster County." PoetL (72:2) Sum 77, p. 58.

NEMOIANU, Virgil
"Capital Punishment" (tr. of Nina Cassian, w. Laura Schiff). AmerPoR (6:6) N-D 77, p. 29.
"The Doors" (tr. of Nina Cassian, w. Laura Schiff). AmerPoR (6:6) N-D 77, p. 29.
"Lady of Miracles" (tr. of Nina Cassian, w. Laura Schiff). AmerPoR (6:6) N-D 77, p. 29.
"Thanks" (tr. of Nina Cassian, w. Laura Schiff). AmerPoR (6:6) N-D 77, p. 29.

NEMSER, Paul
"Monumental Landscape" (tr. of Bohdan Antonych). Bound (5:2)
    Wint 77, p. 604.
"Polaria" (tr. of Bohdan Antonych). Bound (5:2) Wint 77, p. 603.
"Ritual Dance" (tr. of Bohdan Antonych). Bound (5:2) Wint 77,
    p. 604.
"To Those Who Have Been Executed" (tr. of Bohdan Antonych).
    Bound (5:2) Wint 77, p. 603.

NEPO, Mark
"Alan's Death." HangL (29) Wint 76-77, p. 22.

NERSESIAN
"(For My Father)." HangL (29) Wint 76-77, p. 74.

NERUDA, Pablo
"Death" (tr. by Stephen Kessler). Chowder (8) Spr-Sum 77,
    p. 44.
"Ode to the Birds of Chile" (tr. by Stephen Kessler). Bleb (12)
    77, p. 28.

NESTI, Faith
"No Escaping." CarouselQ (2:3) Wint 77, p. 10.

NETO, Agostinho
"Fire and Rhythm" (tr. by Victor M. di Suvero). Kayak (46) O
    77, p. 4.
"The Path of the Stars" (tr. of Victor M. di Suvero). Kayak
    (46) O 77, p. 5.
"Western Civilization" (tr. by Victor M. di Suvero). Kayak (46)
    O 77, p. 3.

NEUFELDT, Leonard
"The Chiaroscurist at the Basilica in Padua." SewanR (85:3)
    Sum 77, p. 433.
"Sandstorm." Ascent (3:2) 77, p. 39.
"Teaching John Berryman in Texas." KanQ (9:2) Spr 77, p. 52.

NEUGROSCHEL, Joachim
"Homesickness" (tr. of Else Lasker-Schüler). Hand (1) 77,
    p. 186.

NEVO, Ruth
"Here" (tr. of Yehuda Amichai). TriQ (39) Spr 77, p. 246.
"Samson Rends His Clothes" (tr. of Anadad Eldan). TriQ (39)
    Spr 77, p. 259.
Travels of a Latter-Day Benjamin of Tudela (tr. of Yehuda
    Amichai). WebR (3:3) Sum 77. Entire issue.
"We shall live forever" (tr. of Yehuda Amichai). TriQ (39) Spr
    77, p. 244.
"When I was a child" (tr. of Yehuda Amichai). TriQ (39) Spr
    77, p. 245.
"When the Waves Fell Silent" (tr. of Anadad Eldan). TriQ (39)
    Spr 77, p. 259.

NEWELL, G. Michael
"Magnetic North." DeKalb (10:2) Wint 77, p. 49.
"The Overweight." DeKalb (10:2) Wint 77, p. 48.

NEWLIN, Margaret
"Generation Gap." AndR (3:1) Spr 76, p. 42.

NEWMAN, Felice
"Madrigal." Gra (12) 77, p. 13.

NEWMAN, P. B.
"Changing Anchor." SouthernPR (17:1) Spr 77, p. 56.
"Irish Ballad." NewRivR (2:1) 77, p. 26.
"The Mathematics of Flight." ColEng (38:6) F 77, p. 592.
"Opera." KanQ (9:4) Aut 77, p. 26.
"Squeezing Plutonium." KanQ (9:4) Aut 77, p. 26.
"Walking Rock." SouthernPR (17:1) Spr 77, p. 57.

NEWTH, Rebecca
"Alone with Her." PoNow (14/18) 77, p. 134.
"Fishermen." PoNow (14/18) 77, p. 134.

NGO Chan Luu
"The Uncarved Block" (tr. by Graeme Wilson). WestHR (31:1)
Wint 77, p. 57.

NIATUM, Duane
"Healing Song" (for Audrey). Hand (1) 77, p. 16.
"His Teacher." PoNow (14/18) 77, p. 135.
"Timebird." PoNow (14/18) 77, p. 135.
"White Writings." ConcPo (10:1) Spr 77, p. 23.

NIBBELINK, Cynthia
"Driving Down the Road." GRR (8:1/2) 77, p. 15.
"I Ate Her." GRR (8:1/2) 77, p. 8.
"Like the Ocean." GRR (8:1/2) 77, p. 11.
"The Room That Is Mexico." GRR (8:1/2) 77, p. 12.
"There Was Laughing in the Face of Someone." GRR (8:1/2) 77,
p. 14.
"The Warrior's Mistress." GRR (8:1/2) 77, p. 5.
"Who Knows." GRR (8:1/2) 77, p. 10.

NICHOLAS, Jeff
"Consolations." BerksR (12:1) Spr 77.
"A Favorable Spring." BerksR (12:1) Spr 77.
"Their Breath Hissing." BerksR (12:1) Spr 77.
"Trout Season." BerksR (12:1) Spr 77.

NICHOLS, Bob
"Poems (As If) Written by Ausonius." TransR (58/59) F 77,
p. 94.
"Poems (As If) Written by Robert McNamara." TransR (58/59)
F 77, p. 95.

NICHOLS, Jeanette
"Creative Poverty" (tr. of László Szabedi).   ModernPS (8:2) Aut
    77, p. 99.
"The Deserted Angel" (tr. of Anna Hajnal).   ModernPS (8:2) Aut
    77, p. 103.
"Family Tree" (tr. of Attila Horvath).   ModernPS (8:2) Aut 77,
    p. 100.
"Irrationale" (tr. of László Szabedi).   ModernPS (8:2) Aut 77,
    p. 99.
"The Marriage of Death" (tr. of László Szabedi).   ModernPS
    (8:2) Aut 77, p. 100.
"Seals" (tr. of Anna Hajnal).   ModernPS (8:2) Aut 77, p. 103.
"To the Creator of My Bones" (tr. of Anna Hajnal).   ModernPS
    (8:2) Aut 77, p. 102.

NICK, Dagmar
"Morgen Am Meer."   ChiR (29:3) Wint 78, p. 86.

NICOLETTA, Peter
"Father Finds His Mother."   Vaga (26) 77, p. 13.
"Meeting an Old Friend on the Street."   Vaga (26) 77, p. 14.
"The Old Time Radio Hour."   Vaga (25) 77, p. 88.
"Something to Say."   Vaga (25) 77, p. 86.

NIDER, Barry Leonard
"Ex Camera."   HangL (29) Wint 76-77, p. 75.
"In D. C."   HangL (29) Wint 76-77, p. 75.

NIDITCH, B. Z.
"Buber."   CarouselQ (2:1) Spr 77, p. 12.
"Chagall."   CarouselQ (2:1) Spr 77, p. 11.
"The Festival of Weeks."   Xa (4) 77, p. 9.
"Negev."   Xa (4) 77, p. 8.

NIEDECKER, Lorine
"His Carpets Flowered."   Hand (1) 77, p. 95.

NIFLIS, Michael
"Brown Radios."   SenR (8:2) D 77, p. 92.
"Making August Rain in Cactus Arizona."   LitR (21:1) Aut 77,
    p. 24.

NIMMO, Kurt
"Anarchist's Prayer."   Sam (59) 77, p. 41.
"Dogs."   Sam (59) 77, p. 40.

NIMNICHT, Nona
"Lakeshore Manor."   HangL (30) Sum 77, p. 52.

NIMS, John Frederick
"Cardiological."   Poetry (129:5) F 77, p. 256.

NIST, John
"The Child's Mouth."   TexQ (20:4) Wint 77, p. 141.

"Easter." Poem (31) N 77, p. 8.
"From Ars(e) Poetica." SouthernPR (17:1) Spr 77, p. 35.
"Good Love, Chaste Love." Poem (31) N 77, p. 5.
"Hatching an Egg." Poem (31) N 77, p. 7.
"I Knew a Man." TexQ (20:4) Wint 77, p. 141.
"Poet in Extremis" (In Memory of Dylan Thomas). ArizQ (33:2)
    Sum 77, p. 155.
"Sunday Morning in a Minor Key." Poem (31) N 77, p. 6.
"You, Tongue That Always Will Be Talking." Poem (31) N 77,
    p. 9.

NITZSCHE, Jane Chance
"Bricklayer." LitR (20:4) Sum 77, p. 433.
"Memento." Qt (57/58) Wint-Spr 77, p. 16.
"Prairie." KanQ (9:1) Wint 77, p. 130.
"Rumpus Room." Qt (57/58) Wint-Spr 77, p. 16.

NIXON, Colin
"Cardboard Box." ChrC (94:1) 5-12 Ja 77, p. 13.
"Love Song." ChrC (94:38) 23 N 77, p. 1089.

NOLAN, J.
"Reading Yeats in the Laundromat." YellowBR (9) 77, p. 34.

NOLAN, Pat
"Music." SunM (4) Aut 77, p. 123.

NOLD, Ellen W.
"Quatrains for Crocuses." EngJ (66:5) My 77, p. 53.

NORD, CarolAnn Russell
"Hand-to-Mouth." MontG (6) Aut 77, p. 41.

NORDHAUS, Jean
"The Aunts." CentR (21:2) Spr 77, p. 156.
"Light." SouthernPR (17:2) Aut 77, p. 22.

NORMAN, Howard A.
"The Bee Dice Game" (tr. of Paulé Bartón). ParisR (70) Sum
    77, p. 96.
"The Bowl Seller" (tr. of Paulé Bartón). ParisR (70) Sum 77,
    p. 95.
"The Honey Seller" (tr. of Paulé Bartón). Nat (225:22) 24 D 77,
    p. 700.
"The Sleep Bus" (tr. of Paulé Bartón). ParisR (70) Sum 77,
    p. 97.

NORRIS, Gunilla B.
"A Dream of Self." TransR (58/59) F 77, p. 141.
"The Rock Gardener" (for Barbara O'Neil). SouthernPR (17:2)
    Aut 77, p. 55.
"Rowing through the House." SouthernPR (17:2) Aut 77, p. 54.

NORRIS, Leslie
"Young Devon Shorthorn Bull." Atl (239:3) Mr 77, p. 36.

NORTH, Charles
"All-Time All Star Team Honorable Mention." LaB (9) N-D 77,
    p. 44.
"Little Poem in July." LaB (9) N-D 77, p. 43.
"Non-Verbs." LaB (9) N-D 77, p. 43.

NORTH, Michael
"California 99." SewanR (85:4) Aut 77, p. 607.
"Curtis and the Kwakiutl." SewanR (85:4) Aut 77, p. 606.
"Without Glasses." Iowa (8:3) Sum 77, p. 30.

NORTH, Susan
"Nobody Tells You." Glass (2:2/3) Wint-Spr 77, p. 91.
"Starvation." Glass (2:2/3) Wint-Spr 77, p. 90.
"Stray." HangL (31) Aut 77, p. 59.

NORTHSUN, Nila
"barrel-racer cowboy-chaser." Wind (24) 77, p. 50.
"Be Careful." WormR (65/66) 77, p. 18.
"floriculturist." Wind (24) 77, p. 50.
"Go West." WormR (65/66) 77, p. 18.
"Indian Money." Vaga (25) 77, p. 7.
"once a week." Juice (4) 77.
"Prepared for Journey." WormR (65/66) 77, p. 18.
"rewrite." Juice (4) 77.

NORTON, Rachel
"Echogram." PoetryNW (18:1) Spr 77, p. 46.

NOVAK, Michael
"'Well, Let Him Out!'" ArkRiv (3:4/4:1) 77, p. 43.

NOVAK, R.
"A Found Poem: The Macedonian Succession." WindO (27) Aut
    76.
"like a fish out of water." WindO (29) Sum 77, p. 39.
"19-Syllable Haiku." WindO (27) Aut 76.
"Someone in New Mexico No Longer Writes Me." WindO (29)
    Sum 77, p. 38.
"there are no trivial subjects." WindO (29) Sum 77, p. 38.

NOVOTNY, Christine
"Aphrodisia." Agni (7) 77, p. 83.

NOWAK, Nancy
"Acknowledgement." SenR (8:2) D 77, p. 70.

NOWLAN, Alden
Sixteen poems. Peb (16) Wint 76-77, pp. 59-70.

NUKADA, Princess
"Longing for you" (tr. by Kenneth Rexroth). ParisR (69) Spr 77, p. 120.

NURMI, Earl
"Death Be More." Wind (27) 77, p. 42.

NYHART, Nina
"A Tall Girl." AndR (3:1) Spr 76, p. 46.

OAKLAND, Sam
"Burnt Ships" (tr. of Henrik Ibsen). PortR (23) 77, p. 85.

OATES, Joyce Carol
"Disfigured Woman." MichQR (16:3) Sum 77, p. 262.
"First Death, 1950." GeoR (31:3) Aut 77, p. 598.
"Footprints." Nat (224:15) 16 Ap 77, p. 475.
"Former Movie Queen, Dying of Cancer, Watches an Old Movie of Hers at a Film Festival in San Francisco." SouthernR (13:4) Aut 77, p. 757.
"Hauled from River, Sunday 8 A.M." SouthernR (13:4) Aut 77, p. 756.
"The Lovers." CalQ (11/12) Wint-Spr 77, p. 44.
"Night Driving, New Year's Eve 1976." Hudson (30:4) Wint 77-78, p. 544.
"Pretty Death." OhioR (18:1) Wint 77, p. 12.
"Resurrection of the Dead." SouthernR (13:4) Aut 77, p. 754.
"Skyscape." NewRep (176:6) 5 F 77, p. 27.
"A Survivor's Tale." CalQ (11/12) Wint-Spr 77, p. 45.
"That." Nat (225:1) 2 Jl 77, p. 23.
"What Has Been Your Life?" MichQR (16:3) Sum 77, p. 261.

O'BRIEN, Donna
"Dürer's Owl and Mine." PortR (23) 77, p. 118.

O'BRIEN, John
"Carnival Dream." Madrona (4:13/14) 77, p. 38.

O'BRIEN, Michael
"Arrival in Liberal, Kansas." Wind (25) 77, p. 49.
"Dust Storm." Wind (25) 77, p. 49.
"For an 'Homage to Rimbaud,' after Montale." LaB (7) My 77, p. 35.
"Saturday Afternoon." Wind (25) 77, p. 50.

O'BRIEN, Muriel
"Behind the Hill." CarouselQ (2:2) Aut 77, p. 2.

O'BRIEN, William P.
"Just Before Closing." KanQ (9:1) Wint 77, p. 105.

OCHESTER, Ed
"America Is Running." SouthernPR (17:2) Aut 77, p. 57.

from The End of the Ice Age: "For My Daughter." <u>Rapp</u> (10)
   77, p. 104.
"History." <u>PoNow</u> (14/18) 77, p. 135.
"how it is in Indiana, Pa." <u>MidwQ</u> (18:3) Spr 77, p. 263.
"The Man Who Tried on Emerson's Hat." <u>PoNow</u> (14/18) 77,
   p. 199.
"Some Poets." <u>Drag</u> (16) 77.
"This Poem Is for Roger." <u>KanQ</u> (9:1) Wint 77, p. 54.
"Toward the Splendid City." <u>NoAmR</u> (262:3) Aut 77, p. 73.

OCKERSE, Tom
   "Velocity." <u>AmerPoR</u> (6:4) Jl-Ag 77, p. 21.

O'CONNELL, Richard
   "Epigrams" (tr. of Martial). <u>Playb</u> (24:7) Jl 77, p. 151.
   Twelve "Jarchas" (tr.). <u>LitR</u> (20:3) Spr 77, p. 346.

O'DALY, Bill
   "Catfishing." <u>PortR</u> (23) 77, p. 58.
   "Our Names Returning after Rain" (for Patti). <u>PortR</u> (23) 77,
   p. 59.

ODAM, Joyce
   "Ann in the Red Kimona." <u>13thM</u> (3:2) 77, p. 7.
   "From Unlived Country." <u>SmPd</u> (14:2) Spr 77, p. 17.
   "The Pure Observer." <u>CimR</u> (40) Jl 77, p. 64.
   "Women of Bones Come Off the Mountain." <u>13thM</u> (3:2) 77,
   p. 6.

ODERMAN, Kevin
   "Doubting Iconoclast to Jessup." <u>Sam</u> (52) Ap 77, p. 30.

O'DONNELL, Mark
   "The Yeti." <u>Ploughs</u> (3:3/4) 77, p. 122.

ÓFEIGSDÓTTIR, Ragnhildur
   from Hvsil: Eight poems (tr. by Thomas N. Grove). <u>GRR</u>
   (8:1/2) 77, p. 57.

O'GRADY, Desmond
   "The End of the Conclave" (tr. of Giuseppe Gioacchino Belli).
   <u>MalR</u> (43) Jl 77, p. 99.
   "The Explanation of the Conclave" (tr. of Giuseppe Gioacchino
   Belli). <u>MalR</u> (43) Jl 77, p. 97.
   "The Limp College (of Cardinals)" (tr. of Giuseppe Gioacchino
   Belli). <u>MalR</u> (43) Jl 77, p. 96.
   "The New Election" (tr. of Giuseppe Gioacchino Belli). <u>MalR</u>
   (43) Jl 77, p. 98.
   "The Sacred College of Cardinals" (tr. of Giuseppe Gioacchino
   Belli). <u>MalR</u> (43) Jl 77, p. 95.

O'HARA, Frank
   Eight poems. <u>ParisR</u> (69) Spr 77, p. 176.

"Poem During Poulenc's Gloria. " PartR (44:1) 77, p. 85.
Seventeen poems. AmerPoR (6:3) My-Je 77, p. 3.
"She, Has She Bathed in Sound. " PartR (44:1) 77, p. 86.
Twelve poems. Poetry (130:2) My 77, p. 63.

O'HARA, J. D.
"A Poet's Day. " VirQR (53:1) Wint 77, p. 54.

Ó HEHIR, Diana
"Besieged. " PoetryNW (18:1) Spr 77, p. 23.
"How to Forgive. " SouthernPR (17:1) Spr 77, p. 24.
"In the Basement of My First House. " PoetryNW (18:1) Spr 77,
    p. 22.
"January Class: It Hasn't Rained for Seven Months. " Columbia
    (1) Aut 77, p. 35.
"Living on the Earthquake Fault. " Kayak (45) My 77, p. 34.
"Maude's Bar. " SouthernPR (17:2) Aut 77, p. 4.
"New Tenants. " Kayak (45) My 77, p. 35.
"Northern Countries. " SouthernPR (17:1) Spr 77, p. 25.
"Reprieved. " SouthernPR (17:2) Aut 77, p. 3.
"Returned, in a Dream. " PoetryNW (18:1) Spr 77, p. 22.
"Victim. " PoetryNW (18:1) Spr 77, p. 24.

OJAIDE, Tanure
"Elegy of the Waters. " Hand (1) 77, p. 186.
"I Am Odjelabo" (tr. of an Urhobo udje dance song). Nimrod
    (21:2/22:1) 77, p. 206.
"Indirect Song. " Nimrod (21:2/22:1) 77, p. 205.

O'KEEFE, Richard
"From the Unconscious Family Photo Album. " PoNow (14/18)
    77, p. 135.

OKURA, Yamanoue no
"Children" (tr. by Graeme Wilson). DenQ (11:4) Wint 77, p. 172.
"The Pass at Ashigawa" (tr. by Graeme Wilson). DenQ (11:4)
    Wint 77, p. 165.

OLACK, Frances G.
"Anthracite Men" (for J. J. O.). StoneC (77:2) My 77, p. 15.
"Peg. " Gra (12) 77.
"Sprung Housewife. " Gra (12) 77.

OLDHAM, Edith G.
"Plea for Plants. " Wind (27) 77, p. 43.
"Surrender. " Wind (27) 77, p. 43.

OLDHAM, Perry
"The Angel Heurtebise" (tr. of Jean Cocteau). WebR (3:1) Wint
    77, p. 37.

OLDKNOW, Antony
"Before the Rain. " PoNow (14/18) 77, p. 135.

"By the River." PoNow (14/18) 77, p. 136.
"Crucifixion." MinnR (NS8) Spr 77, p. 38.
"Picasso: Factory in the Desert." SouthernPR (17:1) Spr 77,
    p. 33.
"The Shadowed Earth." PoNow (14/18) 77, p. 135.

OLDS, Sharon
"The Domesticators" (L. O. C. [1909-1976]). SouthernPR (17:2)
    Aut 77, p. 42.
"Feared Drowned." AmerS (46:3) Sum 77, p. 350.
"Late." Kayak (46) O 77, p. 13.
"One Night." Kayak (46) O 77, p. 12.
"Republican Living Room." Kayak (46) O 77, p. 10.
"The Shrink's Wife." Aspect (69) O-D 76, p. 20.
"The Shrink's Wife." CalQ (11/12) Wint-Spr 77, p. 150.
"That Year." Kayak (46) O 77, p. 11.
"Your Presence in My Life" (for Muriel Rukeyser). Waters (5)
    77, p. 21.

OLES, Carole
Eleven poems. Peb (16) Wint 76-77, pp. 23-38.
"Four Parts of a Thousand-Part Poem." Ploughs (3:3/4) 77,
    p. 82.
"The Green Violinist." Ploughs (3:3/4) 77, p. 84.
"A Manifesto for the Faint-Hearted." PoetryNW (18:4) Wint 77-
    78, p. 8.
"Old Text." PoetryNW (18:4) Wint 77-78, p. 5.
"Response to A. J. Daly, Specialist in 'Permanizing,' Post-
    marked Provincetown." PoetryNW (18:4) Wint 77-78, p. 7.
"The Unteaching." PoetryNW (18:4) Wint 77-78, p. 6.

OLIPHANT, Dave
"Eugene Wukasch, Texas Architect." TexQ (20:4) Wint 77,
    p. 187.
from Five Versions of the Twelfth Street Rag: "Count Basie and
    His Orchestra featuring Lester Young (1939)." NewL (44:2)
    Wint 77, p. 56.
from Five Versions of the Twelfth Street Rag: "Fats Waller and
    His Rhythm (1935)." NewL (44:2) Wint 77, p. 56.
"A Little Something for William Whipple." NewL (44:2) Wint 77,
    p. 52.
"A Mexican Scrapbook." NewL (44:2) Wint 77, p. 54.
"Texas Indian Rock Art." NewL (44:2) Wint 77, p. 53.

OLIVER, Mary
"Bats." MichQR (16:4) Aut 77, p. 402.
"The Lamps." AmerS (46:2) Spr 77, p. 192.
"Meat." Comm (104:15) 22 Jl 77, p. 455.
"Mussels." Atl (240:4) O 77, p. 83.
"Small Animal Paths." PoetryNW (18:2) Sum 77, p. 34.
"Two Horses." MichQR (16:4) Aut 77, p. 403.
"Winter Sleep." PoetryNW (18:2) Sum 77, p. 33.
"You Know How It Feels." Comm (104:23) 11 N 77, p. 710.

OLIVER, Raymond
"Around Mon Louis Island." SouthernHR (11:4) Aut 77, p. 384.
"Responsibilities." SouthernHR (11:4) Aut 77, p. 396.
"Travelogue." SouthernR (13:3) Sum 77, p. 572.

OLSON, Toby
"Aesthetics-29." Hand (1) 77, p. 20.
"Aesthetics-32 (from Krafft-Ebing)." Hand (1) 77, p. 21.
"Sitting in Gusevik." Bound (5:2) Wint 77, p. 533.
"Standard-5, I Can't Get Started (The Fan)." Montra (3) Spr 77,
    p. 148.

O'MEALLY, Robert G.
"There Is a Band." Obs (3:3) Sum 77, p. 57.

O'MEARA, Anick
"In Heat." Bleb (12) 77, p. 8.

O'NEAL, Louise
"Vigil." PoetL (72:2) Sum 77, p. 53.

O'NEILL, Laurence
"In Memory of a Love." DeKalb (10:2) Wint 77, p. 51.

O'NEILL, Patrick
"Brother Jed & Ma's Cat." YellowBR (9) 77, p. 27.

OOSTERHUIS, Huub
"Father" (rendered into poetry by Jean Valentine, from tr. by
    Judith Herzberg). AmerPoR (6:2) Mr-Ap 77, p. 21.
"Orpheus" (rendered into poetry by Jean Valentine, from tr. by
    Judith Herzberg). AmerPoR (6:2) Mr-Ap 77, p. 21.

OPALOV, Leonard
"Around the Clock." Wind (27) 77, p. 39.
"Toy Boat." Wind (27) 77, p. 39.

OPENGART, Bea
"The Argument." CutB (9) Aut-Wint 77, p. 17.

OPPEN, George
"Image." Montra (3) Spr 77, p. 6.
"Strange Are the Products." Montra (3) Spr 77, p. 8.

ORBAN, Ottó
"The Face of Creation" (tr. by Jascha Kessler). MassR (18:2)
    Sum 77, p. 282.
"A Summer on the Lake" (tr. by Jascha Kessler). MassR (18:2)
    Sum 77, p. 284.

O'REILLY, Terry
"High Pressure." AmerPoR (6:3) My-Je 77, p. 36.

ORLEN, Steve
"The Biplane." Iowa (8:2) Spr 77, p. 68.
"The Question Was." Field (17) Aut 77, p. 24.
"Six Persimmons." AntR (35:2/3) Spr-Sum 77, p. 263.
"The Solace of Poetry." AntR (35:2/3) Spr-Sum 77, p. 262.
"Two Obsessive Sonnets." MissR (6:1) 77, p. 51.

ORR, David T.
"Early Moon." SmPd (14:3) Aut 77, p. 11.

ORR, Gregory
"Arriving on Foot." Pequod (2:3) Sum 77, p. 6.
"Beggar's Song." Pequod (2:3) Sum 77, p. 5.
"The Explorer." Drag (16) 77.
"For Peter." Field (16) Spr 77, p. 44.
"Four Biblical Songs." Shen (29:1) Aut 77, p. 106.
"Friday Lunchbreak." Pequod (2:3) Sum 77, p. 1.
"Ghosts at Her Grandmother's House." Field (16) Spr 77, p. 46.
"Solitary Confinement." Pequod (2:3) Sum 77, p. 3.
"Spring Floods." Field (16) Spr 77, p. 45.
"Swamp Songs" (for Trisha). Field (16) Spr 77, p. 43.
"Trakl in Hell." Pequod (2:3) Sum 77, p. 2.
"What Descends." Pequod (2:3) Sum 77, p. 4.
"Work Gloves." Field (16) Spr 77, p. 42.

ORR, Thomas
"Making a Buck." SenR (8:2) D 77, p. 60.
"Taking Your Medicine." SenR (8:2) D 77, p. 59.

ORRINGER, Jeff
"A car is like a buffalo." AAR (27) 77, p. 116.

OSBORNE, Raymond
"Riddle." Agni (7) 77, p. 116.

OSERS, Ewald
"Domenico Di Bartolo" (tr. of Walter Helmut Fritz). ChiR
    (29:3) Wint 78, p. 103.
"Michelangelo" (tr. of Walter Helmut Fritz). ChiR (29:3) Wint
    78, p. 101.
"On Reading Leonardo's Philosophical Diaries" (tr. of Walter
    Helmut Fritz). ChiR (29:3) Wint 78, p. 105.

O Sin-hye
"Hilltop Slum" (tr. by Graeme Wilson). VirQR (53:3) Sum 77,
    p. 452.

OSTERLUND, Steven
"The Old Pedestrian" (For Maria Blair). Aspen (4) Aut 77,
    p. 36.

OSTERMAIER, Larkin
"At the Window." SmPd (14:1) Wint 77, p. 20.

OSTRIKER, Alicia
"As in a Gallery It May Happen." US1 (10) Wint 77-78, p. 9.
"Don't Be Afraid." US1 (10) Wint 77-78, p. 8.
from A Dream of Springtime: "Somebody is very thoughtfully
    making love. That's all." AmerPoR (6:4) Jl-Ag 77, p. 22.
"The Exchange." Columbia (1) Aut 77, p. 13.
"The Fool Stands Up to Teach King Lear Again." US1 (9) Spr 77,
    p. 1.
"The Hospital." AmerPoR (6:4) Jl-Ag 77, p. 22.
"The Killing." MinnR (NS8) Spr 77, p. 39.
"Night Music." US1 (9) Spr 77, p. 1.
"One Marries" (For my son: "To fear himself, and love all
    human kind."--Shelley). US1 (10) Wint 77-78, p. 8.
"The Pleiades in December: Line of Sight from a Frozen Lake."
    HangL (31) Aut 77, p. 60.

OSTROFF, Anthony
"Love." NewL (44:1) Aut 77, p. 64.
"War." NewL (44:1) Aut 77, p. 65.

O'SULLIVAN, Lily
"Sleight-of-Hand." LadHJ (94:1) Ja 77, p. 124.
"So Nice to Know You." LadHJ (94:12) D 77, p. 20.
"Summer Quintessence." LadHJ (94:12) D 77, p. P.S. 16.

OTERO, Blas de
"Bietz-Begietan" (tr. by Michele Hester). PortR (23) 77, p. 79.
"Far Away" (tr. by Michele Hester). PortR (23) 77, p. 78.
"Let everyone bring what he knows" (tr. by Geoffrey R. Barrow).
    Stand (18:2) 77, p. 43.
"World" (tr. by Geoffrey R. Barrow). Stand (18:2) 77, p. 42.

OTIS, Clarence, Jr.
"On Present and Future Comfort." BerksR (12:1) Spr 77.

OTIS, Emily
"Names." Bits (6) Jl 77.

OTTO, Lon Jules
"The Old People." MichQR (16:1) Wint 77, p. 73.

OU-YANG Hsui
"Yearning" (tr. by Graeme Wilson). DenQ (12:2) Sum 77,
    p. 394.

OVERTON, Ron
"First Love." Shen (28:2) Wint 77, p. 101.
"The George Mikan Story." ThRiPo (10) 77, p. 33.
"Love on the Alexander Hamilton" (for Katherine, wherever).
    Salm (38/39) Sum-Aut 77, p. 106.
"Race Driver" (For Albert Drake). PoNow (14/18) 77, p. 136.
"A Short History of the Polish Air Force, 1914-1956." Kayak
    (46) O 77, p. 7.

"Testimony on the Axe." HangL (29) Wint 76-77, p. 31.
"Vacation." Glass (2:2/3) Wint-Spr 77, p. 35.
"Why We Came Over." Some (7/8) 76.

OVIATT, Phil
   "After Seeing a Live Circus." YaleLit (145:3) 77, p. 35.
   "I Want to Live." YaleLit (145:3) 77, p. 36.
   "The Lady Downstairs." YaleLit (145:5) 77, p. 9.
   "On Poetry." YaleLit (146:4/5) 77, p. 57.
   "Poem: When we lived in Palatine Illinois." YaleLit (146:4/5)
      77, p. 57.

OWEN, Maureen
   a brass choir approaches the burial ground and The No-Travels
      Journal. BigD (5) 77. Entire issue.

OWEN, Steve
   "A Mei-P'i Lake Song" (tr. of Tu Fu). YaleLit (145:5) 77,
      p. 17.
   "Song for a Falcon, Whose Beak Hangs Open" (tr. of Tu Fu).
      YaleLit (145:5) 77, p. 18.

OWEN, Sue
   "More Pie." CalQ (11/12) Wint-Spr 77, p. 52.
   "Pastoral." Epoch (27:1) Aut 77, p. 75.
   "Those Magic Herbs." Epoch (27:1) Aut 77, p. 76.

OWENS, Rochelle
   from The Book of King Lugalannemundu: "Opening Poem."
      PoNow (14/18) 77, p. 136.
   "Have You Ever." PoNow (14/18) 77, p. 136.
   "I'm Sharp as a Shark." PoNow (14/18) 77, p. 136.
   "Self Interest." PoNow (14/18) 77, p. 136.

OWER, John
   "Fable for Old Ladies." LittleR (12) 77, p. 15.
   "Kahoutek." Wind (26) 77, p. 45.
   "Pet Python." ParisR (70) Sum 77, p. 33.
   "Rapunzel's Latest Lover." TexQ (20:4) Wint 77, p. 162.
   "Sic Transit...." Wind (26) 77, p. 45.
   "To His Pregnant Wife." SouthernHR (11:3) Sum 77, p. 268.
   "Wild Grapes." KanQ (9:1) Wint 77, p. 75.

OZAROW, Kent Jorgensen
   "Belonging." Shen (28:4) Sum 77, p. 75.

PACERNICK, Gary
   "O Mao." StoneC (77:1) F 77, p. 17.

PACK, Robert
   "Guardians." PoNow (14/18) 77, p. 138.
   "The Map." PoNow (14/18) 77, p. 138.
   "Sorrow." GeoR (31:4) Wint 77, p. 829.

PADGETT, Ron
   from Toujours l'amour: "Baby Rollin." PoNow (14/18) 77,
     p. 137.
   from Toujours l'amour: "Gentlemen Prefer Carrots." PoNow
     (14/18) 77, p. 137.
   from Toujours l'amour: "Poetic License." PoNow (14/18) 77,
     p. 137.
   from Toujours l'amour: "Voice." PoNow (14/18) 77, p. 137.

PADHI, Bibhu Prasad
   "Sea Breeze." Poetry (129:5) F 77, p. 270.

PAGANELLI, Marilyn J.
   "All in Compliance." BallSUF (18:3) Sum 77, p. 61.

PAGE, William
   "The Ocean." KanQ (9:1) Wint 77, p. 132.
   "Touching the Past." Falcon (14) 77, p. 39.

PAGIS, Dan
   "Armchairs" (tr. by Robert Friend). TriQ (39) Spr 77, p. 284.
   "Autobiography" (tr. by Robert Friend). TriQ (39) Spr 77,
     p. 285.
   "The Elephant" (tr. by Robert Friend). TriQ (39) Spr 77,
     p. 284.
   "Fragments of an Elegy" (tr. by Stephen Mitchell). TriQ (39)
     Spr 77, p. 291.
   "Fossils" (tr. by Robert Friend). TriQ (39) Spr 77, p. 286.
   "In the Laboratory" (tr. by Robert Friend). TriQ (39) Spr 77,
     p. 287.
   "The Last" (tr. by Robert Friend). TriQ (39) Spr 77, p. 287.
   "The Portrait" (tr. by Robert Friend). TriQ (39) Spr 77,
     p. 286.
   from Selected Poems: "A Lesson in Observation" (tr. by Stephen
     Mitchell). TriQ (39) Spr 77, p. 288.
   "Twelve Faces of the Emerald" (tr. by Stephen Mitchell). TriQ
     (39) Spr 77, p. 289.

PAK Hyo-kwan
   "Crows" (tr. by Graeme Wilson). DenQ (12:2) Sum 77, p. 397.

PAK In-no
   "Iron Rope" (tr. by Graeme Wilson). DenQ (12:2) Sum 77,
     p. 304.

PAKSOY, Belgi
   "Desert Pain" (tr. of Tahsin Sarac). WebR (3:1) Wint 77, p. 36.
   "In Anatolia" (tr. of Tahsin Sarac). WebR (3:1) Wint 77, p. 35.

PALEN, John
   "For My Son in February." GRR (8:1/2) 77, p. 137.
   "Old Woman's Farm House." GRR (8:1/2) 77, p. 136.
   "Thanksgiving." GRR (8:1/2) 77, p. 138.

"Washing Windows. " GRR (8:1/2) 77, p. 136.

PALEY, Nora
"The Function of X. " TransR (60) Je 77, p. 97.
"Kate says. " TransR (58/59) F 77, p. 145.
"My dear garden, it is a privilege for me to. " TransR (58/59)
    F 77, p. 145.

PALEY, Roberta
"February Thaw. " RemR (5) 77, p. 100.
"I Will Send You This Poem. " NewL (44:2) Wint 77, p. 47.
"In the Dream Mama. " NewL (44:2) Wint 77, p. 47.
"Looking for Water in Kansas. " RemR (5) 77, p. 100.
"Rain for Two Days. " NewL (44:2) Wint 77, p. 48.

PALFFY, Jan
"Cautionary Filthy Limerick. " Mouth (13) D 77, p. 71.
"Song for the Outgoing Male. " Mouth (13) D 77, p. 71.

PALLAIS, Marcel
"Ella. " BerksR (12:1) Spr 77.

PALMA, Michael
from All the Conquerors: (3-4). Northeast (3:4) Aut-Wint 77-78,
    p. 16.

PALMER, Leslie
"Birthcry Echo. " Wind (26) 77, p. 46.
"Coleridge, Cactus, Fish and Boy. " Wind (26) 77, p. 46.
"Elegy for Howard Hughes. " NewOR (5:3) 77, p. 273.
"Fingers Forth. " StoneC (77:1) F 77, p. 10.
"This Lost Friend's Birthdate. " CarouselQ (2:3) Wint 77, p. 35.

PALMER, Michael
"For Voice. " ChiR (29:2) Aut 77, p. 38.
"The Meadow. " ChiR (29:2) Aut 77, p. 41.
"Tenth Symmetrical Poem. " ChiR (29:2) Aut 77, p. 40.

PALMER, Opal
"Ethiopia under a Jamaican Mango Tree. " Nimrod (21:2/22:1)
    77, p. 208.

PALMER, Pamela Lynn
"The Circles. " TexQ (20:4) Wint 77, p. 123.

PALMER, Thelma
"Rite of Purification. " EngJ (66:5) My 77, p. 58.
"Saturday Odyssey. " EngJ (66:5) My 77, p. 59.

PANTOS, Spiros
"Homozygote Hominies. " Pig (3) 77, p. 58.
"Muscae Voliantes Muraenoid. " Pig (3) 77, p. 59.

PAO Chao
"The Prince of Huai-Nan" (tr. by Graeme Wilson). DenQ (12:2)
Sum 77, p. 47.

PAPE, Greg
"And There You Are." OP (23) Spr-Sum 77, p. 14.
"Drill" (for John Skoyles). OP (23) Spr-Sum 77, p. 17.
"The Flower Farm." OP (23) Spr-Sum 77, p. 16.
"The Light" (for my brother, Kevin Woodman). Field (17) Aut
77, p. 100.
"A Man in the Street." Field (17) Aut 77, p. 99.
"Notes from a Reunion" (for Lance and Margaret). OP (23) Spr-
Sum 77, p. 18.
"On Obregón." Iowa (8:3) Sum 77, p. 60.
"An Ordinary Bed." OP (23) Spr-Sum 77, p. 20.
"Starlings" (for Keith Althaus). PoNow (14/18) 77, p. 139.

PARADIS, Phil
"The Hole Story Concerning the Ark." SmPd (14:1) Wint 77,
p. 31.

PARHAM, R. R.
"Go West, My Luv, Go West." NewC (8:1) 76-77, p. 15.

PARINI, Jay
"Coal Train." NewYorker (53:16) 6 Je 77, p. 38.
"This Reaping." Atl (239:5) My 77, p. 62.

PARISH, Barbara Shirk
"Making Amends." SmPd (14:2) Spr 77, p. 13.

PARKER, Elizabeth
"September." PoetL (72:2) Sum 77, p. 60.
"The Vacation." PoetL (72:2) Sum 77, p. 60.

PARKER, Jacqueline
"Thin Poem." 13thM (3:2) 77, p. 53.

PARKS, Patricia
"Voices." BallSUF (18:4) Aut 77, p. 28.

PARLATORE, Anselm
"Refraction." Rapp (10) 77, p. 47.
"The Voyage." Drag (16) 77.

PARLETT, Jim
"After the Fact." Waters (5) 77, p. 23.
"The Cemetery." Waters (5) 77, p. 22.
"For Geoffrey Knight, Royal Dragoon Guards, Dublin, Northern
Ireland." EnPas (5) 77, p. 27.
"The Fraternal Order." Waters (5) 77, p. 21.
"The Green Returns." Waters (5) 77, p. 25.
"The Majestic Theater." Waters (5) 77, p. 20.

"Nearing Tijuana Whorehouses." <u>Waters</u> (5) 77, p. 24.
"Seasons." <u>EnPas</u> (5) 77, p. 26.

PARLOW, Lela
"moments." <u>MalR</u> (43) Jl 77, p. 83.

PARRISH, Wendy Louise
"The Fortunate Pianist." <u>Agni</u> (7) 77, p. 56.

PARSHALL, Linda
"'Dô der sumer komen was'" (tr. of Walther von der Vogelweide).
   <u>PortR</u> (23) 77, p. 88.
"'In einem zwîvellîchen wân'" (tr. of Walther von der Vogel-
   weide). <u>PortR</u> (23) 77, p. 89.
"'Mir hât her Gerhart Atze ein pfert'" (tr. of Walther von der
   Vogelweide). <u>PortR</u> (23) 77, p. 87.
"'Wir suln den kochen râten'" (tr. of Walther von der Vogel-
   weide). <u>PortR</u> (23) 77, p. 87.

PASTAN, Linda
"After." <u>Ploughs</u> (3:3/4) 77, p. 68.
"Arithmetic Lesson: Infinity." <u>Poetry</u> (129:4) Ja 77, p. 211.
"Because." <u>ThRiPo</u> (10) 77, p. 32.
"Birthday Card." <u>AndR</u> (3:1) Spr 76, p. 56.
"The City." <u>NewYorker</u> (53:9) 18 Ap 77, p. 135.
"Consolations." <u>AntR</u> (35:2/3) Spr-Sum 77, p. 261.
"Egg." <u>Poetry</u> (129:4) Ja 77, p. 213.
"The Five Stages of Grief." <u>ChiR</u> (28:4) Spr 77, p. 128.
"Funerary Tower: Han Dynasty." <u>AmerS</u> (46:2) Spr 77, p. 213.
"In the Dream." <u>SouthernPR</u> (16:SI) 77, p. 64.
"It Is Still Winter Here." <u>Iowa</u> (8:3) Sum 77, p. 59.
"The Last Food Poem." <u>Field</u> (16) Spr 77, p. 39.
"Letter to a Son at Exam Time." <u>Ploughs</u> (3:3/4) 77, p. 69.
"March." <u>OhioR</u> (18:2) Spr-Sum 77, p. 34.
"Memorial Banquet." <u>SouthernPR</u> (17:2) Aut 77, p. 45.
"The Mirror" (for Marvin Bell). <u>ChiR</u> (28:4) Spr 77, p. 129.
"The Mirror" (for Marvin Bell). <u>ChiR</u> (29:1) Sum 77, p. 128.
"Postcard from Cape Cod." <u>PoNow</u> (14/18) 77, p. 139.
"Setting the Table." <u>Field</u> (16) Spr 77, p. 38.
"A Short History of Judaic Thought in the Twentieth Century."
   <u>NewRep</u> (177:6/7) 6-13 Ag 77, p. 35.
"Terminal." <u>AmerS</u> (46:4) Aut 77, p. 457.

PASTERNAK, Boris
"'To Love, to Go in Endless Thunder'" (tr. by Mark Rudman and
   Bohdan Boychuk). <u>Some</u> (7/8) 76.

PASTIOR, Oskar
"Carnal Pleasure (senior) and Carnal Pleasure (junior) are
   rowing" (tr. by Christopher Middleton). <u>ChiR</u> (29:3) Wint 78,
   p. 95.
"The effect groundlessness has when points of concentration are"
   (tr. by Christopher Middleton). <u>ChiR</u> (29:3) Wint 78, p. 94.

"The gourmet is a tormented man" (tr. by Christopher Middleton). ChiR (29:3) Wint 78, p. 97.

PASTOR, Ricardo
"Diá Domingo." GRR (8:3) 77, p. 200.
"Forever." GRR (8:3) 77, p. 203.
"Nosotros los de ayer." GRR (8:3) 77, p. 196.
"Siempre." GRR (8:3) 77, p. 202.
"Sunday." GRR (8:3) 77, p. 201.
"Us, Those of Yesterday." GRR (8:3) 77, p. 197.

PATRICCA, Nicholas A.
"There are some things a hand can do." Mouth (13) D 77, p. 18.

PATRICK, W. B.
"The Moon Turned to Blood." CarolQ (29:2) Spr-Sum 77, p. 99.

PATTEN, Karl
"Dead of Winter, Northern England." LitR (20:3) Spr 77, p. 296.
"A Dream: Farewell and Hail for D. I." LitR (20:3) Spr 77, p. 295.
"The Saxon Church, Lower Escombe, ca. 675." LitR (20:3) Spr 77, p. 297.
"Wreathmakertraining." NewL (44:1) Aut 77, p. 98.

PATTERSON, Raymond R.
"Man, My Man!" Nimrod (21:2/22:1) 77, p. 210.

PATTERSON, Thomas
"wounded soldier." Confr (15) Aut 77-Wint 78, p. 72.

PATTON, Lee
"The Monologist." EngJ (66:5) My 77, p. 55.

PAUGH, Bart
"Breaking the Bathroom Mirror." KanQ (9:3) Sum 77, p. 120.

PAUL, James
"The Green Bottle, the Road, the Dream." AmerS (46:3) Sum 77, p. 383.

PAUL, Jay S.
"Cancer." StoneC (77:3) S 77, p. 5.
"Caretaker." WindO (30) Aut 77, p. 12.
"Fantasia on Broken Leg (For Two Hands)." WindO (30) Aut 77, p. 13.
"I Am." WindO (30) Aut 77.
"On the Leaf." StoneC (77:1) F 77, p. 4.
"Pale Old Man." WindO (30) Aut 77.
"Radnóti's Wife." StoneC (77:3) S 77, p. 4.
"Whites." WindO (30) Aut 77, p. 14.

PAUL, Martin
"The Angel of Mystery" (tr. of Rafael Alberti, w. Jose A.
    Elgorriaga). PortR (23) 77, p. 81.
"Days. " QW (4) Aut 77, p. 47.
from Entre el Clavel y la Espada: (29) (tr. of Rafael Alberti,
    w. Jose A. Elgorniaga). PortR (23) 77, p. 81.

PAULSEN, Wynn
"I Like to Think of You as. " QW (2) Wint 77, p. 64.

PAULY, Bill
"Carol. " ChrC (94:42) 21 D 77, p. 1187.
Three Haiku. WindO (29) Sum 77, p. 3.

PAVLOV, Konstantin
"Capriccio for Goya" (tr. by Atanas Slavov). PartR (44:4) 77,
    p. 600.
"Flotation" (tr. by Atanas Slavov). PartR (44:4) 77, p. 599.
"Second Capriccio for Goya" (tr. by Atanas Slavov). PartR (44:4)
    77, p. 601.
"Singing Contest" (tr. by Atanas Slavov). PartR (44:4) 77,
    p. 602.

PAYACK, Paul J. J.
"New Wisdom. " NewL (43:4) Sum 77, p. 54.
"On the Nature of History. " NewL (43:4) Sum 77, p. 54.
Solstice III. Sam (57) 77. Entire issue.
"What the Seers of the Past Have Told Us about the Present. "
    Sam (59) 77, p. 19.

PAYACK, Peter
"The Barrel & Beyond. " ParisR (71) Aut 77, p. 169.
"A Dog's World. " Juice (4) 77.
The Evolution of Death. Sam (51) 77. Entire issue.
"My Pet Trilobite. " Chelsea (36) 77, p. 48.
"The Poverty of Philosophy. " Juice (4) 77.
"The Proffessor--A Reply. " AndR (3:2) Aut 76, p. 13.

PAYNE, John Burnett
"Their Ancestors Were Foxes. " Wind (25) 77, p. 51.

PAZ, Octavio
"Salamander" (tr. by Thomas J. Knight). PoetL (72:1) Spr 77,
    p. 32.
"Vuelta" (a José Alvarado). Montra (3) Spr 77, p. 180.

PEACOCK, Tom
"Waynahbozho and the Bia" (to Dan Wyman). AmerPoR (6:2) Mr-
    Ap 77, p. 32.

PEARCE, Brian Louis
"Birch Trees, Bushy Park. " GRR (8:1/2) 77, p. 129.
"Cedar. " GRR (8:1/2) 77, p. 126.

"Sequoia." GRR (8:1/2) 77, p. 128.
"Yew." GRR (8:1/2) 77, p. 127.

PEARLSTEIN, Darlene
"Yield." Glass (2:2/3) Wint-Spr 77, p. 41.

PEARSON, E. Malcolm
"For a Homecoming." YaleLit (145:5) 77, p. 11.

PEASE, Deborah
"Geography Lesson." ParisR (70) Sum 77, p. 177.

PEASE, Roland
"Held Up for Answers." ParisR (71) Aut 77, p. 176.
"The Only Sound." ParisR (71) Aut 77, p. 177.

PECK, John
"Family Burying Ground." Salm (38/39) Sum-Aut 77, p. 45.
"Fog Burning Off at Cape May." Salm (38/39) Sum-Aut 77,
    p. 42.
"Ground Observer Corps." Salm (38/39) Sum-Aut 77, p. 43.
"Lines for a Daughter." Salm (38/39) Sum-Aut 77, p. 44.

PECKENPAUGH, Angela
"Letters from Lee's Army" (seven poems). VirQR (53:3) Sum
    77, p. 501.

PEDRICK, Jean
"The Empress-Makers." NewRena (9) F 77, p. 87.

PEFFER, Randall
"Appalachian Born." AndR (4:1) Spr 77, p. 14.

PELL, Derek
"The Invention of Style." MontG (6) Aut 77, p. 42.

PELOSI, A. J., Jr.
"Heir." StoneC (77:1) F 77, p. 9.

PENCE, Susan
"Together in a Summer." CarouselQ (2:2) Spr 77, p. 5.

PENFOLD, Gerda
"Always the Same Death." Vaga (25) 77, p. 53.
"The Good Little Gingerbread Girls." Vaga (26) 77, p. 32.
"I Walk in the Financial District" (for Garrett McEnerney II).
    Vaga (26) 77, p. 31.
"In the Dream I Lived." Vaga (25) 77, p. 51.
"Meeting for the First Time." Vaga (26) 77, p. 28.
"The Part of Her That Is Silent" (for Carla and Stephanie). Vaga
    (25) 77, p. 50.
"They Accuse Me of Riding." Vaga (26) 77, p. 29.
"Wasn't Only My Mother Gave Birth to Me." Vaga (25) 77, p. 52.

"White Enamel Bathtub" (for Eileen Russo).   Vaga (26) 77,
    p. 30.

PENN, Rick
"Continuation Record." Icarus (5:1) Spr 77, p. 8.

PENN, W. S.
"Tryptych." SouthernHR (11:3) Sum 77, p. 266.

PENNA, Sandro
"If the summer night yields, just a little" (tr. by Ian Young and
    M. J. Shakley). Mouth (11/12) Mr-Je 77, p. 64.

PENNANT, Edmund
"J & Z." BelPoJ (27:4) Sum 77, p. 27.
"Retreat." LitR (20:4) Sum 77, p. 477.
"Talking to Walls." Comm (104:26) 23 D 77, p. 814.

PENNES, Rickey
"My Brothers." SeC (5:2) 78, p. 26.

PENZAVECCHIA, James
"After One Too Many of Everything." SmPd (14:3) Aut 77,
    p. 12.
"Keys." SmPd (14:3) Aut 77, p. 13.
"Myrtiotissa." Wind (26) 77, p. 64.   Corrected version.

PENZI, James
"night of an insomniac: a visit to the house of john digby."
    MontG (5) Wint 77, p. 8.
"the song of the siren." MontG (5) Wint 77, p. 7.

PERCHIK, Simon
"Every Bone Found." SouthwR (62:2) Spr 77, p. 181.
"The hat oval." HolCrit (14:3) Je 77, p. 12.
"How Did I This Growl?" CalQ (11/12) Wint-Spr 77, p. 117.
"I Can Forget." SoDakR (15:4) Wint 77-78, p. 79.
"I immolate myself with news." WindO (29) Sum 77, p. 35.
"*." PoNow (14/18) 77, p. 139.
"*." Rapp (10) 77, p. 62.
"*." Rapp (10) 77, p. 63.

PEREL, Jane L.
"The Car Wash." Wind (24) 77, p. 52.
"light" (a song for C.T.). Wind (24) 77, p. 52.
"optic nerve." Wind (24) 77, p. 52.

PERELMAN, Bob
"The Classics." Hills (4) 77.
"Self Taught." Hills (4) 77.
"Straight." Hills (4) 77.
"Tract." Hills (4) 77.

PÉRET, Benjamin
"A Bunch of Carrots" (tr. by Keith Hollaman). Field (16) Spr
    77, p. 35.
"Gone without Leaving an Address" (tr. by Keith Hollaman).
    Field (16) Spr 77, p. 32.
"In the Whites of Eyes" (tr. by Jane Barnard and A. F. Mortiz,
    w. Margaret Schaus). Aieee (5/6) 77, p. 19.
"My Last Misfortunes" (To Yves Tanguy) (tr. by Jane Barnard
    and A. F. Moritz, w. Margaret Schaus). Aieee (5/6) 77,
    p. 17.
"Portrait of Andre Breton" (tr. by Jane Barnard and A. F.
    Moritz, w. Margaret Schaus). Aieee (5/6) 77, p. 18.
"Stale Bread" (tr. by Keith Hollaman). Field (16) Spr 77, p. 35.
"To Sleep Standing Up" (tr. by Keith Hollaman). Field (16) Spr
    77, p. 36.
"To Wash Your Hands" (tr. by Keith Hollaman). Field (16) Spr
    77, p. 33.
"Under a Beating Rain" (tr. by Jane Barnard and A. F. Moritz,
    w. Margaret Schaus). Aieee (5/6) 77, p. 20.

PERKINS, David
"The Horizon." ArkRiv (3:4/4:1) 77, p. 13.

PERKINS, D. N.
"Archaeopteryx Fallen." RemR (5) 77, p. 94.
"Grandfather's Bedtime Story." RemR (5) 77, p. 95.
"The Roofs of Houses." GRR (8:1/2) 77, p. 150.

PERKINS, James Ashbrook
"An Unexpected Postcard from Miss Dickinson of Amherst" (for
    DeWolfe, who introduced us). Wind (27) 77, p. 45.

PERLBERG, Mark
"Watercolor: April." Nat (225:4) 6-13 Ag 77, p. 122.

PERLMAN, Anne S.
"A Dying." CalQ (11/12) Wint-Spr 77, p. 46.
"Easter Snow." Hudson (30:1) Spr 77, p. 79.
"An Encounter on Exmoor." Ploughs (4:1) 77, p. 78.
"What Counts." PoNow (14/18) 77, p. 139.

PERLMAN, Jim
"Skyscape." DacTerr (14) Spr-Sum 77, p. 71.

PERRINE, Laurence
"Epitaph on Parnaasus' Side." CEACritic (39:4) My 77, p. 30.
"A Haiku for Emily Dickinson." CEACritic (39:4) My 77, p. 21.
"On Reading T. S. Eliot." CEACritic (39:4) My 77, p. 38.
"Vision." CEACritic (39:4) My 77, p. 30.

PESCHEL, Enid Rhodes
"Villanelle: Chanson Rustique Moderne." SouthernHR (11:4) Aut
    77, p. 346.

PETERFREUND, Stuart
  "Gasoline: A Vision." PoNow (14/18) 77, p. 140.
  "Snow Maiden." Falcon (14) 77, p. 37.
  "Unemployed." PoNow (14/18) 77, p. 140.

PETERS, Nancy
  "A Poem Brought Back to Life." PraS (51:1) Spr 77, p. 87.
  "Three Things to Do When the Baby Will Not Sleep." PraS
    (51:1) Spr 77, p. 86.

PETERS, Robert
  "Abraham's Gift." Hand (1) 77, p. 208.
  "The American Arctic Explorer Elisha Kent Kane Observes Two
    of His Men Making Love (August 1854)." Mouth (13) D 77,
    p. 54.
  "Bronze Chains." Mouth (11/12) Mr-Je 77, p. 5.
  "Closure." Stonecloud (6) 76, p. 131.
  "Louis Fourteen." Stonecloud (6) 76, p. 70.
  "Ludwig Quarrels with Richard Hornig." Mouth (11/12) Mr-Je
    77, p. 6.
  "New Year's Day, 1775." Hand (1) 77, p. 208.
  "Nude." Mouth (11/12) Mr-Je 77, p. 4.
  "Nude Father Cradles Sleeping Children" (for kate and john
    barnard). Stonecloud (6) 76, p. 13.
  "Richard." Mouth (11/12) Mr-Je 77, p. 4.
  "Simple Projection." Stonecloud (6) 76, p. 105.
  "Song." Mouth (11/12) Mr-Je 77, p. 3.
  "A Wasp in Love with Bedrooms." Mouth (11/12) Mr-Je 77,
    p. 7.
  "The Whelks of Death." Stonecloud (6) 76, p. 132.

PETERSON, Elizabeth
  "Sand Castle." Wind (27) 77, p. 44.

PETERSON, James
  "Foal." SouthernPR (17:2) Aut 77, p. 66.

PETERSON, Kathleen
  "Trophies." PortR (23) 77, p. 104.

PETESCH, Donald
  "A Family Album." Rapp (10) 77, p. 66.
  "Father and Son." Rapp (10) 77, p. 67.
  "Father Remembering Other Roads." Rapp (10) 77, p. 68.

PETRAKOS, Chris
  "These Are the Only Clothes I Have." DacTerr (14) Spr-Sum 77,
    p. 31.

PETRIE, Paul
  "Adventure." Hudson (30:3) Aut 77, p. 366.
  "The Gardener." Comm (104:10) 13 My 77, p. 296.
  "Good Day." CentR (21:1) Wint 77, p. 70.

"The Miracle." MichQR (16:3) Sum 77, p. 285.
"The Romantics." Hudson (30:3) Aut 77, p. 367.
"A Toast to Christmas." CentR (21:1) Wint 77, p. 69.

PETROSKI, Henry
    "Appointments." Shen (28:3) Spr 77, p. 73.
    "A Twist in Time." FourQt (27:1) Aut 77, p. 40.

PETROSKY, Tony
    "Late Morning." ModernPS (8:3) Wint 77, p. 254.
    "The Old Stories." ModernPS (8:3) Wint 77, p. 253.

PETSKA, Darrell
    "Pretty Shells." Pig (3) 77, p. 84.

PETT, Stephen
    "Muted to Shadows, To Pines." QW (2) Wint 77, p. 15.

PETTIT, Michael
    "The Old Cowboy." HolCrit (14:2) Ap 77, p. 8.
    "Surely Warm." QW (2) Wint 77, p. 74.

PFINGSTON, Roger
    "Getting Unplugged, a Celebration." Confr (15) Aut 77-Wint 78,
        p. 150.
    "Snow/A Dream of Russia." NewL (44:1) Aut 77, p. 106.
    "Spring on Stoutes Creek Road." Rapp (10) 77, p. 88.
    "Squash Pie." Rapp (10) 77, p. 86.

PHILBRICK, Stephen
    "Left Out." PoNow (14/18) 77, p. 140.

PHILLIPS, Jayne Anne
    "Hagar." NewL (44:1) Aut 77, p. 42.

PHILLIPS, Louis
    "After Midnight Jazz Is the Sweetest Music of All." CimR (41)
        O 77, p. 45.
    "Capriole." StoneC (77:2) My 77, p. 16.
    "Foreplay." TexQ (20:4) Wint 77, p. 114.
    "In the Preserve of Scholars." AAUP (64:4) N 77, p. 316.
    "The Song of My Chains." CimR (41) O 77, p. 28.
    "Theater of Ideas." TexQ (20:4) Wint 77, p. 182.

PHILLIPS, Robert
    "'Affections Harden.'" Shen (28:4) Sum 77, p. 35.
    "Books." Confr (14) Spr-Sum 77, p. 69.
    "Giacometti's Race" (For Herbert Lust). ModernPS (8:1) Spr 77,
        p. 49.

PHILLIPS, Walt
    "A Portion of the Oral History." StoneC (77:1) F 77, p. 29.

PHINEAS-BEDONNA, Issac
"Balling of the Queen." Mouth (13) D 77, p. 24.
"Mesomorphs" (for A. R. S.). Mouth (11/12) Mr-Je 77, p. 20.
"Spelunker." Mouth (11/12) Mr-Je 77, p. 21.
"Studley Shoulders." Mouth (11/12) Mr-Je 77, p. 19.

PICCIONE, Anthony
"Drinking with My Father on My Birthday." OhioR (18:3) Aut 77,
   p. 22.
"Government Film Shown On Television By Mistake." Bleb (12)
   77, p. 26.
"Outside, Naked." Bleb (12) 77, p. 27.

PICCIONE, Sandi
"Walking with My Daughter." OhioR (18:1) Wint 77, p. 24.

PICKETT, Tom
"Why She Laughs." Poem (30) Jl 77, p. 23.

PIDOT, Diane
"Summer Tracing." Confr (14) Spr-Sum 77, p. 85.

PIERCE, Edith Lovejoy
"Risk-Taking." ChrC (94:10) 23 Mr 77, p. 269.
"Terminal" (for G. T.). ChrC (94:3) 26 Ja 77, p. 58.

PIERCY, Marge
"Armed Combat in a Cafe." TransR (60) Je 77, p. 96.
"Ask Me for Anything Else." PoNow (14/18) 77, p. 141.
"Crows." PoNow (14/18) 77, p. 141.
"A Gift of Light." MinnR (NS8) Spr 77, p. 24.
"Going In." Gra (12) 77, p. 53.
"Inertia Is a Kind of Death." OP (24) Aut-Wint 77, p. 35.
"Jay." PoNow (14/18) 77, p. 141.
"The Lansing Bad Penny Doug Come Again Blues." OP (24) Aut-
   Wint 77, p. 30.
from Living in the Open: "To the Pay Toilet." PoNow (14/18)
   77, p. 137.
"Martha as the Angel Gabriel." 13thM (3:2) 77, p. 5.
"The Rose and the Eagle." PoNow (14/18) 77, p. 142.
"Snow in May." OP (24) Aut-Wint 77, p. 34.
"There Is No Known Way to Tickle a Clam." PoNow (14/18) 77,
   p. 137.
"The Twelve-Spoked Wheel Flashing." OP (24) Aut-Wint 77,
   p. 32.

PIERMAN, Carol J.
"The Passenger." CarolQ (29:1) Wint 77, p. 28.
"Possibilities of Light and the Forest." CarolQ (29:1) Wint 77,
   p. 26.

PIERSON, Philip
"Beyond Rock Road." CarlMis (16:1/2) Aut-Wint 76-77, p. 121.

"Caboose Graveyard." CarlMis (16:1/2) Aut-Wint 76-77, p. 122.
"The Cowboy." Rapp (10) 77, p. 22.
"Homecoming." CarlMis (16:1/2) Aut-Wint 76-77, p. 120.
"The Junkman's Prayer." CarolQ (29:2) Spr-Sum 77, p. 29.
"Lazarus." DeKalb (10:3) Spr 77, p. 43.
"Picking Fruit." NewOR (5:3) 77, p. 259.
"2nd Shift Waitress." CarolQ (29:2) Spr-Sum 77, p. 27.
"Snapshot for My Mother." SewanR (85:4) Aut 77, p. 609.
"Sometimes, Nails." SouthernPR (17:1) Spr 77, p. 29.
"Southern Directions." CarolQ (29:2) Spr-Sum 77, p. 28.
"Testing the New Roof." KanQ (9:1) Wint 77, p. 50.
"Thinning." DeKalb (10:3) Spr 77, p. 44.
"Treehouse." SouthernHR (11:3) Sum 77, p. 269.
"Weatherclock." Rapp (10) 77, p. 20.

PIJEWSKI, John
    "The Ardennes Forest" (tr. of Zbigniew Herbert). Field (17)
        Aut 77, p. 5.
    "Dancing Dad." ParisR (70) Sum 77, p. 32.
    "The Garden in Sêlinkonowica." SenR (8:2) D 77, p. 83.
    "A Little Box Called Imagination" (tr. of Zbigniew Herbert).
        Field (17) Aut 77, p. 7.
    "Our Father." ParisR (70) Sum 77, p. 31.
    "Sunday Dinner with Uncle Józef." SenR (8:2) D 77, p. 85.

PILINSZKY, János
    "The Desert of Love" (tr. by Ted Hughes). AmerPoR (6:3) My-
        Je 77, p. 24.
    "Under the Winter Sky" (tr. by Ted Hughes). AmerPoR (6:3)
        My-Je 77, p. 23.

PILLIN, William
    "A Lamp on the Plain." MontG (5) Wint 77, p. 25.

PINSKER, Sanford
    "Consuming Farrah-Fawcett." JnlOPC (11:2) Aut 77, p. 357.
    "Dreaming about Lettuce Cigarette, I Muse over the Future As
        Well." Salm (38/39) Sum-Aut 77, p. 116.
    "In Dreams." KanQ (9:1) Wint 77, p. 47.
    "It Is Getting Harder to Live Here." PoNow (14/18) 77, p. 144.
    "The Last Person in America Not Indicted." PoNow (14/18) 77,
        p. 144.
    "Matthew at Play." Confr (15) Aut 77-Wint 78, p. 16.
    "On Richard Wilbur, About Sylvia Plath." KanQ (9:2) Spr 77,
        p. 80.

PINSKY, Robert
    "Lair." NewYorker (53:35) 17 O 77, p. 157.

PIPPIN, R. Gene
    "In Herculaneum." Poetry (130:1) Ap 77, p. 17.

PISARETZ, Jim
    "6 am." Wind (27) 77, p. 34.

PITCHFORD, Kenneth
"Balcony Scene" (To Robin Morgan in the year of our fifteenth
anniversary). Poetry (130:6) S 77, p. 311.

PITKIN, Anne
"E Pluribus Unum." MalR (42) Ap 77, p. 112.
"A Good Friday Poem." Nat (225:16) 12 N 77, p. 502.
"Notes for Continuing the Performance." Nat (225:2) 9-16 Jl 77,
p. 57.
"River." Nat (225:15) 5 N 77, p. 476.

PLANTEEN, Pete
"For Rebels with Bad Complexions." Sam (56) Sum 77, p. 22.

PLANZ, Allen
"Down the Road." Hand (1) 77, p. 193.

PLAYER, William
"Endless Waiting." Madrona (4:13/14) 77, p. 33.
"Wealthy." Bits (6) Jl 77.
"Welcome." YellowBR (8) 77, p. 3.

PLUMLY, Stanley
"Early Meadow-Rue." OhioR (18:2) Spr-Sum 77, p. 20.
"Ghazal/Insomnia." OhioR (18:2) Spr-Sum 77, p. 21.
"Say Summer/For My Mother." NewYRB (24:6) 14 Ap 77, p. 7.
"This Poem." OhioR (18:2) Spr-Sum 77, p. 20.
"The Tree." Iowa (8:1) Wint 77, p. 38.

PLUMPP, Sterling
from Clinton: "Dick Tracy chases Eighty-Eight Keys." Nimrod
(21:2/22:1) 77, p. 212.
from Clinton: "The sixties." Nimrod (21:2/22:1) 77, p. 211.

PLUNKETT, Eugenia
"On the Pier." FourQt (27:1) Aut 77, p. 32.

POAGE, Michael
"The Beggar." MontG (6) Aut 77, p. 78.
"Laurel." MontG (6) Aut 77, p. 76.
"Requiem." MontG (6) Aut 77, p. 75.
"Somatic: 'shocked by a flower, dismembered by a kiss' (Dupin)."
MontG (6) Aut 77, p. 77.
"The Window." MontG (6) Aut 77, p. 79.
"Yes." MontG (5) Wint 77, p. 6.

POBO, Kenneth G.
"Ennui." Wind (27) 77, p. 20.
"Purgatory." Wind (27) 77, p. 20.
"Sullen Manitoba Warning." NewC (7:3) 75-76, p. 24.
"To John Gould Fletcher." Poem (31) N 77, p. 13.

POBST, Carol B.
"morning of the Dream in scorpio." Chomo (3:3) Spr 77, p. 24.

PO Chu-i
"Reminder" (tr. by Graeme Wilson). DenQ (12:2) Sum 77,
    p. 398.

POE, Edgar Allan
"Annabel Lee." PoNow (14/18) 77, p. 96.

POLIZZOTTI, Mark
"Belfast Photograph." YaleLit (145:4) 77, p. 19.
"Four Women." YaleLit (146:2) 77, p. 7.
"Ozone." YaleLit (145:5) 77, p. 3.
"Pivot" (w. Shelley Reinhardt). YaleLit (145:4) 77, p. 2.
"Voices from Love's Afternoon." YaleLit (146:2) 77, p. 8.

POLLAK, Felix
"Concerning Survival." Sparrow (33) Ja 77, p. 20.
"Of Nightmares and White Canes." BelPoJ (28:2) Wint 77-78,
    p. 17.
"Talking Books." NoAmR (262:1) Spr 77, p. 58.

POLLENS, David
"My Story." Atl (239:5) My 77, p. 61.

POLLITT, Katha
"Intimation." NewRep (176:6) 5 F 77, p. 26.
"Moon and Flowering Plum." NewYorker (53:4) 14 Mr 77,
    p. 34.
"Nettles." Atl (239:2) F 77, p. 63.
"Onion." Atl (239:2) F 77, p. 63.
"Potatoes." Atl (239:2) F 77, p. 63.
"Whose Sleeves?" NewYorker (53:4) 14 Mr 77, p. 34.
"Wild Orchids." NewYorker (53:4) 14 Mr 77, p. 34.

POLLY, Natale S.
"Describing the Depression When It's Not 1929" (for Me and Day).
    Gra (12) 77.
"Sundown Easter." Gra (12) 77, p. 26.

PONDER, Leanne
"The Furniture Mover." Esq (88:5) N 77, p. 12.

PONIKVAR, Dale
"Cruel Assortments" (tr. of Renê Char, w. Helen Bishop and
    Reiner Schürmann). Bound (5:3) Spr 77, p. 755.

POPA, Vasko
"Broken Horns" (tr. by Charles Simic). Field (16) Spr 77,
    p. 28.
"The Other World" (tr. by Charles Simic). Field (16) Spr 77,
    p. 27.
"Shadow of a Shewolf" (tr. by Charles Simic). Field (16) Spr 77,
    p. 25.
"Stepfather of Wolves" (tr. by Charles Simic). Field (16) Spr
    77, p. 26.

POPPINO, Kathryn
  "I Fear the Laundromat after Eleven." YellowBR (9) 77, p. 36.
  "Primitive Telling." ChiR (29:1) Sum 77, p. 57.
  "Untitled." ChiR (29:1) Sum 77, p. 56.
  "The wind tackles the." HangL (31) Aut 77, p. 61.

PORTEGUÉS, Paul
  "wire." Gra (12) 77, p. 6.

PORTER, Caryl
  "Keeping Busy Outside the Gates." Wind (25) 77, p. 53.

PORTER, Peter
  "The Third Man in the Boat." AmerS (46:1) Wint 76-77, p. 85.

PORTUGES
  "césar vallejo" (for JAH). Chelsea (36) 77, p. 74.

POSEY, Lawton W.
  "Three Questions to Tutankhumun at the Display of His Treasures
    in Washington." ChrC (94:15) 27 Ap 77, p. 402.
  "Winter Communion." ChrC (94:40) 7 D 77, p. 1133.

POTTLE, Kathy
  "The Illness." AntR (35:4) Aut 77, p. 399.
  "Letter." AntR (35:4) Aut 77, p. 401.
  "Utopia." AntR (35:4) Aut 77, p. 400.

POULIN, A., Jr.
  "The Angels of Poetry." PraS (51:4) Wint 77-78, p. 400.
  "Brothers." PoNow (14/18) 77, p. 144.
  "Cemetery" (tr. of Rainer Maria Rilke). ParisR (69) Spr 77,
    p. 117.
  "Saltimbanques" (tr. of Rainer Maria Rilke). ParisR (69) Spr 77,
    p. 116.
  "Small Notebook" (tr. of Rainer Maria Rilke). ParisR (69) Spr
    77, p. 116.
  from Sonnets to Orpheus: "First Series (19, 22, 23)" (tr. of
    Rainer Maria Rilke). OhioR (18:1) Wint 77, p. 14.
  from Sonnets to Orpheus: "Second Series (8)" (In memory of
    Egon von Rilke) (tr. of Rainer Maria Rilke). OhioR (18:1)
    Wint 77, p. 15.
  from Sonnets to Orpheus: Twelve poems (tr. of Rainer Maria
    Rilke). AmerPoR (6:1) Ja-F 77, p. 17.

POWELL, Pamela Leslie
  "First Star." Vaga (26) 77, p. 9.
  "Reyes Peak" (for Gary Snyder). Vaga (25) 77, p. 55.
  "Susan." Vaga (25) 77, p. 54.

POWELL, Tony
  "My Experience at Belvin: As I Walk Along." AmerPoR (6:2)
    Mr-Ap 77, p. 32.

POWERS, Arthur
"Two Poems from Juan del Encina." TexQ (20:2) Sum 77,
     p. 33.

POWERS, Jeffrey
"That Distance Is Correct." QW (3) Spr-Sum 77, p. 95.

PRASSINOS, Gisèle
"A Nice Family" (tr. by Ellen Nations). ParisR (69) Spr 77,
     p. 121.

PRATT, Annis
"Women, Sewing." 13thM (3:2) 77, p. 8.

PREIL, Gabriel
"From a Late Diary" (tr. by Robert Friend). TriQ (39) Spr 77,
     p. 294.
"Romantic Reminder" (tr. by Robert Friend). TriQ (39) Spr 77,
     p. 293.
"A Somewhat Clouded Study" (tr. by Robert Friend). TriQ (39)
     Spr 77, p. 292.
"Sunset Possibilities" (tr. by Robert Friend). TriQ (39) Spr 77,
     p. 292.

PREJSNAR, Mark
"Epiphany." BerksR (12:1) Spr 77.
"Iron Music." BerksR (12:1) Spr 77.
"A Troupe." BerksR (12:1) Spr 77.

PRESS, John
"At Sete." SouthernR (13:4) Aut 77, p. 750.

PRESTON, Gordon
"Dawn." CutB (8) Spr 77, p. 6.
"Sunday without Rain." CutB (8) Spr 77, p. 7.

PRETTYMAN, A. E.
"For Julie." Nimrod (21:2/22:1) 77, p. 213.

PREVERT, Jacques
"Marriages" (tr. by Eve Merriam). NewRep (177:2/3) 9-16 Jl
     77, p. 26.
"My Little Lioness" (tr. by Eve Merriam). NewRep (177:2/3)
     9-16 Jl 77, p. 26.
"To Laugh in Society" (tr. by Eve Merriam). NewRep (177:2/3)
     9-16 Jl 77, p. 26.
"War" (tr. by Eve Merriam). NewRep (177:2/3) 9-16 Jl 77,
     p. 26.
"The Wheelbarrow or Great Inventions" (tr. by Eve Merriam).
     NewRep (177:2/3) 9-16 Jl 77, p. 26.

PRICE, Darryl
"Lovesong." Pig (3) 77, p. 36.

PRICE, John
    from Death Segments: "for Buddha's claws." BelPoJ (28:2)
        Wint 77-78, p. 3.

PRINGLE, Tamarah Jane
    "He is on the mountain at the very point" (for Doug). PortR (23)
        77, p. 103.
    "You hear some nights the creak" (for Maranda). PortR (23) 77,
        p. 103.

PRIVETT, Katharine
    "Rites of Passage, Rites of Spring." MidwQ (18:3) Spr 77,
        p. 264.

PROBECK, William R.
    "On Our Way They Stopped." KanQ (9:3) Sum 77, p. 112.

PROCHAK, Michael S.
    "Morning." Gra (12) 77.

PROCTOR, James W.
    "Bedtime Story." Wind (24) 77, p. 54.
    "City Cousins." Wind (24) 77, p. 54.
    "The Winter Season." Wind (24) 77, p. 56.

PROHART, Timothy
    "Day Dreamed Days." DeKalb (10:3) Spr 77, p. 45.

PROSEN, Rose Mary
    Nine poems. CalQ (11/12) Wint-Spr 77, p. 28.

PROST, Ronald
    "black." WormR (65/66) 77, p. 42.
    "dove tail." WormR (65/66) 77, p. 44.
    "white." WormR (65/66) 77, p. 43.

PROVOST, George
    "New World." NewWR (45:4) Jl-Ag 77, p. 3.

PRUNTY, Wyatt
    "The Anesthetic Tenor." TexQ (20:2) Sum 77, p. 63.
    "The Effervescent Mrs. G." VirQR (53:2) Spr 77, p. 334.
    "Failed Suicide: An Ophthalmologist." TexQ (20:2) Sum 77,
        p. 62.
    "The Insurance Agent." VirQR (53:2) Spr 77, p. 333.
    "Letter." SouthernR (13:3) Sum 77, p. 589.
    "The Man with Change." VirQR (53:2) Spr 77, p. 333.
    "The Men of Sad Age." VirQR (53:2) Spr 77, p. 334.
    "Murals in a Greek Museum." SewanR (85:3) Sum 77, p. 434.
    "Not to Fear Falling But to Fear the Dive." Poem (31) N 77,
        p. 45.
    "The Salesman." Poem (31) N 77, p. 46.
    "The Shade Tree." KanQ (9:4) Aut 77, p. 12.

"The Waiting Room. "   Poem (31) N 77, p. 44.

PRYBYZERSKI, Richard
"I wandered in and took a seat. "   Mouth (13) D 77, p. 83.
"Jesus Loves Me. "   Mouth (13) D 77, p. 15.
"An old man reads a poem of mine and weeps. "   Mouth (13) D
    77, p. 83.

PURDY, Al
"Deprivations. "   MalR (41) Ja 77, p. 100.

PURENS, Ilmars
"On the Sadness in President Lincoln's Eyes. "   PoNow (14/18)
    77, p. 144.

QABBANI, Nazar
"You Want" (tr. by Sargon Boulus).   Mund (10:1) 77, p. 72.

al-QASIM, Sameeh
"And Then" (tr. by Sargon Boulus).   Mund (10:1) 77, p. 60.
"Feast" (tr. by Sargon Boulus).   Mund (10:1) 77, p. 60.
"The Last Line in the Poem" (tr. by Sargon Boulus).   Mund
    (10:1) 77, p. 59.

QUASIMODO, Salvatore
"Letter" (tr. by Jeffrey Gantz).   MichQR (16:1) Wint 77, p. 11.

QUINN, John
"Epithalamium" (for Bill and Myrna).   PortR (23) 77, p. 149.
"Fleshing Hide. "   PortR (23) 77, p. 148.

QUINN, John Robert
"Alone. "   Wind (24) 77, p. 57.
"Consensus. "   Wind (24) 77, p. 57.
"Plaint without Rancor. "   Wind (24) 77, p. 57.

QUINN, Sister Bernetta
"Adam Thoroughgood House. "   PoNow (14/18) 77, p. 145.

QUINTANA, Mârio de Miranda
"Minha morte nasceu quando eu nasci. "   TexQ (19:4) Wint 76,
    p. 98.

RAAB, Esther
"Folk Tune" (tr. by Robert Friend and Shimon Sandbank).   TriQ
    (39) Spr 77, p. 294.
"Today I Am Modest" (tr. by Robert Friend and Shimon Sand-
    bank).   TriQ (39) Spr 77, p. 295.

RAAB, Lawrence
"After Edward Hopper. "   NewYorker (53:21) 11 Jl 77, p. 75.
"The Confessions of Doctor X. "   BerksR (12:1) Sum 76, p. 4.
"A Night's Museum" (for Joseph Cornell).   VirQR (53:4) Aut 77,
    p. 729.

RABB, Margoret
"Reaping. " CarolQ (29:1) Wint 77, p. 78.

RABBITT, Thomas
"The Casino Beach. " Esq (87:5) My 77, p. 58.
"Psalm. " Shen (28:2) Wint 77, p. 98.
"Sirocco. " Shen (28:2) Wint 77, p. 97.

RABKIN, David
"I swan down a well into the sea. " AAR (27) 77, p. 115.

RABLIN, Perry J.
"Tribute to e e cummings. " EngJ (66:5) My 77, p. 55.

RACHEL, Naomi
"america the brave. " Wind (25) 77, p. 55.
"not another poem to sylvia plath. " Wind (25) 77, p. 55.
"a room of her own. " Wind (25) 77, p. 54.
"Through Mirrors. " StoneC (77:3) S 77, p. 13.
"tomorrow. " Wind (25) 77, p. 54.

RACHFORD, Fred
"Gone Aztec" (for MVS). Mouth (13) D 77, p. 68.

RACINES, Anthony
"Old Age. " SeC (5:2) 78, p. 27.

RACKSTRAW, Richard
"At Interlochen. " NoAmR (262:3) Aut 77, p. 54.
"Drift" (for Paul and June Shepard). NoAmR (262:3) Aut 77,
    p. 54.
"For Theodore Roethke. " NoAmR (262:3) Aut 77, p. 54.
"The Peaceable Kingdom. " NoAmR (262:3) Aut 77, p. 56.
"Setting the Poem by Hand. " NoAmR (262:3) Aut 77, p. 55.
"'Your Absence, and the Gathering Lake'" (for Loree). NoAmR
    (262:3) Aut 77, p. 55.

RADIN, Doris
"Elegy. " Drag (16) 77.
"In Memory of Danny Warner. " Confr (14) Spr-Sum 77, p. 31.

RADNOTI, Miklós
"Elegy, or Icon, Nailless" (tr. by Emery George). WebR (3:4)
    Aut 77, p. 49.
"Four Poems" (tr. by David Brewster). Madrona (4:13/14) 77,
    p. 30.

RAFFA, Joseph L.
"Sunrise Lesson in a Campus Graveyard: Knowledge Emeritus. "
    WindO (29) Sum 77, p. 8.

RAGAN, Sam
"Sandhills Summer. " SouthernPR (16:SI) 77, p. 65.

RAGLAND, T. L.
  "Floodplain. " Wind (27) 77, p. 46.
  "Harvest. " Wind (27) 77, p. 47.
  "Perception. " Wind (27) 77, p. 46.

RAIL, DeWayne
  "The Drowning. " HiramPoR (22) Aut-Wint 77, p. 30.

RAINE, Kathleen
  "Untitled. " ChiR (28:4) Spr 77, p. 78.

RAINES, Bill
  "Allow my loneliness to be generated at 20 lumens per hour. "
      QW (2) Wint 77, p. 61.

RAINES, Charlotte A.
  "The Summer Magician. " PoetL (72:2) Sum 77, p. 77.
  "25 Lines to a Dead Friend. " PoetL (72:2) Sum 77, p. 78.

RAKOSI, Carl
  "The Avocado Pit. " NewL (43:3) Spr 77, p. 86.
  "Facts. " MoonsLT (2:3) 77, p. 38.
  "Incident. " MoonsLT (2:3) 77, p. 35.
  "Scene with a Gorgon. " NewL (43:3) Spr 77, p. 86.
  "Zzzzzz. " Nat (224:14) 9 Ap 77, p. 438.

RAMANUJAN, A. K.
  "Chicago Zen. " CarlMis (16:1/2) Aut-Wint 76-77, p. 102.

RAMES, David
  "Edelman's Laundromat. " YellowBR (9) 77, p. 12.

RAMINGTON, John
  "Ode to Luther Sperberg. " NewRep (177:6/7) 6-13 Ag 77, p. 34.

RAMIREZ, Eleanor
  "The Politicians. " CarouselQ (2:2) Aut 77, p. 28.

RAMIREZ, Orlan
  "I'm bored. " SeC (5:2) 78, p. 29.
  "life is good. " SeC (5:2) 78, p. 28.

RAMKE, Bin
  "Anopheles. " Salm (36) Wint 77, p. 48.
  "Any Brass Ring" (Eight poems). OhioR (18:3) Aut 77, pp. 33-46.
  "The Channel Swimmer. " GeoR (31:4) Wint 77, p. 811.
  "Confessio Amantis: for Frederick Rolfe, Baron Corvo. " AmerR
      (26) N 77, p. 233.
  "The Dangers of the Domestic. " SouthernPR (17:1) Spr 77,
      p. 28.
  "Martyrdom: A Love Poem. " GeoR (31:4) Wint 77, p. 812.
  "Secrets of the Saints: First Glimmerings. " Poetry (130:2) My
      77, p. 81.

RAMSEY, Jarold
"The Kit." Iowa (8:2) Spr 77, p. 19.
"Pisgah." Atl (239:3) Mr 77, p. 79.
"The Tally Stick." NowestR (16:3) 77, p. 89.

RAMSEY, Paul
"An American Silence near Jasper, Tennessee." SouthernPR
   (17:1) Spr 77, p. 17.
"For a Ceremony for the Order of the Holy Cross." SouthernPR
   (17:2) Aut 77, p. 31.
"The Lords of Quiet Waters." SouthernPR (16:SI) 77, p. 66.

RAND, Harry
"Entropy." Humanist (37:6) N-D 77, p. 59.

RANDALL, Julia
"Another Part of the County." SouthernPR (16:SI) 77, p. 67.

RANKIN, Paula
"The Decoy Carver." ColEng (38:5) Ja 77, p. 514.
"For the Workers in Wood and Dirt Among Us." Poem (29) Mr
   77, p. 31.
"For Vacationers at Endless Caverns Campground." Poem (29)
   Mr 77, p. 39.
"Hazards: Night Driving on Ice." Poem (29) Mr 77, p. 33.
"The Hurricane Watchers." Poem (29) Mr 77, p. 37.
"The Man Who Invented Fireworks." PoetryNW (18:4) Wint 77-
   78, p. 28.
"Progging." Poem (29) Mr 77, p. 41.
"Taking All We Can With Us." Poem (29) Mr 77, p. 38.
"Testing the Ice at Lake Maury." Poem (29) Mr 77, p. 35.
"The Whittlers." ThRiPo (10) 77, p. 40.

RANKIN, Ricky
"Autobiographical #2." Mouth (13) D 77, p. 79.
"Can I Get You Anything Else?" Mouth (13) D 77, p. 26.

RANKIN, Rush
"Genius: A Lament." SenR (8:1) My 77, p. 80.
"Glee." Chelsea (36) 77, p. 8.
"The Lady Waiting." Stand (18:2) 77, p. 62.
"Snails, Octopus, Doves." SenR (8:2) D 77, p. 45.

RANSOM, W. M.
"Autobiography: A Dream in Five Faces." MontG (5) Wint 77,
   p. 40.
"Last Rites." PortR (23) 77, p. 160.

RAPHAEL, Dan
"To Reverse Is to Repeat." Aieee (5/6) 77, p. 24.

RAPOPORT, Janis
"Io and Argus." MalR (41) Ja 77, p. 50.

"Rosedale Valley Ravine 3." MalR (41) Ja 77, p. 51.

RAPPA, Pavitra
"The Nest." RemR (5) 77, p. 96.

RAS, Barbara
"At Sea Level." Confr (14) Spr-Sum 77, p. 126.
"Blinded." CalQ (11/12) Wint-Spr 77, p. 109.
"Cuzco: Reflections." Epoch (26:2) Wint 77, p. 107.
"Espera!" (for Eduardo). Epoch (26:2) Wint 77, p. 106.
"Living with Insects." NowestR (16:3) 77, p. 75.

RASMUSSEN, Rosemary
"Weekend Guest." 13thM (3:2) 77, p. 56.

RASNIC, Steve
"Changes." Wind (24) 77, p. 59.
"Girl in the Photograph." Wind (24) 77, p. 59.

RATCLIFFE, Stephen
"Pause, Pico Blanco." Poetry (129:4) Ja 77, p. 210.
"Summer Rain." Poetry (129:4) Ja 77, p. 208.
"Thomas Campion: Epigrammatum Liber Primus." Poetry
    (130:2) My 77, p. 90.
"Thomas Campion: Epigrammatum Liber Secundus." Poetry
    (130:2) My 77, p. 92.
"The View from Mono Pass." Poetry (129:4) Ja 77, p. 209.
"Waterfall." Poetry (129:4) Ja 77, p. 207.

RATNER, Rochelle
"The Aliens." PoNow (14/18) 77, p. 145.
"Daughter." HangL (29) Wint 76-77, p. 45.
"The Game." Glass (2:2/3) Wint-Spr 77, p. 93.
"Hearing Bronk" (for JW). Hand (1) 77, p. 64.
"Love Chant." Glass (2:2/3) Wint-Spr 77, p. 94.
"Minhah." Hand (1) 77, p. 63.
"Powers of the Hands--1930." Confr (14) Spr-Sum 77, p. 110.
"Taking Home the Matzos." PoNow (14/18) 77, p. 145.
"Thunder." HangL (29) Wint 76-77, p. 34.
"To a Deafmute." Hand (1) 77, p. 64.
"Proving Grounds." PoNow (14/18) 77, p. 145.

RATTI, John
"Centipede." BelPoJ (28:2) Wint 77-78, p. 2.

RAUSKIN, J. A.
"Idleness Is the Size of a Net." KanQ (9:1) Wint 77, p. 23.

RAVIKOVITCH, Dahlia
"Distant Land" (tr. by A. C. Jacobs). TriQ (39) Spr 77,
    p. 298.
"Hard Winter" (tr. by Chana Bloch). TriQ (39) Spr 77, p. 296.
"Hills of Salt" (tr. by Chana Bloch). TriQ (39) Spr 77, p. 296.

"How Hong Kong Was Destroyed" (tr. by Chana Bloch).   TriQ
   (39) Spr 77, p. 299.
"Memory" (tr. by Chana Bloch).   Chowder (8) Spr-Sum 77,
   p. 45.
"Pride" (tr. by Marcia Falk).   TriQ (39) Spr 77, p. 297.

RAVIN, Andrea
   "Self-Portrait One Eared and Smoking."   YaleLit (146:4/5) 77,
   p. 14.

RAWLS, Isetta Crawford
   "'Trouble the Waters.'"   PraS (51:2) Sum 77, p. 191.

RAY, David
   "Climbing Mt. Hood."   Nat (225:12) 15 O 77, p. 374.
   "Farmers' Market."   ArkRiv (3:4/4:1) 77, p. 12.
   "A Few Words about Robert Frost."   PoNow (14/18) 77, p. 146.
   "For Nicholas Born, German Poet."   SunM (4) Aut 77, p. 146.
   "The Lady with the Pomeranian Dog."   Ascent (3:1) 77, p. 49.
   "Meeting the Boat."   ParisR (71) Aut 77, p. 54.
   "A Memory of West Tulsa and Long Beach."   Esq (88:5) N 77,
   p. 16D.
   "The Monastery in Scotland."   AmerR (26) N 77, p. 258.
   "Mulberries."   CutB (8) Spr 77, p. 94.
   "Mummies & Others."   NoAmR (262:1) Spr 77, p. 58.
   "My Bitterness."   ParisR (71) Aut 77, p. 55.
   "My Mission."   ParisR (71) Aut 77, p. 56.
   "News."   Bits (6) Jl 77.
   "A Swedish Postcard."   CornellR (1) Spr 77, p. 77.
   "Writing to Alice."   QW (4) Aut 77, p. 86.

RAY, Sam
   "Haiku."   NewL (44:1) Aut 77, p. 100.

RAY, Sapphina
   "The Train."   NewL (44:1) Aut 77, p. 100.

RAY, Wesley
   "A Sister Is Making Mischief."   NewL (44:1) Aut 77, p. 101.

RAYFORD, Julian Lee
   "Boom."   NewL (44:1) Aut 77, p. 43.
   "Buddha."   NewL (44:1) Aut 77, p. 45.
   "Comprehension."   NewL (44:1) Aut 77, p. 44.
   "Harmony."   NewL (44:1) Aut 77, p. 46.
   "Wonderful Things."   NewL (44:1) Aut 77, p. 43.
   "Yellow-Bellied Tomcat."   NewL (44:1) Aut 77, p. 45.

RAYMOND, Kathy
   "-ception My per-."   CarouselQ (2:2) Aut 77, p. 17.

RAYMOND, Monica
   "Lullaby."   HangL (29) Wint 76-77, p. 46.

REA, Steven
"The Coast of Brittany." Chelsea (36) 77, p. 52.

REA, Tom
"C. Y. Avenue." PortR (23) 77, p. 108.
"That Same Father." PortR (23) 77, p. 106.
"When the Phone Rings at Night." CutB (8) Spr 77, p. 91.
"The Wolfer." MontG (5) Wint 77, p. 5.

READER, Dennis J.
"Dr. Bell." TexQ (20:2) 77, p. 64.
"Note Found in a Bottle." NewL (43:4) Spr 77, p. 100.

REARDON, Marsha
"Oklahoma Woman." Chomo (3:3) Spr 77, p. 11.

REARDON, Patrick
"Rita." Sparrow (33) Ja 77, p. 15.

RECHTMAN, Janet
"To Ann and John on the Perils of Domesticity." Poem (31) N
    77, p. 10.

RECTOR, Ron
"Looks That Are Planet." LaB (8) Jl-Ag 77, p. 47.
"Weather" (to Elizabeth). LaB (8) Jl-Ag 77, p. 46.

REDMOND, Eugene B.
"Carryover." Nimrod (21:2/22:1) 77, p. 228.

REED, Angela
"I am in the 6th grade, I really don't know why. I wish I was."
    AAR (27) 77, p. 113.

REED, Ishmael
from Flight to Canada: "The Saga of Third World Belle."
    AmerPoR (6:1) Ja-F 77, p. 26.

REED, James
"Don't Trust the Face." NewOR (5:3) 77, p. 248.
"When I Was an Accountant." NewOR (5:3) 77, p. 248.

REED, John R.
"Adoration of the Magi, the Uffizi." CentR (21:1) Wint 77,
    p. 67.
"Cartography." CimR (40) Jl 77, p. 58.
"Local Astronomy." CimR (40) Jl 77, p. 59.

REED, Monica
"Calendars." Sam (55) 77, p. 46.

REEDY, Charlotte E.
"Spring, 1974." EngJ (66:5) My 77, p. 57.

REES, Daniel G.
"Freak Poem." KanQ (9:1) Wint 77, p. 25.
"One Poem Seventy Four." KanQ (9:1) Wint 77, p. 24.

REES, Earl
"History According to Pao Cheng" (tr. of Salvador Elizondo).
    PortR (23) 77, p. 82.
"The Man Who Cries" (tr. of Salvador Elizondo).   PortR (23) 77,
    p. 82.

REIBSTEIN, Regina
"Aged Father." Poem (31) N 77, p. 52.
"Bear the Unspeakable." SoDakR (15:2) Sum 77, p. 63.
"George Washington." SoDakR (15:2) Sum 77, p. 65.
"The Good Days." Poem (31) N 77, p. 54.
"With Certainty." SoDakR (15:2) Sum 77, p. 64.
"World I Never Made." Poem (31) N 77, p. 53.

REID, Alastair
"The Academy." NewYorker (53:5) 24 Mr 77, p. 34.
"A Blind Man" (tr. of Jorge Luis Borges). NewYRB (24:19) 24
    N 77, p. 47.
"The Blind Man" (tr. of Jorge Luis Borges). NewYRB (24:19)
    24 N 77, p. 47.
"Browning Resolves to Be a Poet" (tr. of Jorge Luis Borges).
    NewYRB (24:19) 24 N 77, p. 47.
"Brunanburh, A.D. 937" (tr. of Jorge Luis Borges).
    NewYorker (53:9) 18 Ap 77, p. 42.
"Hengist Wants Men" (tr. of Jorge Luis Borges). NewYorker
    (53:18) 20 Je 77, p. 34.
"I Am" (tr. of Jorge Luis Borges). AmerPoR (6:6) N-D 77,
    p. 40.
"Inventory" (tr. of Jorge Luis Borges). AmerPoR (6:6) N-D 77,
    p. 40.
"The Keeper" (tr. of Jorge Luis Borges). NewYorker (53:29) 5
    S 77, p. 26.
"My Books" (tr. of Jorge Luis Borges). AmerPoR (6:6) N-D 77,
    p. 40.
"The Palace." NewYorker (53:32) 26 S 77, p. 38.
"Talismans" (tr. of Jorge Luis Borges). NewYorker (53:25) 8
    Ag 77, p. 26.
"To the German Language" (tr. of Jorge Luis Borges). NewYRB
    (24:19) 24 N 77, p. 47.
"To the Nightingale" (tr. of Jorge Luis Borges). NewYorker
    (53:12) 9 My 77, p. 42.
Twenty poems (tr. of Jorge Luis Borges). NewRep (177:21) 19
    N 77, p. 26.
"You" (tr. of Jorge Luis Borges). AmerPoR (6:6) N-D 77,
    p. 40.

REIFF, Sandra
"Elegy." TexQ (20:4) Wint 77, p. 165.
"Excommunicated." Kayak (44) F 77, p. 27.

"Sometimes." Wind (24) 77, p. 60.
"Summer on the Island." Wind (24) 77, p. 60.
"Tiger Tiger." Wind (24) 77, p. 60.

REIGEL, Joanne
"Custom Made." LitR (21:1) Aut 77, p. 34.

REINHARDT, Marc
"Vacant Lot." BerksR (12:1) Spr 77.
"Winter 1958." BerksR (12:1) Spr 77.

REINHARDT, Shelley
"And why don't you write so hot no more?" YaleLit (145:4) 77,
    p. 13.
"Night Watch." YaleLit (145:3) 77, p. 10.
"Pivot" (w. Mark Polizzotti). YaleLit (145:4) 77, p. 2.

REIS, Marcos Konder
"Letter from the Boy I Was at That Time" (tr. by Jean R. Long-
    land). LitR (21:2) Wint 78, p. 259.
"Solitude" (tr. by Jean R. Longland). LitR (21:2) Wint 78,
    p. 260.

REISS, James
"American Gothic." PoNow (14/18) 77, p. 147.
"Arigato Means Thank You." AmerR (26) N 77, p. 344.
"By the Steps of the Metropolitan Museum of Art." NewYorker
    (53:11) 2 My 77, p. 44.
"The Song of the Vacuum Cleaner Salesman." PoNow (14/18) 77,
    p. 147.

REITER, Thomas
"Black Bass Will Take Them in Bad Weather." PoetryNW (18:3)
    Aut 77, p. 41.
"The Day Before Opening Day" (for Peter). PoetryNW (18:3) Aut
    77, p. 40.
"It's Not Bad Once the Water Goes Down." PoetryNW (18:3) Aut
    77, p. 39.
"Snapshot of the Virgin Islands." Comm (104:13) 24 Je 77,
    p. 391.

REITTER, Rose
"Newsprint Rabbi." StoneC (77:3) S 77, p. 26.
"Tai Chi." Hand (1) 77, p. 189.
"Three Quatrains." HiramPoR (22) Aut-Wint 77, p. 31.

REKOW, Nancy
"Delivery." 13thM (3:2) 77, p. 17.

RENARD, Jean-Claude
from Le Dieu de Nuit: "The First Word" (tr. by Anthony
    Rudolf). GRR (8:1/2) 77, p. 26.
from Le Dieu de Nuit: "The Third Word" (tr. by Anthony
    Rudolf). GRR (8:1/2) 77, p. 26.

from Le Dieu de Nuit: "The Fifth Word" (tr. by Anthony
    Rudolf). GRR (8:1/2) 77, p. 27.

RENDLEMAN, Danny L.
"En Famille." PoNow (14/18) 77, p. 148.
"Purge." Drag (16) 77.

RENFRO, Sally Jo
"The Calling." Atl (239:5) My 77, p. 61.
"Daughters of God." 13thM (3:2) 77, p. 39.

RENNER, Bruce
"Fog off the Lake." LittleR (12) 77, p. 8.

REPETTO, Joanne
"Crazy Jane." SeC (5:2) 78, p. 54.

RESTREPO, Lucy
"One day actually Feb. 14 a new girl came to our class. Her
    name." AAR (27) 77, p. 123.

REVELL, Donald
"Animaux." Poetry (129:4) Ja 77, p. 196.
"The Mambo on the Moon." Poem (30) Jl 77, p. 14.
"Motel View." Poetry (129:4) Ja 77, p. 197.
"Rodeo Aesthetique." Poetry (129:4) Ja 77, p. 195.

REVIS, Jennifer
"Emily." PoNow (14/18) 77, p. 148.

REWAK, William J.
"Le Morte D'Arthur." CEACritic (39:2) Ja 77, p. 12.

REXROTH, Kenneth
"As the first spring mists appear" (tr. of Lady Ise). ParisR
    (69) Spr 77, p. 119.
"Evening darkens until" (tr. of Anonymous). Agni (7) 77, p. 110.
"Following the roads" (tr. of Ono no Komachi). Agni (7) 77,
    p. 110.
"I Fire at the Face of the Country Where I Was Born" (tr. of
    Shiraishi Kazuko). PortR (23) 77, p. 92.
"In the summer, by the river" (tr. of Anonymous). Falcon (14)
    77, p. 92.
"Longing for you" (tr. of Princess Nukada). ParisR (69) Spr 77,
    p. 120.
"The Man Root" (tr. of Shiraishi Kazuko). PortR (23) 77, p. 94.
"Marichi." Ploughs (4:1) 77, p. 73.
"My lover I have lost" (tr. of Anonymous). Falcon (14) 77,
    p. 91.
"Shall I come to see" (tr. of Lady Ise). ParisR (69) Spr 77,
    p. 119.
"Silently" (tr. of Hatsui Shizue). ParisR (69) Spr 77, p. 120.
"The snow falls and falls" (tr. of Okuro Ichijitsu). Falcon (14)
    77, p. 91.

"This world of ours" (tr. of Shami Mansei). Falcon (14) 77,
    p. 92.
"Winter" (tr. of Shiraishi Kazuko). Epoch (26:2) Wint 77,
    p. 164.

REYES, Carlos
"Phone Call from a Stranger." PoNow (14/18) 77, p. 148.

REYNOLDS, Gayle
"Disillusionment." EngJ (66:5) My 77, p. 49.

REYNOLDS, J.
"The Rusted Cat." LaB (8) Jl-Ag 77, p. 51.

REYNOLDS, Tim
"Basho stood on this same bridge." Ploughs (4:1) 77, p. 72.
"A Heiroglyph for Rexroth." Ploughs (4:1) 77, p. 72.
"Untitled" (for Bartolomeu Dos Santos). Ploughs (4:1) 77, p. 71.

REZMERSKI, John Calvin
"The Lost Soldier." PoNow (14/18) 77, p. 148.
"The Collector." PoNow (14/18) 77, p. 149.

RHODES, Dennis E.
"Beach Scene." Aspect (70) Ja-Mr 77, p. 30.

RHYMER, Parke
"Smug Verse." ArizQ (33:1) Spr 77, p. 46.

RIBAR, Joe
"My Popsicle on the Beach." PoNow (14/18) 77, p. 149.

RICAPITO, J. V.
"The Concièrge." SouthernR (13:2) Spr 77, p. 350.
"Two Poems." SouthernR (13:2) Spr 77, p. 349.

RICARDO, Cassiano
"The Cactus" (tr. by Jean R. Longland). LitR (21:2) Wint 78,
    p. 222.
"Sun and Showers" (tr. by Jean R. Longland). LitR (21:2) Wint
    78, p. 223.
"The Taste of Your Kiss" (tr. by Jean R. Longland). LitR
    (21:2) Wint 78, p. 221.

RICE, David L.
"For a Moment Losing Touch." PraS (51:3) Aut 77, p. 238.

RICE, Paul
"A Bucolic: Driving in the Country with a Friend." LittleR
    (12) 77, p. 15.
"Conservation and Maintenance at Canterbury Cathedral."
    LittleR (12) 77, p. 11.

RICE, Ray
"Narrative Passage for K. C." Mouth (11/12) Mr-Je 77, p. 75.
"Shamanical Animal I, for R. D." Mouth (11/12) Mr-Je 77, p. 74.

RICHARDS, I. A.
"In Want." AmerS (46:3) Sum 77, p. 313.

RICHARDS, Jill
"Jeff." EngJ (66:5) My 77, p. 49.

RICHARDSON, Dorothy Lee
"For Van Gogh." LitR (20:3) Spr 77, p. 352.
"Incident at a Cocktail Party." TexQ (20:4) Wint 77, p. 107.
"The LARK." TexQ (20:4) Wint 77, p. 177.
"Moment of Twilight." TexQ (20:4) Wint 77, p. 97.
"A Piece of Toast." LitR (20:3) Spr 77, p. 352.
"Pioneer Wife after Thirty Years." LitR (20:3) Spr 77, p. 351.

RICHARDSON, James
"Less of the Same." Ploughs (3:3/4) 77, p. 167.

RICHMOND, Steve
"Gagaku: flap your long pointed ears." Vaga (26) 77, p. 36.
"Gagaku: going through shit I." Vaga (26) 77, p. 36.
"Gagaku: her arms dangle." Vaga (25) 77, p. 96.
"Gagaku: I despise inspiration." Juice (5) 77.
"Gagaku: my prison is beautiful." Vaga (26) 77, p. 37.
"Gagaku: no fight here." Juice (5) 77.
"Gagaku: oh the demons are howling today." Juice (5) 77.
"Gagaku: their hands are big." Vaga (25) 77, p. 96.
"Gagaku: they'll stop me here someday." Juice (5) 77.
"Gagaku: understand." Vaga (25) 77, p. 97.
"Gagaku: what my cares if my soul's core is." Juice (5) 77.

RICHTER, Harvena
"Seven Scenes from Meditation." SoDakR (15:4) Wint 77-78,
    p. 29.

RICHTER, Ricky
"The Wind." AAR (27) 77, p. 94.

RICKEL, Boyer
"A Crack in Spring." MissR (6:1) 77, p. 70.

RICKS, Tom
"Oh, Canada." YaleLit (146:2) 77, p. 12.
"Persian Miniatures: Morning in Herat." YaleLit (146:4/5) 77,
    p. 30.

RIDER, Brent
"Into the Warm Soil." QW (4) Aut 77, p. 22.

RIDGE, Diana
"Invocation." HangL (31) Aut 77, p. 64.

"Rain Poem. " HangL (31) Aut 77, p. 62.
"Richmond. " HangL (31) Aut 77, p. 63.

RIDL, Jack
"After Four Weeks. " Salm (36) Wint 77, p. 45.
"The Revolution in Ward B. " SouthernPR (17:1) Spr 77, p. 38.

RIDLEY, Tom
"Mime Talk. " NewL (43:4) Sum 77, p. 26.

RIEUR, Ellen
"Twenty. " YaleLit (145:3) 77, p. 12.

RIFKIN, Arthur
"The Hero's Progress. " PoetL (72:2) Sum 77, p. 59.

RIFQAH, Fou'ad
"And Who Are You" (tr. by Sargon Boulus). Mund (10:1) 77,
    p. 70.

RIGGS, Dionis Coffin
"Your lips are pink" (tr. of Cahit Kulebi, w. Ozcan Yal'm and
    William Fielder). DenQ (12:2) Sum 77, p. 230.

RIGSBEE, David
"A Hanging. " AmerPoR (6:2) Mr-Ap 77, p. 19.
"The Stone House" (in memoriam Edmund Wilson). AmerPoR
    (6:2) Mr-Ap 77, p. 18.
"The Thames at Chelsea" (tr. of Joseph Brodsky). NewYorker
    (53:41) 28 N 77, p. 56.
"When We All Split Up. " AmerPoR (6:2) Mr-Ap 77, p. 19.

RILEY, John
"Stalin Ode Sequence: Five Poems from the Second Voronezh
    Notebook" (tr. of Osip Mandelstam). Stand (18:2) 77, p. 28.

RILEY, William J.
"Butts of Boys. " Mouth (13) D 77, p. 53.
"I Came of Age in the Sauna. " Mouth (13) D 77, p. 52.

RILKE, Rainer Maria
"Archaic Torso of Apollo" (tr. by John Felstiner). DenQ (11:4)
    Wint 77, p. 44.
"Autumn" (tr. by Burton Raffel). DenQ (11:4) Wint 77, p. 44.
"The Carousel" (tr. by John Felstiner). DenQ (11:4) Wint 77,
    p. 45.
"Cemetery" (tr. by A. Poulin, Jr.). ParisR (69) Spr 77,
    p. 117.
"The Courtesan" (tr. by James L. Dana). DenQ (11:4) Wint 77,
    p. 47.
"Ninth Elegy" (tr. by David Young). MoonsLT (2:3) 77, p. 77.
"The Panther" (tr. by James L. Dana). DenQ (11:4) Wint 77,
    p. 42.

"The Panther" (tr. by John Felstiner). DenQ (11:4) Wint 77,
    p. 43.
"The Raising of Lazarus" (tr. by Franz Wright). Field (16) Spr
    77, p. 14.
"Saltimbanques" (tr. by A. Poulin, Jr.). ParisR (69) Spr 77,
    p. 116.
"Small Notebook" (tr. by A. Poulin, Jr.). ParisR (69) Spr 77,
    p. 116.
from Sonnets to Orpheus: "First Series (19, 22, 23)" (tr. by A.
    Poulin, Jr.). OhioR (18:1) Wint 77, p. 14.
from Sonnets to Orpheus: "Second Series (8)" (In memory of
    Egon von Rilke) (tr. by A. Poulin, Jr.). OhioR (18:1) Wint
    77, p. 15.
from Sonnets to Orpheus: Twelve poems (tr. by A. Poulin, Jr.).
    AmerPoR (6:1) Ja-F 77, p. 17.
"Spanische Tanzerin. " DenQ (12:1) Spr 77, p. 154.
"Spanish Dancer" (tr. by James L. Dana). DenQ (11:4) Wint 77,
    p. 46.
from Vergers: (16, 35, 55) (tr. by Neil Baldwin). SunM (4) Aut
    77, p. 70.
"A Woman's Fate" (tr. by James L. Dana). DenQ (11:4) Wint
    77, p. 41.

RIMBAUD
from Illuminations: Twenty-two poems (tr. by Katherine Staples).
    DenQ (11:4) Wint 77, p. 49.
"Ophelia" (tr. by Jonathan Griffin). GRR (8:3) 77, p. 224.
"The Spell-Bound" (tr. by Jonathan Griffin). GRR (8:3) 77,
    p. 225.

RIMMON, Shlomit
"Friends" (tr. of Meir Wieseltier, w. Shirley Kaufman). TriQ
    (39) Spr 77, p. 315.
from Gazelle, I'll Send You: "Prologue" and (1-15) (tr. of Amir
    Gilboa, w. Shirley Kaufman). TriQ (39) Spr 77, p. 261.
"March" (tr. of Meir Wieseltier, w. Shirley Kaufman). TriQ
    (39) Spr 77, p. 315.
"Niagara Falls" (tr. of Avner Treinin, w. Shirley Kaufman).
    TriQ (39) Spr 77, p. 304.
"Observation at Dawn" (tr. of Abba Kovner, w. Shirley Kaufman).
    TriQ (39) Spr 77, p. 283.
"A Request" (tr. of Meir Wieseltier, w. Shirley Kaufman). TriQ
    (39) Spr 77, p. 313.
"The Secret of Authority" (tr. of Meir Wieseltier, w. Shirley
    Kaufman). TriQ (39) Spr 77, p. 311.
"To My City Jerusalem, 1967" (tr. of Amir Gilboa, w. Shirley
    Kaufman). TriQ (39) Spr 77, p. 266.

RINALDI, Nicholas
"Goodbye. " LitR (20:4) Sum 77, p. 461.
"Nothing. " BallSUF (18:3) Sum 77, p. 79.
"Overkill. " LitR (20:4) Sum 77, p. 462.

"Thomas Edison Considers the Past & the Future and Goes Off
in Search of Something Else:::" LitR (20:4) Sum 77, p. 461.

RIND, Sherry
"Last Year Our Building Broke in Half." CutB (9) Aut-Wint 77,
p. 13.
"Poet as Office Coolie." SouthernPR (17:1) Spr 77, p. 30.
"Who's Harley-Davidson?" PoetryNW (18:4) Wint 77-78, p. 42.

RINGO, Stephen
"Interstate Penitentiary." ChrC (94:30) 28 S 77, p. 839.

RIPPY, Bob
"Wool Gathering." PoNow (14/18) 77, p. 149.

RIPS, Geoffrey
"Small Fires" (For My Mother). CalQ (11/12) Wint-Spr 77,
p. 148.

RISTAU, Harland
"Late Paradox." ChrC (94:2) 19 Ja 77, p. 38.
"Winter Night." Northeast (3:3) Sum 77, p. 9.

RITCHIE, Elisavietta
"Apple Country." Wind (27) 77, p. 48.
"Bread-Making." PoNow (14/18) 77, p. 150.
"Instructions for a Story." AAR (27) 77, p. 3.
"Searching for Morels." Wind (27) 77, p. 48.
"Silkworms." AAR (27) 77, p. 3.

RITSOS, Yannis
"The Earthen Adolescent" (tr. by Kimon Friar and Kostas
Myrsiades). Epoch (27:1) Aut 77, p. 82.
"Hyalography of the Bath" (tr. by Kimon Friar and Kostas
Myrsiades). Epoch (27:1) Aut 77, p. 82.
"Incense" (tr. by Edmund Keeley). BosUJ (25:3) 77, p. 64.
"In the Ruins of an Ancient Temple" (tr. by Edmund Keeley).
BosUJ (25:3) 77, p. 63.
"The Meaning of Simplicity" (tr. by Edmund Keeley). BosUJ
(25:3) 77, p. 62.
"Miniature" (tr. by Edmund Keeley). BosUJ (25:3) 77, p. 62.
"On the Television Screen" (tr. by Kimon Friar and Kostas
Myrsiades). DenQ (12:2) Sum 77, p. 268.
"Opposition" (tr. by Kimon Friar and Kostas Myrsiades). DenQ
(12:2) Sum 77, p. 268.
"Reconstruction" (tr. by Edmund Keeley). BosUJ (25:3) 77,
p. 64.
"Surveillance" (tr. by Kimon Friar and Kostas Myrsiades).
AntR (35:4) Aut 77, p. 407.
Twelve poems (for Louis Aragon) (tr. by Kimon Friar and Kostas
Myrsiades). Falcon (15) 77, p. 4.
"Women" (tr. by Edmund Keeley). BosUJ (25:3) 77, p. 63.

RIVERS, Ann
"A Mock-Feminist Poem." StoneC (77:3) S 77, p. 15.

RIXON, Robert
"Lunch Hour at the Great Falls." StoneC (77:3) S 77, p. 11.

RIZZA, Peggy
"The Concert." Salm (38/39) Sum-Aut 77, p. 103.
"The Sorrowful Mysteries." NewRep (176:6) 5 F 77, p. 27.

RIZZO, Mary C.
"Untitled." CarouselQ (2:3) Wint 77, p. 2.

ROBB, Christina
"Carol's Thank-You Note." LittleR (12) 77, p. 20.
"JR's Birthday." LittleR (12) 77, p. 7.

ROBBINS, Martin
"Electroencephalogram to My E-Coli." StoneC (77:2) My 77,
    p. 19.
"Go-between" (tr. of Kurt Bauchwitz). GRR (8:3) 77, p. 219.
"In Late September." PoNow (14/18) 77, p. 150.
"Off-Key Poem." PoNow (14/18) 77, p. 150.
"On the Graph Towards Winter." StoneC (77:2) My 77, p. 19.
"Spring Dawn: 1999." GRR (8:1/2) 77, p. 149.
"Time Lapse Photo: Falling Waters Trail." GRR (8:1/2) 77,
    p. 151.

ROBBINS, Rick
"The Patron of the Garden." PoetryNW (18:3) Aut 77, p. 26.
"Report to a Friend North." QW (4) Aut 77, p. 108.
"The Well." PoetryNW (18:3) Aut 77, p. 27.

ROBERSON, Ed
"I Have Opened Six of Ti's Nine Knots." Nimrod (21:2/22:1) 77,
    p. 226.

ROBERTS, Caroline
"When I Come In." CalQ (11/12) Wint-Spr 77, p. 149.

ROBERTS, Cynthia Day
"To My Father." LitR (20:4) Sum 77, p. 434.

ROBERTS, George
"déjà vu." Drag (16) 77.
"The Fourteenth Visit." Northeast (3:4) Aut-Wint 77-78, p. 25.
"Poem: these new planets weave in the wind." Drag (16) 77.
"The Sixth Visit." Northeast (3:4) Aut 77-78, p. 23.
"Tree Climbing in Pequot Lakes." SoDakR (15:4) Wint 77-78,
    p. 55.
"The Twelfth Visit." Northeast (3:4) Aut-Wint 77-78, p. 24.
"Visitor." Drag (16) 77.

ROBERTS, Hortense Roberta
"Crows." PoNow (14/18) 77, p. 152.

ROBERTS, Len
"Easier in Winter." Pig (3) 77, p. 35.
"4,000 Indians." Xa (4) 77, p. 22.
"The Same Door." StoneC (77:1) F 77, p. 24.
"Summer Is My Blood. Winter Knows My Reason." KanQ (9:4)
     Aut 77, p. 54.
"Yes No." Gra (12) 77.

ROBERTS, Marguerite H.
"The Picture." QW (3) Spr-Sum 77, p. 41.
"The Wish." QW (3) Spr-Sum 77, p. 42.

ROBERTS, Peter
"landscapes with love & ruins." Confr (15) Aut 77-Wint 78,
     p. 144.

ROBERTSON, Kirk
"Acoma Love Charm." WormR (65/66) 77, p. 35.
"April Flies." Madrona (4:13/14) 77, p. 28.
"At Least a Blue Guitar Would Be Cooler." WormR (65/66) 77,
     p. 38.
"Coyote Tries to Get Laid." WormR (65/66) 77, p. 36.
"'i don't know what love has got to do with happiness.'" Vaga
     (26) 77, p. 35.
"Ketchup in Ketcham." WormR (65/66) 77, p. 37.
"listening to a child & his fantasies." Juice (4) 77.
"The Most Beautiful Woman Pancho Almost Ever Saw." Juice
     (4) 77.
"new year's eve." Vaga (26) 77, p. 35.
"On the Wagon/Laundermat Blues." YellowBR (9) 77, p. 7.
"Pecan Pies." Vaga (26) 77, p. 34.
"Snake Dancer." Vaga (25) 77, p. 90.
"some myths." Juice (4) 77.
"A Stitch in Time." Madrona (4:13/14) 77, p. 27.
"Success." WormR (65/66) 77, p. 36.
"Vacation." Vaga (25) 77, p. 91.
"What She Did with the Silverware Given to Her by a U.S. Con-
     gressman Desiring to Civilize and Christianize the Zuni
     Indians." YellowBR (8) 77, p. 24.
from Woodrat's Tales, Pulled Off: "What Torngit's Husband Was
     Asked upon Entering the House." WormR (65/66) 77, p. 35.
from Woodrat's Tales, Pulled Off: "What Torngit's Husband
     Replied." WormR (65/66) 77, p. 35.
"A Wormy Day." Madrona (4:13/14) 77, p. 28.

ROBINETT, Jane
"Suicide Note." Sparrow (33) Ja 77, p. 4.

ROBINSON, Andy
"Nebulous City Yer Anything But." DeKalb (10:3) Spr 77, p. 46.

ROBINSON, Edward R.
"Hymn for Soldiers Who Have Lain in the Snow." Poetry (129:5)
F 77, p. 284.

ROBINSON, Frank K.
"amsterdam: departure" (for klaus). Mouth (13) D 77, p. 64.
"At the Elevator." Mouth (13) D 77, p. 64.
"Harmonics." Mouth (11/12) Mr-Je 77, p. 36.

ROBINSON, Jeannette
"I'm Gonna Always." BlackF (2:1) Wint 77-78, p. 25.
"Lady Dressed in Blue." Obs (3:1) Spr 77, p. 66.

ROBINSON, Kit
"Pink Slip." Hills (4) 77.
"Doorbells." Hills (4) 77.

ROBINSON, Margaret A.
"Tongue." CarlMis (17:1) Wint 77-78, p. 61.

ROBINSON, Sondra Till
"Blue Bread." SoDakR (15:2) Sum 77, p. 53.
"The Line of Time." SoDakR (15:2) Sum 77, p. 54.

ROBLES, Mary Lou
"1974." ArizQ (33:3) Aut 77, p. 248.

ROBSON, Evelyn
Eight poems (tr. of Andre Frenaud, w. John Montague). MalR
(43) Jl 77, p. 77.

ROBSON, Ros
"Bullfight." SmPd (14:1) Wint 77, p. 16.

ROCHA, Adrian
"Silver Saddle." Sam (59) 77, p. 57.

ROCHELLE, Larry
"Craft." SmPd (14:1) Wint 77, p. 19.

RODGERS, Katherine
"A Piece of May." CarouselQ (2:3) Wint 77, p. 7.
"The Rainstorm." CarouselQ (2:3) Wint 77, p. 7.

RODRIGUES, Manolo
"sitting here alone in." SeC (5:2) 78, p. 30.

RODRIGUEZ, Shawn
"Crazy John." SeC (5:2) 78, p. 32.
"My Grandmother." SeC (5:2) 78, p. 31.

RODRIGUEZ, William Robert
"The Cop." Epoch (26:3) Spr 77, p. 272.

"crazy horse." Icarus (5:2) Aut 77, p. 7.

ROGERS, Pattiann
"Cannon." KanQ (9:1) Wint 77, p. 95.

ROGERS, W. E.
"Sculpture at an Exhibition." ConcPo (10:2) Aut 77, p. 34.

ROGOFF, Jay
"Sister." Shen (29:1) Aut 77, p. 79.

ROHRER, Jane
"Going to Kerkyra." AmerPoR (6:5) S-O 77, p. 47.
"In the Kitchen before Dinner." AmerPoR (6:5) S-O 77, p. 48.
"Mennonite Funeral in the Shenandoah Valley." AmerPoR (6:5)
    S-O 77, p. 47.

ROKEAH, David
"Abdath" (tr. by Ruth and Matthew Mead). TriQ (39) Spr 77,
    p. 301.
"You Know" (tr. by Ruth and Matthew Mead). TriQ (39) Spr 77,
    p. 301.
"You Let Me Go" (tr. by Ruth and Matthew Mead). TriQ (39)
    Spr 77, p. 302.

ROLLINS, Heather
"A kite is like a wagon." AAR (27) 77, p. 116.

ROMAN, Howard
"Bird." Gra (12) 77, p. 16.
"Bird of Brief Paradise." AAR (27) 77, p. 80.
"A Chinese Saucer." StoneC (77:2) My 77, p. 22.
"For Mars and Beyond." PoetL (72:2) Sum 77, p. 77.
"Horseshoe Crabs." Gra (12) 77, p. 50.
"Prophecy." StoneC (77:2) My 77, p. 22.

ROMNEY, Walter
"Sadness Is Sad." QW (3) Spr-Sum 77, p. 31.

RONAN, John
"afternoons." Focus (12:76) Jl-Ag 77, p. 25.
"Boston Marathon, April 1976." SouthernPR (17:2) Aut 77,
    p. 7.
"the hospital." Focus (12:76) Jl-Ag 77, p. 25.
"tidal pool." Focus (12:76) Jl-Ag 77, p. 25.

RONAN, Richard
"Drag." Mouth (11/12) Mr-Je 77, p. 43.
"The History of Kabuki." Mouth (13) D 77, p. 33.
"hither he huts it." Mouth (11/12) Mr-Je 77, p. 49.
"Mud Dancing." Mouth (13) D 77, p. 10.
"one night." Mouth (13) D 77, p. 11.
"Le Pont." Mouth (11/12) Mr-Je 77, p. 45.

"Tonight. " Mouth (11/12) Mr-Je 77, p. 41.
"Violet Eye. " Mouth (11/12) Mr-Je 77, p. 37.

RONAN, Richard L.
"Gacela. " US1 (9) Spr 77, p. 10.
"Journeys. " US1 (9) Spr 77, p. 11.
"White. " US1 (9) Spr 77, p. 10.

RONCI, Ray
"The Drunk. " Iowa (8:4) Aut 77, p. 64.
"Racing. " Iowa (8:4) Aut 77, p. 63.
"The Time It Will Take. " Iowa (8:4) Aut 77, p. 63.

RONDIN, Leslie
"Come Put Your Hand. " Field (17) Aut 77, p. 17.
"Heraclitus. " Field (17) Aut 77, p. 18.

RONEY, K. E.
"Letter to Yeats. " MontG (5) Wint 77, p. 42.

ROOSEVELT, Lisa
"My friend, Sandra, is like spice. " AAR (27) 77, p. 123.

ROOT, Judith C.
"The Real Thing. " ParisR (71) Aut 77, p. 40.
"To Pose a Chicken" (after Norman Rockwell). ParisR (71) Aut
77, p. 39.

ROOT, William Pitt
"Arctic. " Nat (225:15) 5 N 77, p. 472.
"Coot Tells It Like It Never Was. " NewYRB (24:6) 14 Ap 77,
p. 7.
"Dreamwalker. " Bits (6) Jl 77.
"Sometimes Heaven Is a Mean Machine" (for Wayne). Nat
(225:20) 10 D 77, p. 633.
"Song of the Dawncock" (For Lisalotte). MontG (5) Wint 77,
p. 52.

ROPER, Renee
"All by Hisself. " Nimrod (21:2/22:1) 77, p. 229.

ROSE, Diane
"I died last night and awoke. " Pig (3) 77, p. 60.

ROSE, Harriet
"Little Sister of the Flesh. " Confr (14) Spr-Sum 77, p. 127.

ROSE, Lynne Carol
"Christmas Eve. " GRR (8:1/2) 77, p. 48.
"The End of the Story. " GRR (8:3) 77, p. 184.
"The Fawn" (for Imogen Cunningham [1883-1976]). EnPas (4) 76,
p. 32.
"The Habit of Doubt. " GRR (8:3) 77, p. 182.

"The Housekeeper." GRR (8:3) 77, p. 186.
"Looking up at the Stars." GRR (8:3) 77, p. 180.
"Revelation." GRR (8:1/2) 77, p. 49.
"The Sideshow." HiramPoR (23) Wint 77, p. 30.
"Summer Solstice." GRR (8:1/2) 77, p. 119.
"Surviving the Winter." GRR (8:1/2) 77, p. 48.
"This Man I Carry On My Back." BelPoJ (28:2) Wint 77-78, p. 25.
"Trying to Solve The Mystery." GRR (8:3) 77, p. 188.
"The View from the Hill." HiramPoR (22) Aut-Wint 77, p. 32.

ROSE, Wendy
"Dancing with the New Katcina." Waters (6) 77, p. 36.
"Magic Marker." Waters (6) 77, p. 31.
"Netsuke" (for Ron Tanaka, Sacramento, 1974). Waters (6) 77, p. 13.

ROSELIEP, Raymond
"Enter Flowergarden, Ant Couple." Bits (6) Jl 77.
"House." NewL (43:4) Sum 77, p. 56.
"Marianne Moore." HolCrit (14:2) Ap 77, p. 13.
"My Country 'Tis." NewL (43:4) Sum 77, p. 57.
"Night Piece." PoNow (14/18) 77, p. 150.
"Noël." ChrC (94:41) 14 D 77, p. 1157.
"Postcard." PoNow (14/18) 77, p. 150.
"Rose-Breasted Grosbeak." ChrC (94:18) 18 My 77, p. 470.
"A Sequence of Bells." ChrC (94:42) 21 D 77, p. 1189.
"Skid Row." ChrC (94:37) 16 N 77, p. 1058.
"Song." PoNow (14/18) 77, p. 150.
Two Haiku. WindO (28) Spr 77, p. 21.

ROSEN, Kenneth
"Color." KanQ (9:1) Wint 77, p. 102.

ROSEN, Michael
"Iceage." Icarus (5:1) Spr 77, p. 7.
"Into the Heartland." Focus (12:77) S-O 77, p. 29.
"Is Forever Longer Than Always." Focus (12:77) S-O 77, p. 29.

ROSENBAUM, Harriet
"This Woman." StoneC (77:2) My 77, p. 10.

ROSENBERG, Betsy
"I Left" (tr. of Tuvia Ruebner). TriQ (39) Spr 77, p. 303.

ROSENBERG, D. M.
"The Old Hotel Metropole." CentR (21:2) Spr 77, p. 154.
"Vachel Lindsay's America." BallSUF (18:2) Spr 77, p. 2.

ROSENBERG, David
"Job Speaks" (tr. from the third chapter of the Hebrew Book of Job). NewRep (176:16) 16 Ap 77, p. 22.

ROSENBERG, Jeffrey
"Weekend." Mouth (13) D 77, p. 73.

ROSENBERG, Paul
"The Wait." DeKalb (10:3) Spr 77, p. 47.

ROSENBERGER, Francis Coleman
"On Literary Quality and Fame." SouthwR (62:3) Sum 77,
    p. 257.
"On the Economics of Publishing Poetry." ArizQ (33:2) Sum 77,
    p. 180.

ROSENFELD, June
"Late." Aspen (3) Spr 77, p. 128.
"Sundays in March Any Year But Not This One." Aspen (3) Spr
    77, p. 127.

ROSENMAN, John B.
"Gorilla." SouthernHR (11:4) Aut 77, p. 371.

ROSENSTOCK, Carl Paul
"The Great Gothic Scam." US1 (9) Spr 77, p. 3.

ROSENTHAL, Abby
"The Loaf." Gra (12) 77.

ROSENTHAL, M. L.
"A Friend in Hospital." Nat (224:5) 5 F 77, p. 158.
"Intimacy." Humanist (37:2) Mr-Ap 77, p. 55.
"Through Streets Where Smiling Children." ModernPS (8:2) Aut
    77, p. 134.

ROSENZWEIG, Phyllis
"There's a little beast." SunM (4) Aut 77, p. 111.

ROSHEIM, David L.
"Shorthand Novels." HiramPoR (23) Wint 77, p. 31.

ROSKOLENKO, Harry
"Baguio Poems." SoDakR (15:2) Sum 77, p. 6.
"Come unto Us Who Are ... laden." NewL (43:3) Spr 77,
    p. 72.
"Final Poem." NewL (43:3) Spr 77, p. 74.
"Nationalism." NewL (44:1) Aut 77, p. 73.
from Once Upon an Island: "The River." NewL (43:4) Sum 77,
    p. 24.
"Only God Can Make Me...." NewL (43:3) Spr 77, p. 73.
"Symbols." NewL (43:3) Spr 77, p. 75.
"View." NewL (44:1) Aut 77, p. 73.
"Waiting for God." NewL (43:3) Spr 77, p. 72.

ROSS, John
"Darcy's Ogre at the Arcata Hotel." LaB (7) My 77, p. 37.

ROSS, Martin W.
"Two Phosphorescent Verbs, by Definition. " StoneC (77:3) S 77, p. 22.

ROSS, Mary Nelson
"She Writes. " DeKalb (10:3) Spr 77, p. 48.
"The Three-Minute Affair. " DeKalb (10:3) Spr 77, p. 48.

ROSTEN, Norman
"Mandelstam. " NewYorker (52:48) 17 Ja 77, p. 108.

ROSTON, Ruth
"Folktale. " DacTerr (14) Spr-Sum 77, p. 9.
"Juggler. " DacTerr (14) Spr-Sum 77, p. 8.

ROTHENBERG, Jerome
"A Poem to Celebrate the Spring & Diane Rothenberg's Birthday. " Montra (3) Spr 77, p. 176.

ROWE, L. Bruce
"Summer, Platteville. " EngJ (66:5) My 77, p. 48.

ROWELL, Charles H.
"After Forty. " Nimrod (21:2/22:1) 77, p. 231.
"Alone. " Obs (3:3) Wint 77, p. 62.
"For a 'Gentleman. '" Obs (3:3) Wint 77, p. 62.
"Of Humankind" (for my students in English 313 who saw man as stasis--October 1975). SouthernHR (11:2) Spr 77, p. 144.
"Singing" (for verda talton who will not listen). Nimrod (21:2/22:1) 77, p. 233.
"Soft. " Obs (3:2) Sum 77, p. 50.

ROWL, Wayne
"Being Not There. " ArkRiv (3:4/4:1) 77, p. 68.

ROYSTER, Philip M.
"The Child in My Heart. " Obs (3:2) Sum 77, p. 37.
"Even in chains. " Obs (3:2) Sum 77, p. 38.
"Primeval. " Obs (3:2) Sum 77, p. 37.

ROZEWICZ, Tadeusz
"The Dream of John" (tr. by Victor Contoski). Chowder (9) Aut-Wint 77, p. 44.
"In Haste" (tr. by John M. Gogol). WebR (3:4) Aut 77, p. 37.
"Méliès" (tr. by Magnus Krynski and Robert Maguire). NewRep (176:12) 19 Mr 77, p. 34.

RUBENFELD, Andrew
"Chassis. " Mouth (11/12) Mr-Je 77, p. 64.
"Tandem. " Mouth (11/12) Mr-Je 77, p. 63.

RUBENSTEIN, Carol
"Prayer for Calling the Eagles" (tr. of Anonymous). Hand (1) 77, p. 162.

"Rite of Naming the Child" (tr. of Anonymous).   Hand (1) 77,
     p. 43.
"Spell to Speed Childbirth" (tr. of Anonymous).   Hand (1) 77,
     p. 43.

RUBENSTEIN, Elaine
"Father." Waters (5) 77, p. 15.

RUBIN, Larry
"Among the Missing." SouthernPR (16:SI) 77, p. 69.
"Apocalypse." CarlMis (16:1/2) Aut-Wint 76-77, p. 139.
"The Consolation of Philosophy." DenQ (12:2) Sum 77, p. 105.
"Diagnosis for a Time of Storm." SouthernPR (17:2) Aut 77,
     p. 43.
"The Extortioner." PoNow (14/18) 77, p. 151.
"Ghosts." Poem (31) N 77, p. 18.
"The Guest." KanQ (9:1) Wint 77, p. 45.
"In Emily's Garden." Poem (31) N 77, p. 17.
"Lessons of the Beach: Art and Seduction." FourQt (27:1) Aut
     77, p. 31.
"Lines for an Elderly Ex-Marine, in Remission." AmerR (26)
     N 77, p. 45.
"Lines to a Christian Friend, at Yuletide." CarlMis (16:1/2)
     Aut-Wint 76-77, p. 138.
"Notes on Art, Considered as an Antidote to Love." Wind (27)
     77, p. 50.
"The Photographer." KanQ (9:1) Wint 77, p. 44.
"The Poet's Harvest." Wind (27) 77, p. 51.
"Registered at the Bordello Hotel (Vienna)." NewL (43:3) Spr 77,
     p. 99.
"The Roots of Terror." PraS (51:2) Spr 77, p. 154.
"Seedtime and Harvest." MichQR (16:3) Sum 77, p. 330.
"Space Travel." Wind (27) 77, p. 51.
"The Surfers." PraS (51:2) Sum 77, p. 154.
"Survival in the Flood." SouthernPR (16:SI) 77, p. 69.
"To a Scottish Girl, Living in Saudi Arabia" (For Anne). FourQt
     (27:1) Aut 77, p. 30.
"A View from the Broadwalk." Wind (27) 77, p. 50.
"When the Bough Breaks." CarlMis (16:1/2) Aut-Wint 76-77,
     p. 138.

RUBIN, Stan
"My Three Year Old Coughing at Night." CarolQ (29:3) Aut 77,
     p. 89.

RUBY, Michael
"These Novembers" (for David Robert Herfort). HarvAd (111:2)
     D 77, p. 10.

RUCKER, Marlice Y.
"Flower Pretty." BlackF (2:1) Wint 77-78, p. 33.

RUDD, Jonathan
"The Moon." QW (3) Spr-Sum 77, p. 31.

RUDMAN, Mark
"Abilene." ParisR (71) Aut 77, p. 174.
"The House Beyond the Star" (tr. of Bohdan Antonych). Bound
    (5:2) Wint 77, p. 601.
"Houses" (tr. of Bohdan Antonych). Bound (5:2) Wint 77, p. 600.
"A Reprieve." Pequod (2:3) Sum 77, p. 51.
"Signals." VirQR (53:4) Aut 77, p. 719.
"Sunset" (tr. of Bohdan Antonych). Bound (5:2) Wint 77, p. 602.
"'To Love, to Go in Endless Thunder'" (tr. of Boris Pasternak,
    w. Bohdan Boychuk). Some (7/8) 76.
"A Village" (tr. of Bohdan Antonych). Bound (5:2) Wint 77,
    p. 600.
"Winter" (tr. of Bohdan Antonych). Bound (5:2) Wint 77, p. 602.

RUDOLF, Anthony
from Le Dieu de Nuit: "The First Word" (tr. of Jean-Claude
    Renard). GRR (8:1/2) 77, p. 26.
from Le Dieu de Nuit: "The Third Word" (tr. of Jean-Claude
    Renard). GRR (8:1/2) 77, p. 26.
from Le Dieu de Nuit: "The Fifth Word" (tr. of Jean-Claude
    Renard). GRR (8:1/2) 77, p. 26.

RUEBNER, Tuvia
"Among Iron Fragments" (tr. by Robert Friend). TriQ (39) Spr
    77, p. 302.
"I Left" (tr. by Betsy Rosenberg). TriQ (39) Spr 77, p. 303.
"Waking Up" (tr. by S. F. Chyet). TriQ (39) Spr 77, p. 303.

RUEFLE, Mary
"Smith River." CutB (8) Spr 77, p. 54.

RUFF, John
"Trying to Cash a Check" (for Sheridan Philip Reilly). DacTerr
    (14) Spr-Sum 77, p. 51.

RUFFIN, Paul D.
"The antiChrist." LittleR (12) 77, p. 20.
"Crossing the Andes." TexQ (20:4) Wint 77, p. 101.
"Grandma Arnold and the Bomb." NewRivR (2:1) 77, p. 17.
"Grandma Arnold at the Skin Flick." NewRivR (2:1) 77, p. 18.
"Manhunt." SouthernPR (16:SI) 77, p. 70.
"Patsy's Transfiguration." Qt (57/58) Wint-Spr 77, p. 37.
"A Sign in April." TexQ (20:4) Wint 77, p. 100.

RUGGIERI, Helen
"Peony Sequence I." NewC (7:3) 75-76, p. 26.

RUGGLES, Eugene
"An Opening" (For My Mother). NewYorker (52:49) 24 Ja 77,
    p. 38.

RUHL, Steven
"Two Postcards from Cedar Springs, Pennsylvania." SmPd
    (14:2) Spr 77, p. 16.

RUIZ, Anita
"A hundred years from now." SeC (5:2) 78, p. 56.

RUIZ, Dolly
"Bubble Gum." SeC (5:2) 78, p. 58.
"A hundred years from now there will." SeC (5:2) 78, p. 57.

RUMI
"The Coat" (tr. by John Eskow). Some (7/8) 76.
"Ghazal" (tr. by W. S. Merwin, w. Talat Sait Halman). Nat
    (224:6) 12 F 77, p. 190.
"The Singing Reed" (tr. by Jascha Kessler, w. Amin Banani).
    CentR (21:1) Wint 77, p. 72.
"Words for the Doorman (At the Tavern of the Void)" (tr. by
    John Eskow). Some (7/8) 76.

RUMMEL, Mary Kay
"Antique Table." StoneC (77:2) My 77, p. 12.

RUNCIMAN, Alexander, Jr.
"Why You Give to the American Cancer Society." CarolQ (29:1)
    Wint 77, p. 91.

RUNCIMAN, Lex
"Damages." Antaeus (27) Aut 77, p. 114.
"The Possum on Oleson Road." Antaeus (27) Aut 77, p. 116.

RUSSELL, Norman H.
"the dream which is mine." PoNow (14/18) 77, p. 151.
"the eyes of the child." KanQ (9:1) Wint 77, p. 121.
"a lesson for you." PoNow (14/18) 77, p. 151.

RUSSELL, Peter
"Brock." MalR (42) Ap 77, p. 81.

RUSSELL, R. Stephen
"Eating from a Sack of Oranges" (for Nancy). KanQ (9:4) Aut
    77, p. 4.

RUSSELL, Randy
"An Apology." MidwQ (18:3) Spr 77, p. 265.
"Exultation." MidwQ (18:3) Spr 77, p. 266.

RUSSELL, Timothy
"To the Fifteen Miners Not Accounted For in Kentucky." SenR
    (8:2) D 77, p. 89.

RUSSO, George
"The Tunnel Called Hubbard's Cave." DeKalb (10:2) Wint 77,
    p. 52.

RUST, Gary
"In Kansas." ArkRiv (3:4/4:1) 77, p. 42.

"State Fair." ArkRiv (3:4/4:1) 77, p. 40.

RUTH, Barbara
"mindbodyrush." Paunch (48/49) S 77, p. 123.
"The Undertaste." Paunch (48/49) S 77, p. 124.

RUTLEDGE, Steve
"Hourglass." Poem (30) Jl 77, p. 4.
"Morning." Poem (30) Jl 77, p. 3.

RUTSALA, Vern
"Clukov and Rambian." PoetryNW (18:1) Spr 77, p. 54.
"Disappearing." OhioR (18:3) Aut 77, p. 62.
"Double." PoNow (14/18) 77, p. 151.
"Footsie." ThRiPo (10) 77, p. 35.
"Gravel, Roads, Fathers, Idaho, Hobos, Memory." MissR (6:1)
    77, p. 90.
"Killers." PoNow (14/18) 77, p. 151.
"The Mystery of Lost Shoes." ParisR (70) Sum 77, p. 41.
"Not Listening to Canadian Radio." ChiR (29:1) Sum 77, p. 30.
"On a Binge with Dakota Slim." PoetryNW (18:1) Spr 77, p. 52.
"Snow." ChiR (29:1) Sum 77, p. 31.
"Thank You Note." ThRiPo (10) 77, p. 36.
"The War of the Worlds." Drag (16) 77.

RYAN, Heather
"Double Date--Driver Unidentified." HangL (29) Wint 76-77,
    p. 77.
"Here's to You, and Here's to Me!" (for J. R.). HangL (29)
    Wint 76-77, p. 76.
"Reaching for the Sky." HangL (30) Sum 77, p. 78.

RYAN, Margaret
"Arachne." Madem (83:5) My 77, p. 195.
"Stitching." KanQ (9:3) Sum 77, p. 86.

RYAN, Michael
"Consider a Move." NewYorker (53:34) 10 O 77, p. 102.
"Gangster Dreams." Atl (239:5) My 77, p. 62.
"Nameless." Ploughs (3:3/4) 77, p. 76.
"1976." PoNow (14/18) 77, p. 151.
"Poem at Thirty." Antaeus (27) Aut 77, p. 73.
"You Can Thank." Ploughs (3:3/4) 77, p. 77.

RYDER, Salmon
"The Argo Merchant." US1 (9) Spr 77. p. 12.
"Glass Objects Clouded and Crazed Inside." US1 (9) Spr 77,
    p. 11.
"Naked." US1 (9) Spr 77, p. 12.

RYDER, Vanessa
"Finial." Salm (38/39) Sum-Aut 77, p. 48.
"Illumination from a Psalter." Ploughs (3:3/4) 77, p. 54.

"Marconi among the Angels." Salm (38/39) Sum-Aut 77, p. 47.
"Provincetown: February." Ploughs (3:3/4) 77, p. 53.
"The Steerage, 1907." Salm (38/39) Sum-Aut 77, p. 48.

RYOKAN
  "Offering" (tr. by Graeme Wilson). WestHR (31:1) Wint 77,
    p. 60.

SABATIUK, Lynn
  "January 30, 1977 ... The body of." Waters (5) 77, p. 9.

al-SABOUR, Salah Abd
  "Exodus" (tr. by Sargon Boulus). Mund (10:1) 77, p. 58.

SACHS, Nelly
  "I Saw You Again" (tr. by D. G. H. Schramm). WebR (3:4) Aut
    77, p. 16.

SADAIE, Fujiwara no
  Five Waka (tr. by Erskine Lane). Bleb (12) 77, p. 50.

SADAYORI, Fujiwara no
  "Rat" (tr. by Graeme Wilson). WestHR (31:1) Wint 77, p. 57.

SADEH, Pinhas
  "In the Forest" (tr. by Harris Lenowitz). QW (3) Spr-Sum 77,
    p. 58.
  "In the Garden of the Turkish Consulate" (tr. by Harris Lenowitz).
    QW (3) Spr-Sum 77, p. 59.

SADOFF, Ira
  "Alienation from Nature." Esq (87:1) Ja 77, p. 43.
  "Disaster Viewed from an Airplane." Salm (36) Wint 77, p. 40.
  "Open the Window." MissR (6:1) 77, p. 17.
  "Poem for the Lost." PoNow (14/18) 77, p. 152.
  "Pure Intelligence." Salm (36) Wint 77, p. 39.
  "Romance of the Religious." Gra (12) 77.
  "Romance of the Reluctant." Gra (12) 77.
  "Shelter Island, 1952." Hudson (30:3) Aut 77, p. 368.
  "Someone Plays the Piano." MissR (6:1) 77, p. 18.
  "Suite Française" (after Poulenc). Hudson (30:3) Aut 77, p. 370.
  "Windows." Hudson (30:3) Aut 77, p. 369.

SAFFORD, June Billings
  "On Making Tuna Sandwiches Before 7 A. M." EngJ (66:5) My 77,
    p. 56.

SAGAN, Miriam
  "At the Wedding." Sam (59) 77, p. 80.
  "The Bag of Waters." Madem (83:11) N 77, p. 106.
  "Girl in the Mirror." Chomo (4:2) Aut-Wint 77, p. 3.
  "Lovers in a Garden." Ploughs (3:3/4) 77, p. 105.
  "Montage" (for Martha). Chomo (4:2) Aut-Wint 77, p. 4.

"Riddle. " Sam (55) 77, p. 4.
"Thank You. " Sam (59) 77, p. 81.
"Wave. " Sam (59) 77, p. 81.

SAGER, Bonnie
"Writing is very hard to do. " AAR (27) 77, p. 98.

SAGSTETTER, Karen
"Half the Story. " Paunch (48/49) S 77, p. 193.
"Half the Story. " Shen (29:1) Aut 77, p. 66.

SAHA, P. K.
"Language Lessons. " Bits (6) Jl 77.

SAHA, Pamela
"Halloween. " YaleLit (146:4/5) 77, p. 39.

SAIGYO
"Approaching Death and Enlightenment" (tr. by Robert G. Sewell).
    DenQ (12:2) Sum 77, p. 126.
"Becoming a Priest and Escape into Nature" (tr. by Robert G.
    Sewell). DenQ (12:2) Sum 77, p. 124.
"Deep in the mountains" (tr. by William R. LaFleur). DenQ
    (12:2) Sum 77, p. 128.
"Desolation" (tr. by Graeme Wilson). DenQ (12:2) Sum 77,
    p. 358.
"Dewdrop" (tr. by Graeme Wilson). WestHR (31:1) Wint 77,
    p. 58.
"The Maturing Landscape" (tr. by Robert G. Sewell). DenQ
    (12:2) Sum 77, p. 125.
"Patter of pathos--" (tr. by William R. LaFleur). DenQ (12:2)
    Sum 77, p. 127.
"Plum Trees" (tr. by Graeme Wilson). DenQ (12:2) Sum 77,
    p. 367.
"Propped up by my cane" (tr. by William R. LaFleur). DenQ
    (12:2) Sum 77, p. 128.
"Pushed along by wind" (tr. by William R. LaFleur). DenQ
    (12:2) Sum 77, p. 127.
"Reality" (tr. by Graeme Wilson). TexQ (20:4) Wint 77, p. 147.
"Secular Attachments and Religious Convictions" (tr. by Robert
    G. Sewell). DenQ (12:2) Sum 77, p. 124.
"Soulscape" (tr. by Graeme Wilson). DenQ (12:2) Sum 77, p. 56.
"The Sound of water" (tr. by William R. LaFleur). DenQ (12:2)
    Sum 77, p. 127.
"Stragglers" (tr. by Graeme Wilson). DenQ (12:2) Sum 77,
    p. 368.
"That night when we met" (tr. by William R. LaFleur). DenQ
    (12:2) Sum 77, p. 128.
"Unrequited Love" (tr. by Robert G. Sewell). DenQ (12:2) Sum
    77, p. 123.
"The wisps of smoke from Fuji" (tr. by William R. LaFleur).
    DenQ (12:2) Sum 77, p. 128.

ST. JOHN, Bruce
    "Truth." Nimrod (21:2/22:1) 77, p. 232.

ST. JOHN, David
    from The Notebook: "Orizaba, IV. 26." VirQR (53:4) Aut 77,
        p. 728.
    "A Sense of Things." AntR (35:2/3) Spr-Sum 77, p. 252.
    "The Shore." NewYorker (53:12) 9 My 77, p. 46.

ST. JOHN, Primus
    "Bedding Down." PoNow (14/18) 77, p. 152.
    "Eloma." AmerPoR (6:1) Ja-F 77, p. 28.
    from Notes on a Painter's Palette: (V). PortR (23) 77, p. 166.
    from Post Cards: (VII). PortR (23) 77, p. 167.
    from Skins on the Earth: "Lynching and Burning." PoNow
        (14/18) 77, p. 153.
    from Skins on the Earth: "Oluranti." PoNow (14/18) 77,
        p. 153.
    from Skins on the Earth: "The Morning Star." PoNow (14/18)
        77, p. 153.

ST. MAWR, Erin
    "Queen of Spades." Pig (3) 77, p. 95.
    "Requisition of the Winter Soldier." Pig (3) 77, p. 56.
    "Zen Heroin." Aieee (5/6) 77, p. 3.

ST. ROMAIN, Madeleine A.
    "arachnid." DeKalb (10:4) Sum 77, p. 47.
    "may first, 1973." DeKalb (10:4) Sum 77, p. 48.
    "Short Chant At Moonrise As Sung by One Who Has Never Before
        Beheld the Moon." DeKalb (10:4) Sum 77, p. 49.

ST VINCENT, Paul
    "Adult Education." MinnR (NS8) Spr 77, p. 13.
    "Blaxploitation." MinnR (NS8) Spr 77, p. 13.
    "The Dressing Gown." WormR (65/66) 77, p. 33.
    "Everyman and His Woman." MinnR (NS8) Spr 77, p. 14.
    "Lambchops Has a Problem." MinnR (NS8) Spr 77, p. 12.
    "Ode on the Death of a Rich Man." MinnR (NS8) Spr 77, p. 11.
    "Philpot Embarasses the Headmaster." WormR (65/66) 77,
        p. 32.
    "Top of the Tree." WormR (65/66) 77, p. 31.
    "200 Percent Black." WormR (65/66) 77, p. 33.

SAKANOE, Otomo no
    "Understanding" (tr. by Graeme Wilson). DenQ (11:4) Wint 77,
        p. 164.

SAKUTARO, Hagiwara
    "Blue Sky" (tr. by Graeme Wilson). DenQ (12:2) Sum 77, p. 62.
    "Ear" (tr. by Graeme Wilson). DenQ (12:2) Sum 77, p. 63.
    "Group of Three Persons" (tr. by Graeme Wilson). DenQ (12:2)
        Sum 77, p. 289.

"When I Awoke" (tr. by Graeme Wilson). TexQ (20:4) Wint 77,
    p. 144.
"Winter" (tr. by Graeme Wilson). WestHR (31:3) Sum 77,
    p. 214.

SALAAM, Kalamu ya
    "Hard News for Hip Harry. " Nimrod (21:2/22:1) 77, p. 238.
    "Like Brothers Do. " Nimrod (21:2/22:1) 77, p. 236.
    "Unfinished Business. " Nimrod (21:2/22:1) 77, p. 234.

SALEH, Dennis
    from 100 Chameleons: "Chameleon Ranch. " ParisR (69) Spr 77,
    p. 158.

SALERNO, Joseph
    "After Working. " MichQR (16:2) Spr 77, p. 196.

SALERNO, Salvatore, Jr.
    "Coffee? Wine!?" WormR (65/66) 77, p. 2.
    "Koan. " WormR (65/66) 77, p. 4.

SALKEY, Andrew
    "Deep Footprints" (On Ho Chi Minh's Birthday, May 19th 1975).
    Nimrod (21:2/22:1) 77, p. 242.
    "Dry River Bed. " Nimrod (21:2/22:1) 77, p. 240.
    "Postcard from Jamaica, 9.1.1976" (for Genevieve Eckenstein).
    Nimrod (21:2/22:1) 77, p. 243.

SALLAR, William
    "Frontispiece. " KanQ (9:2) Spr 77, p. 18.

SALSMAN, Marcia
    "Winning. " ArkRiv (3:4/4:1) 77, p. 4.
    "Wrenning Day. " ArkRiv (3:4/4:1) 77, p. 5.

SALTER, Mary Jo
    "The Aquarium Lesson. " Ploughs (3:3/4) 77, p. 86.

SALTMAN, Benjamin
    "Fish Gutting. " PoNow (14/18) 77, p. 152.

SALZMANN, Jerome
    "Horses. " Rapp (10) 77, p. 85.

SAMPERI, Frank
    "The Kingdom. " Hand (1) 77, p. 130.

SAMPSON, Dennis
    "Mornings My Uncle Couldn't Work, He Would. " PoNow (14/18)
    77, p. 152.

SAMUELSON, Janet
    "Expedition. " NewOR (5:3) 77, p. 203.

SANCHEZ, Sonia
 "Kwa Mama Zetu Waliotuzaa. " Nimrod (21:2/22:1) 77, p. 245.
 "Notes from a Journal. " AmerPoR (6:5) S-O 77, p. 30.
 "Poem No. 7. " Nimrod (21:2/22:1) 77, p. 244.
 "Present. " AmerPoR (6:1) Ja-F 77, p. 27.
 "Rebirth. " AmerPoR (6:1) Ja-F 77, p. 27.

SANDBANK, Shimon
 "Folk Tune" (tr. of Esther Raab, w. Robert Friend). TriQ (39)
 Spr 77, p. 294.
 "Today I Am Modest" (tr. of Esther Raab, w. Robert Friend).
 TriQ (39) Spr 77, p. 295.

SANDERS, Scott
 "Bats. " Aspen (4) Aut 77, p. 63.
 "The Dog Who Wanted to Be Human. " Aspen (4) Aut 77, p. 62.

SANDLER, Linda
 "Collage for Lady Oracle. " MalR (41) Ja 77, p. 146.

SANDLER, Suellen
 "The Bruise. " SenR (8:2) D 77, p. 78.
 "Dear Dad. " SenR (8:2) D 77, p. 77.

SANDRY, Ellen
 "Doors and Windows. " CarouselQ (2:2) Aut 77, p. 15.

SANDY, Stephen
 "Bunkers. " PoNow (14/18) 77, p. 154.
 "Condensation. " Iowa (8:4) Aut 77, p. 92.
 "The Hunt. " PoNow (14/18) 77, p. 154.
 "Nacelle. " Bits (6) Jl 77.
 "Prefect. " Atl (240:1) Jl 77, p. 45.

SANER, Reg
 "Clarissima Lumina Mundi: Visiting New York. " Iowa (8:2)
 Spr 77, p. 17.
 "Clear Night, Small Fire, No Wind. " Poetry (131:2) N 77,
 p. 76.
 from Climbing into the Roots: "Cony Creek. " PoNow (14/18)
 77, p. 153.
 from Climbing into the Roots: "Stoning the River. " PoNow
 (14/18) 77, p. 153.
 from Climbing into the Roots: "The Delicate Breathing of Small
 Animals. " PoNow (14/18) 77, p. 153.
 "The Day the Air Was on Fire. " Iowa (8:2) Spr 77, p. 14.
 "Let's Say You Are This Page. " Iowa (8:2) Spr 77, p. 18.
 "Milking the Snowbank. " Poetry (131:2) N 77, p. 73.
 "Neither Lions Ravens nor White Toads. " Poetry (131:2) N 77,
 p. 75.
 "One for the Deer. " PoetryNW (18:1) Spr 77, p. 49.
 "Prayer to St. Francis Among Others. " Epoch (27:1) Aut 77,
 p. 51.

"Return to Tundra at Bighorn Flats: For Anne." ThRiPo (10)
     77, p. 27.
"Stitchwork." Poetry (131:2) N 77, p. 74.
"Traverse." Iowa (8:2) Spr 77, p. 15.

SANGE, Gary
"Real Santa." PoNow (14/18) 77, p. 155.
"Whirling Lawn." Shen (29:1) Aut 77, p. 62.

SANTOS, Lynne McMahon
"Late at Night, with Asthma and a Book of Chinese Poems."
     PortR (23) 77, p. 68.
"You Want to Call Her Name." PortR (23) 77, p. 69.

SANTOS, Victor R., Jr.
"Leper's Wish." Mouth (13) D 77, p. 80.

SARAC, Tahsin
"Desert Pain" (tr. by Belgi Paksoy). WebR (3:1) Wint 77, p. 36.
"In Anatolia" (tr. by Belgi Paksoy). WebR (3:1) Wint 77, p. 35.

SARGENT, Dana
"The Facile Repenter." ChrC (94:20) 1 Je 77, p. 526.
"The Sleeping Divinity Student." ChrC (94:4) 2-9 F 77, p. 82.

SARGENT, Robert
"Request to the Old Forerunners." HolCrit (14:3) Je 77, p. 13.
"Satan, Second Thoughts." KanQ (9:1) Wint 77, p. 112.

SATO, Hiroaki
"Age" (tr. of Taeko Tomioka). DenQ (12:2) Sum 77, p. 227.
"Fine Day" (tr. of Taeka Tomioka). DenQ (12:2) Sum 77,
     p. 228.
"Nights" (tr. of Taeko Tomioka). DenQ (12:2) Sum 77, p. 226.
"Skylark Nest" (tr. of Sakutaro Hagiwara). Montra (3) Spr 77,
     p. 37.
Twenty poems (tr. of Kotaro Takamura). Montra (3) Spr 77,
     pp. 107-29.

SAUL, George Brandon
"The Herdsman's Lament: Fifteenth Century." ArizQ (33:4)
     Wint 77, p. 318.
"In Borrowed Light." ArizQ (33:1) Spr 77, p. 25.

SAUL, Julie
"Old Record." QW (3) Spr-Sum 77, p. 94.

SAULS, Roger
"A History of Snow Late at Night." Kayak (44) F 77, p. 24.
"In the Mirror." Kayak (44) F 77, p. 25.
"Looking for Help in the Sea, in the Sky." Kayak (44) F 77,
     p. 26.
"Our Lady of the Snow." CarolQ (29:1) Wint 77, p. 68.

"Photograph, 1951." CarolQ (29:1) Wint 77, p. 70.

SAUNDERS, Virginia A. W.
"To My Husband." DeKalb (10:3) Spr 77, p. 50.

SAVAS, Kristen
"At night I hear my dog barking." AAR (27) 77, p. 108.

SAVITT, Lynne
"Dry Dream." YellowBR (9) 77, p. 9.
"I Keep Thinking of Your Hands as Feet." Gra (12) 77, p. 21.
"Summer Romance." Gra (12) 77.

SAYEGH, Tawfig
"No, and Why" (tr. by Sargon Boulus). Mund (10:1) 77, p. 71.

SAYRES, William
"Hercule Poirot and Maigret and Miss New Jersey City." WormR
  (65/66) 77, p. 1.
"King Kong Revisited." WormR (65/66) 77, p. 2.

al-SAYYAB, Badr Shakir
"Mirage City" (tr. by Sargon Boulus). Mund (10:1) 77, p. 62.

SCAMMACCA, Nat
"Longly I Sit" (tr. by Jack Hirschman). LaB (7) My 77, p. 36.

SCANTLEBURY, Linda
"Losing Argument." Poem (29) Mr 77, p. 2.
"Water Beauty Down." Poem (29) Mr 77, p. 1.

SCARBROUGH, George
"Daddy." SouthernPR (16:SI) 77, p. 71.
"Pied Beauty." PoNow (14/18) 77, p. 155.
"Root Cellar." PoNow (14/18) 77, p. 155.

SCATES, Maxine
"The Visit." CutB (8) Spr 77, p. 76.

SCHACTER, Mark
"A Panegyric on the Pencil." YaleLit (145:5) 77, p. 8.

SCHAEFER, Ted
"Pop Quiz." Sam (59) 77, p. 78.
"Sentenced to 120 Years, the Prisoner Escapes 63 Years Early."
  NewL (43:4) Sum 77, p. 64.
"The Testament of Abigail Williams." WebR (3:4) Aut 77, p. 63.
"Your Dream" (For Tricia). NewL (43:4) Sum 77, p. 64.
"The Youth Hostel." NewL (43:4) Sum 77, p. 65.

SCHAEFFER, Chere
"Hallway." EngJ (66:5) My 77, p. 48.

SCHAEFFER, Elizabeth
"I wish I was a flower." AAR (27) 77, p. 113.

SCHAEFFER, Susan Fromberg
"Accomplishments." EnPas (4) 76, p. 9.
"Alleys, Etc." CalQ (11/12) Wint-Spr 77, p. 139.
"Alphabet: F." Epoch (26:2) Wint 77, p. 136.
"Alphabet: S." Epoch (26:2) Wint 77, p. 137.
"As One." ColEng (39:2) O 77, p. 217.
"The Bible of the Beasts of the Little Field." CentR (21:3) Sum
    77, p. 273.
"By Her Own Hand." ColEng (39:2) O 77, p. 218.
"The Child." Juice (5) 77.
"Child in the Woods." Bound (5:3) Spr 77, p. 879.
"Country Store." PoNow (14/18) 77, p. 156.
"The Creatures." Juice (5) 77.
"The Exit." CarlMis (17:1) Wint 77-78, p. 66.
"For Elizabeth Taylor." Juice (5) 77.
"Here." KanQ (9:3) Sum 77, p. 10.
"In Flight." Bound (5:3) Spr 77, p. 880.
"The King's Melancholy." CarlMis (17:1) Wint 77-78, p. 64.
"Lady at Night." DacTerr (14) Spr-Sum 77, p. 25.
"Lady with a Floating Bird." DacTerr (14) Spr-Sum 77, p. 24.
"Messages in Bottles." MoonsLT (2:3) 77, p. 71.
"The Moles: Twitchell Cemetery, Vermont." DenQ (12:1) Spr 77,
    p. 184.
"The Months and Their Phases." DenQ (12:1) Spr 77, p. 179.
"The Old Diaries." Bound (5:3) Spr 77, p. 882.
"The Service." PoNow (14/18) 77, p. 157.
"Sign." DenQ (12:1) Spr 77, p. 183.
"Sonora." ColEng (39:2) O 77, p. 214.
"The Stream." MoonsLT (2:3) 77, p. 70.
"Two People at Christmas." Bound (5:3) Spr 77, p. 885.
"Weather." Bound (5:3) Spr 77, p. 878.
"Where." ColEng (39:2) O 77, p. 216.
"Whom." ColEng (39:2) O 77, p. 213.

SCHAPER, Jo
"Anti-Howl." Sam (56) Sum 77, p. 53.
"Silver Dream." Sam (52) Ap 77, p. 32.

SCHARPER, Diane
"One." Stonecloud (6) 76, p. 142.

SCHAUBROEK, Beth
"For Anna Akhmatova." NewL (44:1) Aut 77, p. 105.

SCHAUS, Margaret
"In the Whites of Eyes" (tr. of Benjamin Peret, w. Jane Barnard
    and A. F. Moritz). Aieee (5/6) 77, p. 19.
"My Last Misfortunes" (To Yves Tanguy) (tr. of Benjamin Peret,
    w. Jane Barnard and A. F. Moritz). Aieee (5/6) 77, p. 17.

"Portrait of Andre Breton" (tr. of Benjamin Peret, w. Jane
    Barnard and A. F. Moritz). Aieee (5/6) 77, p. 18.
"Under a Beating Rain" (tr. of Benjamin Peret, w. Jane Barnard
    and A. F. Moritz). Aieee (5/6) 77, p. 26.

SCHEELE, Roy
    "A Counterpoise." Comm (104:19) 16 S 77, p. 583.
    "The Day Trip." Comm (104:9) 29 Ap 77, p. 264.
    Eight poems. SmF (6) Aut 77, p. 29.
    "A Fresh Slant." Comm (104:3) 4 F 77, p. 75.
    "Ryder's The Wood Road." Northeast (3:4) Aut-Wint 77-78,
        p. 5.

SCHEIBLI, Silvia
    "Goldfish on the Prowl" (tr. of Karl Krolow). Agni (7) 77,
        p. 109.
    "Terns in June." AAR (27) 77, p. 47.

SCHELL, Susan
    "Favorable Thoughts in an Unfavorable Time." KanQ (9:4) Aut
        77, p. 119.

SCHEMM, Ripley
    "Mapping My Father." OhioR (18:2) Spr-Sum 77, p. 66.

SCHIFF, Laura
    "Capital Punishment" (tr. of Nina Cassian, w. Virgil Nemoianu).
        AmerPoR (6:6) N-D 77, p. 29.
    "The Doors" (tr. of Nina Cassian, w. Virgil Nemoianu).
        AmerPoR (6:6) N-D 77, p. 29.
    "Lady of Miracles" (tr. of Nina Cassian, w. Virgil Nemoianu).
        AmerPoR (6:6) N-D 77, p. 29.
    "Notes on Saint Maurice" (tr. of Judit Tóth). AmerPoR (6:3)
        My-Je 77, p. 26.
    "Thanks" (tr. of Nina Cassian, w. Virgil Nemoianu). AmerPoR
        (6:6) N-D 77, p. 29.

SCHLOSS, David
    "The White Room." ParisR (70) Spr 77, p. 38.

SCHLOSSER, Robert
    "Stars Overhead." Sam (59) 77, p. 24.

SCHMID, Vernon
    "Dance Me the Epic of Ireland." ChrC (94:27) 31 Ag-7 S 77,
        p. 747.
    "Gallow Waltz." ChrC (94:27) 31 Ag-7 S 77, p. 750.
    "In from the Irish Fog." ChrC (94:27) 31 Ag-7 S 77, p. 749.

SCHMIDT, Tom
    "Spring, Northern California." HiramPoR (22) Aut-Wint 77,
        p. 33.
    "Wild Rosehips." PoNow (14/18) 77, p. 157.

SCHMITZ, Dennis
"Divining." Iowa (8:3) Sum 77, p. 58.
from Goodwill, Inc.: "The Chalk Angel." PoNow (14/18) 77,
    p. 158.
from Goodwill, Inc.: "The Mole." PoNow (14/18) 77, p. 158.
from Goodwill, Inc.: "Widow." PoNow (14/18) 77, p. 158.
"Hard Labor." PoNow (14/18) 77, p. 157.
"Making a Door." Iowa (8:3) Sum 77, p. 58.

SCHMONSEES, Richard
"Thrumming." Mouth (13) D 77, p. 81.

SCHNEIDER, Steven
"Craftsman." PortR (23) 77, p. 133.

SCHNELL, David
"Searching for Rocks." CarouselQ (2:3) Wint 77, p. 34.

SCHNELL, Hartmut
"Poem: 'The sea' is an entertaining excuse" (tr. of Rolf Dieter
    Brinkmann). NewL (43:3) Spr 77, p. 22.
"Red Tomatoes" (tr. of Rolf Dieter Brinkmann). NewL (43:3)
    Spr 77, p. 20.
"Tarzan" (tr. of Rolf Dieter Brinkmann). NewL (43:3) Spr 77,
    p. 20.
"To hear one of those" (tr. of Rolf Dieter Brinkmann). NewL
    (43:3) Spr 77, p. 22.
"Well, somehow" (tr. of Rolf Dieter Brinkmann). NewL (43:3)
    Spr 77, p. 19.

SCHOEBERLEIN, Marion
"Night and His Friend." CarouselQ (2:2) Aut 77, p. 16.
"Tell Me, What Are the Trees?" CarouselQ (2:2) Aut 77, p. 16.

SCHOR, Starry
"Risings." YaleR (67:2) Wint 78, p. 249.
"Sestina: Tegucigalpa." YaleLit (147:1) 77, p. 18.

SCHORB, E. M.
"No." NewL (44:1) Aut 77, p. 22.
"To a Rat." Chelsea (36) 77, p. 75.
"Winter Waking." HiramPoR (22) Aut-Wint 77, p. 34.

SCHOTT, Gordie
"I here footsteps." AAR (27) 77, p. 121.

SCHOTT, John
"Mushroom Man." Bits (6) Jl 77.

SCHOTT, Penelope Scambly
"Exploration and Discovery." YellowBR (9) 77, p. 28.

My Grandparents Were Married for Sixty-Five Years. JnlONJP
    (1:3, part 1) 76. Entire issue.
"Prologue to a Feminist Poetry Reading. " Shen (29:1) Aut 77,
    p. 59.
"7 Ways of Looking at a Blackbird. " CEACritic (39:2) Ja 77,
    p. 13.

SCHRAMM, D. G. H.
"Conversation with My Mother. " Mouth (11/12) Mr-Je 77,
    p. 102.
"I Saw You Again" (tr. of Nelly Sachs). WebR (3:4) Aut 77,
    p. 16.

SCHREIBER, Ron
"The Alphabet Poems. " Mouth (13) D 77, cover.
"Doing Shitwork. " Sparrow (33) Ja 77, p. 11.
"To G--. " Aspect (69) O-D 76, p. 18.

SCHREVENS, Linda
"In Conversation How to Say. " NoAmR (262:3) Aut 77, p. 42.

SCHROEDER, Evelyn R.
"Bells of September. " EngJ (66:5) My 77, p. 60.

SCHRYVER, Danny
"The Bus Ride. " AAR (27) 77, p. 104.

SCHUCHMAN, Dorothy
"Godiva in the Nursery. " Harp (254:1520) Ja 77, p. 29.

SCHULER, Ruth Wildes
"Craft. " Sam (55) 77, p. 20.
"Simpleton. " Sam (55) 77, p. 20.
"Window Shopping along Sausalito Streets. " YellowBR (8) 77,
    p. 24.

SCHULTE, Rainer
"Every day. " NewL (44:2) Wint 77, p. 46.
"Spoleto. " NewL (44:2) Wint 77, p. 46.
"Today. " NewL (44:2) Wint 77, p. 46.

SCHULTZ, Philip
"For the Wandering Jews. " NewYorker (53:2) 28 F 77, p. 30.
"Like Wings. " NewYorker (52:51) 7 F 77, p. 32.
"Main Streets. " Pequod (2:3) Sum 77, p. 12.

SCHULTZ, Robert
"Libretto: For the Fall of the Year. " CutB (8) Spr 77,
    p. 92.
"Nov. 1. " RemR (5) 77, p. 23.
"Of Bottles. " RemR (5) 77, p. 23.

SCHULZ, Bill
"Concrete. " KanQ (9:3) Sum 77, p. 121.
"Grace. " SenR (8:1) My 77, p. 62.

SCHURCH, Maylan
"The North Side of Central. " BallSUF (18:3) Sum 77, p. 50.

SCHÜRMANN, Reiner
"Cruel Assortments" (tr. of René Char, w. Helen Bishop and
    Dale Ponikvar). Bound (5:3) Spr 77, p. 755.

SCHUTTING, Jutta
"Häuser. " ChiR (29:3) Wint 78, p. 108.
"Namen. " ChiR (29:3) Wint 78, p. 106.

SCHWARTZ, Delmore
from The Studies of Narcissus: Three Unpublished Poems.
    SouthernR (13:3) Sum 77, p. 591.

SCHWARTZ, Donna
"Once I was walking and I met my. " AAR (27) 77, p. 124.

SCHWARTZ, Hillel
"A Tour of the City. " PraS (51:4) Wint 77-78, p. 387.

SCHWARTZ, Howard
"Beginning. " Bleb (12) 77, p. 49.
"Esha. " Bleb (12) 77, p. 47.
"Eve. " Bleb (12) 77, p. 46.
"Jacob's Blessing. " WebR (3:2) Spr 77, p. 63.
"Legend. " WebR (3:2) Spr 77, p. 65.
"The Nameless. " Bleb (12) 77, p. 45.
"The Sailors. " Bleb (12) 77, p. 48.
"A Song" (for Reena). Hand (1) 77, p. 210.
"A Tale of Two Sisters" (for Carol Baum). WebR (3:2) Spr 77,
    p. 66.
"The Temple Vessels" (for Gershom Sholem). WebR (3:2) Spr
    77, p. 64.

SCHWARTZ, Jeffrey
"Of Dreams & Bathrooms & Death" (-for Jeff Katz). HangL (31)
    Aut 77, p. 65.

SCHWARTZ, Lloyd
"Childhood. " AmerR (26) N 77, p. 192.
"Double Life. " SenR (8:1) My 77, p. 74.
"Theocritus Schwartz. " SenR (8:1) My 77, p. 77.

SCOTELLARO, Robert
"Gramma. " Vaga (26) 77, p. 69.
"'he's read them all. '" Vaga (26) 77, p. 70.
"the junkies. " Vaga (26) 77, p. 70.
"The Pigeons. " Vaga (26) 77, p. 69.

SCOTT, Dennis
   "Homesong." Nimrod (21:2/22:1) 77, p. 255.
   "I-Song." Nimrod (21:2/22:1) 77, p. 256.
   "Lemonsong" (for Moncada, and my son). Nimrod (21:2/22:1) 77,
      p. 252.

SCOTT, Herbert
   from Groceries: Ten poems. PoNow (14/18) 77, pp. 159-160.
   "The Man Who Would Be a Mother." MissR (6:1) 77, p. 109.

SCULLY, James
   "Postscript." MinnR (NS8) Spr 77, p. 40.

SEABURG, Alan
   "Emily and Henry." KanQ (9:3) Sum 77, p. 50.
   "Henry Reading." KanQ (9:3) Sum 77, p. 50.
   "The Spring of '62." BallSUF (18:2) Spr 77, p. 66.
   "Two Women." KanQ (9:4) Aut 77, p. 4.

SEARS, Peter
   "Horse Head Swamp." Field (16) Spr 77, p. 12.
   "The Man Who Reads Your Whole Library." DacTerr (14) Spr-
      Sum 77, p. 23.
   "The Road." PoNow (14/18) 77, p. 161.
   "Time of Mud." Field (16) Spr 77, p. 13.
   "We Went Dreaming the Valley of the Black Soil." Chowder (8)
      Spr-Sum 77, p. 12.

SEATON, Esta
   "Love." Wind (24) 77, p. 61.
   "October." Wind (24) 77, p. 61.
   "The Poet from Amherst." Wind (24) 77, p. 61.

SEATON, J. P.
   "The Day" (ad. from Tufu). CarolQ (29:2) Spr-Sum 77, p. 122.
   from Drinking Wine: "I built my hut within man's sphere" (tr.
      of T'ao Ch'ien). CarolQ (29:2) Spr-Sum 77, p. 121.
   from Drinking Wine: "The orchid, hidden, growing, in the
      court" (tr. of T'ao Ch'ien). CarolQ (29:2) Spr-Sum 77,
      p. 121.
   "Fording the Han" (tr. of Li P'in). CarolQ (29:2) Spr-Sum 77,
      p. 120.
   "Going This Path" (tr. of Anonymous). CarolQ (29:2) Spr-Sum
      77, p. 120.

SEBENTHALL, R. E.
   "Cellars." Northeast (3:4) Aut-Wint 77-78, p. 15.
   "History." Northeast (3:4) Aut-Wint 77-78, p. 14.
   "The Village Idiots." PoNow (14/18) 77, p. 161.

SEERY, Janet
   "How He Caught the Rainbow." Juice (4) 77.

SEHNERT, Russell
   from The Mower Poems: "Fall Poem." QW (2) Wint 77, p. 23.
   from The Mower Poems: "McCallum $5. 00." QW (2) Wint 77,
      p. 20.
   from The Mower Poems: "Message." QW (2) Wint 77, p. 20.
   from The Mower Poems: "Mrs. Ivans $6. 00." QW (2) Wint 77,
      p. 22.
   from The Mower Poems: "Ms. Morrison." QW (2) Wint 77,
      p. 21.
   from The Mower Poems: "Noon $15. 00." QW (2) Wint 77,
      p. 21.
   from The Mower Poems: "The Luciano Brothers." QW (2)
      Wint 77, p. 22.

SEIDMAN, Clifford
   "Audio Play for 2 Actors." Mouth (11/12) Mr-Je 77, p. 116.
   "on my bed." Mouth (11/12) Mr-Je 77, p. 111.

SEIFERLE, Rebecca
   "a Greek sense." TexQ (20:4) Wint 77, p. 163.
   "reading." TexQ (20:4) Wint 77, p. 175.

SELF, Mark
   "Love." AmerPoR (6:2) Mr-Ap 77, p. 34.
   "Snake Dream." AmerPoR (6:2) Mr-Ap 77, p. 31.
   "Take the tree morning deer and bathe your soul spirit."
      AmerPoR (6:2) Mr-Ap 77, p. 33.

SELLERS, Bettie M.
   "After the Bath." GRR (8:1/2) 77, p. 152.
   "Moment at Dusk." Poem (31) N 77, p. 11.
   "Not Anything More Fair." HolCrit (14:3) Je 77, p. 10.
   "Of Stories Told in a Garden." Poem (31) N 77, p. 12.
   "Terrace by the Museum of Man." GRR (8:1/2) 77, p. 153.

SELLINGER, Alan
   "Once we went on a trip." AAR (27) 77, p. 126.

SELVAGGIO, Leni
   "Etna." Wind (27) 77, p. 23.

SEMENOVICH, Joseph
   "hunger." DeKalb (10:3) Spr 77, p. 53.
   "mr. lucky." CarouselQ (2:3) Wint 77, p. 11.
   "to me the alcoholic." NewL (43:4) Sum 77, p. 55.

SEMONES, Charles
   "The Piedmont" (for Bruce Bennett Brown). Wind (24) 77,
      p. 62.

SENG-TSAN
   "The Believing Mind" (tr. by Graeme Wilson). DenQ (12:2) Sum
      77, p. 47.

SEQUIN, Iliassa
"Love Quintet." PartR (44:2) 77, p. 257.
"Quintet 5." PartR (44:2) 77, p. 255.
"remember them." PartR (44:2) 77, p. 255.

SERCHUK, Peter
"For the Woman Whose Sister Is Dead." Ascent (3:2) 77, p. 31.
"Tired of the Road." Epoch (27:1) Aut 77, p. 59.

SETTERBERG, Ruth
"Loss." PoetL (72:2) Sum 77, p. 61.
"Seasonal Mystery." PoetL (72:2) Sum 77, p. 61.

SEVERY, Bruce
"Learning How to Count." Esq (87:1) Ja 77, p. 130.
"Working for the W. P. A." DacTerr (14) Spr-Sum 77, p. 38.

SEVICK, Joan
"Trompe L'Oeil." MissR (6:1) 77, p. 53.

SEWELL, Robert G.
"Approaching Death and Enlightenment" (tr. of Saigyo). DenQ
    (12:2) Sum 77, p. 126.
"Becoming a Priest and Escape into Nature" (tr. of Saigyo).
    DenQ (12:2) Sum 77, p. 124.
"The Maturing Landscape" (tr. of Saigyo). DenQ (12:2) Sum 77,
    p. 125.
"Secular Attachments and Religious Convictions" (tr. of Saigyo).
    DenQ (12:2) Sum 77, p. 124.
"Unrequited Love" (tr. of Saigyo). DenQ (12:2) Sum 77, p. 123.

SEYFRIED, Robin H.
"Hanging On" (For Mother). PoetryNW (18:3) Aut 77, p. 32.

SHABO, Gary
"Old Men." RemR (5) 77, p. 69.

SHAFER, Margaret
"A Dream of Beautiful Cookies." PoetryNW (18:3) Aut 77, p. 6.
"Jean." PoetryNW (18:3) Aut 77, p. 7.
"Untitled Poem." PoetryNW (18:3) Aut 77, p. 8.

SHAFNER, Rhondala
"A Letter to Catherine." DenQ (11:4) Wint 77, p. 117.
"A Letter to the Editor of Logic." DenQ (12:2) Sum 77, p. 389.
"Three Ways of Looking at Dying." DenQ (12:2) Sum 77,
    p. 387.
"Unloved Women Have No Biographies, They Have Histories,
    Says F. Scott Fitzgerald." DenQ (12:2) Sum 77, p. 390.

SHAHRYAR
"A Poem: Again the nights" (tr. by Muhammad Umar Memon).
    DenQ (12:2) Sum 77, p. 242.

SHAKELY, Lauren
"Away." Pequod (2:3) Sum 77, p. 79.
"Giving Birth." PoNow (14/18) 77, p. 161.
"Practical Joke." Pequod (2:3) Sum 77, p. 77.
"St. Joan in California." Pequod (2:3) Sum 77, p. 78.
"Stars." Pequod (2:3) Sum 77, p. 80.

SHAKLEY, M. J.
"If the summer night yields, just a little" (tr. of Sandro Penna,
    w. Ian Young). Mouth (11/12) Mr-Je 77, p. 64.

SHANNON, Ed
"Rite of Passage." DacTerr (14) Spr-Sum 77, p. 39.

SHANNON, Jeanne
"Area Code 703." PoetL (72:2) Sum 77, p. 65.

SHANTIRIS, Kita
"Monomy." PoetryNW (18:1) Spr 77, p. 34.

SHAPIRO, Harvey
"47th Street." PoNow (14/18) 77, p. 161.

SHAPIRO, Norman R.
"Atavism" (tr. of Leon Laleau). DenQ (11:4) Wint 77, p. 131.
"Cannibal" (tr. of Leon Laleau). DenQ (11:4) Wint 77, p. 130.
"Heredities" (tr. of Leon Laleau). DenQ (11:4) Wint 77,
    p. 131.
"Voodoo" (tr. of Leon Laleau). DenQ (11:4) Wint 77, p. 130.

SHAPIRO, Susan
"To Elizabeth." Rapp (10) 77, p. 36.

SHARONI, Edna G.
"Be Not Far" (tr. of Zelda). TriQ (39) Spr 77, p. 325.
"Time" (tr. of Zelda). TriQ (39) Spr 77, p. 322.

SHARP, David Joshua
"I Will Take Me Away." Poetry (130:3) D 77, p. 132.
"Self-Definitions." Poetry (130:3) D 77, p. 130.
"Transformations." Poetry (130:3) D 77, p. 131.
"Voyage Off and Out." Poetry (129:6) Mr 77, p. 317.

SHAW, Dale
"How to Boil Water." SmPd (14:2) Spr 77, p. 14.

SHAW, Maxine
"issue." Gra (12) 77, p. 18.

SHAW, R. W.
"Trust." StoneC (77:1) F 77, p. 8.

SHECK, Laurie
"Brides." AntR (35:1) Wint 77, p. 68.

SHEEHAN, Marc J.
"Dream Girl." Madrona (4:13/14) 77, p. 23.
"Homesteading." RemR (5) 77, p. 92.
"Shantytown." Wind (26) 77, p. 55.

SHEEHAN, Susan
"Night Bodies." Xa (4) 77, p. 48.

SHEFFIELD, Anne
"Alaska Super 8." SmPd (14:1) Wint 77, p. 27.
"Mrs. R." SmPd (14:1) Wint 77, p. 28.
"Totem." SmPd (14:1) Wint 77, p. 26.

SHEFTEL, Harry B.
"Weights." Xa (4) 77, p. 47.

SHEGOLEFF, Vera
"Gary Gilmore." SeC (5:2) 78, p. 62.

SHELLER, Barbara King
"Anniversary." PoetL (72:1) Spr 77, p. 8.
"Sestina on the Beach." PoetL (72:1) Spr 77, p. 15.

SHELTON, Richard
"Landscape with a Woman." Iowa (8:3) Sum 77, p. 31.
"The Messenger." Chowder (9) Aut-Wint 77, p. 7.
"The Prophet." NewYorker (53:30) 12 S 77, p. 138.
"The Star." Chowder (9) Aut-Wint 77, p. 9.
"The Swimmers." Chowder (9) Aut-Wint 77, p. 6.

SHEN Hsiu
"The Headmonk's Poem" (tr. by Graeme Wilson). WestHR (31:3)
    Sum 77, p. 209.

SHEPHARD, Michael
"The Gunfight." DeKalb (10:4) Sum 77, p. 69.
"The Poet." DeKalb (10:4) Sum 77, p. 70.
"Tornado." DeKalb (10:4) Sum 77, p. 71.

SHEPHERD, J. Barrie
"Advent." ChrC (94:39) 30 N 77, p. 1113.
"Corkscrew." ChrC (94:12) 6 Ap 77, p. 324.
"Four-Letter-Word Tree." ChrC (94:12) 6 Ap 77, p. 318.
"January." ChrC (94:1) 5-12 Ja 77, p. 14.
"The Messiah." ChrC (94:42) 21 D 77, p. 1189.
"Pilgriming." ChrC (94:11) 30 Mr 77, p. 293.
"September." ChrC (94:30) 28 S 77, p. 837.
"Star-Crossing." ChrC (94:40) 7 D 77, p. 1134.

SHEPPARD, Simon
"Mr. Orton Was Murdered in 1967." Mouth (13) D 77, p. 41.
"A Night Like This." Mouth (13) D 77, p. 60.
"Obsessed by the Myth of the Road." Mouth (11/12) Mr-Je 77,
    p. 79.

SHEPPERD, Walt
"Journalist's Prayer." SenR (8:1) My 77, p. 84.
"Power to the People." SenR (8:1) My 77, p. 85.
"Survey." SenR (8:1) My 77, p. 86.

SHERIDAN, Michael
"By a Lake in the Sierras." SouthernPR (17:2) Aut 77, p. 56.
"Turning Back" (for my brother). Iowa (8:4) Aut 77, p. 65.

SHERIFF, Bat-Sheva
"When You Gave Light" (tr. of Anadad Eldan, w. Jon Silkin).
    TriQ (39) Spr 77, p. 260.

SHERMAN, John
"Rooms." TexQ (20:2) Sum 77, p. 59.

SHERRARD, Philip
"The Bandaged Shoulder" (tr. of Constantine Cavafy, w. Edmund
    Keeley). NewYRB (24:2) 17 F 77, p. 33.
"Ionic" (tr. of Constantine Cavafy, w. Edmund Keeley). NewYRB
    (24:2) 17 F 77, p. 33.
"Kaisarion" (tr. of Constantine Cavafy, w. Edmund Keeley).
    NewYRB (24:2) 17 F 77, p. 33.

SHERWIN, Judith Johnson
"The Alarm" (for the Secretary of State). MinnR (NS8) Spr 77,
    p. 31.
"Dance, Spin, Show Yourself." PoNow (14/18) 77, p. 162.
"Do You Hear/Organ Music." PoNow (14/18) 77, p. 162.
"Earths" (For Bob Castro). PoNow (14/18) 77, p. 162.
"How We Changed." PartR (44:3) 77, p. 407.
"The Imitation of Death." NewRep (176:6) 5 F 77, p. 27.
"The Intellectual Pilgrim." Salm (36) Wint 77, p. 45.
"Noon." Nat (225:15) 5 N 77, p. 470.
"The Resting Place." CalQ (11/12) Wint-Spr 77, p. 153.
"A Slow, Traditional Measure." LitR (20:4) Sum 77, p. 456.
"Sonnet: On Women's Business." MissR (6:1) 77, p. 48.
"Statement." Nat (225:19) 3 D 77, p. 606.
"With a Silver Comb." MissR (6:1) 77, p. 47.
"Words for Grandma Clara." SouthwR (62:4) Aut 77, p. 360.

SHETTERLY, Susan Hand
"First Born." BelPoJ (28:2) Wint 77-78, p. 8.

SHEVCHENKO, Tony
"Presidents." SeC (5:2) 78, p. 17.

SHEVIN, David
"Avoiding the Bicentennial." PoNow (14/18) 77, p. 162.
"Doo Dah Downs." DeKalb (10:3) Spr 77, p. 54.
"The Greater Metropolitan Antarctica Telephone Directory."
    Waters (5) 77, p. 16.
"Guys I Used to Know." CalQ (11/12) Wint-Spr 77, p. 106.

"Hearing Lesson." KanQ (9:1) Wint 77, p. 96.
"The Midnight Train to Georgia." DeKalb (10:3) Spr 77, p. 54.
"A Note to Keep Things Straight." CalQ (11/12) Wint-Spr 77,
    p. 105.
"The Road from Celeryville." DeKalb (10:3) Spr 77, p. 55.
"Spearfishing in the Elevator." MontG (5) Wint 77, p. 39.

SHIHAB, Naomi
    "Basketball with the Swami." YellowBR (8) 77, p. 15.
    "Harvey Street, St. Louis." Glass (2:2/3) Wint-Spr 77, p. 84.
    "My Grandmother Has Tattooed Feet." YellowBR (8) 77, p. 15.
    "On This Side of the World." Glass (2:2/3) Wint-Spr 77, p. 85.

SHIHI, Granny
    "Stories" (w. Empress Jito) (tr. by Graeme Wilson). DenQ
    (12:2) Sum 77, p. 372.

SHIHIBU, Izumi
    "Death Poem" (tr. by Graeme Wilson). DenQ (12:2) Sum 77,
    p. 54.
    "Folly" (tr. by Graeme Wilson). DenQ (12:2) Sum 77, p. 368.

SHINDER, Jason
    "After Watching Television." WindO (28) Spr 77, p. 12.
    "The Bleeder." WindO (28) Spr 77, p. 11.

SHIPLEY, Margaret
    "Marin in Taos." SouthwR (62:3) Sum 77, p. 300.

SHISHIN-GOSHIN
    "Talking: seven steps, eight falls" (tr. by Lucien Stryk). ChiR
    (29:2) Aut 77, p. 88.

SHIVELY, Charley
    "Travel." PoNow (14/18) 77, p. 162.

SHIZUE, Hatsui
    "Silently" (tr. by Kenneth Rexroth). ParisR (69) Spr 77, p. 120.

SHOEMAKER, Lynn
    "Doghouse." Epoch (26:2) Wint 77, p. 163.
    "God's Word Is Blue." Hand (1) 77, p. 166.
    "The Gold Horse Nomad." Hand (1) 77, p. 165.
    "Gravity and Grace." Hand (1) 77, p. 166.
    "The Song of Songs/The Song of Red." HangL (31) Aut 77, p. 66.
    "Unisex." Epoch (26:2) Wint 77, p. 162.

SHOLL, Betsy
    "Shades of Gray." HangL (30) Sum 77, p. 53.
    "We Keep Her in a Box." Ploughs (3:3/4) 77, p. 111.

SHORB, Michael
    "Canoe People." MichQR (16:4) Aut 77, p. 424.

"Whale Walker's Morning." MichQR (16:3) Sum 77, p. 307.

SHORE, Jane
"Constantly." Ploughs (3:3/4) 77, p. 169.
"Witness." NewRep (177:10) 3 S 77, p. 25.

SHORT, Clarice
"By Their Right Names: Bird Groups, Circa 1250." WestHR (31:1) Wint 77, p. 68.
"The Common Gallinule." WestHR (31:1) Wint 77, p. 67.
"White on Green: Egret." WestHR (31:1) Wint 77, p. 66.

SHORT, Frank X.
"Contest." SmPd (14:1) Wint 77, p. 30.

SHUMAKER, Peggy
"The Clay Pot and the Iron Pot." Glass (2:2/3) Wint-Spr 77, p. 101.
"Mastectomy." Bits (6) Jl 77.

SHUMAN, R. Baird
"Protective Custody." NewC (7:2) 75-76, p. 13.

SHU NING LIU, Stephen
"A Mid-July Invitation." CalQ (11/12) Wint-Spr 77, p. 104.

SHUNTARO, Tanikawa
"August" (tr. by Harold P. Wright). DenQ (12:2) Sum 77, p. 281.
"August and February" (tr. by Harold P. Wright). DenQ (12:2) Sum 77, p. 285.
"Battle Scene from the Comic Fantastic Opera, 'The Seafarer'" (for Paul Klee) (tr. by Harold P. Wright). DenQ (12:2) Sum 77, p. 284.
"Before the Snow" (for Paul Klee) (tr. by Harold P. Wright). DenQ (12:2) Sum 77, p. 284.
"Child and Train Tracks" (tr. by Harold P. Wright). DenQ (12:2) Sum 77, p. 281.
"Homework" (tr. by Graeme Wilson). DenQ (12:2) Sum 77, p. 63.
"I See a Woman" (tr. by Carol Tenny). Field (17) Aut 77, p. 39.
"Nero" (to a loved little dog) (tr. by Harold P. Wright). DenQ (12:2) Sum 77, p. 282.
"Sadness" (tr. by Harold P. Wright). DenQ (12:2) Sum 77, p. 282.

SHUTTLEWORTH, Paul
"After a Drawing by Suzuki Harunobu (1725-1770)." KanQ (9:4) Aut 77, p. 120.
"After Teaching in a Dark Classroom." Rapp (10) 77, p. 38.
"The Boxer on Canvas." PoNow (14/18) 77, p. 163.
"Disguises in the Sky." Chowder (8) Spr-Sum 77, p. 23.

"The Dog in the Cemetery." Rapp (10) 77, p. 37.
"A Few Flakes of Snow Collapse." DacTerr (14) Spr-Sum 77,
    p. 57.
"Often in Silence." DacTerr (14) Spr-Sum 77, p. 58.
"There'll Be Some Chuck-Holes Made Tonight." KanQ (9:4) Aut
    77, p. 120.
"Wyatt Earp as Utility Infielder." DacTerr (14) Spr-Sum 77,
    p. 58.

SIBCY, Paul R.
    "A Man's Gotta Talk." EngJ (66:5) My 77, p. 60.

SIEGEL, Robert
    "Barney Bodkin" (for Sabina, in a state ward for the senile).
        PraS (51:1) Spr 77, p. 66.
    "Bull." Poetry (130:2) My 77, p. 96.
    "Christmas Eve." PraS (51:1) Spr 77, p. 67.
    "Fen Churches." ConcPo (10:1) Spr 77, p. 86.
    "Hog Heaven" (for NA & KP). Poetry (130:2) My 77, p. 98.
    "Knave of Hearts." Poetry (130:2) My 77, p. 101.
    "Like Butter" (for SJ). PraS (51:1) Spr 77, p. 65.
    "TV Documentary." Poetry (130:2) My 77, p. 100.
    "Them." Poetry (130:2) My 77, p. 97.
    "Wandlebury." ConcPo (10:1) Spr 77, p. 86.

SIEGEL, Rochelle
    "Afterward." Nat (224:19) 14 My 77, p. 602.

SIGSTEDT, Val
    "A Loom, a Horse, and a Rose." Stonecloud (6) 76, p. 121.
    "To Lolita Libran, Whom I Only Know from Her Poets."
        Stonecloud (6) 76, p. 130.

SILBERMAN, Cathleen Medwick
    "Hen." Madem (83:5) My 77, p. 34.

SILBERT, Layle
    "Afterlife." Gra (12) 77.
    "Stickup." Gra (12) 77.

SILESKY, Barry
    "Winter Oaks." DacTerr (14) Spr-Sum 77, p. 43.

SILK, Dennis
    "Beginning." Harp (254:1522) Mr 77, p. 99.
    "Bug." Harp (255:1526) Jl 77, p. 82.
    "Epilogue for Soldier Schweik." Harp (254:1522) Mr 77, p. 99.
    "Forlorn Hope." Harp (254:1522) Mr 77, p. 99.

SILKIN, Jon
    from Against Parting: "Sergeant Weiss" (tr. of Natan Zach, w.
        Abraham Birman). TriQ (39) Spr 77, p. 317.
    "As Sand" (tr. of Natan Zach). TriQ (39) Spr 77, p. 321.

"At Nightfall. " Iowa (8:1) Wint 77, p. 61.
"Entropy at Hartburn. " Iowa (8:1) Wint 77, p. 59.
"He Apologizes" (tr. of Natan Zach). TriQ (39) Spr 77, p. 318.
"The Holy Island of St. Aidan. " Iowa (8:1) Wint 77, p. 60.
"King Solomon's Camel" (tr. of Natan Zach). TriQ (39) Spr 77,
    p. 319.
"Shades. " Iowa (8:1) Wint 77, p. 58.
"Shadowing. " Iowa (8:1) Wint 77, p. 61.
"A Song for the Wise Lovers" (tr. of Natan Zach). TriQ (39)
    Spr 77, p. 320.
"When You Gave Light" (tr. of Anadad Eldan, w. Bat-Sheva
    Sheriff). TriQ (39) Spr 77, p. 260.

SILKO, Leslie
"Deer Dance/For Your Return" (February, 1977). Columbia (1)
    Aut 77, p. 9.
"Story from Bear Country. " Antaeus (27) Aut 77, p. 62.

SILLIMAN, Ron
from The Chinese Notebook: "1.   Wayward, we weigh words. "
    Bound (5:2) Wint 77, p. 539.
"I Am Marion Delgado. " Hills (4) 77.

SILVA, Jeff
"Green, a Chance. " Ploughs (3:3/4) 77, p. 162.

SILVERMAN, Eugene
"For No Rewards. " BallSUF (18:3) Sum 77, p. 31.
"1936-1939. " BallSUF (18:2) Spr 77, p. 24.

SILVERMAN, Stuart
"Poem Poem. " WindO (27) Aut 76.

SILVERTON, Michael
"'Feeling Wonderful!' He continues: 'Argh. '" PoNow (14/18)
    77, p. 163.
"The King of All the Mice, lurking. " PoNow (14/18) 77,
    p. 163.

SIMIC, Charles
"Bread. " SenR (8:1) My 77, p. 6.
"Broken Horns" (tr. of Vasko Popa). Field (16) Spr 77, p. 28.
"December Trees. " NewYorker (53:43) 12 D 77, p. 52.
"Dimly Outlined by a Police Artist. " Ploughs (4:1) 77, p. 54.
"The Great Anonymous Eye and Ear. " Ploughs (4:1) 77, p. 55.
"The Guest. " CornellR (2) Aut 77, p. 74.
"History. " SenR (8:1) My 77, p. 5.
"The Other World" (tr. of Vasko Popa). Field (16) Spr 77,
    p. 27.
"Patriarchs. " Pequod (2:3) Sum 77, p. 81.
"Peaceful Kingdom. " VirQR (53:4) Aut 77, p. 718.
"Photographer's Hood. " Pequod (2:3) Sum 77, p. 82.
"Photographer's Hood. " Ploughs (4:1) 77, p. 56.

"Religious Miniatures. " SenR (8:1) My 77, p. 9.
"Sewing Machine. " SenR (8:1) My 77, p. 8.
"Shadow of a Shewolf" (tr. of Vasko Popa). Field (16) Spr 77,
    p. 25.
"Shirt. " SenR (8:1) My 77, p. 7.
"Stepfather of Wolves" (tr. of Vasko Popa). Field (16) Spr 77,
    p. 26.
"Window Washer. " VirQR (53:4) Aut 77, p. 718.

SIMON, John Oliver
from Excavating the Great Mother Shrine: (14, 35, 41).
    Stonecloud (6) 76, pp. 106, 112.
"1959. " PoNow (14/18) 77, p. 163.

SIMONS, Louise
"June and the Pay Telephone. " 13thM (3:2) 77, p. 35.

SIMPSON, Louis
"Cold Cereal. " OhioR (18:2) Spr-Sum 77, p. 63.
"Peter. " Iowa (8:1) Wint 77, p. 37.

SIMPSON, Mary Scott
"In the Empyrean. " ChrC (94:36) 9 N 77, p. 1028.

SINCLAIR, Iain
"Coban, the Unknown the Unknowable. " Montra (3) Spr 77,
    p. 170.

SINENI, Carole
"Watermelon Incense. " Pig (3) 77, p. 7.

SINGH, G.
"The Ghost" (tr. of Eugenio Montale). NewYRB (24:10) 9 Je 77,
    p. 36.
"A Letter" (tr. of Eugenio Montale). NewYRB (24:10) 9 Je 77,
    p. 36.
"Lights and Colours" (tr. of Eugenio Montale). NewYRB (24:10)
    9 Je 77, p. 36.

SIN Hum
"Pomegranates" (tr. by Graeme Wilson). DenQ (12:2) Sum 77,
    p. 292.
"Twine" (tr. by Graeme Wilson). WestHR (31:1) Wint 77,
    p. 58.
"What Power" (tr. by Graeme Wilson). WestHR (31:3) Sum 77,
    p. 212.

SINISGALLI, Leonardo
"Antefatti. " GRR (8:1/2) 77, p. 18.
"Due Poeti Ai Giardini. " GRR (8:1/2) 77, p. 22.

SISE, Charlie
"Two Crows Feasting. " RemR (5) 77, p. 39.

SISSMAN, L. E.
   "Homage to Clotho: A Hospital Suite. " NewYorker (53:17) 13 Je
     77, p. 34.
   "Negatives. " NewYorker (53:17) 13 Je 77, p. 34.
   "Under the Rose: A Granfalloon for Kurt Vonnegut, Jr. "
     NewYorker (53:17) 13 Je 77, p. 35.

SJOBERG, John
   Ten poems. Spirit (2:2/3) 77, pp. 118-27.

SKEEN, Anita
   "City Park: March Sunday. " 13thM (3:2) 77, p. 29.
   "In Tune" (for Marlene). 13thM (3:2) 77, p. 31.
   "Laying Stone. " KanQ (9:2) Spr 77, p. 20.
   "Sunrise. " ArkRiv (3:4/4:1) 77, p. 53.

SKEETER, Sharyn Jeanne
   "Free the Three. " Nimrod (21:2/22:1) 77, p. 258.
   "Junior. " Nimrod (21:2/22:1) 77, p. 260.
   "Played Cops and Robbers. " Nimrod (21:2/22:1) 77, p. 259.

SKELTON, Robin
   "Landmarks. " Poetry (130:3) D 77, p. 148.

SKILES, Don
   "The Chicken Poem. " SunM (4) Aut 77, p. 152.
   "The Painting of Jack Tworkov. " SunM (4) Aut 77, p. 151.
   "This Is the Rain. " SunM (4) Aut 77, p. 153.

SKINNER, Knute
   "Using Her Head, or How to Salvage an Evening. " PoNow
     (14/18) 77, p. 163.

SKLAR, Morty
   Ten poems. Spirit (2:2/3) 77, pp. 55-67.

SKLAREW, Debbie
   "To Pablo Neruda. " Box (5) Spr 77, p. 17.

SKLAREW, Myra
   "Highway. " PoNow (14/18) 77, p. 163.
   "Unnatural Silences: when a writer doesn't write. " SouthernPR
     (16:SI) 77, p. 73.

SKLOOT, Floyd
   "Circling. " Icarus (5:1) Spr 77, p. 14.
   "The Face. " Vaga (26) 77, p. 8.
   "Fair. " PoNow (14/18) 77, p. 164.
   "A Family Hike. " StoneC (77:1) F 77, p. 25.
   "Max. " CutB (9) Aut-Wint 77, p. 148.
   "The Namings. " KanQ (9:1) Wint 77, p. 66.
   "Sestina: An Appeal to My Father. " Chowder (8) Spr-Sum 77,
     p. 32.

"Triolets for the Wind. " Icarus (5:2) Aut 77, p. 9.
"Wily Hansel. " ConcPo (10:1) Spr 77, p. 77.

SKOLFIELD, Dana F.
"Interstate 80: 1976. " Mouth (11/12) Mr-Je 77, p. 77.

SKOYLES, John
"Burlesque. " OhioR (18:1) Wint 77, p. 77.
"Conviction. " Ploughs (3:3/4) 77, p. 126.
"No Thank You. " OhioR (18:1) Wint 77, p. 77.

SKUJA, Harij
"Lyric" (tr. by John M. Gogol). WebR (3:4) Aut 77, p. 36.

SKY-PECK, Kathryn
"Nine Holes in a Body. " Ascent (3:1) 77, p. 29.

SLADE, Kenneth Sean
"I am obsessed by this cheap. " YaleLit (145:3) 77, p. 11.

SLATE, Ron
"Living Among People with Many Faults. " Ploughs (3:3/4) 77,
    p. 117.
"My Best Friend. " DacTerr (14) Spr-Sum 77, p. 32.
"Pastorale. " PoetryNW (18:4) Wint 77-78, p. 19.
"A Travel Agent's Guide to the Off Season. " DacTerr (14) Spr-
    Sum 77, p. 33.

SLAVITT, David R.
"Garbage. " Hudson (30:3) Aut 77, p. 397.
"Lobsters. " MissR (6:1) 77, p. 111.
"Night Thoughts. " Poetry (131:2) N 77, p. 91.
"Poison. " Poetry (131:2) N 77, p. 90.

SLAVOV, Atanas
"Capriccio for Goya" (tr. of Konstantin Pavlov). PartR (44:4)
    77, p. 600.
"Flotation" (tr. of Konstantin Pavlov). PartR (44:4) 77, p. 599.
"Second Capriccio for Goya" (tr. of Konstantin Pavlov). PartR
    (44:4) 77, p. 601.
"Singing Contest" (tr. of Konstantin Pavlov). PartR (44:4) 77,
    p. 602.

SLEGMAN, Ann
"The Old Man at the Club Royale. " Wind (27) 77, p. 55.

SLOAN, Benjamin
"An Interview with Frank O'Hara. " LaB (7) My 77, p. 45.
"Not Being Impressed" (for Terence Winch). LaB (7) My 77,
    p. 46.
"On and Off the Road. " LaB (7) My 77, p. 44.
"Poem for My Lover's Other Lover, Peter. " LaB (7) My 77,
    p. 45.
"Postmortem. " LaB (7) My 77, p. 44.

SLOSS, Henry
"The Wedding at Vernazzano" (For James Merrill).   Poetry
(131:1) O 77, p. 21.

SMALL, Michael
"Clouds" (for the asp workshop).   Glass (2:2/3) Wint-Spr 77,
p. 38.
"The Next Day."   Glass (2:2/3) Wint-Spr 77, p. 40.
"Thunderstorm."   Glass (2:2/3) Wint-Spr 77, p. 39.

SMALLWOOD, Randy
"The Journey" (for John Unterecker).   Wind (27) 77, p. 52.
"Realization."   Wind (27) 77, p. 52.
"Thought in Early Morning."   Wind (27) 77, p. 53.
"To Another Donor."   Wind (27) 77, p. 53.

SMARIO, Tom
"Don Quixote Come Home for Dinner."   Vaga (25) 77, p. 16.

SMITH, Arthur
"Like Always."   YellowBR (8) 77, p. 19.

SMITH, Bruce
"'Can I Call the Police Against My Own Family?'"   HiramPoR
(23) Wint 77, p. 32.
"The Fourth Letter."   CutB (9) Aut-Wint 77, p. 113.
"Second Trout Fishing Poem."   Wind (27) 77, p. 54.
"West Branch. Fishing at Thirty."   Wind (27) 77, p. 54.

SMITH, C. A.
"To Katherine, Sometime Too Late."   DacTerr (14) Spr-Sum 77,
p. 75.

SMITH, Chris
"The Perfect Lover."   Some (7/8) 76.

SMITH, Christopher
"Ann."   AAR (27) 77, p. 107.
"I Dreamed."   AAR (27) 77, p. 107.

SMITH, Daren
"Movie Projector."   QW (3) Spr-Sum 77, p. 30.

SMITH, Dave
"Apples in Early October."   Poetry (131:1) O 77, p. 24.
"August, on the Rented Farm."   NewYorker (53:28) 29 Ag 77,
p. 40.
"Azaleas."   ThRiPo (10) 77, p. 11.
"Between the Moon and the Sun."   AmerPoR (6:6) N-D 77, p. 48.
"Choking on Fish Bones."   Kayak (44) F 77, p. 34.
"Convulsion."   AmerPoR (6:6) N-D 77, p. 47.
"Dandelions."   ThRiPo (10) 77, p. 12.

"A Day in Which You and I, Having Nothing to Do, Steal an Old
  Lady's Rowboat." KanQ (9:1) Wint 77, p. 37.
"A Day with No Clouds." ThRiPo (10) 77, p. 17.
"Dreaming the Child's Dream." WestHR (31:3) Sum 77, p. 226.
"Dreams in Sunlit Rooms." Poetry (131:1) O 77, p. 28.
"Elk Ghosts: A Birth Memory." WestHR (31:3) Sum 77,
  p. 224.
"Goshawk, Antelope." NewYorker (53:30) 12 S 77, p. 45.
"Hath the Drowned Nothing to Dream." Nat (225:2) 9-16 Jl 77,
  p. 54.
"Hole, Where Once in Passion We Swam." NowestR (16:3) 77,
  p. 79.
"Lovesong after Flood." ThRiPo (10) 77, p. 14.
"North of Rock Springs, Snow Falling in Late Spring, the Wreck-
  age of a Ranch Looms." ThRiPo (10) 77, p. 16.
"Out of the Sea, at Hatteras." SouthernPR (17:1) Spr 77, p. 46.
"Pond." Nat (225:1) 2 Jl 77, p. 25.
"Sometime I Think I Will Ride into St. Louis." NowestR (16:3)
  77, p. 78.
"The Sound of a Silk Dress." Iowa (8:3) Sum 77, p. 64.
"Treehouse." NewYorker (53:28) 29 Ag 77, p. 40.
"Two Memories of a Rented House in a Southern State."
  SouthernPR (16:SI) 77, p. 74.
"Waking among Horses." WestHR (31:3) Sum 77, p. 244.
"Willows, Pond Glitter." Poetry (131:1) O 77, p. 26.

SMITH, Frederick
  "Pappy Shiffer." EngJ (66:5) My 77, p. 53.

SMITH, Gary
  "Mourning Doves." Poetry (129:6) Mr 77, p. 318.
  "Mourning Doves 6." PortR (23) 77, p. 137.
  "The Solitary in Bruegel." PortR (23) 77, p. 138.
  "The Spirit of the Dead Watches (Manao Tupapau)." Icarus (5:2)
    Aut 77, p. 20.
  "Swelter." Poetry (129:6) Mr 77, p. 319.
  "The Yellow Christ." Icarus (5:2) Aut 77, p. 20.

SMITH, Harry
  "On the Attersee" (for Lloyd Van Brunt). NewC (7:2) 75-76,
    p. 24.

SMITH, Holly
  "Dying." AmerPoR (6:2) Mr-Ap 77, p. 34.

SMITH, Jared
  "Also Being an Odyssey." Juice (5) 77.
  "Dallas." Vaga (26) 77, p. 16.
  "La Guardia." Vaga (26) 77, p. 18.
  "Message Left at the Breakfast Table." Juice (5) 77.
  "Nebulous Pinwheel." Juice (5) 77.
  "The Turning Off of Lights." DeKalb (10:3) Spr 77, p. 56.

SMITH, Joan
"What's Money Good For Anyway but to Spend?" Vaga (25) 77,
    p. 77.

SMITH, Ken
    from Tristan Crazy: "Four, Being a Prayer to the Western
        Wind. " GRR (8:3) 77, p. 189.
    from Tristan Crazy: "Five, Which Is Here by the River. " GRR
        (8:3) 77, p. 190.
    from Tristan Crazy: "Six: The Wife's Complaint. " GRR (8:3)
        77, p. 191.
    from Tristan Crazy: "Nine: Shorty's Advice to the Players. "
        GRR (8:3) 77, p. 194.

SMITH, Larry R.
"Sinners Never Forgive or Quitters are Winners" (for James
    Tate). MontG (6) Aut 77, p. 59.

SMITH, Llwelleyn H.
"I. September 10, 1963. " Wind (27) 77, p. 56.

SMITH, Margoret
"Arbitrate. " BosUJ (25:1) 77, p. 22.
"Bufo Americanus. " Ploughs (3:3/4) 77, p. 61.
"Considerations. " CentR (21:3) Sum 77, p. 280.

SMITH, Mike
"Poem on the Reopening of the Water-Mill of Little Salkeld,
    Cumbria. " Stand (18:3) 77, p. 28.

SMITH, Patrick
"Basho the Mountain Leaps. " CalQ (11/12) Wint-Spr 77, p. 121.
"Hermes Speaks. " CalQ (11/12) Wint-Spr 77, p. 120.

SMITH, Peter
"Waynahbozho Comes to the City. " AmerPoR (6:2) Mr-Ap 77,
    p. 32.

SMITH, R. T.
"The Guggenheim Vision. " GRR (8:1/2) 77, p. 76.
"Heart's Map. " GRR (8:3) 77, p. 236.
"Superimposed. " Poem (29) Mr 77, p. 24.

SMITH, Ray
"Homestead Barn. " SouthernHR (11:3) Sum 77, p. 268.
"Jeffers at Tor. " SouthernHR (11:3) Sum 77, p. 290.

SMITH, Richard Bogaert
"At first, in the Dream. " Mouth (11/12) Mr-Je 77, p. 57.

SMITH, Rick
"sequence in a lobby. " Aspect (70) Ja-Mr 77, p. 27.
"Vacation. " Aspect (70) Ja-Mr 77, p. 26.

SMITH, Ronald
"Opening a New Box of Stars." Kayak (45) My 77, p. 26.

SMITH, Stephen E.
"The Cat and the Wind." Wind (25) 77, p. 57.
"Slagel's Poem." Wind (25) 77, p. 57.

SMITH, W. A., II.
"Doing Clothes in D. C." PoetL (72:2) Sum 77, p. 51.

SMITH, William Jay
"The Etruscan Sarcophagus" (tr. of István Vas). AmerPoR (6:3)
  My-Je 77, p. 23.
"Saint Médard" (tr. of István Vas). AmerPoR (6:3) My-Je 77,
  p. 22.
"While the Record Plays" (tr. of Gyula Illyés). AmerPoR (6:3)
  My-Je 77, p. 21.

SMOKEWOOD, Elaine
"A Sort of a Sonnet for my Mother." MidwQ (18:3) Spr 77,
  p. 267.

SMYTH, Gerard
"She Hates Life on Wet Days." Confr (14) Spr-Sum 77, p. 71.
"Today Is Not Enough." DenQ (12:1) Spr 77, p. 96.

SMYTH, Gjertrud Schnackenberg
Twenty poems. MissR (6:2) 77, p. 4.

SMYTH, Paul
"A Box Turtle." Poetry (130:6) S 77, p. 337.
"Drug Store Phone." LittleR (12) 77, p. 10.
"An Elm Leaf" (for Keith Berven). Poetry (130:6) S 77, p. 339.
"A Frame for the Angels." BelPoJ (28:1) Aut 77, p. 1.
"The Love Poems." MissR (6:1) 77, p. 50.
"A Marriage Toast" (To Trude). MichQR (16:2) Spr 77, p. 194.
"Monads." LittleR (12) 77, p. 13.
"A Paperweight." Poetry (130:6) S 77, p. 341.
"They." Poetry (130:6) S 77, p. 340.

SMYTH, Rick
"'Falling into Heaven.'" Focus (12:77) S-O 77, p. 29.

SNELLER, Del
"For Love Is Strong as Death." StoneC (77:1) F 77, p. 16.
"On Quitting a Little College." StoneC (77:1) F 77, p. 15.

SNEYD, Steve
"New Master." Sam (56) Sum 77, p. 49.
"tepid warm old." WindO (27) Aut 76, p. 3.

SNIDER, Clifton
"This Time." StoneC (77:1) F 77, p. 23.

SNIVELY, Susan
    "Moving. " MassR (18:2) Sum 77, p. 226.

SNODGRASS, W. D.
    "Dr. Joseph Goebbels--19 April, 1945. " SenR (8:1) My 77,
        p. 23.
    "Dr. Joseph Goebbels--22 April, 1945. " SenR (8:1) My 77,
        p. 33.
    "Dr. Joseph Goebbels--1 May, 1945, 1800 hours. " SenR (8:1)
        My 77, p. 39.
    from The Führer Bunker: "Adolf Hitler--1 April, 1945. "
        AmerPoR (6:1) Ja-F 77, p. 3.
    from The Führer Bunker: "Adolf Hitler--20 April, 1945; 1900
        hours. " AmerPoR (6:1) Ja-F 77, p. 4.
    from The Führer Bunker: "Adolf Hitler--30 April, 1945; 1520
        hours. " AmerPoR (6:1) Ja-F 77, p. 8.
    from The Führer Bunker: "Albert Speer--18 April 1945. " GeoR
        (31:2) Sum 77, p. 316.
    from The Führer Bunker: "Albert Speer--20 April 1945; 2200
        Hours. " GeoR (31:2) Sum 77, p. 318.
    from The Führer Bunker: "Eva Braun--22 April, 1945. "
        AmerPoR (6:1) Ja-F 77, p. 5.
    from The Führer Bunker: "Eva B. Hitler, geb. Braun--30 April,
        1945. " AmerPoR (6:1) Ja-F 77, p. 7.
    from The Führer Bunker: "Hermann Fegelein--29 April, 1945;
        0200 hours. " AmerPoR (6:1) Ja-F 77, p. 6.
    "Magda Goebbels--19 April, 1945. " SenR (8:1) My 77, p. 29.
    "Magda Goebbels--22 April, 1945. " SenR (8:1) My 77, p. 36.
    "Magda Goebbels--27 April, 1945. " SenR (8:1) My 77, p. 38.

SNYDER, Gary
    "Bows to Drouth. " OhioR (18:3) Aut 77, p. 107.
    "Talking Late with the Governor about the Budget. " OhioR (18:3)
        Aut 77, p. 106.
    "Walked Two Days in Light Snow, Then it Cleared for Five" (for
        Masa). OhioR (18:3) Aut 77, p. 108.

SNYDER, Richard
    "The Aging Poet, on a Reading Trip to Dayton, Visits the Air
        Force Museum and Discovers There a Plane He Once Flew. "
        Comm (104:8) 15 Ap 77, p. 231.
    "Blue Sparks in Dark Closets" (for P. T. P. , 1896-1975). AndR
        (3:2) Aut 76, p. 20.

SOBIN, A. G.
    "Arthur's Last Movie. " BelPoJ (27:3) Spr 77, p. 15.

SOBIN, Gustav
    "Fossilized Light: Fragments. " Kayak (44) F 77, p. 5.
    "That the Universe Is Chrysalid. " Kayak (44) F 77, p. 3.

SOBOSAN, Jeffrey
    "Clowns. " ChrC (94:43) 28 D 77, p. 1212.

SOCOLOW, Liz
"The Swimmer" (Frances Irene Goldberg Sussman 1910-1971).
    US1 (10) Wint 77-78, p. 11.
"The Testing Stick." US1 (10) Wint 77-78, p. 10.

SOLDOFSKY, Alan
"Intercoast." Stonecloud (6) 76, p. 124.

SOLOMON, Andy
"On His Kindness." Atl (240:6) D 77, p. 112.

SOLT, Mary Ellen
"Forsythia." AmerPoR (6:4) Jl-Ag 77, p. 21.
"Poem" (tr. of Augusto De Campos, w. Heitor Martins and Jon
    M. Tolman). LitR (21:2) Wint 78, p. 276.
"se len cio" (tr. of Haroldo de Campos, w. Jon M. Tolman).
    LitR (21:2) Wint 78, p. 208.

SOLVIN, Lois C.
"Richmond, Kentucky." Wind (26) 77, p. 4.

SOLWAY, Arthur
"Star Shepherd." Waters (5) 77, p. 26.

SOLYN, Paul
"Chasing Dragons." Northeast (3:4) Aut-Wint 77-78, p. 22.
"I Remember Kent." NewL (43:4) Sum 77, p. 57.
"Weeds." WindO (27) Aut 76.
"Why I Don't Like Fireworks." RemR (5) 77, p. 28.

SOMLYÓ, György
"Fairy Tale of the Cosmos" (tr. by Daniel Hoffman). NewRep
    (176:13) 26 Mr 77, p. 30.
"Tale of the Double Helix" (tr. by Daniel Hoffman). NewRep
    (176:13) 26 Mr 77, p. 30.

SONG Si-yol
"Gently" (tr. by Graeme Wilson). DenQ (12:2) Sum 77, p. 304.

SONG Sun
"Zen Road" (tr. by Graeme Wilson). TexQ (20:4) Wint 77,
    p. 146.

SONIAT, Katherine
"In Another Mold." PoetryNW (18:4) Wint 77-78, p. 33.
"Interludes in the Backwoods." HiramPoR (23) Wint 77, p. 33.
"To My Birthday Child." GeoR (31:4) Wint 77, p. 874.

SORRELL, John Edward
"April, Afternoon to Evening." NewC (7:2) 75-76, p. 18.
Clenched Horizon. NewC (8:2) 77. Entire issue.
"Landlocked." NewC (7:3) 75-76, p. 21.
"Lilith." NewC (7:3) 75-76, p. 20.

"Market Day." NewC (7:2) 75-76, p. 3.
"Stillborn." NewC (7:3) 75-76, p. 19.
"Twelfth Bombing of Drussberg." NewC (7:3) 75-76, p. 23.

SORRELLS, Helen
"Infantry Man." CarlMis (16:1/2) Aut-Wint 76-77, p. 59.
"Old Women of Spain." PraS (51:3) Aut 77, p. 247.

SORRENTINO, Gilbert
"Orange Sonnet." Columbia (1) Aut 77, p. 14.

SOSEKI, Natsume
"Natural World" (tr. by Graeme Wilson). DenQ (12:2) Sum 77,
   p. 61.
"Original Faces" (tr. by Graeme Wilson). DenQ (12:2) Sum 77,
   p. 61.

SOTHERLAND, Karen
"In Ohio." BallSUF (18:3) Sum 77, p. 72.

SOTO, Gary
"Antigua." Poetry (130:3) Je 77, p. 153.
"Braly Street." PoNow (14/18) 77, p. 164.
"Catalina Trevino Is Really from Heaven." ParisR (69) Spr 77,
   p. 41.
"The Cellar." Poetry (129:5) F 77, p. 254.
"The Drought." Poetry (130:3) Je 77, p. 152.
"The First." Poetry (130:3) Je 77, p. 150.
"Graciela." ParisR (69) Aut 77, p. 40.
"Harvest." Nat (224:13) 2 Ap 77, p. 413.
"History." PoNow (14/18) 77, p. 164.
"The Leaves." PoetryNW (18:1) Spr 77, p. 24.
"The Little Ones." NewYorker (53:37) 31 O 77, p. 114.
"The Map." NewYorker (53:46) 3 Ja 77, p. 69.
"Mitla." Poetry (130:3) Je 77, p. 149.
"El Niño." SenR (8:1) My 77, p. 71.
"The Pockets." Nat (224:18) 7 My 77, p. 568.
"The Point." Antaeus (27) Aut 77, p. 109.
"Tampamachoco." Poetry (130:3) Je 77, p. 151.
"A Small Boy, Once Lost and Found." Poetry (129:6) Mr 77,
   p. 320.
"The Starlings." Poetry (130:3) Je 77, p. 154.
"The Vision That Should Begin with a Beer." ParisR (69) Spr
   77, p. 42.
"The Wound." SenR (8:1) My 77, p. 69.

SOUTHARD, Larry L.
"A Walk in Early Winter." CarolQ (29:1) Wint 77, p. 74.

SOUTHARD, Samuel C., Jr.
"Each and Every Beauty." PoetL (72:1) Spr 77, p. 9.

SOUTHWICK, Marcia
"The Arsonist." Ploughs (4:1) 77, p. 101.

"Kaspar Hauser. " OhioR (18:2) Spr-Sum 77, p. 19.
"My Husband and I Share a Nightmare. " NewL (44:1) Aut 77,
    p. 18.
"The Train Wreck. " Ploughs (4:1) 77, p. 100.

SOVEREIGN, Bobbi
"Here. " Glass (2:2/3) Wint-Spr 77, p. 83.
"Pompeii Two. " CentR (21:3) Sum 77, p. 278.

SOZAN-KYONIN
"A rootless tree" (tr. by Lucien Stryk). ChiR (29:2) Aut 77,
    p. 84.

SPACKS, Barry
"Be Nice. " Salm (38/39) Sum-Aut 77, p. 115.
"Imagining a Unicorn" (After the Unicorn Tapestries at the
    Cloisters): "Theoretically, there exists a perfect possibility
    of happiness: to believe in the indestructible element in one-
    self and not strive after it. "--Kafka, Parables and Paradoxes.
    Poetry (130:5) Ag 77, p. 276.
"In Memory of L. E. Sissman. " Atl (240:6) D 77, p. 84.
"New Copley in the Gallery. " Shen (28:4) Sum 77, p. 33.
"The News. " Salm (38/39) Sum-Aut 77, p. 115.
"The Parent Birds. " BosUJ (25:3) 77, p. 38.
"The Slogan. " ColEng (39:1) S 77, p. 66.
"Spacks Street. " GeoR (31:4) Wint 77, p. 906.
"Starting Up the Keen. " ColEng (39:1) S 77, p. 66.
"Working Title. " Nat (225:21) 17 D 77, p. 662.

SPAFFORD, Roswell
"Sleeping Beauty. " MissR (6:1) 77, p. 133.

SPEAR, Roberta
"Building a Small House. " QW (3) Spr-Sum 77, p. 37.
"Terremoto: Antigua 1976. " Field (16) Spr 77, p. 29.
"Tonsils. " QW (3) Spr-Sum 77, p. 39.

SPEARS, Woodridge
"The House across the Water. " Wind (27) 77, p. 57.

SPEER, Laurel
"Loners. " GRR (8:1/2) 77, p. 46.
"My Teacher. " PoetL (72:2) Sum 77, p. 65.
"Playing Myself with Bombast. " RemR (5) 77, p. 90.
"The Rock. " GRR (8:1/2) 77, p. 47.
"Sleeping with Guarneri. " CutB (8) Spr 77, p. 33.
"Whores Do Not Play Beethoven. " CutB (8) Spr 77, p. 32.
"Winter Sports. " RemR (5) 77, p. 91.

SPEILMAN, Burge Lee
"3:30 at Badger Mine No. 13. " SouthernPR (17:1) Spr 77, p. 15.

SPENDER, Stephen
"Late Stravinsky Listening to Late Beethoven. " AmerPoR (6:6)

N-D 77, p. 13.
"The Mythical Life of D. H. Lawrence." NewYRB (24:21/22) 26
    Ja 78, p. 16.
"Winter No Winter (London, January 1975)." AmerPoR (6:6) N-D
    77, p. 13.

SPICER, David
    "The Child Who Lives." Juice (4) 77.
    "The Day Is Rare." Juice (4) 77.
    "the jacket." Juice (4) 77.

SPICER, Jack
    "An Exercise" (arr. by Robin Blaser and John Granger). Bound
        (6:1) Aut 77, p. 3.

SPIEGEL, Robert M.
    "Oakland County Jail." Wind (27) 77, p. 29.
    "Sara Susan." Wind (27) 77, p. 60.

SPILMAN, Richard
    "A Convoluted Love Poem." WindO (30) Aut 77, p. 9.
    "Janet, Poem for Poem." TexQ (20:4) Wint 77, p. 164.
    "Primum Mobile." KanQ (9:3) Sum 77, p. 110.

SPINELLI, Jerry
    "Well Enough Alone...." CarolQ (29:2) Spr-Sum 77, p. 77.

SPIRES, Elizabeth
    "Brenda Starr in Hollywood." CarlMis (16:1/2) Aut-Wint 76-77,
        p. 40.
    "Flashback." ColEng (38:5) Ja 77, p. 513.
    "Florida 1969." CarlMis (16:1/2) Aut-Wint 76-77, p. 41.
    "Geisha." AmerPoR (6:3) My-Je 77, p. 37.
    "The Love." CarlMis (16:1/2) Aut-Wint 76-77, p. 39.
    "We Interrupt This Program to Bring You--." AmerR (26) N 77,
        p. 359.

SPIRITUS, January
    "Draft" (for Violette Morgan). YaleLit (146:4/5) 77, p. 40.

SPIVACK, Kathleen
    "Flowers." Ploughs (3:3/4) 77, p. 90.
    "The Fourth of July Which Is Meant to Celebrate Independence."
        PoNow (14/18) 77, p. 165.
    "january thaw." Atl (239:3) Mr 77, p. 44.
    "The Seed." CalQ (11/12) Wint-Spr 77, p. 103.

SPRIGGS, William
    "A Negro Sharecropper's Photograph." BerksR (12:1) Spr 77.
    "On Henry O. Tanner's 'The Banjo Lesson.'" BerksR (12:1) Spr
        77.

SQUIRES, Radcliffe
    "Burning the Books." MalR (44) O 77, p. 139.

STACH, Carl
"Inconspicuous, by Choice, in Kansas." ArkRiv (3:4/4:1) 77,
    p. 28.

STAFFORD, Kim
"two gestures." Drag (16) 77.

STAFFORD, Kim Robert
"Civil War Cemetery." KanQ (9:3) Sum 77, p. 41.
"Dear Bird Banders." CutB (8) Spr 77, p. 37.
"Driving Through the Storm." CutB (8) Spr 77, p. 38.
"The Moon." MontG (5) Wint 77, p. 58.
"Old Penny." KanQ (9:3) Sum 77, p. 41.

STAFFORD, William
"Acoma Mesa." Nat (225:11) 8 O 77, p. 348.
"After Space Travel: A Report to the Academy." CornellR (1)
    Spr 77, p. 79.
"All of Us." CEACritic (40:1) N 77, p. 27.
"Assignment." ModernPS (8:2) Aut 77, p. 173.
"At the Conference on Cold." Nat (224:21) 28 My 77, p. 665.
"Beyond the John Haines Place." OP (24) Aut-Wint 77, p. 29.
"Beyond What the Stock Market Says--A Minifesto for Poets and
    Artists--" ConcPo (10:1) Spr 77, p. 32.
"Campus Portraits." WestHR (31:1) Wint 77, p. 53.
"Class Reunion." CEACritic (40:1) N 77, p. 26.
"Duet for Typewriters." CEACritic (40:1) N 77, p. 28.
"A Face." PartR (44:3) 77, p. 405.
"Forgetting Places." OP (24) Aut-Wint 77, p. 28.
"Found Written on the Sand." Drag (16) 77.
"Inside Lincoln's Head in the Black Hills." OP (24) Aut-Wint
    77, p. 25.
"Little Night Stories." Nat (224:16) 23 Ap 77, p. 507.
"Living on the Plains." ArkRiv (3:4/4:1) 77, p. 45.
"On an Un-Named Mountain." Nat (225:6) 3 S 77, p. 184.
"A Poem with Parts Stolen from a Student's Poem." ThRiPo
    (10) 77, p. 22.
"Reading the Golden Treasury." MissR (6:1) 77, p. 58.
"A Report on the Young." CEACritic (40:1) N 77, p. 26.
"Roadside Markers for West of Dodge." ArkRiv (3:4/4:1) 77,
    p. 44.
"Simple Talk." CornellR (1) Spr 77, p. 80.
"Slave on the Headland." NewYorker (53:24) 1 Ag 77, p. 24.
"Starting a Reading at Stephens." OP (24) Aut-Wint 77, p. 26.
"Still Life" (--For a Daughter Now in College--). CEACritic
    (40:1) N 77, p. 26.
"There Is Blindness." ThRiPo (10) 77, p. 23.
"They Carved an Animal." AmerS (46:2) Spr 77, p. 189.
"Vespers." Hand (1) 77, p. 212.
"Watching a Candle." Nat (225:6) 3 S 77, p. 184.
"Ways of Seeing." Nat (225:6) 3 S 77, p. 184.
"What Ever Happened to the Beats?" ModernPS (8:2) Aut 77,
    p. 173.

"What She Left." CornellR (1) Spr 77, p. 80.
"A Window to Let Pride Out." Nat (224:22) 4 Je 77, p. 697.

STAINTON, Albert
  "Brief Report." DacTerr (14) Spr-Sum 77, p. 55.
  "My Great Aunt Lies Down with a Serpent." Gra (12) 77, p. 41.
  "The Shining Island." Gra (12) 77, p. 5.
  "When the Movie Theater Closed." ParisR (69) Spr 77, p. 36.

STAMBLER, Peter
  "Composition." CimR (38) Ja 77, p. 24.
  "Housekeeping." LittleR (12) 77, p. 13.

STANCE, Derek
  "The Noble Order of the K. B. P." SouthernPR (17:1) Spr 77,
    p. 43.

STANDIFORD, Les
  "Surveillance, Denver." KanQ (9:3) Sum 77, p. 31.

STANDING, Sue
  "Convict's Mirror." Ploughs (4:1) 77, p. 157.
  "Swimming." PraS (51:4) Wint 77-78, p. 393.
  "Wanderlust." PraS (51:4) Wint 77-78, p. 393.

STANECKI, Ken
  "Towel." EngJ (66:5) My 77, p. 57.

STANFORD, Ann
  "After September." SouthernR (13:1) Wint 77, p. 167.
  "The Four Horsemen." SouthernR (13:1) Wint 77, p. 163.
  "I Thought Back and." SouthernR (13:1) Wint 77, p. 166.
  "Lake Glimmerglass." SouthernR (13:1) Wint 77, p. 165.
  "Returning Once More." SouthernR (13:1) Wint 77, p. 164.
  from The Women of Perseus: "Danaë;" "The Graeae;" "Medusa."
    SouthernR (13:1) Wint 77, p. 155.

STANSBERGER, Rick
  "August 1975." Aspect (70) Ja-Mr 77, p. 56.
  "Werewolf" (for Quinn). HiramPoR (23) Wint 77, p. 34.

STANTON, Edward
  "Breakfast at the Hilton." Chelsea (36) 77, p. 49.
  "The Guitar" (tr. of Federico García Lorca). AntR (35:2/3) Spr-
    Sum 77, p. 248.

STANTON, Judith
  "After English Examinations." CarolQ (29:1) Wint 77, p. 66.
  "This Is the Hard Part." CarolQ (29:1) Wint 77, p. 67.

STANTON, Maura
  "At the Landing." AmerPoR (6:2) Mr-Ap 77, p. 3.
  "Bathroom Walls." Ploughs (3:3/4) 77, p. 56.

"Circles." Ploughs (3:3/4) 77, p. 57.
"Depth." MoonsLT (2:3) 77, p. 13.
"The Detective." MoonsLT (2:3) 77, p. 15.
"Maple Tree." Esq (88:5) N 77, p. 94.
"New Neighbors in the South." Ploughs (3:3/4) 77, p. 55.
"The Other House." AmerPoR (6:2) Mr-Ap 77, p. 3.
"Prisoners of the Sun." Esq (88:5) N 77, p. 16 H.
"Snowflake." MoonsLT (2:3) 77, p. 14.
"Visit to Miami." PoNow (14/18) 77, p. 165.

STAP, Don
"Fever." TexQ (20:4) Wint 77, p. 99.
"The Kalamazoo River." QW (4) Aut 77, p. 96.
"Prayers Said Quickly." TexQ (20:4) Wint 77, p. 98.
"These Birds, This Life." QW (4) Aut 77, p. 97.

STAPLES, Katherine
from Illuminations: Twenty-two poems (tr. of Rimbaud). DenQ
(11:4) Wint 77, p. 49.

STAPLETON, Wilson
"dill pickled." Paunch (48/49) S 77, p. 49.

STARR, Meg
"Falling off the human tree." YaleLit (145:4) 77, p. 12.

STEAD, Dom Julian
"December Night." Comm (104:7) 1 Ap 77, p. 199.

STEELE, Frank
"Berry Picking." SmF (6) Aut 77, p. 24.
"Elms." SmF (6) Aut 77, p. 26.
"Markings." SmF (6) Aut 77, p. 27.
"My Mother at the Chapel." SmF (6) Aut 77, p. 25.
"Traveling South." SmF (6) Aut 77, p. 28.

STEELE, Nancy
"Recovering." MontG (5) Wint 77, p. 66.
"Two Nights Approaching Winter." MontG (5) Wint 77, p. 67.
"Worship." MontG (5) Wint 77, p. 65.

STEELE, Paul Curry
"Crux et Corpus." LittleR (12) 77, p. 9.

STEELE, Timothy
"Evening, after the Auction." SouthernR (13:4) Aut 77, p. 775.
"History of a Friendship in Mattapoisett." SouthernR (13:4) Aut
77, p. 777.
"The Messenger." SouthernR (13:4) Aut 77, p. 775.
"Poet at the Christmas Tree." SouthernR (13:4) Aut 77, p. 778.
"Sunday Afternoon" (for Mary Baron, adapting a line from
Alexander Barclay). SouthernR (13:4) Aut 77, p. 774.
"Three Notes Toward Definition." Poetry (130:4) Jl 77, p. 218.

STEFANILE, Felix
"Dawn." Comm (104:7) 1 Ap 77, p. 205.
"The Flight." Wind (27) 77, p. 58.
"Genoveffa." Sparrow (33) Ja 77, p. 20.
"James Higginson of Long Island, 1686-1709." Wind (27) 77,
    p. 58.
"Power Failure." Sparrow (33) Ja 77, p. 18.
"Power Failure." Wind (27) 77, p. 58.
"Saying Sorry to You." Comm (104:3) 4 F 77, p. 86.
"Wintering." Northeast (3:4) Aut-Wint 77-78, p. 6.

STEFANILE, Selma
"Three Haiku." Sparrow (33) Ja 77, p. 22.

STEIER, Rod
"After Monday." Falcon (14) 77, p. 72.

STEIN, Dona
"Because it is finally spring." Epoch (27:1) Aut 77, p. 84.
"Poppies in Siena." Epoch (27:1) Aut 77, p. 83.
"Putting Mother By." Ploughs (3:3/4) 77, p. 127.

STEIN, Mark
"Even if you had said." Confr (15) Aut 77-Wint 78, p. 149.

STEIN, Paul
"Legionaires." Madrona (4:13/14) 77, p. 21.

STEINBERG, Alan
"Ebstein at Night." TexQ (20:1) Spr 77, p. 61.
"Ebstein at the Shore." TexQ (20:1) Spr 77, p. 62.
"Ebstein at the Theater." TexQ (20:1) Spr 77, p. 59.
"The Last Wolf in Washington." GRR (8:1/2) 77, p. 144.
"Night Prayer." WebR (3:4) Aut 77, p. 28.

STEINER, Jörg
"Basilikum, Zu Deutsch Hirnkraut." ChiR (29:3) Wint 78, p. 98.

STEINGASS, David
"The Imponderable Beginning of Poetry." PoNow (14/18) 77, p. 166.
"New England." Chowder (8) Spr-Sum 77, p. 6.
"Sorrento Maine '75." PoNow (14/18) 77, p. 166.
"Those Days." Chowder (8) Spr-Sum 77, p. 7.

STEIR, Pat
"The Last Love Poem." UnmOx (15) 77, p. 69.

STEPANCHEV, Stephen
"At Sea." SouthernPR (17:1) Spr 77, p. 8.
"Rada Dobrich." PoNow (14/18) 77, p. 166.

STEPANIAK, Marcia
"I wish the boys were frogs." AAR (27) 77, p. 95.

STEPHENS, Alan
"At Los Olivos and Alameda Padre Serra." SouthernR (13:1)
    Wint 77, p. 172.

STEPHENS, Carolyn
"His Mother loved him." SeC (5:2) 78, p. 60.
"Poetry." SeC (5:2) 78, p. 59.

STEPHENS, Michael
"Lost Objects" (w. Okhee Stephens). ParisR (70) Sum 77,
    p. 101.
"Merle Oberon's Eyes" (w. Okhee Stephens). ParisR (70) Sum 77,
    p. 101.
"The Old Woman Recalls the Time around the Last Dynasty and
    Her Husband's Departure" (w. Okhee Stephens). ParisR (70)
    Sum 77, p. 99.
"On the Air" (w. Okhee Stephens). ParisR (70) Sum 77, p. 100.

STEPHENS, Okhee
"Lost Objects" (w. Michael Stephens). ParisR (70) Sum 77,
    p. 101.
"Merle Oberon's Eyes" (w. Michael Stephens). ParisR (70) Sum
    77, p. 101.
"The Old Woman Recalls the Time around the Last Dynasty and
    Her Husband's Departure" (w. Michael Stephens). ParisR
    (70) Sum 77, p. 99.
"On the Air" (w. Michael Stephens). ParisR (70) Sum 77,
    p. 100.

STEPHENS, Rosemary
"Nostalgia." SouthernPR (16:SI) 77, p. 76.

STEPHENSON, Shelby
"Grandpa's Gobbler." TexQ (20:4) Wint 77, p. 133.
"Grandpa Manly." Bits (6) Jl 77.
"Harvest Out." WindO (30) Aut 77.
"Katie's Play." WindO (30) Aut 77, p. 6.
"Lesson in Kudzu." WindO (30) Aut 77, p. 7.
"Losing a Gobbler." HiramPoR (22) Aut-Wint 77, p. 35.
"No Rabbit for Dinner." DeKalb (10:3) Spr 77, p. 57.
"October, Turning." SouthernPR (16:SI) 77, p. 76.
"Raccoon Den." DeKalb (10:3) Spr 77, p. 57.
"Where I." WindO (30) Aut 77, p. 6.

STERN, Gerald
"Honey Locust." ThRiPo (10) 77, p. 21.
"96 Vandam." NewYorker (53:20) 4 Jl 77, p. 26.
"The Sweetness of Life." Columbia (1) Aut 77, p. 36.
Twelve poems. AmerPoR (6:2) Mr-Ap 77, p. 23.

STERN, J.
"The Eye of the Deer." MichQR (16:4) Aut 77, p. 404.

STERN, Lee
"Jesus Christ and the Easter Vacation. " StoneC (77:3) S 77,
     p. 12.

STERNBERG, Ricardo da Silveira Lobo
"Gifts. " Nat (225:16) 19 N 77, p. 535.
"Questions. " Ploughs (3:3/4) 77, p. 133.
"Science Fiction" (tr. of Carlos Drummond DeAndrade). Drag
     (16) 77.
"Thumb. " ParisR (70) Sum 77, p. 45.

STERNLIEB, Barry
"The Cure. " Xa (4) 77, p. 6.
"Growing to Ask of Flames. " Xa (4) 77, p. 5.
"Lady Ch'eng. " Rapp (10) 77, p. 18.
"Still Life: Dissecting the Shark. " Xa (4) 77, p. 4.
"Tea Master. " Rapp (10) 77, p. 16.

STESSEL, Harry
"Advice for the Pickers. " WindO (29) Sum 77, p. 12.
"A Hiker's Mountain. " KanQ (9:1) Wint 77, p. 68.
"In the Munch Museum in Oslo. " WindO (29) Sum 77, p. 13.
"Speech for an Abdication. " KanQ (9:1) Wint 77, p. 67.
"Stripped. " SouthernPR (17:2) Aut 77, p. 35.

STEVENS, Alex
"Hat of August. " NewYorker (53:26) 15 Ag 77, p. 36.
"A Rare History. " NewYorker (53:39) 14 N 77, p. 52.

STEVENS, Elisabeth
"Maine Summer. " CentR (21:3) Sum 77, p. 278.

STEWART, Dawnie
"To My Son. " DeKalb (10:3) Spr 77, p. 59.

STEWART, Frank
"Consolation. " Northeast (3:3) Sum 77, p. 18.

STEWART, Marie Vogl
"Recollection. " EngJ (66:5) My 77, p. 45.

STEWART, Pamela
"Above the Tobacco Fields of South Deerfield, Massachusetts. "
     NewYorker (53:8) 11 Ap 77, p. 134.
"The Attic Formalities. " MissR (6:1) 77, p. 124.
"Camera Lucida. " Field (16) Spr 77, p. 40.
"The Fathers. " YellowBR (8) 77, p. 16.
"Henry VIII on the Eve of Anne Boleyn's Execution. " MissR
     (6:1) 77, p. 123.
"The Luminist at Age Eleven. " Ploughs (3:3/4) 77, p. 59.
"My Only Photograph of Cesar Vallejo. " Chowder (9) Aut-Wint
     77, p. 4.
"The Orbit:" AntR (35:2/3) Spr-Sum 77, p. 256.

"Vigil." NewYorker (53:39) 14 N 77, p. 166.

STEWART, Robert J.
"Deborah Is a Short Girl, 16." Focus (12:76) Jl-Ag 77, p. 26.
"The Tree." WebR (3:2) Spr 77, p. 56.
"Walking Away from the Job." DacTerr (14) Spr-Sum 77, p. 16.
"Winter Coming." Bleb (12) 77, p. 7.

STEWART, Susan
"Terror." PoetryNW (18:4) Wint 77-78, p. 37.
"The Way the Milkweed Pods." PoetryNW (18:4) Wint 77-78,
    p. 38.

STEWART, Wayne
"Letting the Fires Go Out." Poem (30) Jl 77, p. 24.

STIELER, George
"The Goose Hunter." Shen (29:1) Aut 77, p. 45.
"It Is Early." PoetL (72:1) Spr 77, p. 22.
"Look at Me Look at You." Shen (28:4) Sum 77, p. 95.

STILL, Gloria
"Alone." WindO (27) Aut 76.
"dewberries dead-." WindO (29) Sum 77, p. 43.
"may." WindO (29) Sum 77, p. 43.
"A Poverty of Everything but Winter." WindO (27) Aut 76.

STILLDAY, Dan
"The Difference between Jim and the White Teachers." AmerPoR
    (6:2) Mr-Ap 77, p. 32.

STILLINGER, Tom
"Singing Pipes & Dancing Stems." YaleLit (146:4/5) 77, p. 56.

STILWELL, Elizabeth
"Where the sun still dares to rise." DeKalb (10:3) Spr 77,
    p. 60.

STILWELL, Robert
"Ellen's Verse." AAR (27) 77, p. 86.
"A Hammer of Ice." AAR (27) 77, p. 85.
"Listening Again to the Seventh Symphony of Sibelius (For Edwin
    Ahearn)." MichQR (16:4) Aut 77, p. 381.
"Loneliness." AAR (27) 77, p. 87.
"October 7 1849." MichQR (16:4) Aut 77, p. 378.
"Once More Looking at a Color Plate of Van Gogh's The Painter
    on His Way to Work." MichQR (16:4) Aut 77, p. 380.
"Once More Seeing A Haystack at Sunset Giverny." MichQR
    (16:4) Aut 77, p. 379.

STIVER, Mary Weeden
"All Minor Ecstasies." CarouselQ (2:1) Spr 77, p. 6.
"Birthplace." CarouselQ (2:1) Spr 77, p. 7.

"The Fat and the Lean." CarouselQ (2:1) Spr 77, p. 8.
"Love's Dual Nature." CarouselQ (2:1) Spr 77, p. 6.

STOCK, Ray
"The Paupers' Prayer." GRR (8:1/2) 77, p. 130.

STOCK, Robert
"Man-Giraffe." MichQR (16:1) Wint 77, p. 47.
"Slaughtering the Cow." Humanist (37:4) Jl-Ag 77, p. 53.

STOKELY, Jim
"Redworm." AndR (4:1) Spr 77, p. 55.

STOKES, Frank
"Scene from a Carousel." KanQ (9:3) Sum 77, p. 105.

STOKES, John
"The Patterning Eye." TexQ (19:4) Wint 76, p. 130.
"To a Bright Illusion." TexQ (19:4) Wint 77, p. 129.

STOKES, Terry
"The Blood Supply in New York City is Low." Some (7/8) 76.
"Night: Fruit Dreams." PoNow (14/18) 77, p. 168.
"Night: The Cuttlefish Scandal." PoNow (14/18) 77, p. 168.
"Passing Out." NewYorker (52:47) 10 Ja 77, p. 32.
"Rochester: Four Times in One Year." Some (7/8) 76.
"The Short-Sighted Matron of Mercy." Some (7/8) 76.
"The Wristwatch." Some (7/8) 76.

STOLOFF, Carolyn
"Behind the Hour." PoNow (14/18) 77, p. 168.
"Holiday." PoNow (14/18) 77, p. 169.
"Noon." PoNow (14/18) 77, p. 168.
"When Uncles Leave." PoNow (14/18) 77, p. 169.

STONE, Arlene
"Chairs in a Field." Chelsea (36) 77, p. 31.
"Meeting for Lunch Oh Yes." PoNow (14/18) 77, p. 169.
"The Rape." Icarus (5:1) Spr 77, p. 9.
"War Marriage." Icarus (5:1) Spr 77, p. 9.

STONE, Bradley
"X." LittleR (12) 77, p. 3.

STONE, Joan
"Dry Gardens." TexQ (20:4) Wint 77, p. 91.
"What's Left to Be Said." PoNow (14/18) 77, p. 170.
"Writing Poems to Keep Warm." TexQ (20:4) Wint 77, p. 169.
"Your Laugh at Wrong Times." TexQ (20:4) Wint 77, p. 151.

STONE, John
"Brain." AmerS (46:1) Wint 76-77, p. 18.
"Dreaming Awake." SouthernPR (16:SI) 77, p. 77.

"He Takes the Course in Advanced Cardiac Life Support. " DenQ
   (12:1) Spr 77, p. 236.
"The Words. " AmerS (46:4) Aut 77, p. 505.

STONE, Mead
   "The Dance. " MinnR (NS8) Spr 77, p. 33.

STORNI, Alfonsina
   "Crossed Out" (tr. by Carolyne Wright). EnPas (5) 77, p. 19.

STOTT, William R. , Jr.
   "For William Carlos Williams. " Thought (52:205) Je 77, p. 204.

STOUT, Robert Joe
   "The Curve of the Earth. " Juice (5) 77.
   "The Personnel Office. " PoNow (14/18) 77, p. 169.
   "Teenagers. " Northeast (3:3) Sum 77, p. 19.

STOUTENBURG, Adrien
   "The Brotherhood. " Kayak (44) F 77, p. 18.
   "Dusk. " Bits (6) Jl 77.
   "Rest Home. " PoNow (14/18) 77, p. 170.
   Thirteen poems. Peb (16) Wint 76-77, pp. 89-104.

STRAND, Mark
   "About a Man. " NewYorker (53:34) 10 O 77, p. 44.
   "For Her. " NewYorker (53:34) 10 O 77, p. 44.
   "For Jessica, My Daughter. " NewYorker (53:34) 10 O 77, p. 44.
   "The House in French Village: For Elizabeth Bishop. "
      NewYorker (53:34) 10 O 77, p. 44.
   "The Late Hour. " NewYorker (53:34) 10 O 77, p. 44.
   "Lines for Winter" (for Ros Krauss). Field (16) Spr 77, p. 24.
   "Night Piece. " NewYorker (53:40) 21 N 77, p. 58.
   "Pot Roast. " NewYorker (52:46) 3 Ja 77, p. 26.
   "Where Are the Waters of Childhood?" NewYorker (53:43) 12 D
      77, p. 48.

STRAPAROLA, Giovanni Francesco
   "Ariana" (tr. by John G. Dickson). Playb (24:10) O 77, p. 175.
   "Clara" (tr. by John G. Dickson). Playb (24:10) O 77, p. 175.
   "Floriana" (tr. by John G. Dickson). Playb (24:10) O 77,
      p. 175.
   "Leonora" (tr. by John G. Dickson). Playb (24:10) O 77,
      p. 175.
   "Lucrezia" (tr. by John G. Dickson). Playb (24:10) O 77,
      p. 175.

STRATIDAKIS, Eileen
   "Ledge. " CimR (41) O 77, p. 64.
   "Nightwalk. " SoCaR (9:2) Ap 77, p. 38.

STREIF, Jan
   "Haiku. " Sparrow (33) Ja 77, p. 2.

"Three Haiku." Sparrow (33) Ja 77, p. 23.
"Wearing Open the Land." Wind (24) 77, p. 27.

STRICKLIN, Robert
"The Final Hope." CarouselQ (2:2) Aut 77, p. 25.

STRINGER, Chip
"Dead Reckoning." QW (2) Wint 77, p. 58.

STRINGHAM, Katy
"I believe shoes learn how to walk." QW (2) Wint 77, p. 61.

STRIPLING, Kathryn
"Afternoon." Iowa (8:3) Sum 77, p. 35.
"Alma." Iowa (8:2) Spr 77, p. 43.
"Daughter." Iowa (8:1) Wint 77, p. 40.
"Drought." SouthernPR (16:SI) 77, p. 78.
"Extremity." Iowa (8:3) Sum 77, p. 34.

STROBLAS, Laurie
"Week-Night Party Plot." Glass (2:2/3) Wint-Spr 77, p. 66.

STRONG, Connie
"The eyes of the Eagle are in me." AmerPoR (6:2) Mr-Ap 77, p. 33.

STRONGWATER, Diane
"Foxy Lady." StoneC (77:2) My 77, p. 29.

STRYK, Dan
"Bethlehem St., Chicago." DeKalb (10:3) Spr 77, p. 62.
"Don's Cafe." WindO (30) Aut 77.

STRYK, Lucien
"Earth, river, mountain" (tr. of Dangai). ChiR (29:2) Aut 77, p. 89.
Eight Haiku (tr. of Japanese Masters, w. Takashi Ikemoto). NewL (43:3) Spr 77, p. 56.
"The Face." AmerPoR (6:4) Jl-Ag 77, p. 32.
"Haiku of the Japanese Masters" (tr., w. Takashi Ikemoto). NowestR (16:3) 77, p. 98.
"Joshu's 'Oak in the courtyard'" (tr. of Eian). ChiR (29:2) Aut 77, p. 85.
"Joshu's word--Nothingness" (tr. of Kuchu). ChiR (29:2) Aut 77, p. 83.
"Lap Dog" (tr. of Shinkichi Takahashi, w. Takashi Ikemoto). Bleb (12) 77, p. 9.
"Mount Sumeru--my fist!" (tr. of Kiko). ChiR (29:2) Aut 77, p. 87.
"Rain." AmerPoR (6:4) Jl-Ag 77, p. 32.
"A rootless tree" (tr. of Sozan-Kyonin). ChiR (29:2) Aut 77, p. 84.
"Sixty-five years" (tr. of Un Bun-etsu). ChiR (29:2) Aut 77, p. 90.

"Talking: seven steps, eight falls" (tr. of Shishin-Goshin).
    ChiR (29:2) Aut 77, p. 88.
Thirteen poems (Zen poems, after Shinkichi Takahashi).
    AmerPoR (6:4) Jl-Ag 77, p. 31.
"Traceless, no more need to hide" (tr. of Suian). ChiR (29:2)
    Aut 77, p. 86.

STUART, Dabney
    "An Anthology of Gripes, Cures, Extractions, Provocative High-
        lights, Censorious Deviations, And I Don't Know What-All
        Elogious Material." SouthernPR (16:SI) 77, p. 80.
    "It Takes One to Know One." MichQR (16:1) Wint 77, p. 26.
    "Plowing It Under." Poetry (130:3) D 77, p. 141.
    "The Top of the Forest." Poetry (130:3) D 77, p. 141.

STUART, Floyd C.
    "Chopping Ice." RemR (5) 77, p. 21.
    "Dawn Horse." Poem (31) N 77, p. 50.
    "A Ritual for the Season." Poem (31) N 77, p. 48.
    "You Are in My Jungle." BelPoJ (27:3) Spr 77, p. 36.

STUART, Jane
    "Sea Poem." Wind (25) 77, p. 59.
    "Traveller's Prayer." Wind (25) 77, p. 59.
    "Vacation." Wind (25) 77, p. 60.

STULL, Dalene Workman
    "Midsummer Night's Dream." PoetL (72:1) Spr 77, p. 13.

STULL, Jonathan
    "Mary of Egypt." KanQ (9:1) Wint 77, p. 81.

STULL, Richard
    "Content." Poetry (130:1) Ap 77, p. 27.
    "Fame." Poetry (130:1) Ap 77, p. 26.
    "The First Year." Poetry (130:1) Ap 77, p. 25.

STURROCK, June
    "Above Ontario." GRR (8:1/2) 77, p. 31.
    "Immigrants." GRR (8:1/2) 77, p. 30.

STYLE, Colin
    "Porches of Bones." SewanR (85:2) Spr 77, p. 214.
    "Rhodes's Bed." SewanR (85:2) Spr 77, p. 213.

SUBHAS, Jeannette Spavieri
    "'In the Night of Audacious Stars.'" CarouselQ (2:1) Spr 77,
        p. 13.
    "Sagamore of the Eastern Tribes." CarouselQ (2:1) Spr 77,
        p. 14.

SUDERMAN, Elmer F.
    "Dreiser and Freud." KanQ (9:2) Spr 77, p. 51.

SUHOR, Charles
"The Slogan." EngJ (66:5) My 77, p. 52.

SUIAN
"Traceless, no more need to hide" (tr. by Lucien Stryk). ChiR
(29:2) Aut 77, p. 86.

SUK, Julie
"Into the Hub." Shen (29:1) Aut 77, p. 64.

SUKENICK, Lynn
"All That Water." Hand (1) 77, p. 109.
"Beatrice Remembers, November 1, 1926." Hand (1) 77, p. 108.
"He's At." Hand (1) 77, p. 107.
"How It Went." Hand (1) 77, p. 107.
"She Goes." Hand (1) 77, p. 108.

SUKUNAMARO, Otomo no
"Heartbreaks" (tr. by Graeme Wilson). DenQ (12:2) Sum 77,
p. 374.

SULKIN, Sidney
"For a Poet We Used to Read." ArizQ (33:4) Wint 77, p. 338.
"In the Beginning." LitR (20:4) Sum 77, p. 364.

SULLIVAN
"cook" (for Kathleen). DeKalb (10:3) Spr 77, p. 63.
"red white red." DeKalb (10:3) Spr 77, p. 64.
"song." DeKalb (10:3) Spr 77, p. 65.
"the thing begun." BallSUF (18:4) Aut 77, p. 71.

SULLIVAN, Bob
"Queen of the Five Points Laundromat." YellowBR (9) 77, p. 8.

SULLIVAN, Chuck
"Early This Bright Morning I Saw a Sunbeam." SouthernPR
(16:SI) 77, p. 82.
"Passing Through" (for Ti Jean). CarolQ (29:3) Aut 77, p. 62.
"The Rosary of Dachau: For Pius XII." SouthernPR (17:2) Aut
77, p. 26.

SULLIVAN, Francis
"Church's Rome Again." DenQ (12:1) Spr 77, p. 250.
"Conference. Not for the Record." DenQ (12:1) Spr 77, p. 251.
Eight poems. Peb (16) Wint 76-77, pp. 73-85.
"Holy Land: 1st Study." DenQ (12:1) Spr 77, p. 256.
"Holy Land: 3rd Study." DenQ (12:1) Spr 77, p. 257.
"Oratorio for an Apocalypse." DenQ (12:2) Sum 77, p. 77.
"Psalm." DenQ (12:1) Spr 77, p. 249.
"Roma. Museo Delle Terme. 1976." DenQ (12:1) Spr 77,
p. 253.
"Zen Narrative." DenQ (12:1) Spr 77, p. 254.

SULLIVAN, James
"Men on Trees. " Comm (104:14) 8 Jl 77, p. 433.

SULLIVAN, Joseph
"Route One. " StoneC (77:1) F 77, p. 31.

SULLIVAN, Walter
"I'm Game. " Aspect (69) O-D 76, p. 33.

SULTZ, Phillip
"Dry Garden. " WebR (3:2) Spr 77, p. 71.

SUMMERS, Anthony
"Compassion. " Vaga (25) 77, p. 49.

SUMMERS, Hollis
"From the Capitol the Entomologist Reports Back Home. "
    SouthernPR (17:2) Aut 77, p. 64.
"Grace/Before Calling the Nursing Home and the Jail. "
    SouthernPR (16:SI) 77, p. 83.
"The Minister Orders His Sermon. " PoNow (14/18) 77, p. 170.
from Occupant Please Forward: "Energy. " PoNow (14/18) 77,
    p. 158.
from Occupant Please Forward: "I Know a Man Who Loved. "
    PoNow (14/18) 77, p. 158.
from Occupant Please Forward: "The Telephones. " PoNow
    (14/18) 77, p. 158.
"The Penitent. " PoetryNW (18:4) Wint 77-78, p. 41.
"Petroglyphs. " PoetryNW (18:4) Wint 77-78, p. 41.

SUMNER, Carolyn
"Reverie in the Garden. " Bound (5:3) Spr 77, p. 783.

SUNG Chung
"Coast" (tr. by Graeme Wilson). DenQ (12:2) Sum 77, p. 49.

SUPERVIELLE, Jules
"Alarm" (tr. by Geoffrey Gardner). VirQR (53:4) Aut 77,
    p. 679.
"47 Boulevard Lannes" (tr. by Geoffrey Gardner). VirQR (53:4)
    Aut 77, p. 677.
"In the Forest" (tr. by Frederick Morgan). Humanist (37:1) Ja-
    F 77, p. 56.
"La Mer secrete. " QW (2) Wint 77, p. 44.
"Projection" (tr. by Geoffrey Gardner). VirQR (53:4) Aut 77,
    p. 681.
"Vivre encore. " QW (2) Wint 77, p. 44.

SURDAS
"(Addressing Krishna)" (tr. by Vasant B. Joshi). DenQ (12:2)
    Sum 77, p. 91.
"The beloved of Krishna" (tr. by Vasant B. Joshi). DenQ (12:2)
    Sum 77, p. 93.

"Where else could my mind" (tr. by Vasant B. Joshi). DenQ
    (12:2) Sum 77, p. 92.

SURVANT, Joe
    "Changes. " WebR (3:4) Aut 77, p. 53.

SU Shun-ch'in
    "My Late Father's Favorite Horse Fell Ill and Was Sent to a
        Separate Stable--Now It Has Died" (tr. by Jonathan Chaves).
        DenQ (12:2) Sum 77, p. 68.
    "That year we got drunk together" (tr. by Jonathan Chaves).
        DenQ (12:2) Sum 77, p. 68.

SUTHERLAND-SMITH, James
    "Definition. " Stand (18:3) 77, p. 26.
    "A Sensuous Language" (for B. E. H.). Stand (18:3) 77, p. 26.

SU Tung-po
    "Mount Lu" (tr. by Graeme Wilson). TexQ (20:4) Wint 77,
        p. 146.
    "Remembrance" (tr. by Graeme Wilson). DenQ (12:2) Sum 77,
        p. 393.

SVOBODA, Robert J.
    "Ms. Mistresses. " SmPd (14:2) Spr 77, p. 17.
    "Whiz Kid. " SmPd (14:3) Aut 77, p. 9.

SVOBODA, Terese
    "Dust Storm. " Nat (225:17) 19 N 77, p. 540.

SWANDER, Mary
    "From an Album. " AntR (35:4) Aut 77, p. 408.
    "In a Dream. " Poetry (129:5) F 77, p. 273.
    "Letter. " Poetry (129:5) F 77, p. 272.
    "Lynching, 1493. " AntR (35:4) Aut 77, p. 410.
    "Oktoberfest. " Nat (224:15) 16 Ap 77, p. 472.
    "Song" (RLS, 1916-74). Poetry (129:5) F 77, p. 275.
    "Winter, 1975. " Nat (224:10) 12 Mr 77, p. 310.

SWANGER, David
    "Horsemanship. " MalR (43) Jl 77, p. 120.
    "Probity. " NewL (44:1) Aut 77, p. 24.
    "The Toad Who Mounts a Horse Becomes a Prince: No Kiss
        Required. " CutB (9) Aut-Wint 77, p. 145.

SWANN, Brian
    from L'Aria secca del fuoco: "Like a Trickle of Watered Blood"
        (tr. of Bartolo Cattafi, w. Ruth Feldman). Some (7/8) 76.
    "The Art of the Past. " YaleR (66:3) Spr 77, p. 404.
    "The Autumn Countryside" (tr. of Bartolo Cattafi, w. Ruth
        Feldman). WebR (3:1) Wint 77, p. 8.
    "Blue Sequence. " SunM (4) Aut 77, p. 117.
    "The Descent to the Throne" (tr. of Bartolo Cattafi, w. Ruth
        Feldman). WebR (3:1) Wint 77, p. 7.

"Eyes. " <u>Falcon</u> (14) 77, p. 77.
"Final Solution. " <u>Pan</u> (18) 77, p. 5.
"Five Physiological Riddles. " <u>Agni</u> (7) 77, p. 120.
"Fragment from a Confucian Fable. " <u>KanQ</u> (9:4) Aut 77, p. 119.
"In Those Small Lakes" (tr. of Melih Cevdet Anday, w. Talat
    Halman). <u>WebR</u> (3:4) Aut 77, p. 51.
"The Luftmensch. " <u>MinnR</u> (NS8) Spr 77, p. 16.
"Magic. " <u>Iowa</u> (8:1) Wint 77, p. 65.
"My Mistakes" (tr. of Bartolo Cattafi, w. Ruth Feldman).
    <u>Confr</u> (14) Spr-Sum 77, p. 141.
"Piranha. " <u>Pan</u> (18) 77, p. 9.
"Red Sequence. " <u>SunM</u> (4) Aut 77, p. 118.
"Riddle. " <u>Agni</u> (7) 77, p. 123.
"Skids. " <u>NewYorker</u> (52:52) 14 F 77, p. 54.
"Stalling. " <u>Pan</u> (18) 77, p. 8.
"A Sumerian Tablet" (tr. of Melih Cevdet Anday, w. Talat
    Halman). <u>WebR</u> (3:4) Aut 77, p. 51.
"These Myths" (tr. of Bartolo Cattafi, w. Ruth Feldman). <u>WebR</u>
    (3:1) Wint 77, p. 7.
"3 Riffs for Keith Jarrett. " <u>WebR</u> (3:1) Wint 77, p. 9.
"Totem Loss. " <u>Agni</u> (7) 77, p. 36.
"Tourist. " <u>YaleR</u> (66:3) Spr 77, p. 404.
"The Traveller Is Outward Bound. " <u>Glass</u> (2:2/3) Wint-Spr 77,
    p. 44.
"Visit" (tr. of Bartolo Cattafi, w. Ruth Feldman). <u>Some</u> (7/8) 76.
"Viva Cuba. " <u>Pan</u> (18) 77, p. 7.
"X. " <u>Pan</u> (18) 77, p. 6.
"With the War Over" (tr. of Bartolo Cattafi, w. Ruth Feldman).
    <u>WebR</u> (3:1) Wint 77, p. 8.

SWARD, Robert
    "Letter to a Straw Hat. " <u>Hand</u> (1) 77, p. 78.

SWEATT, Lisa
    "The Tour. " <u>Wind</u> (24) 77, p. 66.

SWEENEY, Matthew
    "Distraught. " <u>GRR</u> (8:1/2) 77, p. 117.
    "Garden. " <u>GRR</u> (8:3) 77, p. 175.
    "Icarus. " <u>GRR</u> (8:3) 77, p. 176.
    "Nightfall. " <u>GRR</u> (8:1/2) 77, p. 116.
    "Spaceships. " <u>GRR</u> (8:3) 77, p. 178.
    "Was Hast Du Mit Mond Getan?" <u>GRR</u> (8:1/2) 77, p. 118.

SWEET, Nanora
    "After the Sirloin. " <u>ConcPo</u> (10:2) Aut 77, p. 23.
    "Eleven Line Poem. " <u>ConcPo</u> (10:2) Aut 77, p. 24.

SWENSON, Karen
    "Coney Island. " <u>Aspen</u> (4) Aut 77, p. 44.
    "Leftover. " <u>PraS</u> (51:3) Aut 77, p. 245.
    "A Persian Lover. " <u>Columbia</u> (1) Aut 77, p. 18.
    "The Red Turtleneck. " <u>Aspen</u> (4) Aut 77, p. 45.

SWENSON, May
"A Navajo Blanket." CornellR (1) Spr 77, p. 78.
"October." NewYorker (53:37) 31 O 77, p. 45.
"View to the North." NewYorker (52:49) 24 Ja 77, p. 83.

SWETS, R. D.
"fin de siecle." Aspect (70) Ja-Mr 77, p. 28.
"For My Roller Derby Queen." Aspect (70) Ja-Mr 77, p. 28.
"A Miner Explains His Early Retirement." Madrona (4:13/14)
    77, p. 32.
"reality mobius." BallSUF (18:4) Aut 77, p. 52.
"Tonight in the Nightmare." NoAmR (262:4) Wint 77, p. 52.
"Two Ways of Meaning." KanQ (9:2) Spr 77, p. 86.
"Winter Prys." NoAmR (262:4) Wint 77, p. 52.

SWIFT, Joan
"Plankton." PoetryNW (18:1) Spr 77, p. 16.
"Sea Urchin Shell." Chowder (9) Aut-Wint 77, p. 30.
"Sutil Point." PortR (23) 77, p. 62.

SWIGART, Rob
"Bone Poem." PoetryNW (18:1) Spr 77, p. 15.

SWILKY, Jody
"Close to the Earth." OhioR (18:2) Spr-Sum 77, p. 22.

SWISS, Thom
"Bathers." Ascent (3:2) 77, p. 42.
"Marble." Ascent (3:2) 77, p. 41.

SWIST, Wally
"Morning." YaleLit (145:5) 77, p. 12.

SWOPE, Mary
"Loaded." 13thM (3:2) 77, p. 43.
"Soap Opera." 13thM (3:2) 77, p. 42.

SYLVESTER, William
"your father tells." Aspect (69) O-D 76, p. 37.

SZABEDI, László
"Creative Poverty" (tr. by Jeanette Nichols). ModernPS (8:2)
    Aut 77, p. 99.
"Irrationale" (tr. by Jeanette Nichols). ModernPS (8:2) Aut 77,
    p. 99.
"The Marriage of Death" (tr. by Jeanette Nichols). ModernPS
    (8:2) Aut 77, p. 100.

SZERLIP, Barbara
"Japanese in Three Weeks: Daily Conversation Made Easy (Re-
    vised 1961)" (found poem). Kayak (45) My 77, p. 30.
"Terra Incognita." Kayak (45) My 77, p. 29.
"24." Kayak (45) My 75, p. 28.

TABITO, Otomo no
"Absurdity" (tr. by Graeme Wilson). DenQ (11:4) Wint 77,
    p. 168.
"Birth Wish" (tr. by Graeme Wilson). DenQ (12:2) Sum 77,
    p. 372.

TABORI, Paul
"After the Flood" (tr. of Zoltan Keszthelyi). ModernPS (8:2)
    Aut 77, p. 106.
"Letter to My Mother" (tr. of Géza Képes). ModernPS (8:2) Aut
    77, p. 104.

TADAMINE, Mibu no
"Dreams" (tr. by Graeme Wilson). DenQ (12:2) Sum 77, p. 54.

TADAON, Suga no
"Heart" (tr. by Graeme Wilson). DenQ (12:2) Sum 77, p. 366.

TAGAMI, Jeff
"Dream of the Philippines. " GreenR (6:1/2) Spr 77, p. 61.
"Grandmother. " GreenR (6:1/2) Spr 77, p. 63.

TAGGART, John
from Dodeka: "a third plait, a bracelet. " Montra (3) Spr 77,
    p. 47.

TAGLIABUE, John
"Anita remembering the 2nd Meeting, on the Grand Pavilion of
    Paradiso, World's Fair. " Aspect (70) Ja-Mr 77, p. 11.
"By My School Office Window, after the Rain, Very Bright and
    Cool and Much Green, June, July and August. " AndR (3:1)
    Spr 76, p. 69.
"Could Adam and Eve Have Known Better?" Icarus (5:2) Aut 77,
    p. 3.
"The decisions by streams and mountains without end. " SunM
    (4) Aut 77, p. 22.
"Faberge Decorated with the Medal of the Legion of Honor, the
    Richmond Museum, Virginia. " NewL (43:4) Sum 77, p. 51.
"From the top of the Eiffel Tower. " Stonecloud (6) 76, p. 10.
"Landscape in the style of Fan K'uan. " SunM (4) Aut 77, p. 23.
"Man of Amorous Integrity. " Kayak (45) My 77, p. 32.
"March 1963; The Month after the Death of Robert Frost. "
    AndR (3:1) Spr 76, p. 68.
"My Zia Anita. " CentR (21:2) Spr 77, p. 157.
"The Restoration. " Kayak (45) My 77, p. 33.
"Specks, Spectacles, Impressions or Dialogue between the Sun
    and an Impressionist Painter. " Stonecloud (6) 76, p. 11.
"The Survival of the Passing of Time. " Stonecloud (6) 76,
    p. 10.
"Three in the Gugenheim Museum. " NewL (43:4) Sum 77, p. 52.
"The Traveller's Rescue by the Rukh. " SunM (4) Aut 77, p. 20.
"Two Poems. " PoNow (14/18) 77, p. 170.
"The Valley Rite" (Five Poems from the Noh Journal). NewL
    (43:3) Spr 77, p. 47.

"While the Young Pianist Practices Intensely for Her Great
Performance We Look at the Paintings of Marsden Hartley,
Thomas Eakins, Whistler, Winslow Homer." AndR (4:1) Spr
77, p. 63.

TAKACS, Nancy
"Grandpa in English." DenQ (12:3) Aut 77, p. 66.
"July 18th, the Old House, and Birds." CutB (9) Aut-Wint 77,
p. 76.
"The Old Country" (for Aunt Mary). CutB (9) Aut-Wint 77,
p. 77.
"Your Winter Visit." CutB (9) Aut-Wint 77, p. 75.

TAKAHASHI, Shinkichi
"Lap Dog" (tr. by Takashi Ikemoto and Lucien Stryk). Bleb (12)
77, p. 9.
Thirteen poems (Zen poems, rendered into English by Lucien
Stryk). AmerPoR (6:4) Jl-Ag 77, p. 31.

TAKAMURA, Kotaro
Twenty poems (tr. by Hiroaki Sato). Montra (3) Spr 77,
pp. 107-29.

TAKUBOKU, Ishikawa
"Prayers" (tr. by Graeme Wilson). WestHR (31:1) Wint 77,
p. 60.

TALARICO, Ross
"After Becoming an Image of Christ Outstretched on a Rock,
Beautiful and Temporarily Dead, in a Lover's Dream." QW
(4) Aut 77, p. 107.
"Learning to Ride." Shen (28:2) Wint 77, p. 96.
"The Metal Detector." PoNow (14/18) 77, p. 171.
"Night Flight." PraS (51:3) Aut 77, p. 234.
"Prayer for Myself." PoetryNW (18:1) Spr 77, p. 27.
"Romance." PoetryNW (18:1) Spr 77, p. 26.
"Sitting in the VD Clinic." Iowa (8:1) Wint 77, p. 69.
"Ten Years." SouthernPR (17:2) Aut 77, p. 10.
"Trying to Get Back." NoAmR (262:3) Aut 77, p. 62.
"The Way." PoNow (14/18) 77, p. 171.

TALCOTT, Rita
"I live in the sun. My name is cold." AAR (27) 77, p. 122.

TALL, Deborah
"The Appointment." Epoch (26:2) Wint 77, p. 111.
"Ninth Life." YaleR (67:1) Aut 77, p. 71.
"The Performance." Epoch (26:2) Wint 77, p. 110.
"'Touched Three Times....'" Nat (224:19) 14 My 77, p. 604.

TALL MOUNTAIN, Mary
"Grandmother's Dream." PoetryNW (18:3) Aut 77, p. 25.

TALMADGE, Jeffrey D.
"Versions." TexQ (20:4) Wint 77, p. 102.

TALNEY, Ron
"The Broken World." PortR (23) 77, p. 119.
"The Hunter." PortR (23) 77, p. 120.

TAMBUZI
"I Betcha Ain't Never...." NewRena (9) F 77, p. 61.
"Sister Nikki Is a Real Bad Poet." NewRena (9) F 77, p. 60.

TAMMARO, Thom
"Where West Is." QW (2) Wint 77, p. 3.

TAMMENGA, Michael J.
"Weavers War" (for Eva). NewC (7:2) 75-76, p. 10.

TANG Yin
"Afterworlds" (tr. by Graeme Wilson). WestHR (31:3) Sum 77,
    p. 210.

TANKA, Hoto
"The Grasshopper." LittleR (12) 77, p. 7.

TAN Yew-kee
"The Way" (tr. by Graeme Wilson). TexQ (20:4) Wint 77, p. 145.

T'AO Ch'ien
    from Drinking Wine: "I built my hut within man's sphere" (tr.
        by J. P. Seaton). CarolQ (29:2) Spr-Sum 77, p. 121.
    from Drinking Wine: "The orchid, hidden, growing, in the
        court" (tr. by J. P. Seaton). CarolQ (29:2) Spr-Sum 77,
        p. 121.
    "Inwardness" (tr. by Graeme Wilson). TexQ (20:4) Wint 77,
        p. 148.
    "On Reading the Shan Hai Ching" (tr. by Christopher Howell).
        PortR (23) 77, p. 99.

TAO-Li
    Two Haiku. WindO (27) Aut 76.

TAPSCOTT, Stephen
    "Afterglow." Drag (16) 77.
    "another October, the green." Epoch (26:2) Wint 77, p. 196.
    "The Man Who Stutters Says Goodbye to the Finches." Epoch
        (26:2) Wint 77, p. 193.
    "The Momentous." PoNow (14/18) 77, p. 171.
    "Monday Morning." Epoch (26:2) Wint 77, p. 192.
    "The Voice Underfoot." Epoch (26:2) Wint 77, p. 195.

TARACHOW, Michael
    "Another View from the Third Floor." DacTerr (14) Spr-Sum
        77, p. 69.

TARGAN, Barry
"River Towns. " PoNow (14/18) 77, p. 171.

TARVER, Stanley
"Black Rivers. " NegroHB (40:5) S-O 77, p. 750.

TATE, James
"Daydreaming in the Forge. " BosUJ (25:1) 77, p. 62.
"Dream of a Prose Poem. " Some (7/8) 76.
"In a Motel on Lake Erie. " Some (7/8) 76.
"Leaving Montana in a Flash. " PoNow (14/18) 77, p. 172.
"Lost Illusions. " Some (7/8) 76.
"Move It. " BosUJ (25:1) 77, p. 62.
"My First Bloomers. " Some (7/8) 76.
"Rooster. " BosUJ (25:1) 77, p. 60.
"The Sun Never Forgets. " BosUJ (25:1) 77, p. 61.

TAYLOR, Alexander
"Sheila. " PoNow (14/18) 77, p. 172.

TAYLOR, Brian
"Ducky. " ParisR (71) Aut 77, p. 170.
"Just Good Friends in Pecos. " ParisR (71) Aut 77, p. 172.
"Play Time. " ParisR (71) Aut 77, p. 171.

TAYLOR, Bruce Edward
"The Woman Next Door. " KanQ (9:3) Sum 77, p. 112.

TAYLOR, Charles B.
"Insurance. " LitR (20:4) Sum 77, p. 397.

TAYLOR, Davis
"Love Poem. " CarlMis (16:1/2) Aut-Wint 76-77, p. 118.
"Model. " CarlMis (16:1/2) Aut-Wint 76-77, p. 118.
"Mother. " CarlMis (16:1/2) Aut-Wint 76-77, p. 119.
"Swimming Pool. " CarlMis (16:1/2) Aut-Wint 76-77, p. 117.

TAYLOR, Eleanor Ross
"Va. Sun. A.M. Dec. '73. " NewYorker (53:22) 18 Jl 77,
    p. 89.

TAYLOR, Henry
"Bathing in Lightning. " HolCrit (14:1) F 77, p. 12.
"The Muse Once More. " SouthernPR (16:SI) 77, p. 84.

TAYLOR, I. P.
"The Hollow Places. " Stand (18:2) 77, p. 64.

TAYLOR, Jay
"The Washo. " Waters (6) 77, p. 11.

TAYLOR, John
Eleven poems. DenQ (12:2) Sum 77, p. 345.

"Insomnia." Stonecloud (6) 76, p. 31.
"Letter to Someone I Once Knew." Stonecloud (6) 76, p. 120.
"Roses Gone Wild." NewL (44:1) Aut 77, p. 103.
"A Shot of Old Taylor" (on being asked to judge another womans-
    club poetry contest). BallSUF (18:2) Spr 77, p. 64.

TAYLOR, K. P. A.
"Manter's Point." SewanR (85:2) Spr 77, p. 215.
"Requiescant." SewanR (85:2) Spr 77, p. 217.
"Tropic of Cancer." SewanR (85:2) Spr 77, p. 216.

TAYLOR, Kent
"Round Trip from San Francisco." Vaga (25) 77, p. 57.

TAYLOR, Laurie
"Excavation at L'Anse Amour." WebR (3:4) Aut 77, p. 56.
"Night Terrors." WebR (3:4) Aut 77, p. 57.

TAYLOR, Leah
"Letter from the Asylum." Gra (12) 77.

TAYLOR, Les
"Boxwood." Poetry (130:3) D 77, p. 142.

TAYLOR, Marion
"Fishes." Ploughs (3:3/4) 77, p. 153.

TAYLOR, Ross
"Self Portrait." SouthernPR (17:2) Aut 77, p. 20.

TAYLOR, Ruie
"Dryest Winter." PortR (23) 77, p. 156.
"Outside the Window." PortR (23) 77, p. 155.
"A Poem for Rheva." PortR (23) 77, p. 154.

TAYLOR, William E.
"Eastward to the Royal Towers." NewRivR (2:1) 77, p. 28.
"A Life of Crime." NewRivR (2:1) 77, p. 29.
"The Runners." SouthernPR (16:SI) 77, p. 86.
"Winter." SouthernPR (17:2) Aut 77, p. 25.

TELLES, Paul
"Overture." Wind (24) 77, p. 22.

TEMPLETON, Fiona
"Quotations." PartR (44:2) 77, p. 265.

TENNY, Carol
"I See a Woman" (tr. of Tanikawa Shuntarō). Field (17) Aut 77,
    p. 39.

TERRILL, Mildred K.
"Abraham's Servant." TexQ (20:3) Aut 77, p. 60.

"Grackles at Sunrise." TexQ (20:3) Aut 77, p. 60.
"Grendel: Dragon Dicta." TexQ (20:3) Aut 77, p. 61.
"Rehearsal." TexQ (20:3) Aut 77, p. 61.

TERRIS, Virginia
"The Beetle." ParisR (70) Sum 77, p. 187.
"Driving." ParisR (70) Sum 77, p. 188.
"Generations." Gra (12) 77.
"Identification." ParisR (70) Sum 77, p. 186.

TESH, Jack
"On Watching Football Practice from a Car." EngJ (66:5) My
    77, p. 52.

THACKER, Julia
"The Grape Pickers." Antaeus (27) Aut 77, p. 108.
"Johns Hopkins Leukemic Center." NoAmR (262:4) Wint 77.

THALMAN, Mark
"My Old Man." Qt (57/58) Wint-Spr 77, p. 17.

THOMAS, D. M.
"Hymen." TransR (60) Je 77, p. 111.
"Orpheus in Hell" (in memory O. M.). AmerS (46:4) Aut 77,
    p. 481.
"Vienna. Zürich. Constance." AmerS (46:4) Aut 77, p. 479.

THOMAS, David
"Fungus History." MontG (6) Aut 77, p. 13.
"Seasons in Prairie Blood." MontG (6) Aut 77, p. 10.
"What the Bi-Centennial Means to Me." MontG (5) Wint 77,
    p. 36.

THOMAS, F. Richard
"Dream." Wind (26) 77, p. 48.
"One Night the Family Man Goes Out on His Own." Wind (26)
    77, p. 47.
"The Party." Wind (26) 77, p. 47.

THOMAS, Harry
"Seasonal Poem" (For Adriana). SouthernR (13:4) Aut 77,
    p. 767.

THOMAS, Janet
"The Cat That Ate the Flower That I Bought to Grace the Kitch-
    en Has Not Been Outside in Five Years." Ploughs (4:1) 77,
    p. 162.

THOMAS, Jim
"Hawk's Wheel." NewRivR (2:1) 77, p. 20.
"Leck's Goodbye." NewRivR (2:1) 77, p. 21.
"The Use of Concrete." KanQ (9:1) Wint 77, p. 84.

THOMAS, Joyce Carol
  "Hide the Children." AmerPoR (6:1) Ja-F 77, p. 28.

THOMAS, Lisa
  "All Morning." DeKalb (10:3) Spr 77, p. 68.
  "Counting My Sister." PoetL (72:2) Sum 77, p. 52.
  "Evening" (in memory of Anne Sexton). Vaga (26) 77, p. 88.
  "Hours." DeKalb (10:3) Spr 77, p. 69.
  "Old Man at the Go Board." NewOR (5:3) 77, p. 223.

THOMAS, Mary Ann Ruhl
  "LeRoy, Michigan." GRR (8:1/2) 77, p. 123.

THOMPSON, Agnes
  "Cash Transactions." KanQ (9:3) Sum 77, p. 44.

THOMPSON, Hunter
  "Collect Telegram from a Mad Dog." Aspen (3) Spr 77, p. 39.

THOMPSON, Jeanie
  "Marie Laurencin's Portrait of Appollinaire." Antaeus (27) Aut
      77, p. 118.

THOMPSON, Joanna
  "Jim Thorpe." CimR (41) O 77, p. 14.

THOMPSON, Phyllis Hoge [see also HOGE]
  "Death and Memory." PoNow (14/18) 77, p. 172.
  "Jade." NewYorker (53:14) 23 My 77, p. 111.

THOMSON, Sharon
  "Without Dark Tinted Glasses." Aspect (70) Ja-Mr 77, p. 49.

THORINGTON, Helen
  "The story hasn't started yet." Chelsea (36) 77, p. 72.

THORN, Arline R.
  "Termination Letter." AAUP (64:4) N 77, p. 300.

THORN, Lee
  "Celluloid." Mouth (11/12) Mr-Je 77, p. 70.

THORPE, Dwayne
  "Four Demons." Shen (28:2) Wint 77, p. 86.
  "The Moon Is the Square of All Distances." ConcPo (10:2) Aut
      77, p. 8.

THORPE, John
  "Between Villon." Hills (4) 77.
  "Men's Shelter." Hills (4) 77.
  "Z." Hills (4) 77.

THULANI
   "he didn't give up/he was taken. " Nimrod (21:2/22:1) 77,
      p. 290.
   "he was taken. " Obs (3:2) Sum 77, p. 56.
   "Rogue & Jar. " Nimrod (21:2/22:1) 77, p. 288.
   "song to some other man. " Obs (3:2) Sum 77, p. 57.

TIETZ, Steve
   "Every Foot of Ground Is Dirt Cheap. " WindO (29) Sum 77,
      p. 9.

TIFFT, Doug
   "Memory's Triad. " YaleLit (146:2) 77, p. 4.

TILLINGHAST, David
   "The Pinkeyville Rabbits. " PoetL (72:2) Sum 77, p. 59.
   "Space Mountain Rocketship Ride. " PoetL (72:2) Sum 77, p. 64.

TILLINGHAST, Richard
   "The Knife" (for David Tillinghast). NewRep (177:10) 3 S 77,
      p. 26.
   "A Poem to Go Before Eight Lines by Jalal-ud-din-Rumi. "
      Ploughs (4:1) 77, p. 76.

TIMMERMAN, John
   "Green Ridge. " PoetL (72:2) Sum 77, p. 48.

TINGLEY, Cindy
   "Storm. " QW (2) Wint 77, p. 29.

TINKLE, Harold
   "Black River Farm. " Bits (6) Jl 77.

TIPTON, James
   "Fields. " PoNow (14/18) 77, p. 172.

TIROLIEN, Guy
   "Prayer of a Little Black Manchild" (tr. by Jim Barnes).
      Nimrod (21:2/22:1) 77, p. 291.

TITT, Kenneth W.
   "Too Long Hiatus, Terminated. " CarouselQ (2:3) Wint 77, p. 8.

TOBEN, Deborah Dobkins
   "Conestoga. " KanQ (9:4) Aut 77, p. 118.

TOBIN, David
   "Deer Bound. " ModernPS (8:2) Aut 77, p. 136.
   "Nightfall in the Unknown Woods. " ModernPS (8:2) Aut 77,
      p. 135.

TOBIRA, Ato
   "Obsession" (tr. by Graeme Wilson). DenQ (12:2) Sum 77,
      p. 372.

TODD, Alexander
"Meat Rack. "   Mouth (11/12) Mr-Je 77, p. 93.

TODD, Patrick
"Country Wedding. "   MontG (5) Wint 77, p. 28.

TODD, Theodora
"In the Center of Wichita. "   ArkRiv (3:4/4:1) 77, p. 10.
"Sunday I Was the Only One to Catch Anything. "   ArkRiv (3:4/4:1)
     77, p. 11.
"3 A. M. "   KanQ (9:4) Aut 77, p. 67.

TOKUHAMA, Tracey
"Top hat on the table, smiling because the opera just left town. "
     HangL (30) Sum 77, p. 79.

TOLMAN, Jon M.
"Poem" (tr. of Augusto de Campos, w. Mary Ellen Solt and Jon
     M. Tolman).   LitR (21:2) Wint 78, p. 276.
"se len cio" (tr. of Haroldo de Campos, w. Mary Ellen Solt).
     LitR (21:2) Wint 78, p. 208.

TOLNAY, Thomas
"Hooray, We're Cripples!"   LitR (20:4) Sum 77, p. 431.
"The Rowboat and the Knife. "   LitR (20:4) Sum 77, p. 432.

TOLSON, Melvin B.
"Augustus Lence. "   NewL (43:3) Spr 77, p. 14.
"Chittling Sue. "   NewL (43:3) Spr 77, p. 11.
"Flora Murdock. "   NewL (43:3) Spr 77, p. 15.
"Lena Lovelace. "   NewL (43:3) Spr 77, p. 13.
"Pearl Tripplett. "   NewL (43:3) Spr 77, p. 12.
"The Underdog. "   NewL (43:3) Spr 77, p. 17.

TOMASSON, Verna Safran
"The Shrinking Man. "   Gra (12) 77.

TOMIOKA, Taeko
"Age" (tr. by Hiroaki Sato).   DenQ (12:2) Sum 77, p. 227.
"Fine Day" (tr. by Hiroaki Sato).   DenQ (12:2) Sum 77, p. 228.
"Nights" (tr. by Hiroaki Sato).   DenQ (12:2) Sum 77, p. 226.

TOMLINS, Jack
"Ceramics" (tr. of Carlos Drummond de Andrade).   LitR (21:2)
     Wint 78, p. 168.
"Confession" (tr. of Carlos Drummond de Andrade).   LitR (21:2)
     Wint 78, p. 166.
"The Dead Horse" (tr. of Cecília Meireles).   LitR (21:2) Wint
     78, p. 205.
"Dead Men in Their Frock Coats" (tr. of Carlos Drummond de
     Andrade).   LitR (21:2) Wint 78, p. 169.
"Death in the Absolute" (tr. of Manuel Bandeira).   LitR (21:2)
     Wint 78, p. 218.

"Discovery" (tr. of Carlos Drummond de Andrade). LitR (21:2) Wint 78, p. 168.
"Heptagonal Poem" (tr. of Carlos Drummond de Andrade). LitR (21:2) Wint 77, p. 166.
"I'm Off at Last for Passargadae" (tr. of Manuel Bandeira). LitR (21:2) Wint 78, p. 214.
"International Congress of Fear" (tr. of Carlos Drummond de Andrade). LitR (21:2) Wint 78, p. 167.
"The Last Poem" (tr. of Manuel Bandeira). LitR (21:2) Wint 78, p. 218.
"The Man from Itabira Tells His Secret" (tr. of Carlos Drummond de Andrade). LitR (21:2) Wint 78, p. 169.
"Psychology of Composition" (tr. of João Cabral de Melo Neto). LitR (21:2) Wint 78, p. 240.
"Seated Woman" (tr. of João Cabral de Melo Neto). LitR (21:2) Wint 78, p. 240.
"The Table" (tr. of João Cabral de Melo Neto). LitR (21:2) Wint 78, p. 239.

TOMLINSON, Charles
"At Dawn" (In Memoriam F. M. D.). Hudson (30:1) Spr 77, p. 15.
"Below Tintern. " Hudson (30:4) Wint 77-78, p. 522.
"Embassy. " Hudson (30:4) Wint 77-78, p. 523.
"The Faring. " Hudson (30:1) Spr 77, p. 14.
"The Gap. " Hudson (30:1) Spr 77, p. 15.
"In the Balance. " Hudson (30:4) Wint 77-78, p. 522.
"The Metamorphosis. " Hudson (30:4) Wint 77-78, p. 523.
"Providence. " Hudson (30:1) Spr 77, p. 13.
"Rhymes. " Hudson (30:1) Spr 77, p. 14.
"The Roe Deer. " Hudson (30:1) Spr 77, p. 13.
"The Scar. " Hudson (30:4) Wint 77-78, p. 524.

TOMLINSON, Russanne
"Just last night. " SeC (5:2) 78, p. 61.

TOMPKINS, B. A. , III.
"National Theatre. " Stonecloud (6) 76, p. 108.

TOMPKINS, Elise
"Hesitancies. " HarvAd (110:3) Mr 77, p. 29.
"Poem: Clouds accoppiato in cerulean of the evening. " HarvAd (111:1) N 77, p. 17.

TORGERSEN, Eric
"In a Subdivision. " PoNow (14/18) 77, p. 173.
"No Hands. " PoNow (14/18) 77, p. 173.
"Owl Gift. " DacTerr (14) Spr-Sum 77, p. 67.
"Poem for Nettie Collins. " PoNow (14/18) 77, p. 172.
"Poem for You Now. " DacTerr (14) Spr-Sum 77, p. 66.

TORNAI, József
"Mr. T. S. Eliot Cooking Pasta" (tr. by Richard Wilbur). NewYorker (53:2) 28 F 77, p. 35.

TORNES, Beth
  "Nocturnal. " Field (17) Aut 77, p. 37.
  "Sleep. " Field (17) Aut 77, p. 36.

TORODE, Mary R.
  "After They Return from Angola Maybe. " Pig (3) 77, p. 92.

TORREGIAN
  "Horse Dregs on the Road. " Chelsea (36) 77, p. 70.

TOTH, Judit
  "Notes on Saint Maurice" (tr. by Laura Schiff). AmerPoR (6:3)
    My-Je 77, p. 26.
  "Seine Wharves Southeast" (tr. by Jascha Kessler). ParisR (69)
    Spr 77, p. 133.

TOTH, Steve
  Eleven poems. Spirit (2:2/3) 77, pp. 128-34.

TOWLE, Barbara Bloom
  "The Myths Do Not Tell Us. " SouthernPR (17:2) Aut 77,
    p. 68.

TOWNER, Daniel
  "The House Plants. " SouthernPR (17:1) Spr 77, p. 43.
  "Mesopotamia. " PoNow (14/18) 77, p. 173.
  "Mother, Mother, Mother. " Bits (6) Jl 77.

TRACHTENBERG, Paul Jon
  "Alter Ego. " Stonecloud (6) 76, p. 13.

TRAKAS, Deno
  "Old Easom. " KanQ (9:1) Wint 77, p. 94.
  "Symmetry. " DenQ (12:1) Spr 77, p. 48.

TRAKL, Georg
  "Abendland: The Occident" (for Else Lasker-Schüler in admira-
    tion). TransR (58/59) F 77, p. 164.
  "At Night" (tr. by Felix de Villiers). TransR (58/59) F 77,
    p. 165.
  "Grodek" (tr. by Felix de Villiers). TransR (58/59) F 77,
    p. 166.

TRAN Te Xuong
  "The Frenchman's Concubine" (tr. by Graeme Wilson). WestHR
    (31:3) Sum 77, p. 213.
  "Jailed Priest" (tr. by Graeme Wilson). DenQ (12:2) Sum 77,
    p. 62.

TRAN Thai Tong
  "The Future Buddha" (tr. by Graeme Wilson). WestHR (31:1)
    Wint 77, p. 58.

TRAXLER, Patricia
  from Blood Calendar: "Blood Calendar." PoNow (14/18) 77,
    p. 174.
  from Blood Calendar: "Note to the Neighbors." PoNow (14/18)
    77, p. 174.
  from Blood Calendar: "The Twister." PoNow (14/18) 77,
    p. 174.
  "The Glass Woman." HangL (30) Sum 77, p. 64.
  "Suppers." PoNow (14/18) 77, p. 175.
  "To the Tombstone Maker." PoNow (14/18) 77, p. 175.

TREADWELL, George
  "Reading Your Letter Saturday Morning." Wind (27) 77, p. 59.

TREBBE, Gail
  "Penelope" (for Gary). CarlMis (17:1) Wint 77-78, p. 98.

TRECHOCK, Mark
  "After a Photograph of Hans Küng." ChrC (94:20) 1 Je 77,
    p. 530.
  "Private Communion." NewOR (5:3) 77, p. 270.

TREFETHEN, Florence
  "Bombay: The Towers of Silence." PoetL (72:1) Spr 77, p. 30.
  "Remembering Miranda." PoetL (72:1) Spr 77, p. 31.
  "The Secretary." PoetL (72:1) Spr 77, p. 31.
  "To Adam in Africa." PoetL (72:1) Spr 77, p. 30.

TREININ, Avner
  "Niagara Falls" (tr. by Shirley Kaufman and Shlomit Rimmon).
    TriQ (39) Spr 77, p. 304.
  "Really" (tr. by E. A. Levenston). TriQ (39) Spr 77, p. 306.
  from Songs of Leonardo: (1-7) (tr. by Shirley Kaufman and Judy
    Levy). TriQ (39) Spr 77, p. 306.

TREITEL, Margot
  "The Student Nurse Is Having a Breakdown." ModernPS (8:3)
    Wint 77, p. 220.
  "The Tigris and Euphrates Days." ModernPS (8:3) Wint 77,
    p. 216.
  "Vermeer's Two Rooms in Delft." Xa (4) 77, p. 38.

TREJO, Ernesto
  "The Day of Vendors." Kayak (44) F 77, p. 59.
  "It's Your Name and It's Also December." Nat (224:21) 28 My
    77, p. 662.
  "The President Is Up before the Fruit Vendor." Kayak (44) F
    77, p. 58.

TRELAWNY, Victor
  "Conversation with a Woman." PortR (23) 77, p. 40.
  "North/South." CutB (9) Aut-Wint 77, p. 83.
  "Redeeming Landscape." PortR (23) 77, p. 41.

"What the Land Offers. " PoetryNW (18:4) Wint 77-78, p. 11.
"The Whirl. " CutB (9) Aut-Wint 77, p. 84.
"Winter Landscape, 1840. " PortR (23) 77, p. 41.

TREMBLAY, Bill
"Carrying an Oar Inland. " MidwQ (19:1) Aut 77, p. 68.
"Evening With Novelists at Crown Point Estates. " MidwQ (19:1)
    Aut 77, p. 65.
"Hogback. " MidwQ (19:1) Aut 77, p. 67.
"Taking Down the Tree. " MidwQ (19:1) Aut 77, p. 64.

TRIEM, Eve
"The Antidote. " Wind (25) 77, p. 63.
"Birthday Gifts from Poland. " Wind (25) 77, p. 62.
"Black Laughter. " Wind (25) 77, p. 62.
"Bordello, Revisited." PoNow (14/18) 77, p. 175.
"For Paul. " Wind (25) 77, p. 63.
"Is This Poem Necessary?" Wind (25) 77, p. 64.
"Tomorrow Very Brightly. " Wind (25) 77, p. 64.
"Woodcarving: Owl Family" (Philip McCracken). PoNow (14/18)
    77, p. 176.

TRIFILIO, Jim
"The Preparation of the Outer Man. " CutB (9) Aut-Wint 77,
    p. 101.
"The Wisdom of Yoga on the Plains of Abraham. " CutB (9) Aut-
    Wint 77, p. 99.

TRIMBLE, Mary H.
"Solstice" (for Ralph Mills). NewC (8:1) 76-77, p. 3.

TROLL, Tim
"Apricot Mush. " KanQ (9:4) Aut 77, p. 55.

TROPMAN, Sarah
"I am a picture hanging on the wall. " AAR (27) 77, p. 114.

TROUPE, Quincy
"The Day Duke Raised: May 24, 1974" (for Duke Ellington).
    Epoch (26:3) Spr 77, p. 244.
"The Day Duke Raised: May 24, 1974" (for Duke Ellington).
    Nimrod (21:2/22:1) 77, p. 293.
"Four, And More: for Miles Davis. " Epoch (26:3) Spr 77,
    p. 246.

TROW, Lisa Beth
"Planting. " TexQ (20:4) Wint 77, p. 94.

TROWER, Peter
"The Reclaimed. " Poetry (129:5) F 77, p. 250.

TRUCK, Fred
"Stone Pilared Family Tree. " LaB (5) Ja 77, p. 17.

TRUDELL, Dennis
"A Fable." Chowder (8) Spr-Sum 77, p. 31.
"Idyll." PoNow (14/18) 77, p. 176.

TRUESDALE, C. W.
from Pope John's Motel: "I am thinking of two words." Paunch
(48/49) S 77, p. 155.

TRUSTMAN, Deborah
"Clearing." Poetry (129:4) Ja 77, p. 200.
"The Fall." Poetry (129:4) Ja 77, p. 199.
"Shelling." Poetry (129:1) Ja 77, p. 201.
"Watercolor." Poetry (129:4) Ja 77, p. 198.

TSURAYUKI, Ki no
"Crane" (tr. by Graeme Wilson). DenQ (12:2) Sum 77, p. 367.
"Travelling to Azuma" (tr. by Graeme Wilson). DenQ (12:2)
Sum 77, p. 357.

TSURUTA, Dorothy Jane Randall
"Bicentennial Woman." NegroHB (40:3) My-Je 77, p. 704.
"Bicentennial Woman II." NegroHB (40:3) My-Je 77, p. 704.

TUCKER, Liza
"A Brief Meditation on an Old Woman and a Puschcart" (tr. of
Miroslav Holub, w. Michael Kraus). Field (16) Spr 77,
p. 76.
"A Brief Meditation on Brief Meditations" (tr. of Miroslav Holub,
w. Michael Kraus). Field (16) Spr 77, p. 77.

TUDOR, Stephen
"Burial Ground near Celilo Falls." Waters (6) 77, p. 28.
"Gold Statue of Chief Kandiyohi, First National Bank, Willmar,
Minnesota." Waters (6) 77, p. 29.
"Grant and Catron Counties, New Mexico, 1939." Waters (6) 77,
p. 22.
"Viewing the Indian Mounds on the Bluffs above the Mississippi
River at Quincy, Illinois." Waters (6) 77, p. 27.

TUEL, Kristen
"nightmares are funny." AAR (27) 77, p. 110.

TU Fu
"The Day" (ad. by J. P. Seaton). CarolQ (29:2) Spr-Sum 77,
p. 122.
"A Mei-P'i Lake Song" (tr. by Steve Owen). YaleLit (145:5) 77,
p. 17.
"Song for a Falcon, Whose Beak Hangs Open" (tr. by Steve
Owen). YaleLit (145:5) 77, p. 18.

TULLOSS, Rod
"The Gunslinger in Winter." Columbia (1) Aut 77, p. 26.
"In the Back of the Refrigerator." US1 (9) Spr 77, p. 8.

"In the Midst of Reading Wang Wei. " <u>US1</u> (10) Wint 77-78,
　　p. 11.
from Molested Oafs: "Fuses in a Little Blood" (tr. of Mikhail
　　Kuzmin). <u>Some</u> (7/8) 76.
from The North Carolina Rent-a-Car Hunger Poems: (2, 4, 5,
　　7). <u>US1</u> (9) Spr 77, p. 8.

TURBYFILL, Mark
　　"Am I then your estranged creator. " <u>ChiR</u> (28:4) Spr 77, p. 39.
　　"The Builder. " <u>ChiR</u> (28:4) Spr 77, p. 35.

TURCO, Lewis
　　"The Bears in the Land-Fill. " <u>PoetryNW</u> (18:3) Aut 77, p. 45.
　　"The Colony. " <u>GeoR</u> (31:2) Sum 77, p. 473.
　　"The Cooperage. " <u>NewC</u> (7:3) 75-76, p. 9.
　　"Dybbuk. " <u>GeoR</u> (31:1) Spr 77, p. 235.
　　"Juggernaut. " <u>Poem</u> (31) N 77, p. 1.
　　"The Maple Works. " <u>GeoR</u> (31:2) Sum 77, p. 474.
　　"Melancholy Love. " <u>NewC</u> (7:2) 75-76, p. 6.
　　"Minotaur. " <u>NewC</u> (7:3) 75-76, p. 3.
　　"Phoenix and Salamander. " <u>Poem</u> (31) N 77, p. 2.
　　"The Recurring Dream" (for Stanley Kunitz). <u>Hudson</u> (30:3) Aut
　　　　77, p. 400.
　　"The Silo. " <u>Nat</u> (224:8) 26 F 77, p. 248.
　　"The Stable. " <u>MichQR</u> (16:3) Sum 77, p. 287.
　　"Troglodyte. " <u>CalQ</u> (11/12) Wint-Spr 77, p. 144.
　　"The Trolley. " <u>Comm</u> (104:18) 2 S 77, p. 551.
　　"The Wind Carol. " <u>MissR</u> (6:1) 77, p. 100.

TURGEON, Gregoire
　　"At Home. " <u>Poetry</u> (130:2) My 77, p. 79.
　　"Before the Rain. " <u>Epoch</u> (27:1) Aut 77, p. 57.
　　"Wind. " <u>Epoch</u> (27:1) Aut 77, p. 56.

TURNER, Alberta
　　"Anyone, Lifting. " <u>ThRiPo</u> (10) 77, p. 34.
　　"Elm Street. " <u>ThRiPo</u> (10) 77, p. 34.

TURNER, Jamie
　　"America. " <u>SeC</u> (5:2) 78, p. 34.

TURNER, Willis
　　"At Road Camp Twenty. " <u>HolCrit</u> (14:1) F 77, p. 14.

TURNSEN, Michael
　　"Sparrow. " <u>Juice</u> (4) 77.

TUSSMAN, Malka Heifetz
　　"Songs of the Priestess" (trans. by Marcia Falk). <u>Hand</u> (1) 77,
　　　　p. 54.

TUTOR, Glennray
　　"Next to an Orchard. " <u>WestHR</u> (31:3) Sum 77, p. 246.

"October Rows." WestHR (31:3) Sum 77, p. 205.
"The Turtle Killer." WestHR (31:3) Sum 77, p. 261.

TU Wei-ming
  "Release" (tr. of Wang Yang-ming, w. Leonard Nathan).
     Chowder (8) Spr-Sum 77, p. 47.

TWICHELL, Chase
  "Angst." PortR (23) 77, p. 131.
  "The North." PortR (23) 77, p. 130.
  "Sisters" (for Eliza). PraS (51:2) Sum 77, p. 150.
  "Snow Light" (for Rick). PraS (51:4) Wint 77-78, p. 411.
  "A Stone from the Bottom." PraS (51:2) Sum 77, p. 152.
  "This Was a Farm." PraS (51:2) Sum 77, p. 149.

TWISS, Dorothy
  "But You Know All That." CalQ (11/12) Wint-Spr 77, p. 140.

TYLER, Susan G.
  "Heatwave." Chomo (4:2) Aut-Wint 77, p. 54.

TYRE, William E.
  "used to catch flies." Glass (2:2/3) Wint-Spr 77, p. 42.

TZELTAL (Tenejapa)
  "Story of the Ants and Grasshoppers" (tr. by W. S. Merwin, w.
     Santiago Mendez Zapata and Kathy Branstetter). Nat (225:14)
     29 O 77, p. 444.

UKON, Lady
  "Betrayal" (tr. by Graeme Wilson). DenQ (12:2) Sum 77,
     p. 357.

ULLMAN, Leslie
  "Ceremony." OP (24) Aut-Wint 77, p. 17.
  "Each Year." OP (24) Aut-Wint 77, p. 13.
  "Eventually, You." Nat (225:3) 23-30 Jl 77, p. 86.
  "The Immaculate Stairs." OP (24) Aut-Wint 77, p. 16.
  "Nostalgia." OP (24) Aut-Wint 77, p. 14.
  "On Vacation a Woman Mistakes Her Leg." NewYorker (53:30)
     12 S 77, p. 40.
  "Plumage." Madem (83:1) Ja 77, p. 56.
  "Roots." OP (24) Aut-Wint 77, p. 12.

UN Bun-etsu
  "Sixty-five years" (tr. by Lucien Stryk). ChiR (29:2) Aut 77,
     p. 90.

UNDERWOOD, Jane
  "Homing." QW (2) Wint 77, p. 75.

UNGARETTI, Giuseppe
  from L'allegria: "One night all night" (tr. by Justin Vitiello).
     PoetL (72:2) Sum 77, p. 62.

UNGER, Barbara
  "Cold Wash." YellowBR (9) 77, p. 20.
  "Collections." StoneC (77:3) S 77, p. 14.
  "Mother-Root." Glass (2:2/3) Wint-Spr 77, p. 102.
  "Touch." KanQ (9:3) Sum 77, p. 111.

UNOKU
  "Words" (tr. by Graeme Wilson). DenQ (12:2) Sum 77, p. 57.

UNTERECKER, John
  "Aprils." Kayak (44) F 77, p. 21.
  "The Betrayal." NewL (44:1) Aut 77, p. 89.
  "English 3 (1938)" (for Mary Walz, Corine Palmerton, and all
    the others). Salm (36) Wint 77, p. 42.
  "Friends, Lovers, at Pohoiki, Hawaii." PoNow (14/18) 77,
    p. 177.
  "The Garden." SouthernR (13:2) Spr 77, p. 343.
  "Genesis." Wind (27) 77, p. 60.
  "Hospital." Poetry (130:3) Je 77, p. 134.
  "January 23: Fragment" (for John Logan). Salm (36) Wint 77,
    p. 41.
  "Lava Tubes." PoNow (14/18) 77, p. 176.
  "Listening to the Night." SouthernR (13:2) Spr 77, p. 344.
  "Night Piece." PoetryNW (18:4) Wint 77-78, p. 10.
  "Nothing Soft, Nothing Loved." PoetryNW (18:4) Wint 77-78,
    p. 11.
  "The Roof." Epoch (26:2) Wint 77, p. 184.
  "The Sleepers." Kayak (46) O 77, p. 34.
  "Song for Emily, 91 Years After." Bits (6) Jl 77.
  "Still Life: Hawaii." Pequod (2:3) Sum 77, p. 25.
  "Summer." Kayak (44) F 77, p. 20.
  "Talking to the Darkness." Kayak (44) F 77, p. 22.
  "Waiting" (for Maxine Hong Kingston). GeoR (31:4) Wint 77,
    p. 881.
  "... Within, Into, Inside, Under, Within...." Poetry (129:6)
    Mr 77, p. 311.

UPDIKE, John
  "Dream and Reality." NewYorker (52:49) 24 Ja 77, p. 34.
  "The Melancholy of Storm Windows." BosUJ (25:1) 77, p. 30.
  "Rats." Atl (239:2) F 77, p. 34.

UPTON, Lee
  "So Much." SmPd (14:2) Spr 77, p. 5.
  "Somewhere So Lush." ChiR (29:2) Aut 77, p. 102.
  "Whispers." SmPd (14:3) Aut 77, p. 17.

URDANG, Constance
  "The Brother Poems: Hide and Seek." NewL (43:4) Sum 77,
    p. 79.
  "In the Suburbs." NewL (43:4) Sum 77, p. 78.
  "Living in the Third World." AmerPoR (6:2) Mr-Ap 77,
    p. 48.

URIOSTE, Pat Keuning
"Laundromat Literature." YellowBR (9) 77, p. 6.

UZOARU, Onyegbule C.
"For the Lady in Cubicle B." Nimrod (21:2/22:1) 77, p. 301.
"I Was Away...." Nimrod (21:2/22:1) 77, p. 302.

VACHA, Koke
"Men." Mouth (13) D 77, p. 78.

VACHON, Ann
"Singsong." WebR (3:2) Spr 77, p. 55.

VAJDA, David
"Advanced Forest Husbandry: 401." CarouselQ (2:3) Wint 77,
   p. 31.
"Auden and Lemonade." SmPd (14:3) Aut 77, p. 4.
"Breton Has Gone to the Dry-Cleaning Closet." CarouselQ (2:3)
   Wint 77, p. 31.
"Heraclitus at Steiner's Diner." CarouselQ (2:3) Wint 77, p. 31.

VALENTINE, Jean
"Father" (based on tr. of Huub Oosterhuis by Judith Herzberg).
   AmerPoR (6:2) Mr-Ap 77, p. 21.
"Orpheus" (based on tr. of Huub Oosterhuis by Judith Herzberg).
   AmerPoR (6:2) Mr-Ap 77, p. 21.
"Turn" (for F. & P. L.). TransR (58/59) F 77, p. 97.

VALERIN, Ron
"A View from the Pond." BerksR (12:1) Spr 77.

VALLEE, Lillian
"Diary of a Naturalist" (tr. of Czeslaw Milosz, w. the author).
   Chowder (8) Spr-Sum 77, p. 48.
Fifteen poems (tr. of Czeslaw Milosz, w. the author). AmerPoR
   (6:4) Jl-Ag 77, p. 23.

VALLEJO, César
   from Payroll of Bones: "Alphonso, you keep looking at me, I
      see" (tr. by Clayton Eshleman and José Rubia Barcia).
      Bound (5:3) Spr 77, p. 748.
   from Payroll of Bones: "Chances are, I am another; walking,
      at dawn, another who moves" (tr. by Clayton Eshleman and
      José Rubia Barcia). Bound (5:3) Spr 77, p. 751.
   from Payroll of Bones: "Farewell Remembering a Goodbye" (tr.
      by Clayton Eshleman and José Rubia Barcia). Bound (5:3)
      Spr 77, p. 750.
   from Payroll of Bones: "I stayed on to warm up the ink in
      which I drown" (tr. by Clayton Eshleman and José Rubia
      Barcia). Bound (5:3) Spr 77, p. 747.
   from Payroll of Bones: "Oh bottle without wine! Oh wine the
      widower of this bottle!" (tr. by Clayton Eshleman and José
      Rubia Barcia). Bound (5:3) Spr 77, p. 745.

from Payroll of Bones: "This" (tr. by Clayton Eshleman and
    José Rubia Barcia). Bound (5:3) Spr 77, p. 746.
from Payroll of Bones: "Upon reflecting on life, upon reflecting"
    (tr. by Clayton Eshleman and José Rubia Barcia). Bound
    (5:3) Spr 77, p. 744.

Van BEENAN, Barton B.
"The Last Look." Wind (27) 77, p. 67.

Van BRUNT, H. L.
"America--Part I." PoNow (14/18) 77, p. 177.

VANDER MOLEN, Robert
"Circumstances: Richard." Wind (27) 77, p. 40.
"Doilies." NewL (43:4) Sum 77, p. 76.
"Squinting." Drag (16) 77.
"Strawberries in the White Bowl." NewL (43:4) Sum 77, p. 76.
"The Sun." GRR (8:1/2) 77, p. 62.
"Susan." Wind (27) 77, p. 40.
"Up the Hill Road." Wind (27) 77, p. 41.

VANDERSEE, Charles
"Civilian." Bound (5:2) Wint 77, p. 613.
"Dead of Summer." Bound (5:2) Wint 77, p. 612.
"Elysian Fields by Cary Wasserman." SewanR (85:4) Aut 77,
    p. 611.
"Leaving." SouthernPR (17:2) Aut 77, p. 61.
"Still Life with Flowers by Thomas Taggart." SewanR (85:3) Sum
    77, p. 435.

Van DUYN, Mona
"At Père Lachaise." NewYorker (53:6) 28 Mr 77, p. 44.

Van DYKE, Cheryl
"Indian Pipe (Monotropa uniflora)." MontG (5) Wint 77, p. 57.
"Kuhn Spit." MontG (5) Wint 77, p. 56.

VAN Hanh
"Doctrine" (tr. by Graeme Wilson). DenQ (12:2) Sum 77, p. 54.

Van SANT, C. L.
"My Sleeping Family." ChrC (94:14) 20 Ap 77, p. 380.

Van SPANCKEREN, Kathryn
"Capitalist Bestiary I: Yankee Trader." Ploughs (3:3/4) 77,
    p. 139.
"The Sea's Side." EnPas (5) 77, p. 32.
"Slow Weathering Down to Where the Changes Are." EnPas (5)
    77, p. 28.

Van WINCKEL, Nance
"Amorgan Triptych." ArkRiv (3:4/4:1) 77, p. 64.
"Letter to Eleanor in Denver." ArkRiv (3:4/4:1) 77, p. 62.

VÁRADY

"Ophelia Gathers Garlands, Accepts the Night." MalR (42) Ap 77, p. 53.
"Water Witching." MissR (6:1) 77, p. 135.

VÁRADY, Szabolcs
"Chairs above the Danube" (tr. by Richard Wilbur). NewYorker (53:2) 28 F 77, p. 34.

VARGIN, Georgii
"City Streets" (tr. by Daniel Weissbort). DenQ (11:4) Wint 77, p. 24.

VARNER, Carol
"Work and Sleep." Box (5) Spr 77, p. 14.

VARTNAW, Bill
"Doin' Time." YellowBR (9) 77, p. 30.

VAS, István
"The Deaf Mute Girl" (tr. by Charles A. Wagner). ModernPS (8:2) Aut 77, p. 114.
"The Etruscan Sarcophagus" (tr. by William Jay Smith). AmerPoR (6:3) My-Je 77, p. 23.
"Insult" (tr. by Thomas Kabdebo). ModernPS (8:2) Aut 77, p. 115.
"Saint Médard" (tr. by William Jay Smith). AmerPoR (6:3) My-Je 77, p. 22.

VEAZEY, Mary
"Pygmalion Revisited." CimR (38) Ja 77, p. 12.

VECCHARELLI, Ann
"To My Yet Unrealized Daughter or Son." PoetL (72:1) Spr 77, p. 34.

VEENENDAAL, Cornelia
"The Carpenter and His Child." HangL (30) Sum 77, p. 73.
"Consider Anything, Only Don't Cry." HangL (30) Sum 77, p. 72.
"Must It Be? It Must Be." HangL (30) Sum 77, p. 74.

VEGA, Janine Pommy
"Stargazer" (for John Eskow). MontG (6) Aut 77, p. 74.
"Tale of the Hunter." MontG (6) Aut 77, p. 72.
"The Traveler" (for Susan & Martin Carey). Falcon (14) 77, p. 36.

VENIT, James
"Home Movies." PartR (44:4) 77, p. 554.
"Little Chapter." PartR (44:4) 77, p. 555.

VENTADOUR, Fanny
"I Shall Roll Amongst You." NewC (7:2) 75-76, p. 23.

"Son Hurt in a Ski Race." Qt (57/58) Wint-Spr 77, p. 34.

VERMEIRE, Drew
"Quivira Saddle Club." EngJ (66:5) My 77, p. 50.

VEST, Quentin
"Background Material." VirQR (53:4) Sum 77, p. 722.
"Le Grand Éléphant de Tours." Antaeus (27) Aut 77, p. 98.
"If the Right One Don't Get You Then the Left One Will."
    VirQR (53:4) Aut 77, p. 723.
"Tracing My Name." Antaeus (27) Aut 77, p. 101.

VIANT, William
"May Fly." StoneC (77:3) S 77, p. 9.

VIERA, Ricardo
"A Short Story" (w. Ken Fifer). Juice (4) 77.

VIERECK, Peter
from Applewood: "Fourth Gate." BosUJ (25:3) 77, p. 36.
from Applewood: "Story of Man." GRR (8:1/2) 77, p. 77.
"Backtalk." PraS (51:1) Spr 77, p. 96.
"The Three Days Underground." MichQR (16:2) Spr 77, p. 171.

VILAS, Bob
"Cool as I Am, I Do Give a Damn." AmerPoR (6:2) Mr-Ap 77,
    p. 33.

VILLANUEVA, Alfredo
"Carpe Diem with a Twist." Mouth (13) D 77, p. 85.
"Leo is upstairs." Mouth (13) D 77, p. 77.
"Yesterday, in the subway." Mouth (13) D 77, p. 77.

VILLASIS-FLORES, Bobby
"Three for D. D. V." Mouth (11/12) Mr-Je 77, p. 112.

VILLIERS, Felix de
"Abendland: The Occident" (for Else Lasker-Schüler in admira-
    tion) (tr. of Georg Trakl). TransR (58/59) F 77, p. 164.
"At Night" (tr. of Georg Trakl). TransR (58/59) F 77, p. 165.
"Georg Trakl" (tr. of Else Lasker-Schüler). TransR (58/59) F
    77, p. 166.
"Grodek" (tr. of Georg Trakl). TransR (58/59) F 77, p. 166.
"Homesickness" (tr. of Else Lasker-Schüler). TransR (58/59) F
    77, p. 167.
"My People" (tr. of Else Lasker-Schüler). TransR (58/59) F 77,
    p. 168.
"Styx" (tr. of Else Lasker-Schüler). TransR (58/59) F 77,
    p. 168.

VILLON, François
"Ballade I" (tr. by Galway Kinnell). ParisR (70) Sum 77,
    p. 102.

"Ballade II" (tr. by Galway Kinnell). ParisR (70) Sum 77, p. 103.
from The Testament: "In the thirtieth year of my time" (tr. by
   Galway Kinnell). AmerPoR (6:5) S-O 77, p. 23.

VINCE, Michael
   "The Awakening." SouthernR (13:4) Aut 77, p. 773.
   "The Memorial Trees." SouthernR (13:4) Aut 77, p. 772.

VINING, James Whitfield
   "Condor." Wind (27) 77, p. 15.
   "The Sun and the Sea." Wind (27) 77, p. 15.

VINOGRAD, Julia
   from Street Pieces: "Freshman." PoNow (14/18) 77, p. 179.
   from Street Pieces: "The Heat." PoNow (14/18) 77, p. 179.
   from Street Pieces: "Love Story." PoNow (14/18) 77, p. 179.
   from Street Pieces: "Well?" PoNow (14/18) 77, p. 179.

VINZ, Mark
   "Bicentennial Minute." Northeast (3:3) Sum 77, p. 3.
   "Death Wish." MontG (5) Wint 77, p. 54.
   "Gladys and Alma." Chowder (8) Spr-Sum 77, p. 43.
   "Hometown Blues." CutB (9) Aut-Wint 77, p. 150.
   "Invitation." MontG (5) Wint 77, p. 55.
   from Letters to the Poetry Editor: "Dear Editor." PoNow
      (14/18) 77, p. 179.
   from Letters to the Poetry Editor: "Dear Shithead." PoNow
      (14/18) 77, p. 179.
   from Letters to the Poetry Editor: "Dear Sir." PoNow (14/18)
      77, p. 179.
   "Poet, Seeking Credentials, Pulls Daring Daylight Robbery of
      Small Town Iowa Bank." CutB (9) Aut-Wint 77, p. 151.
   "Recluse." ThRiPo (10) 77, p. 37.
   "Resolution." PoetryNW (18:1) Spr 77, p. 44.
   "Survival Manual." PoNow (14/18) 77, p. 177.
   "Swimmer." Northeast (3:3) Sum 77, p. 28.
   "The World's Greatest Two-Piece Band." Focus (12:76) Jl-Ag
      77, p. 26.

VIOLI, Paul
   from Harmatan: Eight poems. LaB (5) Ja 77, p. 19.
   "Index." PoNow (14/18) 77, p. 178.
   "Snorkeling with Captain Bravo." Some (7/8) 76.

VITIELLO, Justin
   from L'allegria: "One night all night" (tr. of Giuseppe
      Ungaretti). PoetL (72:2) Sum 77, p. 62.
   "To the Great Zero" (two versions) (tr. of Antonio Machado).
      PoetL (72:2) Sum 77, p. 62.

VOGELWEIDE, Walther von der
   "'Dô der sumer komen was'" (tr. by Linda Parshall). PortR
      (23) 77, p. 88.

"'In einem zwîvellîchen wân'" (tr. by Linda Parshall). PortR
(23) 77, p. 89.
"'Mir hât hêr Gêrhart Atze ein pfert'" (tr. by Linda Parshall).
PortR (23) 77, p. 87.
"'Wir suln den kochen râten'" (tr. by Linda Parshall). PortR
(23) 77, p. 87.

VOGT, Petra
from The Torment of Al Hallaj: "1. As a Young Man" (tr. of
Abd al-Wahab al-Bayyati, w. Ira Cohen). MontG (6) Aut 77,
p. 30.

VOIGT, Ellen Bryant
"Seizure." NewYorker (53:10) 25 Ap 77, p. 46.

VOLK, Craig
"Rodeo Rocko." Northeast (3:4) Aut-Wint 77-78, p. 58.

VO Ngon-thong
"On a Sealing Mind" (tr. by Graeme Wilson). DenQ (12:2) Sum
77, p. 51.

VOZNESENSKY, Andrei
"Monologue of the World's Last Poetry Reader (Poetry Day,
1999)" (tr. by Guy Daniels). AmerR (26) N 77, p. 389.

WAAGE, Fred
"Lead." StoneC (77:1) F 77, p. 21.

WADE, John Stevens
"Aviary." Wind (26) 77, p. 50.
from Each to His Own Ground: "Each to His Own Ground."
PoNow (14/18) 77, p. 180.
from Each to His Own Ground: "Spark Plugs." PoNow (14/18)
77, p. 180.
from Each to His Own Ground: "Upstairs." PoNow (14/18) 77,
p. 180.
"Forecast." BallSUF (18:1) Wint 77, p. 23.
"Hard Cider." Wind (26) 77, p. 50.
"January." AAR (27) 77, p. 71.
"Landfill." Aspect (70) Ja-Mr 77, p. 8.
"Life-Style." Aspect (70) Ja-Mr 77, p. 7.
"Pig Swill." AAR (27) 77, p. 73.
"Spring Plans." Icarus (5:2) Aut 77, p. 22.
"Tall Pine." AAR (27) 77, p. 72.

WAGNER, Anneliese
"village night." Ploughs (4:1) 77, p. 160.

WAGNER, Charles A.
"The Deaf Mute Girl" (tr. of István Vas). ModernPS (8:2) Aut
77, p. 113.

WAGNER, Linda
  "Light Grows." ModernPS (8:3) Wint 77, p. 226.
  "Love Poem." NewL (44:1) Aut 77, p. 102.

WAGONER, David
  "After the Speech to the Librarians." WestHR (31:4) Aut 77,
    p. 326.
  from Collected Poems 1956-1976: "The Uncanny Illusion of the
    Headless Lady." PoNow (14/18) 77, p. 180.
  from Collected Poems: 1956-1976: "Walking in a Swamp."
    PoNow (14/18) 77, p. 180.
  "Cutting Down a Tree." Poetry (130:3) Je 77, p. 158.
  "The Death of the Moon." Poetry (130:3) Je 77, p. 155.
  "Dirge for a Player-Piano." WestHR (31:4) Aut 77, p. 324.
  "Elegy for a Minor Poet." Poetry (130:3) Je 77, p. 160.
  "The Gift." Poetry (130:3) Je 77, p. 157.
  "How Coyote Become Young Coyote." PraS (51:4) Wint 77-78,
    p. 397.
  "How Coyote Learned the Five Songs of Water." Chowder (9)
    Aut-Wint 77, p. 21.
  "How Young Fox and Young Coyote Went Hungry." PraS (51:4)
    Wint 77-78, p. 396.
  "Jeremiad." WestHR (31:4) Aut 77, p. 321.
  "Judging Logs." Shen (29:1) Aut 77, p. 42.
  "Lament for the Non-Swimmers." Atl (239:6) Je 77, p. 69.
  "My Father's Wall." NewYorker (53:1) 23 F 77, p. 97.
  "My Flying Circus." WestHR (31:4) Aut 77, p. 324.
  Nine poems. ChiR (29:1) Sum 77, p. 5.
  "Pile-Driver." Atl (240:5) N 77, p. 74.
  "Stunts." Kayak (46) O 77, p. 52.
  "Thawing a Birdbath on New Year's Day." Antaeus (27) Aut 77,
    p. 56.
  "Thistledown." Poetry (130:3) Je 77, p. 156.
  "Touched-by-the-Moon." Iowa (8:4) Aut 77, p. 67.
  "Waterfall." WestHR (31:4) Aut 77, p. 326.

WAHLE, F. Keith
  "The Muse of Television." Waters (5) 77, p. 13.
  "Theory of Knowledge." Waters (5) 77, p. 11.

WAINO, Ken
  "Hunting Voices." MontG (6) Aut 77, p. 7.
  "The Red Machines." MontG (6) Aut 77, p. 8.

WAKOSKI, Diane
  "The Hitchhikers." Poetry (130:3) Je 77, p. 128.
  "Life Is Like a Game of Cards, Or Another One of Those Meta-
    physical Statements from a Distant Reader" (for Al Green-
    berg and Wendy Parish). CentR (21:4) Aut 77, p. 385.
  "A Poem in Response to Rexroth, Irish Coffee, a Day Alone,
    Forgiving Men, For They Have No Wombs, No Treasury,
    No Sense of the Infinite Possession of Self" (to the Librari-
    an). CentR (21:4) Aut 77, p. 382.

"The Ring." Poetry (130:3) Je 77, p. 125.
"Running Men." CornellR (1) Spr 77, p. 81.
"Tearing Up My Mother's Letters." Poetry (130:3) Je 77,
    p. 126.
"To the Thin and Elegant Woman Who Resides Inside of Alix
    Nelson." Gra (12) 77, p. 8.

WALCOTT, Derek
    from The Schooner, Flight: (I, VI, VIII). MassR (18:4) Wint
        77, p. 795.

WALD, Diane
    "I Was Awake All Night." Rapp (10) 77, p. 70.
    "She-Beast." Kayak (44) F 77, p. 42.
    "Signed Confession." Kayak (44) F 77, p. 43.
    "Take Yourself Back." Iowa (8:2) Spr 77, p. 39.
    "To One of Good Memory & Manners." Rapp (10) 77, p. 71.

WALD, Susana
    from Los placeres de Edipo: "XIV. Everything in That Sphere"
        (tr. of Ludwig Zeller, w. John Robert Colombo). MontG
        (6) Aut 77, p. 33.
    from The Rules of the Game: "Guess or I Get You" (tr. of
        Ludwig Zeller, w. John Robert Colombo). MontG (6) Aut
        77, p. 34.
    from The Rules of the Game: "Landscape for the Blind" (tr. of
        Ludwig Zeller, w. John Robert Colombo). MontG (6) Aut
        77, p. 37.
    from The Rules of the Game: "Riches to Register" (tr. of
        Ludwig Zeller, w. John Robert Colombo). MontG (6) Aut
        77, p. 36.
    from The Rules of the Game: "The Smugglers' Laws" (tr. of
        Ludwig Zeller, w. John Robert Colombo). MontG (6) Aut
        77, p. 35.

WALDEN, William
    "Riposte." NewYorker (53:14) 23 My 77, p. 40.

WALDROP, Keith
    "Falling in Love While Asleep." OP (24) Aut-Wint 77, p. 55.
    "A Picture Postcard of the Queen of Sheba." OP (24) Aut-Wint
        77, p. 52.

WALDROP, Rosmarie
    "The Senses Touchingly." LaB (7) My 77, p. 47.
    "We talk as long as we can." Bits (6) Jl 77.

WALKER, Alice
    "'Good Night, Willie Lee, I'll See You in the Morning.'"
        Nimrod (21:2/22:1) 77, p. 298.
    "The Instant of Our Parting." Nimrod (21:2/22:1) 77, p. 297.
    "light baggage" (for Nella, Zora, Jean). AmerPoR (6:1) Ja-F
        77, p. 28.

"on crying in public" (for June, sister of mercy). AmerPoR
(6:1) Ja-F 77, p. 29.
"On stripping bark from myself" (for Jane, who said trees die
from it). AmerPoR (6:1) Ja-F 77, p. 28.
"When We Held Our Marriage." Nimrod (21:2/22:1) 77, p. 296.
"Your Soul Shines." Nimrod (21:2/22:1) 77, p. 295.

WALKER, Brian
"Heavy Date." GRR (8:1/2) 77, p. 120.
"Robin." GRR (8:1/2) 77, p. 120.
"Self Serving." GRR (8:1/2) 77, p. 120.

WALKER, Carol
"Observation." WindO (30) Aut 77, p. 19.

WALKER, David
"Catching Up." NewL (44:1) Aut 77, p. 75.
"Father and Son." PoNow (14/18) 77, p. 178.
"Footnote to Wolfe." NewL (44:1) Aut 77, p. 74.
"Washing Day and a High Wind in March." SouthernPR (17:2)
Aut 77, p. 58.
"Winter Storm, Maine Coast." ColEng (38:7) Mr 77, p. 721.

WALKER, Isaac
"Ode to a Nightingrackle or, Mucking the Muse in Mudflat
Heights." TexQ (20:2) Sum 77, p. 60.

WALKER, Jeanne Murray
"After the Suicide." Aspen (4) Aut 77, p. 47.
"Complaint: To William Carlos Williams." BallSUF (18:2) Spr
77, p. 23.
"Housewife." Aspen (4) Aut 77, p. 46.
"How This World Needs Keys." Shen (29:1) Aut 77, p. 43.
"On the Language Which Writes the Lecturer." AmerS (46:2)
Spr 77, p. 214.
"Villanelle to Wake My Love." ArizQ (33:1) Spr 77, p. 86.

WALKER, Joseph
"A Good Time Dying." CarouselQ (2:3) Wint 77, p. 26.

WALKER, Lois
"Reflecting." Wind (26) 77, p. 64. Corrected version.

WALKER, Lyn
"State Fair." CarlMis (16:1/2) Aut-Wint 76-77, p. 149.

WALKER, Ted
"Moving." NewYorker (53:9) 18 Ap 77, p. 46.
from A Zodiac Suite: "The bull." BosUJ (25:3) 77, p. 29.
from A Zodiac Suite: "The goat." BosUJ (25:3) 77, p. 31.
from A Zodiac Suite: "The lion." BosUJ (25:3) 77, p. 30.
from A Zodiac Suite: "The ram." BosUJ (25:3) 77, p. 29.
from A Zodiac Suite: "The scorpion." BosUJ (25:3) 77, p. 31.

from A Zodiac Suite: "The virgin." BosUJ (25:3) 77, p. 30.

WALLACE, Robert
"More Than There Is." Comm (104:6) 18 Mr 77, p. 175.

WALLACE, Ronald
"April." QW (4) Aut 77, p. 58.
"Art Work." PoetryNW (18:4) Wint 77-78, p. 13.
"Bingo." SouthernPR (17:2) Aut 77, p. 11.
"Buying the Color TV." BelPoJ (27:4) Sum 77, p. 37.
"City Slicker." CutB (8) Spr 77, p. 97.
"Conversation with the Maker of Cliches." PoetryNW (18:4)
    Wint 77-78, p. 14.
"Devil's Lake." NewRivR (2:1) 77, p. 53.
"Drought." PraS (51:3) Aut 77, p. 277.
"Elm." BelPoJ (27:4) Sum 77, p. 36.
"Every Friday." PoNow (14/18) 77, p. 181.
"Feline." QW (4) Aut 77, p. 56.
"Fence." QW (4) Aut 77, p. 57.
"Getting to Sleep." PoNow (14/18) 77, p. 181.
"God's Wonderful Drowning Machine." PoNow (14/18) 77, p. 198.
"Grief." PraS (51:3) Aut 77, p. 276.
"In the Arboretum." Nat (224:3) 22 Ja 77, p. 93.
"The Medicine Man's Confession." Chowder (9) Aut-Wint 77,
    p. 20.
"Nightcrawlers." NewRivR (2:1) 77, p. 52.
"On Learning That the Most Recurrent Image in Contemporary
    Poetry Is 'Dark.'" PoetC (10:1) 77, p. 24.
"On the Riviera." KanQ (9:3) Sum 77, p. 12.
"Spring." PoetryNW (18:4) Wint 77-78, p. 13.
"Spring Again." QW (4) Aut 77, p. 58.
"Tossa: Celebration." Epoch (26:2) Wint 77, p. 143.
"Trapping the Last Fox." PoNow (14/18) 77, p. 181.
"Triumphs of a Three-Year-Old." PoetryNW (18:1) Spr 77,
    p. 54.
"Trout." PoetC (10:1) 77, p. 28.
"Trout." PraS (51:3) Aut 77, p. 275.
"Underwear." NewRivR (2:1) 77, p. 54.

WALLACE-CRABBE, Chris
"Orpheus." Poetry (130:1) Ap 77, p. 10.
"Parthia." Poetry (130:1) Ap 77, p. 11.

WALLACH, Yona
"Cradle Song" (tr. by Leonore Gordon). TriQ (39) Spr 77,
    p. 310.
"The House Is Empty" (tr. by Warren Bargad). TriQ (39) Spr
    77, p. 310.
"When the Angels Are Exhausted" (tr. by Leonore Gordon).
    TriQ (39) Spr 77, p. 309.
"Yonatan" (tr. by Leonore Gordon). TriQ (39) Spr 77, p. 309.

WALLICH, Paul
"Victor, Victor." YaleLit (146:2) 77, p. 19.

WALLIN, Stephen
 "Planting." PortR (23) 77, p. 39.

WALSER, Robert
 "Snowdrops" (tr. by Tom Whalen and Trudi Anderegg). ParisR
  (71) Aut 77, p. 138.

WALSH, Chad
 "Courtesy." MissR (6:1) 77, p. 122.
 "Goodness Bare." KanQ (9:1) Wint 77, p. 24.
 "I Have Been Here Before." CarolQ (29:1) Wint 77, p. 24.
 "In Memory of W. H. Auden--September 28, 1973." CarolQ
  (29:2) Spr-Sum 77, p. 47.
 "Zihuatanejo." MissR (6:1) 77, p. 121.

WALSH, Joy
 "Edge of Generation." Paunch (48/49) S 77, p. 50.

WALSH, Keith K.
 "Big Apple Blues." Mouth (11/12) Mr-Je 77, p. 110.

WALTER, Eugene
 "My Good Angel." TransR (58/59) F 77, p. 115.
 "The Stone Guest." TransR (58/59) F 77, p. 116.
 "3 Songs." TransR (58/59) F 77, p. 114.

WANG Chi
 "Carnations" (tr. by Graeme Wilson). DenQ (12:2) Sum 77,
  p. 48.

WANG Chi-wu
 "The Gourd of Hsu Yu" (tr. by Graeme Wilson). WestHR (31:1)
  Wint 77, p. 59.

WANG Shih-chen
 "Temple" (tr. by Graeme Wilson). WestHR (31:1) Wint 77,
  p. 59.

WANG Wei
 "Dwelling in the Mountains: Impromptu Lines" (tr. by Pauline
  R. Yu). DenQ (12:2) Sum 77, p. 353.
 "The End of Spring" (tr. by Graeme Wilson). DenQ (12:2) Sum
  77, p. 391.
 "Goodbye" (tr. by Lenore Mayhew and William McNaughton).
  DenQ (12:2) Sum 77, p. 326.
 "Hua-Tzu Hill" (tr. by Pauline R. Yu). DenQ (12:2) Sum 77,
  p. 355.
 "In Response to the Visit of Several Gentlemen" (tr. by Pauline
  R. Yu). DenQ (12:2) Sum 77, p. 354.
 "In the Mountains" (tr. by Graeme Wilson). WestHR (31:1) Wint
  77, p. 35.
 "Lake Yi" (tr. by Pauline R. Yu). DenQ (12:2) Sum 77, p. 355.

"Lamenting Yin Yao" (tr. by Pauline R. Yu).   DenQ (12:2) Sum
    77, p. 353.
"Magnolia Bank" (tr. by Pauline R. Yu).   DenQ (12:2) Sum 77,
    p. 355.
"Mirror" (tr. by Graeme Wilson).   DenQ (12:2) Sum 77, p. 50.
"Visiting the Temple of Gathered Fragrance" (tr. by Pauline R.
    Yu).   DenQ (12:2) Sum 77, p. 353.

WANG Yang-ming
    "Release" (tr. by Tu Wei-ming and Leonard Nathan).   Chowder
        (8) Spr-Sum 77, p. 47.

WANG Yen-hing
    "Brief Parting" (tr. by Graeme Wilson).   DenQ (12:2) Sum 77,
        p. 396.

WANG Yu-cheng
    "In the Provinces" (tr. by Graeme Wilson).   DenQ (12:2) Sum
        77, p. 400.

WANN, David
    "52 Die in Middle East Skirmish--Better Total Expected."   Sam
        (52) Ap 77, p. 51.

WARD, Candice
    "Halfway Home."   DenQ (12:1) Spr 77, p. 195.
    "The Plot."   DenQ (12:1) Spr 77, p. 199.
    "Poem for a Dead Child."   DenQ (12:1) Spr 77, p. 198.
    "Solitary Confinement."   DenQ (12:1) Spr 77, p. 197.
    "What I Feel For You."   DenQ (12:2) Sum 77, p. 356.

WARD, Donald
    "Standjkka."   Stand (18:3) 77, p. 9.
    "Thoughts on a Country Station."   Stand (18:3) 77, p. 9.

WARD, Jerry W.
    "Breaking the Blues" (for Alvin Aubert).   Obs (3:2) Sum 77,
        p. 48.
    "Breaking the Blues" (for Alvin Aubert).   SouthernPR (16:SI) 77,
        p. 87.
    "Presences."   Nimrod (21:2/22:1) 77, p. 299.
    "Trueblood."   Nimrod (21:2/22:1) 77, p. 300.

WARDEN, Marine
    "I Give You This Land."   Sam (55) 77, p. 16.

WARE, Beth
    "I look out the window."   HangL (31) Aut 77, p. 73.
    "The Sea."   HangL (31) Aut 77, p. 73.

WARE, Freddie
    "Unpublished."   BlackF (2:1) Wint 77-78, p. 24.

WARE, Patricia
"I Write This Sonnet to Speak for the Living." PortR (23) 77,
    p. 159.
"Necessary Light." PortR (23) 77, p. 157.
"Sweetbriar, 1894." PortR (23) 77, p. 158.

WARGO, Allen
"Many Voices." ArizQ (33:2) Sum 77, p. 164.

WARNER, Joan
"The Reply of Penelope to Odysseus." HarvAd (110:4) Ap 77,
    p. 30.

WARNHOFF, S. M.
"Wishes." WebR (3:2) Spr 77, p. 69.

WARREN, Danny
"My grandma and grandpa heard my uncle who was killed."
    AmerPoR (6:2) Mr-Ap 77, p. 32.

WARREN, Eugene
"A Dawn." WebR (3:2) Spr 77, p. 74.

WARREN, James E., Jr.
"Goalkeeper." StoneC (77:2) My 77, p. 30.

WARREN, Peter Whitson
"Mammoth & Other Dinosaurs." Stonecloud (6) 76, p. 71.
"Mexican Gulch." Stonecloud (6) 76, p. 15.

WARREN, Robert Penn
"Ah, Anima!" Atl (240:4) O 77, p. 86.
"Amazing Grace in the Back Country." OhioR (18:1) Wint 77,
    p. 32.
"Departure." OhioR (18:1) Wint 77, p. 31.
"Dream." Atl (240:4) O 77, p. 85.
"Dream of a Dream." SouthernR (13:1) Wint 77, p. 147.
"A Few Axioms for a Young Man." GeoR (31:4) Wint 77,
    p. 785.
"First Dawn Light." NewYorker (53:7) 4 Ap 77, p. 38.
"Heart of Autumn." Atl (240:4) O 77, p. 84.
"Little Black Heart of the Telephone." NewYorker (53:14) 23
    My 77, p. 34.
"Love at First Sight." OhioR (18:1) Wint 77, p. 34.
"The Mission." OhioR (18:1) Wint 77, p. 30.
"Orphanage Boy (Octosyllabics)." NewYRB (24:3) 3 Mr 77,
    p. 12.
"Red-Tail Hawk and Pyre of Youth." NewYorker (53:22) 18 Jl
    77, p. 32.
"When the Tooth Cracks--Zing!" OhioR (18:1) Wint 77, p. 35.

WARREN, Rosanna
"Last Days in a Hospital." SouthernR (13:4) Aut 77, p. 749.

"Letter from the First Day." SouthernR (13:4) Aut 77, p. 748.
"Marine Exhibit on Bathroom Rack." SouthernR (13:4) Aut 77,
  p. 747.
"Snow Day." SouthernR (13:4) Aut 77, p. 746.
"Weekend on the Loire." SouthernR (13:4) Aut 77, p. 745.

WATERMAN, Charles
  "Disappointment." MoonsLT (2:3) 77, p. 65.
  "The Powerline Poles." DacTerr (14) Spr-Sum 77, p. 30.
  "Spring Chores." DacTerr (14) Spr-Sum 77, p. 29.
  "To Bed." MoonsLT (2:3) 77, p. 64.
  "To Cary." DacTerr (14) Spr-Sum 77, p. 29.
  "Visiting Bridgeport with You." DacTerr (14) Spr-Sum 77,
    p. 28.

WATERS, Chocolate
  "All Day Poem." Chomo (4:1) Sum 77, p. 22.
  "Openings and Closings." Chomo (4:1) Sum 77, p. 23.

WATERS, Michael
  "Beta." NewRivR (2:1) 77, p. 44.
  "If I Die." Poetry (130:3) Je 77, p. 144.
  "Mausoleum." FourQt (27:1) Aut 77, p. 39.
  "Negative." SouthernPR (17:1) Spr 77, p. 27.
  "Not Just Any Death." Poetry (130:3) Je 77, p. 143.
  "Preserves." Poetry (130:3) Je 77, p. 145.
  "The Rehearsal." KanQ (9:4) Aut 77, p. 127.
  "Religion Comes to Dumb Animals." Chowder (8) Spr-Sum 77,
    p. 11.
  "Remembering the Oak." FourQt (26:4) Sum 77, p. 12.
  "Since Nothing Is Impossible." Ploughs (4:1) 77, p. 96.
  "What the Dead Forget." HiramPoR (23) Wint 77, p. 35.

WATKINS, William Jon
  "The Scholar." SouthernHR (11:1) Wint 77, p. 61.

WATSON, Celia
  "Essences" (for John Crowe Ransom). BallSUF (18:3) Sum 77,
    p. 80.
  "In the Night." BallSUF (18:1) Wint 77, p. 79.

WATSON, Lawrence
  "In My Daughter's Room" (for Elly). NewRivR (2:1) 77, p. 45.
  "Slope Village, Mandan, North Dakota." Waters (6) 77, p. 25.

WATSON, Robert
  "Distance." Shen (28:4) Sum 77, p. 36.
  "Down, Down, Down." SouthernPR (16:SI) 77, p. 88.

WATSON, Tamara
  "For a Prostitute Found Murdered at Age Fifteen." 13thM (3:2)
    77, p. 59.
  "No Advice for the Lovelorn." ParisR (70) Sum 77, p. 174.

WATTS, Harriett
    "Craft and Industry" (tr. of H. C. Artmann).   BosUJ (25:3) 77,
        p. 3.

WATTS, W. Glenn
    "Parking Shelter Forest. "   DeKalb (10:2) Wint 77, p. 53.

WAUGH, William R.
    "Motel Manager. "   CimR (41) O 77, p. 54.

WAX, Judith
    "That Was the Year That Was. "   Playb (24:1) Ja 77, p. 112.
    "To a Flasher. "   Playb (24:12) D 77, p. 176.
    "To a Jogger. "   Playb (24:12) D 77, p. 175.
    "To a Sexual Memoirist. "   Playb (24:12) D 77, p. 175.
    "To an Imminent Transsexual. "   Playb (24:12) D 77, p. 175.
    "To Our Nation's Polluters. "   Playb (24:12) D 77, p. 176.

WAYMAN, Tom
    "New Year's at Ken Tyler Graphics, Route 22 Near Mt. Kisco,
        New York" (for P.).   ParisR (71) Aut 77, p. 77.
    "Ten Years. "   ParisR (71) Aut 77, p. 76.

WEATHERS, Ed
    "Shining His Shoes. "   PoetL (72:2) Sum 77, p. 56.

WEAVER, Gordon
    "Pale Blue Bunk Poem After Forty Years. "   HolCrit (14:2) Ap
        77, p. 9.

WEAVER, Roger
    "Recovering the Mystery. "   ConcPo (10:2) Aut 77, p. 74.
    "Skin Talk. "   ConcPo (10:2) Aut 77, p. 73.

WEBB, Bernice Larson
    "Garter Snake. "   StoneC (77:3) S 77, p. 27.

WEBB, Charles
    "After Blowing the Audition. "   MontG (5) Wint 77, p. 44.
    "All This Blood. "   YellowBR (8) 77, p. 4.
    "Choctaw Creek. "   Wind (27) 77, p. 61.
    "Dream. "   KanQ (9:3) Sum 77, p. 106.
    "Errand. "   Wind (27) 77, p. 61.
    "Getting the Job. "   ConcPo (10:2) Aut 77, p. 82.
    "Given the Bird. "   LittleR (12) 77, p. 9.
    "Heat Addict. "   RemR (5) 77, p. 87.
    "Just at Midnight. "   ConcPo (10:2) Aut 77, p. 81.
    "Lack of Cat. "   Sam (52) Ap 77, p. 63.
    "My Dwarf Marigolds. "   WindO (28) Spr 77, p. 33.
    "No Kind of Deal at All. "   Agni (7) 77, p. 37.
    "Parties. "   Agni (7) 77, p. 38.
    "A Whole New Ballgame. "   PoNow (14/18) 77, p. 181.
    "Wonders Never Cease. "   YellowBR (8) 77, p. 4.

WEBBER, Jan Farnum
  "Losing Sight." NowestR (16:3) 77, p. 81.

WEBBER, Joan
  "Above Snowline." BelPoJ (27:4) Sum 77, p. 11.
  "After the Death That Couldn't Happen." BelPoJ (27:4) Sum 77,
      p. 9.
  "Huckleberry Mountain." BelPoJ (27:4) Sum 77, p. 10.
  "New Snow." Shen (28:2) Wint 77, p. 105.

WEBER, Marc
  "A Shape." PoNow (14/18) 77, p. 181.

WEBER, Mike
  "Silences." Chowder (8) Spr-Sum 77, p. 21.

WEBER, R. B.
  "'A Charming Place, This South.'" PoNow (14/18) 77, p. 182.
  "Dear Abbey." Confr (14) Spr-Sum 77, p. 153.
  "A Musicale." PoNow (14/18) 77, p. 182.
  "The Only Man I Ever Cared For." PoNow (14/18) 77, p. 197.

WEBER, Robert
  "Night Mood" (tr. by John M. Gogol). WebR (3:4) Aut 77, p. 35.
  "On Perseverence" (tr. by John M. Gogol). WebR (3:4) Aut 77,
      p. 34.

WEBER, Ron
  "The Translation." PoNow (14/18) 77, p. 182.

WEBSTER, W. G.
  "Ambergris." LittleR (12) 77, p. 11.

WECHSLER, Shoshana
  "For Years Afterward, Kalfain Could Be Seen by His Many
      Friends on Reruns." MontG (6) Aut 77, p. 68.

WEEDEN, Craig
  "Bedtime Story." EnPas (4) 76, p. 10.
  "The Laundress Removes Your Stain." YellowBR (9) 77, p. 14.
  "The Reaping of Lily Yarnell." RemR (5) 77, p. 61.

WEEKS, Ramona
  "Sonja Henie." Confr (15) Aut 77-Wint 78, p. 122.

WEIDAW, Desirée
  "The Self for What It Is." Rapp (10) 77, p. 19.

WEIGAL, Paul H.
  "Two Thoughts of Death." Epoch (26:2) Wint 77, p. 134.

WEIGL, Bruce
  "Painting on a T'Ang Dynasty Water Vessel." Field (16) Spr 77,
      p. 37.

WEIL, James L.
  "One for One." PoNow (14/18) 77, p. 182.
  "The Tomb of the Cappelletti." Sparrow (33) Ja 77, p. 17.
  "Jenny's, from Seed." Sparrow (33) Ja 77, p. 17.
  "Merlin." Sparrow (33) Ja 77, p. 17.

WEINBERG, Bennett
  "Sète" (to C. D. , 1948-1974). Columbia (1) Aut 77, p. 20.

WEINBERGER, Eliot
  "Return" (for José Alvarado) (tr. of Octavio Paz). Montra (3)
      Spr 77, p. 181.
  "7 Poems" (tr. of Homero Aridjis). Montra (3) Spr 77, p. 133.
  "6 Songs." Montra (3) Spr 77, p. 142.

WEINBERGER, Florence
  "A New Place." FourQt (26:2) Wint 77, p. 21.

WEINERMAN, Chester
  "Rainclouds." PartR (44:3) 77, p. 414.

WEINGARTEN, Roger
  "Celebrations on the Granite-Marble Road." MissR (6:2) 77,
      p. 50.
  "The Death of Two Sonnets, 7/9 of a Sestina, and Uncle Villanelle
      and a Sneak Preview of: Volunteer Sonnet." MissR (6:2) 77,
      p. 57.
  "The Flight of the Stonecutter I. Indictment in Marble." MissR
      (6:2) 77, p. 39.
  "The Flight of the Stonecutter II. Mary's Day." MissR (6:2) 77,
      p. 47.
  "The Magistrate Version." MissR (6:2) 77, p. 54.
  "Magnetic Waters." MissR (6:2) 77, p. 59.
  "Omassum." Ploughs (3:3/4) 77, p. 136.
  "Picaresque." SenR (8:1) My 77, p. 59.
  "A Preview of the Vermont Suicides." MissR (6:2) 77, p. 38.
  "Tentative Mary, Roger and Sophy." SenR (8:1) My 77, p. 56.
  "The Vermont Suicides." MissR (6:2) 77, p. 49.

WEINLEIN, Greg Thomas
  "Drained from This Field." Wind (26) 77, p. 52.
  "You Are the Body." Wind (26) 77, p. 52.

WEINMAN, Paul
  "All Together Now." Pig (3) 77, p. 100.

WEINS, John
  "At the Scene." CutB (8) Spr 77, p. 98.
  "Glowing in Five O'Clock Traffic." PortR (23) 77, p. 53.

WEISMAN, Ann
  "It Happened in Andy's Trading Post, Billings" (for Andy Clair
      de Lune). CutB (8) Spr 77, p. 51.

WEISS, Sigmund
  "The Poetry of Gentle Souls." CimR (40) Jl 77, p. 26.

WEISSBORT, Daniel
  "City Streets" (tr. of Georgii Vargin). DenQ (11:4) Wint 77,
    p. 24.
  "Not in an airplane's wing" (tr. of Natalya Gorbanevskaya).
    DenQ (11:4) Wint 77, p. 24.

WEISSMANN, David
  "A Dutch Painting." Shen (28:2) Wint 77, p. 102.

WEISZ, Gabriel
  "The Skin of the Planets." MontG (6) Aut 77, p. 66.
  "Tuatha de Danann." MontG (6) Aut 77, p. 65.

WEITZEL, Allen Field
  "cordially, the editors." Aspect (70) Ja-Mr 77, p. 58.

WELBORN, Carol B.
  "Eleventh Month." ChrC (94:35) 2 N 77, p. 1004.

WELCH, Don
  "The Hunt." PraS (51:1) Spr 77, p. 12.
  "In the Sandhills, Horse Dreams." PraS (51:1) Spr 77, p. 14.
  "Walking a Pit South of Gothenburg." PraS (51:1) Spr 77,
    p. 15.

WELCH, John
  "The Drops of Wind." PartR (44:2) 77, p. 261.
  "In the Streets." PartR (44:2) 77, p. 261.
  "Millions." PartR (44:2) 77, p. 262.

WELCH, Liliane
  "Conques." StoneC (77:3) S 77, p. 18.
  "Two glacier crevasses." StoneC (77:3) S 77, p. 18.

WELCH, Louise
  "Kinds of Quiet." LadHJ (94:2) F 77, p. 66.

WELCH, Wayne
  "dream." HangL (29) Wint 76-77, p. 47.

WELISH, Marjorie
  "Smooth and Rough." PartR (44:3) 77, p. 413.

WELLMAN, John
  "Batrachomyomachia." Chelsea (36) 77, p. 40.

WELLMAN, Wade
  "Milton Envisioned." CEACritic (39:2) Ja 77, p. 17.

WELLS, Robert
  "Contadino." SouthernR (13:4) Aut 77, p. 769.

"Four Epigrams." SouthernR (13:4) Aut 77, p. 771.
"The Mill." SouthernR (13:4) Aut 77, p. 770.

WELLS, Will
   "Farming the River." PoetryNW (18:4) Wint 77-78, p. 22.
   "The Long Shift." PoetryNW (18:1) Spr 77, p. 43.
   "Troy, Ohio." PoetryNW (18:4) Wint 77-78, p. 21.
   "Twenty-Six Dead in Scotia Number One." PoetryNW (18:1) Spr
      77, p. 43.

WELLS-POWERS, Jeffrey
   "A Little of What Mad Peggy's Letter from Mexico Said."
      Madrona (4:13/14) 77, p. 16.

WELT, Bernard
   "Swans" (for Doug Lang). LaB (6) Mr 77, p. 36.

WENDT, Ingrid
   "Found Poem: Spelling Test, Grade 3." AndR (4:1) Spr 77,
      p. 96.

WEÖRES, Sándor
   "Antithin" (tr. by Richard Lourie). AmerPoR (6:3) My-Je 77,
      p. 23.
   "Twentieth-Century Fresco" (tr. by Adam Makkai). ModernPS
      (8:2) Aut 77, p. 118.

WERNER, Henry O.
   "morning becomes electra." Mouth (11/12) Mr-Je 77, p. 82.

WERTH, Tim
   "See the bird." AAR (27) 77, p. 127.

WESCOTT, Roger W.
   "Suspended City." StoneC (77:1) F 77, p. 19.

WEST, Michael
   "Asparagus." CalQ (11/12) Wint-Spr 77, p. 108.

WESTBROOK, Max
   "Going Back Home for a Visit." SouthernHR (11:4) Aut 77,
      p. 345.

WESTENHAVER, James Conway
   "Working Out of the Basement." Wind (26) 77, p. 53.

WESTERFIELD, Hargis
   "Short-Line Railroad History." Wind (27) 77, p. 63.
   "The Writing of History." Wind (27) 77, p. 63.

WESTERFIELD, Nancy G.
   "Class of '46 Reunion." AAUP (68:1) F 77, p. 16.
   "On the G&LW Railroad." Wind (27) 77, p. 65.

"Sitting the Night Through with Dinky, Dying." WestHR (31:2)
    Spr 77, p. 142.

WESTERN, Daniel
    "A Poet Must Know." AmerPoR (6:2) Mr-Ap 77, p. 31.
    "Sacred Songs I." AmerPoR (6:2) Mr-Ap 77, p. 33.

WESTON, John
    "Exempli Gratia." CEACritic (39:3) Mr 77, p. 8.

WESTWOOD, Norma J.
    "Legacy." ChrC (94:36) 9 N 77, p. 1027.
    "Woman of Magdala." ChrC (94:12) 6 Ap 77, p. 326.

WETHERBY, Terry
    "At Stonehenge." Confr (14) Spr-Sum 77, p. 159.

WEYMOUTH, Dan
    "If I Had a 3rd Eye." AAR (27) 77, p. 118.

WEYMOUTH, Mark
    "At night." AAR (27) 77, p. 108.
    "Tasmanian dodos are found in the Bula" (w. Steve Monto). AAR
    (27) 77, p. 101.

WHALEN, Tom
    "Snowdrops" (tr. of Robert Walser, w. Trudi Anderegg). ParisR
    (71) Aut 77, p. 138.

WHALEY, Bill
    "The Mountain." SouthwR (62:3) Sum 77, p. 294.

WHEATCROFT, John
    "First Day Down In." SouthernHR (11:1) Wint 77, p. 28.
    "Lancelot, Tonsured, Walks the Field at Dover." FourQt (27:1)
        Aut 77, p. 13.
    "On Hearing of a Recent Suicide." Wind (27) 77, p. 66.
    "Pisanello's Studies of Men Hanging on Gallows." NewL (44:1)
        Aut 77, p. 97.
    "Two Visitations." Wind (27) 77, p. 66.

WHEELER, Sylvia
    "Vennishay: No Such Word." Focus (12:75) My-Je 77, p. 25.

WHISLER, Robert F.
    "The Guitarist." CarouselQ (2:3) Wint 77, p. 32.
    "Laughing Girl." CarouselQ (2:2) Aut 77, p. 28.

WHITCOMB, Pineapple
    "portrait: woman with piano." Stonecloud (6) 76, p. 70.

WHITE, Gail
    "The Blind Man's Search for the Sun." PoetL (72:1) Spr 77,
    p. 18.

"I Imagine I Am Not My Mother's Child." WebR (3:4) Aut 77,
    p. 58.
"The Implications of Emptiness." HiramPoR (23) Wint 77,
    p. 37.
"The Lion Who Ate the Sun." HiramPoR (23) Wint 77, p. 36.
"Poetry in Strange Places." SmPd (14:2) Spr 77, p. 19.
"Reply to the Old Man." PoetL (72:1) Spr 77, p. 29.
"The Shropshire Lad's Fiancée." CEACritic (39:2) Ja 77,
    p. 16.
"The Student." ChrC (94:33) 19 O 77, p. 943.

WHITE, Gina
"Glossary of Terms for Chapter Forty." Ploughs (3:3/4) 77,
    p. 119.

WHITE, James
"The Ordinary Composure" (for Kate Green). Chowder (9) Aut-
    Wint 77, p. 97.

WHITE, James L.
"Navajo Moon." Drag (16) 77.

WHITE, Jay
"Song Dog." QW (2) Wint 77, p. 71.

WHITE, Patrick
"Cameo for a Contemporary." TexQ (19:4) Wint 76, p. 53.
"Hunters." TexQ (19:4) Wint 76, p. 55.
"Imperatives." TexQ (19:4) Wint 76, p. 54.
"Make-Up." TexQ (19:4) Wint 76, p. 56.
"Saviors." TexQ (19:4) Wint 76, p. 54.
"Toward the End." TexQ (19:4) Wint 76, p. 52.

WHITE, Steven
"About My Invention." BerksR (12:1) Spr 77.
"Divination." BerksR (12:1) Spr 77.
"A Mime's Elegy." BerksR (12:1) Spr 77.
"Pravāsa." BerksR (12:1) Sum 76, p. 23.
"Tattoo." BerksR (12:1) Spr 77.

WHITE, William M.
"January 23, 1841" (A found poem from Thoreau's journals).
    SouthernPR (16:SI) 77, p. 91.
"The Lost Sheep." LittleR (12) 77, p. 14.
"Maidens Plaint to Her New Brave." CarolQ (29:2) Spr-Sum 77,
    p. 78.
"Mother." CarouselQ (2:3) Wint 77, p. 29.
"Susan at the Gate." SouthernR (13:2) Spr 77, p. 347.
"Susan upon Her Bed." SouthernR (13:2) Spr 77, p. 346.
"Susan upon the Rock." SouthernR (13:2) Spr 77, p. 345.
"Three Found Poems from Thoreau's Journals" (March 10, 1856;
    February 28, 1857; August 28, 1856). SouthernPR (17:2)
    Aut 77, p. 74.

WHITED, David Lloyd
"there is a shimmering voice of glass." Wind (27) 77, p. 68.

WHITEHEAD, James
"The Alabama Man Remembers All He Can about the Battered
    Children and the Woman with Almost Perfect Skin in Mobile
    Seven Years Ago." SouthernPR (16:SI) 77, p. 92.

WHITEHEAD, Jett W.
"Cycle." SmPd (14:1) Wint 77, p. 17.

WHITENER, Barbara
"Harold's Wife She Just Don't Understand Him." CarouselQ
    (2:2) Aut 77, p. 26.

WHITFIELD, Tony
"Wintering." TransR (60) Je 77, p. 97.

WHITING, Nathan
"Atheistic Ballad for the Nighthawk." Hand (1) 77, p. 175.
from Running: "The G. W." PoNow (14/18) 77, p. 183.
from Running: "Homage." PoNow (14/18) 77, p. 183.
"Wax? Wax! Anybody Want to Buy My Wax?" Hand (1) 77,
    p. 82.

WHITMAN, Ruth
"Flying Home." Hand (1) 77, p. 190.
"Tamsen Donner Crosses the Great Salt Desert, September
    1846." Ploughs (3:3/4) 77, p. 113.
"yellow." NewRep (177:10) 3 S 77, p. 28.

WHITMAN, Walt
"I Hear It Was Charged Against Me." PoNow (14/18) 77, p. 99.

WHITNEY, Eugene
"On the Green." Drag (16) 77.

WHITTEMORE, Reed
"Meditative Stomp on the State of Something." AmerPoR (6:5)
    S-O 77, p. 9.
"Mother's Past." AmerPoR (6:5) S-O 77, p. 10.
"Smiling Through." AmerPoR (6:5) S-O 77, p. 10.

WHITTINGTON, Gary
"Villanelle with No Makeup." Kayak (46) O 77, p. 61.

WHYATT, Frances
"The Craft of Their Hands" (for Erika & Diane who build domes
    and Egges). Hand (1) 77, p. 57.
"The Throat As Letter Read Dear God." Hand (1) 77, p. 167.

WIEBE, Dallas
"Red Norder's Poem to Robert Frost." Waters (5) 77, p. 10.

WIEGEL, Nancy J.
"Columbus." DeKalb (10:3) Spr 77, p. 71.

WIEGNER, Kathleen
"The Fate of the Bees." HangL (29) Wint 76-77, p. 48.
"The Little Deaths." HangL (29) Wint 76-77, p. 52.
"Posthumous Fame." HangL (29) Wint 76-77, p. 51.

WIENERMAN, Chester
"Long Daze and Knights." SouthernPR (17:2) Aut 77, p. 52.

WIENERS, John
from Behind the State Capitol or Cincinnati Pike: "After a Poem
    for Cocksuckers (Patsy's)." PoNow (14/18) 77, p. 183.
from Behind the State Capitol or Cincinnati Pike: "Broken
    Hearted Memorys." PoNow (14/18) 77, p. 183.
from Behind the State Capital or Cincinnati Pike: "To Sink
    Love." PoNow (14/18) 77, p. 183.

WIER, Dara
"If for a Night My Tongue Would Sleep." HolCrit (14:2) Ap 77,
    p. 13.
"In This Case, Distance." NewRivR (2:1) 77, p. 30.
"Shed." NewRivR (2:1) 77, p. 32.
"There Is Nothing." NewRivR (2:1) 77, p. 30.

WIESELTIER, Meir
"Friends" (tr. by Shirley Kaufman and Shlomit Rimmon). TriQ
    (39) Spr 77, p. 315.
"March" (tr. by Shirley Kaufman and Shlomit Rimmon). TriQ
    (39) Spr 77, p. 315.
"A Request" (tr. by Shirley Kaufman and Shlomit Rimmon).
    TriQ (39) Spr 77, p. 313.
"The Secret of Authority" (tr. by Shirley Kaufman and Shlomit
    Rimmon). TriQ (39) Spr 77, p. 311.

WIGRA, Ripa
"Friday, and We Careen." WindO (29) Sum 77, p. 17.
"St Francis." WindO (29) Sum 77, p. 17.

WILBUR, Richard
"Chairs above the Danube" (tr. of Szabolcs Várady). NewYorker
    (53:2) 28 F 77, p. 34.
"Mr. T. S. Eliot Cooking Pasta" (tr. of József Tornai).
    NewYorker (53:2) 28 F 77, p. 35.

WILCOX, Patricia
"Comfort Specific." Wind (26) 77, p. 55.
"A First Lesson." Wind (26) 77, p. 54.
"Transfiguration." Wind (26) 77, p. 54.

WILD, Peter
"Alligator Junipers." PoNow (14/18) 77, p. 186.

"The Ballinger Affair. " NowestR (16:3) 77, p. 45.
"Barn Fires. " Iowa (8:1) Wint 77, p. 63.
"Buehman Canyon. " PoNow (14/18) 77, p. 186.
"Cowboy. " QW (3) Spr-Sum 77, p. 68.
"The Farmer's Wife. " PoNow (14/18) 77, p. 186.
"For Carol Wise. " Glass (2:2/3) Wint-Spr 77, p. 52.
"Glenwood. " Glass (2:2/3) Wint-Spr 77, p. 51.
"In the Old Suburbs. " PraS (51:3) Aut 77, p. 246.
"John Muir. " Ploughs (4:1) 77, p. 80.
"Miner. " ThRiPo (10) 77, p. 39.
"Painting. " Iowa (8:1) Wint 77, p. 62.
"Pediatrician. " Epoch (26:2) Wint 77, p. 161.
"Pork Sausage. " CutB (9) Aut-Wint 77, p. 103.
"Salvation. " ThRiPo (10) 77, p. 38.
"Succotash. " PoNow (14/18) 77, p. 186.
"Temperate Zone. " Iowa (8:3) Sum 77, p. 29.

WILDE, Ina Chadwick
"Engineering Feats. " Shen (29:1) Aut 77, p. 65.
"In the Small Space That Is Left. " Gra (12) 77, p. 27.
"Mr. Woods and the Children. " Gra (12) 77, p. 38.
"There Is a Closet Full of Clothes. " AntR (35:4) Aut 77,
    p. 405.
"The World Traveler. " ParisR (71) Aut 77, p. 132.

WILDER, Amos N.
"From Carnival to Christ-Mass. " ChrC (94:42) 21 D 77,
    p. 1208.

WILDFANG, F. B.
"Spring/74/Copenhagen. " Wind (26) 77, p. 56.

WILK, David
"A Future" (for Paul Kahn). Hand (1) 77, p. 22.
"Signs" (for John Yau). Hand (1) 77, p. 23.

WILKINS, W. R.
"Call the Operator. " Wind (26) 77, p. 53.

WILKINSON, Carol Lynn
"Cold Spring Day. " Wind (25) 77, p. 5.
"Sickness. " Wind (25) 77, p. 5.

WILKINSON, Constance
"Only Yesterday. " MissR (6:1) 77, p. 140.

WILL, Frederic
from Epics of America: (XXII): "Milktoast. " PoNow (14/18)
    77, p. 187.
"Epics of America XXIV: Captain Sagenhaft Rises to the
    Occasion. " KanQ (9:1) Wint 77, p. 45.
"Epics of America LXXII: Homing. " Chelsea (36) 77, p. 26.
"Epics of America LXXIII: The Noble Fifty. " Chelsea (36) 77,
    p. 27.

"A Few Words to Poopus before a Commercial Christmas."
MinnR (NS8) Spr 77, p. 29.
"A fire a simple fire." NewL (43:4) Sum 77, p. 63.
"For Beston's Cabin: Eastham Beach." KanQ (9:1) Wint 77,
p. 46.
"How I decided to settle in New Hampshire." Ploughs (3:3/4) 77,
p. 132.
"The Indian Teacher." SouthwR (62:3) Sum 77, p. 238.
"Lines form on the sides of my face." CarlMis (17:1) Wint
77-78, p. 60.
"A Little Overnight Trip." Kayak (45) My 77, p. 52.
"An old dream that keeps recurring." CarlMis (17:1) Wint 77-
78, p. 60.
"Parts of a Play." ModernPS (8:3) Wint 77, p. 222.
"Ways We Get Up." Kayak (45) My 77, p. 52.

WILLARD, Nancy
"Being Mended." Field (16) Spr 77, p. 22.
"Bones, Scales, Etc." Field (16) Spr 77, p. 19.
"The Child. The Ring. The Road." Field (16) Spr 77, p. 18.
"Country Scene." Field (16) Spr 77, p. 21.
"The Generous Body." Field (17) Aut 77, p. 97.
"How the Hen Sold Her Eggs to the Stingy Priest." Field (16)
Spr 77, p. 17.
"Left-Handed Poem." Field (16) Spr 77, p. 16.
"Maundy Thursday." PoNow (14/18) 77, p. 187.
"Origin" (tr. of German Bleiberg). Salm (38/39) Sum-Aut 77,
p. 104.
"The Photographer Gives the Moon a Dark Room." Field (17)
Aut 77, p. 98.
"Poison Ivy." PoNow (14/18) 77, p. 187.
"Small Classical Poem." PoNow (14/18) 77, p. 187.
"Small Pastoral Poem." AntR (35:2/3) Spr-Sum 77, p. 255.
"Two Allegorical Figures." Field (17) Aut 77, p. 96.

WILLEMS, J. Rutherford
from The Fugues: "Five." Hand (1) 77, p. 159.

WILLIAMS, Benjamin
"A Black Martyr Cries." NegroHB (40:4) Jl-Ag 77, p. 721.
"Roots." NegroHB (40:4) Jl-Ag 77, p. 721.

WILLIAMS, David
"Chronicle." Nimrod (21:2/22:1) 77, p. 304.

WILLIAMS, G. Rutherford
"A Torn Sleeve." Chelsea (36) 77, p. 55.

WILLIAMS, Gil
"Beneath a Protective Wall." Glass (2:2/3) Wint-Spr 77, p. 28.
"From an Engraving of John Sartain." Glass (2:2/3) Wint-Spr
77, p. 29.

WILLIAMS, Helen J.
  "Death and -. " DenQ (12:3) Aut 77, p. 108.
  "Eve. " DenQ (12:3) Aut 77, p. 104.
  "Ghost Sonata in Three Moods. " DenQ (12:3) Aut 77, p. 106.
  "March. " DenQ (12:3) Aut 77, p. 105.
  "The Waiting. " DenQ (12:3) Aut 77, p. 103.

WILLIAMS, Miller
  "A Game of Marbles. " PoNow (14/18) 77, p. 188.
  "Husband. " PoetryNW (18:4) Wint 77-78, p. 27.
  "In Love in Ovid's Lounge at 3 PM. " SouthernPR (17:1) Spr 77,
      p. 26.
  "The Inmate from the State Hospital Tells His Hostage How He
      Was Told to Talk Plain. " PoNow (14/18) 77, p. 188.
  "WW I. " ChiR (29:1) Sum 77, p. 108.

WILLIAMS, Norm
  "Clam Flats off Wales: A Theory. " YaleLit (146:4/5) 77,
      p. 48.
  "The Family Jewels. " YaleLit (146:4/5) 77, p. 8.
  "Giants of the Midwest. " YaleLit (146:4/5) 77, p. 9.
  "Low Clouds at Evening off Nova Scotia. " YaleLit (145:5) 77,
      p. 2.

WILLIAMS, Norman
  "Ancient Rites and Mysteries. " NewYorker (53:40) 21 N 77,
      p. 218.

WILLIAMS, Phil
  "Wassily Kandinsky (1866-1944). " KanQ (9:1) Wint 77, p. 114.

WILLIAMS, Randy
  "Untitled. " CarouselQ (2:3) Wint 77, p. 33.

WILLIAMS, R. Leroy
  "A Plea for Me. " CarouselQ (2:3) Wint 77, p. 2.

WILLIAMS, Rena
  "My Two Fine Sisters and I. " Poem (30) Jl 77, p. 47.
  "Resurrection Fern. " SouthernPR (17:2) Aut 77, p. 41.

WILLIAMS, Shirley
  "Becky start the stories. " Nimrod (21:2/22:1) 77, p. 308.
  "Generations. " Nimrod (21:2/22:1) 77, p. 305.
  "I contemplate insanity. " Nimrod (21:2/22:1) 77, p. 306.
  "More Straight Talk from Plain Women. " Nimrod (21:2/22:1) 77,
      p. 307.
  "Someone Sweet Angel Child" (for Carlos and Iris Blanco).
      MassR (18:3) Aut 77, p. 572.
  from Someone's Sweet Angel Chile: Bessie Smith: "down torrey
      pines road. " AmerPoR (6:1) Ja-F 77, p. 30.
  from Someone's Sweet Angel Chile: Bessie Smith: "recollec-
      tions. " AmerPoR (6:1) Ja-F 77, p. 30.

from Someone's Sweet Angel Chile: Bessie Smith: "39. Bessie
on my wall. " AmerPoR (6:1) Ja-F 77, p. 29.
"Straight Talk from Plain Women. " Nimrod (21:2/22:1) 77,
p. 307.
"Tellin the Hundred. " Nimrod (21:2/22:1) 77, p. 308.

WILLIAMSON, Alan
"In the Military Museum. " Shen (28:4) Sum 77, p. 72.

WILLIAMSON, Kim
"From B. , in Fairness. " WindO (30) Aut 77, p. 17.
"Guipure. " Epoch (26:3) Spr 77, p. 228.

WILLIS, Irene
"To My Mother Solo-ing at Sixty-three. " LitR (20:4) Sum 77,
p. 429.

WILLOUGHBY, Robert Louis
"Dry Land Sailor. " CarouselQ (2:3) Wint 77, p. 6.

WILLSON, Robert
"Nixon to Haldeman: A Found Poem. " CarlMis (17:1) Wint 77-
78, p. 42.
"Putsch--1923. " NewL (44:2) Wint 77, p. 94.

WILLY, Todd Gray
"The Proselyte. " Waters (6) 77, p. 33.

WILMER, Clive
"The Dedication" (E. W. , 1882-1948). SouthernR (13:4) Aut 77,
p. 779.

WILSON, Cynthy
"Pieces of Me. " LadHJ (94:8) Ag 77, p. 104.
"Your Breathing Makes No Hurricanes. " LadHJ (94:7) Jl 77,
p. 162.

WILSON, Dave
"12:17 AM. " EngJ (66:5) My 77, p. 57.

WILSON, Edward
"Lot's Wife. " BelPoJ (28:2) Wint 77-78, p. 20.
"Thimble. " BelPoJ (28:2) Wint 77-78, p. 19.

WILSON, Graeme
"Abandoned Temple" (tr. of Yuan Mei). WestHR (31:3) Sum 77,
p. 213.
"Absurdity" (tr. of Otomo no Tabito). DenQ (11:4) Wint 77,
p. 168.
"Accidie" (tr. of Yi Hwang). DenQ (12:2) Sum 77, p. 303.
"Afterworlds" (tr. of Tang Yin). WestHR (31:3) Sum 77, p. 210.
"Aging" (tr. of Anonymous). DenQ (11:4) Wint 77, p. 173.
"Alba" (tr. of Anonymous). DenQ (12:2) Sum 77, p. 392.

"Apricot Wine" (tr. of Anonymous). DenQ (12:2) Sum 77,
  p. 305.
"Assignation" (tr. of Anonymous). DenQ (12:2) Sum 77, p. 370.
"At Court" (tr. of Yamabe no Akahito). DenQ (12:2) Sum 77,
  p. 374.
"At Karu" (tr. of Kakinomoto no Hitomaro). DenQ (11:4) Wint
  77, p. 171.
"At Yu-Chou Terrace" (tr. of Chen Tzu-ang). DenQ (12:2) Sum
  77, p. 49.
"Autumn" (tr. of Hwang Hwi). DenQ (12:2) Sum 77, p. 305.
"Autumn Nights" (tr. of Anonymous). DenQ (12:2) Sum 77,
  p. 373.
"Bamboo Fence" (tr. of Otomo no Yakamochi). DenQ (11:4)
  Wint 77, p. 169.
"Barking at the Moon" (tr. of Chon Gum). DenQ (12:2) Sum 77,
  p. 306.
"Beginnings" (tr. of Manzan). WestHR (31:3) Sum 77, p. 212.
"The Believing Mind" (tr. of Seng-tsan). DenQ (12:2) Sum 77,
  p. 47.
"Bell in the Mountain Mist" (tr. of Anonymous). TexQ (20:4)
  Wint 77, p. 145.
"Betrayal" (tr. of Lady Ukon). DenQ (12:2) Sum 77, p. 357.
"Birth Wish" (tr. of Otomo no Tabito). DenQ (12:2) Sum 77,
  p. 372.
"Black Man's Bride" (tr. of Gottfried Benn). DenQ (11:4) Wint
  77, p. 40.
"Blown" (tr. of Anonymous). DenQ (12:2) Sum 77, p. 370.
"Blue Sky" (tr. of Hagiwara Sakutaro). DenQ (12:2) Sum 77,
  p. 62.
"Brief Parting" (tr. of Wang Yen-hing). DenQ (12:2) Sum 77,
  p. 396.
"Buddhism" (tr. of Anonymous). DenQ (12:2) Sum 77, p. 357.
"Buddhist Priest" (tr. of Ho Xuan Hong). DenQ (12:2) Sum 77,
  p. 59.
"Butterfly" (tr. of Chuang Tzu). WestHR (31:3) Sum 77, p. 207.
"Cancer Ward" (tr. of Gottfried Benn). DenQ (11:4) Wint 77,
  p. 37.
"Candle" (tr. of Yi Gae). VirQR (53:3) Sum 77, p. 454.
"Capital" (tr. of Kim Su-jang). DenQ (12:2) Sum 77, p. 308.
"Carnations" (tr. of Wang Chi). DenQ (12:2) Sum 77, p. 48.
"Cat" (tr. of Anonymous). DenQ (12:2) Sum 77, p. 300.
"Chairs" (tr. of Sakutaro Hagiwara). WestHR (31:2) Spr 77,
  p. 156.
"Ch'an Sermon" (tr. of Hsuan-chien). DenQ (12:2) Sum 77,
  p. 53.
"Children" (tr. of Yamanoue no Okura). DenQ (11:4) Wint 77,
  p. 172.
"Coast" (tr. of Sung Chung). DenQ (12:2) Sum 77, p. 49.
"Cold Mountain" (tr. of Han Shan). WestHR (31:1) Wint 77,
  p. 56.
"Coming Clear" (tr. of Chen Yu-yi). DenQ (12:2) Sum 77,
  p. 55.
"Common Humanity" (tr. of Ikkyu). DenQ (12:2) Sum 77, p. 359.

"The Condition of Man" (tr. of Anonymous). DenQ (12:2) Sum 77, p. 299.

"Cow" (tr. of Anonymous). DenQ (12:2) Sum 77, p. 292.

"Crane" (tr. of Ki no Tsurayuki). DenQ (12:2) Sum 77, p. 367.

"Crazy Crazy Crazy Love" (tr. of Hwang Chi-ni). DenQ (12:2) Sum 77, p. 399.

"Crescent Moon" (tr. of Otomo no Yakamochi). DenQ (12:2) Sum 77, p. 371.

"Crows" (tr. of Pak Hyo-kwan). DenQ (12:2) Sum 77, p. 397.

"Curse" (tr. of Anonymous). TexQ (20:4) Wint 77, p. 147.

"Cycles" (tr. of Gottfried Benn). DenQ (11:4) Wint 77, p. 39.

"Damages" (tr. of Anonymous). DenQ (12:2) Sum 77, p. 373.

"Dear Lady" (tr. of Otomo no Miyori). DenQ (12:2) Sum 77, p. 369.

"Death" (tr. of Sakutaro Hagiwara). WestHR (31:2) Spr 77, p. 110.

"The Death of Prince Iwata" (tr. of Prince Yamakuma). DenQ (12:2) Sum 77, p. 377.

"Death Poem" (tr. of Izumi Shikibu). DenQ (12:2) Sum 77, p. 54.

"Delivering the Hostages" (tr. of Hong So-bong). DenQ (12:2) Sum 77, p. 293.

"Descending Moon" (tr. of Nanei). DenQ (12:2) Sum 77, p. 57.

"Desolation" (tr. of Saigyo). DenQ (12:2) Sum 77, p. 358.

"Dewdrop" (tr. of Saigyo). WestHR (31:1) Wint 77, p. 58.

"Dialogue of Wind and Rose" (tr. of the Daughter of the Governor of Kazura). DenQ (12:2) Sum 77, p. 358.

"Dirge for Heng Chien" (tr. of Anonymous). WestHR (31:3) Sum 77, p. 207.

"Doctrine" (tr. of Van Hanh). DenQ (12:2) Sum 77, p. 54.

"Doll" (tr. of Anonymous). DenQ (12:2) Sum 77, p. 367.

"Dream Road" (tr. of Yi Myong-han). DenQ (12:2) Sum 77, p. 305.

"Dreams" (tr. of Mibu no Tadamine). DenQ (12:2) Sum 77, p. 54.

"Drowned Man" (tr. of Anonymous). DenQ (11:4) Wint 77, p. 174.

"Ear" (tr. of Hagiwara Sakutaro). DenQ (12:2) Sum 77, p. 63.

"The End of Spring" (tr. of Wang Wei). DenQ (12:2) Sum 77, p. 391.

"Entreaty" (tr. of Yi Myong-han). DenQ (12:2) Sum 77, p. 309.

"Extraordinary World" (tr. of Ikkyu). DenQ (12:2) Sum 77, p. 59.

"Face" (tr. of Fujiwara no Kinto). DenQ (12:2) Sum 77, p. 367.

"Falcon" (tr. of Kim Chang-op). VirQR (53:3) Sum 77, p. 453.

"Fallen Petals" (tr. of Chong Min-gyo). VirQR (53:3) Sum 77, p. 453.

"Fame" (tr. of Kim Chang-so). DenQ (12:2) Sum 77, p. 297.

"Fan" (tr. of Anonymous). DenQ (12:2) Sum 77, p. 301.

"Fidelity" (tr. of Young Woman of Harima). DenQ (12:2) Sum 77, p. 373.

"Fishing" (tr. of Cho Chon-song). DenQ (12:2) Sum 77, p. 299.

"Fishing Lanterns" (tr. of Anonymous). DenQ (11:4) Wint 77, p. 167.

"The Flesh" (tr. of Yosano Akiko). WestHR (31:3) Sum 77,
    p. 214.
"Fly" (tr. of Yang Wan-li). DenQ (12:2) Sum 77, p. 399.
"Folly" (tr. of Izumi Shikibu). DenQ (12:2) Sum 77, p. 368.
"The Frenchman's Concubine" (tr. of Tran Te Xuong). WestHR
    (31:3) Sum 77, p. 213.
"Fringed Pinks" (tr. of Otomo no Yakamochi). DenQ (11:4) Wint
    77, p. 175.
"The Future Buddha" (tr. of Tran Thai Tong). WestHR (31:1)
    Wint 77, p. 58.
"The Gateway of the Sword" (tr. of Lu Yu). DenQ (12:2) Sum
    77, p. 398.
"Gently" (tr. of Song Si-yol). DenQ (12:2) Sum 77, p. 304.
"Girl in the Rain" (tr. of Anonymous). VirQR (53:3) Sum 77,
    p. 454.
"Girls" (tr. of Kim Su-jang). DenQ (12:2) Sum 77, p. 297.
"Gossip" (tr. of Anonymous). DenQ (11:4) Wint 77, p. 167.
"The Gourd of Hsu Yu" (tr. of Wang Chi-wu). WestHR (31:1)
    Wint 77, p. 59.
"The Great Bell of Silla" (tr. of Chong Chol). DenQ (12:2) Sum
    77, p. 396.
"Grief" (tr. of Yen Chi-tao). DenQ (12:2) Sum 77, p. 393.
"Group of Three Persons" (tr. of Hagiwara Sakutaro). DenQ
    (12:2) Sum 77, p. 289.
"Habit" (tr. of Anonymous). DenQ (12:2) Sum 77, p. 391.
"Hand" (tr. of Kawahigashi Hekigodo). DenQ (12:2) Sum 77,
    p. 62.
"Hands" (tr. of Anonymous). DenQ (11:4) Wint 77, p. 164.
"Happy Childhood" (tr. of Gottfried Benn). DenQ (11:4) Wint 77,
    p. 36.
"The Harvest of the Heart" (tr. of Princess Hirokawa). DenQ
    (11:4) Wint 77, p. 166.
"The Headmonk's Poem" (tr. of Shen Hsiu). WestHR (31:3) Sum
    77, p. 209.
"Heart" (tr. of Suga no Tadaon). DenQ (12:2) Sum 77, p. 366.
"Heartbreaks" (tr. of Otomo no Sukunamaro). DenQ (12:2) Sum
    77, p. 374.
"Hero" (tr. of Yi Sun-sin). DenQ (12:2) Sum 77, p. 308.
"Hilltop Slum" (tr. of O Sin-hye). VirQR (53:3) Sum 77, p. 452.
"Holy Man" (tr. of Han Shan). DenQ (12:2) Sum 77, p. 51.
"Homework" (tr. of Tanikawa Shuntaro). DenQ (12:2) Sum 77,
    p. 63.
"House by the Highway" (tr. of Chong Chol). DenQ (12:2) Sum
    77, p. 300.
"House in the Woods" (tr. of Minamoto no Yorizane). DenQ
    (12:2) Sum 77, p. 359.
"Idealism" (tr. of Sakutaro Hagiwara). WestHR (31:2) Spr 77,
    p. 156.
"The Identity of Contrarieties" (tr. of Yu Hsin). WestHR (31:3)
    Sum 77, p. 208.
"Ignorance" (tr. of Kukai). DenQ (12:2) Sum 77, p. 52.
"In Case" (tr. of Anonymous). DenQ (12:2) Sum 77, p. 397.
"In the Mountains" (tr. of Wang Wei). WestHR (31:1) Wint 77,
    p. 55.

"In the Provinces" (tr. of Wang Yu-cheng). DenQ (12:2) Sum 77, p. 400.

"In the Season of Yellow Plums" (tr. of Chao Shih-hsu). DenQ (12:2) Sum 77, p. 395.

"Invitation" (tr. of Anonymous). DenQ (12:2) Sum 77, p. 375.

"Inwardness" (tr. of Tao Chien). TexQ (20:4) Wint 77, p. 148.

"Iron Rope" (tr. of Pak In-no). DenQ (12:2) Sum 77, p. 304.

"Jade" (tr. of Yun Du-so). DenQ (12:2) Sum 77, p. 308.

"Jailed Priest" (tr. of Tran Te Xuong). DenQ (12:2) Sum 77, p. 62.

"Kamunabi" (tr. of Anonymous). DenQ (11:4) Wint 77, p. 165.

"Kisaeng" (tr. of Anonymous). DenQ (12:2) Sum 77, p. 301.

"Lake" (tr. of Anonymous). DenQ (12:2) Sum 77, p. 58.

"Lament" (tr. of Anonymous). DenQ (11:4) Wint 77, p. 170.

"Lao Tzu" (tr. of Kitahara Hakushu). TexQ (20:4) Wint 77, p. 145.

"Last Night" (tr. of Anonymous). DenQ (12:2) Sum 77, p. 303.

"Last Night's Work" (tr. of Anonymous). DenQ (12:2) Sum 77, p. 371.

"The Last of the Serious Drinkers" (tr. of Prince Nang-won). DenQ (12:2) Sum 77, p. 307.

"The Law" (tr. of Hue Minh). DenQ (12:2) Sum 77, p. 55.

"Learning" (tr. of Juan Chi). DenQ (12:2) Sum 77, p. 45.

"Leaving the Temple" (tr. of Liu Chang-chui). DenQ (12:2) Sum 77, p. 392.

"Lespedezas" (tr. of Yo Myogun). DenQ (12:2) Sum 77, p. 370.

"Letter" (tr. of Anonymous). DenQ (12:2) Sum 77, p. 297.

"Letter" (tr. of Li Pang-ling). DenQ (12:2) Sum 77, p. 400.

"Letter to a Ch'an Master" (tr. of Han Wo). DenQ (12:2) Sum 77, p. 53.

"Lies" (tr. of Kim Sang-yong). DenQ (12:2) Sum 77, p. 310.

"Long November Night" (tr. of Hwang Chi-ni). DenQ (12:2) Sum 77, p. 303.

"Love" (tr. of Anonymous). DenQ (12:2) Sum 77, p. 368.

"Love" (tr. of Anonymous). VirQR (53:3) Sum 77, p. 452.

"Love" (tr. of Ono no Koma). DenQ (12:2) Sum 77, p. 366.

"Love" (tr. of Ono no Komachi). WestHR (31:3) Sum 77, p. 209.

"Love Token" (tr. of Lady Heguri). DenQ (12:2) Sum 77, p. 376.

"Lover" (tr. of Kaun Han-ching). DenQ (12:2) Sum 77, p. 395.

"Loyalty" (tr. of Chong Mong-ju). DenQ (12:2) Sum 77, p. 298.

"Magic Mountain" (tr. of An Chong). WestHR (31:3) Sum 77, p. 211.

"Marriage" (tr. of Kim Sang-yong). VirQR (53:3) Sum 77, p. 451.

"The Meaning of Existence" (tr. of Fujiwara no Yoshitsune). DenQ (12:2) Sum 77, p. 56.

"Men of Affairs" (tr. of Chen Tzu-ang). DenQ (12:2) Sum 77, p. 49.

"Mind" (tr. of Okuma Kotomichi). DenQ (12:2) Sum 77, p. 61.

"The Mind of Man" (tr. of Kim Su-jang). DenQ (12:2) Sum 77, p. 304.

"Mirror" (tr. of Wang Wei). DenQ (12:2) Sum 77, p. 50.

"The Mirror of the Heart" (tr. of Choe Chi-won). TexQ (20:4)
    Wint 77, p. 149.
"Mister Moon" (tr. of Japanese Child's Song). TexQ (20:4) Wint
    77, p. 144.
"Modalities of Dream" (tr. of Ikkyu). WestHR (31:3) Sum 77,
    p. 211.
"Moonlight" (tr. of Anonymous). DenQ (12:2) Sum 77, p. 373.
"Moss Green Pathway" (tr. of Anonymous). DenQ (12:2) Sum 77,
    p. 375.
"Mother" (tr. of Gottfried Benn). DenQ (11:4) Wint 77, p. 38.
"Mount Lu" (tr. of Su Tung-po). TexQ (20:4) Wint 77, p. 147.
"Natural World" (tr. of Natsume Soseki). DenQ (12:2) Sum 77,
    p. 61.
"Neighbourliness" (tr. of Anonymous). DenQ (11:4) Wint 77,
    p. 169.
"New Year" (tr. of Chu Ui-sik). DenQ (12:2) Sum 77, p. 296.
"Nitwit Love" (tr. of Anonymous). DenQ (12:2) Sum 77, p. 377.
"Nocturne" (tr. of Juan Chi). DenQ (12:2) Sum 77, p. 392.
"Obsession" (tr. of Ato Tobira). DenQ (12:2) Sum 77, p. 372.
"Offering" (tr. of Ryokan). WestHR (31:1) Wint 77, p. 60.
"Old Woman" (tr. of Lady Ishikawa). DenQ (12:2) Sum 77,
    p. 368.
"On a Sealing Mind" (tr. of Vo Ngon-thong). DenQ (12:2) Sum
    77, p. 51.
"One That Got Away" (tr. of Anonymous). DenQ (12:2) Sum 77,
    p. 371.
"Orange Tree" (tr. of Anonymous). DenQ (11:4) Wint 77, p. 175.
"Original Faces" (tr. of Natsume Soseki). DenQ (12:2) Sum 77,
    p. 61.
"Out of Office" (tr. of Kim Sam-hyon). DenQ (12:2) Sum 77,
    p. 296.
"The Palace Road" (tr. of Anonymous). DenQ (12:2) Sum 77,
    p. 371.
"Partings" (tr. of Fan Yen-long). DenQ (12:2) Sum 77, p. 391.
"Party Song" (tr. of Prince Hozumi). DenQ (11:4) Wint 77,
    p. 169.
"The Pass at Ashigaw" (tr. of Yamanoue no Okura). DenQ (11:4)
    Wint 77, p. 165.
"Per Incuriam" (tr. of Kim Su-jang). DenQ (12:2) Sum 77,
    p. 301.
"Plum Trees" (tr. of Saigyo). DenQ (12:2) Sum 77, p. 367.
"Politician" (tr. of Prince In-pyong). DenQ (12:2) Sum 77,
    p. 293.
"Pomegranates" (tr. of Sin Hum). DenQ (12:2) Sum 77, p. 292.
"Pony" (tr. of Anonymous). DenQ (12:2) Sum 77, p. 371.
"Prayer at Mitarashi" (tr. of Anonymous). WestHR (31:1) Wint
    77, p. 57.
"Prayers" (tr. of Ishikawa Takuboku). WestHR (31:1) Wint 77,
    p. 60.
"Priest of the Mountain Temple" (tr. of Anonymous). DenQ
    (12:2) Sum 77, p. 63.
"The Prince of Huai-Nan" (tr. of Pao Chao). DenQ (12:2) Sum
    77, p. 47.

"Principle" (tr. of Hsiao Yen). WestHR (31:3) Sum 77, p. 208.
"Property" (tr. of Kim Kwang-uk). DenQ (12:2) Sum 77, p. 306.
"Quintessence" (tr. of Ban Tinh). DenQ (12:2) Sum 77, p. 52.
"Radiance" (tr. of Honen). WestHR (31:3) Sum 77, p. 211.
"Rainbow" (tr. of Anonymous). DenQ (12:2) Sum 77, p. 369.
"Rat" (tr. of Fujiwara no Sadayori). WestHR (31:1) Wint 77,
     p. 57.
"Real World" (tr. of Anonymous). DenQ (12:2) Sum 77, p. 60.
"Realist" (tr. of Kim Chang-op). DenQ (12:2) Sum 77, p. 300.
"Reality" (tr. of Saigyo). TexQ (20:4) Wint 77, p. 148.
"Recall" (tr. of Anonymous). DenQ (11:4) Wint 77, p. 173.
"Red Skirt" (tr. of Anonymous). DenQ (11:4) Wint 77, p. 168.
"Remembrance" (tr. of Su Tung-po). DenQ (12:2) Sum 77,
     p. 393.
"Reminder" (tr. of Po Chu-i). DenQ (12:2) Sum 77, p. 398.
"Riding for a Fall" (tr. of Anonymous). DenQ (12:2) Sum 77,
     p. 378.
"River Parting" (tr. of Huang Ting-chien). DenQ (12:2) Sum 77,
     p. 394.
"The Road of Love" (tr. of Kakinomoto no Hitomaro). DenQ
     (11:4) Wint 77, p. 168.
"Royal Audience" (tr. of Prince Yu-chon). DenQ (12:2) Sum 77,
     p. 307.
"Runaway" (tr. of Anonymous). DenQ (12:2) Sum 77, p. 393.
"Rural Economy" (tr. of Yi Chae). DenQ (12:2) Sum 77, p. 302.
"Sailor" (tr. of Man Jang). DenQ (12:2) Sum 77, p. 294.
"The Scullion's Reply" (tr. of Lu Hsing-che). WestHR (31:3)
     Sum 77, p. 209.
"The Seasonal Marvels" (tr. of Yi Hwang). DenQ (12:2) Sum 77,
     p. 306.
"Self Discovery" (tr. of Anonymous). WestHR (31:3) Sum 77,
     p. 210.
"Self Seeking" (tr. of Lu Chi). DenQ (12:2) Sum 77, p. 46.
"Shan-shan" (tr. of Hui-chi). WestHR (31:1) Wint 77, p. 56.
"Shrimp Sleep" (tr. of Anonymous). DenQ (12:2) Sum 77, p. 295.
"Slander" (tr. of Anonymous). DenQ (12:2) Sum 77, p. 369.
"Sleep for Loveliness" (tr. of Yi Cho-nyon). DenQ (12:2) Sum
     77, p. 309.
"Small Aster" (tr. of Gottfried Benn). DenQ (11:4) Wint 77,
     p. 35.
"Small Request" (tr. of A Woman of Bizen). DenQ (11:4) Wint
     77, p. 172.
"Song" (tr. of Gottfried Benn). DenQ (11:4) Wint 77, p. 36.
"Soulscape" (tr. of Saigyo). DenQ (12:2) Sum 77, p. 56.
"Sparrows" (tr. of Anonymous). DenQ (12:2) Sum 77, p. 396.
"Spring" (tr. of Chen Yu-yi). DenQ (12:2) Sum 77, p. 56.
"Spring" (tr. of Hwang Hwi). DenQ (12:2) Sum 77, p. 302.
"Spring Snow" (tr. of Anonymous). DenQ (12:2) Sum 77, p. 374.
"Stories" (tr. of Empress Jito and Granny Shihi). DenQ (12:2)
     Sum 77, p. 372.
"Stragglers" (tr. of Saigyo). DenQ (12:2) Sum 77, p. 368.
"Such Cold Case" (tr. of Kim Chon-taek). DenQ (12:2) Sum 77,
     p. 398.

"Summer Grass" (tr. of Anonymous). DenQ (12:2) Sum 77,
p. 375.

"Sundown" (tr. of Anonymous). DenQ (12:2) Sum 77, p. 310.

"Sunrise" (tr. of Anonymous). DenQ (12:2) Sum 77, p. 366.

"Sword" (tr. of Kim Chin-tae). DenQ (12:2) Sum 77, p. 299.

"Talk" (tr. of Chu Ui-sik). DenQ (12:2) Sum 77, p. 310.

"Tamana" (tr. of Anonymous). DenQ (12:2) Sum 77, p. 376.

"Temple" (tr. of Wang Shih-chen). WestHR (31:1) Wint 77,
p. 59.

"The Temple of the Peak" (tr. of Li Po). DenQ (12:2) Sum 77,
p. 50.

"Tenure" (tr. of Archbishop Jien). DenQ (12:2) Sum 77, p. 358.

"Things That Comply with the Wind" (tr. of Ryojin Hissho).
DenQ (12:2) Sum 77, p. 359.

"Time to Be Writing Songs" (tr. of Kim Su-jang). DenQ (12:2)
Sum 77, p. 293.

"Transcience" (tr. of Otomo no Yakamochi). DenQ (12:2) Sum 77,
p. 51.

"Travelling to Azuma" (tr. of Ki no Tsurayuki). DenQ (12:2)
Sum 77, p. 357.

"The Tree of Happiness" (tr. of Kim Sang-yong). DenQ (12:2)
Sum 77, p. 298.

"Troth" (tr. of Anonymous). DenQ (12:2) Sum 77, p. 369.

"Truth Is a Mountain" (tr. of Anonymous). DenQ (12:2) Sum 77,
p. 48.

"Twine" (tr. of Sin Hum). WestHR (31:1) Wint 77, p. 58.

"Two Stone Buddhas" (tr. of Chong Chol). VirQR (53:3) Sum 77,
p. 451.

"The Uncarved Block" (tr. of Ngo Chan Luu). WestHR (31:1)
Wint 77, p. 57.

"Understanding" (tr. of Otomo no Sakanoe). DenQ (11:4) Wint 77,
p. 164.

"The Use of Nothingness" (tr. of Lao Tzu). WestHR (31:1) Wint
77, p. 55.

"Vigil" (tr. of Chou Pang-yen). DenQ (12:2) Sum 77, p. 395.

"Vision" (tr. of Kuo Pu). DenQ (12:2) Sum 77, p. 46.

"Visiting a Taoist" (tr. of Li Po). DenQ (12:2) Sum 77, p. 50.

"Visiting the Master" (tr. of Chia Tao). TexQ (20:4) Wint 77,
p. 149.

"Waiting" (tr. of Anonymous). DenQ (11:4) Wint 77, p. 166.

"The Way" (tr. of Tan Yew-kee). TexQ (20:4) Wint 77, p. 145.

"The Way" (tr. of Yi Hwang). DenQ (12:2) Sum 77, p. 397.

"What Power" (tr. of Sin Hum). WestHR (31:3) Sum 77, p. 212.

"When China Was a Child" (tr. of Choe Chung). DenQ (12:2) Sum
77, p. 298.

"When I Awoke" (tr. of Hagiwara Sakutaro). TexQ (20:4) Wint
77, p. 144.

"Whetstone Mountain" (tr. of Kao Chi). DenQ (12:2) Sum 77,
p. 57.

"White Bird" (tr. of Yosano Akiko). TexQ (20:4) Wint 77,
p. 146.

"Who?" (tr. of Sany Chigami). DenQ (11:4) Wint 77, p. 167.

"Who Says I'm Old" (tr. of Yi Chung-jip). DenQ (12:2) Sum 77,
    p. 292.
"Widow" (tr. of Chong Chol). DenQ (12:2) Sum 77, p. 294.
"Wildest Dream" (tr. of Anonymous). DenQ (12:2) Sum 77,
    p. 372.
"Willow Cuttings" (tr. of Hong-nang). DenQ (12:2) Sum 77,
    p. 295.
"Winter" (tr. of Hagiwara Sakutaro). WestHR (31:3) Sum 77,
    p. 214.
"Winter Landscape" (tr. of Yun Son-do). DenQ (12:2) Sum 77,
    p. 60.
"Within the Dewdrop" (tr. of Kobayashi Issa). DenQ (12:2) Sum
    77, p. 59.
"Words" (tr. of Unoku). DenQ (12:2) Sum 77, p. 57.
"World Enough" (tr. of Anonymous). TexQ (20:4) Wint 77,
    p. 148.
"Yasumiko" (tr. of Fujiwara no Kamatari). DenQ (12:2) Sum 77,
    p. 374.
"Yearning" (tr. of Otomo no Yakamochi). DenQ (11:4) Wint 77,
    p. 164.
"Yearning" (tr. of Ou-yang Hsui). DenQ (12:2) Sum 77, p. 394.
"Yin" (tr. of Lao Tzu). DenQ (12:2) Sum 77, p. 45.
"Zen Death" (tr. of Zumon). TexQ (20:4) Wint 77, p. 149.
"Zen Road" (tr. of Song Sun). TexQ (20:4) Wint 77, p. 146.
"Zen Teaching" (tr. of Anonymous). DenQ (12:2) Sum 77, p. 58.

WILSON, Keith
    "Summer Meadows" (for Aurel Rau). PoNow (14/18) 77, p. 188.

WILSON, Miles
    "Claire, if You Come." SouthernPR (17:2) Aut 77, p. 34.
    "You, Theodore Roethke." NewOR (5:3) 77, p. 272.

WILSON, Patrice M.
    "Disco: Last Dance, First Dance." Nimrod (21:2/22:1) 77,
        p. 310.
    "Earthworm." Nimrod (21:2/22:1) 77, p. 311.
    "My Family" (to my father on his birthday). Nimrod (21:2/22:1)
        77, p. 311.

WILSON, Reuel
    "I John the Almoner ..." (tr. of Jan Kulka). NewYRB (24:7) 28
        Ap 77, p. 37.
    "Patients Take a Walk on a Sunday Afternoon" (tr. of Jan Kulka).
        NewYRB (24:7) 28 Ap 77, p. 37.

WILSON, Robley, Jr.
    "The Black Cat." PoetryNW (18:2) Sum 77, p. 11.
    "The Diver." PoetryNW (18:2) Sum 77, p. 9.

WIMBERLY, Gerard
    "The Secret of Time." Epoch (26:2) Wint 77, p. 142.
    "Winding Sheets." Epoch (26:2) Wint 77, p. 140.

WIMMER, Lynne
  "Lost and Old Rivers." QW (2) Wint 77, p. 30.

WIMMER, Soraya
  "He who now brings me the steely bread" (tr. of Christine
      Lavant, w. M. Deen Larsen). ChiR (29:3) Wint 78, p. 9.
  "It smells much less like fruit and grain" (tr. of Christine
      Lavant, w. M. Deen Larsen). ChiR (29:3) Wint 78, p. 13.
  "Keep twisting the heart-spindle for me" (tr. of Christine
      Lavant, w. M. Deen Larsen). ChiR (29:3) Wint 78, p. 15.
  "The moon leapt up and a toad fell" (tr. of Christine Lavant, w.
      M. Deen Larsen). ChiR (29:3) Wint 78, p. 11.

WINANS, A. D.
  "America." PoNow (14/18) 77, p. 188.
  Eighteen poems. SeC (5:1) 77, pp. 47-76.
  "For Gene Ruggles." Stonecloud (6) 76, p. 12.
  "The Perfect Poem." Stonecloud (6) 76, p. 12.
  "San Francisco." Stonecloud (6) 76, p. 14.

WINCHELL, Margaret
  "Ethiopian Village." HolCrit (14:3) Je 77, p. 11.

WINDAHL, Gibb
  "The Children." AntR (35:2/3) Spr-Sum 77, p. 259.

WINDER, Barbara
  "July." PoetC (10:1) 77, p. 26.

WINDHAM, Revish
  "It's Okay to Play Sometimes." BlackF (2:1) Wint 77-78, p. 33.

WINEBERG, A. M.
  "Back Home Death." NewC (7:3) 75-76, p. 5.

WINK, Johnny
  "Jack Butler: Split End in Space." WindO (28) Spr 77, p. 19.

WINN, Howard
  "After the Romantics." KanQ (9:1) Wint 77, p. 83.
  "Father or Mother of Us All." KanQ (9:1) Wint 77, p. 82.
  "Matter-of-Fact." GRR (8:1/2) 77, p. 43.
  "My Father Talks Politics in Poughkeepsie 1976." GRR (8:1/2)
      77, p. 44.
  "Point of View." KanQ (9:3) Sum 77, p. 104.
  "Truth." GRR (8:1/2) 77, p. 45.

WINNER, Robert
  "Horses." TransR (58/59) F 77, p. 144.
  "Miss Alderman." NewL (44:1) Aut 77, p. 24.

WINSHIP, George P., Jr.
  "On the Ordination of Women." ChrC (94:25) 3-10 Ag 77, p. 683.

WINSTON, Sarah
"Renoir: Nude in Brook. " LitR (20:3) Spr 77, p. 310.
"Soutine: Le Gourdon. " LitR (20:3) Spr 77, p. 310.

WINTERS, Anne
"The Armada. " Shen (29:1) Aut 77, p. 60.
"Demolition Crane. " Poetry (130:5) Ag 77, p. 280.
"The Hall of Armor. " Poetry (130:5) Ag 77, p. 281.
"Readings in the Navigators. " Poetry (130:5) Ag 77, p. 283.
"Still Life with Pots. " Poetry (130:5) Ag 77, p. 282.

WINTERS, Nancy
"In the Catacombs. " SouthernR (13:4) Aut 77, p. 762.
"Mad Person's Epitaph. " SouthernR (13:4) Aut 77, p. 763.
"On a Piece of Fifteenth-Century Embroidery. " SouthernR (13:4)
    Aut 77, p. 761.
"The Proposed Book of Common Prayer. " SouthernR (13:4) Aut
    77, p. 763.
"With Stanley in Darkest Africa. " SouthernR (13:4) Aut 77,
    p. 760.

WISOFF, Ellen
"Getting Out of Brooklyn. " DenQ (12:2) Sum 77, p. 363.
"Oil on Canvas. " DenQ (12:2) Sum 77, p. 360.
"Polymer. " DenQ (12:2) Sum 77, p. 363.
"A Reader's Tale. " DenQ (12:2) Sum 77, p. 362.
"Subway Sallay. " DenQ (12:2) Sum 77, p. 361.

WITSCHEL, John
"At the Cape. " Glass (2:2/3) Wint-Spr 77, p. 82.
"Four Days Without Food. " BelPoJ (28:2) Wint 77-78, p. 18.
"Hog Groomer. " YellowBR (8) 77, p. 20.
"In the Grotto. " YellowBR (8) 77, p. 20.
"Night in the Desert. " Glass (2:2/3) Wint-Spr 77, p. 80.

WITT, Harold
"Aerosol. " NewL (43:4) Sum 77, p. 25.
"Commercial. " PoetryNW (18:3) Aut 77, p. 19.
"Cow. " PoetryNW (18:3) Aut 77, p. 19.
Fourteen poems. PoNow (14/18) 77, pp. 189-193.
"Frankenstein. " Drag (16) 77.
"Hot Air Balloon. " PoetryNW (18:1) Spr 77, p. 54.
"Muir's House. " PoetryNW (18:3) Aut 77, p. 18.

WITTE, John C.
"Catfish Reunion. " Epoch (26:2) Wint 77, p. 159.
"Chasing Hamlet. " ParisR (70) Sum 77, p. 141.
"Mowing a Roadside in Woodbury, Connecticut. " Epoch (26:2)
    Wint 77, p. 157.
"My Neighbor Hosing Her Lawn in the Dark. " PoetryNW (18:4)
    Wint 77-78, p. 20.
"Power Failure. " PoetryNW (18:4) Wint 77-78, p. 20.
"To a Friend in Vermont. " Epoch (26:2) Wint 77, p. 158.

"Uncle Steph. " Falcon (14) 77, p. 59.

WITTE, Phyllis
   "Attraction-One. " DenQ (12:2) Sum 77, p. 334.
   "Warning. " DenQ (12:2) Sum 77, p. 333.

WITTENBERG, Rudolf
   "In the Wintercloset. " DeKalb (10:3) Spr 77, p. 72.

WITZEL, Murry V. , Jr.
   "Rationale. " TexQ (20:2) Sum 77, p. 25.
   "Seascape. " TexQ (20:2) Sum 77, p. 24.

WOESSNER, Warren
   "Blue Lake. " PoNow (14/18) 77, p. 193.
   "The Colossal Horned Owl" (for David Hilton). Drag (16) 77.

WOFFORD, Phillip
   "The Dogs of West Hebron. " PoNow (14/18) 77, p. 193.
   "The Silences: Father and Son. " PoNow (14/18) 77, p. 194.

WOIWODE, Larry
   "Horses. " Atl (240:5) N 77, p. 63.
   "How It Came. " Harp (255:1527) Ag 77, p. 80.
   "Quail. " Harp (255:1527) Ag 77, p. 80.
   "The Rib. " Harp (255:1527) Ag 77, p. 80.

WOJAHN, David
   "Heaven for Railroad Men. " CutB (8) Spr 77, p. 101.
   "Home from Work, Unbandaging. " HangL (31) Aut 77, p. 67.
   "On a Clear Night You Can Pick Up Austin, Texas. " HangL (31)
      Aut 77, p. 70.
   "A White Suit, the Rain" (for the suicide of Thomas James,
      1946-74). HangL (31) Aut 77, p. 68.

WOLF, Leslie
   "Santa's Soliloquy. " SenR (8:2) D 77, p. 90.
   "Thin Tissue. " SenR (8:2) D 77, p. 91.
   "Under the Rainbow. " PartR (44:2) 77, p. 402.

WOLFE, Gary K.
   "Entropy. " SouthernPR (17:1) Spr 77, p. 53.

WOLFE, Michael
   "Wordsworth" (for Keith and Rosemarie). AndR (3:2) Aut 76,
      p. 27.

WOLFERT, Adrienne
   "Sunset over Memorial Park. " PoetL (72:2) Sum 77, p. 66.

WOLFERT, Helen
   "The Crescent and the Dark. " LittleR (12) 77, p. 5.

WOLFF, Whitney
  "As I fall asleep my head grows and grows." TransR (60) Je
    77, p. 99.
  "Everything has been outlined with a blue crayon." TransR (60)
    Je 77, p. 98.

WOLVEN, Fred
  "The Same Notes Again & Again" (for Valerie [& Sarah & Sharon]).
    AAR (27) 77, p. 13.

A WOMAN of BIZEN
  "Small Request" (tr. by Graeme Wilson). DenQ (11:4) Wint 77,
    p. 172.

WONG, Shawn Hsu
  "Peach." GreenR (6:1/2) Spr 77, p. 58.

WOOD, Gayle E.
  "Divorce." CalQ (11/12) Wint-Spr 77, p. 151.

WOOD, Peter
  "Letter to Diane Wakoski." US1 (9) Spr 77, p. 8.
  "The Quick Brown Fox Jumps Over the Lazy Dog." US1 (9) Spr
    77, p. 7.

WOOD, Renate
  Nine poems. Aspen (3) Spr 77, p. 98.

WOOD, Robert E.
  "Agatha." Poem (31) N 77, p. 39.
  "Boutique." Poem (31) N 77, p. 40.
  "Decadence." DeKalb (10:2) Wint 77, p. 54.
  "For Laura Who Is Deaf." WindO (29) Sum 77, p. 4.
  "Sensibility." DeKalb (10:2) Wint 77, p. 55.

WOOD, Susan
  "Bazaar: After Calvino." NewYorker (53:39) 14 N 77, p. 193.
  "What We Really Are We Really Ought to Be" (for Beverly
    Lowry). Antaeus (27) Aut 77, p. 119.

WOOD, Wilbur
  "White Man." MontG (5) Wint 77, p. 61.

WOODARD, Deborah
  "Alice at Tea Time." AntR (35:4) Aut 77, p. 402.
  "The Nettle Spinner's Brothers." BelPoJ (28:2) Wint 77-78, p. 5.
  "Story of the Youngest." BelPoJ (28:2) Wint 77-78, p. 4.

WOODCOCK, George
  "Mutational Blessing" (For Margaret Atwood). MalR (41) Ja 77,
    p. 99.

WOODS, Carl
  "Dionysus." TexQ (19:4) Wint 77, p. 127.

"Ebbtide. " EnPas (4) 76, p. 26.
"Eternal Garden. " Wind (26) 77, p. 59.
"He Who Waits. " Wind (26) 77, p. 57.
"Instructions for a Portrait. " DeKalb (10:2) Wint 77, p. 56.
"Passacaglia. " Wind (26) 77, p. 58.
"Religion in America. " TexQ (19:4) Wint 76, p. 128.
"Small Elegy. " Wind (26) 77, p. 58.
"Thirteen. " Wind (26) 77, p. 57.
Thirteen poems. EnPas (5) 77, p. 5.
"Unknown Child. " StoneC (77:3) S 77, p. 29.
"Wedding. " NewC (8:1) 76-77, p. 7.
"The Whores at the Beach. " Poem (29) Mr 77, p. 3.
"Within. " Poem (29) Mr 77, p. 4.

WOODS, John
    "Pose Proem. " MissR (6:1) 77, p. 79.

WOOLDRIDGE, Easter S.
    "Pictures and Poems from Vermont. " PoetL (72:2) Sum 77,
        p. 76.

WOOLFOLK, Ann
    "Exit. " US1 (9) Spr 77, p. 3.
    "The Mummy at Atacama. " US1 (9) Spr 77, p. 3.

WORLEY, James
    "Below the Picture Window. " ChrC (94:28) 14 S 77, p. 780.
    "Living Room. " ChrC (94:37) 16 N 77, p. 1060.
    "Ruined Rattler on a Florida Path. " ChrC (94:18) 18 My 77,
        p. 475.

WORLEY, Jeff
    "Poem for Anne. " KanQ (9:1) Wint 77, p. 111.

WORSLEY, Alice
    "It Is Not Easy to Say Why I Left You. " Stonecloud (6) 76,
        p. 111.

WORTH, Douglas
    "breakthrough. " Aspect (69) O-D 76, p. 22.
    "Orpheus, Turning. " Aspect (69) O-D 76, p. 22.

WORTH, Valerie
    "Leaving the Grass. " NewL (44:1) Aut 77, p. 68.
    "The Rose and the Fly. " NewL (44:1) Aut 77, p. 66.
    "The Ways of the Grass. " NewL (44:1) Aut 77, p. 68.

WORTHINGTON, Mark P.
    "Portrait of Another Artist. " SouthernPR (17:1) Spr 77,
        p. 59.

WRIGHT, A. J.
    "Three Haiku. " KanQ (9:3) Sum 77, p. 104.

WRIGHT, Brenda
"Beautifully as a chorus." AmerPoR (6:2) Mr-Ap 77, p. 34.
"Trees and trees and open fire." AmerPoR (6:2) Mr-Ap 77,
    p. 31.

WRIGHT, Carolyne
"Bicycle Abandoned in the Rain" (tr. of Miguel Arteche). EnPas
    (4) 76, p. 36.
"Crossed Out" (tr. of Alfonsina Storni). EnPas (5) 77, p. 19.
"The Discipline of Becoming Invisible." HolCrit (14:4) O 77,
    p. 14.
"I promise myself three joys this fall." NewC (7:2) 75-76, p. 9.
"Indian Woman on Socabaya Street." QW (4) Aut 77, p. 30.
"Quevedo Speaks of his Sores" (tr. of Francisco Gómez De
    Quevedo). EnPas (4) 76, p. 37.
"Rain" (tr. of Miguel Arteche). EnPas (4) 76, p. 35.
"Re-Entry." ThRiPo (10) 77, p. 28.
"613." PoetryNW (18:3) Wint 77-78, p. 15.
"'When my life runs out...'" (for Julia Alvarez). Chomo (4:1)
    Sum 77, p. 3.

WRIGHT, Charles
"April." Atl (239:4) Ap 77, p. 45.
"Autumn." AmerPoR (6:3) My-Je 77, p. 16.
"Clear Night." NewYorker (53:11) 2 My 77, p. 123.
"Edvard Munch." NewYorker (53:7) 4 Ap 77, p. 42.
"Homage to Paul Cézanne." NewYorker (53:44) 19 D 77, p. 36.
"Mount Caribou at Night." Field (17) Aut 77, p. 86.
from Le Occasioni: "Motets" (tr. of Eugenio Montale). Pequod
    (2:2) Wint 77, pp. 10-19.
"Reply to Lapo Gianni." Iowa (8:1) Wint 77, p. 39.
"Saturday 6 a.m." AmerPoR (6:3) My-Je 77, p. 16.
"Self-Portrait." SenR (8:2) D 77, p. 36.

WRIGHT, Charles David
"Amnesiac" (for Sonnyman, third cousin, disappeared eighteen
    years ago). Field (17) Aut 77, p. 14.
"The Deputy Fills Out the Report on His Estranged Wife."
    LittleR (12) 77, p. 22.
"The End at the Bath House." Field (17) Aut 77, p. 15.
"Going Down." SouthernPR (17:2) Aut 77, p. 19.
"There Comes a Wind." NowestR (16:3) 77, p. 74.
"Woman Looking Through a Viewmaster." Field (17) Aut 77,
    p. 13.

WRIGHT, DKe.
"The Suburbs." CarouselQ (2:1) Spr 77, p. 19.
"The Suburbs Cont." CarouselQ (2:1) Spr 77, p. 19.
"The Suburbs Cont. (Again)." CarouselQ (2:1) Spr 77, p. 19.

WRIGHT, Franz
"The Raising of Lazarus" (tr. of Rainer Maria Rilke). Field
    (16) Spr 77, p. 14.

"St. Paul's Greek Orthodox Church Minneapolis, 1960." Field
(17) Aut 77, p. 25.

WRIGHT, G. T.
"In Zurich." Esq (87:4) Ap 77, p. 36.

WRIGHT, Harold P.
"August" (tr. of Tanikawa Shuntaro). DenQ (12:2) Sum 77,
p. 281.
"August and February" (tr. of Tanikawa Shuntaro). DenQ (12:2)
Sum 77, p. 285.
"Battle Scene from the Comic Fantastic Opera, 'The Seafarer'"
(for Paul Klee) (tr. of Tanikawa Shuntaro). DenQ (12:2) Sum
77, p. 284.
"Before the Snow" (for Paul Klee) (tr. of Tanikawa Shuntaro).
DenQ (12:2) Sum 77, p. 284.
"Child and Train Tracks" (tr. of Tanikawa Shuntaro). DenQ
(12:2) Sum 77, p. 281.
"Nero" (to a loved little dog) (tr. of Tanikawa Shuntaro). DenQ
(12:2) Sum 77, p. 282.
"Sadness" (tr. of Tanikawa Shuntaro). DenQ (12:2) Sum 77,
p. 282.

WRIGHT, James
"Beautiful Ohio." OhioR (18:2) Spr-Sum 77, p. 40.
"By the Ruins of a Gun Emplacement: Saint-Benoît-sur-Loire."
NewYorker (53:25) 8 Ag 77, p. 22.
"How Spring Arrives in Rome." OhioR (18:2) Spr-Sum 77, p. 42.
"Ohioan Pastoral." OhioR (18:2) Spr-Sum 77, p. 41.
"Reflections in Rome." OhioR (18:2) Spr-Sum 77, p. 43.
"With the Shell of a Hermit Crab." NewYorker (53:27) 22 Ag 77,
p. 30.
"Written in a Copy of Swift's Poems" (for Wayne Burns).
Paunch (46/47) Ap 77, p. 10.

WRIGHT, Jay
"Love's Dozen." MassR (18:4) Wint 77, p. 716.
"The Sanctuary." AmerPoR (6:1) Ja-F 77, p. 30.
"The Sunset's Widow." AmerPoR (6:1) Ja-F 77, p. 30.

WRIGHT, Thomas L.
"To a Colleague Departing: N.B." SouthernHR (11:2) Spr 77,
p. vi.

WRIGHT, Tim
"Percipio." SmPd (14:3) Aut 77, p. 4.

WRIGLEY, Robert
"For the Nuclear Power Plant." Wind (26) 77, p. 60.
"Future." Wind (26) 77, p. 60.
"In the Great Bear." Chowder (9) Aut-Wint 77, p. 23.
"Moving Away." Wind (26) 77, p. 60.

WROBEL, Sylvia
"After Hours." Shen (28:4) Sum 77, p. 74.
"Leaving Versailles: a love song." HolCrit (14:2) Ap 77, p. 14.
"Myth." HiramPoR (22) Aut-Wint 77, p. 36.

WYATT, David
"A Place." PoetC (10:1) 77, p. 18.
"The Rest Home." CutB (8) Spr 77, p. 75.

WYNAND, Derk
from Green-Sealed Messages: (88) (tr. of H. C. Artmann).
    WebR (3:1) Wint 77, p. 60.
"Knowing How to Seek" (tr. of Ernst Jandl). ChiR (29:3) Wint
    78, p. 131.
"odysseus variations" (tr. of Friederike Mayröcker). ChiR (29:3)
    Wint 78, p. 132.
"on a sea of air" (tr. of Friederike Mayröcker). ChiR (29:3)
    Wint 78, p. 134.
"Poetic Renown" (tr. of Jeannie Ebner). ChiR (29:3) Wint 78,
    p. 116.
"Threatening Letter" (tr. of Maria Luise Kaschnitz). WebR (3:1)
    Wint 77, p. 51.

XENOS, Stephanos
"For My Lady" (tr. by Rachel Hadas). EnPas (6) 77, p. 36.
"International Sculpture Exhibit, Philopappos Hill" (tr. by Rachel
    Hadas). EnPas (6) 77, p. 33.
"Kalamita" (tr. by Rachel Hadas). EnPas (6) 77, p. 35.
"Old Men of Democracy" (tr. by Rachel Hadas). EnPas (6) 77,
    p. 34.

YAKAMOCHI, Otomo no
"Bamboo Fence" (tr. by Graeme Wilson). DenQ (11:4) Wint 77,
    p. 169.
"Crescent Moon" (tr. by Graeme Wilson). DenQ (12:2) Sum 77,
    p. 371.
"Fringed Pinks" (tr. by Graeme Wilson). DenQ (11:4) Wint 77,
    p. 175.
"Transcience" (tr. by Graeme Wilson). DenQ (12:2) Sum 77,
    p. 51.
"Yearning" (tr. by Graeme Wilson). DenQ (11:4) Wint 77,
    p. 164.

YAL'M, Ozcan
"Your lips are pink" (tr. of Cahit Kulebi, w. William Fielder
    and Dionis Coffin Riggs). DenQ (12:2) Sum 77, p. 230.

YAMAKUMA, Prince
"The Death of Prince Iwata" (tr. by Graeme Wilson). DenQ
    (12:2) Sum 77, p. 377.

YANG Wan-li
"Fly" (tr. by Graeme Wilson). DenQ (12:2) Sum 77, p. 399.

YATES, J. Michael
  "From Poem of the Endless." MalR (42) Ap 77, p. 50.

YATES, Peter
  "Authority." OP (23) Spr-Sum 77, p. 47.
  "The Garden Prospect." OP (23) Spr-Sum 77, p. 40.
  "Marvelling on the Eve of My 65th Birthday." OP (23) Spr-Sum
      77, p. 48.
  "Whoever Cannot Believe the Good." OP (23) Spr-Sum 77, p. 46.
  "Zoo: In Memory of the Black Gibbon, Bimbo." OP (23) Spr-
      Sum 77, p. 50.

YAU, John
  "Another Installment." AmerPoR (6:6) N-D 77, p. 46.
  "Forensic Foliage." AmerPoR (6:6) N-D 77, p. 45.
  "The Motel Owner and His Wife." Agni (7) 77, p. 35.
  "Poughkeepsie." Some (7/8) 76.
  "Recent Survey." AmerPoR (6:6) N-D 77, p. 45.
  "Robert Herrick." AmerPoR (6:6) N-D 77, p. 45.

YEAGER, Peter E.
  "Under the Porch." SoDakR (15:2) Sum 77, p. 21.

YEAGER, R. F.
  "Grandaddy Describes New Year's Eve in Minnesota." Madrona
      (4:13/14) 77, p. 35.
  "Grandaddy on Unrequited Love." Madrona (4:13/14) 77, p. 36.

YEH, I-Tien
  "propped by an oak tree." YaleLit (145:3) 77, p. 26.

YEN Chi-tao
  "Grief" (tr. by Graeme Wilson). DenQ (12:2) Sum 77, p. 393.

YENKAVITCH, Joseph
  "Late August." Poem (31) N 77, p. 60.

YENSER, Stephen
  "Notebook Entry (Pau, 1971)." NewYorker (53:4) 14 Mr 77,
      p. 68.

YEVTUSHENKO, Yevgeny
  "Poem: Do you think of her, geranium Yelabuga?" (tr. by Elaine
      Feinstein). Stand (18:3) 77, p. 16.
  "Safari in Ulster" (tr. by Jan Butler). TransR (60) Je 77,
      p. 154.

YI Chae
  "Rural Economy" (tr. by Graeme Wilson). DenQ (12:2) Sum 77,
      p. 302.

YI Cho-nyon
  "Sleep for Loveliness" (tr. by Graeme Wilson). DenQ (12:2) Sum
      77, p. 309.

YI Chung-jip
  "Who Says I'm Old" (tr. by Graeme Wilson). DenQ (12:2) Sum
    77, p. 292.

YI Gae
  "Candle" (tr. by Graeme Wilson). VirQR (53:3) Sum 77, p. 454.

YI Hwang
  "Accidie" (tr. by Graeme Wilson). DenQ (12:2) Sum 77, p. 303.
  "The Seasonal Marvels" (tr. by Graeme Wilson). DenQ (12:2)
    Sum 77, p. 306.
  "The Way" (tr. by Graeme Wilson). DenQ (12:2) Sum 77,
    p. 397.

YI Myong-han
  "Dream Road" (tr. by Graeme Wilson). DenQ (12:2) Sum 77,
    p. 305.
  "Entreaty" (tr. by Graeme Wilson). DenQ (12:2) Sum 77, p. 309.

YI Sun-sin
  "Hero" (tr. by Graeme Wilson). DenQ (12:2) Sum 77, p. 308.

YORIZANE, Minamoto no
  "House in the Woods" (tr. by Graeme Wilson). DenQ (12:2) Sum
    77, p. 359.

YOSHITSUNE, Fujiwara no
  "The Meaning of Existence" (tr. by Graeme Wilson). DenQ (12:2)
    Sum 77, p. 56.

YOUMANS, Marlene
  "Another Explanation." SoCaR (9:2) Ap 77, p. 42.

YOUNG, David
  "The Names of a Hare in English." Poetry (131:2) N 77, p. 78.
  "Ninth Elegy" (tr. of Rainer Maria Rilke). MoonsLT (2:3) 77,
    p. 77.

YOUNG, Gary
  "The Cold Did Not Break." Nat (225:14) 29 O 77, p. 440.
  "Out of the Mines." CalQ (11/12) Wint-Spr 77, p. 85.
  "Winter Drought." Poetry (130:3) D 77, p. 144.
  "Winter Solstice." Poetry (130:3) D 77, p. 144.

YOUNG, Ian
  "If the summer night yields, just a little" (tr. by Sandro Penna,
    w. M. J. Shakley). Mouth (11/12) Mr-Je 77, p. 64.
  "Standing and Kneeling Figures." Mouth (11/12) Mr-Je 77, p. 66.

YOUNG, Sal
  "Po Tree." Juice (5) 77.

YOUNG, Thomas
  "After Dionysus." GRR (8:1/2) 77, p. 80.

"For a Previously Infatuated Friend." GRR (8:1/2) 77, p. 121.

YOUNG, Virginia Brady
"The Broomstick Bit." KanQ (9:1) Wint 77, p. 75.
"Every Friday Night." Poem (29) Mr 77, p. 45.
"Frightened." Bound (5:2) Wint 77, p. 610.
"In the Attic." Bound (5:2) Wint 77, p. 611.
"In the Light of a Tiffany Lamp." HiramPoR (22) Aut-Wint 77,
    p. 37.
"Moody in Our Flesh" (For Ruth Lisa). Poem (29) Mr 77, p. 44.
"No One Sees." Poem (29) Mr 77, p. 43.
"Politician's Wife." PoNow (14/18) 77, p. 194.

YOUNG WOMAN of HARIMA
"Fidelity" (tr. by Graeme Wilson). DenQ (12:2) Sum 77, p. 373.

YOUNT, Lisa
"Study for a Portrait Mary R." Chomo (3:3) Spr 77, p. 45.

YU, Pauline R.
"Dwelling in the Mountains: Impromptu Lines" (tr. of Wang
    Wei). DenQ (12:2) Sum 77, p. 353.
"Hua-Tzu Hill" (tr. of Wang Wei). DenQ (12:2) Sum 77, p. 355.
"In Response to the Visit of Several Gentlemen" (tr. of Wang
    Wei). DenQ (12:2) Sum 77, p. 354.
"Lake Yi" (tr. of Wang Wei). DenQ (12:2) Sum 77, p. 355.
"Lamenting Yin Yao" (tr. of Wang Wei). DenQ (12:2) Sum 77,
    p. 353.
"Magnolia Bank" (tr. of Wang Wei). DenQ (12:2) Sum 77,
    p. 355.
"Visiting the Temple of Gathered Fragrance" (tr. of Wang Wei).
    DenQ (12:2) Sum 77, p. 353.

YUAN Mei
"Abandoned Temple" (tr. by Graeme Wilson). WestHR (31:3)
    Sum 77, p. 213.

YU-CHON, Prince
"Royal Audience" (tr. by Graeme Wilson). DenQ (12:2) Sum 77,
    p. 307.

YU Hsin
"The Identity of Contrarieties" (tr. by Graeme Wilson). WestHR
    (31:3) Sum 77, p. 208.

YUN Du-so
"Jade" (tr. by Graeme Wilson). DenQ (12:2) Sum 77, p. 308.

YUN Son-do
"Winter Landscape" (tr. by Graeme Wilson). DenQ (12:2) Sum
    77, p. 60.

YUSIF, Sa'di
"The Five Crosses" (tr. by Sargon Boulus). Mund (10:1) 77, p. 67.

"A Stone" (tr. by Sargon Boulus). Mund (10:1) 77, p. 68.
"The Whole of Night" (tr. by Sargon Boulus). Mund (10:1) 77,
    p. 68.

YUSPEH, Denise
"Renunciation. " YaleLit (145:5) 77, p. 20.

YVONNE
"Encounters (1). " Hand (1) 77, p. 99.
"The Gift. " Hand (1) 77, p. 97.

ZABLE, Jeffrey A. Z.
"Imagine. " SoDakR (15:2) Sum 77, p. 55.
"Teachers. " CarouselQ (2:3) Wint 77, p. 24.
"Wound. " CarouselQ (2:3) Wint 77, p. 24.

ZACH, Natan
from Against Parting: "Sergeant Weiss" (tr. by Jon Silkin and
    Abraham Birman). TriQ (39) Spr 77, p. 317.
"As Sand" (tr. by Jon Silkin). TriQ (39) Spr 77, p. 321.
"He Apologizes" (tr. by Jon Silkin). TriQ (39) Spr 77, p. 318.
"I Saw" (tr. by Robert Friend). TriQ (39) Spr 77, p. 316.
"King Solomon's Camel" (tr. by Jon Silkin). TriQ (39) Spr 77,
    p. 319.
"Samson's Hair" (tr. by S. F. Chyet). TriQ (39) Spr 77,
    p. 316.
"A Song for the Wise Lovers" (tr. by Jon Silkin). TriQ (39)
    Spr 77, p. 320.

ZADE, Wayne
"Poem to My Son. " AmerPoR (6:6) N-D 77, p. 41.

ZADRAVEC, Katharine
"Echoes. " Wind (25) 77, p. 43.

ZAMBARAS, Vassilis
"Melodrama. " Madrona (4:13/14) 77, p. 58.
"On the Beach. " Madrona (4:13/14) 77, p. 57.
"Poem full of Life. " Madrona (4:13/14) 77, p. 59.
"Printer's Devil: Archetype. " Madrona (4:13/14) 77, p. 56.
"Small Street Song. " Madrona (4:13/14) 77, p. 55.

ZANDER, William
"Dogs. " Wind (26) 77, p. 63.
"Jacking Off with a Hammer. " Wind (26) 77, p. 62.
"Trying to Be Faithful. " Wind (26) 77, p. 62.

ZAPATA, Santiago Mendez
"Story of the Ants and Grasshoppers" (tr. of the Tzeltal, w. W.
    S. Merwin and Kathy Branstetter). Nat (225:14) 29 O 77,
    p. 444.

ZARANKA, William
"The Graveyard Swallows. " SouthernPR (17:2) Aut 77, p. 24.

"A Mirror Driven Through Nature." HolCrit (14:5) D 77, p. 12.

ZARZYSKI, Paul
   "The Farmers at Smitty's Bar and Antiques." PoNow (14/18) 77,
      p. 194.
   "Hunting." OhioR (18:3) Aut 77, p. 20.
   "Zarzyski Curses Izaak Walton for All His Rotten Luck."
      Madrona (4:13/14) 77, p. 13.
   "Zarzyski's Futile Love with the Farmer's Rich City Daughter."
      Madrona (4:13/14) 77, p. 12.

ZAUNBRECHER, Judy
   "What Happened?" CarouselQ (2:2) Spr 77, p. 4.

ZAVATSKY, Bill
   "Pencil Poems" (a poem on a pencil and a broadside). Some
      (7/8) 76.

ZAWADIWSKY, Christine
   "Before You Were Born." OP (24) Aut-Wint 77, p. 10.
   "Christine." OP (24) Aut-Wint 77, p. 11.
   "For No Apparent Reason." Epoch (26:2) Wint 77, p. 183.
   "The Glass House." OP (24) Aut-Wint 77, p. 8.
   "Growing Old." DacTerr (14) Spr-Sum 77, p. 19.
   "In My Body." Icarus (5:1) Spr 77, p. 24.
   "Just Before We Crossed the Border." Stonecloud (6) 76,
      p. 114.
   "Kings and Queens." Stonecloud (6) 76, p. 113.
   "Kisses." Stonecloud (6) 76, p. 117.
   "My Age Saddens Me." DacTerr (14) Spr-Sum 77, p. 18.
   "The Night I Guarded the Wounded Angel." Stonecloud (6) 76,
      p. 115.
   "The Night Surrenders." Icarus (5:1) Spr 77, p. 25.
   "Out-of-Step." CutB (9) Aut-Wint 77, p. 28.
   "A Party." EnPas (4) 76, p. 22.
   "Rising." MontG (6) Aut 77, p. 56.
   "Secrecy." OP (24) Aut-Wint 77, p. 5.
   "Sleep." MontG (6) Aut 77, p. 57.
   "Surrounded." Icarus (5:2) Aut 77, p. 11.
   "Targets." OP (24) Aut-Wint 77, p. 3.
   "Touch and Go." MontG (6) Aut 77, p. 58.
   "Valentine's Day." OP (24) Aut-Wint 77, p. 4.
   "Way Up There." OP (24) Aut-Wint 77, p. 6.
   "With the Rest of My Body." Stonecloud (6) 76, p. 116.

ZDANYS, Jonas
   "Night Watch" (tr. of Leonardas Andriekus). Rapp (10) 77,
      p. 13.
   "Reed Grass" (tr. of Leonardas Andriekus). Rapp (10) 77,
      p. 11.
   "Rivers" (tr. of Leonardas Andriekus). Rapp (10) 77, p. 14.
   "The Window" (tr. of Leonardas Andriekus). Rapp (10) 77,
      p. 12.

ZEIDNER, Lisa
"Freud Is Dead." AntR (35:2/3) Spr-Sum 77, p. 254.
"How to Give Blood." Epoch (26:3) Spr 77, p. 226.
"If You Could See This." Epoch (26:3) Spr 77, p. 227.

ZEIGER, L. L.
"Correction." PoNow (14/18) 77, p. 195.
"Kisses." DacTerr (14) Spr-Sum 77, p. 45.
"Possession." PoNow (14/18) 77, p. 195.
"The Ultimate Reality." DacTerr (14) Spr-Sum 77, p. 46.

ZEIGLER, Paul S.
"Can I Get You Anything?" MontG (5) Wint 77, p. 43.

ZELDA
"Be Not Far" (tr. by Edna G. Sharoni). TriQ (39) Spr 77,
    p. 325.
"From the Songs of Childhood" (tr. by Chana Hoffman). TriQ
    (39) Spr 77, p. 324.
"I Stood in Jerusalem" (tr. by Zvi Jagendorf). TriQ (39) Spr 77,
    p. 322.
"The Seamstress" (tr. by Zvi Jagendorf). TriQ (39) Spr 77,
    p. 323.
"Time" (tr. by Edna G. Sharoni). TriQ (39) Spr 77, p. 322.
"When you were here" (tr. by Zvi Jagendorf). TriQ (39) Spr 77,
    p. 324.

ZELENOCK, Kathy
"I wish I had a bottle that." AAR (27) 77, p. 96.

ZELK, Zoltán
"Alone" (tr. by Daniel Hoffman). NewRep (176:13) 26 Mr 77,
    p. 30.
"Moment" (tr. by Daniel Hoffman). NewRep (176:13) 26 Mr 77,
    p. 30.
"The Way" (tr. by Barbara Howes). AmerPoR (6:3) My-Je 77,
    p. 22.

ZELLER, Ludwig
from Los placeres de Edipo: "XIV. Everything in That Sphere"
    (tr. by John Robert Colombo and Susana Wald). MontG (6)
    Aut 77, p. 33.
from Los placeres de Edipo: (XVI) (tr. by Keith Ellis). MontG
    (6) Aut 77, p. 33.
from The Rules of the Game: "Guess or I Get You" (tr. by
    John Robert Colombo and Susana Wald). MontG (6) Aut 77,
    p. 34.
from The Rules of the Game: "Landscape for the Blind" (tr. by
    John Robert Colombo and Susana Wald). MontG (6) Aut 77,
    p. 37.
from The Rules of the Game: "Riches to Register" (tr. by John
    Robert Colombo and Susana Wald). MontG (6) Aut 77,
    p. 36.

from The Rules of the Game: "The Smugglers' Laws" (tr. by
   John Robert Colombo and Susana Wald). MontG (6) Aut 77,
   p. 35.

ZELVIN, Elizabeth
   "The Rhododendron." 13thM (3:2) 77, p. 27.

ZIEGLER, Alan
   "The Great Wall." Agni (7) 77, p. 104.
   "In a Clearing." CarolQ (29:1) Wint 77, p. 93.
   "A Mutual Friend Gave Me Your Number, Etc." CarolQ (29:1)
      Wint 77, p. 92.

ZIEMBA, Frank
   "How Old Men Wind Up." Vaga (26) 77, p. 71.
   "I like the sun in yr beard." Vaga (26) 77, p. 72.

ZIENTARA, Jerry
   "Abraham." Mouth (11/12) Mr-Je 77, p. 32.
   "Bob, For Apple." Mouth (11/12) Mr-Je 77, p. 31.
   "David." Mouth (11/12) Mr-Je 77, p. 80.
   "January Thaw." Mouth (13) D 77, p. 82.
   "Memo #2: Re: Previous Memo." Mouth (11/12) Mr-Je 77,
      p. 33.
   "Passing On Poem, Pass It On Poem." Mouth (13) D 77, p. 75.

ZIMMER, Paul
   "Dear Wanda." QW (4) Aut 77, p. 78.
   "Gus in the Streets." Rapp (10) 77, p. 42.
   "A Month Ago." PoetryNW (18:3) Aut 77, p. 16.
   "Rollo's Miracle." OhioR (18:2) Spr-Sum 77, p. 79.
   "Thurman's Slumping Blues." QW (4) Aut 77, p. 79.
   "Wanda Being Beautiful." Rapp (10) 77, p. 39.
   "Wanda Drinking." QW (4) Aut 77, p. 78.
   "Worrying about You." PoetryNW (18:3) Aut 77, p. 15.
   "Zimmer in Fall." PoNow (14/18) 77, p. 195.
   "Zimmer in Woods, in Dark Times." PoNow (14/18) 77, p. 195.
   "Zimmer's Last Gig." Rapp (10) 77, p. 40.
   "Zimmer's Lincoln Poem." PoNow (14/18) 77, p. 195.
   "Zumer Is Icumen In." PoNow (14/18) 77, p. 195.

ZIMMERMAN, Toni Ortner
   "Japanese Stone Garden 18." Glass (2:2/3) Wint-Spr 77, p. 70.

ZIMROTH, Evan
   "The Lesson." DenQ (12:4) Wint 78, p. 67.

ZINNES, Harriet
   "Accident." PoNow (14/18) 77, p. 196.
   "White Swan." PoNow (14/18) 77, p. 196.

ZIRLIN, Larry
   "Friction." Madrona (4:13/14) 77, p. 10.

ZITO, Eleanor Shiel
"Final Countdown." FourQt (26:3) Spr 77, p. 12.

ZIVLEY, Sherry
"Committee Meeting." ColEng (38:7) Mr 77, p. 749.

ZORN, Marilyn
"Dialogue Before a Broken Mirror." DenQ (12:4) Wint 78, p. 18.
"Mother and Child." DenQ (12:4) Wint 78, p. 16.

ZU-BOLTON, Ahmos, II.
"April Dawn over Galveston." Nimrod (21:2/22:1) 77, p. 313.
"Footnotes." Nimrod (21:2/22:1) 77, p. 312.
"# Two from the Fatherhood Series." PoNow (14/18) 77,
    p. 196.
"One from the Fatherhood Series." Nimrod (21:2/22:1) 77,
    p. 313.

ZUCKER, Jack
"Elegy for Annie." CEACritic (39:3) Mr 77, p. 35.

ZULAUF, Sander
"Anecdote of the Car." Madrona (4:13/14) 77, p. 29.
"Onions." KanQ (9:3) Sum 77, p. 84.

ZUMON
"Zen Death" (tr. by Graeme Wilson). TexQ (20:4) Wint 77,
    p. 149.

ZWEIBEL, Kenneth
"Visit." US1 (9) Spr 77, p. 5.

ZWEIG, Martha
"Dialectic." PartR (44:3) 77, p. 401.
"No Child." CarlMis (16:1/2) Aut-Wint 76-77, p. 77.
"Over Again." PoNow (14/18) 77, p. 196.

ZWISOHN, Van
"It Is Always Better (Quieter) to Live on the Upper Floors."
    Glass (2:2/3) Wint-Spr 77, p. 48.
"Upstairs, Working." Glass (2:2/3) Wint-Spr 77, p. 50.

ZYDEK, Fredrick
"Birds to Hold the Sky" (for Laura). KanQ (9:3) Sum 77, p. 77.
"Casting My Pearls (For My Last Congregation)." CarolQ (29:3)
    Aut 77, p. 13.
"House II." MichQR (16:3) Sum 77, p. 333.
"Ichthyosaurus I." SouthwR (62:4) Aut 77, p. 409.
"Wilkenson Graveyard." CarolQ (29:3) Aut 77, p. 11.